10 760 9263

Entertainers in British Films

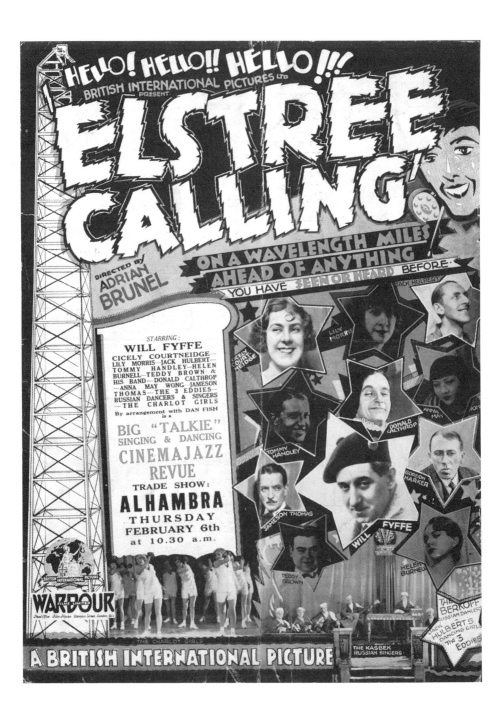

Entertainers in British Films

A Century of Showbiz in the Cinema

Denis Gifford

FLICKS
BOOKS

A CIP catalogue record for this book is available from the British Library.

ISBN 0 948911 76 X

First published in 1998 by

Flicks Books
29 Bradford Road
Trowbridge
Wiltshire BA14 9AN
England
tel   +44 1225 767728
fax +44 1225 760418

An edition of this book is published in North and South America by Greenwood Press, Westport, CT.

Printed and bound in Great Britain by Bookcraft (Bath) Ltd.

Contents

Introduction

This book represents the first attempt to compile a complete catalogue of nearly 4000 entertainers who have appeared on film in Great Britain, from the invention of cinema in the mid-1890s to the present day.

Over a century of cinema is covered in this volume, beginning with the first film produced for pure entertainment in this country, a recording on film of the then very famous cartoonist, Tom Merry (whose real name was William Machin), performing his "Lightning Cartoons" act in front of a film camera invented by pioneer producer/director/photographer, Birt Acres. Incredibly, considering the impermanent nature of early nitrate film, a fragment of this 60-second performance remains with us, preserved in the National Film and Television Archive. It is only the last few frames, but shows Tom Merry leaving the stage on the completion of a caricature of Kaiser Wilhelm II, while an assistant stands by admiringly.

The date of this little film, one of four such "cartoons" made at the same time, is still not pinpointed as to actual production, but evidence indicates the closing months of 1895, as the live-action films it was clearly intended to support were photographed in Germany in June of that year, and featured the Kaiser opening the Kiel Canal.

From this first fragment stems the great parade of performers from the entertainment industry – "showbiz" – who performed for their moment in front of the camera, and who are documented for the first time in this reference book: comedians, singers, impressionists, dancers, bands, pop groups, contortionists, acrobats, circus performers, xylophonists, strip-teasers, ventriloquists, poseurs, and even a "human billiard table" (Joe Adani). All are here, and more!

The arrangement of information is simple. The entertainers are listed alphabetically by surname, or full name where they form a team, troupe or group, followed by their speciality where known. Only those who physically appear in films are listed; where voice performances only apply (as in title songs and animated cartoons), the entertainer is not listed. Each entertainer's appearances are listed chronologically by year, giving the film's title, with production or distribution company in parentheses, and a note as to whether the film was of feature length (30 minutes), which is indicated by F. Otherwise the film is a short. Then follows a list of titles of songs, sketches or pieces of music sung, played or danced to, where it has been possible to trace these. Although many years of research has gone into this seemingly simple book, much remains undiscovered regarding these songs.

The films included in the catalogue are not only the main feature films in which entertainers performed. For the first time in any book are listed appearances in shorts, and especially series of shorts. These include such once-popular titles as *Ace Cinemagazine*, *Eve's Film Review*, *Pathe Pictorial*, *Pathetone Weekly* and other regular pre-war series of "cinemags" or magazine films. Although mainly containing factual items, these series frequently concluded with an act from the variety stage or radio studio. Newsreel performances are also included. Although the films listed are all produced in Britain, the entertainers are not necessarily British. Visitors from the

United States, France, Italy, Spain and elsewhere are included.

The term "British film" here primarily means a film registered in and/or produced in Great Britain. Reissues under a new title are included (for example, the *Music Hall Personalities* series), with reference to the original film. Compilation films using material from earlier pictures (such as *That's Carry On*) are not included. Films included are those on 35mm made for cinema release, rather than those on what was known as a "sub-standard" gauge (16mm, 8mm and 9.5mm).

Research for what would eventually become this book began back in the 1960s, when for six months I was the "Compilation Department" of Associated British-Pathé Pictures. When not compiling short films from material in their archives, I spent my time going through the somewhat tatty and occasionally incomplete listings of their many past productions, which at times included up to three series of short cinemags per week. Whilst the films themselves had not always survived – many in the talkie period were recut into annual 'B' movies for cinema supporting programmes – the listings provided a unique record of popular radio and variety stars of the period. Information from these lists became the basis of this catalogue.

A pioneering book of this nature, whilst representing the author's every effort to make it complete, must inevitably fall short of perfection. Therefore any errors and omissions will be gratefully received by the author, care of the publisher, and will be included in any further edition.

Denis Gifford
Sydenham · March 1998

Abbreviations

ADVERT	advertising short	COI	Central Office of Information
F	feature-length (over 35 minutes)	CWS	Co-operative Wholesale Society
		DUK	Do-U-Know Film Productions
NS	New Series	EMI	Electrical and Musical Industries
S	series		
		FBO	Film Booking Offices
ABFD	Associated British Film Distributors	GFD	General Film Distributors
		GTO	Gem-Toby Organisation
ABP	Associated British-Pathe	ICC	International Cine Corporation
ABPC	Associated British Picture Corporation	ICI	International Chemical Industries
AIP	American International Pictures	IFD	Independent Film Distributors
	Associated Independent Producers	ITC	Incorporated Television Corporation
APD	Associated Producers and Distributors	LIP	London Independent Producers
		MGM	Metro-Goldwyn-Mayer Pictures
ASFI	Associated Sound Film Industries	MOI	Ministry of Information
		NPFD	National Provincial Film Distributors
ATP	Associated Talking Pictures		
B&C	British and Colonial Kinematograph Company	NSS	National Screen Service
		PDC	Producers Distributing Corporation
B&D	British and Dominions Film Corporation	RCA	Radio Corporation of America
BBC	British Broadcasting Corporation	RKO	RKO-Radio Pictures
		TCF	20th Century Fox
BFI	British Film Institute	UA	United Artists
BHE	British Home Entertainments	UFA	Universum Film Aktiengesellschaft
BIF	British Instructional Films		
BIP	British International Pictures	UIP	United International Pictures
BSFP	British Sound Film Productions	UK	United Kingdom Photoplays
BSS	British Screen Service	W&F	Woolf & Freedman Film Service
C&M	Cricks and Martin Films		
CFF	Children's Film Foundation	WP	Williams and Pritchard Films
CIC	Cinema International Corporation		

EKOW ABBAN (singer)
1986　*Absolute Beginners*
　　　(Palace) F
　　　"Santa Lucia"

ABE AND MAWRUSS (Hebrew comedians)
1936　*Pathetone 334*
　　　"Another Misunderstanding"

LOU ABELARDO (singer)
1930　*Pathetone 11*
　　　"Springtime in the Rockies"

SHIRLEY ABICAIR (songs with zither)
1954　*One Good Turn*
　　　(Rank) F
　　　"Botany Bay"

THE ACE QUINTET (band)
1938　*Heavy Sleepers*
　　　(Ace Cinemagazine)
　　　"Christopher Columbus's Sister"

THE ACE TONES (group)
1982　*Local Hero*
　　　(UK) F

HARRY ACRES AND HIS BAND
1937　*Let's Make a Night of It*
　　　(ABPC) F

THE ACT SUPERB (poses)
1936　*Stars On Parade*
　　　(Butcher) F

THE ADAJIO TRIO (dancers)
1930　*Classic v Jazz*
　　　(Gainsborough)
1930　*Toyland*
　　　(Gainsborough)
　　　"Nila"
1930　*Gypsy Land*
　　　(Gainsborough)
　　　"Harlequin Dance"

PAUL ADAM AND HIS MAYFAIR MUSIC
(band)
1951　*London Entertains*
　　　(New Realm) F

THE ADAMS SISTERS (dancers)
1929　*Pathe Magazine 1*
　　　"Fan Dance"

JOE ADANI (human billiard table)
1932　*Ideal Cinemagazine 297*
1934　*Pathe Pictorial 879*

ADELPHI GIRLS (dancers)
1930　*Elstree Calling*
　　　(BIP) F
　　　"My Heart Is Saying"

LARRY ADLER (harmonica)
1937　*Calling All Stars*
　　　(British Lion) F
　　　"Stardust"
　　　"St Louis Blues"
1938　*Saint Martin's Lane*
　　　(ABPC) F
　　　"Wear a Straw Hat in the Rain"

JEAN ADRIENNE (singer)
1934　*The Broken Rosary*
　　　(Butcher) F
　　　"Somewhere a Voice is Calling"
　　　"Speak to Me of Love"

ADZIDO PAN-AFRICAN DANCE COMPANY
1991　*Ama*
　　　(Efiri) F

AFRIQUE (impersonator)
1935　*Pathetone 256*
　　　(as Richard Tauber, Paul Robeson)
1935　*Pathe Pictorial 906*
1936　*Pathe Pictorial NS 21*
1936　*Grand Finale*
　　　(Paramount) F
　　　(as Richard Tauber, George Robey)
1936　*Digging for Gold*
　　　(Ace) F
　　　(as Richard Tauber, George Robey,
　　　Wallace Beery)
1937　*Let's Make a Night of It*
　　　(ABPC) F
　　　(as Richard Tauber, Wallace Beery,
　　　Arthur Tracy)
1939　*Discoveries*
　　　(Vogue) F
　　　(as Richard Tauber, G B Shaw)
1940　*Pathetone 523*
　　　(as G B Shaw, Maurice Chevalier,
　　　Adolf Hitler)
1944　*English Without Tears*
　　　(GFD) F

AIDA'S DOGS (animal act)
1902　*Mademoiselle Aida and Her Troupe*
　　　of Performing Dogs
　　　(Warwick)

MEG AIKMAN (busker)
1968　*Popdown*
　　　(New Realm) F

CHERIE AND DON ALASANDRO (dancers)
1937　*It's a Twist*
　　　(Ace Cinemagazine)
　　　"Rumba"

ROSE ALBA (singer)
1955　*Shadow of a Man*
　　　(New Realm) F
　　　"Shadow of the Man I Love"
　　　"Blow the Man Down"

THE ALBERTS (comedy band)
    1967 *Bang!*
         (Godfrey)

ROBERT ALBINI (singer)
    1938 *Now Beat It*
         (Ace Cinemagazine)
         "Willow in the Rain"

EDITH ALBORD AND FRANK ROWE
(singers)
    1906 *Home to Our Mountains*
         (Chronophone)
    1906 *Miserere*
         (Chronophone)

BOBBIE ALDERSON (singer)
    1929 *Song Copation*
         (BIP)
         "Walking With Susie"
         "Funny That Way"
         "You Can't Make Me Feel Blue"
    1929 *Musical Medley*
         (BIP)
    1939 *Pathetone 494*

CECIL ALDIN (cartoonist)
    1931 *Ideal Cinemagazine 272*

BARRY ALDIS (broadcaster)
    1963 *Blind Corner*
         (Mancunian) F

ALENE AND EVANS (acrobats)
    1933 *Ideal Cinemagazine 368*

**ALEC ALEXANDER AND HIS MELODY
BOYS** (band)
    1931 *Stepping Stones*
         (Benstead) F
         "Lady of the Crinoline"
         "Ladies of the Night"

ALEXIS AND DORRANO (dancers)
    1934 *Pathe Pictorial 870*
         "Danse Apache"

ALEXIS AND ISOLDE (adagio)
    1936 *Pathe Pictorial NS 36*
         "You Are My Song Divine"

ALFREDO AND HIS GYPSY BAND
    1931 *Pathetone 91*
         "The Blue Danube"
         "You Will Remember Vienna"
    1932 *Maid of the Mountains*
         (BIP) F
    1934 *Pathetone 208*
         "Black Eyes"

ALHAMBRA GIRLS (dancers)
    1896 *Dancing Girls*
         (Paul)

    1896 *Trilby Burlesque*
         (Paul)

ALAN ALLAN (escapologist)
    1950 *New Pictorial 295*
    1951 *New Pictorial 340*

AMELIA ALLEN (ballerina)
    1925 *Eve's Film Review*

**CHARLOTTE ALLEN AND JOHNNY
BRODERICK** (comedy singers)
    1937 *Calling All Stars*
         (British Lion) F
         "The Last Rose of Summer"

CHESNEY ALLEN
see **BUD FLANAGAN AND CHESNEY
ALLEN** and **THE CRAZY GANG**

DAVID ALLEN AND GANG (group)
    1973 *Glastonbury Fayre*
         (Goodtimes) F

FRITZI AND RUTH ALLEN (aerialists)
    1952 *New Pictorial 385*

JILL ALLEN (singer)
    1946 *Walking On Air*
         (Piccadilly) F

JUDY ALLEN (singer)
    1950 *Rainbow Round the Corner*
         (Sanders)

LES ALLEN (singer)
    1931 *The Rosary*
         (Twickenham) F
         "The Rosary"
    1935 *Heat Wave*
         (Gainsborough) F
         "If Your Father Only Knew"
         "San Felipe"

MAUD ALLEN (dancer)
    1908 *The Great Salome Dance*
         (Tyler)

NAT ALLEN AND HIS BAND
    1944 *Pathe Pictorial 409*
         "On the Beach at Bali Bali"
    1944 *Pathe Pictorial 425*
         "Radio Red Cross Quiz"

RAYMOND ALLEN (tenor)
    1941 *Pathe Pictorial 290*
         "It Is Only a Tiny Garden"
    1943 *Pathe Pictorial 370*
         "I Heard You Singing"

THE ALLEY CATS (group)
    1957 *Pathe Pictorial 133*
         "Listen On"

THE ALLEY CATS (group)
1981 *Urgh! A Music War*
(Whito) Γ
"Nothing Means Nothing Anymore"

NORMAN ALLIN (bass)
1931 *Pathetone 58*
"Song of the Flea"
1938 *Pathe Pictorial NS 111*
"A Sergeant of the Line"

JEAN ALLISTONE
see **MRS MURGATROYD AND MRS
WINTERBOTTOM**

ROBERT ALLSTONE (singer)
1906 *There Is a Green Hill Far Away*
(Chronophone)

ALMA AND BOBBY (entertainers)
1943 *Up With the Lark*
(New Realm) F

ALMOST HUMAN (group)
1982 *Listen to London*
(White) F

ALOMA HAWAIIANS (dancers)
1931 *Ideal Cinemagazine 262*

**ISABELITA ALONSO AND MILO AMADO
ESTUDIANTINA** (singer/band)
1947 *New Pictorial 139*
"Alma Llamera"

GITTA ALPAR (soprano)
1935 *I Give My Heart*
(BIP) F
"I Give My Heart"
"Before We Met"
"Now I Have Found You"
"Good Luck"
"Loneliness"
"The Dubarry"
1936 *Everything In Life*
(Columbia) F
"Everything in Life"
"My First Thought Is You"
"Hearts Never Know"
"In the Spring"
"Take My Hands"
"Everybody's Dancing"
1936 *Guilty Melody*
(ABFD) F

NINA ALVIS AND CAPLA (dancers)
1936 *Murder at the Cabaret*
(Paramount) F

AMADEUS QUARTET (musicians)
1994 *Death and the Maiden*
(Kramer) F
"String Quartet No. 14"

AMAZULU (group)
1986 *Straight to Hell*
(Island) F

JULIE AMBER (singer)
1959 *Sweet Beat*
(Archway) F

AMBROSE AND HIS ORCHESTRA
1934 *Surprise Item*
(International)
1936 *Soft Lights and Sweet Music*
(British Lion) F
"We're Tops on Saturday Night"
"Lost My Rhythm"
"Piccadilly"
"Limehouse Blues"
"Aloha Oe"
"Diga Diga Doo"
"She"
"South American Joe"
"When Day Is Done"
1937 *Calling All Stars*
(British Lion) F
"Peanut Vendor"
"Serenade in the Night"
"Body and Soul"
"Eleven More Months"
"Rhythm's Okay in Harlem"
"When Day Is Done"
1938 *Kicking the Moon Around*
(Vogue) F
"Mayfair Merry Go Round"
"It's the Rhythm in Me"
"Two Bouquets"
1940 *Pathetone 513*
"Franklin D. Roosevelt Jones"

AMBROSIAN SINGERS
1989 *Valmont*
(Burrill) F
"A Knight Riding"
"Love If You Will Come to Me"
"Pity the Fate"

AMELIO (boy accordionist)
1936 *Fare's Fair*
(Ace)

AMERICAN COMEDY FOUR (singers)
1900 *Sally in Our Alley*
(Phono-Bio-Tableaux)

CARLOS AMES (harpist)
1933 *Ideal Cinemagazine 363*
1939 *Pathe Pictorial NS 147*
1950 *Round Rainbow Corner*
(Sanders)

CHARLES ANCASTER (juggler)
1938 *Pathe Pictorial NS 118*

INGA ANDERSEN (singer)
1938 *Take Off That Hat*
(Viking) F

HEDLI ANDERSON (singer)
1940 *Hullo Fame*
(British Films) F
1948 *Colonel Bogey*
(GFD) F

JOSÉ AND HEATHER ANDERSON
(dancers)
1935 *Pathetone 253*

LAWRENCE ANDERSON (impersonator)
1933 *Ideal Cinemagazine 365*

JULES ANDRÉ AND FELICITY GARRATT
(dancers)
1927 *Eve's Film Review 333*

ANDRÉE AND CURTIS (dancers)
1929 *Eve's Film Review 440*
1930 *Eve's Film Review 474*
1938 *Mountains o' Mourne*
(Butcher) F

EAMONN ANDREWS (broadcaster)
1951 *London Entertains*
(New Realm) F
1955 *Three Cases of Murder*
(British Lion) F
1959 *Left Right and Centre*
(British Lion) F

TED ANDREWS AND HIS GIRL FRIEND
(singers)
1938 *Pathe Pictorial NS 103*
"You Can't Stop Me From
Dreaming"

AVRIL ANGERS (comedienne)
1948 *Lucky Mascot*
(UA) F
"Home Sweet Home"
1949 *Skimpy in the Navy*
(Adelphi) F
"That Dusty Western Trail"
"Hibernian Lament"
1950 *Miss Pilgrim's Progress*
(Angel) F
1951 *The Six Men*
(Eros) F
1954 *Don't Blame the Stork*
(Adelphi) F
1956 *Bond of Fear*
(Eros) F
1956 *The Green Man*
(Grenadier) F
1957 *Light Fingers*
(Archway) F
1960 *Dentist in the Chair*
(Renown) F

1964 *Devils of Darkness*
(Planet) F
1965 *Be My Guest*
(Rank) F
1966 *The Family Way*
(British Lion) F
1967 *Two a Penny*
(Worldwide) F
1969 *The Best House in London*
(MGM) F
1970 *There's a Girl in My Soup*
(Columbia) F
1971 *Mr Forbush and the Penguins*
(EMI) F
1973 *Gollocks*
(Target) F
1976 *Confessions of a Driving Instructor*
(Columbia) F

HARRY ANGERS (comedian)
1933 *Oh for a Plumber*
(Delta)
1938 *My Irish Molly*
(ABPC) F

BRUCE ANGRAVE (cartoonist)
1940 *Pathe Pictorial 205*

THE ANIMALS (group)
1964 *UK Swings Again*
(Baim)
"Baby Let Me Take You Home"
1965 *Pop Gear*
(Pathe) F
"The House of the Rising Sun"
"Don't Let Me Be Misunderstood"
1967 *Tonite Let's All Make Love in
London*
(Lorrimer) F
"When I Was Young"

ANITA AND ARMAND (dancers)
1950 *A Ray of Sunshine*
(Adelphi) F

ANITA, CHARLES AND JACK (apache)
1936 *British Lion Varieties 2; 5*

BETTY ANKERS
see **PAT KAYE AND BETTY ANKERS**

ADAM ANT (singer)
1978 *Jubilee*
(Cinegate) F
"Plastic Surgery"

ANTONIO (Spanish dancer)
1960 *Climb Up the Wall*
(New Realm) F

**DAVE APOLLON AND HIS ROMANTIC
SERENADERS** (band)
1935 *In Town Tonight*
(British Lion) F

THE APPLEJACKS (group)
1964 *Just For You*
      (British Lion) F
1964 *UK Swings Again*
      (Baim)
      "Tell Me When"
      "Like Dreamers Do"

ROSIE AQUINALDO (contortionist)
1901 *Mademoiselle Rosie Aquinaldo*
      (Warwick)

ARCHIE AND HIS JUVENILE BAND
1936 *Dodging the Dole*
      (Mancunian) F
1940 *Music Hall Personalities 18*
      (reissue: *Dodging the Dole*)

ARGENTINE ACCORDION BAND
1935 *Pathe Pictorial 910*
      "In a Monastery Garden"

PEARL ARGYLE (dancer)
1934 *Chu Chin Chow*
      (Gainsborough) F
1934 *Adventure Ltd*
      (Paramount) F
1935 *Royal Cavalcade*
      (BIP) F
1936 *Things To Come*
      (UA) F

ARMANDUS (quick-change)
1902 *Armandus, Quick Change Artiste*
      (Warwick)

JOAN ARMATRADING (singer)
1987 *The Secret Policeman's Third Ball*
      (Virgin) F
      "I Love It When You Call Me
      Names"

ARNAUD, PEGGY AND READY (acrobatic
dancers)
1937 *Let's Make a Night of It*
      (ABPC) F

ARNAUT BROTHERS (musical clowns)
1928 *Phototone 14*
1928 *Eve's Film Review 385*
1939 *Music Hall Parade*
      (Butcher) F
1940 *Cavalcade of Variety*
      (reissue: *Music Hall Parade*)

ARNLEY AND GLORIA (dancers)
1945 *Home Sweet Home*
      (Mancunian) F
1946 *Randle and All That*
      (reissue: *Home Sweet Home*)
1971 *Top of the Bill*
      (Butcher) F

DORIS ARNOLD (pianist)
1933 *Radio Parade*
      (BIP) F
1936 *Sunshine Ahead*
      (Baxter) F
      "Six Piano Jazz Symphony"

MAURICE ARNOLD SEXTET
1948 *Jivin' and Jammin'*
      (Piccadilly)
      "Three Blind Mice"
      "Honeysuckle Rose"
      "These Foolish Things"

TOM ARNOLD'S CIRCUS
1948 *The Big Show*
      (Rayant)

THE ARTEMUS BOYS (comedy/songs)
1945 *Here Comes the Sun*
      (Baxter) F
1946 *The Grand Escapade*
      (Baxter) F
1947 *Fortune Lane*
      (Baxter) F

HAZEL ASCOT (child dancer)
1937 *Talking Feet*
      (Baxter) F
      "Talking Feet"
      "Tapping Out Rhythm"
      "Jack's Ashore"
1938 *Stepping Toes*
      (Baxter) F
      "You Must Have This"
      "Rhythm of My Heart"
      "Join the Army"

DUGGIE ASCOT'S DANCING GIRLS
1934 *Love Mirth Melody*
      (Mancunian) F

ARTY ASH (comedian)
1931 *Pathetone 89*
      "Please Mr Constable"

BRYAN ASHBRIDGE (dancer)
1960 *The Royal Ballet*
      (Rank) F
      "Swan Lake"

VIVIAN ASHDOWN (boy drummer)
1937 *Dust Up*
      (Ace Cinemagazine)

IRIS ASHLEY (singer)
1933 *Heads We Go*
      (BIP) F
      "Whistling Under the Moon"

ROBERT ASHLEY (baritone)
1936 *Pathe Pictorial NS 30*
      "Love Remembers Everything"

1936 *Pathetone 313*
"Moon for Sale"
1936 *Such Is Life*
(Incorporated) F
1937 *Pathe Pictorial NS 49*
"Without a Song"
1938 *Pathetone 425*
"My Heart Will Never Sing Again"
1938 *Pathe Pictorial NS 94*
"County Clare"
1938 *Pathe Pictorial NS 127*
"Deep Dream River"
1939 *Pathetone 465*
"Killarney"
1939 *Pathe Pictorial NS 183*
"Garden in Granada"
1940 *Pathe Pictorial 204*
"Lights of London"
1940 *Pathe Pictorial 239*
"Absent Friends"
1941 *Pathe Pictorial 278*
"Room 504"
1941 *Pathe Pictorial 300*
"The London I Love"
1942 *Pathe Pictorial 311*
"I'll Walk Beside You"
1942 *Pathe Pictorial 326*
"The First Lullaby"

FRANCES ASHMAN (singer)
1997 *Nil By Mouth*
(SE8) F
"Peculiar Groove"
"Pandora"
"My Heart Belongs To Daddy"

DOREEN ASHTON'S JUBILEE TROUPE
(dancers)
1943 *Variety Jubilee*
(Butcher) F
"Can-Can"

FREDERICK ASHTON (dancer)
1951 *Tales of Hoffmann*
(London) F
1971 *Tales of Beatrix Potter*
(EMI) F

ASHTON AND RAWSON (singers)
1928 *Ashton and Rawson*
(Phonofilm)

ARTHUR ASKEY (comedian)
1937 *Calling All Stars*
(British Lion) F
1937 *Pathe Pictorial NS 43*
"The Bee Song"
1937 *Pathe Pictorial NS 89*
"The Moth"
1938 *Pathe Pictorial NS 115*
"A Pretty Bird"
"Big Hearted Arthur"
1940 *Band Waggon*
(Gainsborough) F

"A Pretty Bird"
"Big Hearted Arthur"
"The Bee Song"
1940 *Charley's (Big-Hearted) Aunt*
(Gainsborough) F
"Today I Feel So Happy"
1940 *Pathe Gazette 36*
"The Proposal"
1941 *The Ghost Train*
(Gainsborough) F
"The Seaside Band"
1941 *I Thank You*
(Gainsborough) F
"Hello to the Sun"
"Let's Get Hold of Hitler"
"Half of Everything Is Yours"
1942 *Back Room Boy*
(Gainsborough) F
1942 *King Arthur Was a Gentleman*
(Gainsborough) F
"You Know What King Arthur Said"
"Honey On My Mind"
1942 *The Nose Has It*
(Gainsborough)
1943 *Miss London Limited*
(Gainsborough) F
"The Moth"
"I'm Only Me"
1944 *Bees in Paradise*
(Gainsborough) F
"I'm a Wolf on My Mother's Side"
1945 *New Pictorial 48*
1946 *The Rake's Big-Hearted Progress*
ADVERT
1947 *Taking the Chair*
ADVERT
1947 *How to Take Gas*
ADVERT
1955 *The Love Match*
(Group 3) F
1956 *Ramsbottom Rides Again*
(British Lion) F
1959 *Make Mine a Million*
(British Lion) F
1959 *Friends and Neighbours*
(British Lion) F
1972 *The Alf Garnett Saga*
(Columbia) F
1977 *End of Term*
(Oppidan)
1978 *Rosie Dixon Night Nurse*
(Columbia) F

MICHAEL ASPEL (broadcaster)
1962 *Moment of Decision*
(Anglo)
1969 *The Magic Christian*
(Grand) F

THE ASPIDISTRAS (burlesque singers)
1934 *Lilies of the Field*
(B&D) F
1941 *Pathe Pictorial 259*
1941 *Pathe Pictorial 289*

7

1941 *Gert and Daisy's Weekend*
(Butcher) F
"Convent Bells"
1941 *Kipps*
(TCF) F
1941 *The Saving Song*
(National Savings)
"Sailing Sailing"

BETTY ASTELL (song and dance)
(films as actress not listed)
1933 *Pathetone 173*
"What Have We Got to Lose?"
1935 *Sound Advice*
(NFC) ADVERT
"Bubbling Over With Love"
1935 *Pictorial Organ Interludes*
(Ace)
"The Blues"
1935 *Equity Musical Revue Series*
(British Lion)
"No More You"
"Sitting On a Rainbow"
"Something Came and Got Me"
"What Are Little Girls Made Of?"
"You've Got Me Crying Again"
"I've Got the World on a String"
1936 *Jack of All Trades*
(Gainsborough) F
1942 *Pathe Pictorial 331*
1945 *A Holiday Ramble*
(Renown)

JOE ASTON AND RENEE (dancers)
1955 *The Weapon*
(Eros) F

OLLY ASTON AND HIS BAND
1938 *Take Off That Hat*
(Viking) F

A C ASTOR (ventriloquist)
1928 *A C Astor with Sentimental Mac*
(Phonofilm)
1932 *Pathetone 116*
"Wedding Bells Are Ringing for
Sally"
1932 *Pathetone 137*
1936 *Pathe Pictorial NS 20*
"Spike Sullivan's Girl"

ATHLETICO SPIZZ '80 (group)
1981 *Urgh! A Music War*
(White) F
"Where's Captain Kirk?"

THE PERCY ATHOS BEAUTIES (dancers)
1926 *Eve's Film Review 254*

THE PERCY ATHOS FOLLIES (dancers)
1937 *Let's Make a Night of It*
(ABPC) F

CHET ATKINS (American guitarist)
1987 *The Secret Policeman's Third Ball*
(Virgin) Г
"Imagine"

ROWAN ATKINSON (comedian)
1979 *The Secret Policeman's Ball*
(Tigon) F
1982 *The Secret Policeman's Other Ball*
(UIP) F
1983 *Dead on Time*
(Hobbs)
1983 *Never Say Never Again*
(Columbia-EMI-Warner) F
1989 *The Tall Guy*
(Virgin) F
1994 *Four Weddings and a Funeral*
(Working Title) F
1997 *Bean*
(PolyGram) F

WINIFRED ATWELL (pianist)
1953 *It's a Grand Life*
(Mancunian) F
"Dixie Boogie"
"Britannia Rag"

THE AU PAIRS (group)
1981 *Urgh! A Music War*
(White) F
"Come Again"

GUS AUBREY (comedian)
1942 *Somewhere in Camp*
(Mancunian) F
1943 *Somewhere in Civvies*
(Mancunian) F
1947 *When You Come Home*
(Butcher) F

THE BRIAN AUGER TRINITY (group)
1968 *Popdown*
(New Realm) F
"Wheels on Fire"

AURA (soprano)
1930 *Aura 1; 2*
(West)

CHARLES AUSTIN (comedian)
1912 *Lt Daring and the Plans of the
Minefield*
(B&C)
1916 *Parker's Weekend*
(Homeland)
1918 *Exploits of Parker*
(Ruffells)
1927 *Eve's Film Review 295*
"Aladdin"
1928 *Eve's Film Review 362*
1931 *Pathetone 41*
1931 *Hot Heir*
(Gainsborough)
1942 *We'll Smile Again*
(British National) F

AUSTRALIAN AIR ACES (motorcyclists)
1939   *Music Hall Parade*
       (Butcher) F
1940   *Cavalcade of Variety*
       (reissue: *Music Hall Parade*)
1943   *Down Melody Lane*
       F (reissue: *Music Hall Parade*)

AUSTRALIAN BOYS (entertainers)
1936   *Pathe Pictorial NS 14*

FRANKIE AVALON (singer)
1967   *Sumuru*
       (Anglo) F
1969   *Haunted House of Horror*
       (Tigon) F

AVANT BROTHERS (acrobatic dancers)
1940   *Pathetone 541*
       "Dolls on Parade"
1944   *Pathe Pictorial 413*
       "Spirit of Liberty"

NAT D. AYER (singer)
1943   *Variety Jubilee*
       (Butcher) F
       "Song of the Marching Men"
1943   *Highlights of Variety 25*
       (reissue: *Variety Jubilee*)

JANE AYR (singer)
1935   *Equity Musical Revue 1*
       (British Lion)

CHARLES AZNAVOUR (French singer)
1969   *The Games*
       (TCF) F
1973   *The Blockhouse*
       (Galactacus) F
1974   *And Then There Were None*
       (Filibuster) F

DON AZPIAZU AND HIS BAND
1933   *Pathe Pictorial 792*
       "Amor Navigo"

BABETTE (contortioniste)
1934 *Screen Vaudeville*
(Vaudeville)

THE BACHELORS (group)
1963 *It's All Over Town*
(British Lion) F
"The Stars Still Remember"
1964 *Just For You*
(British Lion) F
1965 *I've Gotta Horse*
(Warner) F
"When You're Far Far Away"
"He's Got the Whole World In His Hands"

BACK TO THE PLANET (group)
1996 *Glastonbury: The Movie*
(Starlight) F
"Teenage Turtles"

MAI BACON (comedienne)
1935 *The Public Life of Henry the Ninth*
(Hammer) F
1936 *Cabaret Nights 5*
(Highbury)
1936 *Chick*
(B&D) F
1937 *Heavily Married*
(Krackerjack) F
1938 *Second Best Bed*
(GFD) F
1938 *Double or Quits*
(Warner) F
1950 *Up for the Cup*
(Byron) F
1967 *I Like Birds*
(Border) F

MAX BACON (comedian)
1936 *Soft Lights and Sweet Music*
(British Lion) F
"Cohen the Crooner"
1937 *Calling All Stars*
(British Lion) F
"When Gimble Hits the Cymbal"
1938 *Kicking the Moon Around*
(Vogue) F
1942 *King Arthur Was a Gentleman*
(Gainsborough) F
1943 *Miss London Limited*
(Gainsborough) F
1944 *Bees in Paradise*
(Gainsborough) F
1944 *Give Us the Moon*
(Gainsborough) F
1952 *The Gambler and the Lady*
(Hammer) F
1953 *Take a Powder*
(Apex) F
1960 *The Entertainer*
(UA) F
1962 *Play It Cool*
(Anglo) F

1963 *The Eyes of Annie Jones*
(Rank) F
1963 *Crooks in Cloisters*
(ABPC) F
1966 *The Sandwich Man*
(Rank) F
1966 *The Whisperers*
(UA) F
1967 *Privilege*
(Universal) F
1968 *Chitty Chitty Bang Bang*
(UA) F
1969 *The Nine Ages of Nakedness*
(Orb) F
1973 *Along the Way*
(EMI) F
1974 *Stardust*
(EMI) F

BAD MANNERS (group)
1981 *Dance Craze*
(Osiris) F
"Ne Ne Na Na Nu Nu"
"Wooly Bully"
"Lip Up Fatty"
"Inner London Violence"

ENA BAGA (organ and piano)
1973 *An Acre of Seats in a Garden of Dreams*
(Contemporary) F
1992 *Chaplin*
(Caroleo) F

TARRANT BAILEY JR (banjoist)
1934 *Pathe Pictorial 858*
"Donkey Laugh"
1936 *Pathe Pictorial NS 30*
1937 *Pathetone 400*
1939 *Pathe Pictorial NS 158*
"Snakes and Ladders"
1942 *Pathe Pictorial 303*
1943 *Pathe Pictorial 375*
"Streamline"

SYDNEY BAINES AND HIS BAND
1935 *Royal Cavalcade*
(BIP) F

RAYMOND BAIRD (saxophonist)
1936 *Stars On Parade*
(Butcher) F
"William Tell"
1938 *Highlights of Variety 8*
(reissue: *Stars On Parade*)

BRUCE BAIRNSFATHER (cartoonist)
1924 *Old Bill Through the Ages*
(Ideal) F
1941 *Pathe Pictorial 286*

BELLE BAKER (singer)
1935 *Charing Cross Road*
(British Lion) F
"Roadway of Romance"

CHET BAKER (musician)
1963 *The Stolen Hours*
(UA) F

GEORGE BAKER (baritone)
1929 *Splinters*
(B&D) F
1930 *The Loves of Robert Burns*
(B&D) F
1930 *Peace of Mind*
(B&D)
1932 *Pathe Pictorial 722*
"I Travel the Road"
1932 *Pathe Pictorial 752*
"The Floral Dance"
1933 *Waltz Time*
(Gaumont) F
"A Glass of Golden Bubbles"
1933 *My Lucky Star*
(W&F) F
1936 *Sunshine Ahead*
(Baxter) F
"Faust"
1941 *The Saving Song*
(National Savings)

HYLDA BAKER (comedienne)
1960 *Saturday Night and Sunday Morning*
(Woodfall) F
1962 *She Knows Y' Know*
(Grand National) F
1967 *Up the Junction*
(Paramount) F
1968 *Oliver*
(Columbia) F
1972 *Nearest and Dearest*
(Hammer) F

JOE BAKER (comedian)
1951 *London Entertains*
(New Realm) F
1960 *Girls of Latin Quarter*
(New Realm) F
1961 *Nearly a Nasty Accident*
(Britannia) F
1966 *Where the Bullets Fly*
(Puck) F
1975 *Side By Side*
(GTO) F
1977 *Confessions from a Holiday Camp*
(Columbia) F

JOSEPHINE BAKER (French singer)
1931 *Pathetone 79*
1933 *Pathe Pictorial 810*
"I'll Sing My Way"

KENNY BAKER (American tenor)
1939 *The Mikado*
(GFD) F
"A Wandering Minstrel"
"The Sun Whose Rays"

KENNY BAKER (trumpet)
1954 *Face the Music*
(Hammer) F
"Carnival of Venice"
"I've Got a Man"
"Got You On My Mind"
"Nobody Knows the Trouble I've Seen"
"Melancholy Baby"
1955 *Eric Winstone Band Show*
(Hammer)
1986 *Mona Lisa*
(Palace) F

BAKER, DOVE AND ALLEN (jugglers)
1943 *Pathe Pictorial 386*

JOAN BAKEWELL (television personality)
1968 *The Touchables*
(TCF) F
1980 *The Alternative Miss World*
(Tigon) F

BALAM (violinist)
1930 *Gypsy Land*
(Gainsborough)
"Hungarian Rhapsody"

GEORGES BALANCHINE (dancer)
1929 *Dark Red Roses*
(BSFP) F

BALANESCU QUARTET (musicians)
1995 *Angels and Insects*
(Playhouse) F

LONG JOHN BALDRY (singer)
1971 *Up the Chastity Belt*
(EMI) F

BOBBY BALL
see **(TOMMY) CANNON AND (BOBBY) BALL**

KENNY BALL AND HIS JAZZMEN
1962 *It's Trad Dad*
(Columbia) F
"Beale Street Blues"
"1919 March"
1963 *Live It Up*
(Rank) F
"Rondo"
"Hand Me Down My Walkin' Shoes"
1979 *And All That Jazz*
(Finecord)

MATTHEW BALLESTER (singer)
1996 *Glastonbury: The Movie*
(Starlight) F
"Garage"

BALLET MONTPARNASSE (dancers)
1965 *Carry On Cowboy*
(Anglo) F

BALLIOL AND MERTON (comedy acrobats)
- 1927 *The Arcadians*
  (Gaumont) F
- 1928 *Champagne*
  (BIP) F
- 1932 *Pathe Pictorial 123*
- 1936 *Queen of Hearts*
  (ATP) F

BALLIOL AND TILLER (comedy acrobats)
- 1937 *Old Mother Riley*
  (Butcher) F

ANDRE BALOG (violinist)
- 1934 *Pathe Pictorial 870*
  "Trees"

FREDDIE BAMBERGER (comedy pianist)
- 1936 *Pathe Pictorial 927*
  "Dizzy Fingers"
  "Red Sails in the Sunset"
  "Trees"
- 1940 *Pathe Pictorial 519*
  "Who's Taking You Home Tonight?"

FREDDIE BAMBERGER AND PAM
(comedy)
- 1950 *A Ray of Sunshine*
  (Adelphi) F

BAMBERGER AND BISHOP (comedy
musicians)
- 1935 *Equity Musical Revue 5*
  (British Lion)
- 1935 *Equity Musical Revue 9*
  (British Lion)
- 1935 *Equity Musical Revue 10*
  (British Lion)
  "Happy Go Lucky You"
  "Paradise"

BAND OF ANGELS (group)
- 1964 *Just For You*
  (British Lion) F

BAND OF H.M. COLDSTREAM GUARDS
- 1929 *Armistice*
  (BIP)
- 1943 *Variety Jubilee*
  (Butcher) F
  "Song of the Marching Men"
- 1944 *Dreaming*
  (Baxter) F

BAND OF H.M. GRENADIER GUARDS
- 1931 *Pathetone 82*
- 1940 *You Will Remember*
  (British Lion) F
  "Soldiers of the King"

BAND OF H.M. IRISH GUARDS
- 1945 *Great Day*
  (RKO) F

BAND OF H.M. ROYAL MARINES
- 1937 *Talking Feet*
  (Baxter) F
  "Jack's Ashore"
  "Rule Britannia"
- 1937 *Okay For Sound*
  (Gainsborough) F
  "The Fleet's Not in Port Very Long"

BAND OF H.M. SCOTS GUARDS
- 1935 *Royal Cavalcade*
  (BIP) F
  "God Save the King"

BAND OF H.M. WELSH GUARDS
- 1929 *Armistice*
  (BIP)

BAND OF THE CAMERON HIGHLANDERS
- 1908 *A Visit to the Seaside*
  (Kinemacolor)

BAND OF THE PLYMOUTH ROYAL MARINES
- 1953 *Innocents in Paris*
  (Romulus) F

BAND OF THE ROYAL ARTILLERY
- 1939 *Pathe Pictorial NS 169*
  "Lohengrin"
- 1939 *Pathetone 472*
  "Coronation Bells"

BANJULELE BABIES (dancers)
- 1926 *London's Famous Cabarets*
  (Parkinson)

CHRIS BARBER AND HIS JAZZ BAND
- 1955 *Momma Don't Allow*
  (BFI)
  "Momma Don't Allow"
  "The Blues Knocking On My Door"
- 1956 *Chris Barber's Jazz Band*
  (BFI)
  "Poor Man's Blues"
  "Lead Me On"
  "Lord You've Been Good to Me"
- 1959 *Look Back in Anger*
  (ABPC) F
- 1962 *It's Trad Dad*
  (Columbia) F
  "It's Trad Dad"
  "Yellow Dog"
  "When the Saints Go Marching In"
  "Down By the Riverside"
- 1962 *Chris Barber Bandstand*
  (British Lion)
  "Revival"
  "Little Liza Jane"
  "Mamma He Treats Your Daughter Mean"
  "Can't Afford To Do It"
  "New Orleans Street Parade"
  "Mean Mistreater"

1968 *Popdown*
      (New Realm) F

JOYCE BARBOUR AND CLAY SMITH
(dancers)
1921 *Around the Town 88*
      (Gaumont)

ROY BARBOUR (comedian)
1936 *Dodging the Dole*
      (Mancunian) F
1937 *Music Hall Personalities 1*
      (reissue: *Dodging the Dole*)

THE BARBOUR BROTHERS (stilt-walkers)
1952 *For Your Entertainment 4*
      (Gaumont)
      "Ask a Policeman"
1974 *Mister Quilp*
      (EMI) F

IGO BARCINSKI (dancer)
1950 *The Dancing Years*
      (ABPC) F

WILKIE BARD (comedian)
1928 *The Nightwatchman*
      (BSFP)
1928 *The Cleaner*
      (BSFP)

**DON MARINO BARETTO AND HIS
RHUMBA BAND**
1940 *Under Your Hat*
      (Grand National) F
      "I Won't Do the Conga"
1941 *Pathe Pictorial 267*
      "Tabu"

ERIC BARKER (comedian)
(films as actor not listed)
1937 *Carry On London*
      (Ace) F
1937 *West End Frolics*
      (Ace) F
1937 *Concert Party*
      (Ace) F
1938 *On Velvet*
      (AIP) F
1941 *Seeing Isn't Believing*
      (Solidox) ADVERT
1947 *Pathe News*
      "Waterlogged Spa"

JACK AND DAPHNE BARKER (singers)
1947 *New Pictorial 156*
      "Believe It Or Not"

RONNIE BARKER (comedian)
1958 *Wonderful Things*
      (ABPC) F
1962 *Kill or Cure*
      (MGM) F
1963 *Father Came Too*
      (Rank) F

1963 *The Cracksman*
      (ABP) F
1963 *Doctor in Distress*
      (Rank) F
1964 *The Bargee*
      (Warner) F
1964 *A Home of Your Own*
      (British Lion)
1965 *Runaway Railway*
      (CFF) F
1967 *The Man Outside*
      (Trio) F
1968 *Ghost of a Chance*
      (CFF) F
1970 *Futtocks End*
      (British Lion)
1971 *The Magnificent Seven Deadly Sins*
      (Tigon) F
1979 *Porridge*
      (ITC) F

BARNBOROUGH COLLIERY ORCHESTRA
1932 *Black Diamonds*
      (Hanmer) F

ALMA BARNES (impressionist)
1926 *Alma Barnes*
      (Phonofilm)

BILLIE BARNES (singer)
also known as Binnie Barnes
(films as actress not listed)
1929 *Billie Barnes*
      (BSFP)
      "Sing Me a Baby Song"
1930 *Billie Barnes*
      (Gainsborough)

BINNIE BARNES (singer)
also known as Billie Barnes
(films as actress not listed)
1933 *Pathe Pictorial 782*
      "I Guess I'll Have To Change My
      Plan"
1933 *Their Night Out*
      (BIP) F
      "Love to be Let or Sold"

FRANK BARNES (singer)
1909 *Home Again My Cherry Blossom*
      (Cinephone)

SALLY BARNES (comedienne)
1948 *Holidays With Pay*
      (Mancunian) F
      "The Natural Thing to Do"
1949 *Somewhere in Politics*
      (Mancunian) F
1959 *Make Mine a Million*
      (British Lion) F
1971 *Top of the Bill*
      (Butcher) F

VIOLET BARNES
see **WALLY FRYER AND VIOLET BARNES**

WINNIE BARNES (accordion)
1948 *Lucky Mascot*
(UA) F
"Flight of the Bumblebee"

LADY ISOBEL BARNET (television personality)
1955 *Simon and Laura*
(Rank) F

LUCILLE BARNETTE (singer)
1938 *Pathe Pictorial NS 108*

DOROTHEE BAROONE (singer)
1949 *It's a Wonderful Day*
(Equity) F
"I Like Singing"
"So Near My Heart"

IDA BARR (singer)
1936 *Happy Days Are Here Again*
(Argyle) F
"Fall In and Follow Me"
"Put Me Among the Girls"
1938 *Happy Days Revue*
F (reissue: *Happy Days Are Here Again*)
1940 *Laugh It Off*
(British National) F
"Growing Old Together"
1942 *Let the People Sing*
(British National) F

MICHAEL BARRATT (television personality)
1969 *The Magic Christian*
(Grand) F
1974 *Percy's Progress*
(EMI) F

AMANDA BARRIE (singer)
1965 *I've Gotta Horse*
(Warner) F
"Men"
"Problems"

MAXiNE BARRIE (singer)
1971 *The Fiend*
(Miracle) F
"Wash Me in His Blood"
"We Are One"
"Set Me Free"

THE BARRIE SISTERS/TWINS (song and dance)
1928 *British Screen Tatler 9*
1930 *Black and White*
(Gainsborough)
"Every Day Away from You"
1930 *Classic v Jazz*
(Gainsborough)
"Snake's Hips"
"Mickey Mouse"

1936 *Dodging the Dole*
(Mancunian) F
1938 *Music Hall Personalities 5*
(reissue: *Dodging the Dole*)

JONAH BARRINGTON (journalist)
1940 *Band Waggon*
(Gainsborough) F

RUTLAND BARRINGTON (singer)
1952 *The Story of Gilbert and Sullivan*
(London) F
"I Once Was a Very Abandoned Person"

CURLY PAT BARRY (singer)
1957 *Rock You Sinners*
(Small) F
"Stop It I Like It"

DORIS BARRY AND JOHN STEVENS (singers)
1937 *Footlights*
(Ace) F

JOHN BARRY (musician and composer)
1968 *Deadfall*
(TCF) F

THE JOHN BARRY SEVEN (band)
1958 *6.5 Special*
(Anglo) F
"You've Gotta Way"
"Every Which Way"
1960 *Beat Girl*
(Renown) F
"Beat Girl"
"The Stripper"
"It's Legal"
1963 *The Cool Mikado*
(Baim) F
"The Willow Twist"
1963 *It's All Happening*
(British Lion) F

BARRY AND GRAY (dancers)
1940 *Pathe Pictorial 207*

MICHAEL BARRYMORE (comedian)
1997 *Spice World*
(Fragile) F

DICK AND EDITH BARSTOW (dancers)
1929 *Eve's Film Review 402*

LIONEL BART (composer and musician)
1980 *The Alternative Miss World*
(Tigon) F

MICHAEL BARTLETT (singer)
1937 *The Lilac Domino*
(GFD) F
"You Are My Love Song"
"My Heart Will Be Dancing"

VERNON BARTLETT (broadcaster)
1934 *Death at Broadcasting House*
(Phoenix) F

REGGIE BARTON AND HIS BAND
1938 *Swing*
(Ace) F

SAM BARTON (trick cyclist)
1935 *Variety*
(Butcher) F
1936 *Stars On Parade*
(Butcher) F
1940 *Cavalcade of Variety*
(reissue: *Variety*)
1948 *For Old Times Sake*
(reissue: *Variety*)

JACK BARTY (comedian)
1930 *Pathetone 15*
1933 *This Is the Life*
(British Lion) F
1934 *My Song Goes Round the World*
(BIP) F
1935 *In Town Tonight*
(British Lion) F
1936 *Pathe Pictorial 345*
1936 *It's In the Bag*
(Warner) F
1936 *All In*
(Gainsborough) F
1937 *Take a Chance*
(Grosvenor) F
1937 *Talking Feet*
(Baxter) F
1938 *Stepping Toes*
(Baxter) F
"Kids! Kids!"
"Goodnight"
1939 *What Would You Do, Chums?*
(British National) F
1940 *Gaslight*
(British National) F

KENNETH BARWICK (singer)
1944 *Pathe Pictorial 433*

THE BASHFUL BOYS (comedians)
1935 *Pathe Pictorial 907*
1939 *Pathetone Parade of 1939*
F (reissue: *Pictorial 907*)

A W BASKCOMB (comedian)
1913 *The Staff Dinner*
(Urban)
1922 *Eve's Film Review 65*
"Snap"
1926 *Eve's Film Review 254*
1928 *Eve's Film Review 388*
"Sons of the Sea"
1929 *Eve's Film Review 408*
"Merry Moments"
1929 *Pathe Magazine 1*
1930 *Pathe Pictorial 631*

1930 *Eve's Film Review 488*
"Follow a Star"
1932 *The Lodger*
(Twickenham) F
1932 *The Midshipmaid*
(Gainsborough) F
1933 *The Good Companions*
(Gaumont) F

SHIRLEY BASSEY (singer)
1996 *La Passione*
(WEA) F

BASYL (novelty musician)
1936 *Pathe Pictorial NS 7*
"Love's Old Sweet Song"

H M BATEMAN (cartoonist)
1920 *Around the Town 14*
(Gaumont)
1931 *Gaumont Sound Mirror*

SIMON BATES (broadcaster)
1981 *Take It Or Leave It*
(GTO) F

THORPE BATES (singer)
1926 *Thorpe Bates*
(Phonofilm)
1928 *Chinese Moon*
(Phototone)
1928 *In a Japanese Garden*
(Phototone)
1928 *The Keys of Heaven*
(Phototone)
1935 *The Small Man*
(Baxter) F
1936 *Our Island*
(Alba) S

THE BAVERA TRIO (skaters)
1934 *Pathe Pictorial 826*
1936 *Pathe Pictorial NS 28*
1936 *Pathetone Parade of 1936*
F (reissue: *Pictorial 826*)

ART BAXTER AND HIS ROCKIN' SINNERS
(group)
1957 *Rock You Sinners*
(Small) F
"Rock You Sinners"
"Art's Theme"
"Dixieland Rock"

RAYMOND BAXTER (television personality)
1962 *The Fast Lady*
(Rank) F

STANLEY BAXTER (comedian)
1955 *Geordie*
(British Lion) F
1962 *Crooks Anonymous*
(Anglo) F

1962   *The Fast Lady*
       (Rank) F
1963   *Father Came Too*
       (Rank) F
1965   *Joey Boy*
       (British Lion) F

B.B.C. MYSTERY SINGER
1935   *Pathe Pictorial 881*
       "Thoughts"

B.B.C. SYMPHONY ORCHESTRA
1932   *Pathetone 144*
       "Land of Hope and Glory"
       (conductor Sir Adrian Boult)
1933   *Pathetone 151*
       "The Mastersingers"
1938   *Pathetone 451*
       (conductor Sir Henry Wood)

JEREMY BEADLE (television personality)
1995   *A Fistful of Fingers*
       (Wrightstuff) F

DOREEN BEAHAN
see **CHARLES THEBAULT AND DOREEN BEAHAN**

THE GEORGE BEAN GROUP
1967   *Privilege*
       (Universal) F

HARRY BEASLEY (comedian)
1924   *The Clicking of Cuthbert*
       (Stoll) S

THE BEAT (group)
1981   *Dance Craze*
       (Osiris) F
       "Ranking Full Stop"
       "Big Shot"
       "Twist 'n' Crawl"
       "Mirror in the Bathroom"
       "Roughrider"

THE BEATLES (group)
see also **GEORGE HARRISON, JOHN LENNON, PAUL McCARTNEY** and **RINGO STARR**
1964   *A Hard Day's Night*
       (UA) F
       "A Hard Day's Night"
       "If I Fell"
       "I'm Happy Just to Dance with You"
       "And I Love Her"
       "Tell Me Why"
       "Can't Buy Me Love"
       "I Should Have Known Better"
       "She Loves You"
       "Any Time at All"
       "I'll Cry Instead"
1964   *Sound of a City*
       (Rank)
1965   *Pop Gear*
       (Pathe) F

       "She Loves You"
       "Twist and Shout"
1965   *Help*
       (UA) F
       "Help"
       "I Need You"
       "You're Going to Lose That Girl"
       "Ticket to Ride"
       "The Night Before"
       "You've Got to Hide Your Love Away"
       "Another Girl"
       "She's a Woman"
       "Act Naturally"
       "It's Only Love"
       "You Like Me Too Much"
       "Tell Me What You See"
       "I've Just Seen a Face"
       "Yesterday"
1968   *Yellow Submarine*
       (UA) F (cartoon)
       "Yellow Submarine"
       "Sergeant Pepper's Lonely Hearts Club Band"
       "Lucy in the Sky with Diamonds"
       "Eleanor Rigby"
       "It's All Too Much"
       "Altogether Now"
       "All You Need Is Love"
       "Hey Bulldog"
       "Nowhere Man"
       "Only a Northern Song"
       "When I'm Sixty Four"
1970   *Let It Be*
       (UA) F
       "Let It Be"
       "Don't Let Me Down"
       "Maxwell's Silver Hammer"
       "Two of Us"
       "I've Got a Feeling"
       "Oh Darling"
       "One After 909"
       "Across the Universe"
       "Dig a Pony"
       "Suzy Parker"
       "I, Me, Mine"
       "For You, Blue"
       "Besame Mucho"
       "Octopus's Garden"
       "Really Got a Hold on Me"
       "Long and Winding Road"
       "Shake Rattle and Roll"
       "Kansas City"
       "Lawdy Miss Clawdy"
       "Dig It"
       "Get Back"
       "All I Want Is You"

GEORGE BEATTY (comedian)
1937   *Pathetone 356*

BEBE AND RENEE (dancers)
1933   *Pathetone 179*
       "Perfume Waltz"

GINO BECCHI (tenor)
1950   *Soho Conspiracy*
(New Realm) F

JEFF BECK (guitarist)
see also **THE YARDBIRDS**
1982   *The Secret Policeman's Other Ball*
(UIP) F
"Farther Up the Road"
1989   *Lenny Live and Unleashed*
(Palace) F
1991   *The Pope Must Die*
(Palace) F

EVE BECKE (singer)
1934   *On the Air*
(British Lion) F
1934   *Death at Broadcasting House*
(Phoenix) F
"I Love You So"
1934   *Radio Parade of 1935*
(BIP) F
"No One to Care for Me"
1935   *Equity Musical Revue 1*
(British Lion)
"I Just Couldn't Tell Him"
1939   *Music Hall Parade*
(Butcher) F
"Stop the Clock"
"Angelino Piccolino"
1940   *Cavalcade of Variety*
(reissue: *Music Hall Parade*)
1943   *Highlights of Variety 25*
(reissue: *Music Hall Parade*)

BERNARD BEDFORD (singer)
1936   *Cabaret Nights 5*
(Highbury)

HARRY BEDFORD (comedian)
1934   *Those Were the Days*
(BIP) F
"A Little Bit Off the Top"
"Lily of Laguna"
1936   *Old Timers*
(Warner)
"A Little Bit Off the Top"

THE BEE GEES (group)
1968   *The Bee Gees*
(Associated)

SIR THOMAS BEECHAM (conductor)
1936   *Whom the Gods Love*
(ATP) F
"Marriage of Figaro"
"The Magic Flute"
1951   *Tales of Hoffmann*
(London) F

THE BEGA FOUR (acrobatic dancers)
1937   *Calling All Stars*
(British Lion) F

DOMINIC BEHAN (Irish singer)
1961   *Johnny Nobody*
(Columbia) F

ERNEST BELCHER AND NORAH WALKER
(dancers)
1913   *The Tango Waltz*
(Selsior)

BRUCE BELFRAGE (broadcaster)
1951   *The Galloping Major*
(Romulus) F

BELITA (skater)
1949   *Sports Serenade*
(ABFD)
1953   *Never Let Me Go*
(MGM) F
1956   *Invitation to the Dance*
(MGM) F

BELLING'S DOGS (animal act)
1938   *On Velvet*
(AIP) F

THE BELLS (singers)
1931   *Pathe Pictorial 707*
"Drink To Me Only"
1939   *Pathetone 499*
"South of the Border"
1940   *Pathe Pictorial 216*
"Misty Islands of the Highlands"
1941   *Pathe Pictorial 258*
1941   *Pathe Pictorial 288*
1944   *Pathe Pictorial 419*
"When You Know You're Not
Forgotten"

BENDER (group)
1996   *Glastonbury: The Movie*
(Starlight) F
"People's Army"

THE BENDETTI BROTHERS (musical
clowns)
1930   *Toyland*
(Gainsborough)

SONYA BENJAMIN (belly dancer)
1965   *The Return of Mr Moto*
(TCF) F
1969   *Loving Feeling*
(Piccadilly) F

BILLY BENNETT (comedian)
1927   *Eve's Film Review 303*
1927   *Pathe Pictorial 493*
1928   *Pathe Pictorial 510*
1928   *Almost a Gentleman*
(Phonofilm)
1928   *Eve's Film Review 362*
1929   *Pathe Pictorial 565*
1930   *Pathetone 25*

1930 *Pathetone 33*
"Unnatural History"
1934 *Radio Parade of 1935*
(BIP) F
1936 *Soft Lights and Sweet Music*
(British Lion) F
"Shooting of Dan McGrew"
1937 *Calling All Stars*
(British Lion) F
"Christmas Day in the Cookhouse"
1938 *Pathetone 453*
"On Golf"
1938 *Almost a Gentleman*
(Butcher) F
1939 *Young Man's Fancy*
(Ealing) F

DICKIE BENNETT (singer)
1957 *Rock You Sinners*
(Small) F
"Heartbreak Hotel"
"How Many Times?"
"Cry Upon My Shoulder"

MAVIS BENNETT (singer)
1932 *Pathetone 10*
"Bird of Love Divine"

BENNETT AND WILLIAMS (comedians)
1931 *Ideal Cinemagazine 289*
1936 *Pathe Pictorial NS 6*
"First Call of Spring"
1937 *Pathe Pictorial NS 69*
"Au Revoir"
1937 *Saturday Night Revue*
(Pathe) F
1940 *Pathe Pictorial 216*
"Misty Islands of the Highlands"

**IVY BENSON AND HER ALL GIRLS
ORCHESTRA**
1943 *The Dummy Talks*
(British National) F
"Post Horn Gallop"
"The Roundabout Goes Round"
"The World Belongs To Me"
1950 *A Ray of Sunshine*
(Adelphi) F
"Sabre Dance"
"Leicester Square Rag"

LUCILLE BENSTEAD (singer)
1938 *Cavalcade of the Stars*
(Coronel)

MICHAEL BENTINE (comedian)
1951 *Cookery Nook*
(Regent)
1951 *What's Cooking?*
(Regent) ADVERT
1951 *London Entertains*
(New Realm) F
1952 *Down Among the Z Men*
(New Realm) F

1953 *Loonizoo*
(New Realm)
1953 *Forces Sweetheart*
(New Realm) F
1955 *Raising a Riot*
(London) F
1957 *Fun at the Movies*
(Danziger)
1958 *I Only Arsked*
(Hammer) F
1960 *Climb Up the Wall*
(New Realm) F
1962 *We Joined the Navy*
(Warner) F
1966 *The Sandwich Man*
(Rank) F
1969 *Bachelor of Arts*
(Paramount)
1972 *Rentadick*
(Rank) F

DICK BENTLEY (comedian)
1959 *Desert Mice*
(Rank) F
1960 *And the Same to You*
(Monarch) F
1961 *The Girl On the Boat*
(UA) F
1961 *The Sundowners*
(Warner) F
1961 *In the Doghouse*
(Rank) F
1962 *The Golden Rabbit*
(Rank) F
1962 *Tamahine*
(ABPC) F
1974 *Barry McKenzie Holds His Own*
(EMI) F

HARRY BENTLEY (singer)
1933 *Pathetone 184*
"Japanese Sandman"

HAROLD BERENS (impersonator)
(films as actor not listed)
1940 *Pathe Pictorial 216*

OSCAR BERGER (cartoonist)
1945 *New Pictorial 41*

DAVID BERGLAS (conjurer)
1956 *Invitation to Magic*
(Baim)

BERINOFF AND CHARLOT (dancers)
1932 *Ideal Cinemagazine 318*
1932 *The Face at the Window*
(Realart) F
1933 *Ideal Cinemagazine 356*
1934 *Waltzes from Vienna*
(Gaumont) F

SVETLANA BERIOSOVA (ballerina)
1954　*Harmony Lane*
　　　(Eros)
　　　"Swan Lake"
1964　*The Soldier's Tale*
　　　(BHE) F
1970　*The Enigma Variations*
　　　(Argo)

BELA BERKES AND HIS GYPSY ORCHESTRA
1932　*It's a King*
　　　(B&D) F

THE BERKOFFS (dancers)
1929　*Pot Pourri*
　　　(BIP)
1930　*Elstree Calling*
　　　(BIP) F

MILTON BERLE (American comedian)
1969　*Can Heironymus Merkin Ever Forget Mercy Humppe and Find True Happiness?*
　　　(Universal) F

IRVING BERLIN (American singer)
1943　*This Is the Army*
　　　(Warner) F (British version)
　　　"Oh How I Hate to Get Up in the Morning"
　　　"My British Buddy"

LEN BERMAN (singer)
1935　*Music Hath Charms*
　　　(BIP) F
　　　"There's No Time Like the Present"
1937　*Pathetone 396*
　　　"Leave the Pretty Girls Alone"

SHELLEY BERMAN (American comedian)
1970　*Every Home Should Have One*
　　　(British Lion) F

TONIA BERN (singer)
1956　*Keep It Clean*
　　　(Eros) F
　　　"Keep It Clean"
　　　"Wishing Well"

GEORGE AND BERT BERNARD (American comedians)
1952　*Decameron Nights*
　　　(Eros) F

PETER BERNARD (singer)
1930　*Why Sailors Leave Home*
　　　(BIP) F
　　　"Imagine My Embarrassment"
　　　"I Want to Be Loved"
1933　*Pathetone 159*
1936　*International Revue*
　　　(Medway) F

1937　*Pathetone 395*
　　　"Waiting for the Robert E. Lee"
　　　"Ragtime Cowboy Joe"
1945　*Here Comes the Sun*
　　　(Baxter) F

RITA BERNARD (singer)
1936　*Cabaret Nights 6; 7*
　　　(Highbury) S

THE STAN BERNARD TRIO (musicians)
1955　*I Am a Camera*
　　　(Remus) F

BERNARDI (singer)
1931　*Pathetone 83*
　　　"River Stay Away from My Door"
1932　*Pathetone 100*
　　　"When It's Sleepy Time Down South"
1936　*Dishonour Bright*
　　　(Cecil) F
1936　*Murder at the Cabaret*
　　　(Paramount) F
　　　"Cabaret Rhumba"
1937　*Pathetone 362*

BERNARDI AND BERNICE (dancers)
1936　*Cabaret Nights 3*
　　　(Highbury)

SHEILA BERNETTE (comedienne)
1968　*A Little of What You Fancy*
　　　(Border) F
　　　"Why Do They Always Pick On Me?"

SANDRA BERNHARD (comedienne)
1987　*Track 29*
　　　(Handmade) F

CHUCK BERRY (singer)
1973　*The London Rock and Roll Show*
　　　(Pleasant) F

DAVE BERRY (singer)
1966　*The Ghost Goes Gear*
　　　(Pathe) F

W H BERRY (comedian)
(films as actor not listed)
1924　*Eve's Film Review 174*
　　　"Poppy"
1929　*Eve's Film Review 408*
　　　"Merry Moments"

BERTINI AND THE BLACKPOOL TOWER BAND
1936　*Dodging the Dole*
　　　(Mancunian) F

CHARLES BERTRAM (conjurer)
1897　*The Vanishing Lady*
　　　(Paul)

1897   *Hail Britannia*
      (Paul)
1904   *Famous Conjuring Tricks*
      (Urban)

BERYL AND BOBO
1960   *The Entertainer*
      (UA) F

JULIAN BEST AND HIS ORCHESTRA
1937   *Starlight Parade*
      (Viking)

BEVERLEY SISTERS (singers)
1946   *New Pictorial 121*
      "Her Bathing Suit Never Got Wet"
1947   *New Pictorial 136*
      "Down in the Valley"
1954   *Harmony Lane*
      (Eros)

EVA BEYNON (singer)
1949   *It's a Wonderful Day*
      (Equity) F
1953   *Out of the Bandbox*
      (New Realm)

BIG BROTHER AND THE HOLDING COMPANY (group)
1968   *Petulia*
      (Warner) F

BIL AND BIL (acrobats)
1933   *Pathetone 167*

MR ACKER BILK AND THE PARAMOUNT JAZZ BAND
1962   *It's Trad Dad*
      (Columbia) F
      "In a Persian Market"
      "High Society"
      "Frankie and Johnny"
1962   *Band of Thieves*
      (Rank) F
      "All I Want To Do Is Sing"
      "Kissin'"
1962   *Four Hits and a Mister*
      (British Lion)
      "Stranger on the Shore"
      "In a Persian Market"
      "Gotta See Baby Tonight"
1963   *It's All Over Town*
      (British Lion) F
      "Volga Boatman"
      "Sippin' Cider"
1964   *Jazz All the Way*
      (Rank)
1966   *The Ghost Goes Gear*
      (Pathe) F

JACK BILLINGS (dancer)
1937   *Quick Wick Capers*
      (Ace Cinemagazine)

1946   *Dancing Thru*
      (Angel) F
1946   *Spring Song*
      (British National) F
      "Give Me a Chance to Dance"
1950   *The Body Said No*
      (Angel) F
1951   *Happy Go Lovely*
      (ABP) F
      "Piccadilly Ballet"
1952   *The Wedding of Lili Marlene*
      (Monarch) F
      "Why Did You Say Goodbye?"
1954   *Harmony Lane*
      (Eros)

CELIA BIRD (singer)
1931   *Stepping Stones*
      (Benstead) F

FRANK BIRD (boy soprano)
1939   *Pathe Pictorial NS 174*
      "Bird Song at Eventide"

NICHOLAS BIRD
see **DORA HIBBERT AND NICHOLAS BIRD**

KENNETH BIRREL (song and dance)
1937   *Footlights*
      (Ace) F
1938   *Swing*
      (Ace) F

BILLY BISSETT AND HIS CANADIAN BAND
1936   *Pathetone 351*
      "A Little Robin Told Me"
1939   *Pathe Pictorial NS 177*
      "Crooners' Corner"

JOE BISSETT AND ENID SELLERS (dancers)
1912   *The Turkey Trot*
      (Selsior)

CILLA BLACK (singer)
1964   *Ferry Cross the Mersey*
      (UA) F
      "It's True"
1968   *Work Is a Four-Letter Word*
      (Rank) F
      "Work Is a Four-Letter Word"

STANLEY BLACK AND HIS ORCHESTRA
1950   *Come Dance With Me*
      (Columbia) F

THE BLACK ARABS (group)
1980   *The Great Rock 'n' Roll Swindle*
      (Virgin) F
      "Black Arabs Medley"

THE BLACK KNIGHTS (group)
  1964 *Ferry Cross the Mersey*
        (UA) F
        "I Got a Woman"

BLACK LACE (group)
  1987 *Rita, Sue and Bob Too*
        (Mainline) F
        "Gang Bang"

TONY BLACKBURN (disc jockey)
  1968 *Music*
        (Archibald) F
  1970 *Simon Simon*
        (Tigon) F
  1973 *Radio Wonderful*
        (Goodtimes) F

**RORY BLACKWELL AND THE
BLACKJACKS** (group)
  1957 *Rock You Sinners*
        (Small) F
        "Rockin' with Rory"
        "Intro to the Rock"

THE BLACKWELLS (group)
  1964 *Ferry Cross the Mersey*
        (UA) F
        "Why Don't You Love Me?"

JIMMY BLADES (vibraphone)
  1933 *Ideal Cinemagazine 381*

DAVID BLAIR (ballet dancer)
  1963 *An Evening with the Royal Ballet*
        (BHE) F
  1966 *Romeo and Juliet*
        (Rank) F

JOYCE BLAIR (song and dance)
  1962 *Number Six*
        (Anglo) F
        "A Lifetime Isn't Long Enough"
  1962 *Crooks Anonymous*
        (Anglo) F
  1963 *The Wild Affair*
        (7 Arts) F
  1965 *Be My Guest*
        (Rank) F
        "Gotta Get Away Now"
  1967 *Mister Ten Per Cent*
        (ABP) F
  1969 *Can Heironymus Merkin Ever Forget
        Mercy Humppe and Find True
        Happiness?*
        (Universal) F
  1976 *Intimate Games*
        (Tigon) F

LIONEL BLAIR (dancer)
  1953 *The Limping Man*
        (Eros) F
  1955 *King's Rhapsody*
        (Wilcox) F

  1960 *The World of Suzie Wong*
        (Paramount) F
  1962 *Play It Cool*
        (Anglo) F
        "Take It Easy"
  1962 *The Main Attraction*
        (MGM) F
  1963 *The Cool Mikado*
        (Baim) F
        "Tit Willow"
  1964 *The Beauty Jungle*
        (Rank) F
  1964 *A Hard Day's Night*
        (UA) F
  1966 *Maroc 7*
        (Rank) F
  1969 *The Sandal*
        (Eagle)
  1986 *Absolute Beginners*
        (Palace) F

MAUDIE BLAKE (musical saw)
  1994 *Funny Bones*
        (Hollywood) F

BLAKE AND JACKSON (comedians)
  1929 *Pathe Pictorial 18*

JAMES BLAKELEY (face-puller)
  1911 *Studies in Expression*
        (Gaumont)

PAULA ANNE BLAND (striptease)
  1988 *Tank Malling*
        (Parkfield) F

NORAH BLANEY (singer)
  1922 *Eve's Film Review 54*
        "Midnight Follies"
  1924 *Eve's Film Review 169*
  1929 *Norah Blaney 1*
        (BSFP)
        "He Ain't Done Right by Our Nell"
        "Masculine Women and Feminine
        Men"
  1929 *Norah Blaney 2*
        (BSFP)
        "If You Hadn't Gone Away"
        "All Scotch"
        "What About Me?"
  1932 *Musical Medley 2*
        (reissue: *Norah Blaney 1*)
  1932 *Musical Medley 6*
        (reissue: *Norah Blaney 2*)
  1956 *Who Done It?*
        (Ealing) F

JULES BLEDSOE (American baritone)
  1932 *Pathetone 102*
        "Dear Old Southland"

KITTY BLEWETT (comedienne)
  1949 *What a Carry On*
        (Mancunian) F

JASMINE BLIGH (television personality)
1940 *Band Waggon*
(Gainsborough) F
1940 *Inspector Hornleigh on Holiday*
(Gainsborough) F

BLONDE ON BLONDE (group)
1979 *The Golden Lady*
(Target) F
"Woman Is Free"

BLOS (LEWIS) (cartoonist)
1931 *Ideal Cinemagazine 268*

THE BLOSSOM TOES (group)
1968 *Popdown*
(New Realm) F

WINDY BLOW (balloon act)
1954 *Variety Half Hour*
(Baim)

BEN BLUE (American dancer)
1927 *The Arcadians*
(Gaumont) F

JIMMY BLUE AND HIS BAND
1969 *Country Dance*
(MGM) F

THE BLUE ANGELS (group)
1978 *What's Up, Superdoc?*
(Blackwater) F

THE BLUE BOYS (quartette)
1930 *The Blue Boys 1; 2*
(Gainsborough)

THE BLUES BAND
1981 *The Blues Band*
(ITC)
"Sus Blues"
"Going Home"
"Find Yourself Another Fool"
"Come On In"
"Greenstuff"
"The Cat"
"Lonely Avenue"
"Maggie's Farm"
"Back Door Man"

BLUM AND BLUM (balancers)
1938 *Pathe Pictorial 120*

EDWARD BLUNT AND MARGERY JACKSON (dancers)
1927 *Eve's Film Review 301*
"Black Bottom"

BOBBIE AND VIRGINIA (dancers)
1936 *Limelight*
(Wilcox) F
"Celebrating"
"Farewell Sweet Señorita"
"The Whistling Waltz"

THE BODYSNATCHERS (group)
1981 *Dance Craze*
(Osiris) F
"007"
"Do the Rock-Steady"
"Easy Life"

THE BOJOS (group)
1969 *Moon Zero Two*
(Hammer) F

MARC BOLAN AND T. REX (group)
1972 *Born to Boogie*
(Apple) F
"Marc's Intro"
"Jeepster"
"Baby Strange"
"Children of the Revolution"
"Look to the Left"
"Space Ball Pitcher"
"Telegram Sam"
"Cosmic Dancer"
"Hot Love"
"Get It On"
"The Slider"
"Chariot Choogle"
"Union Hall Poem"
"Tutti Frutti"
"Some People Like to Rock"

AL BOLLINGTON (organ)
1949 *Organ Antics*
(New Realm)

THE BOLSHOI BALLET
1957 *The Bolshoi Ballet*
(Rank) F
"Dance of the Tartars"
"Le Lac des Cygnes"
"Spring Water"
"The Dying Swan"
"Polonaise and Cracovienne"
"Walpurgisnacht"
"Giselle"

GEORGE BOLTON (comedian)
1941 *Bob's Your Uncle*
(Butcher) F

REG BOLTON (comedian)
1937 *Saturday Night Revue*
(Pathe) F

JON BON JOVI (singer)
1996 *The Leading Man*
(J&M) F

THE GRAHAM BOND ORGANISATION (group)
1965 *Gonks Go Beat*
(Anglo) F

GARY (U.S.) BONDS (singer)
1962 *It's Trad Dad*
(Columbia) F
"Seven Day Weekend"

LUIS BONFA (singer)
1968 *Popdown*
(New Realm) F

ALI BONGO (conjurer)
1968 *Popdown*
(New Realm) F

ISSY BONN (comedian)
1939 *Pathetone 475*
"Shake Hands with a Millionaire"
1939 *Discoveries*
(Vogue) F
1941 *I Thank You*
(Gainsborough) F

SONNY BONO (American singer)
1979 *Escape to Athena*
(ITC) F

THE BONZO DOG DOO DAH BAND
1967 *Pathe Pictorial 673*
"Equestrian Statue"

PAT BOONE (singer)
(films as actor not listed)
1962 *The Main Attraction*
(MGM) F
"The Main Attraction"
"Gondola Gondola"
"Si Si Si"
"Amore Baciami"

WEBSTER BOOTH (tenor)
1935 *Musical Medley*
(Mancunian)
1936 *Faust Fantasy*
(Publicity) F
1936 *Pathe Pictorial 932*
"The World Is Mine Tonight"
1936 *The Invader*
(MGM) F
1936 *The Robber Symphony*
(Concordia) F
"Romance"
"Serenata"
1936 *Sunshine Ahead*
(Baxter) F
"Faust"
1937 *Saturday Night Revue*
(Pathe) F
1938 *Georges Bizet Composer of Carmen*
(MGM) F
1944 *Demobbed*
(Mancunian) F
"So Deep Is the Night"
"Love's Old Sweet Song"
"I Hear You Calling Me"
"Until"

1945 *Waltz Time*
(British National) F
"You Will Return to Vienna"
1946 *The Laughing Lady*
(British National) F
"Laugh at Life"
"Love Is the Key"
1952 *The Story of Gilbert and Sullivan*
(London) F

TONI BORELLO AND MIMI (trapezists)
1939 *Pathe Pictorial NS 178*

SHEILA BORRETT (broadcaster)
1934 *Surprise Item*
(International)

THE BORSTAL BOYS (comedians)
1946 *Amateur Night*
(Renown)

REGINALD BOSANQUET (television
personality)
1975 *Flame*
(VPS) F

THE BOSWELL TWINS (dancers)
1939 *Pathe Pictorial NS 155*
"Mirror Dance"
1940 *Pathe Pictorial 223*
"Doll Dance"
1944 *Rainbow Round the Corner*
(Berkeley) F
1945 *I Didn't Do It*
(Columbia) F
"Try Try Again"

CHILI BOUCHIER (singer)
(films as actress not listed)
1937 *The Minstrel Boy*
(Butcher) F
"Love's a Racketeer"
"The Best Things in Life"

PATTI BOULAYE (singer)
1979 *The Music Machine*
(Target) F
"Ready for Love"
"Disco Dancer"
"Get the Feel Right"
1980 *Hussy*
(Boyd) F
"The Best Show in Town"
"No-One is Ever Lost"

SIR ADRIAN BOULT (conductor)
1932 *Pathetone 144*
"Land of Hope and Glory"
1943 *Battle for Music*
(Strand) F
"Cockaigne Overture"

JOHN BOULTER (singer)
1963 *It's All Happening*
(British Lion) F
"Once Upon a Time in Venice"

BOURNEMOUTH MUNICIPAL SYMPHONY ORCHESTRA
1938 *Hungarian Rhapsody*
(Pathe)
1938 *Lohengrin*
(Pathe)
1938 *Tannhäuser*
(Pathe)
1938 *The Damnation of Faust*
(Pathe)
1938 *Pathétique Symphony*
(Pathe)
1938 *Old King Cole*
(Pathe)

BOW WOW WOW (group)
1984 *Scandalous*
(Hemdale)

EDDIE BOWERS (harmonica)
1929 *Eddie Bowers*
(Phonofilm)
"New Colonial March"
1932 *Musical Medley 6*
(reissue: *Eddie Bowers*)

BOWERS AND RUTHERFORD (pianists)
1932 *Ideal Cinemagazine 305*

DAVID BOWIE (singer)
1969 *The Image*
(Border)
1969 *The Virgin Soldiers*
(Columbia) F
1973 *Ziggy Stardust and the Spiders from Mars*
(EMI) F
"Hang On To Yourself"
"Ziggy Stardust"
"Watch That Man"
"The Wild-Eyed Boy from Free Cloud"
"All the Young Dudes"
"Oh! You Pretty Things"
"Moonage Daydream"
"Changes"
"Space Oddity"
"Cracked Actor"
"Time"
"Width of a Circle"
"Suffragette City"
"Rock and Roll Suicide"
"My Death"
"Let's Spend the Night Together"
"White Light/White Heat"
1976 *The Man Who Fell To Earth*
(British Lion) F
1983 *Merry Christmas Mr Lawrence*
(Palace) F

1983 *Yellowbeard*
(Hemdale) F
1986 *Absolute Beginners*
(Palace) F
"Absolute Beginners"
"That's Motivation"
"Volare"
1986 *Labyrinth*
(Henson) F
"Underground"
"Dance Magic"
"Chilling Down"
"As the World Falls Down"
"Within You"

AL BOWLLY (singer)
1931 *Chance of a Night Time*
(B&D) F
"Leave the Rest to Nature"
"I'm So Used to You Now"
1932 *A Night Like This*
(B&D) F
"A Night Like This"
"Considering"
"If Anything Happened to You"
1932 *The Mayor's Nest*
(B&D) F
"Say to Yourself I Will Be Happy"
1934 *Pathetone 227*
"The Very Thought of You"
1936 *Pathe Pictorial NS 25*
"Melancholy Baby"

BOB BOWMAN (broadcaster)
1936 *Olympic Honeymoon*
(RKO) F

PATRICIA BOWMAN (dancer)
1937 *Okay For Sound*
(Gainsborough) F

DOROTHY BOWYER (acrobatic dancer)
1932 *Eve's Film Review 573*

THE BOY CHORISTERS (singers)
1935 *Off the Dole*
(Mancunian) F

JACQUELINE BOYER (dancer)
1945 *New Pictorial 68*

RONNIE BOYER AND JEANNE REVEL
(dancers)
1936 *Pathe Pictorial NS 30*
"The Touch of Your Lips"
1937 *Pathe Pictorial NS 54*
"Some Day"
1937 *Cafe Colette*
(ABFD) F
1937 *Lucky Jade*
(Paramount) F
1940 *Pathe Pictorial 215*
"So Deep Is the Night"

1948 *Noose*
(Pathe) F
1952 *For Your Entertainment 3*
(Gaumont)

CATHERINE BOYLE (Katie Boyle) (television personality)
1957 *Not Wanted on Voyage*
(Renown) F
1958 *The Truth About Women*
(British Lion) F
1958 *Intent to Kill*
(TCF) F

BUDDY BRADLEY'S RHYTHM GIRLS (dancers)
1932 *Ideal Cinemagazine 349*
1934 *On the Air*
(British Lion) F
1934 *Radio Parade of 1935*
(BIP) F
1935 *Joy Ride*
(City) F
1935 *A Fire Has Been Arranged*
(Twickenham) F
"The Fire Brigade"
"It Doesn't Cost a Thing to Smile"
1937 *Film Fare*
(Ambassador)
1957 *Edmundo Ros Half Hour*
(Hammer)

GRACE BRADLEY (dancer)
1937 *O.H.M.S.*
(Gaumont) F
"Turning the Town Upside Down"

JOSEPHINE BRADLEY AND HER FORMATION DANCERS
1937 *Let's Make a Night of It*
(ABPC) F
1942 *Pathe Pictorial 339*

VERA BRADLEY
1944 *Rainbow Round the Corner*
(Berkeley) F
1944 *Night of Magic*
(Berkeley) F

BEATE BRADNA (acrobat)
1931 *Pathe Pictorial 81*
1932 *Eve's Film Review 556*

JACK BRADY AND HIS BAND
1937 *It's a Racquet*
(Ace Cinemagazine)
"The Vicar of Bray"
1937 *How When and Wear*
(Ace Cinemagazine)

PAUL BRADY (singer)
1987 *The Secret Policeman's Third Ball*
(Virgin) F
"El Salvador"

MELVYN BRAGG (television personality)
1979 *Sweet William*
(Kendon) F
1979 *The Kids Are Alright*
(Rose) F
1989 *The Tall Guy*
(Virgin) F

FRANK BRAIDWOOD (singer)
1936 *International Revue*
(Medway) F

DENNIS BRAIN (horn player)
1953 *Beethoven Sonata*
(Anvil)

WARWICK BRAITHWAITE (conductor)
1943 *Battle for Music*
(Strand) F

JOHNNY BRANDON (singer)
1956 *Fun at St Fanny's*
(British Lion) F
"Anyone Can Be a Millionaire"

OWEN BRANNIGAN (singer)
1952 *The Story of Gilbert and Sullivan*
(London) F
"Sentry Song"
"The Mikado"
"The Gondoliers"

THE BREAKAWAYS (group)
1963 *Just For Fun*
(Columbia) F
"What's the Name of the Game?"

PATRICIA BREDIN (singer)
1959 *Make Mine a Million*
(British Lion) F
1959 *The Bridal Path*
(British Lion) F
1959 *Left Right and Centre*
(British Lion) F
1959 *Desert Mice*
(Rank) F
"Christmas Star"
"Till the Right Time Comes"

BOBBY BREEN QUINTET (band)
1965 *The Curse of Simba*
(Gala) F

GLORIA BRENT (singer)
1945 *What Do We Do Now?*
(Grand National) F

TONY BRENT (singer)
1959 *Pathe Pictorial 234*

LYNN BRETON (singer)
1947 *New Pictorial 133*
"I've Got the Eye"

JANET BRETT AND VAL HOADLEY
(dancers)
1975 *I Don't Want to be Born*
(Rank) F

THE BREWSTER TRIO (dancers)
1902 *The Brewster Trio*
(Warwick)
1902 *The Brewster Trio of High Kickers and Dancers*
(Warwick)

LESLIE BRIDGEWATER AND HERBERT LODGE (musicians)
1932 *Pathe Pictorial 717*

LESLIE BRIDGEWATER AND HIS HARP SEPTET
1933 *Pathe Pictorial 816*
"Welsh Medley"

TIM BRINTON (television personality)
1961 *Information Received*
(Rank) F
1963 *Heavens Above*
(British Lion) F
1965 *Bunny Lake Is Missing*
(Columbia) F
1973 *Man At the Top*
(Hammer) F
1978 *Carry On Emmanuelle*
(Hemdale) F

CARL BRISSON (singer)
1927 *The Ring*
(BIP) F
1929 *The Manxman*
(BIP) F
1929 *The American Prisoner*
(BIP) F
1929 *Chelsea Nights*
(BIP)
"My Ideal"
1930 *Song of Soho*
(BIP) F
"Camille"
"There's Something About You"
1930 *Knowing Men*
(UA) F
"Collette"
1933 *Prince of Arcadia*
(Gaumont) F
"A Crown Prince of Arcadia"
"If I Could Only Find Her"
1934 *Two Hearts in Waltz Time*
(Gaumont) F
"Give Her a Little Kiss"
"Two Hearts that Beat in Waltz Time"
"In Old Vienna"
"Your Eyes Are So Tender"

REGGIE BRISTOW AND GEORGE CROW
(pianists)
1937 *Hot Stuff*
(Ace Cinemagazine)

REGGIE BRISTOW AND HIS BAND
1933 *Pathetone 173*
"What Have We Got to Lose?"
1935 *Equity Musical Revue Series*
(British Lion)
"Yes Ma'am"
"That's What Life Is Made Of"
"Sentimental Gentleman from Georgia"
"Peter Peter"
"Stay Out of My Dreams"
"Hold Me"
1937 *Train of Events*
(Ace Cinemagazine)

BRITISH LEGION CITY OF LONDON MILITARY BAND
1935 *Pathe Pictorial 891*
"God Bless Our King"

THE BRITISH STEEL STOCKSBRIDGE BAND
1997 *The Full Monty*
(TCF) F
"The Zodiak"
"Slaidburn"

THE BRITISH WOMEN'S SYMPHONY ORCHESTRA
1934 *Pathetone 210*
"Don Juan"

CECIL BROADHURST (singer)
1937 *The New Frontiersman*
(Positive)
1938 *Youth Marches On*
(New Oxford)
"Wise Old Horsey"

THE BROADWAY BOYS (comedians)
1944 *Night of Magic*
(Berkeley) F

CECIL BROCK (guitarist)
1946 *Caravan*
(Gainsborough) F

JOHNNY BRODERICK
see **CHARLOTTE ALLEN AND JOHNNY BRODERICK**

ESTELLE BRODY (singer)
(films as actress not listed)
1929 *Kitty*
(BIP) F
"Parted"
1929 *Me and the Boys*
(BIP)

THE BROOK BROTHERS (singers)
1962   *It's Trad Dad*
        (Columbia) F
        "Double Trouble"

BROOKINS AND VAN (comedians)
1937   *Pathetone 378*
1937   *Sam Small Leaves Town*
        (BSS) F

DAN BROOKS (singer)
1960   *The Gentle Trap*
        (Butcher) F
        "I Could Go For You"

PETER BROUGH (ventriloquist)
1940   *Cavalcade of Variety*
        (Butcher) F
1943   *Pathe Pictorial 400*
1943   *Pathe Gazette 24*

ARTHUR BROWN AND KINGDOM COME
(group)
1973   *Glastonbury Fayre*
        (Goodtimes) F

BURTON BROWN (pianist)
see also **GEORGE MOON AND BURTON
BROWN**
1938   *Pathe Pictorial NS 124*
        "Wedding of the Painted Doll"
1945   *What Do We Do Now?*
        (Grand National) F

ELSIE BROWN (singer)
1937   *The Penny Pool*
        (Mancunian) F
        "Let's Be in Love"
        "What Lancashire Thinks Today"
1940   *Music Hall Personalities 16*
        (Butcher)

GEORGE BROWN (singer)
1957   *Rock You Sinners*
        (Small) F
        "Calypso Rock 'n' Roll"
1960   *Climb Up the Wall*
        (New Realm) F

HAL BROWN (comedian)
1927   *Hal Brown Lancashire Comedian*
        (Phonofilm)
        "Swistles"

JANET BROWN (impressionist)
1949   *Floodtide*
        (GFD) F
1950   *A Ray of Sunshine*
        (Adelphi) F
1952   *Folly To Be Wise*
        (London) F
1970   *My Lover My Son*
        (MGM) F

1972   *Bless This House*
        (Rank) F
1081   *For Your Eyes Only*
        (UA) F

JOE BROWN (singer)
1961   *Spike Milligan Meets Joe Brown*
        (British Lion)
1963   *Just For Fun*
        (Columbia) F
        "Let Her Go"
        "What's the Name of the Game?"
1963   *What a Crazy World*
        (Hammer) F
        "What a Crazy World"
        "Brothers Brothers"
        "I Feel the Same Way Too"
        "Just You Wait and See"
1964   *The Beauty Jungle*
        (Rank) F
1965   *Three Hats for Lisa*
        (Anglo) F
1968   *Lionheart*
        (CFF) F

LENA BROWN (comedienne)
1939   *Let's Be Famous*
        (ATP) F
        "Whistle If You Want Me"

LOUISE BROWN (singer)
1933   *Pathe Pictorial 783*
        "Charm of Life"

NANCY BROWN (singer)
1932   *Maid of the Mountains*
        (BIP) F
        "Love Will Find a Way"
        "Farewell"
        "The Keys to My Heart"
1933   *Facing the Music*
        (BIP) F
        "Let Me Gaze"
1933   *A Southern Maid*
        (BIP) F
        "Southern Love"
        "Lonely Am I"
1934   *Red Wagon*
        (BIP) F

ROY 'CHUBBY' BROWN (comedian)
1993   *U.F.O.*
        (PolyGram) F

SAXSON BROWN (strong man)
1930   *Pathetone 28*
1932   *Pathe Pictorial 769*
1937   *Pathe Pictorial NS 92*

TEDDY BROWN (xylophonist)
1927   *Syncopated Melodies*
        (Parkinson)
1928   *Phototone 1*
        "Dancing Tambourine"

1928 *Phototone 6*
1929 *Teddy Brown Xylophonist*
(BSFP)
1929 *Musical Medley*
(BIP)
1929 *Pot Pourri*
(BIP)
1930 *Elstree Calling*
(BIP) F
"Ain't Misbehavin'"
1930 *Pathetone 17*
"Dance of the Raindrops"
1932 *Indiscretions of Eve*
(BIP) F
1934 *On the Air*
(British Lion) F
1934 *Pathe Pictorial 844*
"Play to Me Gypsy"
1935 *Equity Musical Revue 7*
(British Lion)
"Star Spangled Banner"
1935 *Equity Musical Revue 9*
(British Lion)
"Cabin in the Pines"
1935 *Radio Pirates*
(Sound City) F
1935 *Clap Hands*
(Fidelity)
"Dancing With My Shadow"
"Winter Wonderland"
1936 *Pathetone 330*
"Buffoon"
1936 *Variety Parade*
(Butcher) F
"Buffoon"
1937 *Starlight Parade*
(Viking)
1938 *Pathetone 413*
"Canadian Capers"
1938 *Convict 99*
(Gainsborough) F
1939 *Pathe Pictorial 194*
"We Must All Stick Together"
1939 *Pathetone Parade of 1940*
F (reissue: *Pathetone 413*)
1941 *Pathetone Parade of 1941*
F (reissue: *Pathe Pictorial 194*)
1942 *Pathe Pictorial 325*
1944 *Dreaming*
(Baxter) F
"Orpheus in the Underworld"
"Let's Have Another One"

BROWN AND LAHORE (skaters)
1930 *The Musical Beauty Shop*
(PDC)

JACKSON BROWNE (singer)
1987 *The Secret Policeman's Third Ball*
(Virgin) F
"El Salvador"
"Voices of Freedom"

PADDY BROWNE (comedienne)
1931 *Splinters in the Navy*
(Twickenham) F
1932 *Hotel Splendide*
(Ideal) F
1932 *Crooked Lady*
(Realart) F
1933 *Born Lucky*
(MGM) F
1936 *Pathe Pictorial NS 39*
1936 *Full Steam*
(Ace) F
1936 *Bottle Party*
(Ace) F
1936 *Song in Soho*
(Ace) F
1936 *Piccadilly Playtime*
(Ace) F
1937 *Windmill Revels*
(Ace) F
1937 *Carry On London*
(Ace) F
1938 *Two Men in a Box*
(Ace) F
1940 *Spy for a Day*
(Two Cities) F
1940 *Contraband*
(British National) F
"Connie You're a Caution"
"Your Face in a Crowd"

SAM BROWNE (singer)
1936 *Variety Parade*
(Butcher) F
"Please Believe Me"
"The Glory of Love"
1937 *Calling All Stars*
(British Lion) F
"Serenade in the Night"
"Peanut Vendor"
"Body and Soul"
1940 *Highlights of Variety 17*
(reissue: *Variety Parade*)
1941 *Hi Gang*
(Gainsborough) F
"We Chose the Air Force"
1951 *Pathe Pictorial 335*
"Last Night's Kisses"

HETTY BROWNING (contortionist)
1932 *Ideal Cinemagazine 327*
1933 *Pathetone 178*
"Oh Mr Hemingway"

JACK BROWNING (dancer)
1936 *Railroad Rhythm*
(Carnival)

BROWNING AND STARR (singers)
1935 *Pathetone 286*

JOHN BROWNLEE (singer)
1933 *The Private Life of Don Juan*
(London) F
"Serenade"

DAVE BRUBECK (musician)
  1962 *All Night Long*
       (Rank) F

**RUBY BRUNEAU AND THE HAWAIIAN
ISLANDERS** (band)
  1937 *Take Your Seat*
       (Ace Cinemagazine)
  1937 *Docks and Keys*
       (Ace Cinemagazine)
  1938 *Beside the Point*
       (Ace Cinemagazine)
  1938 *First at the Post*
       (Ace Cinemagazine)

HARRY BRUNNING (comedian)
  1935 *Royal Cavalcade*
       (BIP) F
       "Mammy"
  1935 *Variety*
       (Butcher) F
       "Get Your Hair Cut"
  1937 *Highlights of Variety 3*
       (reissue: *Variety*)

MURIEL BRUNSKILL (singer)
  1952 *The Story of Gilbert and Sullivan*
       (London) F

RITA BRUNSTROM (character studies)
  1932 *Ideal Cinemagazine 303*
       "The Radio Star"
  1932 *Ideal Cinemagazine 312*
       "A Cockney Lady"

THE BRUVVERS (group)
  1963 *What a Crazy World*
       (Hammer) F
       "What a Crazy World"

HAL BRYAN (comedian)
  1937 *Uptown Revue*
       (Ace) F
  1937 *Footlights*
       (Ace) F
  1937 *Concert Party*
       (Ace) F

JIMMY BRYANT (tap-dancer)
  1934 *Music Hall*
       (Realart) F

MARIE BRYANT (singer)
  1955 *Tiger By the Tail*
       (Eros) F
       "I Know Love"

JACK BUCHANAN (song and dance)
  1931 *Man of Mayfair*
       (Paramount) F
       "Alone With My Dreams"
       "You Forgot Your Gloves"
  1932 *Goodnight Vienna*
       (B&D) F

       "Goodnight Vienna"
       "Living in Clover"
       "Just Heaven"
       "Dear Little Waltz"
       "Marching Song"
  1933 *Yes Mr Brown*
       (B&D) F
       "Yes Mr Brown"
       "Leave a Little Love for Me"
       "If You Would Learn to Live"
  1933 *That's a Good Girl*
       (B&D) F
       "Fancy Our Meeting"
       "Now That I've Found You"
       "So Green"
       "Oo La La"
       "The Battle"
  1935 *Brewster's Millions*
       (B&D) F
       "I Think I Can"
       "One Good Tune Deserves Another"
       "Pull Down the Blind"
       "The Carranga"
  1935 *Come Out of the Pantry*
       (B&D) F
       "Everything Stops for Tea"
       "From One Minute to Another"
  1936 *Limelight*
       (Wilcox) F
       "Goodnight Vienna"
  1936 *When Knights Were Bold*
       (Wilcox) F
       "I'm Still Dreaming"
       "Let's Put Some People to Work"
       "Onward We Go"
  1936 *This'll Make You Whistle*
       (Wilcox) F
       "This'll Make You Whistle"
       "There Isn't Any Limit"
       "I'm in a Dancing Mood"
       "Crazy with Love"
  1937 *Smash and Grab*
       (GFD) F
  1937 *The Sky's the Limit*
       (GFD) F
       "My Beloved"
       "Swing Madame"
       "Just Whisper I Love You"
       "The Montreal"
  1938 *Break the News*
       (GFD) F
       "It All Belongs to You"
  1938 *Cavalcade of the Stars*
       (Coronel)
  1939 *The Gang's All Here*
       (ABPC) F
  1940 *The Middle Watch*
       (ABPC) F
  1940 *Bulldog Sees It Through*
       (ABPC) F
  1955 *As Long As They're Happy*
       (Rank) F
       "I Hate the Morning"
       "Cry"

"I Don't Know Whether to Laugh or Cry"
1955 *Josephine and Men*
(British Lion) F

BUCK AND BUBBLES (dancers)
1937 *Calling All Stars*
(British Lion) F
"Harlem Rhythm"

GEOFFREY BUCKINGHAM (conjurer)
1952 *Say Abracadabra*
(Butcher)

THE BUCKLEYS (novelty act)
1932 *Ideal Cinemagazine 334*
"The Hatters"

SID BUCKMAN (singer)
1935 *Radio Pirates*
(Sound City) F
"Old Faithful"

BETTY BUCKNELL (acrobatic dancer)
1933 *Pathe Pictorial 802*
"Danse Poupette"

BUNG LUNG (group)
1996 *Glastonbury: The Movie*
(Starlight) F
"Jacob's Magic Banana"

SIDNEY BURCHALL (baritone)
1939 *Pathetone 491*
"Pete the Postman"
1939 *Pathetone 465*
"The Open Road"
1939 *Pathetone 500*
"Old Lady of Armentières"
1939 *Pathe Pictorial NS 152*
"The Gay Highway"
1939 *Pathe Pictorial NS 168*
"The Lord Mayor's Coachman"
1940 *Pathe Pictorial 241*
"Song of Empire"
1940 *Laugh It Off*
(British National) F
"What Do They Say of England?"
1941 *Pathetone 565*
"The Skipper"
1941 *Pathetone Parade of 1941*
F (reissue: *Pictorial 241*)
1942 *Pathe Pictorial 318*
"It's a Beautiful Day"
1942 *Pathe Pictorial 338*
"This Is Worth Fighting For"
1943 *Pathe Pictorial 365*
"The Drover"
1943 *Pathe Pictorial 376*
1943 *Pathe Pictorial 402*
"Britain All the Way"
1944 *Pathe Pictorial 428*
"I Travel the Road"

BILLY BURDEN (comedian)
1983 *The Boys in Blue*
(Rank) F

ALBERT BURDON (comedian)
1932 *Maid of the Mountains*
(BIP) F
"Dirty Work at the Crossroads"
1933 *Letting in the Sunshine*
(BIP) F
"Letting in the Sunshine"
1933 *It's a Boy*
(Gaumont) F
1935 *Heat Wave*
(Gainsborough) F
1936 *She Knew What She Wanted*
(ABPC) F
1938 *Oh Boy*
(ABPC) F
1938 *Luck of the Navy*
(ABPC) F
1939 *Jail Birds*
(Butcher) F

ANN BURGESS (singer)
1931 *Pathetone 68*
"Little Brown Owl"

MARIE BURKE (singer)
1929 *Pathe Pictorial 13*
"Sunrise"

PATRICIA BURKE (singer)
1937 *Ship's Concert*
(Warner) F
1946 *Lisbon Story*
(British National) F
"Some Day We Shall Meet Again"
"Paris in My Heart"
"Follow the Drum"
"Song of the Sunrise"

THOMAS (TOM) BURKE (Irish tenor)
1929 *Eve's Film Review 445*
"Dear Love"
1931 *Pathetone 60*
"For You Alone"
1932 *Pathetone 110*
"E Lucevan le Stelle"
1932 *Pathetone 120*
"Pagliacci"
1932 *Pathetone 125*
"Voice in the Old Village Choir"
1932 *Pathetone 134*
"Lullabye of the Leaves"
1933 *Pathetone 145*
"Maire My Girl"
1935 *Father O'Flynn*
(Butcher) F
"Father O'Flynn"
"Ave Maria"
"Macushla"
"Let's Fall in Love"
"I Know Two Bright Eyes"

1937 *Kathleen Mavourneen*
(Butcher) F
"Kathleen Mavourneen"
1938 *My Irish Molly*
(ABPC) F
"Off to Philadelphia"
"The Irish Emigrant"
"Eileen Alanah"
"Ireland, Mother Ireland"
"Come Back to Erin"
"Londonderry Air"
"Kathleen Mavourneen"

DAVY BURNABY (comedian)
(films as actor not listed)
see also **THE CO-OPTIMISTS**
1929 *The Co-Optimists*
(New Era) F
1934 *Screen Vaudeville*
(Vaudeville)
1935 *Equity Musical Revue 4*
(British Lion)
"The Midshipmaid"

HELEN BURNELL (dancer)
1930 *Elstree Calling*
(BIP) F
"My Heart Is Saying"
"The Thought Never Entered My
Head"

AL BURNETT (comedian)
1942 *King Arthur Was a Gentleman*
(Gainsborough) F

GWENDOLINE BURNEY (singer)
1906 *Serenade from Faust*
(Chronophone)

RAY BURNS (singer)
1955 *Cyril Stapleton and the Show Band*
(Hammer)

REX BURROWS AND HIS ORCHESTRA
1938 *On Velvet*
(AIP) F

HUMPHREY BURTON (television presenter)
1967 *Interlude*
(Columbia) F

THERESE BURTON (television personality)
1957 *Not Wanted on Voyage*
(Renown) F

BOB BUSBY (dancer)
1938 *Romance of Dancing*
(Highbury) S

KATE BUSH (singer)
1987 *The Secret Policeman's Third Ball*
(Virgin) F
"Running Up That Hill"

JAN BUSSELL
see **ANNE HOGARTH AND JAN BUSSELL**

ERNEST BUTCHER (singer)
1936 *Song of the Road*
(UK) F
"Turmut Hoeing"

JACK BUTLER (comedian)
1937 *The Penny Pool*
(Mancunian) F
"It's a Sin To Tell a Lie"

SHEILA BUXTON (singer)
1958 *The Golden Disc*
(Butcher) F
"The In Between Age"

MAX BYGRAVES (comedian)
1949 *Bless 'Em All*
(Adelphi) F
"Bless 'Em All"
"I'm Afraid to Love You"
1949 *Nitwits on Parade*
(Adelphi) F
1949 *Skimpy in the Navy*
(Adelphi) F
"Opportunity"
"She Was Poor But She Was
Honest"
1951 *Tom Brown's Schooldays*
(Renown) F
1954 *Harmony Lane*
(Eros)
1954 *Tonight in Britain*
(Pathe)
"Big'ead"
1956 *Charley Moon*
(British Lion) F
"Out of Town"
"Fingers Crossed"
"It Isn't That One"
"The Fabulous Golden Boy"
"Funny Man"
1958 *A Cry from the Streets*
(Eros) F
"Gotta Have Rain"
1959 *Bobbikins*
(TCF) F
"Bobbikins' Lullaby"
"Funny Little Clown"
"Last Night I Dreamed"
"World of Dreams"
1961 *Spare the Rod*
(Bryanston) F
1972 *The Alf Garnett Saga*
(Columbia) F

DOUGLAS BYNG (comedian)
1932 *Pathetone 124*
1934 *Pathetone 246*
"Spring Song"
"I Love Me"

1935 *Opening Night*
      (Olympic) F
1938 *Pathetone 409*
      "The Mayoress"
1938 *Dress Rehearsal*
      (reissue: *Opening Night*)
1941 *Yellow Caesar*
      (Ealing)
1966 *Hotel Paradiso*
      (MGM) F

ALLIE BYRNE (tap-dancer)
1995 *In the Bleak Midwinter*
      (Rank)

DONAL BYRNE (Irish singer)
1993 *Widow's Peak*
      (Rank)
      "Mother Machree"

CABBAGE HEAD (group)
1996 *Glastonbury: The Movie*
(Starlight) F
"12th Caller"
"Mambo Rat"
"Crawl Home"
"Jacob's Magic Banana"

CHARLIE CAIROLI AND PAUL (musical clowns)
1952 *The Secret People*
(Ealing) F

CAIROLI BROTHERS (musical clowns)
1943 *Happidrome*
(Aldwych) F

CALEDONIAN HIGHLANDERS PIPE BAND
1976 *Confessions of a Driving Instructor*
(Columbia) F

CALIGARY BROTHERS
1936 *Beloved Impostor*
(RKO) F

MEL CALMAN (cartoonist)
1980 *Long Shot*
(Mithras) F

EDDIE CALVERT (trumpeter)
1956 *Beyond Mombasa*
(Columbia) F

HOPE AND PENNY CALVERT AND DICKIE MARTIN (dancers)
1949 *Nitwits on Parade*
(Adelphi) F

CAMARO AND HIS BAND
1928 *Phototone 12*

JAMES CAMERON (television personality)
1967 *Tell Me Lies*
(Ronorus) F

COMMANDER A B CAMPBELL (broadcaster)
1943 *B.B.C. Brains Trust*
(Strand)

BIG BILL CAMPBELL AND HIS ROCKY MOUNTAINEERS (band)
1937 *Pathetone 399*
"They're Tough Mighty Tough in the West"
1938 *Pathe Pictorial NS 99*
"Springtime in the Rockies"
"Coming Round the Mountain"
"Across the Great Divide"
1943 *Pictorial Revue of 1943*
F (reissue: *Pictorial 99*)

HERBERT CAMPBELL (comedian)
1900 *The Rats*
(Warwick)

1900 *Burlesque Attack on a Settler's Cabin*
(Warwick)
1900 *Burlesque Fox Hunt*
(Warwick)
1902 *Dan Leno and Herbert Campbell Edit 'The Sun'*
(Biograph)

MURRAY CAMPBELL (trumpeter)
1958 *The Golden Disc*
(Butcher) F
"Balmoral Melody"

ALFREDO CAMPOLI (violinist)
see also **CELEBRITY TRIO**
1938 *Stepping Toes*
(Baxter) F
1938 *Melodies of the Moment*
(Inspiration)
1939 *Tunes of the Times*
(Inspiration)
1940 *Fiddlers All*
(reissue: *Stepping Toes*)
1941 *A Musical Cocktail*
(Inspiration)
1943 *Old Mother Riley Detective*
(British National) F
1944 *Dreaming*
(Baxter) F
"Mendelssohn's Violin Concerto"
1946 *Musical Masquerade*
(Inspiration)
1949 *Music Parade*
(reissue: *title unknown*)
1951 *Mirth and Melody*
(reissue: *title unknown*)

ALFREDO CAMPOLI AND HIS TZIGANE ORCHESTRA
1935 *His Majesty and Co*
(Fox) F
1936 *B.B.C. Musicals 5*
(Inspiration)
1947 *Making the Grade*
(Inspiration)
(reissue: *B.B.C. Musicals 5*)

ALFREDO CAMPOLI AND REGINALD KING (violin)
1934 *Pathe Pictorial 824*
"Kasbek"
1934 *Pathe Pictorial 863*
"Pierrette Cherie"
1940 *Pathetone 529*
"Murmurs of Spring"
1940 *Pathetone 554*
"Autumn Sunshine"

CANADIAN BACHELORS (singers)
also known as The Three Canadian Bachelors
1937 *Calling All Stars*
(British Lion) F
"Painting Rainbows"

1939 *Pathetone 488*
"Sick and Tired of Hillbilly"
1940 *Pathe Pictorial 201*
"Nellie Dean"

CHAN CANASTA (conjurer)
1952 *The Amazing Mr Canasta*
(Butcher)

FREDDY CANNON (singer)
1963 *Just For Fun*
(Columbia) F
"The Ups and Downs of Love"
"Get Up Early in the Morning"

(TOMMY) CANNON AND (BOBBY) BALL
(comedians)
1983 *The Boys in Blue*
(Rank) F

GEORGE CANSDALE (television personality)
1955 *Simon and Laura*
(Rank) F

TONY CAPALDI (accordion)
1932 *Gaumont Sound Mirror 71*

BEBE CAPLAN (child accordionist)
1938 *Pathe Pictorial NS 144*
"Gopak"

LIONEL CARDAC (conjurer)
1913 *How It Is Done*
(Hepworth)

CARDOC BROTHERS (dancers)
1932 *Ideal Cinemagazine 340*

LESLIE CAREWE (singer)
1937 *Calling All Stars*
(British Lion) F
"Eleven More Months"
1938 *Around the Town*
(British Lion) F
1938 *Kicking the Moon Around*
(Vogue) F

CARL CARLISLE (impersonator)
1939 *Pathetone 510*
1940 *Pathe Pictorial 196*
(as Basil Rathbone, Charles Boyer,
Gordon Harker)
1941 *Pathe Pictorial 273*
1943 *Pathe Pictorial 390*
1945 *Sweethearts For Ever*
(Empire) F
1946 *Amateur Night*
(Renown)
1949 *Melody in the Dark*
(Adelphi) F

ELSIE CARLISLE (singer)
1930 *Al Fresco*
(Gainsborough)

1930 *Black and White*
(Gainsborough)
"I Want a Good Time Bad"
1931 *Pathetone 62*
"Alone and Afraid"
"My Canary Has Circles Under His
Eyes"
1933 *Radio Parade*
(BIP) F

DON CARLOS (singer)
1932 *Pathetone 140*
"Gypsy Moon"
1933 *Pathe Pictorial 791*
"Nothing But a Lie"

CARLYLE COUSINS (singing trio)
1932 *For the Love of Mike*
(BIP) F
"Sing Brothers"
1933 *Aunt Sally*
(Gainsborough) F
"The Wind's in the West"
1933 *Radio Parade*
(BIP) F
1934 *Screen Vaudeville*
(Vaudeville)
1934 *Radio Parade of 1935*
(BIP) F
"Good Morning to You"

JOHN CARMICHAEL AND HIS BAND
1994 *Shallow Grave*
(Figment) F
"Shallow Grave"

CARMICHAEL TROUPE (dancers)
1922 *Scottish National Dances*
(Square)

TULLIO CARMINATI (Italian tenor)
1936 *The Three Maxims*
(Wilcox) F
1937 *London Melody*
(Wilcox) F
1937 *Sunset in Vienna*
(Wilcox) F

CARMONA (Spanish dancer)
1935 *She Shall Have Music*
(Twickenham) F

TERRI CAROL (paper-tearer)
1994 *Funny Bones*
(Hollywood) F

EDWARD CARPENTER (dancer)
1931 *Ideal Cinemagazine 263*

FREDDIE CARPENTER (dancer)
1948 *Easy Money*
(Gainsborough) F

HARRY CARPENTER (television personality)
  1969 *The Magic Christian*
       (Grand) F

CARPENTER CORPS DE BALLET (dancers)
  1946 *Carnival*
       (Two Cities) F

CAROLE CARR (singer)
  1952 *Down Among the Z Men*
       (New Realm) F
       "Down Among the Z Men"
       "If This Is Love"
  1959 *Left Right and Centre*
       (British Lion) F

JANE CARR (singer)
(films as actress not listed)
  1932 *Love Me Love My Dog*
       (Warner)
  1934 *On the Air*
       (British Lion) F
  1934 *Those Were the Days*
       (BIP) F
       "As I Take My Morning Promenade"

JEAN CARR (singer)
(*also known as* Jean Kent)
  1940 *Hullo Fame*
       (British) F

JOAN CARR (dancer)
  1926 *London's Famous Cabarets*
       (Parkinson)
       "Metropole Midnight Follies"

MICHAEL CARR (composer)
see also **JIMMY KENNEDY AND MICHAEL CARR**
  1938 *Around the Town*
       (British Lion) F

WILL CARR (juggler)
  1937 *Pathe Pictorial NS 87*

EARL CARROLL AND HIS RADIO BOYS
(band)
  1937 *Spirit of Variety*
       (Exclusive)
  1938 *Pathetone 456*
       "Swing and Sway"

EDDIE CARROLL AND HIS BAND
  1937 *Let's Make a Night of It*
       (ABPC) F
  1939 *Eddie Carroll and his Boys*
       (Inspiration)
       "Harlem"
       "It Ain't Whatcha Do"
       "What Do You Know About Love?"
       "Sweet Sue"
  1947 *Making the Grade*
       (Inspiration)
       (reissue: *Eddie Carroll and his Boys*)

  1949 *Music Parade*
       (reissue: *Eddie Carroll and his Boys*)

FAY CARROLL (singer)
  1934 *Radio Parade of 1935*
       (BIP) F

PAMELA CARROLL (dancer)
  1946 *London Town*
       (GFD) F

RONNIE CARROLL (singer)
  1963 *Blind Corner*
       (Mancunian) F
       "Blind Corner"
       "Where You Goin'?"

CARROLL AND HOWE (comedians)
  1937 *Pathetone 379*

JASPER CARROTT (comedian)
  1987 *Jane and the Lost City*
       (Marcel) F

CHARD CARSON (singer)
  1963 *Farewell Performance*
       (Rank) F

FRANK CARSON (comedian)
  1987 *Testimony*
       (Isolde) F

JEAN (JEANNIE) CARSON (singer)
(films as actress not listed)
  1948 *A Date With a Dream*
       (Grand National) F
       "Unlucky"
       "Let Me Dream"
       "How About Me for You?"
       "Now Is the Time for Love"
  1955 *As Long As They're Happy*
       (Rank) F
       "Crazy Little Mixed Up Heart"
       "Quiet Rendezvous"
  1955 *An Alligator Named Daisy*
       (Rank) F
       "Midnight Madness"
       "I'm in Love for the Very First Time"
       "Your First Love Was Your Last"
  1958 *Rockets Galore*
       (Rank) F
       "Ye Banks and Braes"

CARSON SISTERS (singers)
  1934 *Pathe Pictorial 877*
  1935 *In Town Tonight*
       (British Lion) F
  1936 *Pathe Pictorial NS 8*
  1936 *Pathetone Parade of 1936*
       F (reissue: *Pictorial 877*)
  1936 *British Lion Varieties 6*
       "It's Love"

THE CARSONS (circus act)
1941 *Old Mother Riley's Circus*
(British National) F

HARRY CARTON (singer)
1929 *Mickey Mouse*
(Gainsborough)

CARUSO AND HIS NEW YORK SYNCOPATERS (band)
1929 *Pathe Pictorial 11*
"Just a Little Medley"

BILLY CARYLL AND HILDA MUNDY (comedy)
1930 *Amateur Night in London*
(PDC) F
1935 *Royal Cavalcade*
(BIP) F
1937 *Calling All Mas*
(Fox) F
1938 *Lassie from Lancashire*
(British National) F
1945 *I Didn't Do It*
(Columbia) F
1946 *New Pictorial 72*

CASA AND LENN (novelty act)
1932 *Pathe Pictorial 769*
"Fun and Fancy"

CASA NOVA GIRLS (dancers)
1933 *One Precious Year*
(B&D) F
"A Glad New Year"

SANTOS CASANI (dancer)
1929 *Pathe Magazine 1*
1932 *Pathetone 132*
1933 *Pathetone 147*
"Gaucho Tango"
1933 *Pathetone 194*
"Charleston Blues"

SANTOS CASANI AND JOSE LENNARD (dancers)
1926 *The Flat Charleston*
(Phonofilm)
1927 *British Screen Magazine*
"Charleston"
1927 *Eve's Film Review 307*
"French Tango"
1927 *Eve's Film Review 324*
"The Yale"
1927 *Eve's Film Review 334*
"The New Waltz"
1927 *Eve's Film Review 338*
"The New Foxtrot"
1928 *Eve's Film Review 344*
"Dos and Donts in Dance"
1928 *Eve's Film Review 361*
"Argentine Tango"
1928 *Eve's Film Review 366*
"Sugar Step"

1928 *Eve's Film Review 381*
"Dance Variation"
1929 *Eve's Film Review 434*
"The Six Eight"
1929 *Pathe Magazine 2*
"Ballroom Dancing"
1930 *Eve's Film Review 452*
"The Skater's Waltz"
1930 *Eve's Film Review 490*
"Midway Rhythm"
1931 *Eve's Film Review 541*
"New Tango"

TERENCE CASEY (organist)
1934 *Kentucky Minstrels*
(Realart) F

MORNEY CASH (comedian)
1904 *The Eviction*
(Gaumont)

CASINO DE PARIS CHORUS (dancers)
1923 *Woman to Woman*
(W&F) F

ISABELLA ROSATI CASSERINI (harp)
1927 *A Harp Overture*
(Phonofilm)
"Verdi's March Triumphant"

PETER CASSON (hypnotist)
1952 *New Pictorial 363*

REUBEN CASTANG AND HIS APES (animal act)
1935 *No Monkey Business*
(GFD) F

ROY CASTLE (comedian)
1958 *Hello London*
(Regal) F
"The Way to Make It Hep"
"All the Time"
"Do It For Me"
1964 *Dr Terror's House of Horrors*
(Amicus) F
1965 *Dr Who and the Daleks*
(Regal) F
1967 *Go With Matt Monro*
(Pathe)
1967 *The Plank*
(Rank) F
1968 *Carry On Up the Khyber*
(Rank) F
1969 *The Intrepid Mr Twigg*
(British Lion) F
1975 *Legend of the Werewolf*
(Tyburn) F

WALTER CATLETT (American comedian)
1920 *Around the Town 8*
(Gaumont)

GWEN CATLEY (soprano)
1942 *We'll Smile Again*
      (British National) F
      "Waltz of Delight"
      "Tonight You're Mine"
1943 *Theatre Royal*
      (Baxter) F
      "I Must Be Dreaming"
      "Tell Me Truly"

LAUDERIC CATON AND HIS RHYTHM SWINGTETTE (band)
1946 *Walking On Air*
      (Piccadilly) F
      "Harlem Jamboree"
      "St Louis Blues"
      "Honeysuckle Rose"
      "Ain't She Sweet?"

JEAN CAVALL (singer)
1947 *New Pictorial 165*
      "Darling Je Vous Aime Beaucoup"
1948 *Quartet*
      (Gainsborough) F
      "Alouette"
1949 *The Temptress*
      (Ambassador) F
      "Quand Même"
      "Je Suis Seule Ce Soir"
1951 *Let's Go Crazy*
      (Adelphi) F
      "Until a Few Kisses Ago"
      "Sur le Pont d'Avignon"

PETER CAVANAGH (impersonator)
1943 *Pathe Pictorial 382*
      (as Arthur Askey, Jack Hulbert,
      Cicely Courtneidge, Ronald
      Frankau)
1943 *Pathe Pictorial 401*
1971 *Top of the Bill*
      (Butcher) F

ANDY CAVELL AND THE SAINTS (group)
1963 *Live It Up*
      (Rank) F
      "Don't Take Your Love From Me"

KAY CAVENDISH (songs at the piano)
see also **CAVENDISH THREE**
1945 *New Pictorial 51*
      "I'm Gonna Love That Guy"
1949 *Poet's Pub*
      (GFD) F
      "Half a World Away"

CAVENDISH THREE (singers) (Kay Cavendish, Pat Rignold, Helen Raymond)
1943 *Playtime for Workers*
      (Federated) F
      "Jealousy"
      "And So Do I"
      "It Ain't Whatcha Do"

FRANCISCO CAVEZ AND HIS BAND
1956 *Parade of the Bands*
      (Hammer)

CAYENNE (Latin American band)
1987 *Eat the Rich*
      (Comic Strip) F

CELEBRITY TRIO (musicians) (Alfredo Campoli, Reginald King, Otto Pagotti)
1934 *Pathe Pictorial 863*
      "Pierrette Cherie"
1934 *Pathetone 230*
      "Song of Paradise"

JULIAN CHAGRIN (mime)
1967 *Danger Route*
      (Amicus) F
1967 *Blow-Up*
      (MGM) F
1968 *The Bliss of Mrs Blossom*
      (Paramount) F
1969 *Alfred the Great*
      (Smith) F
1972 *Alice's Adventures in Wonderland*
      (TCF) F
1974 *The Concert*
      (Columbia)
1975 *The Great McGonagall*
      (Tigon) F
1975 *Christmas Tree*
      (Warner)
1977 *The Morning Spider*
      (Warner)

FEODOR CHALIAPIN (Russian singer)
1933 *Don Quixote*
      (UA) F

GLADYS CHALK AND PARTNER
1929 *Pot Pourri*
      (BIP)

HARRY CHAMPION (comedian)
1934 *On the Air*
      (British Lion) F
1935 *Equity Musical Revue 4*
      (British Lion)
1936 *Old Timers*
      (Warner)
      "Any Old Iron"
1941 *Any Old Iron*
      (MOI)
      "Any Old Iron"

LES CHANTELLES (group)
1965 *Dateline Diamonds*
      (Rank) F

EVE CHAPMAN (singer)
1934 *Music Hall*
      (Realart) F
      "An Old-Fashioned Love Song"

GRAHAM CHAPMAN (comedian)
1969   *The Magic Christian*
        (Grand) F
1970   *The Rise and Rise of Michael
        Rimmer*
        (Anglo) F
1970   *Doctor in Trouble*
        (Rank) F
1971   *And Now For Something Completely
        Different*
        (Columbia) F
1975   *Monty Python and the Holy Grail*
        (EMI) F
1976   *Pleasure at Her Majesty's*
        (Amnesty) F
        "Court Room Sketch"
        "Lumberjack Song"
1978   *The Odd Job*
        (EMI)
1979   *Monty Python's Life of Brian*
        (CIC) F
1982   *The Secret Policeman's Other Ball*
        (UIP) F
        "Cash or I'll Strip Sketch"
1983   *Crimson Permanent Assurance*
        (UIP)
1983   *Monty Python's The Meaning of Life*
        (UIP) F
1983   *Monty Python Live at the Hollywood
        Bowl*
        (Handmade) F
1983   *Yellowbeard*
        (Hemdale) F

CHAPMAN'S CIRCUS
1937   *Make Up*
        (ABFD) F

WILLIAM CHAPPELL (dancer)
1951   *Flesh and Blood*
        (London) F

LAWRENCE CHARLES
see **CLAIRE DIVINA AND LAWRENCE
CHARLES**

RAY CHARLES (singer)
1964   *Ballad in Blue*
        (Warner) F
        "Light Out of Darkness"
        "Please Forgive and Forget"

**DICK CHARLESWORTH AND HIS CITY
GENTS** (band)
1963   *Suddenly Its Jazz*
        (British Lion)
        "Brown Skin Girl"
1964   *Jazz All the Way*
        (Rank)

CHARLEY'S BALLET (dancers)
1965   *24 Hours to Kill*
        (Warner) F

CHARLIE (boy xylophonist)
1934   *Pathetone 232*

CHARLIE AND SONIA (group)
see also **CHARLIE CREED-MILES**
1996   *Glastonbury: The Movie*
        (Starlight) F
        "Heaven"

ANDRE CHARLOT GIRLS (dancers)
1929   *Musical Medley*
        (BIP)
1930   *Elstree Calling*
        (BIP) F
        "The Lady's Maid Is Always in the
        Know"
1930   *The New Waiter*
        (PDC)
1930   *The Musical Beauty Shop*
        (PDC)
1935   *Opening Night*
        (Olympic) F

CHAZ CHASE (comedian)
1950   *New Pictorial 286*

DIANA CHASE (dancer)
1946   *Dancing Thru*
        (Angel) F

BARRI CHAT AND TERRI GARDNER (drag
comedians)
1968   *A Little of What You Fancy*
        (Border) F
        "Why Do They Always Say No?"
        "Somebody Loves Me"
        "I Wonder Where My Baby Is
        Tonight"

CHUBBY CHECKER (singer)
1962   *It's Trad Dad*
        (Columbia) F
        "Lose Your Inhibitions Twist"

KEITH CHEGWIN (television personality)
1970   *Egghead's Robot*
        (CFF) F
1971   *The Troublesome Double*
        (CFF)
1972   *Macbeth*
        (Playboy) F
1975   *Robin Hood Junior*
        (CFF) F
1978   *Keith Chegwin Introduces*
        (CFF)
1980   *High Rise Donkey*
        (CFF) F

CHELA AND DORAY (dancers)
1936   *Tropical Trouble*
        (City) F
1936   *Such Is Life*
        (Incorporated) F

CHELSEA (group)
1981 *Urgh! A Music War*
(White) F
"I'm on Fire"

RONALD CHESNEY (harmonica)
1941 *Facing the Music*
(Butcher) F
1943 *They Met in the Dark*
(GFD) F
1944 *Give Me the Stars*
(British National) F
1955 *Value for Money*
(Rank) F
"Gentle Maiden"

BETTY CHESTER (singer)
see also **THE CO-OPTIMISTS**
1926 *Betty Chester, the Well Known Co-Optimist Star*
(Phonofilm)
"Pig Tail Alley"
1929 *The Co-Optimists*
(New Era) F
"The Band Master's Daughter"

CHARLIE CHESTER (comedian)
1945 *Food Flash*
(MOI) S
1947 *Holiday Camp*
(Gainsborough) F
"Bobbing Up and Down Like This"
"Song of the Farmer's Boy"
1971 *Top of the Bill*
(Butcher) F
"Mary From the Dairy"
1979 *Can I Come Too?*
(New Realm) F

MAURICE CHESTER'S PERFORMING DOGS
1930 *Eve's Film Review 481*
1934 *Music Hall*
(Realart) F

BARBARA CHETHAM (dancer)
1921 *Around the Town*
(Gaumont)
"Jockey Dance"

ALBERT CHEVALIER (comedian)
1915 *The Bottle*
(Hepworth) F
1915 *My Old Dutch*
(Turner) F
1915 *The Middleman*
(London) F

ALBERT CHEVALIER JR (comedian)
1948 *For Old Times Sake*
(Butcher)

GUS CHEVALIER (comedian)
1922 *Around the Town 115*
(Gaumont)

"Minstrels of 1922"
1936 *Full Steam*
(Ace) F
1936 *Bottle Party*
(Ace) F
1936 *Song in Soho*
(Ace) F
1937 *Windmill Revels*
(Ace) F
1937 *Carry On London*
(Ace) F
1937 *Uptown Revue*
(Ace) F
1937 *Concert Party*
(Ace) F
1937 *Footlights*
(Ace) F
1938 *Two Men in a Box*
(Ace) F
1938 *Swing*
(Ace) F
1938 *Revue Parade*
(Ace) F
1938 *Behind the Tabs*
(Ace) F
1938 *The Interrupted Rehearsal*
(Ace) F
1938 *Spotlight*
(Ace) F

MAURICE CHEVALIER (French singer)
1936 *Beloved Vagabond*
(Toeplitz) F
"Loch Lomond"
"Tzinga Doodle Day"
"You Look So Sweet Madame"
1938 *Break the News*
(GFD) F
1962 *In Search of the Castaways*
(Disney) F

THE CHEYNES (group)
1964 *Mods and Rockers*
(Anglo)

ROBERT CHIGWELL (singer)
1930 *The Jolly Farmers*
(BIP)
"London"

THE CHIKOLAS (acrobats)
1939 *Pathe Pictorial NS 174*

EDDIE CHILDS (comedian)
1926 *London's Famous Cabarets*
(Parkinson)
"Metropole Midnight Follies"

GILBERT CHILDS (comedian)
see also **THE CO-OPTIMISTS**
1929 *The Co-Optimists*
(New Era) F
"When the Rich Man Rides By"

CHILTON AND THOMAS (comedy dancers)
1937   *Sing As You Swing*
         (Rock) F

G H CHIRGWIN (comedian)
1896   *Chirgwin in his Humorous Business*
         (Paul)
1896   *Chirgwin Plays a Scotch Reel*
         (Paul)
1900   *The Blind Boy*
         (Phono-Bio-Tableaux)
1917   *The Blind Boy*
         (Photoplay) F

GEORGE CHISHOLM (comedian)
1963   *The Mouse on the Moon*
         (UA) F
1965   *The Knack*
         (UA) F
1983   *Superman III*
         (Warner) F

ROBERT CHISHOLM (baritone)
1935   *Cock o' the North*
         (Butcher) F
         "La Rêve Passe"
1935   *Father O'Flynn*
         (Butcher) F
1938   *Highlights of Variety 11*
         (reissue: *Cock o' the North*)

CHOIR OF H.M. WELSH GUARDS
1946   *I'll Turn To You*
         (Butcher) F

ARTHUR CHRISTIANSEN (editor)
1961   *The Day the Earth Caught Fire*
         (British Lion) F
1963   *80,000 Suspects*
         (Rank) F

KEITH CHRISTIE (musician)
1962   *All Night Long*
         (Rank) F

CINGALEE (conjurer)
1935   *Can You Hear Me, Mother?*
         (British Lion) F

PAUL CINQUEVALLI (juggler)
1901   *Cannon Ball Juggling*
         (Warwick)

THE CIRCLE JERKS (group)
1986   *Sid and Nancy*
         (Zenith) F
         "Love Kills"

CITY OF LONDON BOY PLAYERS (band)
1938   *Pathe Pictorial NS 112*

JOHNNY CLAES AND HIS CLAEPIGEONS
(band)
1942   *Escape to Justice*
         (Renown) F
1946   *George in Civvy Street*
         (Columbia) F

LIONEL CLAFF AND HIS BAND
1934   *Love Mirth Melody*
         (Mancunian) F

CLANE MUSICAL SOCIETY
1990   *The Miracle*
         (Palace) F

CHARLIE CLAPHAM (comedian)
1941   *My Wife's Family*
         (ABPC) F

CLAPHAM AND DWYER (comedians)
1929   *Clapham and Dwyer 1; 2*
         (BSFP)
1929   *Pathe Pictorial 564*
1931   *Pathetone 72*
1931   *Ideal Cinemagazine 284*
1932   *Musical Medley 2*
         (reissue: *Clapham and Dwyer 1*)
1933   *Radio Parade*
         (BIP) F
1934   *On the Air*
         (British Lion) F
1934   *Radio Parade of 1935*
         (BIP) F
1935   *Wedding Eve*
         (Astor) F
1935   *B.B.C. the Voice of Britain*
         (New Era) F
1936   *Pathe Pictorial NS 1*
1937   *Variety Hour*
         (Fox) F
1937   *Sing As You Swing*
         (Rock) F
1940   *Music Box*
         (reissue: *Sing As You Swing*)

ERIC CLAPTON (guitarist)
see also **CREAM**
1975   *Tommy*
         (Stigwood) F
         "Eyesight to the Blind"
1982   *The Secret Policeman's Other Ball*
         (UIP) F
         "Farther Up the Road"
1985   *Water*
         (Rank) F

BERNICE CLARE (singer)
1935   *Two Hearts in Harmony*
         (Times) F

TOM CLARE (comedian)
1932   *Pathe Pictorial 733*
         "My Bally Eyeglass"

WYN CLARE (singer)
1936   *B.B.C. Musicals 2*
         (Inspiration)
1947   *Making the Grade*
         (reissue: *B.B.C. Musicals 2*)

DAVE CLARK FIVE (group)
1965   *Catch Us If You Can*
         (Anglo) F
         "Catch Us If You Can"
         "Time"
         "Sweet Memories"
         "When"
         "I Can't Stand It"
         "On the Move"
         "Move On"
         "Wild Weekend"

JOHNSON CLARK (ventriloquist)
1938   *Pathe Pictorial NS 116*

PETULA CLARK (singer)
(films as actress not listed)
1944   *New Pictorial 35*
1948   *Here Come the Huggetts*
         (Gainsborough) F
         "Try Walking Backwards"
1949   *Vote for Huggett*
         (Gainsborough) F
         "In the Shade of the Old Apple
         Tree"
1949   *The Huggetts Abroad*
         (Gainsborough) F
         "Toodle Oodle Ay"
         "House in the Sky"
1949   *Don't Ever Leave Me*
         (Rank) F
         "Don't Ever Leave Me"
         "Not for the Want of Trying"
1951   *Pathe Pictorial 335*
         "Have I Told You Lately That I Love
         You?"
1958   *6.5 Special*
         (Anglo) F
         "Baby Lover"

GEORGE CLARKE (comedian)
1926   *Eve's Film Review 252*
         "Umbrellas and Ice Cream"
1930   *Pathe Magazine 34*
         "The Whiskers Song"
1930   *His First Car*
         (PDC) F
1930   *Pathe Gazette*
         "Darling I Love You"
1931   *Eve's Film Review 506*
         "Blue Roses"

GRACE CLARKE AND COLIN MURRAY
(singers)
1936   *Pathetone 310*
         "The Song That is Calling Me
         Home"

ROMA CLARKE
see **JOSIE SANTOI AND ROMA CLARKE**

JULIAN CLARY (comedian)
1992   *Carry On Columbus*
         (Comedy House) F

THE CLASH (group)
1980   *Rude Boy*
         (Tigon) F
         "Revolution Rock"
         "Garageland"
         "London's Burning"
         "White Riot"
         "White Man at Hammersmith Palais"
         "U.S.A."
         "Janie Jones"
         "The Prisoner"
         "Tommy Gun"
         "All the Young Punks"
         "Rudi Can't Fail"
         "Complete Control"
         "Safe European Home"
         "What's My Name?"
         "Police and Thieves"
         "I Fought the Law"
         "No Reason"
         "Stay Free"

ARTHUR CLAYTON (entertainer)
1936   *Full Steam*
         (Ace) F

ROBINSON CLEAVER (organist)
1944   *Pathe Pictorial 408*
         "The Skater's Waltz"

JOHN CLEESE (comedian)
1967   *Interlude*
         (Columbia) F
1968   *The Bliss of Mrs Blossom*
         (Paramount) F
1969   *The Magic Christian*
         (Grand) F
1969   *The Best House in London*
         (MGM) F
1970   *The Rise and Rise of Michael
         Rimmer*
         (Anglo) F
1971   *And Now For Something Completely
         Different*
         (Columbia) F
1972   *It's a 2'6" Above the Ground World*
         (British Lion) F
1975   *Monty Python and the Holy Grail*
         (EMI) F
1975   *Romance of a Double Bass*
         (CIC)
1976   *Pleasure at Her Majesty's*
         (Amnesty) F
         "Dead Parrot Sketch"
         "Court Room Sketch"
         "Last Supper Sketch"
         "Lumberjack Song"

1979	*Monty Python's Life of Brian* (CIC) F
1980	*The Secret Policeman's Ball* (Tigon) F
1981	*Time Bandits* (UIP) F
1981	*The Great Muppet Caper* (ITC) F
1982	*The Secret Policeman's Other Ball* (UIP) F
1983	*Privates On Parade* (Handmade) F
1983	*Monty Python's The Meaning of Life* (UIP) F
1983	*Monty Python Live at the Hollywood Bowl* (Handmade) F
1983	*Yellowbeard* (Hemdale) F
1985	*Clockwise* (Moment) F
1987	*The Secret Policeman's Third Ball* (Virgin) F
1988	*A Fish Called Wanda* (Prominent) F
1989	*Erik the Viking* (UIP) F
1993	*Splitting Heirs* (Prominent) F
1994	*Mary Shelley's Frankenstein* (TriStar) F
1996	*The Wind in the Willows* (Allied) F
1996	*Fierce Creatures* (Universal) F

CLEMSON AND VALERIE (dancers)
1936	*Pathe Pictorial NS 12* "Nigger Strut"
1936	*Pathe Pictorial NS 29* "Rumba"
1937	*Pathe Pictorial NS 62* "Gold and Silver Waltz"
1937	*Pathe Pictorial NS 66*

LADDIE CLIFF (comedian)
see also **THE CO-OPTIMISTS**
1922	*The Card* (Ideal) F
1925	*Eve's Film Review 224* "Dear Little Billy"
1927	*On With the Dance* (Parkinson)
1929	*Eve's Film Review 410* "Love"
1929	*The Co-Optimists* (New Era) F "My Girl's Face"
1931	*Eve's Film Review 523* "The Millionaire Kid"
1933	*Sleeping Car* (Gaumont) F
1934	*Happy* (BIP) F "Dancing Through Life"

1936	*Sporting Love* (British Lion) F "In the Springtime" "That Coal Black Mammy of Mine"
1937	*Over She Goes* (ABPC) F "We'll Have a Country Wedding" "Side By Side" "Over She Goes"

BERNARD CLIFTON (singer)
1938	*Pathetone 411* "Hold Me Close to Your Heart"
1938	*Pathetone 438*
1938	*Pathe Pictorial NS 129* "So Little Time"
1940	*Pathe Pictorial 240* "A Nightingale Sang in Berkeley Square"

THE CLIPPERS (musicians)
1960	*The Entertainer* (UA) F

JIMMY CLITHEROE (comedian)
1942	*Much Too Shy* (Columbia) F
1943	*Rhythm Serenade* (Columbia) F
1949	*Somewhere in Politics* (Mancunian) F
1949	*School for Randle* (Mancunian) F
1956	*Stars in Your Eyes* (British Lion) F
1960	*Full House* (reissue: *Somewhere in Politics*)
1960	*Teacher's Pest* (reissue: *School for Randle*)
1967	*Jules Verne's Rocket to the Moon* (Anglo) F

DONALD CLIVE (singer)
1949	*Murder at the Windmill* (Grand National) F "I'll Settle for You" "Two Little Dogs" "Life Should Go With a Swing"

JUNE CLYDE (song and dance)
1935	*Dance Band* (BIP) F "Lovey Dovey"
1935	*No Monkey Business* (GFD) F
1935	*She Shall Have Music* (Twickenham) F "Do the Runaround" "My First Thrill" "Nothing on Earth" "May All Your Troubles Be Little Ones"
1935	*Charing Cross Road* (British Lion) F "Roadway of Romance"

1936 *Land Without Music*
(Capitol) F
1936 *King of the Castle*
(City) F
1937 *Let's Make a Night of It*
(ABPC) F
"Let It Rain"
"If My Heart Says Sing"
1937 *Make Up*
(ABFD) F
1937 *Sam Small Leaves Town*
(BSS) F
1938 *Weddings Are Wonderful*
(RKO) F
1938 *His Lordship Goes to Press*
(RKO) F
1952 *Treasure Hunt*
(Romulus) F
1952 *24 Hours of a Woman's Life*
(ABPC) F
1954 *The Love Lottery*
(Ealing) F
1957 *After the Ball*
(Romulus) F
"Her Golden Hair Was Hanging
Down Her Back"

CLYDE VALLEY STOMPERS (band)
1963 *It's All Happening*
(British Lion) F
"Casbah"

THE CO-CREATORS (group)
1996 *Glastonbury: The Movie*
(Starlight) F
"My Life in Politics/The Media"

ERIC COATES (composer)
1934 *Pathetone 218*
"Chasing the Moon"
"London Bridge"
1944 *New Pictorial 5*

PETER COATES (impersonator)
1943 *Pathe Pictorial 373*

CHARLES COBURN (comedian)
1933 *Ideal Cinemagazine 353*
1934 *Pathe Pictorial 836*
"The Man Who Broke the Bank"
1934 *Pathetone 220*
"Two Lovely Black Eyes"
1934 *Say It With Flowers*
(Realart) F
"The Man Who Broke the Bank"
1936 *Pathe Pictorial NS 38*
"He's All Right When You Know
Him"
1936 *Old Timers*
(Warner)
"The Man Who Broke the Bank"
1936 *Pathetone Parade of 1936*
F (reissue: *Pictorial 836*)
1936 *Pictorial Revue*
F (reissue: *Pathetone 220*)

1943 *Variety Jubilee*
(Butcher) F
"The Man Who Broke the Bank"
1944 *Highlights of Variety 26*
(reissue: *Variety Jubilee*)

CHARLES B COCHRAN'S YOUNG LADIES
(dancers)
1930 *The Shaming of the True*
(BIF)
1933 *Pathetone 164*
1936 *Pathetone 323*
"The Greeks Had a Word For It"
1936 *It's In the Bag*
(Warner) F

PEGGY COCHRANE (pianist)
see also **THAT CERTAIN TRIO**
1932 *Pathe Pictorial 719*
"I Found You"
1933 *Pathe Pictorial 799*
"Toy Balloon"
1934 *Radio Parade of 1935*
(BIP) F
"There's No Excusing Susan"
1936 *Pathetone 341*
"Dinah"

COCKNEY REBEL (group)
1976 *Between the Lines*
(EMI)

THE COCKNEYS (group)
1964 *Swinging UK*
(Baim)
"After Tomorrow"

CATHERINE COFFEY (dancer)
1994 *Welcome II the Terrordome*
(Metro Tartan) F
"Ghetto Tension"

DENISE COFFEY (comedienne)
1962 *Waltz of the Toreadors*
(Rank) F
1963 *Farewell Performance*
(Rank) F
1966 *Georgy Girl*
(Columbia) F
1967 *Far From the Madding Crowd*
(Warner) F
1970 *Percy*
(EMI) F
1980 *Sir Henry at Rawlinson End*
(Charisma) F
1983 *Another Time, Another Place*
(Cinegate) F

ALMA COGAN (singer)
1955 *Eric Winstone Band Show*
(Hammer)
1956 *Eric Winstone's Stagecoach*
(Hammer)

HARRIET COHEN (pianist)
1944 *Love Story*
(Gainsborough) F
"Cornish Rhapsody"

LEONARD COHEN (singer)
1972 *Bird on a Wire*
(EMI) F
"Bird on a Wire"
"You Know Who I Am"
"Nancy"
"Sisters of Mercy"
"Famous Blue Raincoat"
"One of Us Can't Be Wrong"
"Tonight Will Be Fine"
"Suzanne"
"Chelsea Hotel"
"That's No Way to Say Goodbye"
"Marianne"
"Partisan"
"Avalanche"

COIN COIN (unicyclist)
1968 *Popdown*
(New Realm) F

COL LING SOO (conjurer)
1952 *Say Abracadabra*
(Butcher)

PATRICK COLBERT (bass)
1935 *Pathe Pictorial 908*
"Rain"
1936 *Pathetone 315*
"Down the Hillbilly Trail"
1937 *Pathetone Parade of 1938*
F (reissue: *Pathetone 315*)
1937 *Pathetone 354*
"Haul the Timber"
1938 *Pathe Pictorial NS 113*
"Deep Waters"
1940 *Pathetone 558*
"River Sing Me a Song"

CHARLES COLE (cartoonist)
1941 *Pathe Pictorial 258*
1943 *Pathe Pictorial 382*

MARY COLE (tap-dancer)
1937 *Mad About Money*
(Morgan) F
"Dusting the Stars"

MAURICE COLE (singer)
1930 *Pathetone 27*
"Liebestraum"

ESTHER COLEMAN (singer)
1935 *Pathetone 268*
1936 *B.B.C. Musicals 2*
(Inspiration)
1938 *Melodies of the Moment*
(reissue: *B.B.C. Musicals 2*)

GEORGIA COLEMAN (singer)
1933 *Pathe Pictorial 800*
"In the Twilight"

JOAN COLERIDGE
1937 *Spirit of Variety*
(Exclusive)

COLERIDGE-TAYLOR ORCHESTRA
1933 *Ideal Cinemagazine 390*
"Dance from Othello"

JEAN COLIN (singer)
1930 *Eve's Film Review 458*
"Here Comes the Bride"
1930 *Compromising Daphne*
(BIP) F
1937 *Mad About Money*
(Morgan) F
"Oh So Beautiful"
"The Little Lost Tune"
"Dusting the Stars"
1939 *The Mikado*
(GFD) F
1940 *Laugh It Off*
(British National) F
"We'll Always Give a Thought To You"
"If You Were the Only Girl in the World"
"There'll Always Be Time for a Song"
"Sing Me Some of the Old Songs"
"The Honeysuckle and the Bee"
1941 *Surprise Broadcast*
(Exclusive)
1941 *Bob's Your Uncle*
(Butcher) F
1941 *Eating Out with Tommy Trinder*
(Strand)

BONAR COLLEANO JR (comedian)
(films as actor not listed)
1944 *Starlight Serenade*
(Federated) F
1944 *We the People*
(Independent)
1948 *Merry Go Round*
(Federated) F

CON COLLEANO (wire-walker)
1935 *Pathetone 256*

CECILIA COLLEDGE (skater)
1934 *Pathetone 244*
(Argo)
1946 *Mind Your Step*
(Argo)
1947 *Top Speed*
(Sherwood)

RAE COLLET (child dancer)
1936 *Ace Cinemagazine*

1937 *Captain's Orders*
(Liberty) F

ALF COLLINS (comedian)
1907 *This Little Girl and That Little Girl*
(Chronophone)
1907 *Won't You Throw Me a Kiss?*
(Chronophone)
1908 *I Get Dizzy When I Do That Twostep Dance*
(Chronophone)

ELGA COLLINS (singer)
1927 *Elga Collins the Versatile Entertainer*
(Phonofilm)
"Ain't It Nice?"
"Tonight You Belong to Me"

JOSÉ COLLINS (singer)
1919 *Nobody's Child*
(B&C) F
1920 *The Sword of Damocles*
(B&C) F
1923 *The José Collins Dramas*
(B&C) S
1933 *Pathe Pictorial*
"The Last Waltz"
1933 *Facing the Music*
(BIP) F
"Jewel Song"

PHIL COLLINS (singer)
see also **GENESIS**
1967 *Calamity the Cow*
(CFF) F
1982 *The Secret Policeman's Other Ball*
(UIP) F
"In the Air Tonight"
1988 *Buster*
(Buster) F
1993 *Calliope*
(Schmitt) F
1993 *Guv'nor*
(Spartan) F

WINNIE COLLINS
see **WALTER WILLIAMS AND WINNIE COLLINS**

COLLINSON AND BREEN (comedians)
1939 *Pathetone 462*
1943 *Pictorial Revue of 1943*
F (reissue: *Pathetone 462*)

COLLINSON AND DEAN (comedians)
1930 *Jerry Builders*
(PDC)
1930 *Pathetone 36*
"One Night Alone With You"
1931 *Pathetone 77*
"A Lying Argument"
1932 *Pathetone 111*
1932 *Pathetone 127*
"A Naval Pact"

1933 *Pathetone 192*
1934 *Pathetone 205*
"At the Bar"
1934 *Pathetone Parade*
F (reissue: *title unknown*)
1935 *Pathe Pictorial 899*
"Business Figures"
1935 *Pathe Pictorial 917*
"Three Feet"
1936 *Pictorial Revue*
F (reissue: *Pictorial 899*)
1937 *Pathe Pictorial NS 44*
1937 *Heavily Married*
(Krackerjack) F
1937 *Pathetone Parade of 1938*
F (reissue: *Pictorial 917*)
1938 *On Velvet*
(AIP) F

EDDIE COLLIS AND THE ARISTOCRATS
(band)
1933 *Pathe Pictorial 787*
"Liebestraum"

KEN COLLYER AND HIS JAZZ BAND
1963 *West Eleven*
(Angel) F

EMILIO COLOMBO'S TZIGANE BAND
1933 *Heads We Go*
(BIP) F
"She's Everybody's Sweetheart Now"
1937 *Gypsy*
(Warner) F

JERRY COLONNA (American comedian)
1962 *The Road to Hong Kong*
(UA) F

MARIE COLORES
see **JEAN PERRIE AND MARIE COLORES**

COLOSSEUM (group)
1970 *Colosseum and Juicy Lucy*
(Warner)

MR AND MRS JACK COLTON (dancers)
1921 *Around the Town 106*
(Gaumont)

NORAH COLTON (singer)
1936 *Cabaret Nights 3; 7*
(Highbury)
"Funiculi Funicula"

COLUMBIA CHOIR
1938 *On Velvet*
(AIP) F

ALA COMA (juggler)
1898 *Juggler*
(Cinematograph)

BOBBIE COMBER (comedian)
- 1930 *Elstree Calling*
  (BIP) F
- 1931 *Hot Heir*
  (Gainsborough)
- 1932 *Pathetone 138*
  "There's Another Trumpet Playing in the Sky"
- 1932 *Brother Alfred*
  (BIP) F
- 1932 *The Fortunate Fool*
  (ABFD) F
- 1934 *Lilies of the Field*
  (B&D) F
- 1934 *There Goes Susie*
  (Pathe) F
- 1935 *Lazybones*
  (Realart) F
- 1935 *Ace of Spades*
  (Realart) F
- 1935 *Be Careful Mr Smith*
  (Apex) F
  "Who Were You With Last Night?"
- 1935 *Sound Advice*
  (NFC) ADVERT
- 1936 *Don't Rush Me*
  (PDC) F
- 1936 *Excuse My Glove*
  (ABFD) F
- 1936 *Sporting Love*
  (British Lion) F
- 1937 *Romance in Flanders*
  (British Lion) F

COMEDIAN HARMONISTS (singers)
- 1932 *Monte Carlo Madness*
  (UFA) F

THE COMMODORES (group)
- 1978 *Natural High*
  (EMI)

LES COMPAGNONS DE LA CHANSON
(French singers)
- 1950 *New Pictorial 327*
  "Jimmy Brown"

FAY COMPTON (singer)
(films as actress not listed)
- 1934 *Song at Eventide*
  (Butcher) F
  "Wandering to Paradise"
  "My Treasure"
  "For You Alone"
  "Dreaming"
  "Gigolette"
  "Vienna City of My Dreams"

CONCHITA AND MALAQUITA (Spanish dancers)
- 1936 *Cabaret Nights 2*
  (Highbury)

FRANZ CONDE AND HIS BEGUINES
(band)
- 1944 *Pathe Pictorial 420*
  "Kiss Me"

CONDOS BROTHERS (pantomime horse)
- 1932 *The Midshipmaid*
  (Gainsborough) F

CONEY ISLAND SIX (singers)
- 1927 *Syncopation and Song*
  (Phonofilm)

BILLY CONNOLLY (Scottish comedian)
- 1976 *Big Banana Feet*
  (Viz) F
- 1978 *Absolution*
  (Bulldog) F
  "Shady Grove"
- 1980 *The Secret Policeman's Ball*
  (Tigon) F
  "The Country and Western Supersong"
- 1982 *The Secret Policeman's Other Ball*
  (UIP) F
- 1983 *Bullshot*
  (Handmade) F
- 1985 *Water*
  (Rank) F
- 1990 *The Big Man*
  (Palace) F
- 1997 *Mrs Brown*
  (BBC) F
- 1997 *The Changeling*
  (High Time) F

EDRIC CONNOR (singer)
- 1947 *New Pictorial 135*
  "Water Boy"
- 1948 *My African People*
  (Best)

ARTHUR CONQUEST (comedian)
- 1902 *Bluebeard*
  (Warwick)
- 1913 *Harnessing a Horse*
  (Hepworth)
- 1914 *Whitewashing the Ceiling*
  (Day)
- 1914 *Building a Chicken House*
  (Sunny South)
- 1914 *The Jockey*
  (Sunny South)
- 1914 *Moving a Piano*
  (Sunny South)
- 1914 *The Showman's Dream*
  (Sunny South)
- 1914 *Tincture of Iron*
  (Sunny South)

JESS CONRAD (singer)
(films as actor not listed)
    1961   *Rag Doll*
            (Butcher) F
            "Why Am I Living?"
    1980   *The Great Rock 'n' Roll Swindle*
            (Virgin) F
    1988   *Tank Malling*
            (Parkfield) F

CONSTANCE, LILYAN AND MALO
    1936   *King of Hearts*
            (Butcher) F

MABEL CONSTANDUROS (comedienne)
    1929   *Ag and Bert*
            (BSFP)
    1932   *Pathe Pictorial 763*
            "The Bugginses"
    1933   *Radio Parade*
            (BIP) F
    1935   *Where's George?*
            (B&D) F
    1936   *Stars On Parade*
            (Butcher) F
    1938   *Highlights of Variety 10*
            (reissue: *Stars On Parade*)
    1939   *Zoo and You*
            (Technique)
    1940   *Food for Thought*
            (Ealing)
    1942   *Rose of Tralee*
            (Butcher) F
    1942   *Salute John Citizen*
            (British National) F
    1944   *Medal for the General*
            (British National) F
    1944   *My Ain Folk*
            (Butcher) F
    1946   *Bad Company*
            (New Realm) F
    1946   *Caravan*
            (Gainsborough) F
    1947   *The White Unicorn*
            (GFD) F
    1948   *Easy Money*
            (Gainsborough) F

ITALIA CONTI'S JUVENILES (song and dance)
    1935   *Kiddies On Parade*
            (Majestic) F

CONTINENTAL TRIO (singers)
    1934   *Pathetone 206*
            "La La La"

JOY CONWAY (singer)
    1941   *Pathe Pictorial 299*
            "All Those in Favour of Swing"

RUSS CONWAY (pianist)
    1960   *Climb Up the Wall*
            (New Realm) F
            "Lucky Five"
    1961   *Weekend With Lulu*
            (Hammer) F
    1963   *It's All Happening*
            (British Lion) F
            "Flamenco"

SHIRL CONWAY (singer)
    1949   *Helter Skelter*
            (Gainsborough) F
            "Without a Shadow of a Doubt"

FRED CONYNGHAM (song and dance)
    1932   *Indiscretions of Eve*
            (BIP) F
            "I'll Be the Lucky One"
            "Get Your Friends to Do It"
            "She's Only Wax"
    1934   *Radio Parade of 1935*
            (BIP) F
            "There's No Excusing Susan"
    1935   *Key to Harmony*
            (B&D) F
    1935   *School for Stars*
            (B&D) F
    1935   *The Crouching Beast*
            (BIP) F
    1936   *Ball At Savoy*
            (RKO) F
    1936   *Beloved Impostor*
            (RKO) F
    1936   *She Knew What She Wanted*
            (ABPC) F
            "Swonderful"
            "Funny Face"
            "My One and Only"
            "Let's Kiss and Make Up"
    1936   *Chick*
            (B&D) F
    1937   *Wake Up Famous*
            (ATP) F
    1937   *Rose of Tralee*
            (Butcher) F
            "The Mountains o' Mourne"
            "Those Endearing Young Charms"
            "Did Your Mother Come From Ireland?"
    1937   *The Minstrel Boy*
            (Butcher) F
            "The Minstrel Boy"
            "I Love the Moon"
            "When Loves Are So Many"
            "MacDougall McNab and McKay"
    1937   *Sam Small Leaves Town*
            (BSS) F
    1947   *When You Come Home*
            (Butcher) F
            "Take a Step"

STEVE COOGAN (comedian)
1989 *Resurrected*
      (Hobo) F
1996 *The Wind in tho Willows*
      (Allied) F

PAUL COOK (drummer)
see also **THE SEX PISTOLS**
1980 *The Great Rock 'n' Roll Swindle*
      (Virgin) F

PETER COOK (comedian)
1966 *The Wrong Box*
      (Columbia) F
1967 *Bedazzled*
      (TCF) F
1967 *A Dandy in Aspic*
      (Columbia) F
1969 *The Bed Sitting Room*
      (UA) F
1969 *Monte Carlo or Bust*
      (Paramount) F
1970 *The Rise and Rise of Michael
      Rimmer*
      (Anglo) F
1976 *Pleasure at Her Majesty's*
      (Amnesty) F
      "Court Room Sketch"
      "Asp"
      "So That's the Way You Like It"
      "Lumberjack Song"
1977 *The Hound of the Baskervilles*
      (Hemdale) F
1980 *The Secret Policeman's Ball*
      (Tigon) F
1983 *Yellowbeard*
      (Hemdale) F
1984 *Supergirl*
      (Columbia) F
1988 *Whoops Apocalypse*
      (Virgin) F

PHIL COOL (comedian)
1987 *The Secret Policeman's Third Ball*
      (Virgin) F

EDWARD COOPER (singer)
1935 *Opening Night*
      (Olympic) F
1941 *Pathe Pictorial 293*
      "Song of the Open Country"
1942 *Pathe Pictorial 342*

JACK COOPER (singer)
1936 *Soft Lights and Sweet Music*
      (British Lion) F
      "Madonna"

TOMMY COOPER (comedian)
1957 *Magic in the Air*
      (Gas) ADVERT
1960 *And the Same to You*
      (Monarch) F

1963 *The Cool Mikado*
      (Baim) F
1967 *The Plank*
      (Rank) F

JOHN COOPER CLARKE (singer and poet)
1981 *Urgh! A Music War*
      (White) F
      "Chicken Town"

THE CO-OPTIMISTS (concert party)
(Melville Gideon, Stanley Holloway, Davy
Burnaby, Peggy Petronella, Elsa MacFarlane,
Laddie Cliff, Phyllis Monkman, Harry S
Pepper, Betty Chester, Gilbert Childs)
1929 *The Co-Optimists*
      (New Era) F
      "Bow Wow"
      "London Town"
      "My Girl's Face"
      "Sam Pick Up Thy Musket"
      "It's For You"
      "Maybe Me Maybe You"
      "If It Weren't for the Likes of Us
      Chaps"
      "Wun Lung Too"
      "You've Gotta Beat Out the Rhythm"
      "When the Rich Man Rides By"
      "Till the Wheel Comes Off"
      "Down Love Lane"
      "My Lady's Eyes"

BERT COOTE (comedian)
1921 *Around the Town*
      (Gaumont)
      "Puss Puss"
1931 *Bracelets*
      (Gaumont) F

MILES COPELAND (musician)
1987 *Eat the Rich*
      (Comic Strip) F

RONNIE CORBETT (comedian)
1952 *You're Only Young Twice*
      (ABFD) F
1956 *Fun at St Fanny's*
      (British Lion) F
1958 *Rockets Galore*
      (Rank) F
1967 *Casino Royale*
      (Columbia) F
1969 *Some Will, Some Won't*
      (ABP) F
1970 *The Rise and Rise of Michael
      Rimmer*
      (Anglo) F
1973 *No Sex Please, We're British*
      (Columbia) F
1996 *Fierce Creatures*
      (Universal) F

SONYA CORDEAU (singer)
1962 *Danger By My Side*

(Butcher) F
"A Simple Girl"

LOLA CORDELL *see* **AL GOLD AND LOLA CORDELL**

LOUISE CORDET (singer)
1963 *Just For Fun*
(Columbia) F
"Which Way the Wind Blows"
1964 *Just For You*
(British Lion) F
"It's So Hard to be Good"

CORNELIA AND EDDIE (comedy acrobats)
1938 *Mountains o' Mourne*
(Butcher) F

MARCEL CORNELIS (mime)
1953 *Master of Laughter*
(Baim)
1954 *Variety Half Hour*
(Baim)

LYN CORNELL (singer)
1963 *Just For Fun*
(Columbia) F
"Kisses Can Lie"

CORNFIELDS QUARTETTE (singers)
1900 *The Cornfields Quartette*
(Phono-Bio-Tableaux)

CORONA BABES (juveniles)
1937 *Talking Feet*
(Baxter) F
1946 *Wot No Gangsters*
(reissue: *Talking Feet*)

CORONA BOYS AND GIRLS (juveniles)
1966 *Finders Keepers*
(UA) F
"The Washerwoman"
"The La La La Song"

CORONA KIDS (juveniles)
1936 *Variety Parade*
(Butcher) F
1940 *Highlights of Variety 17*
(reissue: *Variety Parade*)

CORONETS (singers)
1956 *It's Great To Be Young*
(ABPC) F

CAROL LYNN CORTEZ (striptease)
1988 *Tank Malling*
(Parkfield) F

LEON CORTEZ AND HIS COSTER PALS
(band)
1936 *Pathe Pictorial 35*
"My Old Dutch"
1937 *Calling All Stars*

(British Lion) F
"One of the Ruins Cromwell Knocked About a Bit"
"Whoa Mare"
"The Old Apple Tree"

RAMON CORTEZ AND FLORA HARTE
(dancers)
1930 *Eve's Film Review 487*
"Argentine Tango"

CORTEZ AND PEGGY (dancers)
1931 *Ideal Cinemagazine 277*
"Cuban Rhythm"

COSSACK CHOIR (singers)
1933 *Pathe Pictorial 802*
"Campanella"

SAM COSTA (singer and comedian)
1939 *Pathe Pictorial NS 177*
"Moon at Sea"
1948 *Penny and the Pownall Case*
(GFD) F
1948 *Trouble in the Air*
(GFD) F
"They're Gathering Flowers for Mother"
1948 *A Piece of Cake*
(GFD) F
1950 *New Pictorial 297*
"Much Binding in the Marsh"
1951 *One Wild Oat*
(Eros) F
1952 *The Pickwick Papers*
(Renown) F
1956 *One Wish Too Many*
(Realist) F
1964 *Just For You*
(British Lion) F

BILLY 'POPEYE' COSTELLO (comedian)
1937 *Calling All Stars*
(British Lion) F
"I'm Popeye the Sailor Man"

ELVIS COSTELLO (musician)
1985 *No Surrender*
(Palace) F
1986 *Straight to Hell*
(Island) F
1997 *Spice World*
(Fragile) F

TOM COSTELLO (comedian)
1934 *Pathetone 210*
"At Trinity Church"
1934 *Say It With Flowers*
(Realart) F
"Sons of the Sea"

THE COTRILLOS (jugglers)
1939 *Pathe Pictorial NS 171*

GERRY COTTLE CIRCUS
1976 *World Within a Ring*
(New Decade)

BILLY COTTON AND HIS BAND
1932 *The First Mrs Fraser*
(Sterling) F
1933 *Pathetone 169*
"I'm Just Wild About Harry"
1933 *Pathe Pictorial 818*
"I Found the Right Girl"
1935 *Variety*
(Butcher) F
"Whistle My Love"
"The Man from Harlem"
1937 *Highlights of Variety 1*
(reissue: *Variety*)
1939 *Music Hall Parade*
(Butcher) F
"Somebody Stole My Girl"
"Swing That Music"
"Fall In and Fly"
"Blue Danube Swing"
"Tom the Piper's Son"
1940 *Cavalcade of Variety*
(reissue: *Music Hall Parade*)
1943 *Down Melody Lane*
F (reissue: *Music Hall Parade*)

WAYNE COUNTY AND THE ELECTRIC
CHAIRS (group)
1978 *Jubilee*
(Cinegate) F
"Paranoia Paradise"

DIANA COUPLAND (singer)
(films as actress not listed)
1951 *London Entertains*
(New Realm) F

CICELY COURTNEIDGE (comedienne)
1922 *Eve's Film Review 54*
"Midnight Follies"
1925 *Eve's Film Review 196*
"By the Way"
1928 *British Screen Tatler 10*
"Clowns in Clover"
1930 *Elstree Calling*
(BIP) F
"I've Fallen in Love"
1931 *Eve's Film Review 503*
"Folly to be Wise"
1931 *The Ghost Train*
(Gainsborough) F
1932 *Jack's the Boy*
(Gainsborough) F
"If You Are Out to Give a Party"
1932 *Happy Ever After*
(Gainsborough) F
1933 *Soldiers of the King*
(Gainsborough) F
"There's Something About a Soldier"
"When Old Man Love Comes"
"The Moment I Saw You"

1933 *Falling For You*
(Gainsborough) F
"Why Has a Cow Got Four Legs?"
"Send for Mrs Bartholomew"
1933 *Aunt Sally*
(Gainsborough) F
"We All Go Riding on a Rainbow"
"A Fair and Square Man"
"My Wild Oat"
"The Wind's in the West"
"Ain't She Dainty?"
"Napoleon's Hat"
"You Ought to See Sally on Sunday"
1935 *Things Are Looking Up*
(Gainsborough) F
"Things Are Looking Up"
1935 *Me and Marlborough*
(Gainsborough) F
"All for a Shilling a Day"
1936 *Everybody Dance*
(Gainsborough) F
"Everybody Dance"
"What Does It Get Me?"
"My What a Different Night"
1937 *Take My Tip*
(Gainsborough) F
"Birdie Out of a Cage"
"I Was Anything But Sentimental"
1939 *Pathe Gazette 97*
"The Empire Depends On You"
1940 *Under Your Hat*
(Grand National) F
"Keep It Under Your Hat"
"We Can't Find the Tiger Any More"
"The Empire Depends On You"
"I Won't Do the Conga"
1955 *Miss Tulip Stays the Night*
(Adelphi) F
1956 *How to Sell Your Husband a Washing Machine*
(Beda) ADVERT
1960 *The Spider's Web*
(Danziger) F
1962 *The L-Shaped Room*
(British Lion) F
"Take Me Back to Blighty"
1965 *Those Magnificent Men in Their Flying Machines*
(TCF) F
1966 *The Wrong Box*
(Columbia) F
1972 *Not Now Darling*
(LMG) F

JACK COURTNEY (organist)
1936 *Scenes in Harmony*
(Fidelity)
"Rustle of Spring"
"Lullabye of the Leaves"
1946 *Deep Rivers*
(Renown)

COVENT GARDEN OPERA CHORUS
1936 *Melody of My Heart*
(Butcher) F

JULIE COVINGTON (singer)
1982 *Ascendancy*
(BFI) F

COX TWINS (FREDDIE AND FRANK)
(comedians)
1972 *Alice's Adventures in Wonderland*
(TCF) F
1994 *Funny Bones*
(Hollywood) F

LOL COXHILL (musician)
1983 *The Gold Diggers*
(BFI) F
1986 *Caravaggio*
(BFI) F
1992 *Orlando*
(Electric) F

ARMAND CRABBE (singer)
1933 *Pathe Pictorial 778*
"Ich Liebe Dich My Dear"

CHARLES CRAIG (singer)
1953 *Melba*
(UA) F

DONNA CRAIG (singer)
1938 *Made to Measure*
(Ace Cinemagazine)

FAYE CRAIG (dancer)
1963 *Jungle Street*
(Theatrecraft) F

FRANK CRAM (impressionist)
1936 *Cabaret Nights 7*
(Highbury)
(as Wallace Beery)

THE CRAMPS (group)
1981 *Urgh! A Music War*
(White) F
"Tear It Up"

JESSE CRAWFORD (organist)
1933 *Pathetone 168*

JIMMY CRAWFORD (singer)
1962 *Play It Cool*
(Anglo) F
"Take It Easy"

MIMI CRAWFORD (singer)
1929 *An Old World Garden*
(BIP)
1929 *Chelsea Nights*
(BIP)

DAN CRAWLEY (singer)
1906 *They Can't Diddle Me*
(Chronophone)

CRAZY CAVAN AND THE ROCKERS
(group)
1979 *Blue Suede Shoes*
(Boyd) F

THE CRAZY GANG (comedians) (Bud
Flanagan, Chesney Allen, Jimmy Nervo,
Teddy Knox, Charlie Naughton, Jimmy Gold)
see also **BUD FLANAGAN AND CHESNEY
ALLEN, CHARLIE NAUGHTON AND JIMMY
GOLD, JIMMY NERVO AND TEDDY KNOX**
1933 *Pathetone 196*
1937 *Okay For Sound*
(Gainsborough) F
"Say Tata to Your Tar"
1938 *Alf's Button Afloat*
(Gainsborough) F
"Goodbye Little Yellow Bird"
1939 *The Frozen Limits*
(Gainsborough) F
1940 *Gasbags*
(Gainsborough) F
"Whistle While You Work"
1954 *Tonight in Britain*
(Pathe)
"Ring Out the Bells"
"Underneath the Arches"
1958 *Life Is a Circus*
(British Lion) F
"Life Is a Circus"
"Underneath the Arches"

CRAZY MABEL AND WEB (group)
1971 *Bread*
(Salon) F

CRAZY WORLD OF ARTHUR BROWN
(singer)
1968 *The Committee*
(Planet) F
"Nightmare"

CREAM (group)
1968 *Cream – Last Concert*
(Stigwood) F
"Spoonful"
"Politician"
"I'm Glad"

CHARLIE CREED-MILES (singer)
see also **CHARLIE AND SONIA**
1991 *London Kills Me*
(Rank) F
1991 *Let Him Have It*
(First Independent) F
1993 *The Punk*
(Videodrome) F
"Push the Clouds Away"
"Milton's SexRap"
"Just as Fat"
"Eh Deh Oh"

1994　*The Young Poisoner's Handbook*
　　　(Kinowelt) F
1994　*SuperGrass*
　　　(Partners in Film) F
1997　*Nil By Mouth*
　　　(SE8) F

KNOX CRICHTON (conjurer)
1948　*Things Happen at Night*
　　　(Renown) F

THE CRICKETS (group)
1963　*Just For Fun*
　　　(Columbia) F
　　　"My Little Girl"
　　　"Teardrops Fell Like Rain"

TOMMY CRIDDLE (boy soprano)
1944　*Pathe Pictorial 414*
　　　"Passing By"

HALSTAN CRIMMINS (comedian)
1946　*Amateur Night*
　　　(Renown)

WALTER CRISHAM (comedian)
(films as actor not listed)
1935　*Opening Night*
　　　(Olympic) F

CRITERION REVELLERS (singers)
1932　*Pathetone 114*
　　　"I Love the Moon"
1932　*Pathe Pictorial 753*
　　　"Just Humming Along"

TONY CROMBIE AND HIS ROCKETS
(group)
1957　*Rock You Sinners*
　　　(Small) F
　　　"Brighton Rock"
　　　"Let's You and I Rock"

CROMWELL BROTHERS (trapezists)
1947　*Dual Alibi*
　　　(British National) F

MORRIS CRONIN (juggler)
1896　*Cronin, American Club Manipulator*
　　　(Paul)
1896　*Cronin with Three Clubs*
　　　(Paul)

WILHELM CROSS (composer)
1934　*Pathe Pictorial 861*
　　　"Isle of Capri"

CROSS SECTION (group)
1979　*Quadrophenia*
　　　(Who) F
　　　"Hi Heel Sneakers"
　　　"Dimples"

KEN CROSSLEY (singer)
1935　*Cheerio*
　　　(Fidelity)

GEORGE CROW
see **REGGIE BRISTOW AND GEORGE CROW**

GENE CROWLEY (singer)
1937　*Feather Wait and See*
　　　(Ace Cinemagazine)
　　　"Pride of My Irish Home"
1947　*The Courtneys of Curzon Street*
　　　(Wilcox) F

LESLIE CROWTHER (comedian)
1972　*Always on Saturday*
　　　(CFF)
1972　*Saturday Lovely Saturday*
　　　(CFF)
1972　*Super Saturday*
　　　(CFF)
1973　*Saturday Special*
　　　(CFF)

FREDDIE CRUMP (drummer)
1942　*King Arthur Was a Gentleman*
　　　(Gainsborough) F
1946　*Walking On Air*
　　　(Piccadilly) F

BARRY CRYER (comedian)
1963　*The Mouse on the Moon*
　　　(UA) F
1968　*A Little of What You Fancy*
　　　(Border) F
　　　"The Whiffenpoof Song"
　　　"Oh the Fairies"
1984　*Bloodbath at the House of Death*
　　　(EMI) F

ANN CUBITT (campanologist)
1937　*Modern Daze*
　　　(Ace Cinemagazine)

SMILEY CULTURE (singer)
1986　*Absolute Beginners*
　　　(Palace) F
　　　"So What?"

CULTURE CLUB (group)
1984　*A Kiss Across the Ocean*
　　　(Virgin)
　　　"I'll Tumble 4 Ya"
　　　"Mister Man"
　　　"It's a Miracle"
　　　"Karma Chameleon"
　　　"Black Money"
　　　"Love Twist"
　　　"Do You Really Want To Hurt Me?"
　　　"Miss Me Blind"
　　　"Church of the Poison Mind"
　　　"Victims"
　　　"Time"

"White Boy"
"Melting Pot"

BERYL CUNNINGHAM (dancer)
1965 *The Curse of Simba*
(Gala) F

THE CURE (group)
1987 *The Cure in Orange*
(Fiction) F
"Shake Dog Shake"
"Piggy in the Mirror"
"Play for Today"
"A Strange Day"
"Primary"
"Kyoto Song"
"Charlotte Sometimes"
"In Between Days"
"The Walk"
"A Night Like This"
"Push"
"One Hundred Years"
"A Forest"
"Sinking"
"Close to Me"
"Let's Go To Bed"
"Six Different Ways"
"Three Imaginary Boys"
"Boys Don't Cry"
"Faith"
"Give Me It"
"10.15 Saturday Night"
"Killing an Arab"
1993 *The Cure Show*
(Rank) F
"Tape"
"Open"
"High"
"Trust"
"Doing the Unstuck"
"Friday I'm in Love"
"From the Edge of the Deep Green Sea"
"Cut"
"End"
"Pictures of You"

"Lullaby"
"Fascination Street"
"Just Like Heaven"
"A Night Like This"
"In Between Days"
"The Walk"
"Let's Go To Bed"
"Never Enough"

SAMMY CURTIS (tap-dancer)
1946 *Dancing Thru*
(Angel) F

COUNT CUTELLI (impressionist)
1932 *Pathe Pictorial 750*

RENE CUTFORTH (broadcaster)
1961 *The Queen's Guards*
(TCF) F

IVOR CUTLER (comedian)
1963 *It's All Over Town*
(British Lion) F

IRENE CUTTER (tap-dancer)
1943 *Swingonometry*
(Inspiration)
"Honeysuckle Rose"

CYCLING LYNTONS (specialty)
1937 *Shooting Stars*
(Viking) F
1940 *Showtime*
(reissue: *Shooting Stars*)

CYNTHIA (acrobat)
1940 *Pathe Pictorial 246*

CYNTHIA AND GLADYS (jugglers)
1952 *For Your Entertainment 2*
(Gaumont)

CYNTHIA AND LEROY (jugglers)
1952 *For Your Entertainment 4*
(Gaumont)

British Independent Exhibitors (Distribution) Co. Ltd., present —

Sing as you Swing

WITH

EVELYN DALL & CLAUDE DAMPIER

CLAPHAM & DWYER
FOUR MILLS BROTHERS
MANTOVANI & HIS TIPICAS
NAT GONELLA & GEORGIANS
LU ANNE MEREDITH
SHERMAN FISHER
GIRLS

A JOE ROCK PRODUCTION

TRADE SHOW
PHOENIX THEATRE, Wednesday, July 7,
at 3 p.m.

ALAN D'ALBERT AND THE WINDMILL THEATRE BAND
  1936 *Digging for Cold*
        (Ace) F
  1936 *Full Steam*
        (Ace) F
  1936 *Bottle Party*
        (Ace) F
  1936 *Piccadilly Playtime*
        (Ace) F
  1936 *Song in Soho*
        (Ace) F
  1937 *Windmill Revels*
        (Ace) F
  1937 *Carry On London*
        (Ace) F
  1937 *West End Frolics*
        (Ace) F
  1937 *Uptown Revue*
        (Ace) F
  1937 *Concert Party*
        (Ace) F
  1937 *Footlights*
        (Ace) F
  1938 *Two Men in a Box*
        (Ace) F

CHAPPIE D'AMATO AND HIS BAND
  1937 *Pathetone 391*
        "St Louis Blues"
  1944 *Round Rainbow Corner*
        (Berkeley) F

D'OYLY CARTE OPERA COMPANY
  1967 *The Mikado*
        (BHE) F

ANITA D'RAY (dancer)
  1946 *New Pictorial 109*
  1946 *Pathe News*
        "Television Dress Rehearsal"
  1949 *Murder at the Windmill*
        (Grand National) F
  1951 *Old Mother Riley's Jungle Treasure*
        (Renown) F

RAIE DA COSTA (pianist)
  1933 *Pathe Pictorial 777*
        "Fairies' Gavotte"

RICHARD DABSON AND HIS ORCHESTRA
  1937 *Sweet Art*
        (Ace Cinemagazine)
        "Down Old Lover's Lane"

DACIA (DEANE) (dancer)
  1921 *Celebrities of the Dance*
        (Gaumont)

DAGENHAM GIRL PIPERS (Scottish band)
  1937 *Talking Feet*
        (Baxter) F
        "Call Me Home"

  1944 *One Exciting Night*
        (Columbia) F
  1946 *School for Secrets*
        (Two Cities) F
  1956 *Who Done It?*
        (Ealing) F

ALEC DAIMLER AND DORA EADIE
(comedy)
  1927 *Frivolous Fragments*
        (Phonofilm)

DAISY QUARTETTE (dancers)
  1898 *Sailor's Hornpipe*
        (Levi Jones)
  1898 *Scotch Reel*
        (Levi Jones)
  1898 *Irish Jig*
        (Levi Jones)
  1898 *Dance by the Daisy Quartette*
        (Levi Jones)

W BARRINGTON DALBY (broadcaster)
  1969 *The Magic Christian*
        (Grand) F

JIM DALE (singer)
(films as actor not listed)
  1958 *6.5 Special*
        (Anglo) F
        "Sugartime"
        "The Train Kept Arolling"
  1973 *Adolf Hitler My Part in His Downfall*
        (UA) F
        "It's Gonna Be a Good War"

MARJORIE DALE (singer)
  1938 *Dead Men Tell No Tales*
        (British National)
        "Drifting With the Tide"

DOLORES DALGARNO (dancer)
  1935 *Opening Night*
        (Olympic) F

EVELYN DALL (singer)
  1936 *Soft Lights and Sweet Music*
        (British Lion) F
        "I'm All In"
        "I've Lost My Rhythm"
  1937 *Calling All Stars*
        (British Lion) F
        "Organ Grinder's Swing"
        "I Don't Wanna Get Hot"
  1937 *Sing As You Swing*
        (Rock) F
        "Let's Dance"
        "Sing As You Swing"
        "That's as Far as It Goes"
  1938 *Kicking the Moon Around*
        (Vogue) F
        "It's the Rhythm in Me"
        "No Song About Love"

1940 *Swing Tease*
(reissue: *Sing As You Swing*)
1940 *Pathetone 513*
"Franklin D. Roosevelt Jones"
1941 *He Found a Star*
(GFD) F
"Salome"
"Coster Rhumba"
1942 *King Arthur Was a Gentleman*
(Gainsborough) F
"Honey On My Mind"
"Don't Put a Thing in Writing"
"You'll Love the Army"
1943 *Miss London Limited*
(Gainsborough) F
"A Fine How Do You Do"
"Keep Cool Calm and Collect"
1944 *Time Flies*
(Gainsborough) F
"Big Chief Tom Tom"
"Sitting On a Cloud"
1946 *New Pictorial 76*

LORNA DALLAS (singer)
1975 *Inside Out*
(Warner) F

DALMORA CAN-CAN DANCERS
1935 *She Shall Have Music*
(Twickenham) F

ROGER DALTREY (singer)
see also **THE WHO**
1975 *Lisztomania*
(Warner) F
"Love's Dream"
"Orpheus Song"
"Funerailles"
"Peace at Last"
1975 *Tommy*
(Stigwood) F
"I'm Free"
"Sensation"
"Welcome"
"Mother and Son"
"See Me Feel Me"
"We're Not Gonna Take It"
1978 *The Legacy*
(EMI) F
1980 *McVicar*
(Who) F
1984 *Pop Pirates*
(CFF)
1990 *Buddy's Song*
(Castle) F

JACK DALY (Irish comedian)
1937 *Kathleen Mavourneen*
(Butcher) F
1939 *Pathe Pictorial 198*
"That's How I Spell Ireland"
1945 *I Didn't Do It*
(Columbia) F

CLAUDE DAMPIER (comedian)
1930 *Claude Deputises*
(BIP)
1934 *Radio Parade of 1935*
(BIP) F
1935 *So You Won't Talk*
(Warner) F
1935 *White Lilac*
(Fox) F
1935 *Boys Will Be Boys*
(Gainsborough) F
1935 *No Monkey Business*
(GFD) F
1935 *She Shall Have Music*
(Twickenham) F
1936 *King of the Castle*
(City) F
1936 *Public Nuisance No. 1*
(GFD) F
1936 *She Knew What She Wanted*
(ABPC) F
1936 *Such Is Life*
(Incorporated) F
1936 *All In*
(Gainsborough) F
1937 *Wanted*
(Sound City) F
1937 *Mr Stringfellow Says No*
(Incorporated) F
1937 *Sing As You Swing*
(Rock) F
1937 *Riding High*
(British Lion) F
1940 *The Backyard Front*
(British Films)
1941 *Let the People Laugh*
(reissue: *Sing As You Swing*)
1944 *Don't Take It To Heart*
(GFD) F
1946 *Wot No Gangsters*
(reissue: *Sing As You Swing*)
1950 *Climb Up the Wall*
(reissue: *Sing As You Swing*)
1954 *Meet Mr Malcolm*
(Apex) F

DANA (singer)
1971 *Flight of the Doves*
(Columbia) F
"The Far Off Place"

DANCERS OF THE CENTRE DE DANSE CLASSIQUE
1966 *The Yellow Hat*
(Monarch) F

THE DANCETTES (dancers)
1938 *Pathe Pictorial NS 109*
"Under the Double Eagle"

DANCING DUDES (acrobatic dancers)
1940 *Pathe Pictorial 221*
1941 *Pathe Pictorial 248*

DANDY GEORGE AND ROSIE
1927 *Dandy George and Rosie*
(Phonofilm)

BEBE DANIELS (singer)
(films as actress not listed)
1933 *A Southern Maid*
(BIP) F
"My Southern Maid"
1933 *The Song You Gave Me*
(BIP) F
"The Song You Gave To Me"
"Goodnight"
1936 *Not Wanted on Voyage*
(British Lion) F
1941 *Hi Gang*
(Gainsborough) F
"I'm Singing to a Million"
"My Son"
"The Lady Known as Sal"
"It's a Small World"

JOE DANIELS AND HIS BAND
1938 *Pathe Pictorial NS 102*
"Some of These Days"

JOHNNY DANKWORTH AND HIS BAND
1956 *Parade of the Bands*
(Hammer)
1958 *6.5 Special*
(Anglo) F
"Train Gang"
"What Am I Going to Tell Them
Tonight?"
1962 *All Night Long*
(Rank) F
1963 *The Servant*
(Anglo) F

THE DANSETTES (dancers)
1938 *Pictorial NS 109*

DANTALION'S CHARIOT (group)
1968 *Popdown*
(New Realm) F

PHYLLIS DARE (dancer)
1913 *The Argentine Tango*
(Hepworth)

DARE AND YATES (acrobats)
1932 *Ideal Cinemagazine 338*
1933 *Ideal Cinemagazine 350*
1938 *Pathe Pictorial NS 113*

HERMAN DAREWSKI (musician)
1924 *Eve's Film Review 182*
1929 *Pathe Pictorial 31*
1931 *No Lady*
(Gaumont) F
1931 *Bill and Coo*
(BIP) F
1931 *Pathetone 44*
"Bluebells of Scotland"

1933 *My Lucky Star*
(W&F) F
1933 *Pathetone 192*
"Tappitout"
1935 *Pathe Pictorial 876*
"Wire Ways"

MAX DAREWSKI (boy conductor)
1907 *Nelson's Victory*
(Chronophone)
1907 *The Royal Standard*
(Chronophone)
1907 *March of the Light Cavalry*
(Chronophone)

BOBBY DARIN (American singer)
1967 *Stranger in the House*
(Rank) F

DARKTOWN TROUPE (singers)
1906 *The Whistling Coon*
(Chronophone)

DARMORA BALLET (dancers)
1940 *Gaslight*
(British National) F

YVETTE DARNAC (singer)
1929 *Yvette Darnac*
(Phonofilm)
1934 *Radio Parade of 1935*
(BIP) F
"You're My Everything"

HERMIONE DARNBOROUGH (dancer)
1937 *Wings of the Morning*
(Fox) F

JEFF DARNELL
see **(JACK) WARNER AND (JEFF)
DARNELL**

EVELYN DARVILLE (singer)
1943 *The Dummy Talks*
(British National) F
"The World Belongs to Me"

DARVILLE AND SHIRES (dancers)
1940 *Laugh It Off*
(British National) F
"Anybody Can Dance"

KIM DARVOS (singer)
1962 *Danger By My Side*
(Butcher) F
"Danger By My Side"

GEORGE DAVENPORT (conjurer)
1931 *Ideal Cinemagazine 261*

ALAN DAVID (singer)
1965 *Gonks Go Beat*
(Anglo) F
"Love Is a Dream"

AL DAVIDSON AND HIS BAND
1932 *The New Hotel*
   (PDC) F

MATT DAVIDSON AND ADELE (dancers)
1936 *Strange Cargo*
   (Paramount) F

DAVID DAVIES (singer)
1943 *Pathe Pictorial 396*
   "Bless This House"

GLYN DAVIES (boy singer)
1939 *Discoveries*
   (Vogue) F
   "There'll Always Be an England"

IRVING DAVIES (dancer)
1955 *Value for Money*
   (Rank) F

IWAN DAVIES (Welsh singer)
1932 *Pathe Pictorial 728*
   "Charming Chloe"

LILLIAN DAVIES (singer)
1930 *Just For a Song*
   (Gainsborough) F

MORGAN DAVIES (baritone)
1934 *Pathe Pictorial 859*
   "To You Cherie"

RAY DAVIES (singer)
1986 *Absolute Beginners*
   (Palace) F
   "Quiet Life"

SIOBHAN DAVIES (dancer)
1983 *The Gold Diggers*
   (BFI) F

BERYL DAVIS (singer)
1944 *Pathe Pictorial 421*
   "Room 504"
   "Till the Lights of London Shine
   Again"
1944 *Starlight Serenade*
   (Federated) F
   "Whistling and Whittling"
   "Frenesi"
1946 *London Town*
   (GFD) F
   "So Would I"
1948 *Merry Go Round*
   (Federated) F
   "Loneliness in My Heart"

BILLIE DAVIS (singer)
1965 *Pop Gear*
   (Pathe) F

COLIN DAVIS (conductor)
1968 *Music*
   (Warner-Pathe)

FREDDIE DAVIS (comedian)
1985 *Number One*
   (Lutebest) F
1991 *Funny Bones*
   (Hollywood) F

**JACK DAVIS AND THE HAVANA CLUB
BAND**
1940 *At the Havana*
   (New Realm)

JOAN DAVIS DANCERS
1940 *Laugh It Off*
   (British National) F
   "Anybody Can Dance"

JOAN DAVIS EIGHT ROSE PETALS
(dancers)
1940 *Garrison Follies*
   (Butcher) F

SAMMY DAVIS JR (American singer)
1968 *Salt and Pepper*
   (UA) F
   "Salt and Pepper"
   "I Like the Way You Dance"
1969 *One More Time*
   (UA) F
   "One More Time"
   "Where Do I Go From Here?"
   "When the Feeling Hits You"

SPENCER DAVIS GROUP
1965 *Pop Gear*
   (Pathe) F
1966 *The Ghost Goes Gear*
   (Pathe) F
1967 *Here We Go Round the Mulberry
   Bush*
   (UA) F
   "Every Little Thing"
   "Just Like Me"
   "Taking Out Time"
   "Looking Back"
   "Picture of Her"
   "Possession"
   "Waltz for Caroline"

TUDOR DAVIS (singer)
1933 *The Lost Chord*
   (Butcher) F
   "The Lost Chord"
1936 *Whom the Gods Love*
   (ATP) F

ALAN DAVISON (singer)
1963 *It's All Over Town*
   (British Lion) F
   "Please Let It Happen to Me"

DAWN (dancer)
1941 *A Musical Cocktail*
   (Inspiration)

DOREEN DAWN (model)
  1956 *The Extra Day*
        (British Lion) F
  1959 *Son of Robin Hood*
        (TCF) F
  1959 *Room at the Top*
        (Romulus) F

VIRGINIA DAWN (singer)
  1941 *Pathe Pictorial 272*
        "Moonlight in Mexico"
  1941 *Pathetone 563*

FORBES DAWSON (singer)
  1902 *Biograph Dramatised Songs*
        (Biograph) S

MUSICAL DAWSON AND HIS CANARY CHOIR (animal act)
  1932 *Pathe Pictorial 751*
        "The Bells of St Mary's"
  1938 *Pathe Pictorial NS 112*
        "In a Monastery Garden"

PETER DAWSON (baritone)
  1907 *Bedouin's Love Song*
        (Chronophone)
  1935 *Pathetone 255*
        "The Winding Road"
  1937 *Okay For Sound*
        (Gainsborough) F
        "The Fleet's Not in Port Very Long"
  1938 *Pathetone 427*
        "Old Kettledrum"
  1938 *Chips*
        (BFA) F
        "The Sea Is the Life for Me"

DAPHNE DAY (singer)
  1944 *Rainbow Round the Corner*
        (Berkeley) F
        "Aloha Oe"
        "Sleepy Lagoon"
  1946 *Late at Night*
        (Premier) F

EDITH DAY (singer)
  1925 *Eve's Film Review 203*
        "Rose Marie"

ELSIE DAY
see **RUPERT HAZELL AND ELSIE DAY**

FRANCES DAY (singer)
  1927 *The Price of Divorce*
        (Stoll) F
  1930 *Big Business*
        (Fox) F
  1930 *OK Chief*
        (BIP)
  1932 *The First Mrs Fraser*
        (Sterling) F
  1933 *The Girl from Maxim's*
        (London) F

  1934 *Two Hearts in Waltz Time*
        (Gaumont) F
        "Men Oh How I Hate Them"
  1934 *Temptation*
        (Gaumont) F
        "What Is This Thing?"
        "Show Me the Way to Romance"
  1935 *Oh Daddy*
        (Gainsborough) F
        "Now I Understand"
        "You Bring Out the Savage in Me"
  1936 *Dreams Come True*
        (Reunion) F
        "Love's Melody"
        "So Must Our Love Remain"
  1936 *You Must Get Married*
        (GFD) F
  1936 *Public Nuisance No. 1*
        (GFD) F
        "Between You and Me and the Carpet"
        "Swing"
        "Hotsy Totsy"
        "Me and My Dog"
        "Blue Mediterranean Sea"
  1937 *Who's Your Lady Friend?*
        (ABFD) F
        "Moonlight and Music"
  1937 *The Girl in the Taxi*
        (ABFD) F
        "The Old Dog and the Young Dog"
  1940 *Room for Two*
        (Grand National) F
        "Just for the Fun of It"
  1944 *Fiddlers Three*
        (Ealing) F
        "Caesar's Wife"
        "You Can't Live Without Love"
  1952 *Tread Softly*
        (Apex) F
  1957 *There's Always a Thursday*
        (Rank) F
  1960 *Climb Up the Wall*
        (New Realm) F

JILL DAY (singer)
  1953 *Always a Bride*
        (GFD) F
        "Love Me Little Love Me Long"
  1955 *All For Mary*
        (Rank) F
        "Far Away from Everybody"

LESLIE DAY (boy soprano)
  1933 *Television Follies*
        (English) F
        "Love's Old Sweet Song"
  1935 *Musical Medley*
        (Mancunian)

MARJORIE DAY (dancer)
  1937 *Sum Game*
        (Ace Cinemagazine)
        "Spanish Dance"

TERRY DAY (comedy songs)
1968   *A Little of What You Fancy*
       (Border) F
       "All the World Loves a Fat Girl"
       "Some of These Days"

DE BIERE (musician)
1933   *Pathe Pictorial 785*
       "Stille Nacht"

JEANNE DE CASALIS (comedienne)
(films as actress not listed)
1933   *Radio Parade*
       (BIP) F
1933   *The Feather Bed*
       (BIP)
1935   *Pathetone 272*
1935   *Pathetone 283*
1941   *The Fine Feathers*
       (British Films)
1941   *Pathetone Parade of 1941*
       F (reissue: *Pathetone 283*)
1942   *Pathetone Parade of 1942*
       F (reissue: *Pathetone 272*)
1948   *Mrs Feather Takes the Cake*
       ADVERT

HOWARD DE COURCY (conjurer)
1937   *Pathetone 391*
1938   *Pathe Pictorial NS 96*
1938   *Pathetone 417*
1940   *Pathetone 527*
1940   *At the Havana*
       (New Realm)
1941   *Pathe Pictorial 296*
1942   *Pathe Pictorial 336*
1944   *Pathe Pictorial 412*

YOLA DE FRAINE
1933   *Taking Ways*
       (Sound City) F

**BERNARD DE GAUTIER AND JESSICA
MERTON** (dancers)
1936   *International Revue*
       (Medway) F

DE GROOT (violinist)
1924   *Eve's Film Review 192*
1928   *A Window in Piccadilly*
       (Morgan) F
1932   *Pathe Pictorial 768*
       "Song of Songs"
1933   *Pathe Pictorial 774*
       "Black Eyes"

MARCEL DE HAES AND HIS BAND
1934   *Danny Boy*
       (Butcher) F

BILLY DE HAVEN AND DANDY PAGE
(comedians)
1944   *Starlight Serenade*
       (Federated) F
       "Down Forget-Me-Not Lane"

FLORENCE DE JONG (organist)
1939   *Pathetone 467*
       "Il Travatore"
       "Tannhäuser"
       "Swan Song"
1942   *Pathetone Parade of 1942*
       F (reissue: *Pathetone 467*)

SIDNEY DE JONG (comedian)
1930   *Gaumont Sound Mirror*

JOHNNY DE LITTLE (singer)
1963   *It's All Happening*
       (British Lion) F
       "The Wind and the Rain"

MICHELE DE LYS
1945   *New Pictorial 62*

ANTONIO AND RENEE DE MARCO
(dancers)
1937   *Pathetone 384*

CHRISTIANNE DE MURIN (French singer)
1943   *Candlelight in Algeria*
       (British Lion) F
       "Flamme d'Amour"
       "It's Love"

ANN DE NYS
see **JOHN RIDLEY AND ANN DE NYS**

LYNSEY DE PAUL (singer)
1984   *Gabrielle and the Doodleman*
       (CFF)

MARIO DE PIETRO (musician)
1930   *Pathetone 24*
       "Lollipops"
1931   *Pathetone 58*
       "La Paloma"
1932   *Gaumont Sound Mirror 76*
1933   *Ideal Cinemagazine 361*
1934   *On the Air*
       (British Lion) F
1934   *Pathe Pictorial 871*
1934   *Pathetone 241*
1935   *Equity Musical Revue 2*
       (British Lion)
1935   *Equity Musical Revue 8*
       (British Lion)
       "Londonderry Air"
1939   *Pathe Pictorial 188*
       "Temptation Rag"
1939   *Pathetone Parade of 1939*
       F (reissue: *Pathetone 241*)
1943   *Pathe Pictorial 363*
       "Jealousy"
1944   *Pathe Pictorial 439*

**MARIO DE PIETRO AND HIS
ESTUDIANTINAS** (band)
1936   *B.B.C. Musicals 3*
       (Inspiration)

1939   *Tunes of the Times*
        (reissue: *B.B.C. Musicals 3*)

BEBE DE ROLAND (dancer)
1946   *Carnival*
        (Two Cities) F

AMELIE DE S.
see **R. L. LEONARD AND AMELIE DE S.**

ERIN DE SELFA (singer)
1946   *Caravan*
        (Gainsborough) F

STEPHANIE DE SYKES (singer)
1975   *Side By Side*
        (GTO) F
        "Born With a Smile on My Face"

MARIE DE VERE DANCERS
1952   *For Your Entertainment 1-4*
        (Gaumont)
        "Brazilly Willy"
        "Aloha Oe"
        "Cherokee"
        "Tico Tico"

DE VINARAN, ORLOFF AND CASADO
(dancers)
1928   *Phototone 12*
        "La Cumparsita"

GAU DE VITO AND HIS LADIES BAND
1938   *Pathe Pictorial NS 130*
        "Gypsy Moon"

LOUIS DE VRIES (trumpeter)
1935   *Pathe Pictorial 889*
        "Auntie's Got Ants in Her Pants"

DAPHNE DE WITT (dancer)
1933   *Pathetone 171*
1938   *Pathe Pictorial NS 128*
1938   *Pathe Pictorial NS 132*

THE DEAD KENNEDYS (group)
1981   *Urgh! A Music War*
        (White) F
        "Bleed For Me"

ALAN DEAN (singer)
1949   *Melody in the Dark*
        (Adelphi) F
        "If I Won the Penny Pool"

TESSA DEANE (singer)
1935   *In Town Tonight*
        (British Lion) F
1935   *Variety*
        (Butcher) F
        "Goodbye Dolly Gray"
1936   *British Lion Varieties 5*
1938   *Lassie from Lancashire*
        (British National) F

"Jolly Good Luck"
        "I'll Be Your Sweetheart"
1943   *Variety Jubilee*
        (Butcher) F
        "Keep the Home Fires Burning"
1944   *Highlights of Variety 26*
        (reissue: *Variety Jubilee*)

ANGUS DEAYTON (television presenter)
1989   *The Tall Guy*
        (Virgin) F

THE DEBONAIRS (group)
1973   *That'll Be the Day*
        (EMI) F

MIKI DECIMA (entertainer)
1946   *Wot No Gangsters*
        (New Realm) F

DIANA DECKER (singer)
(films as actress not listed)
1949   *Murder at the Windmill*
        (Grand National) F
        "I'll Settle for You"
        "A Modern Romeo"
1955   *A Yank in Ermine*
        (Monarch) F
        "Honey You Can't Love Two"

DAVE DEE, DOZY, BEAKY, MICK AND TICH (group)
1966   *Pathe Pictorial 619*
        "Bend It"
1980   *The Great Rock 'n' Roll Swindle*
        (Virgin) F

JACK DEE (comedian)
1995   *The Steal*
        (Poseidon) F

KIKI DEE (singer)
1965   *Dateline Diamonds*
        (Rank) F

SIMON DEE (television personality)
1969   *The Italian Job*
        (Paramount) F
1970   *Doctor in Trouble*
        (Rank) F

CAROL DEENE (singer)
1962   *Band of Thieves*
        (Rank) F
1963   *It's All Happening*
        (British Lion) F
        "The Boy on the Beach"

MADAME DEERING (singer)
1909   *Loch Lomond*
        (Cinephone)

OLIVE DEL MAR (dancer)
1936   *Bottle Party*
        (Ace) F
1936   *Piccadilly Playtime*
        (Ace) F
1936   *Song in Soho*
        (Ace) F

YOLANDE DEL MAR (striptease)
1969   *Zeta One*
        (Tigon) F

THE DELACARDOS (group)
1967   *Up the Junction*
        (Paramount) F

ERIC DELANEY AND HIS BAND
1960   *Eric Delaney and his New Band*
        (Anglo)
        "When Lights Are Low"
        "It's a Pity to Say Goodnight"
        "Rollin' the Tymps"
1960   *Blue Tunes*
        (British Lion)
        "My Guy's Come Back"
1960   *Making Music*
        (British Lion)

DOT DELAVINE
1944   *A Night of Magic*
        (Berkeley) F

DAVID DELMONTE (singer)
1939   *Discoveries*
        (Vogue) F

DELYA (singer)
1943   *Pathe Pictorial 364*
        "The Hills of Donegal"

DELYS AND CLARK (singers)
1927   *So Blue*
        (Phonofilm)

ALICE DELYSIA (singer)
1920   *Around the Town 11*
        (Gaumont)
        "Afgar"
1926   *Stage Stars off Stage 4*
        (C&M)
1934   *Evensong*
        (Gaumont) F

SEAN DEMPSEY
1937   *Kathleen Mavourneen*
        (Butcher) F

DORRIE DENE (singer)
1931   *Bull Rushes*
        (Gainsborough)
1931   *Who Killed Doc Robin?*
        (Gainsborough) F
1932   *Pathetone 104*
        "Just in Time"

1932   *Pathetone 118*
1934   *Pathetone Parade*
        F (reissue: *Pathetone 118*)

TERRY DENE (singer)
1958   *The Golden Disc*
        (Butcher) F
        "Charm"
        "The Golden Age"
        "Come In and Be Loved"
        "Candy Floss"

JOHNNY DENIS AND HIS RANCHERS
(cowboy band)
1944   *Starlight Serenade*
        (Federated) F
1945   *Sweethearts For Ever*
        (Empire) F

JOHNNY DENIS AND NETTA ROGERS
(singers)
1951   *New Pictorial 340*
        "Have I Told You Lately That I Love You?"

HERMANOS DENIZ AND HIS CUBAN RHYTHM BAND
1961   *Cuban Melody*
        (Anglo)
1961   *Cuban Rhythm*
        (Anglo)
        "Malgré Tout"
        "Rosita"
        "Maria from Bahia"
1963   *Modern Rhythm*
        (Carisbrooke)
        "The Story of Tina"

IVOR DENNIS (pianist)
1943   *Pathe Pictorial 394*
        "Whispering"

JACKIE DENNIS (singer)
1958   *6.5 Special*
        (Anglo) F
        "La Dee Dah"

DENNIS FAMILY (dancers)
1937   *Pathe Pictorial NS 86*

DINKY DENTON TRIO
1932   *Ideal Cinemagazine 336*

KARL DENVER TRIO (group)
1963   *Just For Fun*
        (Columbia) F
        "Can You Forgive Me?"

DEONZO BROTHERS (acrobats)
1901   *The Deonzo Brothers*
        (Paul)

PETER DESJARDINE (dancer)
1932   *Pathetone 109*

DESLYS AND CLARKE (singers)
1927 *So Blue*
(Phonofilm)
1929 *Pathe Magazine 3*

FLORENCE DESMOND (impressionist)
(films as actress not listed)
1932 *Impromptu*
(Warner)
(as Tallulah Bankhead, Marlene
Dietrich, Gracie Fields)
1933 *Radio Parade*
(BIP) F
(as Greta Garbo, Tallulah
Bankhead)
1933 *My Lucky Star*
(W&F) F
1934 *Gay Love*
(British Lion) F
(as Greta Garbo, Mae West)
"Don't Blame Me"
"The Man for Me"
"Mae Time"
1935 *No Limit*
(ATP) F
"Riding Around on a Rainbow"
"Your Way Is My Way"
1936 *Keep Your Seats Please*
(ATP) F
"On the Tips of My Toes"
1936 *Accused*
(UA) F
"Rendezvous in Paradise"
1939 *Hoots Mon*
(Warner) F
(as Max Miller, Syd Walker, Bette
Davis, Elisabeth Bergner, Cicely
Courtneidge)
1943 *Pathe Pictorial 370*

LORRAE DESMOND (singer)
1955 *Stock Car*
(Butcher) F
"All By Myself"

PEGGY DESMOND (pianist)
1937 *Pathe Pictorial NS 87*
"Under a Banana Tree"
1940 *Pathetone 539*
1941 *Pathe Pictorial 280*
"In the Mood"
1942 *Pathe Pictorial 341*
1943 *Pathe Pictorial 378*
1944 *Pathe Pictorial 406*
"Stardust"

TAMARA DESNI (singer)
1937 *The Squeaker*
(London) F
"He's Gone"
"I Can't Get Along Without You"

DETURA AND MORELL (dancers)
1938 *The Write Stuff*
(Ace Cinemagazine)
"La Siesta"

DAVID DEVANT (conjurer)
1896 *The Mysterious Rabbit*
(Paul)
1896 *The Egg Laying Man*
(Paul)
1896 *Devant's Exhibition of Paper Folding*
(Paul)
1896 *Devant's Hand Shadows*
(Paul)
1903 *David Devant Conjurer*
(Mutoscope)
1903 *David Devant's Laughable Hand
Shadows*
(Mutoscope)
1920 *The Great London Mystery*
(Torquay) S

TOMMY DEVEL AND PARTNER
1963 *Farewell Performance*
(Rank) F

LAURIE DEVINE (dancer)
1930 *Eve's Film Review 489*
1932 *Ideal Cinemagazine 339*
1933 *Ideal Cinemagazine 383*
"Burmese Hand Dance"
1934 *On the Air*
(British Lion) F

DEVITT AND BROWNING (eccentric
dancers)
1932 *Ideal Cinemagazine 323*

DEVO (group)
1981 *Urgh! A Music War*
(White) F
"She's Lost Control"

SHEILA DEXTER (dancer)
1931 *Ideal Cinemagazine 258*
"Eastern Dance"

ALICE AND JIMMY DEY (tap-dancers)
1935 *Cheerio*
(Fidelity)
"Shine"

HUGHIE DIAMOND (singer)
1938 *Pathe Pictorial NS 117*
"The Gypsy"

THE DIAMONDOS
1933 *Pathe Pictorial 793*
"Flirtation"
1936 *Pictorial Revue*
F (reissue: *Pictorial 793*)

DOROTHY DICKSON (singer)
1923   *Eve's Film Review 124*
        "The Beauty Prize"
1924   *Eve's Film Review 182*
        "Patricia"
1934   *Danny Boy*
        (Butcher) F
        "Danny Boy"
        "If You're Walking My Way"
        "Second Chance"
        "Sleepy Boy"
1939   *Sword of Honour*
        (Butcher) F

BO DIDDLEY (singer)
1973   *The London Rock and Roll Show*
        (Pleasant) F

MARLENE DIETRICH (singer)
(films as actress not listed)
1949   *Stage Fright*
        (ABPC) F
        "The Laziest Girl in Town"
        "La Vie en Rose"

ERNEST DILLON (trampolinist)
1938   *Pathe Pictorial NS 101*
1940   *Pathetone 544*
1942   *Somewhere on Leave*
        (Mancunian) F
1943   *Pathe Pictorial 395*

RICHARD DIMBLEBY (broadcaster)
1950   *Twenty Questions Murder Mystery*
        (Grand National) F
1952   *Murder On the Air*
        F (reissue: *Twenty Questions Murder
        Mystery*)
1954   *Berwick on Tweed*
        (Gaumont)
1955   *John and Julie*
        (Group 3) F
1958   *Rockets Galore*
        (Rank) F
1959   *Libel*
        (MGM) F

DIRE STRAITS (group)
see also **MARK KNOPFLER**
1981   *Making Movies*
        (CIC)

LES DISQUES BLEUES (group)
1987   *Souvenir*
        (Fancy Free) F

**CLAIRE DIVINA AND LAWRENCE
CHARLES** (apache dancers)
1923   *Eve's Film Review 133*
1927   *On With the Dance*
        (Parkinson)

PHYLLIS DIXEY (striptease)
1936   *Love Up the Pole*
        (Butcher) F

1944   *New Pictorial 8*
1946   *This Glamour Business*
        (Barralet)
1947   *Dual Alibi*
        (British National) F

ADELE DIXON (singer)
1936   *Calling the Tune*
        (Phoenix) F
        "Solveig's Song"
        "Bird of Love Divine"
1946   *Woman to Woman*
        (British National) F

REG DIXON (comedian)
1953   *Love in Pawn*
        (Eros) F
1955   *No Smoking*
        (Eros) F

ROSINA DIXON
see **THE SINGING COOK**

VAN DOCK (cartoonist)
1928   *Pathe Pictorial*
1933   *Eve's Film Review 633*
1935   *Variety*
        (Butcher) F

KEN DODD (comedian)
1963   *Pathe Pictorial 456*
1996   *Hamlet*
        (Castle Rock) F

ANTON DOLIN (dancer)
1929   *Dark Red Roses*
        (BSFP) F
1930   *Alfs Button*
        (Gaumont) F
        "Scheherazade"
1930   *Eve's Film Review 486*
        "Charlot's Masquerade"
1931   *Ideal Cinemagazine 278*
1934   *Forbidden Territory*
        (Gaumont) F
1935   *Invitation to the Waltz*
        (BIP) F
1952   *Giselle*
        (Exclusive)
1953   *Never Let Me Go*
        (MGM) F

DOLLIE AND BILLIE (dancers)
1924   *The Mating of Marcus*
        (Stoll) F
1925   *We Women*
        (Stoll) F

DOLLY SISTERS (American dancers)
1921   *Around the Town*
        (Gaumont)
        "League of Notions"
1922   *Eve's Film Review 33*
        "Babes in the Wood"

M'LITA DOLORES (dancer)
1922 *Around the Town*
(Gaumont)

LEE DON (pianist)
1931 *Ideal Cinemagazine 280*

DON AND LUIS (comedy acrobats)
1930 *Amateur Night in London*
(PDC) F

JACK DONAHUE (tap-dancer)
1936 *Rhythm in the Air*
(Fox) F
"You're On My Mind All Day"
"Walking the Beam"
"Spring All the Year Round"
1937 *Variety Hour*
(Fox) F
1937 *Ship's Concert*
(Warner) F
1938 *Keep Smiling*
(TCF) F

MARGARET DONALD (soprano)
1929 *Pot Pourri*
(BIP)

LONNIE DONEGAN (singer)
1955 *Momma Don't Allow*
(BFI)
"Momma Don't Allow"
1957 *Light Fingers*
(Archway) F
1958 *6.5 Special*
(Anglo) F
"Jack o' Diamonds"
"Big Grand Coolie Dam"

DONNA SISTERS (dancers)
1938 *Pathe Pictorial NS 136*

DONOVAN (singer)
1971 *The Pied Piper*
(Sagittarius) F
1982 *The Secret Policeman's Other Ball*
(UIP) F
"Catch the Wind"

DAN DONOVAN (singer)
1934 *Music Hall*
(Realart) F
"So Shy"
1935 *B.B.C. the Voice of Britain*
(New Era) F
"Sweetmeat Joe"
1935 *Music Hath Charms*
(BIP) F
"I'm Feeling Happy"
1937 *Let's Make a Night of It*
(ABPC) F
"My Irish Song"
1939 *Pathetone 470*
"With Me Old Clay Pipe"

DONOVAN AND BYL (comedy acrobats)
1945 *Home Sweet Home*
(Mancunian) F
1946 *Randle and All That*
(reissue: *Home Sweet Home*)

DONOVAN OCTETTE
1946 *Under New Management*
(Mancunian) F

DONOVAN SISTERS (dancers)
1927 *The Arcadians*
(Gaumont) F

GEORGE DOONAN (comedian)
1940 *Pathe Pictorial 208*
1941 *Pathe Pictorial 268*
1943 *Somewhere in Civvies*
(Mancunian) F
1960 *The Entertainer*
(UA) F

DORAY AND SHEILA (dancers)
1938 *Pathe Pictorial NS 114*

DORCHESTER GIRLS (dancers)
1936 *Hot News*
(Columbia) F
1936 *The Show's the Thing*
(Fidelity)
1936 *Soft Lights and Sweet Music*
(British Lion) F
"Diga Diga Doo"
1939 *Pathe Pictorial 167*

DOREEN (xylophonist)
also known as Little Doreen
1932 *Ideal Cinemagazine 299*
"The Wonder Child Xylophonist"
1937 *Pathetone 364*
"Goodnight Sweetheart"
1938 *Pathe Pictorial NS 133*
"Raymonde Overture"

DORIS AND HER ZEBRA (specialty)
1936 *Annie Laurie*
(Butcher) F
1940 *Highlights of Variety*
(reissue: *Annie Laurie*)

DAISY DORMER (comedienne)
1914 *Potted Pantomimes*
(Vaudefilms)

RAQUELLE DORNE (singer)
1934 *Pathe Pictorial 857*
"Who Walked In?"

CRAIG DOUGLAS (singer)
1960 *Climb Up the Wall*
(New Realm) F
"Of Love"
"Miss In Between"

1962 *It's Trad Dad*
(Columbia) F
"Rainbows In Your Tears"
"Ring-a-Ding"

JACK DOUGLAS (comedian)
1961 *Nearly a Nasty Accident*
(Britannia) F
1971 *Carry On Matron*
(Rank) F
1971 *The Beauty of Protection*
(Trent) ADVERT
1972 *Carry On Abroad*
(Rank) F
1973 *Carry On Girls*
(Rank) F
1974 *Carry On Dick*
(Rank) F
1976 *Carry On Behind*
(Rank) F
1976 *Carry On England*
(Rank) F
1977 *What's Up, Nurse?*
(Variety) F
1978 *Carry On Emmanuelle*
(Hemdale) F
1980 *Bloody Kids*
(British Lion) F
1983 *The Boys in Blue*
(Rank) F

JOSEPHINE DOUGLAS (television personality)
1958 *6.5 Special*
(Anglo) F
1959 *Left Right and Centre*
(British Lion) F

KEN DOUGLAS (comedian)
1932 *Strip Strip Hooray*
(BIP) F
1936 *Digging for Gold*
(Ace) F
1936 *Full Steam*
(Ace) F
1938 *Revue Parade*
(Ace) F

BEN DOVA (acrobat)
1933 *Pathetone 164*

ANTHONY DOWELL (ballet dancer)
1966 *Romeo and Juliet*
(Rank) F
1967 *Opus*
(COI)

CYRIL DOWLER (comedian)
1971 *Top of the Bill*
(Butcher) F

MORTON DOWNEY (singer)
1933 *Pathe Pictorial 172*
"Stormy Weather"

DOWNTOWN SYNCOPATERS (band)
1962 *Pathe Pictorial 375*

BUNNY DOYLE (comedian)
1941 *Facing the Music*
(Butcher) F
"The Same Old Road"

DESMOND DOYLE (ballet dancer)
1966 *Romeo and Juliet*
(Rank) F

JACK DOYLE (singing boxer)
1935 *McGlusky the Sea Rover*
(BIP) F
1954 *The Belles of St Trinian's*
(British Lion) F

DR. DIDGE (group)
1996 *Glastonbury: The Movie*
(Starlight) F
"Echoes of the Past"

CHARLIE DRAKE (comedian)
1954 *The Golden Link*
(Archway) F
1960 *Sands of the Desert*
(ABP) F
1961 *Petticoat Pirates*
(ABP) F
1962 *What's Cooking?*
(Pathe) ADVERT
1962 *Pathe Pictorial 393*
1963 *The Cracksman*
(ABP) F
1967 *Mister Ten Per Cent*
(ABP) F
1974 *Professor Popper's Problems*
(CFF) S

DRAPER AND LINDEN (dancers)
1939 *Pathe Pictorial 477*
"Waltz"

SEYMOUR DRASI (paper-tearer)
1933 *Eve's Film Review 630*

DREAM BOYS (group)
1997 *Spice World*
(Fragile) F

FRANK DREW
1941 *A Musical Cocktail*
(Inspiration)

PADDY DREW (cartoonist)
1938 *Pathe Pictorial NS 97*
1940 *Pathe Pictorial 236*
1941 *Pathe Pictorial 263*
1941 *Facing the Music*
(Butcher) F
1943 *Pathe Pictorial 393*

TOM DRIBERG (journalist)
1955 *Your Sunday Newspaper*
(CWS) F
1967 *Tell Me Lies*
(Ronorus) F

THE DRIFTERS (group)
1959 *Serious Charge*
(Eros) F

BETTY DRIVER (singer)
1934 *Boots Boots*
(Blakeley) F
1938 *Penny Paradise*
(ATP) F
"Stick Out Your Chin"
"You Can't Have Your Cake"
"Learn How to Sing a Love Song"
1939 *Let's Be Famous*
(ATP) F
"I Ran into Love"
"The Moon Remembers"
"I've Got a Hunch"
"Whistle When You Want Me"
"The Gospel of Love"
1941 *Facing the Music*
(Butcher) F
"You Don't Have to Tell Me I Know"

ELLA DRUMMOND (dancer)
1936 *B.B.C. Musicals 3*
(Inspiration)
1951 *Mirth and Melody*
(reissue: *B.B.C. Musicals 3*)

BERNARD DUDLEY (baritone)
1931 *Pathe Pictorial 712*
"Shovel On a Few More Coals"
1932 *Pathe Pictorial 717*
"Gypsy Dan"
1932 *Pathe Pictorial 737*
"The Longshoreman"
1933 *Taking Ways*
(Sound City) F

CUDDLY DUDLEY (singer)
1960 *Girls of Latin Quarter*
(New Realm) F

ERNEST DUDLEY (broadcaster)
1952 *The Armchair Detective*
(Apex) F

JOHN DUDLEY (singer)
1936 *Love Up the Pole*
(Butcher) F
"I Send My Love With These Roses"

DUDLEY'S MIDGETS (specialty)
1945 *Here Comes the Sun*
(Baxter) F

DUKE OF YORK'S BOYS BAND
1942 *Pathe Pictorial 346*

DUKES OF DIXIELAND (band)
1962 *It's Trad Dad*
(Columbia) F
"In the Sweet Bye and Bye"

ARTHUR DULAY (pianist)
1938 *Melodies of the Moment*
(Inspiration)
1943 *Kings of the Keyboard*
(Inspiration)
1947 *Making the Grade*
(Inspiration)
(reissue: *Melodies of the Moment*)

DUMP AND TONY (comedians)
1939 *Discoveries*
(Vogue) F
"A Shanty in Old Shanty Town"

DUNCAN AND GODFREY (comedians)
1930 *Amateur Night in London*
(PDC) F

HUGH DUNCAN AND NAN HAY (comedy)
1928 *Gaumont Mirror*
"The Tale"

MISS DUNDEE'S DOGS (animal act)
1902 *Trained Dogs*
(Gaumont)

KATHERINE DUNHAM (West Indian dancer)
1952 *New Pictorial 398*

MARTIN DUNNE (singer)
1988 *Joyriders*
(Cannon) F

MARCELLE DUPREY (singer)
1993 *Backbeat*
(Rank)
"Kiss Me Honey Honey"

FRED DUPREZ (comedian)
1933 *Heads We Go*
(BIP) F
1933 *Oh What a Duchess*
(BIP) F
1933 *Meet My Sister*
(Pathe) F
1934 *Without You*
(British Lion) F
1934 *Love Life and Laughter*
(ATP) F
1935 *No Monkey Business*
(GFD) F
1935 *Dark World*
(Fox) F
1935 *Dance Band*
(BIP) F
1936 *Ball At Savoy*
(RKO) F
1936 *A Wife or Two*
(British Lion) F

1936 *Queen of Hearts*
(ATP) F
1936 *You Must Get Married*
(GГD) F
1936 *Reasonable Doubt*
(Morgan) F
1936 *All That Glitters*
(RKO) F
1936 *International Revue*
(Medway) F
1936 *Pathetone 319*
1936 *Pathetone 335*
1937 *Shooting Stars*
(Viking) F
1937 *Cafe Colette*
(ABFD) F
1937 *Head Over Heels*
(Gaumont) F
1937 *Kathleen Mavourneen*
(Butcher) F
1937 *Knights for a Day*
(Pathe) F
1937 *Pathetone 386*
1938 *Pathetone 421*
1938 *Take Off That Hat*
(Viking) F

MAY MOORE DUPREZ (song and dance)
1912 *May Moore Duprez Whilst You Wait*
(Precision)
1920 *Around the Town*
(Gaumont)
1922 *Eve's Film Review 64*

DURAN DURAN (group)
1987 *The Secret Policeman's Third Ball*
(Virgin) F
"Save a Prayer"

JACK DURANT (impressionist)
1948 *No Orchids for Miss Blandish*
(Renown) F
(as Peter Lorre, Sydney
Greenstreet)

GEORGE DURANTE (tightrope)
1932 *Ideal Cinemagazine 302*

JIMMY DURANTE (American comedian)
1936 *Land Without Music*
(Capitol) F

TED AND GEORGE DURANTE (comedy
acrobats)
1952 *For Your Entertainment 4*
(Gaumont)

DURHAM CATHEDRAL CHOIR
1949 *Tinker*
(Citizen) F
"Purcell's Evening Hymn"

VIOLET DURRANT AND PAUL ORAH
(dancers)
1926 *Eve's Film Review 258*
"Simultaneous Steppers"

IAN DURY (singer)
1985 *Number One*
(Lutebest) F
1986 *Rocinante*
(Cinema Action) F
1987 *The Raggedy Rawney*
(Handmade) F
1989 *The Cook, the Thief, His Wife and
Her Lover*
(Allarts) F

LORELY DYER (singer)
1946 *Lisbon Story*
(British National) F

DYKE'S ROMANY MANDOLIN BAND
1938 *Pathe Pictorial NS 116*

RENEE DYMOTT (tap-dancer)
1935 *Pathe Pictorial 895*
"I'm in Love"
1939 *Pathe Pictorial NS 162*

THE DYNAMITES (tap-dancers)
1935 *In Town Tonight*
(British Lion) F

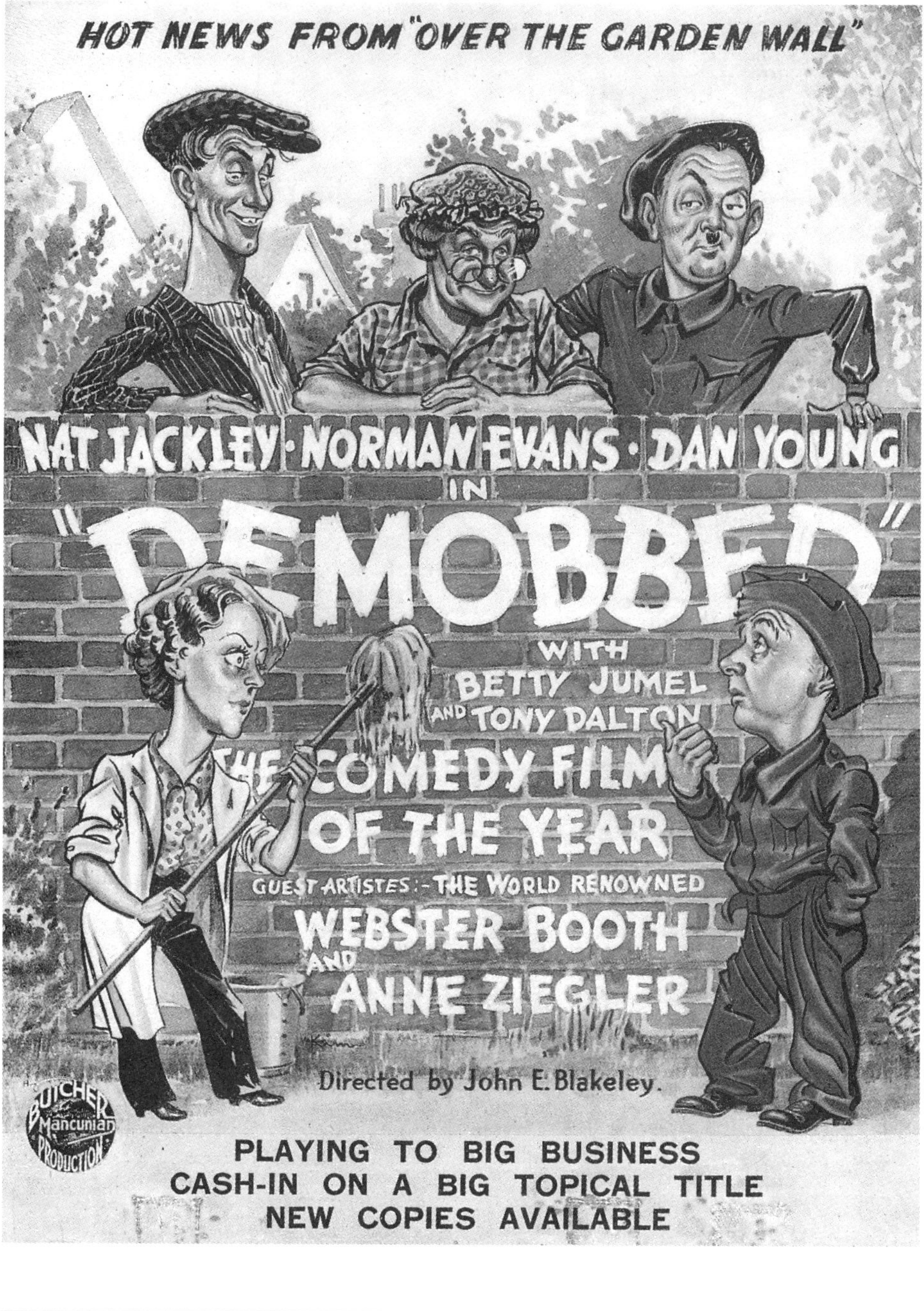
HOT NEWS FROM "OVER THE GARDEN WALL"
NAT JACKLEY · NORMAN EVANS · DAN YOUNG
IN
"DEMOBBED"
WITH
BETTY JUMEL
AND TONY DALTON
THE COMEDY FILM
OF THE YEAR
GUEST ARTISTES:- THE WORLD RENOWNED
WEBSTER BOOTH
AND
ANNE ZIEGLER
Directed by John E. Blakeley.
BUTCHER
Mancunian
PRODUCTION
PLAYING TO BIG BUSINESS
CASH-IN ON A BIG TOPICAL TITLE
NEW COPIES AVAILABLE

DORA EADIE
see **ALEC DAIMLER AND DORA EADIE**

EARL, SACHA AND VICKI (specialty)
1948　*Holidays With Pay*
　　　　(Mancunian) F

JOSEPHINE EARLE (singer)
1929　*Josephine Earle*
　　　　(BSFP)
　　　　"You Have No Idea"
　　　　"Shout Hallelujah"
1930　*Raise the Roof*
　　　　(BIP) F
1932　*Musical Medley 1; 4*
　　　　(reissue: *Josephine Earle*)

EASTBOURNE GIRLS' CHOIR
1951　*London Entertains*
　　　　(New Realm) F

ROBERT EASTON (bass)
1932　*Pathe Pictorial 730*
　　　　"Boots Boots"
1932　*Pathe Pictorial 740*
　　　　"Road to Mandalay"
1932　*Pathe Pictorial 758*
　　　　"Devil May Care"
1932　*Pathe Pictorial 766*
　　　　"In Cellar Cool"
1933　*Pathe Pictorial 792*
　　　　"The Gay Highway"
1933　*Pathetone 190*
　　　　"Shipmates o' Mine"
1934　*Pathetone 207*
　　　　"Tally Ho"
1934　*Pathetone 234*
　　　　"Skipper of the Mary Jane"
1934　*Pathe Pictorial 839*
　　　　"The Old Organ Blower"
1935　*Pathetone 250*
　　　　"The Laughing Cavalier"

SHEENA EASTON (singer)
1982　*The Secret Policeman's Other Ball*
　　　　(UIP) F
　　　　"I Shall Be Released"

MEGGIE EATON (song and dance)
1936　*Pathetone 329*
　　　　"Goodie Goodie"
1936　*Digging for Gold*
　　　　(Ace) F
1936　*Full Steam*
　　　　(Ace) F
1936　*Bottle Party*
　　　　(Ace) F
1936　*Piccadilly Playtime*
　　　　(Ace) F
1936　*Song in Soho*
　　　　(Ace) F
1937　*Windmill Revels*
　　　　(Ace) F

1937　*Carry On London*
　　　　(Ace) F
1937　*West End Frolics*
　　　　(Ace) F
1937　*Uptown Revue*
　　　　(Ace) F
1937　*Concert Party*
　　　　(Ace) F
1937　*Footlights*
　　　　(Ace) F
1938　*Swing*
　　　　(Ace) F
1938　*Revue Parade*
　　　　(Ace) F
1938　*Two Men in a Box*
　　　　(Ace) F
1938　*The Interrupted Rehearsal*
　　　　(Ace) F
1938　*Behind the Tabs*
　　　　(Ace) F
1938　*Spotlight*
　　　　(Ace) F

REX EATON (impressionist)
1938　*Pathe Pictorial NS 98*
　　　　(as Claude Dampier, Popeye)

MARGARET EAVES (soprano)
1943　*Pathe Pictorial 356*

ECHO AND THE BUNNYMEN (group)
1981　*Urgh! A Music War*
　　　　(White) F
　　　　"Puppet"

EDEIRO AND HIS ORCHESTRA
1936　*Cabaret Nights 3*
　　　　(Highbury)

OTTO EDELMANN (bass-baritone)
1962　*Der Rosenkavalier*
　　　　(Rank) F

JACK AND EDDIE EDEN (singers)
1940　*Pathe Pictorial 242*
1940　*Pathe Pictorial 252*
　　　　"Whoopee"
1941　*Pathe Pictorial 271*
　　　　"Turned Out Nice Again"
1941　*Pathe Pictorial 274*
1942　*Pathe Pictorial 304*
1943　*Pathe Pictorial 354*

MARK EDEN (singer)
1968　*A Little of What You Fancy*
　　　　(Border) F

MARRIOTT EDGAR (monologuist)
1935　*Hello Sweetheart*
　　　　(Warner) F
1942　*Pathe Pictorial 335*
　　　　"Albert and the Lion"

JACK EDGE (comedian)
1917 *How's Your Poor Wife?*
(Homeland)

CONNIE EDISON (specialty)
1907 *The Electric Fire Girl*
(Walturdaw)

CONNIE EDISS (comedienne)
1932 *The Temperance Fete*
(MGM) F
1933 *Night of the Garter*
(B&D) F

ADRIAN EDMONDSON (comedian)
1985 *The Supergrass*
(Comic Strip) F
1987 *Eat the Rich*
(Comic Strip) F
1987 *More Bad News*
(Comic Strip) F
1988 *The Strike*
(Palace) F
1988 *The Yob*
(Palace) F
1991 *The Pope Must Die*
(Palace) F

DAVE EDMUNDS (singer)
1974 *Stardust*
(EMI) F

DAVE EDMUNDS AND THE STRAY CATS
(group)
1974 *Stardust*
(EMI) F
"When Will I Be Loved?"
"A Shot of Rhythm and Blues"
"Some Other Guy Now"
"Make Me Good"
"Come On Little Dixie"

JIMMY EDWARDS (comedian)
1948 *Trouble in the Air*
(GFD) F
1949 *Helter Skelter*
(Gainsborough) F
1949 *Murder at the Windmill*
(Grand National) F
1952 *Treasure Hunt*
(Romulus) F
1953 *Innocents in Paris*
(Romulus) F
1955 *An Alligator Named Daisy*
(Rank) F
1956 *Three Men in a Boat*
(Romulus) F
1960 *Bottoms Up*
(ABP) F
1961 *Nearly a Nasty Accident*
(Britannia) F
1967 *The Plank*
(Rank) F

1968 *Ghost of a Chance*
(CFF) F
1968 *Lionheart*
(CFF) F
1969 *The Bed Sitting Room*
(UA) F
1970 *Rhubarb*
(Warner) F
1971 *The Magnificent 6½*
(CFF) SERIAL
1972 *Anoop and the Elephant*
(CFF) F

MAUDIE EDWARDS (Welsh comedienne)
1943 *My Learned Friend*
(Ealing) F
1945 *I'll Be Your Sweetheart*
(Gainsborough) F
1945 *Murder in Reverse*
(British National) F
1946 *Walking On Air*
(Piccadilly) F
1946 *Nest Egg*
(National Savings)
1949 *School for Randle*
(Mancunian) F
1952 *Girdle of Gold*
(Eros) F
1957 *The Key Man*
(Anglo) F
1960 *Teacher's Pest*
(reissue: *School for Randle*)
1960 *Bella's Birthday*
(Mancunian) (reissue: *School for Randle*)
1962 *Band of Thieves*
(Rank) F
1972 *Under Milk Wood*
(Rank) F

PERCY EDWARDS (bird impressionist)
1970 *The Rise and Rise of Michael Rimmer*
(Anglo) F

EFFIE AND HALIMA (specialty)
1938 *Pathe Pictorial NS 143*

MARTA EGGERTH (soprano)
1934 *Unfinished Symphony*
(Cine) F
1935 *The Divine Spark*
(Cine) F
"Occhi Puri Che Incante"
"Una Voce Poco Fa"
"Maddalena"

EIGHT BLACK STREAKS (dancers)
1934 *Night Club Queen*
(Realart) F
1934 *Kentucky Minstrels*
(Realart) F

EIGHT GRAFTON GIRLS (dancers)
1930   *Eve's Film Review 447*

EIGHT MASTERSINGERS (male octet)
1938   *Calling All Crooks*
(Mancunian) F
1940   *Somewhere in England*
(Mancunian) F
"The Beat of the Drum"

EIGHT PIANO SYMPHONY
1935   *Pathe Pictorial 920*
"When the Rain Comes Rolling
Down"

EILEEN (fan dancer)
1937   *Concert Party*
(Ace) F

EL CUBANOS BAND
1936   *Cabaret Nights 2; 5; 6*
(Highbury)
1936   *Below Rio*
(Kinograph)

ELAINE AND DEREK (singers)
1965   *Gonks Go Beat*
(Anglo) F

**TEDDY ELBEN AND THE IRISH
JEWZALEERS** (comedy band)
1926   *Mr Teddy Elben in a Song Scena*
(Phonofilm)
"When That Yiddisher Band Plays
an Irish Tune"

ELDRED'S EQUESTRIANS (animal act)
1902   *Eldred's Great Equestrian Act*
(Warwick)

ELECTRIC ORCHESTRA
1933   *Ideal Cinemagazine 369*

ELEKTRA QUARTET
1991   *Edward II*
(Palace) F
"Divertimento"

GUS ELEN (comedian)
1907   *Wait Till the Work Comes Round*
(Chronophone)
1931   *Pathetone 85*
"Half a Pint of Ale"
1932   *Pathetone 96*
"It's a Great Big Shame"
1932   *Pathetone 119*
"The Postman's Holiday"
1934   *Pathetone Parade*
F (reissue: *Pathetone 96*)

SIR EDWARD ELGAR (composer)
1931   *Pathetone 88*
"Land of Hope and Glory"
1932   *Pathetone 93*
"Nursery Suite"

FRED ELIZALDE AND HIS ORCHESTRA
1928   *Christmas Party*
(BSFP)

DESIREE ELLINGER (singer)
1928   *Chinese Moon*
(Phototone)
1928   *In a Japanese Garden*
(Phototone)
1928   *The Keys of Heaven*
(Phototone)

**DUKE ELLINGTON AND THE COTTON
CLUB BAND**
1933   *Pathetone 145*
"Hot as Hades"

RAY ELLINGTON QUARTET (musicians)
1948   *Stephane Grappelly and His Quintet*
(Inspiration)
1949   *Paper Orchid*
(Columbia) F
1951   *London Entertains*
(New Realm) F
1953   *Super Secret Service*
(New Realm) F
1956   *Eric Winstone's Stagecoach*
(Hammer)
"The Three Bears"
1960   *Ray Ellington and His Quartet*
(British Lion)
"Lucky Strike"
"Waltzing the Blues"
"Flamenco Bongo"
1960   *Free and Easy*
(Grand National)
"Lady of Spain"
"Carina"
"Pet"
1960   *Blue Tunes*
(British Lion)
"I'll Close My Eyes"

ALONZO ELLIOTT (singer)
1937   *Pathetone 398*
"The Long Long Trail"

BERT ELLIOTT (juggler)
1942   *Pathe Pictorial 349*

G H ELLIOTT (singer)
1934   *Music Hall*
(Realart) F
"Lily of Laguna"
"Sue Sue Sue"

JIMMY ELLIOTT (animal impressions)
1932   *Ideal Cinemagazine 319*
1937   *Pathe Pictorial NS 68*

MADGE ELLIOTT
see **CYRIL RITCHARD AND MADGE
ELLIOTT**

ROSE ELLIOTT (singer)
1948 *For Old Times Sake*
(Butcher)

ELLIOTT AND ROCHE (dancers)
1945 *Cabaret*
(Empire) F

THE ELLIOTTS (comedy musicians)
1936 *Pathe Pictorial NS 22*

EDDIE ELLIS (singer)
1961 *Payroll*
(Anglo) F
"It Happens Every Day"

LENA ELLIS (striptease)
1968 *Strip Poker*
(Miracle) F

MARY ELLIS (singer)
1937 *Glamorous Night*
(ABP) F
"Glamorous Night"
"The Gypsy Played"
"Fold Your Wings of Love Around
Me"
"Shine Through My Dreams"
"My Ship"
"Each Night I Make a Song for You"

PATRICIA ELLIS (singer)
1937 *Paradise for Two*
(London) F
"In a Paradise for Two"
"Kiss Me Goodnight"

ANDY ELLISON (singer)
1967 *Here We Go Round the Mulberry
Bush*
(UA) F
"It's Been a Long Time"
1968 *Popdown*
(New Realm) F

JOHN ELLISON (broadcaster)
1955 *Simon and Laura*
(Rank) F

GEORGE ELRICK (singer)
1939 *Pathe Pictorial 191*
"We're Gonna Hang Out the
Washing"
1940 *Pathe Pictorial 244*
1941 *Pathe Pictorial 299*
"All in Favour"

BEN ELTON (comedian)
1987 *The Secret Policeman's Third Ball*
(Virgin) F
1993 *Much Ado About Nothing*
(Entertainment) F

EILEEN ELTON AND KEITH MELVILLE
(dancers)
1953 *Twice Upon a Time*
(London) F

JOE ELVIN (comedian)
1900 *The Rats*
(Warwick)
1900 *Burlesque Attack on a Settler's
Cabin*
(Warwick)

VIOLETTA ELVIN (singer)
1949 *The Queen of Spades*
(ABP) F
1953 *Melba*
(UA) F
1953 *Twice Upon a Time*
(London) F

DAMIEN AND CARRIE ELWES (dancers)
1979 *Yesterday's Hero*
(EMI) F

EMBASSY KIDS (juvenile dancers)
1937 *Pathe Pictorial NS 67*
"One Two Button Your Shoe"

THE EMBERS (group)
1963 *The Yellow Teddy Bears*
(Compton) F

EMERSON, LAKE AND PALMER (group)
1972 *Pictures at an Exhibition*
(Schulman) F
"The Barbarian"
"Take a Pebble"
"Knife Edge"
"Nut Rocker"
"Pictures at an Exhibition"

DICK EMERY (comedian)
1953 *Super Secret Service*
(New Realm) F
1956 *Case of the Mukkinese Battlehorn*
(Archway)
1960 *Light Up the Sky*
(British Lion) F
1960 *A Taste of Money*
(Danziger) F
1962 *Mrs Gibbons Boys*
(British Lion) F
1962 *Crooks Anonymous*
(Anglo) F
1962 *The Wrong Arm of the Law*
(British Lion) F
1962 *The Fast Lady*
(Rank) F
1963 *Just For Fun*
(Columbia) F
1965 *The Big Job*
(Anglo) F
1967 *River Rivals*
(CFF) S

1968 *Baby Love*
(Avco) F
1970 *Loot*
(British Lion) F
1972 *Ooh You Are Awful*
(British Lion) F

EMILIO (accordionist)
1947 *New Pictorial 126*

IVOR EMMANUEL (Welsh baritone)
1963 *Zulu*
(Paramount) F
"Men of Harlech"

E. V. H. EMMETT (newsreel commentator)
1937 *Wings of the Morning*
(Fox) F
1939 *The Arsenal Stadium Mystery*
(GFD) F

FRED EMNEY (comedian)
(films as actor not listed)
1926 *Eve's Film Review 256*
1956 *Emney's Electrical Enterprise*
ADVERT

EMPIRE GIRLS (dancers)
1913 *The Empire Glide*
(Selsior)
1931 *Pathetone 50*
1931 *Pathetone 66*
1940 *Cavalcade of Variety*
(Butcher) F
"Ta-Ra-Ra-Boom-De-Ay"

EMPIRE MILITARY BAND
1940 *Laugh It Off*
(British National) F
"What Do They Think of England Now?"

EMPIRE PLAYERS (piano trio)
1930 *Classic v Jazz*
(Gainsborough)

CHICK ENDOR
see **CHARLES FARRELL AND CHICK ENDOR**

ENGELEN BROTHERS (jugglers)
1931 *Ideal Cinemagazine 272*

FRANKLYN ENGELMAN (broadcaster)
1963 *Heavens Above*
(British Lion) F

PAUL ENGLAND (singer)
1926 *The Sheik of Araby*
(Phonofilm)
1926 *Knee Deep in Daisies*
(Phonofilm)
1929 *An Old World Garden*
(BIP)

1929 *An Arabian Night*
(BIP)

ARTHUR ENGLISH (comedian)
1963 *The Hijackers*
(Butcher) F
1970 *Percy*
(EMI) F
1972 *For the Love of Ada*
(Tigon) F
1973 *The Seaweed Children*
(Supreme) F
1973 *Love Thy Neighbour*
(Hammer) F
1974 *Barry McKenzie Holds His Own*
(EMI) F
1977 *Are You Being Served?*
(EMI) F
1983 *The Boys in Blue*
(Rank) F

DOREEN ENGLISH (singer)
1950 *Round Rainbow Corner*
(Sanders)

ENGLISH QUARTETTE (singers)
1936 *Calling the Tune*
(Phoenix) F
"Thomas and Anne"

BRIAN ENO (musician)
1973 *Eno*
(Teamwork)
"Here Come the Warm Jets"

JOHN ENTWHISTLE (bass player)
see **THE WHO**

ERIKSON (conjurer)
1936 *Bottle Party*
(Ace) F
1936 *Pathetone 336*
1936 *Pathe Pictorial NS 26*
1937 *Pathe Pictorial NS 53*
1941 *Pathe Pictorial 285*
1942 *Pathe Pictorial 315*
1942 *Pathe Pictorial 330*
1952 *For Your Entertainment 1*
(Gaumont)

BERT ERROL (singer)
1935 *Equity Musical Revue 8*
(British Lion)

LINA ESHRARD (dancer)
1902 *Serpentine Dancer*
(Gaumont)

GENE ESSEN AND HIS CHICAGO VELLUM BOYS (banjo band)
1934 *Pathe Pictorial 853*
"Plantation Medley"

1937   *Pathe Pictorial NS 66*
"Turkey in the Straw"
"Stars and Stripes For Ever"

DAVID ESSEX (singer)
1970   *Assault*
(Rank) F
1970   *Carry On Henry*
(Rank) F
1971   *All Coppers Are...*
(Rank) F
1973   *That'll Be the Day*
(EMI) F
"Dream Lover"
1974   *Stardust*
(EMI) F
"Let It Be Me"
"Just a Little Bit Too Long"
"Take It Away"
"You Kept Me Waiting"
"Stardust"
"Americana Stray Cat Blues"
"Dea Sancta"
1980   *Silver Dream Racer*
(Rank) F
"Silver Dream Machine"
"Looking for Someone"

ESTELLE AND LEROY (dancers)
1938   *Pathe Pictorial NS 125*

JAMES ETHERINGTON (singer)
1947   *The Hills of Donegal*
(Butcher) F
"The Hills of Donegal"
"The Low Backed Car"
"The Harp That Once Through
Tara's Halls"
"Eileen Mavourneen"
"Those Endearing Young Charms"

EVAN DANDO AND THE LEMONHEADS
(group)
1996   *Glastonbury: The Movie*
(Starlight) F
"Kitchen"

CONSTANCE EVANS (acrobatic dancer)
1939   *Pathetone Parade of 1939*
F

DAVID EVANS
see **TONY FAYNE AND DAVID EVANS**

LEE EVANS (comedian)
1994   *Funny Bones*
(Hollywood) F

LYLE EVANS (singer)
1940   *Pathe Pictorial 199*
"The Jolly Song"

NORMAN EVANS (comedian)
1937   *Pathe Pictorial NS 81*
"Melody in F"

1937   *Pathe Pictorial NS 88*
1937   *Pathetone 376*
1938   *Pathe Pictorial NS 119*
1941   *Pathetone Parade of 1941*
F (reissue: *Pathe Pictorial*)
1944   *Demobbed*
(Mancunian) F
1946   *Under New Management*
(Mancunian) F
1948   *Honeymoon Hotel*
(reissue: *Under New Management*)
1950   *Over the Garden Wall*
(Mancunian) F
1959   *Evans Above*
(reissue: *Over the Garden Wall*)

REX EVANS (songs at the piano)
1930   *Comets*
(Alpha) F

WILL EVANS (comedian)
1899   *They Do Such Things at Brighton*
(Warwick)
1899   *The Musical Eccentric*
(Warwick)
1899   *Let 'Em All Come*
(Warwick)
1900   *The Rats*
(Warwick)
1907   *On the Doorstep*
(Chronophone)
1907   *The Novelette*
(Chronophone)
1907   *The Jockey*
(Chronophone)
1913   *Harnessing a Horse*
(Hepworth)
1914   *Whitewashing the Ceiling*
(Day)
1914   *Building a Chicken House*
(Sunny South)
1914   *The Jockey*
(Sunny South)
1914   *Moving a Piano*
(Sunny South)
1914   *The Showman's Dream*
(Sunny South)
1914   *Tincture of Iron*
(Sunny South)
1915   *A Study in Skarlit*
(Sunny South)
1915   *Some Fun*
(Sunny South)
1920   *Around the Town 86*
(Gaumont)

EVE (dancer)
1934   *Bella Donna*
(Twickenham) F

KENNY EVERETT (comedian)
1965   *Dateline Diamonds*
(Rank) F

1969 *The Undertakers*
      (Paramount) F
1984 *Bloodbath at the House of Death*
      (EMI) F

THE EVERHARDTS (jugglers)
1902 *The Everhardts Clever Hoop*
      Manipulation
      (Warwick)

EXQUISITE THREE (tap-dancers)
1939 *Pathe Pictorial NS 166*

EYES OF BLUE (group)
1969 *Connecting Rooms*
      (Telstar) F
      "What Happens To Her?"

TOMMY EYTLE'S CALYPSO BAND
1957 *The Tommy Steele Story*
      (Anglo) F
      "Narrative Calypso"

F

F

FABELLA (juggler)
1936 *Pathetone 308*

FABIAN (singer)
1965 *Ten Little Indians*
(Warner) F

FAIRCHILD AND LINDHOLM (pianists)
1931 *Pathetone 45*
"Kitten on the Keys"

LANCE FAIRFAX (baritone)
1931 *Gypsy Blood*
(BIP) F
"Toreador Song"
1931 *Pathetone 45*
"Onaway Awake Beloved"
1931 *Pathetone 48*
"Blue Dragoons"
1931 *Pathetone 67*
"Macushla"
1933 *Pathe Pictorial 805*
"Top of the House"
1933 *Pathe Pictorial 815*
"Danny Boy"
1933 *Pathe Pictorial 829*
"The Deathless Army"
1934 *Pathetone 235*
"The Last Roundup"
1936 *Pathetone 302*
"The Strong Go On"
1936 *Pathe Pictorial NS 24*
"Trumpeter"
1937 *Pathe Pictorial NS 74*
"Life's a Joker"
1937 *Pathetone Parade of 1938*
F (reissue: *title unknown*)
1938 *Pathe Pictorial NS 109*
"Walk Down the Road"
1939 *Pathetone 497*
"The Deathless Army"
1939 *Pathetone 507*
"Roll the Clouds Before You"
1939 *Pathe Pictorial 170*
"Onaway Awake Beloved"

FAIRPORT CONVENTION (group)
1970 *Fairport Convention and Matthews
Southern Comfort*
(Hemdale)
1973 *Glastonbury Fayre*
(Goodtimes) F

ADAM FAITH (singer)
1960 *Beat Girl*
(Renown) F
"Made You"
"I Did What You Told Me"
1960 *Never Let Go*
(Rank) F
1961 *What a Whopper*
(Regal) F
"What a Whopper"
"The Time Has Come"

1961 *What a Carve Up!*
(New World) F
1962 *Mix Me a Person*
(British Lion) F
1974 *Stardust*
(EMI) F
1979 *Yesterday's Hero*
(EMI) F
1980 *McVicar*
(Who) F

MARIANNE FAITHFULL (singer)
1967 *I'll Never Forget Whatsisname*
(Rank) F
1968 *The Girl on a Motorcycle*
(British Lion) F
1969 *Hamlet*
(Columbia) F
1974 *Ghost Story*
(Weeks) F
1979 *Broken English*
(Mainline)
"Witches Song"
"The Ballad of Lucy Jordan"
"Broken English"
1993 *Shopping*
(Rank)
1996 *Crimetime*
(Focus) F
"Time"
"She"
"Sleep"

BERNARD FALK (television personality)
1974 *Percy's Progress*
(EMI) F

KEITH FALKNER (singer)
1937 *Mayfair Melody*
(Warner) F
"San Diego Betty"
"Without the Moon"
"Wings"
"A Song Doesn't Care"
1938 *The Singing Cop*
(Warner) F
"The Soldiers' Chorus"
"Faust"
1938 *Thistledown*
(Warner) F

FALLOW TWINS (dancers)
1934 *Pathe Pictorial 860*
"Coppelia"
1934 *Pathetone 232*

GEORGIE FAME (singer)
1968 *The Mini Affair*
(United) F

FAMILY (group)
1973 *Glastonbury Fayre*
(Goodtimes) F

FAMOUS WALLENDAS (specialty)
1937   *Pathetone 381*

MICHAEL FARADAY (singer)
1931   *Pathetone 90*
        "Thistledown"

CHRIS FARLOWE (singer)
1967   *Tonite Let's All Make Love in
        London*
        (Lorrimer) F

**BOB FARNON AND THE BAND OF THE
AMERICAN EXPEDITIONARY FORCES**
1945   *I Live in Grosvenor Square*
        (ABP) F

**BOB FARNON AND THE CANADIAN ARMY
ORCHESTRA**
1946   *This Man Is Mine*
        (Columbia) F

CHICK FARR (comedian)
1929   *The Fighting Fool*
        (BSFP)
1930   *Pathetone 26*
        "The Parliamentary Candidate"
1937   *Pathe Pictorial NS 17*

FARR AND FARLAND (comedians)
1931   *Ideal Cinemagazine 294*
1934   *Pathe Pictorial 833*
        "A Political Meeting"
1936   *Murder at the Cabaret*
        (Paramount) F

GERALDINE FARRAR (singer)
1946   *Amateur Night*
        (Renown)

GWEN FARRAR (singer and cellist)
1922   *Eve's Film Review 54*
        "Midnight Follies"
1924   *Eve's Film Review 169*
1926   *Gwen Farrar*
        (Phonofilm)
        "Drink To Me Only"
1926   *Gwen Farrar and Billy Mayerl*
        (Phonofilm)
        "I've Got a Sweetie on the Radio"
1929   *Odd Numbers*
        (BIP)
        "Rainbow"
        "It Don't Do Nothin' But Rain"
1929   *Notes and Notions*
        (BIP)
        "An Old-Fashioned Girl"
        "He's a Dangerous Man"
1935   *She Shall Have Music*
        (Twickenham) F
1936   *Beloved Impostor*
        (RKO) F
1937   *Take a Chance*
        (Grosvenor) F

SONNY FARRAR (singer and musician)
1935   *She Shall Have Music*
        (Twickenham) F
        "My First Thrill"
1937   *Talking Feet*
        (Baxter) F
1940   *Band Waggon*
        (Gainsborough) F
1943   *Happidrome*
        (Aldwych) F
        "Nobody Discovers Me"
1970   *Carry On Loving*
        (Rank) F
1972   *Four Dimensions of Greta*
        (Walker) F

CHARLES FARRELL AND CHICK ENDOR
(comedy songs)
1935   *Two Hearts in Harmony*
        (Times) F

ELEANOR FARRELL
see **CHARLES FORSYTHE, ADDIE
SEAMON AND ELEANOR FARRELL**

FRED FARREN (comedian)
1901   *The Captain's Birthday*
        (Paul)
1903   *The Adventurous Voyage of the
        Arctic*
        (Paul)
1913   *The Apache Dance*
        (Motograph)

JOSEPH FARRINGTON (bass-baritone)
1932   *Pathe Pictorial 727*
        "The Rebel"
1932   *Pathe Pictorial 742*
        "Glorious Devon"

DANIEL FARSON (television personality)
1958   *Rockets Galore*
        (Rank) F
1960   *The Angry Silence*
        (British Lion) F

PATRICIA FAYE
1939   *Music Hall Parade*
        (Butcher) F

TONY FAYNE AND DAVID EVANS
(impressionists)
1951   *London Entertains*
        (New Realm) F
1953   *Out of the Bandbox*
        (New Realm)

ELEANOR FAYRE (singer)
1936   *Song of the Forge*
        (Butcher) F
        "Wear a Great Big Smile"
        "Vienna City of My Dreams"

FAYRE SISTERS (singing quartette)
1928 *Phototone 4*
"Mammy's Little Fellow"
1928 *Phototone 0*

FEARLESS FOUR (motorcycle acrobats)
1933 *Pathetone 187*

BUDDY FEATHERSTONEHAUGH AND HIS SEXTET
1946 *Appointment With Crime*
(British National) F

SUTHERLAND FELCE (conjurer)
1931 *Ideal Cinemagazine 287*
1937 *Pathetone 367*
1938 *Pathe Pictorial NS 104*
1939 *Pathetone 469*
1940 *Hullo Fame*
(British Films) F

BERT FELDMAN (composer)
1935 *Royal Cavalcade*
(BIP) F

MARTY FELDMAN (comedian)
1969 *The Bed Sitting Room*
(UA) F
1970 *Every Home Should Have One*
(British Lion) F
1971 *The Magnificent Seven Deadly Sins*
(Tigon) F
1976 *The Adventures of Sherlock Holmes'
Smarter Brother*
(TCF) F
1977 *The Last Remake of Beau Geste*
(Universal) F
1983 *Yellowbeard*
(Hemdale) F

VICTOR FELDMAN (boy drummer)
1942 *King Arthur Was a Gentleman*
(Gainsborough) F
1943 *Theatre Royal*
(Baxter) F
1944 *New Pictorial 21*

JULIE FELIX (folk singer)
1970 *Mediterranean Journey*
(ABP)

ANDREW FENNER (organist)
1944 *Pathe Pictorial 414*
"Passing By"

SHANE FENTON (singer)
also known as Alvin Stardust
1962 *Play It Cool*
(Anglo) F
"Like Magic"
1963 *It's All Happening*
(British Lion) F
"Somebody Else"

SHANE FENTON AND THE FENTONES (group)
1963 *Take Six*
(British Lion)
"Cindy's Birthday"

JIMMY FERGUSON (dancer)
1930 *Eve's Film Review 497*

TANYA FEROVA (striptease)
1975 *The Sexplorers*
(Butcher) F
1978 *Terror*
(Crystal) F

ARTHUR FERRIER (cartoonist)
1931 *Ideal Cinemagazine 268*
(draws Dodo Watts)
1944 *New Pictorial 7*
(with model for "Sally")

THE FESTIVE FELLOWS (singers)
1930 *Pathetone 40*
"Song of the Geese"

LOLA FIELD (skater)
1936 *Pathe Pictorial NS 5*

SID FIELD (comedian)
1940 *That's the Ticket*
(Warner)
1946 *London Town*
(GFD) F
"You Can't Keep a Good Dreamer Down"
"The Hampstead Way"
"You Ought to See Me on Saturday Night"
"Any Way the Wind Blows"
"Any Old Iron"
1949 *Cardboard Cavalier*
(Rank) F

GUY FIELDING (dancer)
1944 *Candles at Nine*
(British National) F
1944 *Give Me the Stars*
(British National) F

BETTY FIELDS (comedienne)
1930 *Pathetone 39*
"Fonso My Hot Spanish Knight"
1932 *Old Spanish Customers*
(BIP) F
1932 *Tonight's the Night*
(BIP) F
"Wake Up"
1934 *Lost in the Legion*
(BIP) F
1936 *On Top of the World*
(City) F
"On Top of the World"
"The Girl in the Clogs and Shawl"
"Little Friend"

"Early in the Morning"
"Hard Times Come Again No More"
"Billykins and His Dinah"

HAPPY FANNY FIELDS (dancer)
1913 *Happy Fanny Fields and the Four
      Little Dutchmen*
      (Selsior)

GRACIE FIELDS (comedienne and singer)
1929 *Eve's Film Review 421*
      "The Show's the Thing"
1931 *Sally in Our Alley*
      (ATP) F
      "Sally"
      "Fall In and Follow the Band"
      "Fred Fanakapan"
      "Lancashire Blues"
1932 *Looking On the Bright Side*
      (ATP) F
      "Looking on the Bright Side"
      "You're More than All the World to
      Me"
      "He's Dead But He Won't Lie Down"
      "I Hate You"
      "After Tonight We Say Goodbye"
1933 *Pathetone 153*
      "Making a Record at HMV"
1933 *This Week of Grace*
      (Realart) F
      "Mary Rose"
      "My Unlucky Day"
      "Happy Ending"
      "Melody at Dawn"
      "When Cupid Calls"
      "Heaven Will Protect an Honest Girl"
1934 *Love Life and Laughter*
      (ATP) F
      "Cherie"
      "Out in the Cold Cold Snow"
      "Riding on the Clouds"
      "I'm a Failure"
      "How Happy the Lover"
      "Love Life and Laughter"
1934 *Sing As We Go*
      (ATP) F
      "Sing As We Go"
      "Love"
      "Just a Catchy Little Tune"
      "My Little Bottom Drawer"
      "Speak to Me Thora"
1935 *Look Up and Laugh*
      (ATP) F
      "Look Up and Laugh"
      "Anna from Anacapresi"
      "Love Is Everywhere"
      "Shall I Be an Old Man's Darling"
1936 *Queen of Hearts*
      (ATP) F
      "Queen of Hearts"
      "My First Love Song"
      "Why Did I Have to Meet You?"
      "Orphans of the Storm"

1937 *The Show Goes On*
      (ATP) F
      "A Song in Your Heart"
      "My Love For You"
      "The Co-Op Shop"
      "You've Got to Smile"
      "I Never Cried So Much in All My
      Life"
      "We're All Good Pals Together"
      "In a Little Lancashire Town"
1938 *Keep Smiling*
      (TCF) F
      "Giddy Up"
      "The Holy City"
      "Mrs Binns's Twins"
      "Peace of Mind"
      "Swing Your Way to Happiness"
      "You've Got to be Smart in the
      Army"
1938 *We're Going To Be Rich*
      (TCF) F
      "Walter, Walter"
      "Ee by Gum"
      "Trek Song"
      "Will You Love Me When I'm
      Mutton?"
      "The Sweetest Song in the World"
      "Oh You Naughty Men"
      "The Man Who Broke the Bank"
      "Ta-Ra-Ra-Boom-De-Ay"
      "Two Lovely Black Eyes"
      "There Is a Tavern in the Town"
1939 *Shipyard Sally*
      (TCF) F
      "Danny Boy"
      "Grandfather's Bagpipes"
      "I've Got the Jitterbugs"
      "Wish Me Luck As You Wave Me
      Goodbye"
1939 *Pathe Gazette 92*
      "Sing As We Go"
      "I'm Sending a Letter to Santa
      Claus"
      "Wish Me Luck As You Wave Me
      Goodbye"
1939 *Gaumont British News 614*
1940 *Pathe Gazette 1*
      "Trek Song"
1940 *Pathe Gazette 4*
      "Sally"
1940 *Gaumont British News 628*
1940 *Pathe Gazette 36*
      "Land of Hope and Glory"
1954 *Pathe Pictorial 532*
      "Christopher Robin"

TOMMY FIELDS (song and dance)
1934 *Pathetone 210*
1935 *Look Up and Laugh*
      (ATP) F
1937 *The Penny Pool*
      (Mancunian) F
1938 *Keep Smiling*
      (TCF) F

FIELDS AND ROSSINI (comedy musicians)
1932   *Ideal Cinemagazine 306*

THE FILBERTS (group)
1996   *Glastonbury: The Movie*
        (Starlight) F
        "Forever"
        "Trouser Snake"

SENORITA FILLIS (balancer)
1903   *Senorita Fillis Queen of the*
        Revolving Globe
        (Urban)

FREDDIE FINCH (trumpeter)
1936   *Pathe Pictorial NS 8*
        "Post Horn Gallop"

PHIL FINCH AND HIS EIGHT PIANO RHAPSODY
1933   *Pathetone 187*
1934   *Pathetone 223*

FINDLAY AND WORTH (dancers)
1939   *Pathe Pictorial NS 157*

JOHNNY FINGERS (pianist)
1982   *The Secret Policeman's Other Ball*
        (UIP) F
        "I Don't Like Mondays"

TOM E FINGLASS (singer)
1940   *You Will Remember*
        (British Lion) F
        "Lily of Laguna"
        "Little Dolly Daydream"
1943   *Variety Jubilee*
        (Butcher) F
        "Lily of Laguna"

FINNISH NATIONAL ORCHESTRA
1934   *Pathe Pictorial 846*
        "Cockaigne Overture"
1940   *Pathetone 516*
        "Finlandia"

FIORENTI AND HIS GAUCHOS (band)
1936   *Pathetone 346*

SIDNEY FIRMAN AND THE LONDON RADIO DANCE BAND
1927   *Syncopated Melodies*
        (Parkinson)

MICHAEL FISH (television personality)
1980   *The Alternative Miss World*
        (Tigon) F

ARCHIE FISHER AND JENNY CLARK (singers)
1986   *Blood Red Roses*
        (Freeway) F

SHERMAN FISHER GIRLS (dancers)
1930   *Big Business*
        (Fox) F
1932   *Ideal Cinemagazine 325*
1934   *Night Club Queen*
        (Realart) F
1934   *Music Hall*
        (Realart) F
1935   *Variety*
        (Butcher) F
1935   *Jimmy Boy*
        (Baxter) F
1935   *Father O'Flynn*
        (Butcher) F
1936   *Stars On Parade*
        (Butcher) F
1936   *Sunshine Ahead*
        (Baxter) F
1936   *Shipmates o' Mine*
        (Butcher) F
        "Hearts of Oak"
        "Sailor's Hornpipe"
        "A Life on the Ocean Wave"
1936   *Variety Parade*
        (Butcher) F
1937   *Highlights of Variety 1*
        (reissue: *Variety*)
1937   *Okay For Sound*
        (Gainsborough) F
1937   *Sing As You Swing*
        (Rock) F
1937   *Shooting Stars*
        (Viking) F
1937   *Captain's Orders*
        (Liberty) F
1938   *Take Off That Hat*
        (Viking) F
1938   *Calling All Crooks*
        (Mancunian) F
1938   *Highlights of Variety 10; 16*
        (reissue: *Variety Parade*)
1940   *Cavalcade of Variety*
        (reissue: *Variety Parade*)
1940   *Band Waggon*
        (Gainsborough) F
1940   *Showtime*
        (reissue: *Shooting Stars*)
1943   *Down Melody Lane*
        F (reissue: *Variety*)

GERRY FITZGERALD (singer)
1934   *Radio Parade of 1935*
        (BIP) F
        "Let Me Go On Dreaming"
1937   *Pathe Pictorial NS 92*
        "The Greatest Mistake of My Life"
1937   *Saturday Night Revue*
        (Pathe) F
1938   *Stepping Toes*
        (Baxter) F
        "Springtime in County Clare"
        "If Night Should Fall"
1939   *Me and My Pal*
        (Pathe) F
        "The Bells of St Mary's"

SCOTT FITZGERALD (singer)
1975   *Never Too Young To Rock*
       (GTO) F
       "Never Too Young To Rock"
       "Shouted Out"

DAVE AND DOROTHY FITZGIBBON
(dancers)
1933   *Pathetone 188*

FIVE AQUAZANIES (comedy divers)
1949   *Sports Serenade*
       (ABFD)

FIVE CHARLADIES (comediennes)
1936   *Soft Lights and Sweet Music*
       (British Lion) F
       "There's Life in the Old Girl Yet"
1943   *Happidrome*
       (Aldwych) F

FIVE SMITH BROTHERS (singers)
1951   *Pathe Pictorial 335*
       "Harbour Lights"

DAVE FLAME AND THE BARBARIANS
(group)
1994   *Funny Bones*
       (Hollywood) F

BUD FLANAGAN (comedian)
1952   *Judgement Deferred*
       (Group 3) F
       "Au Revoir Dear Old Pal"
1963   *The Wild Affair*
       (7 Arts) F

BUD FLANAGAN AND CHESNEY ALLEN
(comedians)
see also **THE CRAZY GANG**
1932   *The Bailiffs*
       (ATP)
1933   *They're Off*
       (ATP)
1933   *The Dreamers*
       (ATP)
       "Dreaming"
       "Underneath the Arches"
1934   *Wild Boy*
       (Gainsborough) F
1935   *A Fire Has Been Arranged*
       (Twickenham) F
       "They're Building Flats Where the
       Arches Used To Be"
1937   *Underneath the Arches*
       (Twickenham) F
       "Underneath the Arches"
       "A Million Tears"
1937   *Okay For Sound*
       (Gainsborough) F
       "Free"
       "There's a Big Day Coming"
1938   *Alf's Button Afloat*
       (Gainsborough) F

1939   *The Frozen Limits*
       (Gainsborough) F
1940   *Gasbags*
       (Gainsborough) F
       "Yesterday's Dreams"
1941   *Pathe Gazette 42*
       "Underneath the Arches"
1942   *We'll Smile Again*
       (British National) F
       "We'll Smile Again"
1942   *Listen to Britain*
       (Crown)
       "Round the Back of the Arches"
1943   *Pathe Pictorial 370*
1943   *Theatre Royal*
       (Baxter) F
       "Roll On Tomorrow"
       "Here's To You, Here's To Me"
       "I'll Always Have Time for You"
1944   *Dreaming*
       (Baxter) F
       "Dreaming"
       "Sing a Song of Tomorrow Today"
       "Home Town"
       "Flying Through the Rain"
       "Underneath the Arches"
1945   *Here Comes the Sun*
       (Baxter) F
       "Here Comes the Sun"
       "Tomorrow Is a Beautiful Day"
       "Linger Awhile"
       "There's a Part of America"
       "You Never Miss Your Mother"
1958   *Dunkirk*
       (Ealing) F
       "We're Gonna Hang Out the
       Washing"
1958   *Life Is a Circus*
       (British Lion) F
       "Life Is a Circus"
       "Underneath the Arches"

MICHAEL FLANDERS (singer)
1963   *Doctor in Distress*
       (Rank) F
1970   *The Raging Moon*
       (EMI) F

THE FLESHTONES (group)
1981   *Urgh! A Music War*
       (White) F
       "Shadow Line"

CYRIL FLETCHER (comedian)
1939   *Pathe Pictorial 187*
1940   *Pathe Pictorial 211*
1940   *Pathe Pictorial 222*
1940   *Pathe Pictorial 228*
       "The Tale of Hilda Hose"
1941   *More and More*
       (MOI)
1942   *Pathe Gazette 6*
       "The Careless Sneezer"
1942   *Pathe Pictorial 331*

1943 *Yellow Canary*
(RKO) F
"The Tale of Queenie Feather"
"Dreaming of Thee"
1945 *Food Flash*
(MOI) S
1947 *Nicholas Nickleby*
(Ealing) F
1948 *A Piece of Cake*
(GFD) F

JIMMY FLETCHER (boy soprano)
1936 *Soft Lights and Sweet Music*
(British Lion) F
"It's My Mother's Birthday Today"

VERA FLORENCE (soprano)
1942 *Pathe Pictorial 329*
"An Old Violin"

FLOTSAM AND JETSAM (comedy songs)
also known as Mr Flotsam and Mr Jetsam
(C Hilliam and Malcolm MacEachern)
1928 *Eve's Film Review 356*
1933 *Radio Parade*
(BIP) F
"The Changing of the Guard"
1936 *The Crimes of Stephen Hawke*
(King) F
1937 *Calling All Stars*
(British Lion) F
"Calling All Stars"
"The Changing of the Guard"
1941 *Pathe Gazette 3*
"The Londoner and the Hun"

THE FLYING SAUCERS (group)
1979 *Blue Suede Shoes*
(Boyd) F

FODEN'S MOTOR WORKS PRIZE BAND
1935 *The Small Man*
(Baxter) F
1938 *Pathetone 426*
"Hunting Melody"
1938 *Pathetone 441*
"Cossack March"
1942 *Pathetone Parade of 1942*
F (reissue: *Pathetone 441*)

THE GREAT (MAURICE) FOGEL (hypnotist)
1966 *Pathe Pictorial 623*

TINO FOLGAR (singer)
1931 *Pathetone 77*
"Señorita"

MARGOT FONTEYN (ballerina)
1947 *The Little Ballerina*
(CFF) F
1960 *The Royal Ballet*
(Rank) F
"Swan Lake"
"Firebird"
"Ondine"

1963 *An Evening with the Royal Ballet*
(BHE) F
"Les Sylphides"
"Aurora's Wedding"
1966 *Romeo and Juliet*
(Rank) F
1972 *I Am a Dancer*
(EMI) F
"Marguerite and Armand"

REGINALD FOORT (organist)
1934 *Pathetone 216*
"Sonny Boy"
1936 *Pathe Pictorial NS 37*
"A Star Fell Out of Heaven"
1937 *Funeral March of a Marionette*
(BSS)
1937 *Lullabye*
(BSS)
1937 *River Folk*
(BSS)
"Eton Boating Song"
"Volga Boatman"
1937 *Songs of the Sign*
(BSS)
"Has Anybody Here Seen Kelly?"
"Yip-I-Addy-I-Ay"
1937 *The Open Road*
(BSS)
1937 *Rustic Moments*
(BSS)
"Trees"
1938 *Irish Medley*
(Visonor)
"Londonderry Air"
1938 *London*
(Visonor)
1938 *The Old Sailor's Story*
(Visonor)
1938 *Pathetone 426*
"William Tell"
1939 *Pathetone 458*
1940 *Let's Get Together*
(Exclusive)
1940 *Let's Sing Again*
(Exclusive)
"I Love a Lassie"
1940 *Let's Sing Something*
(Exclusive)
1940 *Let's Get Together and Sing*
(Exclusive)
1940 *Let's Have a Sing Song*
(Exclusive)
1940 *Shall We Sing?*
(Exclusive)
1944 *Dreaming*
(Baxter) F
"William Tell"

FREDDIE FORBES (comedian)
1936 *Murder at the Cabaret*
(Paramount) F
1939 *Music Hall Parade*
(Butcher) F

1945   *Old Mother Riley at Home*
        (British National) F

MOLLY FORBES (organist)
1941   *Pathe Pictorial 294*
        "Spring Song"

ALLY FORD (comedian)
1930   *Pathe Pictorial 652*
        "Vaudeville's Big Boots"

ANNA FORD (television personality)
1980   *The Secret Policeman's Ball*
        (Tigon) F
1982   *Who Dares Wins*
        (Rank) F

VIC FORD AND CHRIS SHEEN (female impersonators)
1949   *Skimpy in the Navy*
        (Adelphi) F
        "Nobody Loves a Fairy When She's Forty"

FLORRIE FORDE (singer)
1934   *Say It With Flowers*
        (Realart) F
        "Lassie from Lancashire"
        "Has Anybody Here Seen Kelly?"
        "Hold Your Hand Out Naughty Boy"
        "Oh Oh Antonio"
        "The Old Bull and Bush"
        "Pack Up Your Troubles"
        "Tipperary"
1934   *My Old Dutch*
        (Gainsborough) F
1935   *Royal Cavalcade*
        (BIP) F
1948   *For Old Times Sake*
        (reissue: *Say It With Flowers*)

KEITH FORDYCE (television personality)
1961   *Dentist on the Job*
        (Anglo) F

FOREST HILL ACCORDION BAND
1937   *Pathe Pictorial NS 85*

FRANCO FORESTA (tenor)
1933   *For Love of You*
        (Windsor) F
        "The Pearl Fishers"
        "Othello"
        "Pagliacci"
        "Tales of Hoffmann"
        "For Love of You"

REGINALD FORESYTHE AND HIS BAND
1935   *Jimmy Boy*
        (Baxter) F
1936   *The Big Noise*
        (Fox) F
        "The Duke Insists"
1936   *Calling the Tune*
        (Phoenix) F

1956   *Stars in Your Eyes*
        (British Lion) F

FOREVER MORE (group)
1970   *Permissive*
        (Tigon) F

BERYL FORMBY (song and dance)
1934   *Boots Boots*
        (Blakeley) F
        "Chinese Laundry Blues"
        "Red Hot Feet"
        "Maybe Baby"
1935   *Off the Dole*
        (Mancunian) F
        "Surely There's No Harm in a Kiss"
        "Isn't Love a Funny Thing?"

GEORGE FORMBY (comedian)
1915   *By the Shortest of Heads*
        (Barker) F
1934   *Boots Boots*
        (Blakeley) F
        "Maybe Baby"
        "Why Don't Women Like Me?"
        "Sitting On the Ice in the Ice Rink"
        "Chinese Laundry Blues"
        "I Could Make a Good Living at That"
1935   *Off the Dole*
        (Mancunian) F
        "If You Don't Want the Goods"
        "With My Little Ukulele"
        "I Promised to be Home by Nine"
        "I'm Going to Stick by My Mother"
        "Surely There's No Harm in a Kiss"
        "Isn't Love a Funny Thing?"
1935   *No Limit*
        (ATP) F
        "Riding in the TT Races"
        "In a Little Wigan Garden"
        "Riding Around on a Rainbow"
        "Your Way Is My Way"
        "The Isle of Man"
1936   *Keep Your Seats Please*
        (ATP) F
        "Good Night Binkie"
        "Keep Your Seats Please"
        "When I'm Cleaning Windows"
1937   *George Formby 1-4*
        (Mancunian) S
        (reissue: *Boots Boots*; *Off the Dole*)
1937   *Feather Your Nest*
        (ATP) F
        "When We Feather Our Nest"
        "Leaning on a Lamp Post"
        "I'm as Happy as a Sand Boy"
        "You're a Liarty"
1937   *Keep Fit*
        (ATP) F
        "Keep Fit"
        "Biceps Muscle and Brawn"
        "I Don't Like"

1937 *Music Hall Personalities 2*
(reissue: *Boots Boots*)
1937 *Music Hall Personalities 4*
(reissue: *Off the Dole*)
1938 *I See Ice*
(ATP) F
"In My Little Snapshot Album"
"Mother, What'll I Do Now?"
"Noughts and Crosses"
1938 *Cavalcade of the Stars*
(reissue: *Boots Boots*)
1938 *It's In the Air*
(ATP) F
"It's In the Air"
"Our Sergeant Major"
"They Can't Fool Me"
1939 *Trouble Brewing*
(ATP) F
"Hitting the High Spots Now"
"I Can Tell It By My Horoscope"
"Fanlight Fanny"
1939 *Come On George*
(ATP) F
"I Couldn't Let the Stable Down"
"I'm Making Headway Now"
"Goodnight Little Fellow"
"Pardon Me"
1939 *George Formby Cavalcade*
(reissue: *Boots Boots*; *Off the Dole*)
1939 *Pathe Gazette 86*
"Have You Heard This One?"
"Swinging Along"
1940 *Pathe Gazette 17*
"Imagine Me in the Maginot Line"
1940 *Pathe Gazette 25*
"When I'm Cleaning Windows"
1940 *Pathe Gazette 97*
"Guarding the Home of the Home
Guard"
1940 *Let George Do It*
(ATP) F
"Count Your Blessings and Smile"
"Grandad's Flannelette Nightshirt"
"Mr Wu's a Window Cleaner Now"
"Oh Don't the Wind Blow Cold"
1940 *Spare a Copper*
(ATP) F
"On the Beat"
"The Ukulele Man"
"I Wish I Was Back on the Farm"
"I'm Shy"
1940 *The Folks At Home*
(NAAFI)
1941 *Turned Out Nice Again*
(ATP) F
"The Emperor of Lancashire"
"You're Everything to Me"
"Auntie Maggie's Remedy"
"You Can't Go Wrong in These"
1941 *South American George*
(Columbia) F
"Swing Momma"
"I Played on my Spanish Guitar"

"The Barmaid at the Rose and
Crown"
"I'd Do It with a Smile"
1942 *Much Too Shy*
(Columbia) F
"Andy the Handy Man"
"They Laughed When I Started to
Play"
"Delivering the Morning Milk"
"Talking to the Moon About You"
1942 *Get Cracking*
(Columbia) F
"Get Cracking"
"Under the Blasted Oak"
"Home Guard Blues"
1942 *Bell Bottom George*
(Columbia) F
"Bell Bottom George"
"If I Had a Girl Like You"
"It Serves You Right"
"Swim Little Fish"
1943 *He Snoops To Conquer*
(Columbia) F
"Unconditional Surrender"
"Hill Billy Willy"
"Got to Get Your Photo in the
Press"
"When the Water Works Caught
Fire"
1945 *I Didn't Do It*
(Columbia) F
"The Daring Young Man"
"I'd Like a Dream Like That"
"She's Got Two of Everything"
1946 *George in Civvy Street*
(Columbia) F
"Mad March Hare"
"You Don't Need a Licence for That"
"It Could Be"
"I Was Christened with a Horse
Shoe"
"We've Been a Long Time Gone"

GEORGE FORMBY (senior) (comedian)
1914 *No Fool Like an Old Fool*
(GCA)

BRUCE FORSYTH (comedian)
1969 *Can Heironymus Merkin Ever Forget
Mercy Humppe and Find True
Happiness?*
(Universal) F
1971 *The Magnificent Seven Deadly Sins*
(Tigon) F
1985 *Pavlova*
(PMS) F

**CHARLES FORSYTHE, ADDIE SEAMON
AND ELEANOR FARRELL** (comedy and
songs)
1934 *Pathetone 236*
"Every Little Bit of Me"
"Whistle and Blow Your Blues Away"

1941　*I Thank You*
　　　(Gainsborough) F
　　　"Say Hello to the Sun"
　　　"Oh Johnny Teach Me to Dance"
　　　"Let's Get Hold of Hitler"
1943　*Pathe Pictorial 398*
　　　"A Touch of Texas"

AIDA FOSTER GIRLS (dancers)
1930　*Stark Nature*
　　　(BIF) F
1946　*Dancing Thru*
　　　(Angel) F
1950　*Come Dance With Me*
　　　(Columbia) F

PAMELA FOSTER (dancer)
1950　*The Dancing Years*
　　　(ABPC) F

RENEE FOSTER (dancer)
1927　*British Screen Magazine*
　　　"Charleston"

TEDDY FOSTER AND HIS BAND
1949　*Landfall*
　　　(ABP) F

VIVIAN FOSTER (comedian)
1929　*Pathe Magazine 22*
　　　"The Vicar of Mirth"
1931　*Gaumont Sound Mirror*
1933　*This Week of Grace*
　　　(Realart) F

FOUR ACES (comedy and songs)
1936　*Gaumont Magazine*
1936　*British Lion Varieties 2*
1936　*British Lion Varieties 4*
　　　"Hand Me Down My Walking Cane"
1936　*British Lion Varieties 6*
1936　*British Lion Varieties 9*
　　　"Put On Your Old Grey Bonnet"
1937　*Let's Make a Night of It*
　　　(ABPC) F
　　　"Air Raid"
　　　"Take Your Pick"
1938　*Pathetone 410*
　　　"Calling All Cars"
1938　*Pathetone 434*
　　　"Air Raid"
1938　*Pathe Pictorial NS 132*
　　　"Swinging the Pick"
1939　*Pathe Pictorial NS 165*
　　　"John Peel"

FOUR ADMIRALS (singers)
1928　*Phototone 5*
　　　"Melodious Melodies"

FOUR ASTAIRES (dancers)
1938　*Pathe Pictorial NS 95*
　　　"Stilt Dance"

FOUR BRIGHT SPARKS (singers)
1934　*Pathetone 222*
　　　"How Come You Do Me Like You Do?"

FOUR COMETS (skaters)
1937　*Pathetone 388*

FOUR CROTCHETS (dancers)
1935　*Pathe Pictorial 904*
1936　*Stars On Parade*
　　　(Butcher) F
　　　"Heads or Tails"

FOUR FLASH DEVILS (tap-dancers)
1936　*Soft Lights and Sweet Music*
　　　(British Lion) F
　　　"Nola"

FOUR FRANKS (tap-dancers)
1937　*Let's Make a Night of It*
　　　(ABPC) F

FOUR JOKERS (dancers)
1936　*Pathe Pictorial NS 7*
　　　"I'll Never Say Never Again"

FOUR KREMLINS (acrobats)
1939　*Pathe Pictorial NS 182*

FOUR LAZANDERS (acrobats)
1939　*Pathe Pictorial NS 164*

FOUR MUSKETEERS (singers)
1933　*Pathetone 149*
　　　"Sylvia"
1933　*Pathetone 152*
　　　"Fit as a Fiddle"
1933　*Pathe Pictorial 794*
　　　"The World May Pass Me By"
1933　*Pathe Pictorial 808*
　　　"Roll Dem Bones"
1933　*Pathe Pictorial 818*
　　　"Ezekiel Saw the Wheel"
1933　*Pathetone 165*
　　　"In a Cloister Garden"

FOUR NEW YORKERS (singers)
1937　*The Sky's the Limit*
　　　(GFD) F
1938　*Sweet Devil*
　　　(GFD) F

FOUR PENNIES (group)
1964　*Swinging UK*
　　　(Baim)
　　　"Juliette"
　　　"Running Scared"
1965　*Pop Gear*
　　　(Pathe) F
　　　"Juliette"
　　　"Black Girl"

FOUR ROBEYS (jugglers)
1933   *Pathe Pictorial 819*

FOUR ROBINAS (dancers)
1936   *Soft Lights and Sweet Music*
       (British Lion) F

FOUR SPALLAS (acrobats)
1939   *Pathe Pictorial NS 185*
1940   *Pathetone 552*
1942   *Pathe Pictorial 314*

FOUR TROJANS (acrobats)
1935   *Pathe Pictorial 920*

FOURMOST (group)
1964   *Ferry Cross the Mersey*
       (UA) F
       "I Love You Too"
1965   *Pop Gear*
       (Pathe) F
       "A Little Loving"

FOURTEEN THUNDERBOLTS (dancers)
1933   *Pathe Pictorial 818*

FOWLER AND TAMARA (dancers)
1927   *Eve's Film Review 300*
       "Exhibition Waltz"
1932   *Eve's Film Review 599*
       "Paso Doble"

FOX (group)
1975   *Side By Side*
       (GTO) F
       "Imagine Me Imagine You"

HAL FOX AND HIS BAND
1936   *Chinese Cabaret*
       (Bijou) F

ROY FOX AND HIS BAND
1932   *A Night Like This*
       (B&D) F
       "A Night Like This"
       "Considering"
       "If Anything Happened to You"
1932   *Pathetone 115*
       "It Ain't No Fault of Mine"
1932   *Pathetone 124*
1933   *Radio Parade*
       (BIP) F
1933   *Britannia of Billingsgate*
       (Gaumont) F
       "Piccadilly Playground"
       "There'll Still Be Love"
1934   *Pathe Pictorial 839*
1934   *On the Air*
       (British Lion) F
1935   *Equity Musical Revue 1*
       (British Lion)
       "Hunting the Fox"
1935   *Radio Pirates*
       (Sound City) F

"Old Faithful"
"Get Along Little Dogie"
1936   *British Lion Varieties 6*
1940   *Big Ben Calling*
       (Sound City) F (reissue: *Radio Pirates*)

FRAKSON (conjurer)
1936   *King of Hearts*
       (Butcher) F
1941   *Highlights of Variety 23*
       (reissue: *King of Hearts*)

DAI FRANCIS (singer)
1963   *It's All Happening*
       (British Lion) F
       "It's Summer"

DON FRANCISCO (singer)
1937   *Pathetone 377*

FRANCOIS AND ANGELO (tightrope)
1954   *Pathe Pictorial 523*

FRANK'S FAMOUS FOX TERRIERS
(animal act)
1944   *Pathe Pictorial 427*
1952   *Meet Me Tonight*
       (GFD) F

RONALD FRANKAU (comedian)
see also **MURGATROYD AND WINTERBOTTOM**
1930   *Pathetone 35*
       "In a Little Garage"
1931   *Pathetone 59*
       "Colinette"
1931   *Pathetone 70*
       "I'm in Love with Susan"
1931   *Potiphar's Wife*
       (BIP) F
1931   *The Skin Game*
       (BIP) F
1931   *Let's Love and Laugh*
       (BIP) F
1931   *The Other Mrs Phipps*
       (Realart) F
1932   *Pathetone 95*
1932   *Pathe Pictorial 746*
1932   *Pathetone 136*
1933   *Pathetone 148*
1933   *Pathetone 157*
1933   *Pathe Pictorial 813*
       "The Policeman"
1933   *Pathe Pictorial 820*
       "The Preparatory School, the Public School, the Varsity"
1934   *Radio Parade of 1935*
       (BIP) F
       "Let's Go Wild"
1934   *Pathetone Parade*
       F (reissue: *title unknown*)
1935   *Pathe Pictorial 875*
       "Macbeth"

1935	*Pathetone 285*
	"I'm Terribly British"
1936	*Pictorial Revue*
	F (reissue: *title unknown*)
1936.	*Pathetone 304*
	"The Miner from Asia Minor"
1936	*Pathe Pictorial NS 15*
1936	*Pathe Pictorial NS 32*
	"A Political Satire"
1936	*International Revue*
	(Medway) F
1936	*Talking Hands*
	(Harmonicolor)
1936	*The Show's the Thing*
	(Fidelity)
	"Give Me a Mustang and a Rifle"
1937	*Pathe Pictorial NS 47*
	"Faust"
1937	*Hands in Harmony*
	(reissue: *Talking Hands*)
1937	*Pathetone 383*
1937	*Pathetone Parade of 1938*
	F (reissue: *title unknown*)
1938	*Pathe Pictorial NS 102*
	"One in a Crowd"
1938	*Pathetone 431*
	"Pity the Man Who Stands Alone"
1938	*Pathetone 452*
	"Hotcha"
1939	*His Brother's Keeper*
	(Warner) F
1939	*Pathe Pictorial NS 167*
	"1 2 3 4 5 6 7"
1939	*Pathe Pictorial 190*
	"That's How I Write a Love Song"
1940	*Pathe Pictorial 205*
	"Don't Let's Sing About the War"
1941	*Pathe Pictorial 249*
1941	*Pathe Pictorial 288*
	"The Fairy"
1941	*Pathetone Parade of 1941*
	F (reissue: *title unknown*)
1942	*Pathe Pictorial 301*
	"The Crooner"
1943	*Pathe Pictorial 377*
	"After the War"
1945	*What Do We Do Now?*
	(Grand National) F
1946	*Wot No Gangsters*
	(New Realm) F
1947	*Dual Alibi*
	(British National) F
1947	*Ghosts of Berkeley Square*
	(British National) F
1950	*Round Rainbow Corner*
	(Sanders)

FRANK E FRANKS (comedian)
1939	*Music Hall Parade*
	(Butcher) F
1940	*Cavalcade of Variety*
	(reissue: *Music Hall Parade*)

MORTON FRASER AND HIS HARMONICA GANG (comedy band)
1937	*Pathe Pictorial NS 82*
	"I Love a Lassie"
1941	*Pathe Pictorial 251*
1943	*Pathe Pictorial 361*
	"Song of India"
1944	*Pathe Pictorial 410*
	"In the Mood"
1947	*New Pictorial 134*
	"In the Mood"
1950	*A Ray of Sunshine*
	(Adelphi) F
	"Shoe Shine Boy"
1957	*Edmundo Ros Half Hour*
	(Hammer)

MOYRA FRAZER (dancer)
1950	*Madeleine*
	(GFD) F
1950	*The Dancing Years*
	(ABPC) F
	"Leap Year Waltz"
1955	*The Man Who Loved Redheads*
	(British Lion) F
1959	*Left Right and Centre*
	(British Lion) F

FREDDIE AND THE DREAMERS (group)
1963	*What a Crazy World*
	(Hammer) F
	"Twisting the Night Away"
	"Sally Ann"
	"Who Wears Short Shorts?"
	"Camptown Races"
1964	*Every Day's a Holiday*
	(Grand National) F
1964	*Just For You*
	(British Lion) F
1965	*Cuckoo Patrol*
	(Grand National) F

CECIL FREDERICK (comedian)
1943	*Happidrome*
	(Aldwych) F
	"We Three"
1945	*Home Sweet Home*
	(Mancunian) F

ALAN FREEMAN (disc jockey)
1962	*It's Trad Dad*
	(Columbia) F
1963	*Just For Fun*
	(Columbia) F
1964	*Swinging UK*
	(Baim)
1964	*UK Swings Again*
	(Baim)
1964	*Dr Terror's House of Horrors*
	(Amicus) F
1967	*Sebastian*
	(Paramount) F
1973	*Radio Wonderful*
	(Goodtimes) F

1986 *Absolute Beginners*
(Palace) F
1994 *Mad Dogs and Englishmen*
(Moor)

GORDON FREEMAN (comedian)
1929 *Gordon Freeman Novelty Entertainer*
(BSFP)
1929 *Pathe Magazine 1*

LEOPOLDO FREGOLI (protean artiste)
1898 *Fregoli*
(Paul)

DAWN FRENCH (comedienne)
1985 *The Supergrass*
(Comic Strip) F
1987 *Eat the Rich*
(Comic Strip) F
1987 *More Bad News*
(Comic Strip) F
1988 *The Strike*
(Palace) F
1996 *The Adventures of Pinocchio*
(Allied) F

ERNST AND MARY FREY-
BERNHARSGRUTTER (Swiss yodellers)
1929 *Alpine Melodies*
(BIP)
1929 *Pot Pourri*
(BIP)

FREDDIE FRINTON (comedian)
1948 *Trouble in the Air*
(GFD) F
1951 *Penny Points to Paradise*
(Adelphi) F
1953 *Forces Sweetheart*
(New Realm) F
"She Knows Me"
1956 *Stars in Your Eyes*
(British Lion) F
1960 *Make Mine Mink*
(Rank) F
1961 *What a Whopper*
(Regal) F

FRISCO (singer)
1928 *Phototone 12*
"Nobody Knows the Trouble I've
Seen"
1928 *Phototone 13*
"I've Got a Robe"

FRONTLINE ORCHESTRA
1982 *Eddy Grant Live at Notting Hill*
(Hemdale)

DAVID FROST (television personality)
1963 *The VIPs*
(MGM) F

PATRICIA FROST (xylophonist)
1942 *Pathe Pictorial 345*

STEPHEN FRY (comedian)
1986 *The Good Father*
(Greenpoint) F
1987 *A Handful of Dust*
(Premier) F
1987 *The Secret Policeman's Third Ball*
(Virgin) F
1988 *A Fish Called Wanda*
(Prominent) F
1992 *Peter's Friends*
(Renaissance) F
1995 *Cold Comfort Farm*
(BBC) F
1995 *The Steal*
(Poseidon) F
1996 *The Wind in the Willows*
(Allied) F
1997 *Wilde*
(PolyGram) F
1997 *Spice World*
(Fragile) F

WALLY FRYER AND VIOLET BARNES
(dancers)
1950 *Dance Hall*
(Ealing) F

LESLIE FULLER (comedian)
1930 *Not So Quiet on the Western Front*
(BIP) F
1930 *Kiss Me Sergeant*
(BIP) F
1930 *Why Sailors Leave Home*
(BIP) F
1931 *Old Soldiers Never Die*
(BIP) F
1931 *What a Night*
(BIP) F
1931 *Poor Old Bill*
(BIP) F
1931 *Bill's Legacy*
(BIP) F
1932 *Tonight's the Night*
(BIP) F
1932 *The Last Coupon*
(BIP) F
1932 *Old Spanish Customers*
(BIP) F
1933 *Hawleys of High Street*
(BIP) F
1933 *Pride of the Force*
(BIP) F
1934 *A Political Party*
(BIP) F
1934 *The Outcast*
(BIP) F
1934 *Lost in the Legion*
(BIP) F
1934 *Doctor's Orders*
(BIP) F
"I'm So Happy When I Cry"

1935 *Strictly Illegal*
(Fuller) F
1935 *The Stoker*
(Fuller) F
1935 *Captain Bill*
(Fuller) F
1936 *One Good Turn*
(Fuller) F
1937 *Boys Will Be Girls*
(Fuller) F
1940 *Here Comes a Policeman*
(reissue: *Strictly Illegal*)
1940 *Shovel Up a Bit More Coal*
(reissue: *The Stoker*)
1940 *The Middle Watch*
(ABPC) F
1940 *Two Smart Men*
(Equity) F
1941 *My Wife's Family*
(ABPC) F
1942 *Front Line Kids*
(Butcher) F
1945 *What Do We Do Now?*
(Grand National) F

SHEILA FULLER (dancer)
1930 *Toyland*
(Gainsborough)

RIKKI FULTON (Scottish comedian)
1953 *Laxdale Hall*
(ABFD) F
1981 *Dollar Bottom*
(Paramount) F

BILLY FURY (singer)
1962 *Play It Cool*
(Anglo) F
"Play It Cool"
"I Think You're Swell"
"Once Upon a Dream"
"Let's Paint the Town"
"Twist Kid"
1965 *I've Gotta Horse*
(Warner) F
"I've Gotta Horse"
"Wonderful Day"
"I'll Be There to Stand by You"
"Do the Old Soft Shoe"
"Tell Me Why"
"I Like Animals"
"To Find Your Dream"
"You've Got to Look Right for the Part"
1973 *That'll Be the Day*
(EMI) F
"No Other Love Like Yours"
"Long Live Rock"
"The Stars in the Skies"

WILL FYFFE (Scottish comedian)
1930 *Elstree Calling*
(BIP) F
"Twelve and a Tanner a Bottle"
1934 *Happy*
(BIP) F
"Now Ain't That Wonderful?"
1935 *Rolling Home*
(Sound City) F
1936 *King of Hearts*
(Butcher) F
1936 *Debt of Honour*
(British National) F
1936 *Love in Exile*
(GFD) F
1936 *Men of Yesterday*
(Baxter) F
1936 *Annie Laurie*
(Butcher) F
"I'm Ninety Four Today"
1937 *Well Done Henry*
(Butcher) F
1937 *Spring Handicap*
(ABP) F
1937 *Cotton Queen*
(Rock) F
1937 · *Said O'Reilly to McNab*
(Gainsborough) F
"New Year's Day"
1938 *Owd Bob*
(Gainsborough) F
1939 *The Mind of Mr Reeder*
(Grand National) F
1939 *The Missing People*
(Grand National) F
1940 *They Came By Night*
(TCF) F
1940 *Camp Concert*
(reissue: *Men of Yesterday*)
1940 *For Freedom*
(Gainsborough) F
1940 *Neutral Port*
(Gainsborough) F
1941 *Highlights of Variety 23*
(reissue: *King of Hearts*)
1941 *The Prime Minister*
(Warner) F
1943 *Scottish National Savings*
(MOI)
1944 *Heaven Is Round the Corner*
(British National) F
1944 *Give Me the Stars*
(British National) F
1947 *The Brothers*
(GFD) F

CHRISTOPHER GABLE (dancer)
1969 *Women in Love*
(UA) F
1970 *The Music Lovers*
(UA) F
1972 *The Boy Friend*
(MGM) F
1973 *Pianorama*
(MGM)
1976 *The Slipper and the Rose*
(CIC) F
1988 *The Rainbow*
(Vestron) F
1988 *The Lair of the White Worm*
(Vestron) F

PETER GABRIEL
see also **GENESIS**
1987 *The Secret Policeman's Third Ball*
(Virgin) F
"Biko"
"Voices of Freedom"

GAELIC IRISH DANCERS
1947 *The Hills of Donegal*
(Butcher) F

ZOE GAIL (singer)
1948 *No Orchids for Miss Blandish*
(Renown) F
"Still Waters"
"When He Got It Did He Want It?"

SLIM GAILLARD (singer)
1986 *Absolute Beginners*
(Palace) F
"Selling Out"

GAILLARD BROTHERS (dancers)
1939 *Home From Home*
(British Lion) F

GAINSBOROUGH GIRLS (dancers)
1930 *Al Fresco*
(Gainsborough)
"Aloha Oe"
1930 *Black and White*
(Gainsborough)
"Doing the Low Down"
1930 *Toyland*
(Gainsborough)
"Dance of the Wooden Dolls"
1930 *Darkie Melodies*
(Gainsborough)
"Swanee River"
1930 *Gypsy Land*
(Gainsborough)

ARCHIE GALBRAITH (accordionist)
1939 *Discoveries*
(Vogue) F
"Down South"

RORY GALLAGHER (singer)
1975 *Rory Gallagher's Irish Tour*
(New Realm) F

RAY GALTON AND ALAN SIMPSON
(comedy writers)
1967 *Funny Business Is No Joke*
(Rank)

DON GALVAN (singer)
1936 *Pathetone 333*
"The Glory of Love"
1936 *Pathetone 340*
"Is It True What They Say About Dixie?"
1936 *Full Steam*
(Ace) F
1937 *The Gang Show*
(Wilcox) F
1937 *All Change*
(Ace Cinemagazine)
1937 *Pathetone 374*
"I Once Had a Heart, Marguerita"
1938 *Pathetone 447*
"Little Lady Make Believe"

MIGUEL GALVAN (mandolin)
1928 *Phototone 10*
"Don't Be Like That"
1928 *Phototone 11*
"Halfway to Heaven"

TOM GAMBLE (comedian)
1939 *Music Hall Parade*
(Butcher) F
1940 *Sailors Don't Care*
(Butcher) F
1940 *Cavalcade of Variety*
(reissue: *Music Hall Parade*)

GAMBLERS (group)
1965 *I've Gotta Horse*
(Warner) F
"I Cried All Night"

LIONEL GAMLIN (broadcaster)
(films as actor not listed)
1944 *Pathe Pictorial 409*
"Radio Red Cross Quiz"

THE GANG OF FOUR (group)
1981 *Urgh! A Music War*
(White) F
"He's Sent in the Army"

GANJOU BROTHERS AND JUANITA
(acrobatic dancers)
1943 *Variety Jubilee*
(Butcher) F
1944 *Highlights of Variety 28*
(reissue: *Variety Jubilee*)

HENRI GARAT (French singer)
1937   *The Girl in the Taxi*
       (ABFD) F
       "The Sun Will Shine"
       "Here's to You"

**FREDDIE GARDNER AND HIS
ORCHESTRA**
1949   *Skimpy in the Navy*
       (Adelphi) F

TERRI GARDNER
see **BARRI CHAT AND TERRI GARDNER**

ART GARFUNKEL (American singer)
1980   *Bad Timing*
       (Rank) F

JUDY GARLAND (American singer)
1962   *I Could Go On Singing*
       (UA) F
       "Hello Bluebird"
       "You"
       "By Myself"
       "I Could Go On Singing"
       "I Am the Monarch of the Sea"

PROFESSOR GARLAND (conjurer)
1897   *Professor Garland the Conjurer*
       (Prestwich)

VICTOR GARLAND (comedian)
1940   *At the Havana*
       (New Realm)

FELICITY GARRATT
see **JULES ANDRÉ AND FELICITY
GARRATT**

GUS GARRICK (comedian)
1921   *Around the Town*
       (Gaumont)

JOHN GARRICK (singer)
1934   *Lily of Killarney*
       (Twickenham) F
       "Father O'Flynn"
       "The Moon Has Raised Her Lamp
       Above"
       "Hunting Song"
       "Those Endearing Young Charms"
       "Dear Little Shamrock"
       "My Little Irish Gig"
       "Ireland in Spring"
       "My Sheep Dog and I"
1934   *Chu Chin Chow*
       (Gainsborough) F
       "Coraleen"
       "My Tender Flower"
1937   *The Last Rose of Summer*
       (MGM) F
       "The Last Rose of Summer"
       "The Minstrel Boy"
       "Those Endearing Young Charms"
       "Oft in the Stilly Night"

GASTON AND ANDREE (acrobatic dancers)
1926   *Eve's Film Review 280*
       "Terpslchorean Acrobatics"
1932   *Eve's Film Review 553*
1933   *Pathe Pictorial 820*
       "Elfin Folly"
1934   *Pathetone 205*
1935   *Facts and Figures*
       (Zenifilms)
1936   *Pathetone 327*
       "Airs and Graces"
1936   *It's In the Bag*
       (Warner) F
1938   *Pathe Pictorial NS 94*
1943   *Pathe Pictorial 373*

GASTON AND HELEN (dancers)
1946   *Appointment With Crime*
       (British National) F

GEOFFREY GAUNT (pianist)
see also **ARTHUR YOUNG AND GEOFFREY
GAUNT**
1928   *Phototone 13*

MAISIE GAY (comedienne)
1930   *The Shaming of the True*
       (BIF)
1931   *To Oblige a Lady*
       (British Lion) F
       "What Love Means to Girls Like Me"
1931   *The Old Man*
       (British Lion) F

GAY EDWARDIANS (singers)
1969   *Under the Table You Must Go*
       (Butcher) F

LUCILLE GAYE (comedienne)
1950   *A Ray of Sunshine*
       (Adelphi) F

GEDDES BROTHERS (comedy musicians)
1937   *Pathe Pictorial NS 75*
       "Harbour Lights"

GEORGE GEE (comedian)
1928   *Weekend Wives*
       (BIP) F
1929   *Eve's Film Review 422*
       "Hold Everything"
1930   *Eve's Film Review 465*
       "Rio Rita"
1931   *Let's Love and Laugh*
       (BIP) F
1933   *Leave It To Me*
       (BIP) F
1933   *Strike It Rich*
       (British Lion) F
1935   *Pathe Pictorial 912*
1940   *Pathe Pictorial 212*
       "Runaway Love"

BOB GELDOF (singer)
1982 *The Secret Policeman's Other Ball*
      (UIP) F
      "I Don't Like Mondays"
1982 *Pink Floyd: The Wall*
      (UIP) F
1985 *Number One*
      (Lutebest)
1987 *The Secret Policeman's Third Ball*
      (Virgin) F
      "This Is the World Calling"
1997 *Spice World*
      (Fragile) F

MAX GELDRAY (harmonica)
1954 *Winston Lee and his Orchestra*
      (Carisbrooke)
      "Il Bacio"

GENESIS (group)
1976 *Genesis a Band in Concert*
      (EMI) F
      "I Know What I Like"
      "Fly on a Windshield"
      "The Cinema Show"
      "Carpet Crawl"
      "Entangled"
      "Supper's Ready"
      "Los Endos"

GENEVIEVE (singer)
1966 *The Spy With a Cold Nose*
      (Paramount) F
1967 *Tonite Let's All Make Love in
      London*
      (Lorrimer) F
1968 *Wonderwall*
      (Clore) F

BOY GEORGE
see **CULTURE CLUB**

GEORGIAN SINGERS
1937 *Riding High*
      (British Lion) F
      "Dixie"
      "Oh Dem Golden Slippers"
      "Little Brown Jug"
1940 *Laugh It Off*
      (British National) F

**GERALDO AND HIS GAUCHO TANGO
ORCHESTRA**
1931 *Pathetone 46*
      "Caminto"
1931 *Pathetone 56*
      "Adios Muchachos"
1931 *Pathetone 71*
      "Tell Me I'm Forgiven"
1932 *Pathetone 112*
      "My Sunshine Is You"
1932 *Pathe Pictorial 731*
      "Carmelita"
1932 *Pathe Pictorial 735*

"Close Your Eyes"
1932 *Gaumont Sound Mirror*
      "Lady of Spain"

GERALDO AND HIS ORCHESTRA
1934 *Pathetone 216*
      "One Morning in May"
1934 *Road House*
      (Gaumont) F
      "What a Little Moonlight Can Do"
      "Don't Cry When We Say Goodbye"
1934 *Mr Cinders*
      (BIP) F
1935 *School for Stars*
      (B&D) F
1936 *Limelight*
      (Wilcox) F
      "Farewell Sweet Señorita"
      "The Whistling Waltz"
      "Celebrating"
1936 *Fame*
      (Wilcox) F
1936 *Pictorial Revue*
      F (reissue: *Pathetone 216*)
1937 *London Melody*
      (Wilcox) F
      "The Eyes of the World Are On You"
      "Jingle of the Jungle"
1938 *No Parking*
      (Wilcox) F
1940 *Laugh It Off*
      (British National) F
      "Hall of Memory Medley"
1942 *We'll Meet Again*
      (Columbia) F
1944 *I Like Lobsters*
      ADVERT
1950 *Dance Hall*
      (Ealing) F
      "You're Only Dreaming"
      "Sleepy Lagoon"
      "La Cumparsita"
      "There Is a Tavern in the Town"
      "Goodnight Sweetheart"
      "Knees Up Mother Brown"

GILBERT GERARD (imitator)
1906 *Animal Imitations*
      (Chronophone)

GERARDO AND ADAIR (acrobatic dancers)
1926 *Eve's Film Review 268*
1930 *Eve's Film Review 450*

BILLY GERHARDI AND HIS BAND
1932 *Illegal*
      (Warner) F
      "Now That You're Gone"
      "Can't We Talk It Over?"
      "Was That the Human Thing To
      Do?"
      "Too Late"
1937 *Pathe Pictorial NS 48*
      "Two Gun Dan"

97

GERLYS AND LYSIA (dancers)
1931 *Ideal Cinemagazine 267*
1931 *Ideal Cinemagazine 273*
"Golfing Blues"

GENE GERRARD (comedian)
1922 *Around the Town 115*
(Gaumont)
"Minstrels of 1922"
1925 *Eve's Film Review 201*
"Katya the Dancer"
1931 *Let's Love and Laugh*
(BIP) F
1931 *My Wife's Family*
(BIP) F
1931 *Out of the Blue*
(BIP) F
"Out of the Blue"
"Let's Be Sentimental"
"I'm Glad I Met You"
1932 *Brother Alfred*
(BIP) F
1932 *Lucky Girl*
(BIP) F
"This Little Island of Mine"
"For Nothing"
"Peeping Round the Corners"
1932 *Let Me Explain Dear*
(BIP) F
1933 *Leave It To Me*
(BIP) F
"Somebody"
1933 *The Love Nest*
(BIP) F
1934 *There Goes Susie*
(Pathe) F
1935 *It's a Bet*
(BIP) F
1935 *Royal Cavalcade*
(BIP) F
1935 *Joy Ride*
(City) F
1935 *The Guv'nor*
(Gaumont) F
1935 *No Monkey Business*
(GFD) F
1936 *Faithful*
(Warner) F
1936 *Where's Sally*
(Warner) F
1936 *Such Is Life*
(Incorporated) F
1937 *Glamour Girl*
(Warner) F
1945 *Dumb Dora Discovers Tobacco*
(Grand National) F

GERRY GERRARD AND JACKIE RIPPER
(dancers)
1937 *Eat Wave*
(Ace Cinemagazine)

GERRARD QUARTET (singers)
1937 *The Schooner Gang*
(Butcher) F
"A-Roving"
"Billy Boy"

GERRY AND THE PACEMAKERS (group)
1964 *Ferry Cross the Mersey*
(UA) F
"Ferry Cross the Mersey"
"This Thing Called Love"
"Baby You're So Good to Me"
"Fall in Love"
"I'll Wait for You"
"It's Gonna Be Alright"
"My Love Forever"
"You're Good to Me"
"Why Oh Why?"

GERRY, LEE AND LEN (comedy musicians)
1933 *Pathetone 179*

GERSHOM PARKINGTON QUINTET
(musicians)
1934 *Music Hall*
(Realart) F
1934 *Death at Broadcasting House*
(Phoenix) F

**THE G.I. RHYMSTERS HOT RHYTHM
BAND**
1950 *Round Rainbow Corner*
(Sanders)

CARROLL GIBBONS (pianist)
1935 *Hello Sweetheart*
(Warner) F
1939 *Pathetone 510*
1940 *The Folks At Home*
(NAAFI)
1941 *The Common Touch*
(British National) F
1945 *New Pictorial 59*
1946 *Night Boat to Dublin*
(ABPC) F
"I Shall Remember Tonight"

**CARROLL GIBBONS AND HIS
ORCHESTRA**
1929 *Splinters*
(B&D) F
"In Cellar Cool"
"Sweet and Low"
"Hold Your Hand Out Naughty Boy"
"Encore"
"The Old Folks at Home"
"At Gretna Green"
"Since I Fell in Love With You"
"There's Room in My Heart"
"I'll Be Getting Along"
1934 *Falling in Love*
(Vogue) F
"Thanks Very Much"

1937 *Calling All Stars*
(British Lion) F
"Painting Rainbows"
1938 *Saint Martin's Lane*
(ABPC) F
1943 *Pathe Pictorial 358*
"On the Air"
1944 *Pathe Pictorial 416*
"Somebody Soon"
1945 *I Live in Grosvenor Square*
(ABP) F
"If I Had My Way"
1948 *The Blind Goddess*
(Gainsborough) F

CARROLL GIBBONS AND THE SAVOY ORPHEANS (band)
1932 *There Goes the Bride*
(Gainsborough) F
"I'll Stay With You"
"I'm Looking for You"
1933 *I Adore You*
(Warner) F
1933 *Call Me Mame*
(Warner) F
1934 *Romance in Rhythm*
(Allied) F

KATHLEEN GIBSON (singer)
1937 *Cross My Heart*
(Paramount) F
"Blue Devil"
"It's a Sin To Tell a Lie"

LORNE GIBSON TRIO (group)
1966 *The Ghost Goes Gear*
(Pathe) F

WAYNE GIBSON AND THE DYNAMIC SOUNDS (group)
1963 *It's All Over Town*
(British Lion) F
"Come On Let's Go"

MELVILLE GIDEON (songs at the piano)
see also **THE CO-OPTIMISTS**
1929 *The Co-Optimists*
(New Era) F
1932 *Her First Affaire*
(Sterling) F
"When Love Comes My Way"
1933 *Pathetone 177*
"I Wish I Had a Bigger Word Than Love"

GIGGIE AND CORTEZ (comedians)
1930 *Big Business*
(Fox) F

BENJAMINO GIGLI (Italian tenor)
1933 *Pathetone 158*
1935 *Pathe Pictorial 885*
"The Puritans"

1936 *Forget Me Not*
(London) F
"Say You Will Not Forget Me"
"Lullaby"
"Venetian Serenade"
"Come Back to Me"
"Rigoletto"
"Marta"
"L'Africana"
"Elisir d'Amour"
1950 *Soho Conspiracy*
(New Realm) F
"Carmen"

ARTHUR GILBERT (singer)
1907 *Regiment of Frocks and Frills*
(Chronophone)
1908 *We Close at Two on Thursday*
(Chronophone)

OLIVE GILBERT (contralto)
1950 *The Dancing Years*
(ABPC) F
"Wings of Sleep"

GILBERT AND FRENCH (dancers)
1933 *Eve's Film Review 628*

RONALD GILES (cartoonist)
1945 *New Pictorial 58*

CHRIS GILL (tap-dancer)
1939 *Pathe Pictorial NS 161*
1946 *Dancing Thru*
(Angel) F
"Rhumba"

DINH GILLY (singer)
1932 *Insult*
(Paramount) F

JANETTE GILMORE (skater)
1927 *Gaumont Mirror*
1927 *Gaumont Graphic*

DAVID GILMOUR (guitarist)
see also **PINK FLOYD**
1987 *The Secret Policeman's Third Ball*
(Virgin) F
"Running Up That Hill"

JACK GILMOUR (cartoonist)
1932 *Ideal Cinemagazine 336*
(draws G B Shaw)

JOHN GILPIN (dancer)
1953 *The Nutcracker*
(Group 3)
1975 *Theatre of Blood*
(UA) F

FRED GINNETT (equestrian)
1906 *Dick Turpin's Ride to York*
(Warwick)

ALLEN GINSBERG (poet)
1965 *Wholly Communion*
(Lorrimer)

GINTARO (Japanese juggler)
1933 *Ideal Cinemagazine 379*

GIOVANNI (pickpocket)
1929 *Pathe Pictorial 581*
1933 *Pathe Pictorial 779*
1939 *Me and My Pal*
(Pathe) F

WYN GLADWYN (comedy)
1928 *Wyn Gladwyn, One Person Two Personalities*
(Phonofilm)

GLANHOWY SINGERS
1931 *Land of My Fathers*
(BIP)
"Land of My Fathers"
"Sailors Chorus"
"All Through the Night"
"Men of Harlech"

GLASGOW ORPHEUS CHOIR
1930 *Choral Cameos*
(BIP)
"Isle of Mull"
"The Campbells Are Coming"
"Down in a Flowery Vale"
1930 *A Feast of Harmony*
(BIP)
"Faery Chorus"
"Londonderry Air"
"Loch Lomond"
1945 *I Know Where I'm Going*
(Archers) F
1951 *The Glasgow Orpheus Choir*
(Film Traders)
"Isle of Mull"
"Faery Chorus"
"The Dashing White Sergeant"
"Mice and Men"
"Kedron"

GLASGOW PHILHARMONIC MALE VOICE CHOIR
1933 *Pathe Pictorial 800*
"Border Ballad"
1933 *Pathe Pictorial 804*
"Loch Lomond"

SIMON GLASS (card tricks)
1938 *Winning Hands Down*
(Ace Cinemagazine)

RON GLEESON (pianist)
1963 *Pathe Pictorial 456*

ARCHIE GLEN (comedian)
1932 *Ideal Cinemagazine 347*
1932 *The Midshipmaid*
(Gainsborough) F

1936 *Variety Parade*
(Butcher) F
1940 *Highlights of Variety 16*
(reissue: *Variety Parade*)

RAYMOND GLENDENNING (broadcaster)
1942 *Asking for Trouble*
(British National) F
1944 *Dreaming*
(Baxter) F
1951 *The Galloping Major*
(Romulus) F
1952 *Derby Day*
(Wilcox) F
1953 *Small Town Story*
(GFD) F
1954 *The Rainbow Jacket*
(Ealing) F
1956 *Dry Rot*
(Remus) F
1959 *Make Mine a Million*
(British Lion) F
1962 *The Iron Maiden*
(Anglo) F

SHAUN GLENVILLE (Irish singer)
1939 *Jail Birds*
(Butcher) F
1939 *Pathe Pictorial 192*
1940 *Dr O'Dowd*
(Warner) F

GARY GLITTER (singer)
1974 *Remember Me This Way*
(GTO) F
"Remember Me This Way"
"Hello Hello I'm Back Again"
"Leader of the Gang"
"I Love You Love Me Love"

GLITTER BAND
1975 *Never Too Young To Rock*
(GTO) F
"Never Too Young To Rock"
"Angel Face"
"Just For You"
"Let's Get Together Again"
"Shout It Out"

LUCILLE GLOVER (impressionist)
1937 *Talking Feet*
(Baxter) F
(as Sophie Tucker, Albert Whelan)

GLUM (accordionist)
1933 *Ideal Cinemagazine 364*
"The Dancing Accordionist"

LUD GLUSKIN AND HIS AMBASSADORS (band)
1928 *Phototone 13; 16*

BARBARA GOALEN (model)
1958 *Wonderful Things*
(ABPC) F

TITO GOBBI (Italian tenor)
1949 *The Glass Mountain*
(Renown) F
"The Glass Mountain"
"Wayfarer"
"La Montasara"
1950 *Soho Conspiracy*
(New Realm) F
"Largo el Factotum"

SIR DAN GODFREY (conductor)
1931 *Pathetone 76*

LOUISE GOFFIN (singer)
1996 *Glastonbury: The Movie*
(Starlight) F
"Idle Days"

THE GO-GOS (group)
1981 *Urgh! A Music War*
(White) F
"We Got the Beat"

AL GOLD AND LOLA CORDELL (dancers)
1939 *Pathe Pictorial NS 191*
1941 *Pathe Pictorial 254*
1946 *Bedelia*
(GFD) F

JIMMY GOLD
see **(CHARLIE) NAUGHTON AND (JIMMY)
GOLD** and **THE CRAZY GANG**

GOLDEN SERENADERS (band)
1930 *Comets*
(Alpha) F

HORACE GOLDIN (conjurer)
1902 *Goldin's Little Joke*
(Mutoscope)
1905 *Comic Conjuring*
(Mutoscope)
1936 *Stars On Parade*
(Butcher) F

RALPH GOLDSMITH AND HIS BAND
1930 *Piccadilly Nights*
(FBO) F

NAT GONELLA (singer)
1932 *Pathetone 115*
"It Ain't No Fault of Mine"

NAT GONELLA AND HIS GEORGIANS
(band)
1935 *Pity the Poor Rich*
(ABFD)
"Georgia"
"I'm Gonna Wash My Hands of You"
"Troublesome Trumpet"
"Tiger Rag"
1936 *Variety Parade*
(Butcher) F
"Old Cornet"

"Old Man Mose Is Dead"
"Yes Suh"
1937 *Sing As You Swing*
(Rock) F
"Georgia"
1940 *Swing Tease*
(reissue: *Sing As You Swing*)
1940 *Highlights of Variety 14*
(reissue: *Variety Parade*)

ARMAND GONET (boy soprano)
1934 *Pathe Pictorial 855*
"For You Alone"

F C GOODENOUGH (cartoonist)
1932 *Ideal Cinemagazine 339*

GOODFELLOW AND GREGSON
(comedians)
1914 *How Spotted Duff Saved the Squire*
(Vaudefilms)

GEOFFREY GOODHART AND HIS BAND
1934 *Screen Vaudeville*
(Vaudeville)

**MURRAY GOODMAN AND HIS NEW
YORKERS** (band)
1929 *Pathe Magazine 3*
"Just a Little Jazz"

KEN GOODWIN (comedian)
1971 *Top of the Bill*
(Butcher) F

EUGENE GOOSSENS (harpist)
1934 *Surprise Item*
(International)

LEON GOOSSENS (oboe)
1932 *Wedding Rehearsal*
(London) F

ANN GORDON (singer)
1936 *Variety Parade*
(Butcher) F
"When You Smile"

CLIFF GORDON (comedian)
1946 *Nest Egg*
(National Savings)

OTTORINO GORNO MARIONETTES
1928 *The Gorno Marionettes*
(BSFP)
1929 *Dimples and Tears*
(BSFP)
1930 *Don Dougio Fairabanca*
(ASFI)
1930 *Tom Mixup*
(ASFI)
1930 *Kuster Beaton*
(ASFI)

1930 *Kerri Chearton in Jungle Tungle*
(ASFI)
1930 *Anna Went Wrong*
(ASFI)
1930 *Our Dumb Friend*
(ASFI)
1931 *Pathetone 71*
1932 *Camera Cocktales 2*
(Hallmark) (reissue: *The Gorno Marionettes*)
1932 *Camera Cocktales 3*
(reissue: *Dimples and Tears*)

GOTHAM QUARTETTE (singers)
1929 *Under the Greenwood Tree*
(BIP) F
"When King Arthur Rules Our Land"
"The Old Sow"
1930 *Alf's Button*
(Gaumont) F
1930 *Kiss Me Sergeant*
(BIP) F

RONALD GOURLAY (blind pianist)
1932 *Gaumont Sound Mirror 73*
"Dicky Bird Hop"
1943 *Pathe Pictorial 397*
"Dicky Bird Hop"

THE GOVERNMENT (group)
1981 *Burning an Illusion*
(BFI) F

LEONARD GOWINGS (tenor)
1930 *Pathetone 34*
"Murmuring Breezes"
1931 *Pathetone 57*
"Colinette"
1931 *Pathe Pictorial 711*
"The Road That Leads to You"
1932 *Pathe Pictorial 725*
"Song of Songs"

FRANKLYN GRAHAM AND BARBARA
(dancers)
1926 *Eve's Film Review 277*
"Foxtrot"

RONNY GRAHAM (American comedian)
1958 *Hello London*
(Regal) F
"My Four British Tailors"

GRAND BALLET CLASSIQUE DE FRANCE
1968 *Mayerling*
(Warner) F
"Giselle"

ALEXANDER GRANT
see **GERD LARSEN AND ALEXANDER GRANT**

EDDY GRANT (singer)
1982 *Eddy Grant Live at Notting Hill*
(Hemdale)

GILLY GRANT (striptease)
1969 *School for Sex*
(Miracle) F
1969 *Clegg*
(Tigon) F

PAULINE GRANT BALLET COMPANY
1946 *Bad Company*
(New Realm) F
"Can-Can"
"Russian Rhapsody"

GRANT AND MOSELEY (dancers)
1936 *Chinese Cabaret*
(Bijou) F

STÉPHANE GRAPPELLY (violinist)
1944 *Time Flies*
(Gainsborough) F
1946 *Lisbon Story*
(British National) F
1948 *The Flamingo Affair*
(Inspiration) F
1948 *Stephane Grappelly and His Quintet*
(Inspiration)
"Stephane Blues"
"Piccadilly Stomp"
"Sweet Georgia Brown"
1949 *Music Parade*
(Inspiration)
1951 *Mirth and Melody*
(Inspiration)
1952 *Blonde for Danger*
(reissue: *The Flamingo Affair*)

GRATEFUL DEAD (group)
1968 *Petulia*
(Warner) F

GEORGE GRAVES (comedian)
1913 *A Sister to Assist 'Er*
(Kineplastikon)
1914 *The Jockey*
(Sunny South)
1921 *Around the Town*
(Gaumont)
1930 *Jerry Builders*
(PDC)
1932 *Crooked Lady*
(Realart) F
1934 *Those Were the Days*
(BIP) F
1935 *Royal Cavalcade*
(BIP) F
1935 *Honours Easy*
(BIP) F
1936 *Wolf's Clothing*
(Universal) F
1936 *A Star Fell From Heaven*
(BIP) F
1936 *The Robber Symphony*
(Concordia) F

THOMAS GRAVES (singer)
1906   *We All Walked Into the Shop*
(Chronophone)

BILLY GRAY (juggler)
1985   *Hitler's SS: Portrait in Evil*
(Cannon) F
1987   *Little Dorrit*
(Sands) F

CHANTAL GRAY (stripper)
1979   *The Human Factor*
(Rank) F

'MONSEWER' EDDIE GRAY (comedian and juggler)
1930   *Pathe Pictorial 622*
1935   *First a Girl*
(Gaumont) F
1936   *Skylarks*
(Reunion) F
1938   *Keep Smiling*
(TCF) F
1943   *Pathe Pictorial 370*
1945   *Don Chicago*
(British National) F
1954   *Tonight in Britain*
(Pathe)
1958   *Life Is a Circus*
(British Lion) F
1962   *The Fast Lady*
(Rank) F

GRAY, AUSTIN AND WORTH (jugglers)
1941   *Pathe Pictorial 564*

JOHNNY B. GREAT (singer)
1964   *Just For You*
(British Lion) F
"If I Had a Hammer"

JULIETTE GRECO (French singer)
1957   *Naked Earth*
(Foray) F
1957   *Bonjour Tristesse*
(Columbia) F
1966   *Night of the Generals*
(Horizon) F

ALAN GREEN AND HIS BAND
1931   *Pathetone 43*

BENNY GREEN (broadcaster)
1969   *Under the Table You Must Go*
(Butcher) F

BRUCE GREEN (dame comedian)
1929   *Pathe Pictorial M 9*

HARRY GREEN (comedian)
1932   *Marry Me*
(Gainsborough) F
1953   *Glad Tidings*
(Eros) F

1955   *An Alligator Named Daisy*
(Rank) F
"Crocodile Tears"

HUGHIE GREEN (impressionist)
1934   *Pathetone 226*
1934   *Little Friend*
(Gaumont)
1935   *Midshipman Easy*
(Ealing) F
1935   *Radio Pirates*
(Sound City) F
1937   *Melody and Romance*
(British Lion) F
1939   *Music Hall Parade*
(Butcher) F
(as Lionel Barrymore, Nellie Wallace, Jack Buchanan, Claude Dampier, Charles Laughton, Robertson Hare, Vic Oliver, Harry Tate)
1939   *Down Our Alley*
(BSS) F
1940   *Big Ben Calling*
(Sound City) F (reissue: *Radio Pirates*)
1943   *The Gang Show*
(reissue: *Down Our Alley*)
1949   *Paper Orchid*
(Columbia) F
1978   *What's Up, Superdoc?*
(Blackwater) F

MARTYN GREEN (singer)
1939   *The Mikado*
(GFD) F
1952   *The Story of Gilbert and Sullivan*
(London) F
"The Mikado"
"HMS Pinafore"
"Iolanthe"
"Ruddigore"
"The Gondoliers"
"I Have a Song to Sing, O!"

PAMELA GREEN (nude model)
1960   *Peeping Tom*
(Anglo) F
1961   *Naked as Nature Intended*
(Compton) F
1963   *The Chimney Sweeps*
(Compton)
1965   *The Naked World of Harrison Marks*
(Gala) F
1975   *Legend of the Werewolf*
(Tyburn) F
1976   *Under the Bed*
(New Realm)

PAT GREEN
see **PAMELA GREY AND PAT GREEN**

PAULA GREEN (singer)
1938   *Pathetone 440*
"I Double Dare You"

TOPLISS GREEN (bass)
1931 *Pathe Pictorial 714*
"London is a Fine Town"
"The Fortune Hunter"
1931 *Pathetone 41*
"Old Barty"

GREEN FLAG CEILIDH BAND
1947 *The Hills of Donegal*
(Butcher) F

GREEN SISTERS (singers)
1941 *Hi Gang*
(Gainsborough) F
"Hi Gang"

GERTRUDE GREENBANK (singer)
1906 *You'll Remember Me*
(Chronophone)

GREENE SISTERS (dancers)
1930 *Eve's Film Review 449*

PETER GREENWELL (pianist)
1972 *The Boy Friend*
(MGM) F
1972 *Up the Front*
(EMI) F

ART GREGORY AND HIS BAND
1936 *Pathetone 342*
"Nagasaki"

GRESHAM SINGERS
1937 *Pathe Pictorial NS 69*
"Simon the Cellarer"

BERYL GREY (ballerina)
1952 *The Black Swan*
(Stereo)

PAMELA GREY AND PAT GREEN (song and dance)
1935 *Equity Musical Revue 4*
(British Lion)
"This Is the Rhythm for Me"

LITTLE TEDDY GREY (boy singer)
1934 *Love Mirth Melody*
(Mancunian) F

GRIFF (specialty: bubble blower)
1931 *Pathetone 53*
1931 *Pathetone 74*

NORMAN GRIFFITHS AND HIS ORCHESTRA
1947 *Brighton Rock*
(ABP) F

GRIFFITHS BROTHERS (pantomime animal)
1928 *Eve's Film Review 365*
"Trocadero Cabaret"
1937 *Daisy Bell Comes to Town*
(Realist)

GRIMETHORPE COLLIERY BAND
1996 *Brassed Off*
(Prominent) F
"Death or Glory"
"The Floral Dance"
"Jerusalem"
"Danny Boy"
"Colonel Bogey"
"All Things Bright and Beautiful"
"Pomp and Circumstance"
"William Tell"

CHARLES GRIMSHAW
see **PHYLLIS TAYLOR AND CHARLES GRIMSHAW**

EMILE GRIMSHAW BANJO QUARTETTE
1929 *Emile Grimshaw Banjo Quartette*
(BSFP)
1932 *Musical Medley 3*
(reissue: *Emile Grimshaw Banjo Quartette*)
1932 *Music Without Words*
(reissue: *Emile Grimshaw Banjo Quartette*)

MARK GRIVER AND HIS SCOTTISH REVELLERS (band)
1927 *Mark Griver and his Scottish Revellers*
(Phonofilm)

EDDIE GROSS-BART AND HIS BAND
1933 *Pathetone 150*

GEORGE GROSSMITH (comedian)
1909 *A Gaiety Duet*
(Gaumont)
1910 *Winning a Widow*
(Gaumont)
1913 *The Argentine Tango*
(Hepworth)
1928 *Eve's Film Review 356*
"Lady Mary"
1932 *Service for Ladies*
(Paramount) F
1932 *Wedding Rehearsal*
(London) F
1933 *The Girl from Maxim's*
(London) F
1934 *Princess Charming*
(Gaumont) F

FRED GROUTS (musical saw)
1948 *Lucky Mascot*
(UA) F
"Those Endearing Young Charms"

OLIVE GROVES (soprano)
1931 *Gaumont Sound Mirror*
1932 *Pathetone 92*
"An Old Violin"
1932 *Pathetone 132*
"A Song in the Night"

1935 *In Town Tonight*
(British Lion) F

1936 *Radio Favourites*
(Publicity) ADVERT

BILL GRUNDY (television personality)
1974 *Man About the House*
(Hammer) F

THEODORE GUITTER AND HIS GYPSY BAND
1938 *Stick It*
(Ace Cinemagazine)

CORAL GUNNING (singer)
1937 *Business Is Bristling*
(Ace Cinemagazine)

GURLESS AND PARTNER (dancers)
1931 *Ideal Cinemagazine 273*

ANDY GUTHRIE (singer)
1996 *Glastonbury: The Movie*
(Starlight) F
"Marakech"

BRYN GWYN (baritone)
1937 *Pathe Pictorial NS 62*
"Leanin'"

GYPSY REVELLERS (band)
1938 *Calling All Crooks*
(Mancunian) F

NORMAN HACKFORTH (pianist)
1929 *Musical Moments*
(BIP)
1929 *A Song or Two*
(BIP)
1940 *The Great Conway*
(Reynolds)
1950 *Twenty Questions Murder Mystery*
(Grand National) F
1952 *Murder On the Air*
F (reissue: *Twenty Questions Murder Mystery*)

PETER HAIGH (television personality)
1955 *Simon and Laura*
(Rank) F
1962 *Band of Thieves*
(Rank) F
1963 *Live It Up*
(Rank) F

SAMIA HAKIM (dancer)
1952 *South of Algiers*
(Mayflower) F

HALAMAR AND KONARSKI (dancers)
1945 *Flight from Folly*
(Warner) F
1946 *Lisbon Story*
(British National) F
1948 *No Orchids for Miss Blandish*
(Renown) F

BINNIE HALE (singer)
1920 *Around the Town 9*
(Gaumont)
1924 *Eve's Film Review 139*
"Puppets"
1927 *On With the Dance*
(Parkinson)
1931 *Eve's Film Review 507*
"Toy Town Dance"
1933 *This Is the Life*
(British Lion) F
"I'm So Happy to Be Back Home"
1935 *The Phantom Light*
(Gaumont) F
1935 *Hyde Park Corner*
(Grosvenor) F
"Did You Get That Out of a Book?"
"You Don't Know the Half of It"
1937 *Take a Chance*
(Grosvenor) F
1937 *Love From a Stranger*
(UA) F
1939 *Pathe Gazette 93*

SONNIE HALE (comedian)
1924 *Eve's Film Review 158*
"Punch Bowl Revue"
1927 *On With the Dance*
(Parkinson)
1927 *The Parting of the Ways*
(Triangle)

1932 *Happy Ever After*
(Gainsborough) F
1932 *Tell Me Tonight*
(Gaumont) F
1933 *Early to Bed*
(Gaumont) F
1933 *Friday the Thirteenth*
(Gainsborough) F
1934 *Evergreen*
(Gaumont) F
"Tinkle Tinkle Tinkle"
1934 *Wild Boy*
(Gainsborough) F
1934 *Are You a Mason?*
(Twickenham) F
1934 *My Song for You*
(Gaumont) F
1934 *My Heart Is Calling*
(Gaumont) F
1935 *Marry the Girl*
(Gaumont) F
1935 *First a Girl*
(Gaumont) F
1936 *It's Love Again*
(Gaumont) F
1938 *The Gaunt Stranger*
(Ealing) F
1939 *Let's Be Famous*
(ATP) F
"We've Got a Hunch"
1944 *Fiddlers Three*
(Ealing) F
"Sweet Fanny Adams"
1946 *London Town*
(GFD) F

ALEC HALES (comedian)
1932 *Ideal Cinemagazine 317*
"The Big Stiff"

JADE HALES (song and dance)
1931 *Stepping Stones*
(Benstead) F

BILL HALEY AND THE COMETS (band)
1973 *The London Rock and Roll Show*
(Pleasant) F

ADELAIDE HALL (singer)
1939 *Pathetone 510*
1940 *The Thief of Bagdad*
(London) F
1951 *New Pictorial 340*
"The Whole World In His Hands"

BILL HALL TRIO (comedy musicians)
1947 *New Pictorial 138*
"The Canary"

GARDA HALL (singer)
1936 *Twenty-One Today*
(Albany) F

**HENRY HALL AND THE B.B.C. DANCE
ORCHESTRA**
1932 *Pathetone 122*
"This Is the Time for Dancing"
"Here's to the Next Time"
1935 *B.B.C. the Voice of Britain*
(New Era) F
"Piccadilly Ride"
"Sweetmeat Joe"
"Here's to the Next Time"
1935 *Music Hath Charms*
(BIP) F
"Music Hath Charms"
"Many Happy Returns"
"In My Heart of Hearts"
"Big Ship"
"Just Little Bits and Pieces"
"No Time Like the Present"
"Juju"
"I'm Feeling Happy"
"Here's to the Next Time"
1938 *Happy in the Morning*
(Gas) ADVERT
"Happy in the Morning"
"Horsey Horsey"
"Churchmouse on the Spree"
"Swinging In Between"

MISS HALL
see **JACK ROWALL AND MISS HALL**

TONY HALL (broadcaster)
1957 *Rock You Sinners*
(Small) F

WILBUR HALL (comedy violinist)
1940 *Hullo Fame*
(British Films) F

HALLAM HAWAIIAN GUITAR PLAYERS
1935 *Pathe Pictorial 893*
"Aloha Waikiki"

WILSON HALLETT (child impersonator)
1938 *Pathetone 422*

MOLLIE HALLIWELL
1938 *Revue Parade*
(Ace) F

MARK HAMBOURG (pianist)
1930 *Pathetone 32*
"Moonlight Sonata"
1932 *Pathetone 108*
"Prelude in C Sharp Minor"
1937 *Talking Feet*
(Baxter) F
"Polonaise"
"When Day Is Done"
1941 *The Common Touch*
(British National) F
"Piano Concerto No. 1"
1941 *Twinkling Fingers*
(reissue: *Talking Feet*)

1944 *New Pictorial 26*
1946 *Wot No Gangsters*
(reissue: *Talking Feet*)

MICK HAMER (pianist)
1987 *Stormy Monday*
(Palace) F

CHARLES HAMILTON
see **FRANK RICHARDS**

DAVID HAMILTON (television personality)
1972 *Top Gear*
(Butcher's)
1973 *Tiffany Jones*
(Hemdale) F
1975 *Confessions of a Pop Performer*
(Columbia) F
1978 *Home Before Midnight*
(EMI) F

ORD HAMILTON (pianist)
1928 *Phototone 3; 9*
1934 *Death at Broadcasting House*
(Phoenix) F

**ORD HAMILTON AND HIS 20TH CENTURY
BAND**
1934 *Pathetone 246*
"I Couldn't Be Mean To You"

RUSS HAMILTON (singer)
1958 *6.5 Special*
(Anglo) F
"I Had a Dream"

PETE HAMPTON (singer)
1909 *Hannah Won't You Open That Door?*
(Cinephone)

TONY HANCOCK (comedian)
1954 *Orders Are Orders*
(British Lion) F
1961 *The Rebel*
(ABP) F
1962 *The Punch and Judy Man*
(ABP) F
1965 *Those Magnificent Men in Their
Flying Machines*
(TCF) F
1966 *The Wrong Box*
(Columbia) F

TOMMY HANDLEY (comedian)
see also **MURGATROYD AND
WINTERBOTTOM**
1929 *Pathe Magazine 6*
"The Wireless"
1930 *Elstree Calling*
(BIP) F
1931 *Eve's Film Review 548*
"In the Garden"
1933 *Pathe Pictorial 791*

1933 *Making a Christmas Pudding*
(Winads) ADVERT
1935 *Pathe Pictorial 903*
"Hiking"
1936 *B.B.C. Musicals 2*
(Inspiration)
1936 *Pathetone 343*
"The Tramp's Sacrifice"
1936 *Radio Favourites*
(Publicity) ADVERT
1937 *Pathetone 355*
1938 *A Thousand Happy Days*
ADVERT
1943 *Pictorial Revue of 1943*
F (reissue: Pathetone 355)
1943 *It's That Man Again*
(Gainsborough) F
"The Tenderfoot Song"
1944 *Time Flies*
(Gainsborough) F
1944 *New Pictorial 31*
1944 *Bob in the Pound*
(National Savings)
1944 *Get It Off Your Chest*
(Vick) ADVERT
1944 *Poppy Poopah's Pennies*
(National Savings)
1944 *New Pictorial 31*
1946 *It's a Cake Walk*
(Marshall) ADVERT
1947 *Making the Grade*
(Inspiration)
(reissue: B.B.C. Musicals 2)

HANWELL SILVER BAND
1955 *Value for Money*
(Rank) F
"A Life on the Ocean Wave"
"Colonel Bogey"

HAPPY BOYS (comedians)
1930 *Eve's Fall*
(PDC)

HAPPY WANDERERS (buskers band)
1958 *Hello London*
(Regal) F
"Snake Charmer of Old Bagdad"
1963 *What a Crazy World*
(Hammer) F
1966 *The Vanishing Busker*
(Ritz)

PHILIP HARBEN (television personality)
1951 *What's Cooking?*
(Regent) ADVERT
1953 *Meet Mr Lucifer*
(Ealing) F
1955 *Man of the Moment*
(Rank) F

ROBERT HARBIN (conjurer)
1933 *Ideal Cinemagazine 376*
1939 *Pathe Pictorial NS 179*

1940 *Pathe Pictorial 211*
1952 *Say Abracadabra*
(Butcher)
1953 *The Limping Man*
(Eros) F

LEWIS HARDCASTLE'S DUSKY SYNCOPATERS (band)
1930 *Lewis Hardcastle's Dusky Syncopaters*
(Gainsborough)
1930 *Darkie Melodies*
(Gainsborough)
"Cake Walk"
"Swanee River"

GILBERT HARDING (broadcaster)
1952 *What a Husband*
(Regent)
1952 *The Gentle Gunman*
(Ealing) F
1953 *The Oracle*
(Group 3) F
1953 *Behind the Headlines*
(New Realm) F
1953 *Meet Mr Lucifer*
(Ealing) F
1953 *Gilbert Harding Speaking of Murder*
(Danziger) F
1955 *As Long As They're Happy*
(Rank) F
1955 *Simon and Laura*
(Rank) F
1955 *An Alligator Named Daisy*
(Rank) F
1956 *My Wife's Family*
(ABPC) F
1956 *Get Off the Hose*
(ICI) ADVERT
1956 *Into the Light*
(Verity)
1959 *Left Right and Centre*
(British Lion) F
1959 *Expresso Bongo*
(British Lion) F
1961 *Talking About Kitchens*
ADVERT

DUDLEY HARDY (cartoonist)
1920 *Around the Town 16*
(Gaumont)

DORIS HARE (comedienne)
1926 *Eve's Film Review 254*
1935 *Equity Musical Revue 5*
(British Lion)
"Clarence That's My Beau"
1935 *Opening Night*
(Olympic) F
1939 *Discoveries*
(Vogue) F
"I Want to Be Discovered, Mr Levis"
1939 *She Couldn't Say No*
(ABPC) F

1950 *Dance Hall*
(Ealing) F
1958 *Another Time, Another Place*
(Kaydor) F
1960 *The League of Gentlemen*
(Rank) F
1964 *A Place to Go*
(British Lion) F
1971 *On the Buses*
(Hammer) F
1972 *Mutiny On the Buses*
(Hammer) F
1973 *Holiday On the Buses*
(Hammer) F
1975 *Confessions of a Pop Performer*
(Columbia) F
1976 *Confessions of a Driving Instructor*
(Columbia) F
1977 *Confessions from a Holiday Camp*
(Columbia) F
1990 *Nuns on the Run*
(Handmade) F

HARLEQUIN BALLET TRUST (dancers)
1966 *The Yellow Hat*
(Monarch) F

STEVE HARLEY (singer)
1976 *Between the Lines*
(EMI)

APRIL HARLOWE (striptease)
1970 *Night After Night After Night*
(Butcher) F

HARMONICA RASCALS (musicians)
1939 *Home From Home*
(British Lion) F

HARMONY FOUR (singers)
1937 *Press the Button*
(Ace Cinemagazine)

HARMONY KINGS (singers)
1934 *Pathetone 212*
"Sunday Down in Old Caroline"
1934 *Pathetone 229*
"Cabin in the Pines"
1935 *Pathetone 269*
"Caliope Yodel"

CHARLIE HAROLD
see **GEORGE HAROLD**

GEORGE HAROLD (comedy violinist)
also known as Charlie Harold
1932 *Pathe Pictorial 744*
1932 *Ideal Cinemagazine 297*

NORMAN HARPER (cowboy singer)
1948 *International Circus Revue*
(Butcher) F

ROY HARPER (singer)
1972 *Made*
(Janni) F

CECIL HARRINGTON (pianist)
1936 *Pathe Pictorial NS 16*

ANITA HARRIS (singer)
1966 *Pathe Pictorial 600*
"Who's Foolish?"
1966 *Death Is a Woman*
(Pathe) F
1967 *Follow That Camel*
(Rank) F
1967 *Carry On Doctor*
(Rank) F

DINAH HARRIS
see **TED TREVOR AND DINAH HARRIS**

JACK HARRIS AND HIS BAND
1933 *Send 'Em Back Half Dead*
(Fox) F
1933 *Pathetone 172*
"Tony's Wife"
1934 *Pathetone 240*
1935 *Two Hearts in Harmony*
(Times) F
1937 *Let's Make a Night of It*
(ABPC) F
"Said the Spider to the Fly"

JET HARRIS AND THE JETBLACKS
(group)
1963 *Just For Fun*
(Columbia) F
"The Man from Nowhere"
"Hully Gully"

**MARGARET HARRIS AND VALERIE
TANDY** (dancers)
1941 *Pathe Pictorial 283*

MARION HARRIS (singer)
1934 *Falling in Love*
(Vogue) F
"Thanks Very Much"

PEGGY HARRIS
see **CARL HYSON AND PEGGY HARRIS**

ROLF HARRIS (Australian singer)
1955 *You Lucky People*
(Adelphi) F
1959 *Web of Suspicion*
(Danziger) F
1959 *Crash Drive*
(Danziger) F

RONNIE HARRIS (singer)
1955 *Just For You*
(Hammer) F

110

HARRIS SISTERS (dancers)
1929 *Musical Moments*
(BIP)

BEATRICE HARRISON (cellist)
1943 *The Demi-Paradise*
(Two Cities) F

CHARLES HARRISON (comedian)
1933 *Pathetone 196*
"Sewing on a Button"

GEORGE HARRISON (singer)
see also **THE BEATLES**
1972 *Imagine*
(Vaughan) F
1979 *Monty Python's Life of Brian*
(CIC) F
1985 *Water*
(Rank) F
1986 *Shanghai Surprise*
(Handmade) F
"S.S."
"A Breath Away From Heaven"
"Someplace Else"

SYD AND MAX HARRISON (comedians)
1933 *Pathe Pictorial 809*
"Black Eyed Susan Brown"
1936 *Stars On Parade*
(Butcher) F
1938 *Highlights of Variety 10*
(reissue: *Stars On Parade*)
1949 *Somewhere in Politics*
(Mancunian) F
1950 *Soho Conspiracy*
(New Realm) F
1960 *Full House*
(reissue: *Somewhere in Politics*)
1966 *The Sandwich Man*
(Rank) F

HARRY AND GRAY (singers)
1940 *Pathe Pictorial 207*
"Love's Serenade"

JACK HART AND HIS BAND
1936 *Pathetone 345*
"Jazznochracy"
1937 *Captain's Orders*
(Liberty) F

JUNE HART
see **JACK HOLLAND AND JUNE HART**

FLORA HARTE
see **RAMON CORTEZ AND FLORA HARTE**

FRED HARTLEY AND HIS QUINTET (band)
1947 *Life Is Nothing Without Music*
(Inspiration)
"Life Is Nothing Without Music"
"Sleepy Lagoon"
"Shenandoah"

HARTLEY WONDERS (acrobats)
1903 *The Hartley Wonders*
(Urban)
1903 *The Marvellous Hartley Barrel Jumpers*
(Urban)

RUSSELL HARTY (television personality)
1979 *The Kids Are Alright*
(Rose) F

HARVARD, MORTIMER AND KENDRICK
(specialty)
1934 *Music Hall*
(Realart) F
"Football on Wheels"

AL AND BOB HARVEY (singers)
1935 *Pathe Pictorial 892*
"A Street in Old Seville"
1938 *Pathetone 416*
"Here We Go Again"
1938 *Pathe Pictorial NS 98*
"We Like Eliza"
1938 *Pathe Pictorial NS 125*
"The Girl With the Dreamy Eyes"
1938 *Around the Town*
(British Lion) F
1939 *Pathetone Parade of 1939*
F (reissue: *Pictorial 125*)

RICHARD HASSETT (comedian)
1938 *Have Another Glass*
(Ace Cinemagazine)
1938 *The Answer's Know*
(Ace Cinemagazine)
1940 *Pathe Pictorial 218*
1940 *Pathe Pictorial 231*
1941 *Pathe Pictorial 248*

HASTINGS MUNICIPAL ORCHESTRA
1931 *Gaumont Sound Mirror*

IKE HATCH (singer)
1937 *Jericho*
(UA) F
1938 *Pathe Pictorial NS 122*
"Lawd You Made the Night Too Long"
1944 *Starlight Serenade*
(Federated) F

LESLIE HATTON (comedian)
1934 *Kentucky Minstrels*
(Realart) F

WILL HATTON AND ETHEL MANNERS
(comedy)
1936 *Dodging the Dole*
(Mancunian) F
1937 *Music Hall Personalities 1*
(reissue: *Dodging the Dole*)

HAVANA CLUB GIRLS (dancers)
1940   *At the Havana*
        (New Realm)

HARRY HAVER
see **CLAY KEYES**

HAVER AND LEE (comedians)
1934   *Radio Parade of 1935*
        (BIP) F
1935   *The Student's Romance*
        (BIP) F
1936   *Don't Rush Me*
        (PDC) F
1936   *Once in a Million*
        (BIP) F
1936   *Cabaret Nights*
        (Highbury) S
1937   *The Scat Burglars*
        (New Ideal) F
1940   *Pathe Pictorial 227*
1940   *Pathe Pictorial 232*

CHESNEY HAWKES (singer)
1990   *Buddy's Song*
        (Castle) F
        "The One and Only"

LIL HAWTHORNE (singer)
1900   *Kitty Mahone*
        (Phono-Bio-Tableaux)

BESSIE HAY
see **SID TRACEY AND BESSIE HAY**

NAN HAY
see **HUGH DUNCAN AND NAN HAY**

WILL HAY (comedian)
1928   *Eve's Film Review 355*
1933   *Know Your Apples*
        (Publicity) ADVERT
1934   *Those Were the Days*
        (BIP) F
1934   *Radio Parade of 1935*
        (BIP) F
1935   *Dandy Dick*
        (BIP) F
1935   *Boys Will Be Boys*
        (Gainsborough) F
1936   *Where There's a Will*
        (Gainsborough) F
1936   *Windbag the Sailor*
        (Gainsborough) F
1937   *Good Morning Boys*
        (Gainsborough) F
1938   *Convict 99*
        (Gainsborough) F
1938   *Oh Mr Porter*
        (Gainsborough) F
1938   *Hey Hey USA*
        (Gainsborough) F
1938   *Old Bones of the River*
        (Gainsborough) F

1939   *Ask a Policeman*
        (TCF) F
1939   *Where's That Fire*
        (TCF) F
1941   *The Ghost of St Michael's*
        (Ealing) F
1941   *Black Sheep of Whitehall*
        (Ealing) F
1942   *The Big Blockade*
        (Ealing) F
1942   *Go To Blazes*
        (Ealing)
1942   *The Goose Steps Out*
        (Ealing) F
1943   *My Learned Friend*
        (Ealing) F

CHARLES HAYES (comedian)
1932   *Pathetone 105*

ELTON HAYES (singer with guitar)
1948   *A Date With a Dream*
        (Grand National) F
        "Sombrero"
1952   *The Story of Robin Hood*
        (Disney) F
1954   *The Black Knight*
        (Columbia) F

TUBBY HAYES (musician)
1962   *All Night Long*
        (Rank) F
1964   *Dr Terror's House of Horrors*
        (Amicus) F

PHYLLIS HAYLOR AND ALEC MILLAR
(dancers)
1926   *Eve's Film Review 267*
        "Charleston"
1928   *Eve's Film Review 361*
        "Argentine Tango"

ARTHUR HAYNES (comedian)
1945   *Food Flash*
        (MOI) S
1965   *Doctor in Clover*
        (Rank) F

RICHARD HAYWARD (Irish singer)
1935   *Flame in the Heather*
        (Paramount) F
1935   *Luck of the Irish*
        (Paramount) F
        "The Old Man of Killyburn Brae"
        "The Wee Shop"
        "The Bright Silvery Light of the
        Moon"
        "Nelly Bly"
        "Ulster Love Song"
        "The Royal Blackbird"
1935   *The Voice of Ireland*
        (Haddick) F
1936   *The Early Bird*
        (Paramount) F

"Tread on the Tail of My Coat"
"The Comber Ballad"
1936 *Irish and Proud of It*
(Paramount) F
"Sweet Enniskillen"
"Johnny I Hardly Knew You"
"The Harp That Once Through
Tara's Halls"
1936 *Shipmates o' Mine*
(Butcher) F
1938 *Devil's Rock*
(Burger) F
"Rose of Tralee"
1953 *In the Steps of Saint Patrick*
(Hayward)
1953 *Where the Shannon Flows Down to
the Sea*
(Hayward)
1953 *In the Kingdom of Kerry*
(Hayward)

RUXTON HAYWARD (comedian)
1973 *White Cargo*
(Border) F

HY HAZELL (singer)
1950 *Dance Hall*
(Ealing) F
"You're Only Dreaming"
1950 *The Lady Craved Excitement*
(Hammer) F
"The Lady Craved Excitement"
"Ladies of the Gaiety"
1953 *Forces Sweetheart*
(New Realm) F
"I'm Your Sweetheart Maybe"
"I'm the Girl the Forces Fight For"
"All Through the Year"

RUPERT HAZELL AND ELSIE DAY
(comedy)
1933 *Pathetone 191*
1934 *Pathetone 239*
1935 *Pathetone 261*
1936 *Pictorial Revue*
F (reissue: *Pathetone 239*)
1939 *Pathetone Parade of 1939*
F (reissue: *Pathetone 261*)

JOAN HEAL (dancer)
1951 *Happy Go Lovely*
(ABP) F
"Mackintosh's Wedding"
1951 *Flesh and Blood*
(London) F

RICHARD HEARNE (comedian)
1934 *Give Her a Ring*
(BIP) F
1935 *Dance Band*
(BIP) F
1935 *No Monkey Business*
(GFD) F

1936 *Millions*
(Wilcox) F
1937 *Splinters in the Air*
(Wilcox) F
1940 *Pathetone 520*
1942 *Post Early*
(Post Office)
1943 *Miss London Limited*
(Gainsborough) F
1943 *The Butler's Dilemma*
(British National) F
1948 *One Night With You*
(GFD) F
1948 *Woman Hater*
(GFD) F
1949 *Helter Skelter*
(Gainsborough) F
1949 *Passport to Pimlico*
(Ealing) F
1950 *Something in the City*
(Butcher) F
1950 *Mr Pastry Does the Laundry*
(Regent)
1951 *We've Got It Taped*
1951 *Captain Horatio Hornblower RN*
(Warner) F
1951 *Madame Louise*
(Butcher) F
1952 *What a Husband*
(Regent)
1952 *Miss Robin Hood*
(Group 3) F
1955 *The Time of his Life*
(Renown) F
1956 *Tons of Trouble*
(Renown) F
1960 *Pathe Pictorial 291*
"Mr Pastry at the Circus"
1963 *The King's Breakfast*
(FM)

HAROLD HEATH (singer)
1936 *Pal o' Mine*
(RKO) F

HILDA HEATH (contortionist)
1932 *Pathe Pictorial 774*
"Veronica"

TED HEATH AND HIS MUSIC (band)
1948 *Uneasy Terms*
(British National) F
1950 *Dance Hall*
(Ealing) F
"Saturday Nite Drag"
"Palais Jive"
"Dance Hall"
"That Lovely Weekend"
"Post Horn Boogie"
1956 *It's a Wonderful World*
(Renown) F
"Hawaiian War Chant"
"When You Came Along"

1960 *Jazzboat*
(Columbia) F
"Operation Jazzboat"
"Spider's March"
1961 *Listen To My Music*
(Anglo)
"Sidewalks of Cuba"
"The Champ"
"Ill Wind"
1961 *Ted Heath and His Music*
(Anglo)
"Cherokee"
"Bond Street"
"Rockin' in Morocco"
1963 *Modern Rhythm*
(Carisbrooke)
"Paradise"

TED HEATH AND HIS SWING GROUP
1949 *The Small Back Room*
(Archers) F

HEDGEHOPPERS ANONYMOUS (group)
1966 *Run With the Wind*
(Puck) F

PATSY ANN HEDGES (tap-dancer)
1946 *New Pictorial 84*

THE HEDLEY WARD TRIO
see under **W**

MATTIE HEFT (pianist)
1943 *There's a Future In It*
(Strand) F

HEINZ (singer)
1963 *Farewell Performance*
(Rank) F
1963 *Live It Up*
(Rank) F
"Live It Up"
"Don't You Understand?"
1973 *The London Rock and Roll Show*
(Pleasant) F

HELENA TRIO (poseurs)
1936 *Pathe Pictorial NS 21*

HELGA AND JO
1938 *On Velvet*
(AIP) F

HELIO (go-go dancer)
1994 *To Die For*
(Metro)

HELLIWELL GIRLS (step dancers)
1930 *Toyland*
(Gainsborough)

ROBERT HELPMANN (dancer)
1942 *One of Our Aircraft Is Missing*
(British National) F

1945 *Henry V*
(GFD) F
1948 *The Red Shoes*
(Archers) F
1948 *Steps of the Ballet*
(Crown)
1951 *Tales of Hoffmann*
(London) F
1956 *The Iron Petticoat*
(Remus) F
1964 *The Soldier's Tale*
(BHE) F
1966 *The Quiller Memorandum*
(Rank) F
1968 *Chitty Chitty Bang Bang*
(UA) F
1972 *Alice's Adventures in Wonderland*
(TCF) F

HAYDN HEMEREY SINGERS
1935 *Pathe Pictorial 884*
"Peaceful Night"

PERCY HEMMING (singer)
1936 *Whom the Gods Love*
(ATP) F

HARRY HEMSLEY (child impersonator)
1913 *Talking to the Pictures*
1932 *Ideal Cinemagazine 343*
1933 *Pathetone 194*
1933 *Pathe Pictorial 789*
1940 *Pathe Pictorial 207*
1941 *Pathe Pictorial 262*
1941 *Pathe Pictorial 289*
1942 *Pathe Pictorial 328*
1943 *Pathe Pictorial 353*
1943 *Pathe Pictorial 391*

ALEX HENDERSON (Scottish singer)
1947 *Comin' Thro' the Rye*
(Adelphi) F
"My Love She's But a Lassie Yet"
"The Devil's Awa' wi' the Exciseman"

DICK HENDERSON (senior) (comedian)
1926 *Dick Henderson*
(Phonofilm)
"I Love Her All the More"
1926 *Dick Henderson Singing Tripe*
(Phonofilm)
1926 *Dick Henderson in a Song Scena*
(Phonofilm)
"Let's All Go to Mary's House"
1926 *Dick Henderson*
(Phonofilm)
"I Don't Care What You Used To Be"
1926 *Dick Henderson*
(Phonofilm)
"There Are More Heavens Than
One"
1926 *Dick Henderson the Great Yorkshire
Comedian*
(Phonofilm)
"I've Never Seen a Straight Banana"

1926 *Dick Henderson*
(Phonofilm)
"Ain't She Sweet?"
1930 *Dick Henderson*
(Gainsborough)
1930 *Just For a Song*
(Gainsborough) F
1935 *Pathetone 250*
1935 *Things Are Looking Up*
(Gainsborough) F
1936 *Men of Yesterday*
(Baxter) F

DICKIE HENDERSON (comedian)
1935 *Things Are Looking Up*
(Gainsborough) F
1957 *Time Without Pity*
(Eros) F
1959 *Make Mine a Million*
(British Lion) F

ROY HENDERSON (baritone)
1933 *Pathetone 155*
"Who Is Sylvia?"

RUSS HENDERSON STEEL BAND
1964 *Dr Terror's House of Horrors*
(Amicus) F

HENDERSON AND LENNOX (eccentric
dancers)
1931 *Stepping Stones*
(Benstead) F
1933 *Television Follies*
(English) F
"Water Water"
1940 *Music Hall Personalities 16*
(Butcher)

JOHN HENDRIK (tenor)
1934 *Pathe Pictorial 831*
"Memory's Garden"
1935 *Pathe Pictorial 888*
"I Love You Very Much Madame"

BILL AND JOHN HENGLER (acrobats)
1936 *Pathe Pictorial NS 20*

MAY AND FLORA HENGLER (dancers)
1896 *May and Flora Hengler, Specialty
Dancers*
(Paul)

HENGLER'S PLUNGING HORSES (animal
act)
1901 *Tally Ho*
(Bio-Tableaux)

SONJA HENIE (skater)
1930 *Pathetone 35*
1931 *Pathetone 80*
1958 *Hello London*
(Regal) F
"Hello London"

"Black Ice Ballet"
"Girl of My Dreams"
"The Magic of You"

HERSCHEL HENLERE (pianist)
1928 *Phototone 3*
"The Lost Chord"
1928 *Phototone 8*
"Home Sweet Home"
1931 *Pathetone 91*
"Peggy"
1933 *Soldiers of the King*
(Gainsborough) F
1934 *Crazy People*
(British Lion) F
1935 *Pathetone 267*

BROTHERS HENRY (trick cyclists)
1898 *Trick Bicyclists*
(Haydon & Urry)

JOHN HENRY AND BLOSSOM (comedy)
1926 *John Henry Calling*
(Redman) S
1928 *The Superior Sex*
(BSFP)
1932 *Camera Cocktales 1*
(reissue: *The Superior Sex*)

LENNY HENRY (comedian)
1987 *The Secret Policeman's Third Ball*
(Virgin) F
1989 *Lenny Live and Unleashed*
(Palace) F

LEONARD HENRY (comedian)
1929 *Pathe Magazine 17*
1930 *The New Waiter*
(PDC)
1930 *The Musical Beauty Shop*
(PDC)
1931 *Gaumont Sound Mirror*
1933 *Pathe Pictorial 771*
1933 *Radio Parade*
(BIP) F
1934 *Surprise Item*
(International)
1934 *Pathetone 243*
1934 *Pathe Pictorial 837*
"Adventures of Bunny"
1935 *Royal Cavalcade*
(BIP) F
1935 *Pathetone 251*
1935 *The Public Life of Henry the Ninth*
(Hammer) F
1936 *Pathe Pictorial NS 38*
1936 *Sunshine Ahead*
(Baxter) F
1938 *Mountains o' Mourne*
(Butcher) F
1939 *Pathetone Parade of 1939*
F (reissue: *Pictorial 38*)
1939 *The Face at the Window*
(British Lion) F

STUART HENRY (disc jockey)
1970 *Toomorrow*
(Rank) F
1973 *Radio Wonderful*
(Goodtimes) F

TOM HENRY AND HIS TOMBOYS (singers)
1947 *New Pictorial 127*

BOBBIE 'UKE' HENSHAW (ukulele)
1935 *Variety*
(Butcher) F
"Poll Parrot Rag"
"Stars and Stripes For Ever"
1940 *Cavalcade of Variety*
(reissue: *Variety*)

LESLIE HENSON (comedian)
1916 *Wanted a Widow*
(British Actors)
1916 *The Real Thing At Last*
(British Actors)
1916 *The Lifeguardsman*
(British Actors)
1920 *Broken Bottles*
(Gaumont)
1920 *Around the Town 22*
(Gaumont)
1920 *Alf's Button*
(Hepworth) F
1923 *Eve's Film Review 124*
"The Beauty Prize"
1924 *Tons of Money*
(Stoll) F
1926 *Eve's Film Review 248*
"Kid Boots"
1927 *Eve's Film Review 314*
"Lady Luck"
1927 *On With the Dance*
(Parkinson)
1929 *Eve's Film Review 438*
"Follow Through"
1929 *Gaumont Mirror 142*
1930 *Pathe Pictorial 631*
1930 *A Warm Corner*
(Gaumont) F
1931 *The Sport of Kings*
(Gaumont) F
1933 *It's a Boy*
(Gaumont) F
1933 *The Girl from Maxim's*
(London) F
1935 *Oh Daddy*
(Gainsborough) F
1937 *Pathetone 399*
1939 *Pathe Gazette 93*
1943 *The Demi-Paradise*
(Two Cities) F
1956 *Home and Away*
(Eros) F

GRACE AND CHARLES HERBERT
1937 *Pathetone 405*

HARRY HERBERT (comedian)
1940 *Garrison Follies*
(Butcher) F

HERBERT'S DOGS (animal act)
1901 *Tally Ho*
(Bio-Tableaux)

THE HERD (group)
1968 *Otley*
(Columbia) F

HERMAN'S HERMITS (group)
1965 *Pop Gear*
(Pathe) F
"I'm Into Something Good"
1968 *Mrs Brown You've Got a Lovely Daughter*
(MGM) F
"Mrs Brown You've Got a Lovely Daughter"
"It's Nice To Be Out in the Morning"
"Down at Holiday Inn"
"She's Done It Again"
"All Over the World"
"Round the Corner"
"The Most Beautiful Thing in My Life"

DAME MYRA HESS (pianist)
1942 *Listen to Britain*
(Crown)
"Piano Concerto in C Major"
1945 *Myra Hess*
(Crown)
"Sonata Appassionata"
1946 *Diary for Timothy*
(Crown)

WILLIAM HEUGHEN (Scottish singer)
1936 *B.B.C. Musicals 1*
(Inspiration)
"Father O'Flynn"
1937 *Talking Feet*
(Baxter) F
"Call Me Home"

PAT HEYWOOD TROUPE (dancers)
1948 *Holidays With Pay*
(Mancunian) F

STUART HIBBERD (broadcaster)
1935 *Royal Cavalcade*
(BIP) F
1937 *Storm in a Teacup*
(London) F

DORA HIBBERT AND NICHOLAS BIRD
1937 *Leave It To Me*
(British Lion) F

SIR SEYMOUR HICKS (comedian)
(films as actor not listed)
1907 *Seymour Hicks Edits the Tatler*
(Urban)

1913　*Seymour Hicks and Ellaline Terriss*
(Zenith)
"Bumble Bee Sting"
"Alexander's Ragtime Band"
1914　*Always Tell Your Wife*
(Zenith)
1915　*A Prehistoric Love Story*
(Zenith)
1923　*Always Tell Your Wife*
(Hicks)
1930　*Tell Tales*
(BIP)
1930　*Heard This One*
(BIP)

TONY HICKS (singer)
1968　*Popdown*
(New Realm) F

HILDEGARDE (singer)
1933　*Pathe Pictorial 814*
"I Was in the Mood"
1934　*Pathetone 197*
"Trouble in Paradise"
1935　*Pathe Pictorial 896*
"In the Air"
1935　*Music Hath Charms*
(BIP) F
"Honey Coloured Moon"
"In My Heart of Hearts"
1938　*Striking Gold*
(Ace Cinemagazine)

BENNY HILL (comedian)
1956　*Who Done It?*
(Ealing) F
1960　*Light Up the Sky*
(British Lion) F
"Touch It Light"
1965　*Those Magnificent Men in Their
Flying Machines*
(TCF) F
1968　*Chitty Chitty Bang Bang*
(UA) F
1969　*The Italian Job*
(Paramount) F
1969　*The Waiters*
(Paramount)
1974　*The Best of Benny Hill*
(EMI) F

HAMILTON HILL (singer)
1906　*The Fireman's Song*
(Chronophone)
1906　*The Waltz Must Change to a March*
(Chronophone)
1907　*The Fireman*
(Chronophone)

HELEN HILL (soprano)
1945　*For You Alone*
(Butcher) F
"Bless This House"
1945　*Home Sweet Home*
(Mancunian) F

VINCE HILL (singer)
1963　*Take Six*
(British Lion)
"Twisting the Night Away"

THE HILLBILLIES (cowboy singers)
1934　*Pathetone 213*
"Home On the Range"
1934　*Pathe Pictorial 845*
"The Old Town Hall"
1934　*Pathe Pictorial 867*
"Old Faithful"
1935　*Pathe Pictorial 874*
"Hannah"
1936　*Pathetone 322*
"Old Shep"
1937　*Pathetone Parade of 1938*
F (reissue: *Pathetone 322*)
1937　*Saturday Night Revue*
(Pathe) F
1938　*Pathe Pictorial NS 134*
"The Old Pine Tree"
1938　*Around the Town*
(British Lion) F

B C HILLIAM
see **FLOTSAM AND JETSAM**

VERA HILLIARD
see **TOM PAYNE AND VERA HILLIARD**

FAY HILLIER (striptease)
1978　*What's Up, Superdoc?*
(Blackwater) F

RONNIE HILTON (singer)
1972　*Showcase*
(Butcher) F

HINTONI BROTHERS (balancers)
1933　*Pathe Pictorial 821*

HIPPODROME GIRLS (dancers)
1913　*Spanish-American Quickstep*
(Selsior)
1924　*The Cost of Beauty*
(Napoleon) F
1935　*Hello Sweetheart*
(Warner) F
1936　*Limelight*
(Wilcox) F
"Celebrating"
1936　*The Three Maxims*
(Wilcox) F

JOSEPH HISLOP (Scottish tenor)
1930　*The Loves of Robert Burns*
(B&D) F
"Annie Laurie"
"Comin' Thro' the Rye"
"Loch Lomond"
"Auld Lang Syne"
"Go Fetch Me a Pint of Wine"
"Of a' the Airts"

"Bonnie Wee Thing"
"To a Stream"

JESSIE HITTER (singer)
1930 *Amateur Night in London*
     (PDC) F

VAL HOADLEY
see **JANET BRETT AND VAL HOADLEY**

BETTY HOBBS GLOBE GIRLS (balancers)
1952 *For Your Entertainment 1*
     (Gaumont)

LES HOBEAUX (skiffle group)
1958 *The Golden Disc*
     (Butcher) F
     "Dynamo"

McDONALD HOBLEY (television personality)
1950 *No Place for Jennifer*
     (ABP) F
1951 *The Kilties Are Coming*
     (Adelphi) F
1953 *Meet Mr Lucifer*
     (Ealing) F
1953 *Lads and Lassies On Parade*
     (reissue: *The Kilties Are Coming*)
1955 *Man of the Moment*
     (Rank) F
1956 *Checkpoint*
     (Rank) F
1960 *The Entertainer*
     (UA) F
1965 *Primitive London*
     (Searchlight) F

EDMUND (TED) HOCKRIDGE (singer)
1944 *Starlight Serenade*
     (Federated) F
     "Perfidia"
1946 *Piccadilly Incident*
     (Wilcox) F
     "When You Wish Upon a Star"
1950 *Variety Makers*
     (reissue: *Starlight Serenade*)
1954 *For Better For Worse*
     (ABP) F
     "For Better For Worse"
1954 *Bang You're Dead*
     (British Lion) F
1955 *King's Rhapsody*
     (Wilcox) F

JACK HODGES (comedy singer)
1927 *To See If My Dreams Come True*
     (Phonofilm)
1932 *Ideal Cinemagazine 348*
     (musical saw)
1933 *Television Follies*
     (English) F
     "Chinese Nights"
     "Annie Laurie"

1936 *Shipmates o' Mine*
     (Butcher) F
1949 *It's a Wonderful Day*
     (Equity) F
     "The Barrow Song"

WILLIAM HODGSON AND HIS BAND
1930 *Stark Nature*
     (BIF)
     "Blue Nile Blues"
     "Drums of the Desert"

DENNIS HOEY (singer)
(films as actor not listed)
1930 *Pathetone 20*
     "Will She Be Waiting Up?"
1934 *Chu Chin Chow*
     (Gainsborough) F
1936 *Faust Fantasy*
     (Publicity) F

BRUNO HOFFMAN (musical glasses)
1937 *Pathetone 389*
1938 *Two Men in a Box*
     (Ace) F

MICHAEL HOGAN (comedian)
(films as actor not listed)
1929 *Ag and Bert*
     (BSFP)
1932 *Pathe Pictorial 763*
     "The Bugginses"

ANNE HOGARTH AND JAN BUSSELL
(puppeteers)
1952 *Pulling Strings*
     (New Realm)

DOROTHY HOGBEN SINGERS
1937 *Screen Struck*
     (Baxter) F

**DOROTHY HOLBROOK AND HER
HARMONY HUSSARS** (band)
1938 *Pathe Pictorial NS 142*
     "Hungarian Medley"
1938 *Mind the Paint*
     (Ace Cinemagazine)
1938 *Reaching a Pitch*
     (Ace Cinemagazine)

BOSCOE HOLDER (dancer)
1962 *Four Hits and a Mister*
     (British Lion)
1963 *Take Six*
     (British Lion)
     "Let's Twist Again"
     "Twisting the Night Away"
1966 *The Hand of Night*
     (Pathe) F

NODDY HOLDER (musician)
1975 *Flame*
     (VPS) F

GORDON HOLDOM (baritone)
1939 *Pathe Pictorial NS 166*
"Here's to the Ladies"

HOLIDAY ON ICE CORPS DE BALLET
(skaters)
1956 *Who Done It?*
(Ealing) F

DAVE HOLLAND (musician)
1983 *The Gold Diggers*
(BFI) F

JACK HOLLAND AND JUNE HART
(dancers)
1935 *Dance Band*
(BIP) F
"The Valparaiso"

JOOLS HOLLAND (pianist)
1981 *Urgh! A Music War*
(White) F
"Foolish I Know"
1987 *Eat the Rich*
(Comic Strip) F
1997 *Spice World*
(Fragile) F

HOLLAND'S MAGYAR BAND
1936 *Murder at the Cabaret*
(Paramount) F

MICHAEL HOLLIDAY (singer)
1958 *Life Is a Circus*
(British Lion) F
"Life Is a Circus"
"For You"

THE HOLLIES (group)
1963 *It's All Over Town*
(British Lion) F
"Now's the Time"
1964 *UK Swings Again*
(Baim)
"Here I Go Again"
"Baby That's All"

KEN HOLLINS (baritone)
1938 *Showing Their Teeth*
(Ace Cinemagazine)

STANLEY HOLLOWAY (comedian and singer)
(films as actor not listed)
see also **THE CO-OPTIMISTS**
1929 *The Co-Optimists*
(New Era) F
"Sam and his Musket"
"Down Love Lane"
1934 *Lily of Killarney*
(Twickenham) F
"Father O'Flynn"
1935 *In Town Tonight*
(British Lion) F
"Albert and the Lion"

1935 *Play Up the Band*
(City) F
"Play Up the Band"
"Music Hath Charms"
1936 *Song of the Forge*
(Butcher) F
"The Village Blacksmith"
"The Poacher"
"Why Can't We?"
1937 *The Vicar of Bray*
(Twickenham) F
"The Vicar of Bray"
"Here's a Health Unto His Majesty"
"I'm Leaving Dear Old Ireland"
"Down Among the Dead Men"
1937 *Sam Small Leaves Town*
(BSS) F
"Hi De Hi"
1937 *Cotton Queen*
(Rock) F
"Ilkley Moor Baht 'At"
1939 *Co-operette*
(CWS) ADVERT
"Sam Small Goes Shopping"
1939 *Sam Goes Shopping*
(Publicity)
1940 *Albert's Savings*
(National Savings)
1944 *The Way Ahead*
(Two Cities) F
"Lily of Laguna"
1944 *Champagne Charlie*
(Ealing) F
"Strolling in the Park"
"I Do Like a Little Drop of Gin"
"Rum Rum Rum"
"A Glass of Sherry Wine"
"Hunting After Dark"
1945 *The Way to the Stars*
(Rank) F
"MacNamara's Band"
1948 *The Winslow Boy*
(London) F
"Just You Wait and See"
1958 *Hello London*
(Regal) F
"Sing a Song of London"
"Petticoat Lane"
1959 *No Trees in the Street*
(ABPC) F
"Picking All the Big Ones Out"
"Liza You Are My Dona"
1968 *Mrs Brown You've Got a Lovely Daughter*
(MGM) F
"Round the Corner"
"The World Is For the Young"

LESLIE HOLMES (singer)
see also **THE TWO LESLIES**
1932 *Pathetone 106*
"It Always Starts to Rain"
1933 *Pathe Pictorial 783*
"Milano"

119

1933 *Aunt Sally*
(Gainsborough) F
"My Wild Oat"
1934 *Pathe Pictorial 825*
"The Loch Ness Monster"

BOB HOLNESS (television personality)
1984 *The Chain*
(Rank) F

PAUL HOLT (journalist)
1940 *Band Waggon*
(Gainsborough) F

GORDON HONEYCOMBE (television personality)
1978 *The Medusa Touch*
(ITC) F
1986 *Castaway*
(EMI) F
1987 *The Fourth Protocol*
(Rank) F

THE HONEYCOMBS (group)
1965 *Pop Gear*
(Pathe) F

MARY HONRI (accordionist)
1936 *Twenty-One Today*
(Albany) F

PERCY HONRI (accordionist)
1934 *Say It With Flowers*
(Realart) F

PERCY AND MARY HONRI (musicians)
1936 *Pathe Pictorial NS 12*
"Two Lovely Black Eyes"
"Why Did She Fall for the Leader of the Band?"
"Down at the Old Bull and Bush"
1937 *The Schooner Gang*
(Butcher) F
"Davy Jones"
"Oh Papa"
"Home"

ETHEL HOOK (contralto)
1926 *Ethel Hook*
(Phonofilm)
1928 *Phototone 1*
"Love's Old Sweet Song"
1928 *Phototone 7*
"Land of Hope and Glory"

BARRINGTON HOOPER (tenor)
1931 *Pathetone 86*
"Britain I Am With Thee"
1931 *Gaumont Sound Mirror*
1932 *Pathe Pictorial 720*
"Trees"

EDDIE HOOPER (dancer)
1936 *Full Steam*
(Ace) F
1936 *Bottle Party*
(Ace) F
1936 *Song in Soho*
(Ace) F
1937 *West End Frolics*
(Ace) F

KENNETH HORNE (comedian)
1950 *New Pictorial 297*
"Much Binding in the Marsh"

MICHAEL HOROVITS (poet)
1965 *Wholly Communion*
(Lorrimer)

J F HORRABIN (cartoonist)
1945 *New Pictorial 69*

HOT GOSSIP (dancers)
1977 *Adventures of a Private Eye*
(Salon) F
1979 *The Golden Lady*
(Target) F
1981 *Hot Gossip*
(Rank)
"Space Invaders"
"Super Casanova"
"Like Clones"
"Super Nature"

THE HOUSE SHAKERS (group)
1973 *The London Rock and Roll Show*
(Pleasant) F

RENEE HOUSTON (Scottish comedienne)
see also **THE HOUSTON SISTERS**
1932 *Come Into My Parlour*
(GEM) F
1933 *Their Night Out*
(BIP) F
1934 *Lost in the Legion*
(BIP) F
1934 *Mr Cinders*
(BIP) F
1935 *No Monkey Business*
(GFD) F
1937 *Fine Feathers*
(British Films) F
1939 *A Girl Must Live*
(GFD) F
1940 *Old Bill and Son*
(Legeran) F
1944 *2000 Women*
(GFD) F
1951 *Lady Godiva Rides Again*
(London) F
1954 *The Belles of St Trinian's*
(British Lion) F
1955 *Track the Man Down*
(Republic) F

1956 *A Town Like Alice*
(Rank) F
1957 *Time Without Pity*
(Eros) F
1958 *Big Money*
(Rank) F
1958 *The Horse's Mouth*
(Knightsbridge) F
1958 *Them Nice Americans*
(Chelsea) F
1959 *Flesh and the Fiends*
(Triad) F
1960 *And the Same to You*
(Monarch) F
1961 *Watch It Sailor*
(Hammer) F
1961 *No My Darling Daughter*
(Five Star) F
1961 *Three on a Spree*
(Caralan) F
1962 *Twice Round the Daffodils*
(Anglo) F
1962 *Phantom of the Opera*
(Hammer) F
1962 *Out of the Fog*
(Eternal) F
1962 *Tomorrow at Ten*
(Mancunian) F
1962 *Carry on Cruising*
(Anglo) F
1963 *Nurse on Wheels*
(GHW) F
1963 *Rescue Squad*
(CFF) F
1964 *Carry on Spying*
(Adder) F
1965 *Repulsion*
(Compton) F
1965 *Secrets of a Windmill Girl*
(Searchlight) F
1966 *Cul de Sac*
(Compton) F
1966 *The Idol*
(Embassy) F
1967 *River Rivals*
(CFF) S
1971 *Carry On at Your Convenience*
(Rank) F
1975 *Legend of the Werewolf*
(Tyburn) F

SHIRLEY HOUSTON (singer)
1936 *Happy Days Are Here Again*
(Argyle) F

THE HOUSTON SISTERS (RENEE AND BILLIE) (song and dance)
1926 *The Houston Sisters*
(Phonofilm)
1926 *Eve's Film Review 280*
"A Match for Two"
1927 *Blighty*
(Gainsborough) F

1932 *Musical Medleys*
(reissue: *The Houston Sisters*)
1933 *Radio Parade*
(BIP) F
1935 *Variety*
(Butcher) F
"I Don't Want to Climb a Mountain"
1936 *Happy Days Are Here Again*
(Argyle) F
"Happy Days Are Here Again"
"The Toy Drum Major"
"Topsy Turvy Blues"
"A Bench Beneath the Tree"
"Hey There Circus Clown"
"If You Haven't Got a Train"
"Rhythm"
1937 *Highlights of Variety 2*
(reissue: *Variety*)
1938 *Happy Days Revue*
F (reissue: *Happy Days Are Here Again*)
1943 *Down Melody Lane*
F (reissue: *Variety*)

LUCAS HOVINGA (dancer)
1946 *London Town*
(GFD) F

HELEN HOWARD (torch singer)
1937 *Variety Hour*
(Fox) F

JACK HOWARD AND THE ROYAL OPERA HOUSE BAND
1927 *Syncopated Melodies*
(Parkinson)

JENNY HOWARD (comic singer)
1936 *Dodging the Dole*
(Mancunian) F
1938 *Music Hall Personalities 5*
(reissue: *Dodging the Dole*)

MICHAEL HOWARD (comedian)
1944 *A Canterbury Tale*
(GFD) F
1946 *I See a Dark Stranger*
(GFD) F
1948 *A Sister to Assist 'Er*
(Premier) F
1954 *Front Page Story*
(British Lion) F
1955 *Out of the Clouds*
(Ealing) F
1956 *The Baby and the Battleship*
(British Lion) F
1963 *The Handy Manns*
(CWS) ADVERT

SYDNEY HOWARD (comedian)
1929 *Eve's Film Review 445*
"Dear Love"
1929 *Splinters*
(B&D) F

"Sweet Adeline"
"What Has England Done for Him?"
1930 *French Leave*
(Sterling) F
1931 *Tilly of Bloomsbury*
(B&D) F
1931 *Almost a Divorce*
(B&D) F
1931 *Up for the Cup*
(B&D) F
1931 *Splinters in the Navy*
(Twickenham) F
1932 *The Mayor's Nest*
(B&D) F
1932 *It's a King*
(B&D) F
1933 *Up for the Derby*
(B&D) F
1933 *Night of the Garter*
(B&D) F
1933 *Trouble*
(B&D) F
1934 *It's a Cop*
(B&D) F
1934 *Girls Please*
(B&D)
"Music is the Cure"
1935 *Where's George?*
(B&D) F
1936 *Fame*
(Wilcox) F
1936 *Chick*
(B&D) F
1937 *Splinters in the Air*
(Wilcox) F
1937 *What a Man*
(Wilcox) F
1939 *Shipyard Sally*
(TCF) F
1940 *Tilly of Bloomsbury*
(RKO) F
1940 *Pathetone 520*
"Chamber Music"
1941 *Once a Crook*
(TCF) F
1941 *Mr Proudfoot Shows a Light*
(MOI)
1943 *When We Are Married*
(British National) F
1945 *Flight from Folly*
(Warner) F

HOWARD, HARGER AND NALDY (dancers)
1930 *Eve's Fall*
(PDC)
1930 *Amateur Night in London*
(PDC) F

GYULA HOWATH GYPSY BAND
1934 *Unfinished Symphony*
(Cine) F

CATHERINE HOWE (singer)
1974 *Can You Keep It Up For a Week?*
(Target) F
"Keep It For Me"

FRANKIE HOWERD (comedian)
1954 *The Runaway Bus*
(Eros) F
1955 *An Alligator Named Daisy*
(Rank) F
1955 *The Ladykillers*
(Ealing) F
1956 *Jumping for Joy*
(Rank) F
1956 *A Touch of the Sun*
(Eros) F
1958 *Further Up the Creek*
(Hammer) F
1961 *Watch It Sailor*
(Hammer) F
1962 *The Fast Lady*
(Rank) F
1963 *The Cool Mikado*
(Baim) F
"The Flowers That Bloom in the Spring"
"The Lord High Executioner"
1963 *The Mouse on the Moon*
(UA) F
1966 *The Great St Trinian's Train Robbery*
(British Lion) F
1967 *Carry On Doctor*
(Rank) F
1970 *Carry On Up the Jungle*
(Rank) F
1971 *Up Pompeii*
(EMI) F
1971 *Up the Chastity Belt*
(EMI) F
1972 *Up the Front*
(EMI) F
1973 *House in Nightmare Park*
(EMI) F

BOBBY HOWES (comedian)
1926 *London's Famous Cabarets*
(Parkinson)
"Metropole Midnight Follies"
1926 *Eve's Film Review 248*
"Midnight Follies"
1927 *On With the Dance*
(Parkinson)
1928 *The Guns of Loos*
(Stoll) F
1928 *Eve's Film Review 353*
"The Yellow Mask"
1930 *Eve's Film Review 453*
"The Kerb Step"
1930 *Eve's Film Review 476*
"Sons o' Guns"
1931 *Third Time Lucky*
(Gaumont) F
1932 *Lord Babs*
(Gaumont) F

1932 *For the Love of Mike*
(BIP) F
"Got a Date with an Angel"
"Sing Brothers"
1934 *Over the Garden Wall*
(BIP) F
"Why Wasn't I Told?"
1937 *Please Teacher*
(ABP) F
"You Give Me Ideas"
"Mind How You Go Across the Road"
"Temple Bells"
"Hail Women of History"
1938 *Sweet Devil*
(GFD) F
"You Should Be Set to Music"
"What's Going to Happen to Me?"
1938 *Yes Madam*
(ABP) F
"Yes Madam"
"What Are You Going to Do if Love Comes?"
"Something Will Happen Today"
"Czechoslovakian Love"
"Cat Duet"
1945 *The Trojan Brothers*
(British National) F
1951 *Happy Go Lovely*
(ABP) F
1957 *The Good Companions*
(ABPC) F
1961 *Watch It Sailor*
(Hammer) F

ROBERTA HUBY (singer)
1940 *Hullo Fame*
(British Films) F

ROY HUDD (comedian)
1968 *The Blood Beast Terror*
(Tigon) F
1971 *The Magnificent Seven Deadly Sins*
(Tigon) F
1971 *Up the Chastity Belt*
(EMI) F
1971 *Up Pompeii*
(EMI) F
1972 *The Alf Garnett Saga*
(Columbia) F
1973 *An Acre of Seats in a Garden of Dreams*
(Contemporary) F

JOHNNY HUDGINS (dancer)
1927 *Pathe Pictorial 469*
"Feet Fun and Fancy"

HARRY HUDSON AND HIS BAND
1934 *Boots Boots*
(Blakeley) F
"Red Hot Feet"
"Baby"
"Peter Peter"

RODNEY HUDSON GIRLS (dancers)
1927 *Eve's Film Review 333*
1936 *Annie Laurie*
(Butcher) F
1936 *Song of the Forge*
(Butcher) F

LEANORA HUGHES AND M MAURICE (dancers)
1920 *Around the Town 27*
(Gaumont)

CLAUDE HULBERT (comedian)
(films as actor not listed)
1928 *Eve's Film Review 388*
"Sons of the Sea"
1930 *Eve's Film Review 488*
"Follow a Star"
1933 *Radio Parade*
(BIP) F
1941 *Oh You Clever Boy*
(Ford) ADVERT

JACK HULBERT (comedian)
1922 *Eve's Film Review 41*
1922 *Eve's Film Review 54*
"Midnight Follies"
1925 *Eve's Film Review 196*
"By the Way"
1926 *Eve's Film Review 291*
"Lido Lady"
1927 *Eve's Film Review 343*
"Clowns in Clover"
1928 *British Screen Tatler 10*
"Clowns in Clover"
1930 *Eve's Film Review 488*
"Follow a Star"
1930 *Elstree Calling*
(BIP) F
"The Thought Never Entered My Head"
1931 *The Ghost Train*
(Gainsborough) F
1931 *Sunshine Susie*
(Gainsborough) F
"Today I Feel So Happy"
1932 *Jack's the Boy*
(Gainsborough) F
"The Flies Crawled Up the Window"
"I Want to Cling to Ivy"
1932 *Love On Wheels*
(Gainsborough) F
"The Same Old Bus"
"I Hunger For You"
"Wear Gloves"
"Little Girl"
"Find the Lady"
"Two in a Bar"
1932 *Happy Ever After*
(Gainsborough) F
"Keep On the Bright Side"
1933 *Falling For You*
(Gainsborough) F
"Why Has a Cow Got Four Legs?"

"Sweep"
"You Don't Understand"
1934 *Jack Ahoy*
(Gainsborough) F
"My Hat's on the Side of My Head"
"You've Got Everything"
"Goodbye Again"
"Jolly Good Company"
"Taint"
1934 *The Camels Are Coming*
(Gainsborough) F
"Who's Been Polishing the Sun?"
1935 *Bulldog Jack*
(Gainsborough) F
1936 *Jack of All Trades*
(Gainsborough) F
"Tap Your Tootsies"
"You're Sweeter Than I Thought You Were"
"Where There's You There's Me"
1937 *Take My Tip*
(Gainsborough) F
"Birdie Out of a Cage"
"If I Was Anything But Sentimental"
1937 *Paradise for Two*
(London) F
"In a Paradise for Two"
"When You Hear Music"
1938 *Kate Plus Ten*
(Wainwright) F
1939 *Pathe Gazette 97*
"Under Your Hat"
1940 *Under Your Hat*
(Grand National) F
"Keep It Under Your Hat"
"I Won't Do the Conga"
"We Can't Find the Tiger Any More"
1948 *Highwaymen*
(Kinocrat)
1951 *Into the Blue*
(Wilcox) F
1951 *The Magic Box*
(Festival) F
1955 *Miss Tulip Stays the Night*
(Adelphi) F
1956 *How to Sell Your Husband a Washing Machine*
(Beda) ADVERT
1960 *The Spider's Web*
(Danziger) F
1972 *Not Now Darling*
(LMG) F
1972 *The Cherry Picker*
(Rank) F

ROD HULL (comedian)
1978 *In the Projection Box*
(CFF)

BARRY HUMPHRIES (comedian)
1967 *Bedazzled*
(TCF) F
1968 *The Bliss of Mrs Blossom*
(Paramount) F

1974 *Barry McKenzie Holds His Own*
(EMI) F
1974 *Percy's Progress*
(EMI) F
1975 *Side By Side*
(GTO) F
1976 *Pleasure at Her Majesty's*
(Amnesty) F
"Spunk"
"Lumberjack Song"
1981 *Shock Treatment*
(TCF) F
1996 *The Leading Man*
(J&M) F
1997 *Spice World*
(Fragile) F

HUNGARIA GYPSY ORCHESTRA
1953 *Innocents in Paris*
(Romulus) F

ALBERTA HUNTER (singer)
1934 *Radio Parade of 1935*
(BIP) F
"Black Shadows"

BARBARA HUNTER (striptease)
1970 *Sweet and Sexy*
(Miracle) F

JACKIE HUNTER (comedian)
1944 *Give Me the Stars*
(British National) F
1945 *Don Chicago*
(British National) F

GEORGE HURD (juggler)
1934 *Pathe Pictorial 827*
1936 *Pathe Pictorial NS 9*

ALEC HURLEY (singer)
1900 *The Lambeth Walk*
(Phono-Bio-Tableaux)

GEORGE HURLEY
1937 *Footlights*
(Ace) F

DICK HURRAN (tap-dancer)
1937 *West End Frolics*
(Ace) F
1938 *Two Men in a Box*
(Ace) F
1938 *Swing*
(Ace) F

PAT HURRAN
1937 *Spirit of Variety*
(Exclusive)

BUCK HURST (conjurer)
1949 *Conjurer's Party*
(Watsonian)

HARRIETTE HUTCHINS (singer)
- 1936 *British Lion Varieties 4*
  "Dennis the Menace from Venice"
- 1936 *British Lion Varieties 6*
  "Weather Man"
- 1936 *British Lion Varieties 8*
  "What Harlem Means to Me"

LESLIE A HUTCHINSON ('HUTCH') (singer and pianist)
- 1930 *Big Business*
  (Fox) F
- 1932 *Pathetone 116*
  "Close Your Eyes"
- 1932 *Pathetone 131*
  "What Makes You So Adorable?"
- 1933 *Pathetone 146*
  "How Deep Is the Ocean?"
- 1933 *Pathetone 151*
  "Trees"
- 1935 *Cock o' the North*
  (Butcher) F
  "Two Tired Eyes"
  "Wake"
- 1936 *Pathe Pictorial NS 10*
  "Don't Let the River Run Dry"
- 1936 *Beloved Impostor*
  (RKO) F
- 1937 *Pathetone 361*
  "Souvenirs"
- 1937 *Pathetone 402*
  "If It's to Last"
- 1938 *Highlights of Variety 11*
  (reissue: *Cock o' the North*)
- 1939 *Pathe Pictorial NS 145*
  "Two Sinners"
- 1943 *Happidrome*
  (Aldwych) F
  "You Are My Love Song"
  "Take the World Exactly As You Find It"
- 1943 *Pictorial Revue of 1943*
  F (reissue: *Pathe Pictorial 145*)
- 1943 *Melody Lane*
  (reissue: *Cock o' the North*)
- 1948 *Lucky Mascot*
  (UA) F
  "Tomorrow's Rainbow"
- 1959 *Treasure of San Teresa*
  (British Lion) F

JULIAN HUXLEY (broadcaster)
- 1943 *B.B.C. Brains Trust 1; 2*
  (Strand)

PAT HYDE (accordionist)
- 1936 *Stars On Parade*
  (Butcher) F
  "The World Goes Around Just the Same"
- 1937 *Highlights of Variety 7*
  (reissue: *Stars On Parade*)

HYDE SISTERS
- 1928 *The Hyde Sisters*
  (BSFP)
- 1932 *Musical Medley 3*
  (reissue: *The Hyde Sisters*)

WALFORD HYDEN (musician)
- 1946 *Great Expectations*
  (GFD) F
- 1951 *Lady Godiva Rides Again*
  (London) F

WALFORD HYDEN AND HIS CAFE COLETTE ORCHESTRA
- 1937 *Cafe Colette*
  (ABFD) F

WALFORD HYDEN AND HIS CIGANSKIES
- 1933 *Pathetone 193*
- 1935 *Pathetone 266*

WALFORD HYDEN AND HIS MAGYAR ORCHESTRA
- 1933 *Pathetone 173*
  "Autumn Leaves"

JACK HYLTON AND HIS BAND
- 1923 *Eve's Film Review 124*
  "Exhibition One Step"
- 1926 *Eve's Film Review 258*
- 1926 *London's Famous Cabarets*
  (Parkinson)
- 1927 *Syncopated Melodies*
  (Parkinson)
- 1930 *Pathe Sound Magazine 36*
- 1931 *Pathetone 49*
  "Choo Choo"
- 1931 *Pathetone 65*
  "Say Yes"
- 1933 *Pathetone 196*
- 1935 *She Shall Have Music*
  (Twickenham) F
  "She Shall Have Music"
  "The Band That Jack Built"
  "Moaning Minnie"
  "The Blue Danube"
  "Sailing Along on a Carpet of Clouds"
  "Nothing on Earth"
  "Don't Ask Me Any Questions"
  "The Runaround"
  "The Hylton Stromp"
  "May All Your Troubles Be Little Ones"
  "My First Thrill"
  "Why Did She Fall for the Leader of the Band?"
- 1940 *Band Waggon*
  (Gainsborough) F
  "The Melody Maker"
  "Roadhouse Revels"
  "Band Waggon"
  "Boomps-a-Daisy"
  "Heaven Will Be Heavenly"

"The Only One Who's Difficult Is You"

1941   *The Saving Song*
(National Savings)
"Saving Saving"

1943   *Battle for Music*
(Strand) F

MRS JACK HYLTON AND HER BOYS
(band)

1936   *Variety Parade*
(Butcher) F
"We Want a Little Song"
"This Is the Missis"
"Let's All Go Up in the Sky"
"Just an Old Sprig of Shamrock"

"Taking a Stroll Around the Park"

1939   *Highlights of Variety 16*
(reissue: *Variety Parade*)

1940   *Cavalcade of Variety*
(reissue: *Variety Parade*)

CARL HYSON AND PEGGY HARRIS
(dancers)

1922   *Eve's Film Review 63*
"Waltz"

1928   *Eve's Film Review 362*

CARL HYSON DANCERS

1937   *The Street Singer*
(ABPC) F

CONFESSIN'
(THAT I LOVE YOU)

Words by AL J. NEIBERG   Music by DOC DAUGHERTY & ELLIS REYNOLDS

Recorded on Columbia
by
FRANK IFIELD

FRANCIS, DAY & HUNTER LTD, 138-140, CHARING CROSS RD, LONDON W.C.2

ERIC IDLE (comedian)
1971   *And Now For Something Completely
         Different*
         (Columbia) F
1975   *Monty Python and the Holy Grail*
         (EMI) F
1979   *Monty Python's Life of Brian*
         (CIC) F
         "Bright Side of Life"
1983   *Monty Python's The Meaning of Life*
         (UIP) F
1983   *Monty Python Live at the Hollywood
         Bowl*
         (Handmade) F
1983   *Yellowbeard*
         (Hemdale) F
1988   *The Adventures of Baron
         Munchausen*
         (Columbia) F
1990   *Nuns on the Run*
         (Handmade) F
1993   *Splitting Heirs*
         (Prominent) F
         "Someone Stole My Baby"
         "La Mère"
1996   *The Wind in the Willows*
         (Allied) F

IDLE RACE (group)
1968   *Popdown*
         (New Realm) F

FRANK IFIELD (Australian singer)
1965   *Up Jumped a Swagman*
         (Elstree) F
         "Look Don't Touch"
         "I Remember You"
         "I've Got a Hole in My Pocket"
         "I'll Never Feel This Way Again"
         "Cry Wolf"
         "Wild River"
         "Make It Soon"
         "Waltzing Matilda"
         "Lovin' On My Mind"
         "Lovers"
1965   *Pathe Pictorial 565*
         "Lovin' On My Mind"

IMITO (animal mimic)
1932   *Ideal Cinemagazine 346*

IMPERIAL HAWAIIANS
1930   *Pathetone 38*

ROBERTO INGLEZ AND HIS ORCHESTRA
1952   *Melody Time*
         (International)
         "Let's Do the Samba"

JOHN INMAN (comedian)
1977   *Are You Being Served?*
         (EMI) F
1989   *The Tall Guy*
         (Virgin) F

CHARMIAN INNES (singer)
1948   *The Flamingo Affair*
         (Inspiration) F
1948   *Chorus Girl*
         (Renown) F
1948   *Eugene Pini and his Orchestra*
         (Inspiration)
         "Jungle Love"
1950   *Up for the Cup*
         (Byron) F
1950   *Dark Interval*
         (Apex) F
1962   *Band of Thieves*
         (Rank) F
1968   *The Magnificent 6½*
         (CFF) SERIAL

NEIL INNES (comedian)
1975   *Monty Python and the Holy Grail*
         (EMI) F
1976   *Pleasure at Her Majesty's*
         (Amnesty) F
         "Lumberjack Song"
1977   *Jabberwocky*
         (Columbia) F
1979   *Monty Python's Life of Brian*
         (CIC) F
1980   *The Secret Policeman's Ball*
         (Tigon) F
1982   *The Secret Policeman's Other Ball*
         (UIP) F
1983   *Monty Python Live at the Hollywood
         Bowl*
         (Handmade) F
1983   *The Missionary*
         (Handmade) F
1989   *Erik the Viking*
         (UIP) F

INVISIBLE SEX (group)
1981   *Urgh! A Music War*
         (White) F
         "Valium"

IPI-TOMBI COMPANY (African dancers)
1979   *The Human Factor*
         (Rank) F

IRENE (dancer)
1942   *Pathe Pictorial 334*

IRWIN TWINS (dancers)
1930   *Eve's Fall*
         (PDC)

ISIDORO AND CARARINE (accordionists)
1935   *Pathetone 257*

FRANK IVALLO (novelty singer)
1932   *Pathe Pictorial 732*
         "Still as the Night"

IVY LEAGUE (group)
1965   *Our Love is Slipping Away*
         (Monarch) F

JACK JACKIE
1937   *Pathe Pictorial NS 64*

JACKIE AND THE RAINDROPS (group)
1964   *Just For You*
       (British Lion) F
       "The Locomotion"

GEORGE JACKLEY (comedian)
1926   *A Doggy Ditty*
       (Phonofilm)
1932   *Pathetone 97*
1933   *Pathe Pictorial 810*
1935   *Pathetone 250*

NAT JACKLEY (comedian)
1944   *Demobbed*
       (Mancunian) F
1946   *Under New Management*
       (Mancunian) F
       "When We Were in the Forces"
1948   *Honeymoon Hotel*
       (reissue: *Under New Management*)
1956   *Stars in Your Eyes*
       (British Lion) F
1968   *Mrs Brown You've Got a Lovely*
       Daughter
       (MGM) F
       "My Old Man's a Dustman"
       "God Save the Queen"
1979   *Yanks*
       (UA) F
1980   *The Inside Man*
       (ITC) F
1981   *Towers of Babel*
       (EMI) F
1983   *The Ploughman's Lunch*
       (Greenpoint) F
1984   *Return to Waterloo*
       (RCA)

BEE JACKSON (dancer)
1925   *Eve's Film Review*
       "Charleston"

J W JACKSON'S TOE DANCERS
see also **TWELVE JACKSON GIRLS**
1932   *Pathe Pictorial 759*

JACK JACKSON (broadcaster)
1956   *Stars in Your Eyes*
       (British Lion) F
       "A Man and his Music"
1960   *Climb Up the Wall*
       (New Realm) F
1962   *Behave Yourself*
       (Baim) F

JACK JACKSON AND HIS BAND
1933   *Pathetone 188*
1937   *Let's Make a Night of It*
       (ABPC) F
       "Havana"
       "If My Heart Says Sing"

1938   *Pathetone 428*
       "Parade of the Toys"
1941   *Pathetone Parade of 1941*
       F (reissue: *Pathetone 428*)
1941   *War Work News*
       (MOI)

MARGERY JACKSON
see **EDWARD BLUNT AND MARGERY JACKSON**

MILLIE JACKSON (singer)
1979   *Millie Jackson Live*
       (CEE)

MILLIE JACKSON GIRLS (dancers)
1936   *International Revue*
       (Medway) F

THE NORAH JACKSON DANCERS
see **JACKSON GIRLS**

ZAIDEE JACKSON (singer)
1932   *Ideal Cinemagazine 344*
       "I've Got the Wrong Man"
1933   *Ideal Cinemagazine 387*
       "Black Magic"

JACKSON AND BLAKE (comedians)
1929   *Black and White*
       (BIP)

JACKSON GIRLS (dancers)
also known as The Norah Jackson Dancers
1929   *Chelsea Nights*
       (BIP)
1932   *Pathetone 100*
       "When the Guards Go Marching By"

THE JACKSONS (group)
1971   *Gumshoe*
       (Columbia) F

DAVID JACOBS (broadcaster)
1958   *The Golden Disc*
       (Butcher) F
1962   *It's Trad Dad*
       (Columbia) F
1963   *Just For Fun*
       (Columbia) F
1963   *Towers Open Fire*
       (Balch)
1965   *You Must Be Joking*
       (Columbia) F
1974   *Stardust*
       (EMI) F

HOWARD JACOBS AND HIS ORCHESTRA
1934   *Gay Love*
       (British Lion) F
1935   *In Town Tonight*
       (British Lion) F

ERNESTO JACONELLI (musician)
 1933 *Pathe Pictorial 807*
 "Light Cavalry Overture"
 1936 *Pictorial Revue*
 F (reissue: *Pictorial 807*)

JIMMY JADE (comedian)
 1934 *On the Air*
 (British Lion) F

MAX JAFFA (violinist)
 1959 *Music With Max Jaffa*
 (Zonic)

MICK JAGGER (singer)
see also **THE ROLLING STONES**
 1967 *Tonite Let's All Make Love in
 London*
 (Lorrimer) F
 1968 *Sympathy for the Devil*
 (Connoisseur) F
 "Sympathy for the Devil"
 1970 *Ned Kelly*
 (UA) F
 1970 *Performance*
 (Warner) F
 "Memo for Turner"
 1973 *The London Rock and Roll Show*
 (Pleasant) F
 1983 *Undercover*
 (Palace)
 1985 *Running Out of Luck*
 (Nitrate) F

CLIVE JAMES (television personality)
 1974 *Barry McKenzie Holds His Own*
 (EMI) F
 1980 *The Secret Policeman's Ball*
 (Tigon) F

DICK JAMES (singer)
 1948 *London Belongs To Me*
 (GFD) F
 "Little Girl in Blue"
 1973 *Radio Wonderful*
 (Goodtimes) F

ENID JAMES (singer)
 1936 *Whom the Gods Love*
 (ATP) F

JIMMY JAMES (comedian)
 1932 *The Spare Room*
 (PDC) F
 1936 *Stars On Parade*
 (Butcher) F
 1950 *Over the Garden Wall*
 (Mancunian) F
 1953 *Those People Next Door*
 (Mancunian) F

SALLY JAMES (television personality)
 1970 *The Railway Children*
 (MGM-EMI) F

 1975 *Never Too Young To Rock*
 (GTO) F

JAN AND KELLY (singers)
 1963 *It's All Over Town*
 (British Lion) F
 "The Trouble with Man"

JANE (CHRISTABEL LEIGHTON-PORTER)
(model)
 1943 *Pathe Pictorial 395*
 1944 *New Pictorial 23*
 1949 *Adventures of Jane*
 (Eros) F

BERTIE JARRETT
see **JOHNNY WORTHY AND BERTIE
JARRETT**

JACK JARROTT
see **VERA MAXWELL AND JACK JARROTT**

DAVID JASON (comedian)
 1972 *Under Milk Wood*
 (Rank) F
 1973 *White Cargo*
 (Border) F
 1975 *Royal Flash*
 (Two Roads) F
 1978 *The Odd Job*
 (EMI)

JUDY JASON (singer)
 1964 *Just For You*
 (British Lion) F

JAVA'S TZIGANE BAND
 1936 *King of Hearts*
 (Butcher) F

JEAN (contortionist)
 1931 *Ideal Cinemagazine 271*

LITTLE JEAN AND JOAN (dancers)
 1934 *Love Mirth Melody*
 (Mancunian) F

LESLIE JEFFRIES (violinist)
 1938 *Pathetone 429*
 "Operatic Medley"
 1939 *Pathe Pictorial NS 157*
 "Hungarian Dance"

LESLIE JEFFRIES AND HIS ORCHESTRA
 1936 *B.B.C. Musicals 2*
 (Inspiration)
 1938 *Melodies of the Moment*
 (reissue: *B.B.C. Musicals 2*)
 1939 *Radio Nights*
 (Inspiration)
 "The Skater's Waltz"
 1952 *Melodies from Grand Hotel*
 (Inspiration)
 "These Foolish Things"

"Trees"
"I'll Take You Home Again Kathleen"
"Hungarian Rhapsody"

LESLIE JEFFRIES TRIO (musicians)
1942 *Pathe Pictorial 308*
1942 *Pathe Pictorial 339*
1943 *Pathe Pictorial 388*
"The Blue Danube"
1944 *Pathe Pictorial 426*

STANTON JEFFRIES (musician)
1935 *Royal Cavalcade*
(BIP) F

JEFFRIES' FLEA CIRCUS (specialty)
1948 *New Pictorial 187*

WARREN JENKINS (singer)
1940 *Laugh It Off*
(British National) F
"The Twi-Twi-Twilight"

JEREZ BROTHERS (acrobatic dancers)
1926 *Eve's Film Review 265*

JERZIMY (singer)
1980 *The Great Rock 'n' Roll Swindle*
(Virgin) F
"Anarchie pour le UK"

GEORGE JESSEL (American comedian)
1969 *Can Heironymus Merkin Ever Forget Mercy Humppe and Find True Happiness?*
(Universal) F

JESSICA (child impersonator)
1936 *The Show's the Thing*
(Fidelity)
(as Cicely Courtneidge, Zasu Pitts, Jimmy Durante)

JESTERS (impressionists)
1934 *Pathe Pictorial 865*
(as Bing Crosby, Kate Smith, Arthur Tracy)

JOAN JETT (singer)
1981 *Urgh! A Music War*
(White) F
"Bad Reputation"

JIMMY JEWEL (comedian)
see also **JIMMY JEWEL AND BEN WARRISS**
1970 *The Man Who Had Power Over Women*
(Avco) F
1972 *Nearest and Dearest*
(Hammer) F
1986 *Arthur's Hallowed Ground*
(Enigma) F

1986 *Rocinante*
(Cinema Action) F
1990 *The Krays*
(Rank) F
"Balling the Jack"

JIMMY JEWEL AND BEN WARRISS
(comedians)
1943 *Rhythm Serenade*
(Columbia) F
"You Can't Have Everything"
"I Can't Give You Anything But Love"
"Timber"
1949 *What a Carry On*
(Mancunian) F
"Sabre Dance"
1950 *Let's Have a Murder*
(Mancunian) F
1953 *Joining the Army*
(reissue: *What a Carry On*)
1959 *Stick 'Em Up*
(reissue: *Let's Have a Murder*)

JIGSAW (group)
1978 *Home Before Midnight*
(EMI) F
"Home Before Midnight"
"Kick Me When I'm Down"
"The Way We Dance"
"Every Move You Make"

C E M JOAD (broadcaster)
1943 *B.B.C. Brains Trust 1; 2*
(Strand)

JOE AND BUSTER (tap-dancers)
1936 *Play Fare*
(Ace Cinemagazine)

AUD JOHANSEN (dancer)
1972 *Macbeth*
(Playboy) F

ELTON JOHN (singer)
1975 *Tommy*
(Stigwood) F
"Pinball Wizard"
1979 *To Russia with Elton*
(ITC) F
"Crocodile Rock"
"Daniel"
"Better Off Dead"
"Rocketman"
"Back in the USSR"
"Pinball Wizard"
1981 *Elton John in Central Park*
(Barber)
1997 *Spice World*
(Fragile) F

CECIL JOHNSON (comedian)
1937 *Pathe Pictorial NS 66*
"Running Commentary"

KEN SNAKEHIPS JOHNSON AND HIS WEST INDIAN BAND
1939   *Traitor Spy*
     (Pathe) F

TEDDY JOHNSON (singer)
1958   *Girls At Sea*
     (ABP) F
     "Merci Beaucoup"

BOB JOHNSTON (singer)
1931   *Hindle Wakes*
     (Gaumont) F
     "Take a Ride on the Roundabouts"

BRIAN JOHNSTON (broadcaster)
1952   *Derby Day*
     (Wilcox) F

ASTLEY JONES (newsreader)
1978   *Destiny*
     (BBC) F

DAVY JONES AND HIS BAND
1942   *Pathe Pictorial 350*

DES JONES (finger conjurer)
1976   *Pleasure at Her Majesty's*
     (Amnesty) F

DILL JONES AND HIS ALL STARS (band)
1960   *Dill Jones and His All Stars*
     (Grand National)
     "South of the Border"
     "Isle of Capri"
     "Cherokee"
1960   *Blue Tunes*
     (British Lion)
     "The Gypsy"
1961   *Flying Fingers*
     (British Lion)
     "A Nightingale Sang in Berkeley Square"
     "Penny Serenade"

GRACE JONES (American singer)
1985   *View to a Kill*
     (UIP) F
1986   *Straight to Hell*
     (Island) F

GRIFF RHYS JONES (comedian)
1982   *The Secret Policeman's Other Ball*
     (UIP) F
1985   *Morons From Outer Space*
     (EMI) F
1986   *Royal Flush*
     (Linkwood) ADVERT
1989   *Wilt*
     (LWT) F
1992   *As You Like It*
     (Sands) F
1993   *Staggered*
     (Big Deal) F

1996   *The Adventures of Pinocchio*
     (Allied) F
1997   *Up "n" Under*
     (Touchdown) F

GUY JONES AND HIS BAND
1938   *Little Dolly Daydream*
     (Butcher) F

GWEN JONES (singer)
1939   *Eddie Carroll and his Boys*
     (Inspiration)
     "What Do You Know About Love?"

HAL JONES (comedian)
1929   *Splinters*
     (B&D) F
     "I Should Shay Sho"
     "Carrie From Lancasheer"
     "That's What I'm Trying to Say"
1931   *Splinters in the Navy*
     (Twickenham) F

JACK JONES (singer)
1978   *The Comeback*
     (Heritage) F
     "Traces of a Long Forgotten Time"

JACQUELINE JONES (singer)
1963   *The Cool Mikado*
     (Baim) F
     "The Moon and I"
     "Here's a How d'ye Do"

PARRY JONES (Welsh singer)
1933   *Waltz Time*
     (Gaumont) F
1934   *My Heart Is Calling*
     (Gaumont) F

PAUL JONES (singer)
1967   *Privilege*
     (Universal) F
1968   *The Committee*
     (Planet) F
1971   *Demons of the Mind*
     (Hammer) F

RUSSELL JONES (singer)
1932   *Pathetone 96*
     "Eleven More Months"
1932   *Pathe Pictorial 728*
     "You Call It Madness, I Call It Love"

STEVE JONES (guitarist)
see also **THE SEX PISTOLS**
1980   *The Great Rock 'n' Roll Swindle*
     (Virgin) F

TERRY JONES (comedian)
1971   *And Now For Something Completely Different*
     (Columbia) F

1975	*Monty Python and the Holy Grail* (FMI) F	1942	*The Great Mr Handel* (GFD) F

1975 *Monty Python and the Holy Grail*
(FMI) F
1976 *Pleasure at Her Majesty's*
(Amnesty) F
"Court Room Sketch"
"So That's the Way You Like It"
"Lumberjack Song"
1977 *Jabberwocky*
(Columbia) F
1979 *Monty Python's Life of Brian*
(CIC) F
1980 *The Secret Policeman's Ball*
(Tigon) F
1983 *Crimson Permanent Assurance*
(UIP)
1983 *Monty Python's The Meaning of Life*
(UIP) F
1983 *Monty Python Live at the Hollywood Bowl*
(Handmade) F
1989 *Erik the Viking*
(UIP) F
1996 *The Wind in the Willows*
(Allied) F

THUNDERCLAP JONES (pianist)
1961 *Spike Milligan on Treasure Island WC2*
(British Lion)
"Crosshands Boogie"
"Treasure Island"

TOM JONES (violin)
1932 *Ideal Cinemagazine 316*
"Liebestraum"
1932 *Ideal Cinemagazine 326*
"Hungarian Dance"
1933 *Pathetone 155*
"Sylvia"
1933 *Pathe Pictorial 776*
"Violin Song from Tina"

TREFOR JONES (Welsh tenor)
1932 *Pathe Pictorial 749*
"Maire My Girl"
1934 *Pathe Pictorial 850*
"The Hills"
1934 *The Queen's Affair*
(B&D) F
"Fisherman's Waltz"
1935 *Pathe Pictorial 931*
"Shine Through My Dreams"
1935 *Old Roses*
(Fox) F
1937 *Glamorous Night*
(ABP) F
"Glamorous Night"
"Fold Your Wings of Love Around Me"
1938 *Pathetone 415*
"Here's to the Best of Us"
1941 *Pathe Pictorial 292*
"Invictus"

1942 *The Great Mr Handel*
(GFD) F
1947 *Comin' Thro' the Rye*
(Adelphi) F
"My Love Is Like a Red Red Rose"
"Mary Morison"
"Bonnie Wee Thing"
"Ae Fond Kiss"
"Of a' the Airts"
1949 *All Over Town*
(GFD) F
1958 *Hello London*
(Regal) F
"My Four British Tailors"

JORDAN (singer)
1976 *Sebastiane*
(Cinegate) F
1978 *Jubilee*
(Cinegate)
"Rule Britannia"

JOSEPHINE AND PAYNE (dancers)
1949 *Nitwits on Parade*
(Adelphi) F

ARCHIBALD JOYCE (conductor)
1913 *Always Gay*
(Hepworth)

EILEEN JOYCE (pianist)
1943 *Battle for Music*
(Strand) F
"Concerto in A Minor"
1945 *The Seventh Veil*
(GFD) F
1946 *Girl in a Million*
(British Lion) F
"Symphonic Variations"
1952 *Trent's Last Case*
(Wilcox) F
1954 *Behind the Scenes*
(Gas) ADVERT

EMMIE JOYCE (singer)
1927 *I Don't Know*
(Phonofilm)

LIND JOYCE (singer)
1946 *New Pictorial 120*
1947 *New Pictorial 141*
"I Want a Little Doggie"
1947 *Meet Me At Dawn*
(TCF) F
"I Guess I'm Not the Type"
1948 *The Clouded Crystal*
(Butcher) F

TEDDY JOYCE AND HIS BAND
1934 *Radio Parade of 1935*
(BIP) F
"Good Morning"
"There's No Excusing Susan"

1936　*Hearts of Humanity*
　　　(Baxter) F
　　　"I'm Gonna Wash My Hands of You"
1942　*The Crypt*
　　　(reissue: *Hearts of Humanity*)

JUAN AND MARVA (dancers)
1943　*Pathe Pictorial 375*

JUBILEE DUETTISTS (singers)
1933　*Pathe Pictorial 775*
　　　"Twickenham Ferry"
　　　"Cinderella's Wedding"

JACK JUDGE (singer)
1935　*Royal Cavalcade*
　　　(BIP) F
　　　"Tipperary"

JUGGLING DEMONS (jugglers)
1933　*Pathetone 172*

JUICY LUCY (group)
1970　*Colosseum and Juicy Lucy*
　　　(Warner)
　　　"I'm a Little Pimp"
1971　*Bread*
　　　(Salon) F

JULIAS LADIES CHOIR
1940　*Laugh It Off*
　　　(British National) F
　　　"God Send You Back to Me"

BETTY JUMEL (comedienne)
1944　*Demobbed*
　　　(Mancunian) F
1946　*Under New Management*
　　　(Mancunian) F
1948　*Honeymoon Hotel*
　　　(reissue: *Under New Management*)
1948　*Cup Tie Honeymoon*
　　　(Mancunian) F
　　　"Love Is Just a Game"

JUNE (dancer)
1922　*Eve's Film Review 70*
　　　"Phi-Phi"
1923　*Eve's Film Review 112*
　　　"Little Nelly Kelly"
1925　*Eve's Film Review 202*
　　　"Boodle"
1927　*Eve's Film Review 294*
　　　"Happy Go Lucky"

JUNE AND NADIADJA (dancers)
1932　*Ideal Cinemagazine 310*
　　　"Rumba"

ERIC JUPP AND HIS BAND
1956　*Parade of the Bands*
　　　(Hammer)

SENA JURINAC (soprano)
1962　*Der Rosenkavalier*
　　　(Rank) F

HARRY KAHNE (mental marvel)
1938   *Pathe Pictorial NS 144*

DICK KALLMAN (singer)
1963   *It's All Happening*
        (British Lion) F
        "Meeting You"

KALUA ISLANDERS (Hawaiian band)
1947   *New Pictorial 128*

KAM TAI TRIO (entertainers)
1936   *Pathetone 350*

KIRI TE KANAWA (opera singer)
1990   *Meeting Venus*
        (Warner) F
        "Tannhäuser"

ALAN KANE (singer)
1937   *Spirit of Variety*
        (Exclusive)
1943   *Up With the Lark*
        (New Realm) F

EDEN KANE (singer)
1963   *Take Six*
        (British Lion)
        "Forget Me Not"

JASON KANE (singer)
1971   *Gumshoe*
        (Columbia) F

ANTON KARAS (zither)
1949   *The Third Man*
        (London) F
        "Harry Lime Theme"
        "Cafe Mozart Waltz"
1949   *New Pictorial 279*
        "Harry Lime Theme"
        "Cafe Mozart Waltz"
1950   *Come Dance With Me*
        (Columbia) F
        "Harry Lime Theme"

KARINA (ballerina)
1921   *Celebrities of the Dance*
        (Gaumont)
1922   *Eve's Film Review 42*
        "The Dying Swan"

KARINA, VADIO AND HERTZ (acrobatic dancers)
1936   *Soft Lights and Sweet Music*
        (British Lion) F
1937   *Shooting Stars*
        (Viking) F

KARLINS (singers)
1968   *Diamonds for Breakfast*
        (Paramount) F

FRED KARNO (comedian)
1923   *Early Birds*
        (Brouett)
1932   *The Bailiffs*
        (ATP)

MADAME KARSAVANIA (dancer)
1921   *Eve's Film Review 2*
1921   *Celebrities of the Dance*
        (Gaumont)

KASBEK SINGERS
1930   *Elstree Calling*
        (BIP) F

ALEXANDER KASS (singer)
1934   *Pathetone 198*

MADEMOISELLE KAUFMAN (dancer)
1903   *Two Pretty Dances*
        (Paul)

RON KAVANA AND TERRY WOODS
(musicians)
1990   *Hidden Agenda*
        (Hemdale) F
        "Joe McDormell"
        "Young Ned of the Hill"

KATHLEEN KAVANAGH
1940   *Pathetone 561*

BILLY KAY (singer)
1933   *Television Follies*
        (English) F
        "Chinky Blues"

JANET KAY (singer)
1981   *Burning an Illusion*
        (BFI) F
        "Imagine That"

KAY, KATYA AND KAY (adagio dancers)
1937   *Variety Hour*
        (Fox) F

DAVY KAYE (comedian)
1956   *Fun at St Fanny's*
        (British Lion) F
1962   *The Pot Carriers*
        (ABP) F
1962   *The Wrong Arm of the Law*
        (British Lion) F
1963   *The World Ten Times Over*
        (Warner) F
1963   *Crooks in Cloisters*
        (ABPC) F
1965   *Those Magnificent Men in Their Flying Machines*
        (TCF) F
1965   *Carry On Cowboy*
        (Anglo) F
1968   *Chitty Chitty Bang Bang*
        (UA) F

1971   *Top of the Bill*
       (Butcher) F
1971   *Carry On at Your Convenience*
       (Rank) F
1971   *The Magnificent Seven Deadly Sins*
       (Tigon) F
1972   *Alice's Adventures in Wonderland*
       (TCF) F

DINAH KAYE (singer)
1948   *Jivin' and Jammin'*
       (Piccadilly)
       "Honeysuckle Rose"
       "These Foolish Things"
1953   *Betty Slow Drag*
       (Halfmoon)
       "Betty Slow Drag"

EDNA KAYE (singer)
1948   *Third Time Lucky*
       (Rank) F
       "Forgive Me For Dreaming"

IRVING KAYE (whistling violinist)
1940   *Pathe Pictorial 213*
       "The Skater's Waltz"
1941   *Pathe Pictorial 253*

PAT KAYE AND BETTY ANKERS (comedy)
1951   *Let's Go Crazy*
       (Adelphi) F
       "Thinking to Myself About You"
       "This Thing Called Sin"

STUBBY KAYE (American singer)
1963   *The Cool Mikado*
       (Baim) F
       "Make the Punishment Fit the
       Crime"
       "The Flowers That Bloom in the
       Spring"
       "A More Humane Mikado"
1969   *Can Heironymus Merkin Ever Forget
       Mercy Humppe and Find True
       Happiness?*
       (Universal) F
1970   *Cool It Carol*
       (Miracle) F

KEARNEY AND BROWNING (tap-dancers)
1934   *Say It With Flowers*
       (Realart) F
       "Knocked 'em in the Old Kent Road"

ALVIN KEECH (banjoist)
1926   *Eve's Film Review 277*

ALVIN AND KELVIN KEECH
(instrumentalists)
1926   *Alvin and Kelvin Keech*
       (Phonofilm)

BARRY KEEGAN (Irish singer)
1950   *Irish Melody*
       (Barralet)

KATHY KEETON (striptease)
1965   *The Spy Who Came In From the
       Cold*
       (Paramount) F

EDDIE KELLAND (singer)
1935   *Pathe Pictorial 893*
       "Practise What You Preach"
1937   *Uptown Revue*
       (Ace) F
1937   *West End Frolics*
       (Ace) F

JACK AND SYLVIA KELLAWAY (adagio
dancers)
1933   *Ideal Cinemagazine 389*

SYLVIA KELLAWAY AND LESLIE (adagio
dancers)
1940   *Garrison Follies*
       (Butcher) F
1941   *He Found a Star*
       (GFD) F

GRETA KELLER (singer)
1932   *Pathetone 119*
       "Auf Wiedersehen"
1934   *Pathe Pictorial 861*
       "Isle of Capri"

JIMMY KELLEY
see **THE SINGING CARPENTER**

SCOTCH KELLY (comedian)
1928   *Love's Option*
       (WP) F

LARRY KEMBLE (trick cyclist)
1940   *Pathe Pictorial 219*

GARY KEMP (singer)
1972   *Hide and Seek*
       (Eady) F
1990   *The Krays*
       (Rank) F
1991   *Paper Marriage*
       (Forstater) F
1994   *Bad Medicine*
       (Unity) F

LINDSAY KEMP (dancer)
1972   *Savage Messiah*
       (Russell) F
1973   *The Wicker Man*
       (British Lion) F
1973   *The Lindsay Kemp Circus*
       (Scottish Arts)
       "The Ball Dancer"
       "The Flower"
1974   *The Stud*
       (Globebest) F
1976   *Sebastiane*
       (Cinegate) F

1977 *Valentino*
(UA) F
1978 *Jubilee*
(Cinegate) F
1985 *A Midsummer Night's Dream*
(Mainline) F

MARTIN KEMP (singer)
1990 *The Krays*
(Rank) F
1997 *Monk Dawson*
(Warrene) F

PAT AND TERRY KENDAL (song and dance)
1926 *London's Famous Cabarets*
(Parkinson)
1928 *Phototone 6*
"Virginia"
1928 *Phototone 12*
"I Can't Give You Anything But Love"

TERRY AND DORIC KENDAL (dancers)
1936 *B.B.C. Musicals 6*
(Inspiration)
1937 *Pathetone 397*
1938 *Melodies of the Moment*
(reissue: *B.B.C. Musicals 6*)
1939 *Radio Nights*
(Inspiration)
1951 *Mirth and Melody*
(reissue: *Radio Nights*)
1955 *On With the Dance*
(Carisbrooke)
"Samba Sud"

GAIL KENDALL (singer)
1946 *Happy Family*
(British Foundation)

KENNETH KENDALL (television personality)
1962 *Vengeance*
(Stross) F
1967 *They Came From Beyond Space*
(Amicus) F
1968 *2001: A Space Odyssey*
(MGM) F
1979 *Electric Eskimo*
(CFF) F

MARIE KENDALL (comedienne)
1933 *Pathetone 156*
"Just Like the Ivy"
1934 *Say It With Flowers*
(Realart) F
"Did Your First Wife Ever Do That?"
"Just Like the Ivy"
1936 *Happy Days Are Here Again*
(Argyle) F
"Just Like the Ivy"
1938 *Happy Days Revue*
F (reissue: *Happy Days Are Here Again*)

1940s *Variety Follies: Mad As a March Hare*
(reissue: *Happy Days Are Here Again*)

BERTIE KENDRICK (boy soprano)
1937 *Riding High*
(British Lion) F
"Love's Old Sweet Song"

JIMMY KENNEDY AND MICHAEL CARR (composers)
1938 *Around the Town*
(British Lion) F
"Red Sails in the Sunset"
"Harbour Lights"
"Sunset Trail"
"Dinner for One Please, James"

LAURI KENNEDY (singer)
1930 *Pathetone 17*
"Songs My Mother Taught Me"

LUDOVIC KENNEDY (television personality)
1957 *The Lonely House*
(Anglo) F
1963 *Heavens Above*
(British Lion) F

NAN KENNEDY (impressionist)
1931 *Bill and Coo*
(BIP) F
"Down Where the Breezes" (as Maurice Chevalier, Gracie Fields)

VICKI KENNEDY (model)
1963 *It's a Bare, Bare World*
(Antler)

HORACE KENNEY (comedian)
1928 *The Trial Turn*
(BSFP)
1934 *Love Life and Laughter*
(ATP) F
1934 *Road House*
(Gaumont) F
1935 *Cock o' the North*
(Butcher) F
1942 *Let the People Sing*
(British National) F
1942 *We'll Smile Again*
(British National) F
1943 *Theatre Royal*
(Baxter) F
1945 *Here Comes the Sun*
(Baxter) F
1948 *Counterblast*
(British National) F
1950 *Something in the City*
(Butcher) F

KENNY (group)
1975 *Side By Side*
(GTO) F
"Fancy Pants"

KENNY AND THE WRANGLERS (group)
1965 *Be My Guest*
(Rank) F
"Somebody Help Me"

BETTY KENT (singer)
1941 *Pathe Pictorial 269*
1942 *Pathe Pictorial 316*
1943 *Pathe Pictorial 357*
"I Mean You"

JEAN KENT
see **JEAN CARR**

THE KENTONES (singers)
1958 *6.5 Special*
(Anglo) F
"It's Just the Gypsy in My Soul"

KENTUCKY SINGERS
1930 *Pathetone 13*
"All God's Chillun"

NAN KENWAY AND DOUGLAS YOUNG
(comedy)
1937 *Pathe Pictorial NS 91*
1938 *Pathe Pictorial NS 117*
"Our Own Pictorial"
1939 *Pathetone 508*
"Grannie"
1940 *Pathetone 543*
1942 *Pathe Pictorial 323*
"At Home"
1942 *Pathe Pictorial 344*
"Mr Pottle"
1943 *Pathe Pictorial 403*
(with Leslie Bridgemont)

NEIL KENYON (Scottish comedian)
1913 *Golfing*
(Hewitt)

DAVID KERNAN (singer)
1962 *Mix Me a Person*
(British Lion) F
1963 *Zulu*
(Paramount) F
"Men of Harlech"
1967 *I Like Birds*
(Border) F
1971 *Up the Chastity Belt*
(EMI) F
"The Troubadour Song"
1972 *Carry On Abroad*
(Rank) F

BOB KERR'S WHOOPEE BAND
1975 *Never Too Young To Rock*
(GTO) F
"The Cat Crept In"
"Juke Box Jive"
1975 *Bob Kerr's Whoopee Band*
(GTO)

NIK KERSHAW (singer)
1987 *The Secret Policeman's Third Ball*
(Virgin) F
"Wouldn't It Be Good"

KETTERING MADRIGAL MALE VOICE CHOIR
1935 *Pathe Pictorial 887*
"Sailors Chorus"

KEVIN AND GARY (singers)
1968 *Popdown*
(New Realm) F

KEY AND HAWORTH (singers)
1927 *Key and Haworth*
(Phonofilm)

CLAY KEYES (comedian)
also known as Harry Haver
1932 *Pathetone 106*
"It Always Starts to Rain"

LILLIAN KEYES (soprano)
1930 *A Knight in London*
(Warner) F
1934 *Boots Boots*
(Blakeley) F
1935 *Musical Medley*
(Mancunian)

KEYNOTES (singers)
1949 *Melody in the Dark*
(Adelphi) F
"Jingle Jangle Thingamajig"

NELSON KEYS (comedian)
1909 *Drowsy Dick's Dream*
(B&C)
1910 *Drowsy Dick Dreams He's a Burglar*
(B&C)
1914 *Alone I Did It*
(Heron)
1916 *The Real Thing At Last*
(British Actors)
1916 *Judged by Appearances*
(British Oak)
1918 *Once Upon a Time*
(British Actors) F
1922 *Let's Pretend*
(British Super) F
1927 *Tiptoes*
(British National) F
1927 *Madame Pompadour*
(British National) F
1927 *Mumsie*
(Wilcox) F
1928 *The Triumph of the Scarlet Pimpernel*
(B&D) F
1929 *When Knights Were Bold*
(B&D) F
1929 *Splinters*
(B&D) F
"Don't Send My Boy to Prison"

1931 *Pathetone 48*
1931 *Eve's Film Review 503*
       "Folly to be Wise"
1931 *Almost a Divorce*
       (B&D) F
1933 *Send 'Em Back Half Dead*
       (Fox) F
1935 *We've Got to Have Love*
       (B&N)
1935 *Pathe Pictorial 886*
1935 *The Last Journey*
       (Twickenham) F
1936 *Eliza Comes to Stay*
       (Twickenham)
1936 *In the Soup*
       (Twickenham)
1936 *Dreams Come True*
       (Reunion) F
1937 *Wake Up Famous*
       (ATP) F
1937 *Knights for a Day*
       (Pathe) F

BERT AND MICHAEL KIDD
1936 *Happy Days Are Here Again*
       (Argyle) F
1938 *Happy Days Revue*
       F (reissue: *Happy Days Are Here
       Again*)

NOR KIDDIE (comedian)
1932 *The Bad Companions*
       (BIF) F
1936 *Don't Rush Me*
       (PDC) F

JAN KIEPURA (Polish tenor)
1931 *City of Song*
       (ASFI) F
       "Naples Your Song Is Everywhere"
       "Nun Me Sceta"
       "La Donna e Mobile"
1932 *Tell Me Tonight*
       (Gaumont) F
       "Tell Me Tonight"
       "Che Gelida Manina"
       "Ach So Fromm"
       "La Danza"
       "O Sole Mio"
       "My Heart Is Full of Sunshine"
1934 *My Song for You*
       (Gaumont) F
       "My Song for You"
       "Ave Maria"
       "Aida"
       "With All My Heart"
       "Smile At Me Just Once"
       "O Madonna"
1934 *My Heart Is Calling*
       (Gaumont) F
       "My Heart Is Always Calling"
       "You Me and Love"

KIMBERLEY AND PAGE (comedy)
1939 *A Window in London*
       (GFD) F

ALAN KING (American comedian)
1961 *On the Fiddle*
       (Anglo) F

DAVE KING (comedian)
1962 *Go To Blazes*
       (ABP) F
1962 *The Road to Hong Kong*
       (UA) F
1969 *It's the Only Way to Go*
       (Gala)
1971 *Up the Chastity Belt*
       (EMI) F
1976 *The Ritz*
       (Warner) F
1979 *The Long Good Friday*
       (Calendar) F
1985 *Revolution*
       (Goldcrest) F

FRANK KING AND HIS ORCHESTRA
1945 *Sweethearts For Ever*
       (Empire) F
1945 *Cabaret*
       (Empire) F
       "Tears On My Pillow"
       "Cuban Pete"
       "Don't Forget Me"
1946 *Amateur Night*
       (Renown)

HETTY KING (male impersonator)
1923 *Eve's Film Review 108*
1954 *Lilacs in the Spring*
       (Republic) F
1970 *Hetty King Performer*
       (Robinson) F
       "All the Nice Girls Love a Sailor"

JONATHAN KING (television presenter)
1969 *Under the Table You Must Go*
       (Butcher) F
1973 *Radio Wonderful*
       (Goodtimes) F

**NOSMO KING (Vernon Watson) AND
HUBERT (Jack Watson)** (comedy)
see also **JACK WATSON** and **VERNON
WATSON**
1934 *Pathe Pictorial 847*
1935 *Pathe Pictorial 898*
       "Oh You Nasty Man"
1936 *Pathe Pictorial NS 29*
1936 *Pathetone Parade of 1936*
       F (reissue: *Pictorial 898*)
1937 *Pathe Pictorial NS 54*
1939 *Pathetone Parade of 1940*
       F (reissue: *Pictorial 54*)

REGINALD KING (pianist)
see also **ALFREDO CAMPOLI AND REGINALD KING** and **CELEBRITY TRIO**
- 1938 *Pathetone 412*
  "Passing Clouds" (with Albert Sandler)
- 1940 *Pathetone 529*
  "Murmurs of Spring" (with Alfredo Campoli)

REGINALD KING AND HIS ORCHESTRA
- 1934 *Pathe Pictorial 828*
  "The House Beautiful"
- 1934 *Pathe Pictorial 832*
  "Song of the Troubadour"
- 1936 *Pathetone 339*
- 1936 *B.B.C. Musicals 4*
  (Inspiration)
- 1939 *Radio Nights*
  (Inspiration)
  "If You Could Care For Me"

REGINALD KING QUARTET (musicians)
- 1941 *Pathe Pictorial 348*
  "June Night on Marlow Reach"
- 1943 *Pathe Pictorial 371*
  "Minuet"

STANLEY KING (baritone)
- 1940 *Somewhere in England*
  (Mancunian) F
  "Somewhere in England"

KING AND PRINCE (entertainers)
- 1937 *Pathetone 396*

KING BROTHERS (singers)
- 1958 *6.5 Special*
  (Anglo) F
  "Hand Me Down My Walking Cane"
  "The Six Five Jive"

KINGS OF THE CARIBBEAN STEEL BAND
- 1957 *The Heart Within*
  (Rank) F

TOM KINNIBURGH (baritone)
- 1931 *Pathetone 42*
  "Song of the Highway"
- 1931 *Pathetone 50*
- 1931 *Pathetone 61*
  "A Yokel's Philosophy"
- 1931 *Pathe Pictorial 713*
  "March of the Cameron Men"
- 1932 *Pathe Pictorial 726*
  "Rolling Stones"
- 1933 *Pathe Pictorial 812*
  "Song of the Tramp"
- 1934 *Banks and Braes*
  (Pathe)
  "Ye Banks and Braes"

TONY KINSEY QUARTET (musicians)
- 1961 *The Tony Kinsey Quartet*
  (Carisbrooke)

"Dinner for One Please, James"
"The Clock on the Wall"
"Autobahn"
- 1963 *Small Band Jazz*
  (Carisbrooke)
  "The Golden Striker"
  "Little Chick"
  "Didn't We?"
- 1963 *Modern Rhythm*
  (Carisbrooke)
  "The Bluest Kind of Blues"
- 1963 *West Eleven*
  (Angel) F

IVOR KIRCHIN AND HIS BAND
- 1939 *Pathetone 471*
  "Park Parade"
- 1948 *Spring in Park Lane*
  (Wilcox) F
  "The Sheik of Araby"

STANLEY KIRKBY (baritone)
- 1930 *The Jolly Farmers*
  (BIP)
- 1935 *Father O'Flynn*
  (Butcher) F

IRIS KIRKWHITE (tap-dancer)
also known as Iris Whyte; Iris Kirk White
- 1930 *Toyland*
  (Gainsborough)
- 1931 *Ideal Cinemagazine 290*

IRIS KIRKWHITE DANCERS
- 1945 *Here Comes the Sun*
  (Baxter) F

PAT (PATRICIA) KIRKWOOD (song and dance)
- 1938 *Save a Little Sunshine*
  (Pathe) F
  "Save a Little Sunshine"
  "Gentle Flowers"
  "Nothing Can Worry Me Now"
- 1939 *Me and My Pal*
  (Pathe) F
  "Dinah"
  "Some of These Days"
  "I'm Nobody's Sweetheart Now"
- 1939 *Come On George*
  (ATP) F
- 1940 *Band Waggon*
  (Gainsborough) F
  "The Melody Maker"
  "The Only One Who's Difficult Is You"
  "Heaven Will Be Heavenly"
  "Boomps-a-Daisy"
- 1945 *Flight from Folly*
  (Warner) F
  "The Majorca"
- 1950 *Once a Sinner*
  (Butcher) F

1956 *Stars in Your Eyes*
(British Lion) F
"Stars in My Eyes"
"I'd Pick Piccadilly"
"Has Anybody Here Seen Kelly?"
1957 *After the Ball*
(Romulus) F
"The Army of Today's All Right"
"After the Ball"
"Jolly Good Luck to the Girl Who
Loves a Soldier"
"Algy the Piccadilly Johnnie"
"My Word He Is a Naughty Boy"
"Give It to Father"
"Following in Father's Footsteps"
"Scotch and Polly"

FRED KITCHEN (comedian)
1914 *Freddy's Nightmare*
(Premier)
1934 *Wild Boy*
(Gainsborough) F

KITKAT SAXOPHONE RASCALS
(musicians)
1937 *Pathe Pictorial NS 70*
"Colonel Bogey"
"In Cellar Cool"
"Whistling Rufus"

EARTHA KITT (singer)
1960 *Pathe Pictorial 309*
1971 *Up the Chastity Belt*
(EMI) F
"A Knight for My Nights"
1989 *Erik the Viking*
(UIP) F

ELSIE KITT (singer)
1927 *Love's Old Sweet Song*
(Synchrofilms)

ALAN KLEIN AND JULIE SAMUEL (singers)
1963 *Take Six*
(British Lion)
"Come Outside"

KNELLER HALL MILITARY BAND
1932 *Pathetone 98*
"The Two Imps"
1932 *Pathetone 105*
"Let the Bulgine Run"
1935 *In Town Tonight*
(British Lion) F

JUNE KNIGHT (soprano)
1937 *The Lilac Domino*
(GFD) F
"The Lilac Domino Waltz"
"My Heart Will Be Dancing"

MARK KNOPFLER (guitarist)
1987 *The Secret Policeman's Third Ball*
(Virgin) F
"Imagine"

R G KNOWLES (comedian)
1905 *Dreamy Eyes*
(Chronophone)

TEDDY KNOX
see **JIMMY NERVO AND TEDDY KNOX** and
THE CRAZY GANG

BOBBY KNUTT (comedian)
1986 *Coast to Coast*
(Britannia) F
1989 *Ladder of Swords*
(Hobo) F

THE KOOBAS (group)
1966 *Money Go Round*
(Libertas)

KORINGA (snake act)
1944 *Bees in Paradise*
(Gainsborough) F

KOROSENKO (strong man)
1944 *Pathe Pictorial 422*

HARRY KORRIS (comedian)
1940 *Somewhere in England*
(Mancunian) F
1942 *Somewhere in Camp*
(Mancunian) F
1942 *Somewhere on Leave*
(Mancunian) F
1943 *Happidrome*
(Aldwych) F
"Come to the Happidrome"
"We Three"
"Let Me Tell You"

AMAZING KOVACS (circus act)
1948 *International Circus Revue*
(Butcher) F

KRAKOW JAZZ ENSEMBLE (band)
1987 *Stormy Monday*
(Palace) F

BILLY J. KRAMER AND THE DAKOTAS
(group)
1965 *Primitive London*
(Searchlight) F
1965 *Pop Gear*
(Pathe) F
"Little Children"

KREMLIN DANCERS
1939 *Pathe Pictorial NS 182*

KRIS KRISTOFFERSON (American singer)
1976 *The Sailor Who Fell From Grace with
the Sea*
(Fox-Rank) F

KID KRUPA (boy drummer)
1943 *Variety Jubilee*
(Butcher) F

1944 *Highlights of Variety 28*
(reissue: *Variety Jubilee*)

PETER KUBEKE (tap-dancer)
1993 *Friends*
(Metro) F

MAGDA KUN (singer)
1935 *Dance Band*
(BIP) F
"Gypsy Love"

CHARLIE KUNZ (pianist)
1933 *Pathetone 171*
"Goodnight But Not Goodbye"
1933 *Pathetone 184*
"Japanese Sandman"
1934 *Pathe Pictorial 834*
"Poor Butterfly"
"After You've Gone"
"Whispering"
1934 *Pathetone 248*
"I Saw Stars"
"All I Do Is Dream of You"
1935 *Pathetone 279*
"Clap Hands"
"Pink Elephants"
1935 *Pathe Pictorial 913*
"The Very Thought of You"
"Miss Annabelle Lee"
1935 *Clap Hands*
(Fidelity)
"Clap Hands"
"Around and About"
"I Don't Know Why"
"You Were There"

"Miss Annabelle Lee"
"Side By Side"
"I Can't Give You Anything But
Love"
"You're in Kentucky Sure as You're
Born"
"Everything I Have Is Yours"
1936 *Pathetone Parade of 1936*
F (reissue: *Pathetone 279*)
1937 *Pathetone Parade of 1938*
F (reissue: *Pictorial 913*)
1942 *Charlie Kunz Sing Song*
(NSS) S
1944 *Twinkling Fingers*
(reissue: *Clap Hands*)
1946 *New Pictorial 119*
"Bless You for Being an Angel"
1947 *New Pictorial 125*
"Viennese Waltz"
1960 *Climb Up the Wall*
(reissue: *Clap Hands*)

ERICH KUNZ (bass-baritone)
1962 *Der Rosenkavalier*
(Rank) F

SYDNEY KYTE AND HIS BAND
1932 *Pathetone 106*
1933 *Pathetone 167*
"See Me Dance the Polka"
1934 *Pathe Pictorial 856*
"Blue Rhythm"
1934 *Pathetone 228*
"Melody in F"
1937 *Saturday Night Revue*
(Pathe) F

144

BRITISH NATIONAL FILMS present——————

OLD MOTHER RILEY IN SOCIETY

FEATURING

ARTHUR LUCAN & KITTY McSHANE

Directed by JOHN BAXTER

TRADE SHOW: PHOENIX THEATRE, WEDNESDAY, APRIL 24th, at 3 p.m.

Distribution:—

ANGLO-AMERICAN FILM CORPORATION LTD.

123 WARDOUR ST., LONDON, W.1 —————— GERRARD 3202

LORRAINE LA FOSSE (singer)
1936 *Melody of My Heart*
(Dutcher) F
"Melody of My Heart"
"Repeat It Again to Me"
"Habanera"
"Gypsy Song"

JACK LA ROC AND HIS ORCHESTRA
1951 *I'll Get You For This*
(Romulus) F

DANNY LA RUE (comedian)
1972 *Our Miss Fred*
(EMI) F

MARTA LABARR (soprano)
1936 *Ball At Savoy*
(RKO) F
"I Live for Love"
"I'm in Love with my Life"
"A Girl Like Nina"

BRUCE LACEY (comedian)
1960 *The Running Jumping and Standing Still Film*
(British Lion)
1960 *The Battle of New Orleans*
(Biographic)
1962 *It's Trad Dad*
(Columbia) F
1962 *The Plain Man's Guide to Advertising*
(Biographic)
1965 *One Man Band*
(Biographic)
1965 *The Knack*
(UA) F
1965 *Help*
(UA) F
1966 *L'Art Pour l'Art*
(Godfrey)
1967 *Smashing Time*
(Paramount) F
1967 *Bang!*
(Godfrey)
1972 *Adult Fun*
(Maya) F

THE LADYBIRDS (group)
1969 *Connecting Rooms*
(Telstar) F

LAI-FOUN AND HIS CHINESE WONDERS
(jugglers)
1935 *Pathetone 288*
1936 *Chinese Cabaret*
(Bijou) F
1936 *International Revue*
(Medway) F
1939 *Pathetone Parade of 1939*
F (reissue: *Pathetone 288*)
1942 *Pathe Pictorial 312*

1943 *The Dummy Talks*
(British National) F

CHIKA LAINE
see **BILLY RHODES AND CHIKA LAINE**

CLEO LAINE (singer)
1955 *Murder By Proxy*
(Hammer) F
1956 *Parade of the Bands*
(Hammer)
1958 *6.5 Special*
(Anglo) F
"What Am I Going to Tell Them Tonight?"
1961 *The Third Alibi*
(Grand National) F
"Now and Then"
1962 *The Roman Spring of Mrs Stone*
(Warner) F
"Love Is a Bore"

LEW LAKE (comedian)
1912 *The Bloomsbury Burglars*
(Cinema)
1929 *Splinters*
(B&D) F
1930 *The Great Game*
(Gaumont) F
1931 *Splinters in the Navy*
(Twickenham) F
1937 *Splinters in the Air*
(Wilcox) F

LAMBEG FOLK DANCE SOCIETY
1938 *Devil's Rock*
(Burger) F

CONSTANT LAMBERT (composer)
1943 *Battle for Music*
(Strand) F
"Piano Concerto No. 2"

JOHNNY AND SUMA LAMONTE (jugglers)
1974 *Mister Quilp*
(EMI) F

HARRY LAMORE (wire-walker)
1897 *Fun On the Clothes Line*
(Paul)

ROBERT LAMOURET (ventriloquist)
1949 *Helter Skelter*
(Gainsborough) F

BETTY LANCASTER (singer)
1938 *Meet the Mare*
(Ace Cinemagazine)
"Carolina Cotton Town Blues"

ELSA LANCHESTER (comedienne)
1924 *Scarlet Woman*
(Greenidge) F

1928 *Bluebottles*
(Angle)
1928 *Daydreams*
(Angle)
1929 *Mr Smith Wakes Up*
(BSFP) F
1930 *Comets*
(Alpha) F
"Please Sell No More Drink To My Father"
1931 *Officer's Mess*
(Ideal) F
1931 *The Stronger Sex*
(Gainsborough) F
1931 *The Love Habit*
(BIP) F
1931 *Potiphar's Wife*
(BIP) F
1932 *Camera Cocktales 2*
(Hallmark)
"After the Ball"
1933 *The Private Life of Henry VIII*
(London) F
1935 *The Ghost Goes West*
(London) F
1936 *Rembrandt*
(London) F
1936 *Miss Bracegirdle Does Her Duty*
(London)
1938 *Vessel of Wrath*
(Mayflower) F

WALDO LANCHESTER (puppeteer)
1956 *Magic Strings*
(Baim)

LANCY AND ADAMS (clowns)
1902 *Clown Pantaloon and Bobby*
(Gaumont)

CAROLE LANDIS (American singer)
1948 *Lucky Mascot*
(UA) F
"I Know Myself Too Well"

DESMOND LANE (musician)
1958 *6.5 Special*
(Anglo) F
"Midgets"

LAURI LUPINO LANE (comedian)
1957 *A King in New York*
(Archway) F
1970 *Carry On Loving*
(Rank) F
1975 *Side By Side*
(GTO) F
1977 *Confessions from a Holiday Camp*
(Columbia) F

LUPINO LANE (comedian)
1915 *His Cooling Courtship*
(John Bull)

1915 *Nipper's Busy Holiday*
(John Bull)
1915 *Nipper and the Curate*
(John Bull)
1915 *The Man in Possession*
(Homeland)
1916 *Nipper's Busy Bee Time*
(Nipper)
1916 *A Wife in a Hurry*
(Homeland)
1916 *The Dummy*
(Homeland)
1917 *Hello, Who's Your Lady Friend?*
(Homeland)
1917 *The Missing Link*
(Homeland)
1917 *Splash Me Nicely*
(Homeland)
1918 *Unexpected Treasure*
(Kinekature)
1918 *Trips and Tribunals*
(Kinekature)
1918 *His Busy Day*
(Kinekature)
1918 *His Salad Days*
(Kinekature)
1918 *Love and Lobster*
(Kinekature)
1919 *A Dreamland Frolic*
(Globe)
1919 *Clarence Crooks and Chivalry*
(Lane)
1920 *A Lot About a Lottery*
(Ideal)
1920 *A Night Out and a Day In*
(Ideal)
1920 *Around the Town 9*
(Gaumont)
1926 *Eve's Film Review 256*
"Turned Up"
1930 *The Yellow Mask*
(BIP) F
"Personality"
1931 *Never Trouble Trouble*
(PDC) F
"Who Could, We Could, We Two"
1931 *No Lady*
(Gaumont) F
1933 *A Southern Maid*
(BIP) F
1933 *Pathetone 147*
1934 *Pathetone 197*
1935 *Pathe Pictorial 886*
1935 *Who's Your Father?*
(Columbia) F
1935 *The Deputy Drummer*
(Columbia) F
"Old Pal"
"Bread and Cheese and Kisses"
1935 *Trust the Navy*
(Columbia) F
1936 *Hot News*
(Columbia) F

1938 *Pathetone 442*
"The Lambeth Walk"
1939 *The Lambeth Walk*
(MGM) F
"The Lambeth Walk"
"Me and My Girl"
1945 *New Pictorial 50*

MARYON LANE
see **DAVID POOLE AND MARYON LANE**

DON LANG AND HIS FRANTIC FIVE (band)
1958 *6.5 Special*
(Anglo) F
"It's a Crazy World"
"Boy Meets Girl"

HARRY LANGDON (American comedian)
1937 *Mad About Money*
(Morgan) F
"Dusting the Stars"

BONITA (BONNIE) LANGFORD (song and
dance)
1976 *Bugsy Malone*
(TCF) F
1978 *Wombling Free*
(Rank) F

**FRANCIS LANGFORD'S SINGING
SCHOLARS** (juveniles)
1956 *Fun at St Fanny's*
(British Lion) F
"The ABC Song"

LARSEN BROTHERS (accordionists)
1938 *Pathe Pictorial NS 105*
"The Wee MacGregor"

GERD LARSEN AND ALEXANDER GRANT
(dancers)
1948 *Steps of the Ballet*
(Crown)

NIKO LASKI (belly dancer)
1971 *Up the Chastity Belt*
(EMI) F

THE LATELLES (aerialists)
1903 *The Latelles, Aerial High Rope
Cyclists*
(Urban)

FREDDIE LATHAM (baritone)
1935 *Pathetone 265*
"Little Girl What Now?"
1939 *Pathe Pictorial NS 164*
"The Same Old Story"
1939 *Pathe Pictorial NS 182*
"They Say"

LATIN QUARTER LOVELIES (dancers)
1951 *New Pictorial 347*

GEORGE LATOUR (juggler)
1939 *Pathe Pictorial NS 153*

IRENE LATOUR (contortionist)
1901 *Irene Latour Contortionist*
(Warwick)

SIR HARRY LAUDER (Scottish singer)
1907 *I Love a Lassie*
(Chronophone)
1907 *Inveraray*
(Chronophone)
1907 *She Is Ma Daisy*
(Chronophone)
1907 *Stop Your Tickling Jock*
(Chronophone)
1907 *The Wedding of Sandy McNab*
(Chronophone)
1907 *We Parted on the Shore*
(Chronophone)
1908 *Harry Lauder in a Hurry*
(Gaumont)
1913 *Golfing*
(Hewitt)
1921 *Around the Town*
(Gaumont)
1922 *A Trip Down the Clyde*
(Scottish Film Council)
1927 *Hunting Tower*
(Welsh Pearson) F
1929 *Auld Lang Syne*
(Welsh Pearson) F
"The End of the Road"
"It's a Fine Thing to Sing"
"I Love a Lassie"
"A Wee Deoch and Doris"
"Auld Lang Syne"
1931 *I Love a Lassie and The Old Scotch
Songs*
(Gainsborough)
1931 *Somebody's Waiting for Me*
(Gainsborough)
1931 *I Love to Be a Sailor and The Wee
Hoose Among the Heather*
(Gainsborough)
1931 *Roaming in the Gloaming and The
End of the Road*
(Gainsborough)
1931 *Tobermory*
(Gainsborough)
1931 *Nanny*
(Gainsborough)
1931 *The Saftest of the Family*
(Gainsborough)
1931 *She Is Ma Daisy*
(Gainsborough)
1936 *The End of the Road*
(Fox) F
"The End of the Road"

CY LAURIE'S JAZZ BAND
1958 *Bandwagon*
(Ford) ADVERT

HUGH LAURIE (comedian)
1985　*Plenty*
　　　(RKO) F
1987　*The Secret Policeman's Third Ball*
　　　(Virgin) F
1988　*Strapless*
　　　(Granada) F
1992　*Peter's Friends*
　　　(Renaissance) F
1995　*Sense and Sensibility*
　　　(Columbia) F
1997　*The Borrowers*
　　　(PolyGram) F
1997　*Spice World*
　　　(Fragile) F

JAY LAURIER (comedian)
1922　*Eve's Film Review 32*
　　　"Jack and the Beanstalk"
1922　*Eve's Film Review 70*
　　　"Phi-Phi"
1931　*Pathetone 44*
　　　"Stein Stein"
1933　*I'll Stick to You*
　　　(British Lion) F
1933　*Pyjamas Preferred*
　　　(BIP) F
1933　*Waltz Time*
　　　(Gaumont) F
1937　*The Black Tulip*
　　　(Fox) F
1938　*Oh Boy*
　　　(ABPC) F

MARIE LAVARRE (singer)
1937　*Captain's Orders*
　　　(Liberty) F
　　　"Sailors Don't Care"
　　　"Let the Great Big World Keep
　　　Turning"

GABRIEL LAVELLE (singer)
1937　*Pathetone 380*
　　　"The Garden Where the Praeties
　　　Grow"

COOPER LAWLEY
see **HAL YATES AND COOPER LAWLEY**

BRYAN LAWRANCE (singer)
1932　*Marry Me*
　　　(Gainsborough) F
1935　*She Shall Have Music*
　　　(Twickenham) F
　　　"Don't Ask Me Any Questions"
　　　"Sailing Along on a Carpet of
　　　Clouds"
　　　"May All Your Troubles Be Little
　　　Ones"
　　　"She Shall Have Music"
　　　"My First Thrill"
1936　*Fame*
　　　(Wilcox) F

1937　*Variety Hour*
　　　(Fox) F
1937　*Sing As You Swing*
　　　(Rock) F
　　　"The Mountains of Mourne"
1940　*Music Box*
　　　(reissue: *Sing As You Swing*)

EDWIN LAWRENCE (comedian)
1932　*The Midshipmaid*
　　　(Gainsborough) F
1932　*Ideal Cinemagazine 339*
1933　*Ideal Cinemagazine 372*
1936　*Stars On Parade*
　　　(Butcher) F
1938　*Highlights of Variety 9*
　　　(reissue: *Stars On Parade*)

GERTRUDE LAWRENCE (singer)
1931　*Pathetone 84*
　　　"You're My Decline and Fall"
1932　*Women Who Play*
　　　(BIP) F
1932　*Lord Camber's Ladies*
　　　(BIP) F
　　　"What I Do I Do Well"
1932　*Aren't We All?*
　　　(Paramount) F
　　　"My Sweet"
1933　*No Funny Business*
　　　(Stafford) F
　　　"No Funny Business"
1935　*Mimi*
　　　(BIP) F
1936　*Rembrandt*
　　　(London) F
1936　*Men Are Not Gods*
　　　(London) F
　　　"Sing Willow"
1938　*Cavalcade of the Stars*
　　　(Coronel)

JOSIE LAWRENCE (comedienne)
1991　*Enchanted April*
　　　(BBC) F

EVELYN LAYE (singer)
1920　*Around the Town 24*
　　　(Gaumont)
　　　"The Shop Girl"
1921　*Eve's Film Review 24*
　　　"Fun of the Fayre"
1924　*Eve's Film Review 142*
　　　"Madame Pompadour"
1925　*Eve's Film Review 236*
　　　"Betty in Mayfair"
1927　*Luck of the Navy*
　　　(Wilcox) F
1928　*Eve's Film Review 370*
　　　"Blue Eyes"
1933　*Waltz Time*
　　　(Gaumont) F
　　　"A Glass of Golden Bubbles"
　　　"Butterfly Song"

1934 *Princess Charming*
(Gaumont) F
"The Princess Is Awakening"
"Love Is a Song"
"Near and Yet So Far"
"Brave Hearts"
"On the Wings of Dawn"
"When Gay Adventure Calls"
1934 *Evensong*
(Gaumont) F
"I Wait for You"
"La Bohème"
"La Traviata"
"Santa Lucia"
"Tipperary"
"The End of a Perfect Day"
"Keep the Home Fires Burning"
"There's a Long Long Trail
Awinding"
"Without You"
"Love's Old Sweet Song"
"My Home in Tralee"
1954 *Pathe Pictorial 509*
"Wedding in Paris"
1959 *Make Mine a Million*
(British Lion) F
1965 *Theatre of Death*
(Pennea) F
1970 *Say Hello to Yesterday*
(Cinerama) F

ROBERT LAYTON (baritone)
1933 *Pathe Pictorial 773*
"Lighterman Tom"

TURNER LAYTON (songs at the piano)
1936 *Soft Lights and Sweet Music*
(British Lion) F
"My S.O.S. to You"
1937 *Calling All Stars*
(British Lion) F
"East of the Sun"
"These Foolish Things"

DONNA LE BOURDAIS (singer)
1935 *Barnacle Bill*
(Butcher) F

FLORA LE BRETON (singer)
(films as actress not listed)
1929 *Flora le Breton*
(BSFP)
"Poor Little Locked-Up Me"
"The Doll"
"Coseita"
1930 *Comets*
(Alpha) F

JENNIE LE GON (dancer)
1936 *Dishonour Bright*
(Cecil) F

EARL AND JOSEPHINE LEACH (dancers)
1937 *Pathetone 403*
"Big Apple"

1938 *Pathe Pictorial NS 99*
"Drink To Me Only"

PAT LEACOCK (singer)
1996 *Glastonbury: The Movie*
(Starlight) F
"Blow Your Head"

HARRY LEADER AND HIS BAND
1936 *Pot Shots*
(Ace Cinemagazine)

LECUONA CUBAN BOYS (band)
1935 *Heat Wave*
(Gainsborough) F

LED ZEPPELIN (group)
1976 *The Song Remains the Same*
(Columbia) F
"Black Dog"
"Rock and Roll"
"Since I've Been Loving You"
"No Quarter"
"Rain Song"
"Dazed and Confused"
"Stairway to Heaven"
"Moby Dick"
"Heart Breaker"
"Whole Lotta Love"
"Autumn Lake"
"The Song Remains the Same"

ANDRE LEDOR (ethoniumist)
1936 *Pathe Pictorial NS 9*
"O Star of Eve"

LEE (striptease)
1968 *Inadmissible Evidence*
(Paramount) F

DINAH LEE (singer)
1936 *Chinese Cabaret*
(Bijou) F

FRANK LEE'S TARA CEILIDH BAND
1937 *Kathleen Mavourneen*
(Butcher) F

FREDDIE FINGERS LEE (musician)
1979 *Blue Suede Shoes*
(Boyd) F

GERRY LEE AND LEN (novelty musicians)
1933 *Pathetone 179*

LISA LEE (singer)
1951 *Lady Godiva Rides Again*
(London) F
1953 *Out of the Bandbox*
(New Realm)

THELMA LEE
see **AL VERDI AND THELMA LEE**

WINSTON LEE AND HIS ORCHESTRA
1954 *A Musical Medley*
      (Carisbrooke)
1954 *Time for Music*
      (Carisbrooke)
1954 *Hands in Harmony*
      (Carisbrooke)
1954 *Take a Few Notes*
      (Carisbrooke)
1954 *Melody Mixture*
      (Carisbrooke)
1954 *Magic of Music*
      (Carisbrooke)
1954 *Winston Lee and his Orchestra*
      (Carisbrooke)
1955 *On With the Dance*
      (Carisbrooke)
      "Anima-e-Care"

LEE LEE LEE AND LEE (comedians)
1933 *Ideal Cinemagazine 370*

MICHEL LEGRAND (French composer)
1971 *Time for Loving*
      (Hemdale) F

ADELE LEIGH (singer)
1957 *Davy*
      (Ealing) F
      "Voi Che Sapete"

JOE LEIGH (male soprano)
1934 *Give Her a Ring*
      (BIP) F
      "Giving You the Stars"

CHRISTABEL LEIGHTON-PORTER
see **JANE**

LEMMY (singer)
1987 *Eat the Rich*
      (Comic Strip) F
1990 *Hardware*
      (Palace) F

JOSE LENNARD
see **SANTOS CASANI AND JOSE LENNARD**

PAULA LENNARD (singer)
1946 *New Pictorial 118*

ANN LENNER (singer)
1940 *Garrison Follies*
      (Butcher) F
      "Oh Johnny"
      "When the Night Is Through"

SHIRLEY LENNER (singer)
1943 *Swingonometry*
      (Inspiration)
      "Yours"
      "Whistler's Mother-in-Law"

JOHN LENNON (singer)
see also **THE BEATLES**
1967 *How I Won the War*
      (UA) F
1972 *Imagine*
      (Vaughan) F
      "Imagine"
      "Crippled Inside"
      "Jealous Guy"
      "Power to the People"
      "Gimme Some Truth"
      "Oh My Love"
      "It's So Hard"
      "I Don't Want to Be a Soldier"
      "How Do You Sleep?"
      "Oh Yoko"

ANNIE LENNOX (singer)
1985 *Revolution*
      (Goldcrest) F
1991 *Edward II*
      (Palace) F
      "Every Time We Say Goodbye"

LOTTIE LENNOX (singer)
1936 *Old Timers*
      (Warner)

DAN LENO (comedian)
1900 *The Rats*
      (Warwick)
1900 *Burlesque Attack on a Settler's Cabin*
      (Warwick)
1900 *Dan Leno's Attempt to Master the Cycle*
      (Warwick)
1900 *Burlesque Fox Hunt*
      (Warwick)
1900 *Dan Leno's Cricket Match*
      (Acres)
1901 *Dan Leno's Day Out*
      (Warwick)
1901 *Dan Leno Musical Director*
      (Warwick)
1902 *Bluebeard*
      (Warwick)
1902 *Dan Leno and Herbert Campbell Edit 'The Sun'*
      (Biograph)

DAN LENO JR (comedian)
1913 *His Father's Voice*
      (Kineplastikon)
1913 *Mrs Kelly*
      (Kineplastikon)

LOTTE LENYA (German cabaret singer)
1962 *The Roman Spring of Mrs Stone*
      (Warner) F
1963 *From Russia With Love*
      (Danjaq) F

LENZA BROTHERS (specialty)
 1925 *Eve's Film Review*

HARRY LEON (singer)
 1961 *Spike Milligan on Treasure Island WC2*
 (British Lion)
 "You Must Have a Heartache"

JACK LEON AND HIS BAND
 1943 *Pathe Pictorial 374*
 "Concerto for Two"

LEON AND LUCETTE (dancers)
 1937 *Pathe Pictorial NS 63*

BILLY LEONARD (comedian)
 1925 *Eve's Film Review 213*
 "Clo-Clo"
 1929 *Pathe Magazine 15*

MISS DEFOREST LEONARD (dancer)
 1908 *Dances*
 (Hepworth)

R. L. LEONARD AND AMELIE DE S.
(dancers)
 1913 *The Society Tango*
 (Selsior)
 1913 *The Maxixe Brasilienne*
 (Selsior)

THE LEROYS (comedy dancers)
 1952 *For Your Entertainment 4*
 (Gaumont)
 "Waltz of the Flowers"
 1964 *Every Day's a Holiday*
 (Grand National) F

DAWN LESLEY (singer)
 1949 *Melody in the Dark*
 (Adelphi) F
 "My Song of Love"

EDDIE LESLIE (comedian)
 1935 *Equity Musical Revue 1*
 (British Lion)
 1948 *That Golf Game*
 (Comet)
 1948 *That Day of Rest*
 (Comet)
 1951 *Lady Godiva Rides Again*
 (London) F
 1953 *Trouble in Store*
 (Two Cities) F
 1956 *Up in the World*
 (Rank) F
 1957 *Just My Luck*
 (Rank) F
 1958 *The Square Peg*
 (Rank) F
 1959 *Follow a Star*
 (Rank) F

 1965 *The Early Bird*
 (Rank) F

ALFRED LESTER (comedian)
 1920 *Around the Town 13*
 (Gaumont)
 "The Eclipse"
 1920 *Around the Town 24*
 (Gaumont)
 "The Shop Girl"

CLAUDE LESTER (comedian)
 1936 *Dodging the Dole*
 (Mancunian) F
 1938 *Music Hall Personalities 5*
 (reissue: *Dodging the Dole*)

**JOHN LESTER AND HIS COWBOY
SYNCOPATERS** (band)
 1927 *Syncopated Melodies*
 (Parkinson)

KETTY LESTER (singer)
 1963 *Just For Fun*
 (Columbia) F
 "Warm Summer Day"

LEVANDA (balancer)
 1932 *Ideal Cinemagazine 332*
 1934 *Pathe Pictorial 848*
 1935 *Pathe Pictorial 910*
 1943 *Pictorial Revue of 1943*
 F (reissue: *Pictorial 910*)

LEVANDA AND VAN (jugglers)
 1952 *For Your Entertainment 1; 2; 3; 4*
 (Gaumont)

ETHEL LEVEY (singer)
 1922 *Around the Town*
 (Gaumont)

PEARL LEVEY (child dancer)
 1930 *Pathetone 12*

BERNARD LEVIN (television personality)
 1963 *Nothing But the Best*
 (Anglo) F

CARROLL LEVIS (discoverer)
 1939 *Discoveries*
 (Vogue) F
 1940 *Pathetone 513*
 1948 *Lucky Mascot*
 (UA) F
 1948 *A Song Is Born*
 (Coal Board)
 1957 *The Depraved*
 (Danziger) F

IAGO LEWIS (singer)
 1906 *The Captain of the Pinafore*
 (Chronophone)

JACK LEWIS'S SINGING SCHOLARS
(juveniles)
  1937 *The Penny Pool*
         (Mancunian) F
         "Hang On To Happiness"

JERRY LEE LEWIS (singer)
  1965 *Be My Guest*
         (Rank) F
         "No One But Me"
  1973 *The London Rock and Roll Show*
         (Pleasant) F

JOHN LEWIS (singer)
  1948 *Lucky Mascot*
         (UA) F
         "Santa Lucia"

LINDA LEWIS (singer)
  1973 *Glastonbury Fayre*
         (Goodtimes) F

NAT LEWIS
see **JOHN RAKER AND NAT LEWIS**

RAY LEWIS AND THE TREKKERS (group)
  1965 *Gonks Go Beat*
         (Anglo) F

SAMMY LEWIS (dancer)
  1930 *The Musical Beauty Shop*
         (PDC)

TESSA LEWIS (striptease)
  1970 *Sweet and Sexy*
         (Miracle) F

VIC LEWIS AND HIS ORCHESTRA
  1948 *A Date With a Dream*
         (Grand National) F
         "Here Comes the Show"
         "You Made Me Mad"
         "Whose Turn Now?"

NOEL LEYLAND (singer)
  1932 *The First Mrs Fraser*
         (Sterling) F

JOHNNY LEYTON (singer)
  1961 *The Johnny Leyton Touch*
         (Viscount)
         "Wild Wind"
         "Son, This Is She"
         "The Beat of a Brother Heart"
         "Taboo"
  1962 *It's Trad Dad*
         (Columbia) F
         "Lonely City"
  1964 *Every Day's a Holiday*
         (Grand National) F
         "All I Want Is You"
         "A Boy Needs a Girl"
         "The Crazy Horse Saloon"

ALVAR LIDDELL (broadcaster)
  1942 *We'll Meet Again*
         (Columbia) F
  1943 *They Met in the Dark*
         (GFD) F
  1945 *I Live in Grosvenor Square*
         (ABP) F
  1946 *School for Secrets*
         (Two Cities) F
  1947 *Life Is Nothing Without Music*
         (Inspiration)
         "Shenandoah"
  1952 *The Voice of Merrill*
         (Eros) F
  1954 *The Love Lottery*
         (Ealing) F
  1963 *It Happened Here*
         (UA) F
  1973 *Adolf Hitler My Part in His Downfall*
         (UA) F

TERRY LIGHTFOOT AND HIS NEW ORLEANS JAZZ BAND
  1962 *It's Trad Dad*
         (Columbia) F
         "There Is a Tavern in the Town"
         "Maryland"
  1985 *Plenty*
         (RKO) F

SUSIE LIGHTNING (striptease)
  1975 *I Don't Want to be Born*
         (Rank) F

LITTLE MISS LILLIAN (toe-dancer)
  1902 *Little Miss Lillian*
         (Warwick)

BEATRICE LILLIE (comedienne)
  1926 *Eve's Film Review 252*
         "Girls of the Old Brigade"
  1930 *Eve's Film Review 486*
         "Charlot's Masquerade"
  1934 *Pathetone 197*
  1938 *Cavalcade of the Stars*
         (Coronel)
  1941 *On Approval*
         (GFD) F
  1943 *Welcome to Britain*
         (Strand)

LILYAN, DANIA AND MALO (dancers)
  1937 *Pathe Pictorial NS 72*
         "Carnival Nights"

MARIANNE LINCOLN (comedienne)
  1944 *Demobbed*
         (Mancunian) F
  1946 *Under New Management*
         (Mancunian) F
  1948 *Honeymoon Hotel*
         (reissue: *Under New Management*)
  1956 *Stars in Your Eyes*
         (British Lion) F

CELIA LIPTON (singer)
1939 *Meet the Ovaltineys*
      (Ovaltine)
1940 *Old Mother Riley in Society*
      (British National) F
1948 *This Was a Woman*
      (TCF) F
1948 *Calling Paul Temple*
      (Butcher) F
      "Lady on the Loose"
1952 *The Tall Headlines*
      (Grand National) F

DANNY LIPTON AND HIS MILITAIRES
(dancers)
1941 *Pathe Pictorial 274*

DANNY LIPTON TRIO (dancers)
1935 *Pathe Pictorial 915*
      "Round About Regent Street"
1937 *Pathe Pictorial NS 68*
      "Never Say Never Again Again"
1937 *Pathetone Parade of 1938*
      F (reissue: *Pictorial 915*)
1938 *Pathe Pictorial NS 98*
      "Running Wild"
1939 *Pathe Pictorial NS 184*
      "Hornpipe Song"

SIDNEY LIPTON AND HIS BAND
1937 *Let's Make a Night of It*
      (ABPC) F

EMMANUEL LIST (bass)
1928 *Phototone 8*
      "Asleep in the Deep"
1928 *Phototone 10*
      "In Cellar Cool"

EVE LISTER (singer)
1936 *Here and There*
      (Baxter)

MONIA LITER (violinist)
1946 *Lisbon Story*
      (British National) F

GORDON LITTLE (singer)
1936 *Shipmates o' Mine*
      (Butcher) F
1936 *Rhythm of the Road*
      (Ford) ADVERT
      "Rhythm of the Road"
1938 *On Velvet*
      (AIP) F
1940 *Hullo Fame*
      (British Films) F

LENORE LITTLE (striptease)
1972 *The Love Box*
      (Eagle) F

STAN LITTLE
see **STAN PELL AND STAN LITTLE**

LITTLE DOREEN
see **DOREEN**

LITTLE RICHARD (singer)
1973 *The London Rock and Roll Show*
      (Pleasant) F

LITTLE TICH (comedian)
1920 *Around the Town 17*
      (Gaumont)

LITTLEWOODS' GIRLS CHOIR
1952 *New Pictorial 419*
      "Greensleeves"
1953 *New Pictorial 458*
      "At the End of the Day"

BOB LIVELY (singer)
1934 *Pathetone 247*
      "I Found a New Moon"
1935 *In Town Tonight*
      (British Lion) F
1936 *British Lion Varieties 6*
      "I Found a New Moon"

ALICE LLOYD (singer)
1935 *Royal Cavalcade*
      (BIP) F
      "I Can't Forget the Days When I
      Was Young"

JIMMY LLOYD (singer)
1958 *6.5 Special*
      (Anglo) F
      "Ever Since I Met Lucy"

MARIE LLOYD (singer)
1898 *Marie Lloyd an Animated Portrait*
      (Warwick)
1909 *Marie Lloyd's Little Joke*
      (Urban)
1913 *Marie Lloyd at Home and Bunkered*
      (Magnet)

MARIE LLOYD JUNIOR (singer)
1926 *Marie Lloyd Junior*
      (Phonofilm)
1936 *Old Timers*
      (Warner)
      "One of the Ruins Cromwell
      Knocked About a Bit""
1936 *Pal o' Mine*
      (RKO) F
1943 *Variety Jubilee*
      (Butcher) F
      "A Little of What You Fancy"
1944 *Highlights of Variety 26*
      (reissue: *Variety Jubilee*)
1946 *Those Were the Days*
      (reissue: *Variety Jubilee*)
1948 *For Old Times Sake*
      (reissue: *Variety Jubilee*)

LLOYD BROTHERS (acrobats)
1901   *The Lloyd Brothers Double Rope Act*
        (Warwick)

DAVID LOBER (dancer)
1950   *New Pictorial 314*
        "Peanut Polka"
1951   *Happy Go Lovely*
        (ABP) F
        "Piccadilly Ballet"

LOCARNO FOUR (acrobatic dancers)
1931   *Eve's Film Review 531*
1932   *Gaumont Sound Mirror 72*
1933   *Pathe Pictorial 772*
        "Ballet from Faust"
1937   *Pathetone Parade of 1938*
        F (reissue: *Pictorial 772*)

JOSEF LOCKE (Irish baritone)
1948   *Holidays With Pay*
        (Mancunian) F
        "I'll Take You Home Again Kathleen"
        "Moonlight and a Prairie Sky"
1949   *Somewhere in Politics*
        (Mancunian) F
        "Violetta"
        "Oft in the Stilly Night"
        "Macushla"
1949   *What a Carry On*
        (Mancunian) F
        "Goodbye"
        "Ave Maria"
        "Abide With Me"
1991   *Hear My Song*
        (Palace) F
        "Hear My Song Violetta"
        "I'll Take You Home Again Kathleen"
        "Blaze Away"
        "Count Your Blessings"
        "Come Back to Sorrento"
        "Goodbye"

HERBERT LODGE
see **LESLIE BRIDGEWATER AND HERBERT LODGE**

JIMMY LOGAN (Scottish comedian)
1949   *Floodtide*
        (GFD) F
1963   *The Wild Affair*
        (7 Arts) F
1972   *Carry On Abroad*
        (Rank) F
1973   *Carry On Girls*
        (Rank) F

MORRIS LOGAN TRIO (musicians)
1938   *Vanity Ware*
        (Ace Cinemagazine)
        "Stardust"

NANCY LOGAN (singer)
1937   *Getting the Bird*
        (Ace Cinemagazine)
        "Each Hour of Every Day"

CHRISTOPHER LOGUE (poet)
1965   *Wholly Communion*
        (Lorrimer)
1971   *The Devils*
        (Warner) F
1977   *Jabberwocky*
        (Columbia) F
1982   *Moonlighting*
        (White) F

LOLA AND LUIS (dancers)
1927   *The Arcadians*
        (Gaumont) F

LOLITA AND CORTEZ (dancers)
1924   *Eve's Film Review 184*
        "Wildflower"
1926   *Eve's Film Review 251*
        "Romany Tango"

LONDON ACCORDION BAND
1932   *Pathetone 121*
1933   *Pathe Pictorial 781*
        "Bohemian Memories"

LONDON AMATEUR ORCHESTRA
1939   *Pathe Pictorial NS 154*
        "Gopak"

LONDON BRASS BAND
1935   *Play Up the Band*
        (City) F

LONDON CASINO DANCERS
1948   *Easy Money*
        (Gainsborough) F

LONDON FESTIVAL BALLET
1980   *Nijinsky*
        (Paramount) F

LONDON FOUR (singers)
1927   *The London Four*
        (Phonofilm)

LONDON PHILHARMONIC ORCHESTRA
1936   *Whom the Gods Love*
        (ATP) F
        "Marriage of Figaro"
        "The Magic Flute"
1943   *Battle for Music*
        (Strand) F
        "Tristan and Isolde"
        "Romeo and Juliet"
        "Princess Jaune"
        "Cockaigne Overture"
        "Piano Concerto No. 2"
        "Mozart's 10th Symphony"
        "La Colinda"

"Beethoven's Fifth Symphony"
"Carnival Romain"
"Pomp and Circumstance"

LONDON RADIO DANCE BAND
see **SIDNEY FIRMAN AND THE LONDON RADIO DANCE BAND**

LONDON SYMPHONY ORCHESTRA
1935   *B.B.C. the Voice of Britain*
        (New Era) F
1937   *Dreaming Lips*
        (UA) F
        "Concerto in D Major"
1943   *I'll Walk Beside You*
        (Butcher) F
        "Die Fledermaus"
        "Fingal's Cave"
1945   *For You Alone*
        (Butcher) F
        "Merry Wives of Windsor"
        "Tales from the Vienna Woods"
1946   *I'll Turn To You*
        (Butcher) F
1946   *Musical Masquerade*
        (Inspiration)
1946   *Instruments of the Orchestra*
        (Crown)
        "Variations on a Fugue"
1952   *Giselle*
        (Exclusive)
        "Giselle"
1952   *Trent's Last Case*
        (Wilcox) F

LONDON WELSH ASSOCIATION CHORAL SOCIETY
1953   *Valley of Song*
        (ABPC) F
        "Land of My Fathers"
        "Sospen Bach"
        "All Through the Night"
        "Loudly Proclaim" (Messiah)

NORMAN LONG (comedy singer)
1929   *Pathe Magazine 4*
1932   *Pathetone 109*
        "The Barrers in the Walworth Road"
1932   *The New Hotel*
        (PDC) F
1932   *Pathetone 126*
        "Under the Bazunka Tree"
1933   *Pathe Pictorial 784*
1934   *Pathetone 200*
        "When Chelsea Won the Cup"
1934   *Pathetone 238*
        "Firty Fahsand Quid"
1935   *Pathe Pictorial 900*
        "'Oles"
1935   *Royal Cavalcade*
        (BIP) F
        "Down in Our Village in Somerset"
1936   *Pathetone Parade of 1936*
        F (reissue: *Pathetone 238*)

1936   *Pathetone 331*
        "The Bus Conductor"
1937   *Pathe Pictorial NS 76*
        "When Your Television Set Comes Home"
1937   *Starlight Parade*
        (Viking)
1937   *Pathetone Parade of 1938*
        F (reissue: *Pathetone 331*)
1939   *Pathe Pictorial NS 172*
        "Working for the Mayor and Corporation"
1939   *Pathetone Parade of 1940*
        F (reissue: *Pictorial 76*)

LONG AND THE SHORT (group)
1965   *Gonks Go Beat*
        (Anglo) F
        "Take This Train"

LOOT (group)
1995   *Brothers in Trouble*
        (Renegade) F
        "You Really Got Me"

SANTIAGO LOPEZ AND HIS RUMBA BAND
1946   *New Pictorial 118*
1947   *New Pictorial 142*
        "Rumba Batumba"

LYDIA LOPOKOVA (dancer)
1929   *Dark Red Roses*
        (BSFP) F

VIOLET LORAINE (singer)
1920   *Around the Town 8*
        (Gaumont)
        "Eastward Ho"
1926   *Ideal Cinemagazine*
1933   *Britannia of Billingsgate*
        (Gaumont) F
        "Let the World Go Drifting By"
        "There'll Still Be Love"
        "How Does a Fresh Fish Wish?"
        "Piccadilly Playground"
1934   *Road House*
        (Gaumont) F
        "What a Little Moonlight Can Do"
        "Don't You Cry When We Say Goodbye"
        "Let the Great Big World Keep Turning"
1937   *The King's People*
        (Warner)
        "If You Were the Only Girl in the World"
1939   *Pathe Gazette 93*
        "If You Were the Only Girl in the World"

EDITH LORAND (singer)
1931   *Pathetone 64*

JON LORD (musician)
1985   *Water*
        (Rank) F

JACK LORENTZ (impressionist)
1939   *Pathe Pictorial NS 163*
        (as Syd Walker)

MARIO 'HARP' LORENZI (harpist)
1933   *Radio Parade*
        (BIP) F
1939   *Pathe Pictorial NS 178*
        "Highland Swing"
1940   *Pathe Pictorial 244*
        "Medley"
1942   *Pathe Pictorial 306*
1947   *New Pictorial 122*
1947   *New Pictorial 143*
        "Tico Tico"

TOMMY LORNE (comedian)
1927   *Tommy Lorne and Dumplings*
        (Phonofilm)
1927   *The Lard Song*
        (Phonofilm)

VYVYAN LORRAYNE (ballet dancer)
1967   *Opus*
        (COI)

TILLY LOSCH (dancer)
1936   *Limelight*
        (Wilcox) F
        "Nirewana"
        "Wine Women and Song"

JOE LOSS AND HIS ORCHESTRA
1936   *British Lion Varieties 1*
        "Love Is Like a Cigarette"
        "The Wheel of the Wagon"
1936   *British Lion Varieties 2*
        "Treasure Island"
1936   *British Lion Varieties 3*
        "For You Madonna"
1936   *British Lion Varieties 5*
        "My Shadow's Where My Sweetheart
        Used to Be"
1936   *British Lion Varieties 7*
        "My Heart Wouldn't Beat Again"
1936   *British Lion Varieties 8*
        "White Heat"
1936   *British Lion Varieties 10*
        "The General's Fast Asleep"
        "Heads or Tails"
1937   *Pathe Pictorial NS 63*
        "Let's Dance"
1937   *Let's Make a Night of It*
        (ABPC) F
1939   *Pathe Pictorial NS 162*
        "Rhythm in the Alphabet"
1949   *Sports Serenade*
        (ABFD)
1965   *The Mood Man*
        (Baim)
        "In the Mood"

ERNIE LOTINGA (comedian)
1928   *The Raw Recruit*
        (Phonofilm)
1928   *The Orderly Room*
        (Phonofilm)
1928   *Nap*
        (BSFP)
1928   *Joining Up*
        (BSFP)
1929   *Josser KC*
        (BSFP)
1929   *Doing His Duty*
        (BSFP)
1929   *Spirits*
        (BSFP)
1929   *Accidental Treatment*
        (BSFP)
1931   *Pathetone 56*
        "My Wife's Family"
1931   *P. C. Josser*
        (Gainsborough) F
1931   *Dr Josser KC*
        (BIP) F
1932   *Josser Joins the Navy*
        (BIP) F
1932   *Josser on the River*
        (BIP) F
1932   *Josser in the Army*
        (BIP) F
1934   *Josser on the Farm*
        (Fox) F
1935   *Smith's Wives*
        (Fox) F
1936   *Love Up the Pole*
        (Butcher) F

DENNIS LOTIS (singer)
1956   *The Extra Day*
        (British Lion) F
        "The Extra Day"
        "There's a Time and a Place"
1956   *It's a Wonderful World*
        (Renown) F
        "When You Came Along"
        "Rosanne"
        "Girls Girls Girls"
        "A Few Kisses Ago"
1958   *The Golden Disc*
        (Butcher) F
        "I'm Gonna Wrap You Up"
1958   *Pathe Pictorial 160*
1959   *Make Mine a Million*
        (British Lion) F
1960   *City of the Dead*
        (British Lion) F
1962   *She'll Have To Go*
        (Anglo) F
1962   *What Every Woman Wants*
        (Danziger) F

LOTTO, LILLO AND OTTO (trick cyclists)
1900   *Clever and Comic Cycle Act*
        (Williamson)
1903   *Diavolo's Dilemma*
        (Paul)

LUCY LOUPE (dancer)
1937 *Carry On London*
(Ace) F

COURTNEY LOVE (singer)
1986 *Sid and Nancy*
(Zenith) F
1986 *Straight to Hell*
(Island) F

GEOFF LOVE (conductor)
1963 *It's All Happening*
(British Lion) F

ALAN LOVEDAY (violin)
1954 *In Melodious Mood*
(Paramount)

LOW AND WEBSTER (comedians)
1936 *Pathe Pictorial NS 11*

ANITA LOWE (singer)
1935 *Variety*
(Butcher) F
"Lassie from Lancashire"
1937 *Highlights of Variety 3*
(reissue: *Variety*)

LEN AND BILL LOWE (comedians)
1948 *A Date With a Dream*
(Grand National) F
1949 *Melody Club*
(Eros) F

TONY LOWRY AND CLIVE RICHARDSON
(pianists)
1944 *My Ain Folk*
(Butcher) F
"The Campbells Are Coming"
"Eightsome Reel"
1952 *For Your Entertainment 1; 2; 3; 4*
(Gaumont)

ARTHUR LUCAN AND KITTY McSHANE
(comedy)
1936 *Stars On Parade*
(Butcher) F
1937 *Kathleen Mavourneen*
(Butcher) F
1937 *Old Mother Riley*
(Butcher) F
1938 *Old Mother Riley in Paris*
(Butcher) F
1939 *Old Mother Riley MP*
(Butcher) F
1939 *Old Mother Riley Joins Up*
(Butcher) F
1940 *The Return of Old Mother Riley*
(reissue: *Old Mother Riley*)
1940 *Old Mother Riley in Business*
(British National) F
1940 *Old Mother Riley in Society*
(British National) F
1941 *Old Mother Riley's Ghosts*
(British National) F

1941 *Old Mother Riley's Circus*
(British National) F
"A Tear, a Smile, a Sigh"
1941 *The Original Old Mother Riley*
(reissue: *Old Mother Riley*)
1942 *Old Mother Riley Catches a Quisling*
(reissue: *Old Mother Riley in Paris*)
1943 *Old Mother Riley Detective*
(British National) F
1943 *Old Mother Riley Overseas*
(British National) F
1945 *Old Mother Riley at Home*
(British National) F
1949 *Old Mother Riley's New Venture*
(Renown) F
"Galway Bay"
1950 *Old Mother Riley Headmistress*
(Renown) F
1951 *Old Mother Riley's Jungle Treasure*
(Renown) F
1952 *Mother Riley Meets the Vampire*
(Renown) F (Lucan only)

JONATHAN LUCAS (dancer)
1951 *Happy Go Lovely*
(ABP) F
"Piccadilly Ballet"

CLAIRE LUCE (singer)
1937 *Let's Make a Night of It*
(ABPC) F
"Said the Spider to the Fly"
"Havana"
1937 *Over She Goes*
(ABPC) F
"I Breathe on Windows"
1937 *Mademoiselle Docteur*
(UA) F
"Remember Me"

LUCERNE SKATERS
1940 *Showtime*
(Viking)

LUCIENNE AND ASHOUR (adagio)
1933 *Pathetone 167*
"La Midinette"
1937 *Okay For Sound*
(Gainsborough) F

LUCILLE AND FRANK (dancers)
1937 *Pathetone 391*
"St Louis Blues"

OLIVE LUCIUS (singer)
1948 *Noose*
(Pathe) F
"When Love Has Passed You By"

ANNA LUDMILLA (dancer)
1930 *Alf's Button*
(Gaumont) F
"Scheherazade"

LULU (singer)
1966   *To Sir With Love*
        (Columbia) F
        "To Sir With Love"
        "Off and Running"
        "Stealing My Love from Me"
        "It's Getting Harder All the Time"
1972   *The Cherry Picker*
        (Rank) F

LULU AND THE LUVVERS (group)
1964   *UK Swings Again*
        (Baim)
        "Shout"
1965   *Gonks Go Beat*
        (Anglo) F
        "Choc Ice"
        "The Only One"

DONYALE LUNA (model)
1967   *Tonite Let's All Make Love in
        London*
        (Lorrimer) F

LUNA BOYS (buskers)
1938   *St Martin's Lane*
        (ABPC) F
        "Shine On Harvest Moon"

TED LUNE (comedian)
1959   *The Lady Is a Square*
        (ABPC) F
1967   *Berserk*
        (Columbia) F

BARRY LUPINO (comedian)
1931   *Eve's Film Review 523*
        "The Millionaire Kid"
1931   *Never Trouble Trouble*
        (PDC) F
1933   *Song Birds*
        (BIP) F
1934   *Master and Man*
        (BIP) F
1934   *Bagged*
        (BIP) F
1934   *Wishes*
        (BIP) F
1936   *Bed and Breakfast*
        (West) F
1937   *The Sky's the Limit*
        (GFD) F
1940   *Garrison Follies*
        (Butcher) F
1945   *What Do We Do Now?*
        (Grand National) F

MARK LUPINO (comedian)
1928   *The Tallyman*
        (Homeland)

STANLEY LUPINO (comedian)
1920   *Around the Town 9*
        (Gaumont)

1922   *Around the Town*
        (Gaumont)
1922   *Eve's Film Review 70*
        "Phi-Phi"
1924   *Eve's Film Review 139*
        "Puppets"
1929   *Eve's Film Review 410*
        "Love"
1931   *Love Lies*
        (BIP) F
1931   *The Love Race*
        (BIP) F
1932   *Sleepless Nights*
        (BIP) F
        "I Don't Want to Go to Bed"
1933   *King of the Ritz*
        (Gaumont) F
1933   *Pathetone 156*
        "My Awful Past"
1933   *Facing the Music*
        (BIP) F
        "Oh What a Girl"
        "Let Me Gaze"
        "Light as Air"
1933   *You Made Me Love You*
        (BIP) F
        "Miss Whatshername"
        "Why Can't We?"
1934   *Happy*
        (BIP) F
        "Happy"
        "There's So Much I'm Wanting to
        Tell You"
1935   *Honeymoon for Three*
        (Gaiety) F
        "Make Hay While the Moon Shines"
        "I'll Build a Fence Around You"
        "Why Not Madame?"
1936   *Cheer Up*
        (ABFD) F
        "Cheer Up"
        "There's a Star in the Sky"
        "London Town"
1936   *Sporting Love*
        (British Lion) F
        "Living in Clover"
        "In the Springtime"
        "I Lift Up My Finger"
        "After the Ball"
        "It's Derby Day"
1937   *Over She Goes*
        (ABPC) F
        "Over She Goes"
        "Side By Side"
        "Country Wedding"
1938   *Hold My Hand*
        (ABPC) F
        "Hold My Hand"
        "Turn on the Love Light"
        "Spring Time"
1939   *Lucky To Me*
        (ABPC) F

LINDA LUSARDI (model)
  1988 *Consuming Passions*
      (Vestron) F

LUTON BRASS BAND
  1932 *The Mayor's Nest*
      (B&D) F

LUTON GIRLS' CHOIR
  1950 *Old Mother Riley Headmistress*
      (Renown) F
      "Count Your Blessings"
      "I Heard a Robin Singing"
      "Till All Your Dreams Come True"

LUTON SILVER PRIZE BAND
  1931 *Up for the Cup*
      (B&D) F
  1932 *It's a King*
      (B&D) F
  1933 *General John Regan*
      (B&D) F
  1934 *The Queen's Affair*
      (B&D) F
  1935 *Where's George?*
      (B&D) F
      "My Girl's a Yorkshire Girl"
      "Lassie from Lancashire"

JOE LYNCH (comedian)
  1961 *Johnny Nobody*
      (Columbia) F

KENNY LYNCH (singer)
(films as actor not listed)
  1963 *Just For Fun*
      (Columbia) F
      "Crazy Crazes"
      "Monument"
  1964 *Dr Terror's House of Horrors*
      (Amicus) F
      "Everybody's Got Love"
      "Give Me Love"

DAVE LYNN (drag comedian)
  1995 *Beautiful Thing*
      (World) F

LENI LYNN (soprano)
  1944 *Heaven Is Round the Corner*
      (British National) F
      "Heaven Is Round the Corner"
  1944 *Give Me the Stars*
      (British National) F
      "Throughout the Years"
  1946 *Spring Song*
      (British National) F
      "I Love the Moon"
      "Little Grey Home in the West"
  1946 *Gaiety George*
      (Embassy) F
      "Awake Awake"
      "One Love"

VERA LYNN (singer)
  1936 *British Lion Varieties 1*
      "Love Is Like a Cigarette"
  1936 *British Lion Varieties 7*
      "My Heart Wouldn't Beat Again"
  1941 *Gaumont British News 833*
      "Christmas Greetings to Forces
      Everywhere"
  1942 *We'll Meet Again*
      (Columbia) F
      "We'll Meet Again"
      "You'll Never Know"
      "Be Like the Kettle and Sing"
      "Yours Sincerely"
      "After the Rain"
  1943 *Rhythm Serenade*
      (Columbia) F
      "The Sunshine of Your Smile"
      "Home Sweet Home Again"
      "I Love to Sing"
      "It Doesn't Cost a Dime"
      "Bye and Bye"
      "So It Goes On"
      "With All My Heart"
  1944 *One Exciting Night*
      (Columbia) F
      "It's Like Old Times"
      "There's a New World"
      "One Love"
      "My Prayer"
  1946 *New Pictorial 107*
  1951 *New Pictorial 335*
      "My Love For You"
  1954 *Behind the Scenes 4*
      (Gas) ADVERT

GILLIAN LYNNE (dancer)
  1953 *The Master of Ballantrae*
      (Warner) F
  1959 *Make Mine a Million*
      (British Lion) F

THE GILLIAN LYNNE DANCERS
  1964 *Every Day's a Holiday*
      (Grand National) F

HUMPHREY LYTTELTON (trumpeter)
  1950 *New Pictorial 302*
      "Come On and Stomp"
  1955 *Your Sunday Newspaper*
      (CWS) F
  1956 *It's Great To Be Young*
      (ABPC) F
  1957 *The Tommy Steele Story*
      (Anglo) F
      "Bermondsey Bounce"
  1964 *Jazz All the Way*
      (Rank)

PIANO SELECTION

Words and Music by
SAM LERNER,
AL GOODHART
and
AL HOFFMAN

JESSIE MATTHEWS
.. in ..
"GANGWAY"
.. with ..
BARRY MACKAY,
NAT PENDLETON
•
A GAUMONT-BRITISH PICTURE
DIRECTED BY
SONNIE HALE.

GAUMONT
BRITISH
PICTURES

3/-

Cinephonic Music Co., Ltd.
DEAN HOUSE,
2, 3 & 4, DEAN STREET,
W.1.

MOON OR NO MOON . . . . . 6d. net
LORD AND LADY WHOOZIS . . . 6d. net
GANGWAY . . . . 6d. net
WHEN YOU GOTTA SING
YOU GOTTA SING 6d. net
PIANO SELECTION . . . . . . 1/- net

THE M 6 (group)
1966 *The Ghost Goes Gear*
(Pathe) F

EVELYN McCABE (singer)
1948 *A Song for Tomorrow*
(GFD) F
"Danny Boy"
"Abide With Me"

JAMES McCAFFERTY (Irish tenor)
1932 *The Hills of Donegal*
(Heale)
1932 *The Meeting of the Waters*
(Heale)
1932 *The Blue Hills of Antrim*
(Heale)
1932 *The Green Isles of Erin*
(Heale)

ARCHIE McCAIG (Scottish comedian)
1930 *Amateur Night in London*
(PDC) F

JOCK McCARTHY (Scottish singer)
1937 *Capital Tea*
(Ace Cinemagazine)

LINDA McCARTNEY (singer)
1982 *The Cooler*
(UIP)
1984 *Give My Regards to Broad Street*
(UK) F
"Not Such a Bad Boy"
"No Values"
"Ballroom Dancing"
"Silly Love Songs"
"So Bad"

PAUL McCARTNEY (singer)
see also **THE BEATLES**
1980 *Breaking Glass*
(GTO) F
1982 *The Cooler*
(UIP)
1984 *Give My Regards to Broad Street*
(UK) F
"Yesterday"
"Here, There and Everywhere"
"Wanderlust"
"Not Such a Bad Boy"
"No Values"
"Ballroom Dancing"
"Silly Love Songs"
"So Bad"
"For No One"
"Eleanor Rigby"
"Long and Winding Road"
"No More Lonely Nights"
1987 *Eat the Rich*
(Comic Strip) F

PAUL AND LINDA McCARTNEY (singers)
1991 *Get Back*
(Front Page) F

"Band on the Run"
"Rough Ride"
"Put It There"
"This One"
"Coming Up"
"Live and Let Die"
"Got to Get You Into My Life"
"Long and Winding Road"
"Fool on the Hill"
"Sergeant Pepper"
"Good Day Sunshine"
"I Saw Her Standing There"
"Eleanor Rigby"
"Back in the USSR"
"Can't Buy Me Love"
"Let It Be"
"Hey Jude"
"Yesterday"
"Get Back"
"Golden Slumbers"
"Carry That Weight"
"The End"
"Birthday"

JUNE McCOMB (conjurer)
1952 *New Pictorial 378*
1953 *New Pictorial 440*

CAL McCORD (comedian)
1934 *Pathetone 225*
1960 *Too Young to Love*
(Rank) F
1960 *Never Take Sweets From a Stranger*
(Hammer) F
1969 *The Adding Machine*
(Universal) F

JOHN McCORMACK (Irish tenor)
1937 *Wings of the Morning*
(Fox) F
"Killarney"
"Come Back to Erin"
"Those Endearing Young Charms"
"At the Dawning of the Day"

PAT McCORMACK (Irish tenor)
1938 *Around the Town*
(British Lion) F

MOYA McCRACKEN (organ)
1933 *Pathe Pictorial 171*

DEREK McCULLOCH (broadcaster)
1943 *B.B.C. Brains Trust 1; 2*
(Strand)

GENE McDANIELS (singer)
1962 *It's Trad Dad*
(Columbia) F
"Another Tear Falls"

ROBERT McDERMOTT (broadcaster)
1956 *Who Done It?*
(Ealing) F

CHAS McDEVITT SKIFFLE GROUP
1957 *The Tommy Steele Story*
(Anglo) F
"Freight Train"
1958 *The Golden Disc*
(Butcher) F
"Johnny O"

MALCOLM MacEACHERN (bass)
see also **FLOTSAM AND JETSAM**
1931 *Pathetone 88*
"Only an Old Rough Diamond"
1934 *Chu Chin Chow*
(Gainsborough) F
"Chu Chin Chow of China"
"Behold Behold"
"Olive Oil"
1937 *Calling All Stars*
(British Lion) F
"The Changing of the Guard"
1940 *Pathe Pictorial 255*
"Convoy"
1941 *Pathe Pictorial 287*
"Spread Your Wings"
1942 *We'll Smile Again*
(British National) F
"Temple Song"
1944 *Pathe Pictorial 418*
"The Changing of the Guard"

IAN McELHINNEY (Scottish singer)
1995 *Small Faces*
(Skyline) F
"Cod Liver Oil"
"When I Leave Old Glasgow
Behind"

ELSA MacFARLANE (singer)
see also **THE CO-OPTIMISTS**
1926 *London's Famous Cabarets*
(Parkinson)
"Metropole Midnight Follies"
1929 *The Co-Optimists*
(New Era) F
"Down Love Lane"

ALEC McGILL (comedian)
1931 *Pathetone 72*
(with Gwen Vaughan)
1932 *Pathetone 105*
(with Charles Hayes)
1937 *Pathe Pictorial NS 73*
(with Fred Yule)

ROGER McGOUGH (poet)
see also **SCAFFOLD**
1972 *Plod*
(Crown)

TERENCE McGOVERN AND HIS NOVELTY ORCHESTRA
1933 *Musical Film Revue*
(British Lion) S
"How're We Doing?"

"Nobody's Sweetheart"
"Pagan Love Song"
"Tiger Rag"
1935 *Equity Musical Revue Series*
(British Lion)
"It's the Same Old World"
"Crazy People"

SHANE MacGOWAN (singer)
1986 *Straight to Hell*
(Island) F
1987 *Eat the Rich*
(Comic Strip) F

MacGREGOR AND WEST (comedians)
1942 *Pathe Pictorial 310*
1942 *Pathe Pictorial 319*
1942 *Pathe Pictorial 340*
1943 *Pathe Pictorial 367*
1943 *Pathe Pictorial 380*
1943 *Pathe Pictorial 404*
1944 *Pathe Pictorial 431*

BILL McGUFFIE (pianist)
1955 *Cyril Stapleton and the Show Band*
(Hammer)
1960 *The Challenge*
(Alliance) F
"The Challenge"

SCOTTY (ALASTAIR) McHARG (singer)
1946 *London Town*
(GFD) F
"Any Way the Wind Blows"

FLORENCE McHUGH (singer)
1931 *Romany Love*
(MGM) F

JOHN McHUGH (tenor)
1939 *Pathe Pictorial NS 149*
1943 *I'll Walk Beside You*
(Butcher) F
"I'll Walk Beside You"
"Passing By"
1946 *I'll Turn To You*
(Butcher) F
"I'll Turn To You"
"Liebestraum"

KEN MacINTOSH AND HIS BAND
1955 *An Alligator Named Daisy*
(Rank) F
"Midnight Madness"
"Your First Love"
"The Crocodile Crawl"
"In Love for the Very First Time"

JOCK McKAY (Scottish comedian)
1930 *Pathetone 21*
"Bye Bye Blackbird"
1932 *Ideal Cinemagazine 306*
1933 *Television Follies*
(English) F
"Secretive Sarah"

1935 *Rolling Home*
(Sound City) F
1935 *Blue Smoke*
(Fox) F
1936 *King of Hearts*
(Butcher) F
1937 *Underneath the Arches*
(Twickenham) F
1937 *Museum Mystery*
(Paramount) F
1937 *Said O'Reilly to McNab*
(Gainsborough) F
1952 *The Brave Don't Cry*
(ABFD) F

NEIL McKAY (singer)
1935 *Lieutenant Daring RN*
(Butcher) F
"Off to Philadelphia"

THE MacKAY TWINS (THE TWO MacKAYS) (tap-dancers)
1935 *Jimmy Boy*
(Baxter) F
1935 *She Shall Have Music*
(Twickenham) F
"The Runaround"

HELEN McKAYE (singer)
1940 *A Postal Packet*
(British Lion)

MIKE McKENZIE (singer)
1978 *The Stickup*
(Backstage) F
"Friend of Mine"

NINA MAE McKINNEY (singer)
1934 *Kentucky Minstrels*
(Realart) F
"I'm in Love with the Band"
1935 *B.B.C. the Voice of Britain*
(New Era) F
"Dinah"
1935 *Sanders of the River*
(London) F
"My Little Black Dove"
1938 *On Velvet*
(AIP) F
"Swanee River"

MCKOY (group)
1996 *Glastonbury: The Movie*
(Starlight) F
"Fight For Your Rights"

ALICK McLEAN (Scottish comedian)
1932 *Pathetone 119*
"A Nice Quiet Day"

KITTY AND MARIETTA McLEOD (mouth musicians)
1935 *Rob Roy the Highland Rogue*
(Disney) F

TEX McLEOD (comedian)
1922 *Around the Town*
(Gaumont)
1926 *Eve's Film Review 249*
1931 *Pathetone 65*
"Song of Swanee"
1932 *Pathetone 139*
(with Marjorie Tiller)
1933 *Radio Parade*
(BIP) F
1940 *Pathetone 511*
"Whoopee"
1942 *Pathe Pictorial 343*

GRAHAM McPHERSON
see "**SUGGS**"

IAN McPHERSON (Scottish singer)
1936 *Pathe Pictorial NS 23*
"Road to the Isles"

SANDY MacPHERSON (organ)
1939 *Pathetone 463*
"Any Broken Hearts to Mend"
1941 *Pathetone Parade of 1941*
F (reissue: *Pathetone 463*)
1941 *The Common Touch*
(British National) F
1946 *I'll Turn To You*
(Butcher) F
"I'll Turn To You"

STEWART MacPHERSON (broadcaster)
1947 *I'll Leave It To You*
(Butcher)
1950 *Twenty Questions Murder Mystery*
(Grand National) F
1952 *Murder On the Air*
F (reissue: *Twenty Questions Murder Mystery*)

W. MacQUEEN POPE (broadcaster)
1936 *Limelight*
(Wilcox) F

KITTY McSHANE
see **ARTHUR LUCAN AND KITTY McSHANE**

JAMES McSHERRY (trick golf)
1936 *Pathe Pictorial NS 1*

RAY McVAY BAND
1992 *Leon the Pig Farmer*
(Electric) F
"Simon Tov"
"Asher Bara"
"Have Nagila"

MA FU (Chinese juggler)
1939 *Pathetone 484*
1941 *Pathetone Parade of 1941*
F (reissue: *Pathetone 484*)

ANNA MAC (bell ringer)
1938   *Pathe Pictorial NS 93*
        "The Belle with the Bells"
1939   *Pathe Pictorial NS 145*
        "Waltz"

MACARI AND HIS DUTCH SERENADERS
(band)
1934   *Music Hall*
        (Realart)
        "By the Side of the Zuyder Zee"
1937   *The Penny Pool*
        (Mancunian) F
        "Harbour Lights"
1939   *Music Hall Parade*
        (Butcher) F
        "Tulip Time"
        "Le Touquet"
1940   *Cavalcade of Variety*
        (reissue: *Music Hall Parade*)
1943   *Highlights of Variety*
        (reissue: *Music Hall Parade*)

MACARI BROTHERS (accordionists)
1931   *Ideal Cinemagazine 293*

**ERNIE MACK AND THE SATURATED
SEVEN** (group)
1971   *Gumshoe*
        (Columbia) F

JOE MACK (singer)
1906   *Strolling Home with Angelina*
        (Chronophone)

PERCIVAL MACKEY (piano)
1929   *The Percival Mackey Trio*
        (BSFP)
1941   *Pathetone 562*
1943   *Pathetone Revue of 1943*
        (reissue: *Pathetone 562*)

PERCIVAL MACKEY AND HIS BAND
1933   *Pathetone 154*
        "Millions of Kisses"
1933   *This Is the Life*
        (British Lion) F
1934   *Death at Broadcasting House*
        (Phoenix) F
1935   *Honeymoon for Three*
        (Gaiety) F
1936   *Cheer Up*
        (ABFD) F
1937   *The Minstrel Boy*
        (Butcher) F
        "Moonlight Madonna"
        "Sweet Muchacha"
1938   *Mountains o' Mourne*
        (Butcher) F
        "The Mountains o' Mourne"
        "Kerry Dance"
        "Dear Little Shamrock"
1938   *Just Picture It*
        (Ace Cinemagazine)

1938   *Getting Down to Cases*
        (Ace Cinemagazine)
1939   *Pathe Pictorial 189*
        "Roses of Picardy"
1940   *Garrison Follies*
        (Butcher) F
        "Sweet Sue"
1940   *Somewhere in England*
        (Mancunian) F
        "Somewhere in England"
1941   *Facing the Music*
        (Butcher) F
1942   *Somewhere on Leave*
        (Mancunian) F
        "Somewhere on Leave"
        "Boy Meets Girl"
1946   *Under New Management*
        (Mancunian) F
        "Fraternise"
        "Little Sprig of Shamrock"
1948   *Honeymoon Hotel*
        (reissue: *Under New Management*)

HUGHES MACKLIN (tenor)
1930   *Pathe Magazine 34*
        "Sylvia"
1934   *Lily of Killarney*
        (Twickenham) F

FRANCIS MADDOX (entertainer)
1938   *Pathetone 408*

HELENE MADISON (dancer)
1931   *Pathetone 74*

MADNESS (group)
1981   *Dance Craze*
        (Osiris) F
        "The Prince"
        "Razor Blade Alley"
        "Madness"
        "One Step Beyond"
        "Night Boat to Cairo"
1981   *Take It Or Leave It*
        (GTO) F

MADONNA (American singer)
1986   *Shanghai Surprise*
        (Handmade) F

MAESTRO SINGERS (quartette)
1931   *Motley and Melody*
        (Warner)
1931   *Pathe Pictorial 715*
        "I Did Not Know"
1931   *Pathetone 49*
        "Swinging in a Hammock"
1934   *Pathetone 244*
        "Where the Mountains Meet the
        Sea"

MAGAZINE (group)
1981   *Urgh! A Music War*
        (White) F
        "Model Worker"

MAGIC MICHAEL (group)
1973 *Eno*
(Teamwork)
1973 *Glastonbury Fayre*
(Goodtimes) F

WILL MAHONEY (American comedy dancer)
1934 *Pathetone 235*
1937 *Said O'Reilly to McNab*
(Gainsborough) F
"A Little Bit of Heaven"
"Phil the Fluter's Ball"
1939 *Pathetone 509*
"It's Up To You"

MAJOR AND MINOR (comedians)
1937 *Pathe Pictorial NS 73*

MARY MALCOLM (television personality)
1962 *Design for Loving*
(Danziger) F

BOB MALLIN (singer)
1938 *Happy in the Morning*
(Gas) ADVERT
"Horsey Horsey"

JUNE MALO (singer)
1937 *Pathe Pictorial NS 58*
"My Attraction"

THE MALO TRIO (dancers)
1938 *Pathe Pictorial NS 126*

MALOFF, CHIKA AND TONY (acrobats)
1936 *Pathe Pictorial NS 26*

DANNY MALONE (Irish tenor)
1935 *Pathe Pictorial 895*
"Danny Boy"
1936 *Pathe Pictorial NS 27*
"Eileen Ogh"
1937 *Rose of Tralee*
(Butcher) F
"Rose of Tralee"
1938 *Around the Town*
(British Lion) F

KAY MALONE (singer)
1937 *Simply Grandfather*
(Ace Cinemagazine)

PERCY MANCHESTER (tenor)
1934 *Pathe Pictorial 841*
"Maureen O'Dare"
1936 *Pathe Pictorial NS 39*
"Her Name Is Mary"
1936 *Pathetone 339*
"Highgate Hill"
1937 *Saturday Night Revue*
(Pathe) F
1941 *Danny Boy*
(Butcher) F
"The Mountains o' Mourne"
"Dear Old Pals"

**PETE MANDELL AND HIS RHYTHM
MASTERS**
1930 *Pete Mandell No. 1*
(Gainsborough)
1930 *Pete Mandell No. 2*
(Gainsborough)

THE MANGAN TILLERETTES (dancers)
1930 *Just For a Song*
(Gainsborough) F
1932 *The Love Contract*
(B&D) F

THE FRANCIS MANGAN GIRLS (dancers)
1931 *Man of Mayfair*
(Paramount) F

THE HAZEL MANGEAN GIRLS (dancers)
1933 *Pathetone 164*
"Ding Dong Daddy"

MANLEY AND AUSTIN (comedy acrobats)
1943 *The Dummy Talks*
(British National) F
1951 *Let's Go Crazy*
(Adelphi) F

ALICE MANN (singer)
1939 *Pathe Pictorial NS 177*
"Sing Me a Swing Song"

ETHEL MANNERS
see **WILL HATTON AND ETHEL MANNERS**

MARGERY MANNERS (singer)
1968 *Mrs Brown You've Got a Lovely
Daughter*
(MGM) F
"My Old Man's a Dustman"

MERCY MANNERS (dancer)
1913 *Ragtime à la Carte*
(Selsior)
1913 *By the Sea*
(Selsior)
1913 *Spanish-American Quickstep*
(Selsior)

BERNARD MANNING (comedian)
1980 *The Great British Striptease*
(Target) F

IRENE MANNING (American singer)
1945 *I Live in Grosvenor Square*
(ABPC) F
"Home"

MANSELL AND LING (banjos)
1937 *Riding High*
(British Lion) F
"Marche Militaire"

MANTOVANI (violin)
1940 *Fiddlers All*
(reissue: *title unknown*)

1941 *Pathe Pictorial 264*

MANTOVANI AND HIS TIPICA ORCHESTRA
1934 *Pathetone 237*
      "Reginella"
1934 *Pathe Pictorial 843*
      "Vienna City of My Dreams"
1934 *Pathe Pictorial 854*
      "Elvira"
1935 *Pathe Pictorial 878*
      "I Saw Stars"
1936 *Pathetone 338*
      "I Left My Heart in Budapest"
1937 *Pathetone 375*
      "Tipica Stomp"
1937 *Sing As You Swing*
      (Rock) F
      "Black Eyes"
      "Let's Dance"
1939 *Pathetone 502*
      "Violin in Vienna"
1939 *Pathe Pictorial NS 150*
      "Violetta"
1939 *Pathetone Parade of 1939*
      F (reissue: *title unknown*)
1939 *Pathetone Parade of 1940*
      F (reissue: *title unknown*)
1939 *French Without Tears*
      (Two Cities) F
1940 *Pathetone 538*
      "When Dreams Grow Old"
1940 *Music Box*
      (reissue: *Sing As You Swing*)
1941 *Pathetone Parade of 1941*
      F (reissue: *Pathetone 538*)
1941 *Pathe Pictorial 264*

MANTOVANI AND HIS TRIO
1938 *Pathetone 417*
      "Kashmiri Song"

MANUFACTURED ROMANCE (group)
1982 *Listen to London*
      (White) F

MANZ, CHICO AND LOPEZ (clowns)
1949 *Horsecapades*
      (GFD)

LUCILLE MAPP (singer)
1957 *No Time for Tears*
      (ABPC) F
      "Tingaling"

JOSEF MARAIS AND HIS BUSHVELD BOYS (singers)
1942 *Pathe Pictorial 349*
      "Sari Marais"

FRANK MARCUS INDIAN DANCERS
1982 *Priest of Love*
      (Enterprise) F

LIANE MARELLI (striptease)
1960 *The Challenge*
      (Alliance) F

MARGARET AND GUY (singers)
1941 *Pathe Pictorial 250*

MARGHERITA (Spanish dancer)
1947 *New Pictorial 131*

SERGIUS MARGOLINSKI (singer)
1937 *Up to the Hilt*
      (Ace Cinemagazine)
1938 *Romance of Dancing*
      (Highbury) S

MARGUERITE (dancer)
1949 *Horsecapades*
      (GFD)
1949 *Sawdust Cabaret*
      (GFD)

MARIE-LOUISE SISTERS (acrobats)
1937 *The Penny Pool*
      (Mancunian) F

MARILYN (singer)
1979 *Steppin' Out*
      (White)

MARION AND IRMA (dancers)
1936 *Pathetone 323*
      "Symphony in Motion"

ANNA MARITA (ballerina)
1938 *Pathe Pictorial NS 117*

GLORIA MARIVILLA (singer)
1928 *Phototone 11*
      "La Violetera"

ALICIA MARKOVA (ballerina)
1952 *Giselle*
      (Exclusive)

BOB MARLEY AND THE WAILERS (group)
1978 *Bob Marley and the Wailers Live*
      (Blue Mountain) F
      "Trenchtown Rock"
      "I Shot the Sheriff"
      "Lively Up Yourself"
      "Running Away"
      "No More Trouble"
      "Heathen"
      "Jamming"
      "Exodus"
      "Get Up Stand Up"
      "Them Bellyful"
      "Rebel Music"
      "Crazy Baldhead"
      "War"
      "No Woman No Cry"

METIN MARLOW (conjurer)
1995 *Secrets and Lies*
(Ciby) F

MARQUE AND MARQUETE (dancers)
1929 *Pathe Magazine 3*
"Acrobatic Waltz"

MARQUIS TRIO (acrobats)
1939 *Pathe Pictorial 190*
1942 *Pathe Pictorial 351*
1950 *Come Dance With Me*
(Columbia) F

SYLVIA MARRIOTT (soprano)
1943 *I'll Walk Beside You*
(Butcher) F
"I'll Walk Beside You"

GERRY MARSDEN (singer)
see **GERRY AND THE PACEMAKERS**

**KOHALA MARSH AND HIS HAWAIIAN
REVELLERS** (band)
1928 *The Hawaiian Revellers*
(Phonofilm)
1932 *Musical Medley 4*
(reissue: *The Hawaiian Revellers*)
1932 *Music Without Words*
(reissue: *The Hawaiian Revellers*)

ARTHUR MARSHALL (comedian)
1936 *Windbag the Sailor*
(Gainsborough) F
1946 *New Pictorial 78*

ERIC MARSHALL (singer)
1928 *Tannhäuser Act Three*
(BSFP)
1931 *Glamour*
(BIP) F
1932 *Pathe Pictorial 756*
"Love's Glamour"
"Two Grenadiers"

ANITA MARTELL (juggler)
1937 *Pathe Pictorial NS 48*
1937 *Windmill Revels*
(Ace) F

DENIS MARTIN (Irish tenor)
1954 *Happy Ever After*
(ABPC) F
"My Heart Is Irish"

DICKIE MARTIN
see **HOPE AND PENNY CALVERT AND
DICKIE MARTIN**

GEORGES MARTIN (finger dancer)
1933 *Pathetone 152*

JESSICA MARTIN (singer)
1990 *The Garden*
(Basilisk)
"Think Pink"

LORNA MARTIN (singer)
1944 *My Ain Folk*
(Butcher) F
"My Ain Folk"
"Mountain Lovers"
"Will Ye No Come Back Again"
1946 *Amateur Night*
(Renown)

MILLICENT MARTIN (singer)
1959 *Libel*
(MGM) F
1961 *Invasion Quartet*
(MGM) F
1961 *The Girl On the Boat*
(UA) F
1963 *Nothing But the Best*
(Anglo) F
1965 *Those Magnificent Men in Their
Flying Machines*
(TCF) F
1966 *Stop the World I Want to Get Off*
(Warner) F
"Typically English"
"Gloriously Russian"
"Typically Japanese"
"The New York Scene"
1966 *Alfie*
(Paramount) F
1966 *Pathe Pictorial 626*

SKEETS MARTIN (animal mimic)
1938 *Display's the Thing*
(Ace Cinemagazine)

TONY MARTIN (singer)
1957 *Let's Be Happy*
(ABPC) F
"Stan the Man from Idaho"
"Hold on to Love"
"The Golfer's Glide"
"The Piper's Wedding"
"Such a Lonely Number"
"Let's Be Happy"

RAY MARTINE (comedian)
1965 *Primitive London*
(Searchlight) F

NINO MARTINI (Italian tenor)
1948 *One Night With You*
(GFD) F
"One Night With You"
"A Path in the Forest"

MARTINI AND HIS BAND
1930 *Martini and his Band No. 1*
(Gainsborough)
1930 *Martini and his Band No. 2*
(Gainsborough)

FRANK MARX AND IRIS (balancers)
1940 *Pathetone 537*

MASAI TRIBE WAKAMBA TRIBAL DANCERS
1967 *The Last Safari*
(Paramount) F

ERIC MASCHWITZ (composer)
1937 *Pathetone 397*

MASCOT AND MAURICE (dancers)
1937 *The Penny Pool*
(Mancunian) F

JASPER MASKELYNE (conjurer)
1930 *The Dizzy Limit*
(PDC) F
1936 *Terror on Tiptoe*
(New Realm) F
1937 *Pathetone 370*
1939 *Pathetone 473*
1941 *Little White Lies*
(Solidox) ADVERT
1942 *Pathetone Parade of 1942*
F (reissue: *Pathetone 473*)
1940s *Ace of Clubs*
(Luke)

NEVIL MASKELYNE (conjurer)
1896 *Mr Maskelyne Spinning Plates and Basins*
(Paul)

GLEN MASON (singer)
1958 *Man With a Gun*
(Anglo) F
"Fall in Love"
1960 *Climb Up the Wall*
(New Realm) F
"Don't Move"
"What's Cooking?"
1962 *Behave Yourself*
(Baim) F
1963 *The Cool Mikado*
(Baim) F

HARRY MASON (entertainer)
1931 *Pathetone 53*

LYN MASON (singer)
1953 *Out of the Bandbox*
(New Realm)

MELISSA MASON (dancer)
1935 *In Town Tonight*
(British Lion) F

NICK MASON (drummer)
see also **PINK FLOYD**
1987 *The Secret Policeman's Third Ball*
(Virgin) F
"Running Up That Hill"

MASONI (conjurer)
1949 *Passport to Pimlico*
(Ealing) F

LEONIDE MASSINE (dancer)
1926 *London's Famous Cabarets*
(Parkinson)
1948 *The Red Shoes*
(Archers) F
1951 *Tales of Hoffmann*
(London) F

MASSINE AND NIKITINA (dancers)
1932 *The Blue Danube*
(B&D) F

THE MASTERSINGERS (trio)
1932 *Pathe Pictorial 762*
"Pagan Moon"
1933 *Pathetone 163*
"Drake Is Going West"
"Floral Dance"
1933 *Pathetone 166*
"Trumpeter"
1933 *Pathe Pictorial 806*
"Valley of the Moon"
1933 *Pathe Pictorial 814*
"John Peel"
1934 *Pathetone 202*
"St Louis Blues"

MASU (Japanese juggler)
1932 *Ideal Cinemagazine 331*

CLELIA MATANIA (singer)
1936 *Melody of My Heart*
(Butcher) F
"Nubecitas"

MATCHBOX (group)
1979 *Blue Suede Shoes*
(Boyd) F

GLEN MATLOCK (bass player)
see also **THE SEX PISTOLS**
1980 *The Great Rock 'n' Roll Swindle*
(Virgin) F
1986 *Sid and Nancy*
(Zenith) F
"I'm Not Your Stepping Stone"
"God Save the Queen"
"Anarchy in the UK"
"No Feelings"
"Holidays in the Sun"
"Pretty Vacant"
"Problems"
"Oh Bondage Up Yours"
"My Way"
"I Wanna Be Your Dog"

MATTHE AND PARTNER (balancers)
1938 *Pathe Pictorial 127*

BRIAN MATTHEW (broadcaster)
1964 *Swinging UK*
(Baim)
1964 *UK Swings Again*
(Baim)

JESSIE MATTHEWS (song and dance)
1923 *Beloved Vagabond*
(Astra) F
1924 *Straws in the Wind*
(Phillips) F
1924 *This England*
(Napoleon) F
1931 *Out of the Blue*
(BIP) F
"Out of the Blue"
"I'm Glad I Met You"
"Let's Be Sentimental"
1932 *There Goes the Bride*
(Gainsborough) F
"I'll Stay With You"
"I'm Looking for You"
1933 *The Man From Toronto*
(Gainsborough) F
1933 *The Midshipmaid*
(Gainsborough) F
"One Little Kiss from You"
"Tiddley Om Pom Pay"
1933 *The Good Companions*
(Gaumont) F
"Three Wishes"
"Let Me Give My Happiness to You"
"Lucky for Me"
1933 *Friday the Thirteenth*
(Gainsborough) F
1934 *Waltzes from Vienna*
(Gaumont) F
1934 *Evergreen*
(Gaumont) F
"Daddy Wouldn't Buy Me a Bow-Wow"
"My Little Wooden Hut"
"When You've Got a Little Springtime in Your Heart"
"Just By Your Example"
"Tinkle Tinkle Tinkle"
"Dear Dear Dear"
"Over My Shoulder"
"Harlemania"
"Dancing on the Ceiling"
1935 *First a Girl*
(Gaumont) F
"Everything's in Rhythm with My Heart"
"I Can Wiggle My Ears"
"Half and Half"
"Say the Word and It's Yours"
"Little Silkworm"
1936 *It's Love Again*
(Gaumont) F
"It's Love Again"
"Tony's in Town"
"Slipping Through My Fingers"
"Got to Dance My Way to Heaven"

1937 *Head Over Heels*
(Gaumont) F
"Head Over Heels in Love"
"Through the Courtesy of Love"
"Looking Around Corners"
"There's That Look in Your Eye"
"Don't Give a Good Gosh Darn"
"May I Have the Next Romance With You"
1937 *Gangway*
(Gaumont) F
"Gangway"
"When You Gotta Sing"
"Moon or No Moon"
"Lord and Lady Whozis"
1938 *Sailing Along*
(Gaumont) F
"My River"
"Trusting My Luck"
"Souvenir of Love"
"My Heart Skips a Beat"
1939 *Climbing High*
(Gaumont) F
1944 *Candles at Nine*
(British National) F
1947 *Life Is Nothing Without Music*
(Inspiration)
"Life Is Nothing Without Music"
"Sleepy Lagoon"
1947 *Making the Grade*
(Inspiration)
1958 *Tom Thumb*
(MGM) F
"After All These Years"
1977 *The Hound of the Baskervilles*
(Hemdale) F

MATTHEWS' SOUTHERN COMFORT
(group)
1970 *Fairport Convention and Matthews Southern Comfort*
(Hemdale)

EDNA MAUDE (dancer)
1920 *Around the Town*
(Gaumont)
"Spirit of the Dance"
1921 *Around the Town*
(Gaumont)
"Old English Fan Dance"
1922 *Around the Town 166*
(Gaumont)
1924 *Eve's Film Review 168*

GLENDA MAUGHAN (child singer)
1940 *Pathe Pictorial 234*

SUSAN MAUGHAN (singer)
1963 *What a Crazy World*
(Hammer) F
"What a Crazy World"
"I Hate You, Alfie Hitchens"
"This Is My First Romance"
"I Feel the Same Way Too"

1965 *Pop Gear*
(Pathe) F

M MAURICE
see **LEANORA HUGHES AND M MAURICE**

MAURICETTE
1938 *Pathe Pictorial NS 128*
"Vilanelle"

BILLY MAXAM (comedian)
1963 *The Chimney Sweeps*
(Compton)
1977 *Come Play With Me*
(Tigon) F

LOUISE MAXIM (juggler)
1924 *Eve's Film Review 180*
1926 *Eve's Film Review 261*
1934 *Pathe Pictorial 838*
1938 *Pathetone 418*

MAXON AND WOOD (strong act)
1933 *Eve's Film Review 609*

CHARLES MAXWELL (broadcaster)
1942 *They Flew Alone*
(RKO) F

VERA MAXWELL AND JACK JARROTT
(dancers)
1913 *Always Gay*
(Hepworth)

HELEN MAY (dancer)
1922 *Around the Town*
(Gaumont)

RIK MAYALL (comedian)
1981 *An American Werewolf in London*
(Lycanthrope) F
1981 *Eye of the Needle*
(Kings Road) F
1981 *Shock Treatment*
(TCF) F
1981 *Couples and Robbers*
(Flamingo)
1987 *Eat the Rich*
(Comic Strip) F
1987 *More Bad News*
(Comic Strip) F
1988 *Whoops Apocalypse*
(Virgin) F
1988 *The Strike*
(Palace) F
1992 *Carry On Columbus*
(Comedy House) F
1996 *The Wind in the Willows*
(Allied) F
1997 *Bring Me the Head of Mavis Davis*
(Goldcrest) F

BILLIE MAYE
see **HARRY RAYE AND BILLIE MAYE**

NORAH MAYER (dancer)
1898 *Norah Mayer the Quick Change
Dancer*
(Williamson)

BILLY MAYERL (pianist)
1925 *Eve's Film Review 233*
1926 *Gwen Farrar and Billy Mayerl*
(Phonofilm)
1929 *Odd Numbers*
(BIP)
"It Don't Do Nothin' But Rain"
"Marigold"
1929 *Notes and Notions*
(BIP)
"An Old-Fashioned Girl"
1930 *Pathetone 21*
"Syncopation"
1931 *Gaumont Sound Mirror*
1933 *The Lost Chord*
(Butcher) F
"Hilarity"
1934 *Without You*
(British Lion) F
1935 *Pathetone 260*
1938 *Pathetone 449*
"Bats in the Belfry"
1939 *Pathetone 498*
"Runaway Love"
1940 *Pathe Pictorial 212*
1941 *Pathe Pictorial 270*
1942 *We'll Smile Again*
(British National) F
"Marigold"
1943 *Guess What No. 1*
(British Pictorial)
1944 *Pathe Pictorial 411*
"D'Ye Ken John Peel"
"Marigold"
1951 *Billy Mayerl Entertains No. 1*
(Ambassador)
1951 *Billy Mayerl Entertains No. 2*
(Ambassador)
1951 *One Good Turn*
(Ambassador)

CHARLES MAYHEW (baritone)
1933 *Pathetone 174*
"Onaway Awake Beloved"

CLARICE MAYNE (singer)
1916 *Nursie Nursie*
(Samuelson)
1922 *Eve's Film Review 32*
"Jack and the Beanstalk"
1922 *Eve's Film Review 65*
"Snap"
1926 *Eve's Film Review 242*
"Cinderella"
1926 *Eve's Film Review 279*
"A Leaf of Life"
1927 *Eve's Film Review 295*
"Aladdin"

ERNIE MAYNE (comedian)
1906   *Excelsior*
        (Chronophone)
1929   *Pathe Magazine 23*

SAM MAYO (comedian)
1930   *Pathetone 28*
1931   *Pathetone 78*
        "The Whispering Whatnot"
1932   *Pathe Pictorial 759*
        "Where Do Flies Go?"
        "I've Only Come Down for the Day"
        "I'm Gonna Sing a Song"
1934   *Pathetone Parade*
        F (reissue: *Pictorial 759*)

MAYURA (Chinese dancer)
1945   *Cabaret*
        (Empire) F
1945   *Sweethearts For Ever*
        (Empire) F

MARILYN MAZUR (drummer)
1983   *The Gold Diggers*
        (BFI) F

ROBERT MEAD (ballet dancer)
1966   *Romeo and Juliet*
        (Rank) F
1967   *Opus*
        (COI)
1971   *Tales of Beatrix Potter*
        (EMI) F

BUNTY MEADOWS (comedienne)
1943   *Happidrome*
        (Aldwych) F
        "Nobody Discovers Me"
1945   *Home Sweet Home*
        (Mancunian) F
1946   *Under New Management*
        (Mancunian) F
1948   *Honeymoon Hotel*
        (reissue: *Under New Management*)

MEATLOAF (American singer)
1975   *The Rocky Horror Picture Show*
        (TCF) F
1997   *Spice World*
        (Fragile) F

GEORGE MEATON (impressionist)
1939   *Discoveries*
        (Vogue) F
1969   *What's Good for the Goose*
        (Tigon) F

**ANDREA MEAZZA AND CONSTANCE
SEYMOUR** (dancers)
1925   *Eve's Film Review*
        "La Paloma"

MEDLOCK AND MARLOW
1941   *Old Mother Riley's Circus*
        (British National) F

MEDRANO AND DONNE (castanettists)
1935   *Pathe Pictorial 898*
        "Seville"

MEDVEDEFF'S BALALAIKA ORCHESTRA
1929   *Medvedeff's Balalaika Orchestra*
        (BSFP)
1932   *Camera Cocktales 1*
        (reissue: *Medvedeff's Balalaika
        Orchestra*)
1947   *New Pictorial 130*

TONY MEEHAN (singer)
1963   *Just For Fun*
        (Columbia) F
        "Hully Gully"

GEORGE MELACHRINO (singer and piano)
AND HIS ORCHESTRA
1940   *Pathetone 546*
1948   *House of Darkness*
        (British Lion) F
1948   *Things Happen at Night*
        (Renown) F
1950   *Old Mother Riley Headmistress*
        (Renown) F

MELANIE (singer)
1973   *Glastonbury Fayre*
        (Goodtimes) F

KARL MELENE (entertainer)
1936   *International Revue*
        (Medway) F

JACK MELFORD (singer)
(films as actor not listed)
1936   *Radio Lover*
        (ABFD) F
1943   *Theatre Royal*
        (Baxter) F
        "Man About Town"

MAT MELROSE (comedian)
1902   *The Comedian and the Fly Paper*
        (Smith)

MILDRED MELROSE (dancer)
1927   *Eve's Film Review 301*
        "Black Bottom"

THE MELROSE TRIO (dancers)
1902   *The Cakewalk*
        (Smith)

MELTON CLUB ORCHESTRA
1930   *Comets*
        (Alpha) F

JEAN MELVILLE (piano)
see also **PHILIP RIDGEWAY AND JEAN
MELVILLE**
1931   *Pathetone 75*
        (with Billy Thorburn)

1932 *Pathetone 107*
(with Billy Thorburn)
"Smile and Whistle a Love Song"
1933 *Pathe Pictorial 803*
(with Rene Cook)
"Fit as a Fiddle"
1933 *Pathetone 189*
(with Billy Thorburn)
1934 *Pathe Pictorial 869*
(with Billy Thorburn)
"Mixed Melody"
1936 *Pathe Pictorial*
(with Philip Ridgeway)
"Paint and Powder"
1937 *Pathetone 372*

KEITH MELVILLE
see **EILEEN ELTON AND KEITH MELVILLE**

ROSALIND MELVILLE (singer)
1945 *Sweethearts For Ever*
(Empire) F
1945 *Cabaret*
(Empire)
"Tears On My Pillow"
"Don't Forget Me"

THE MELVILLES (comedy jugglers)
1939 *Pathe Pictorial NS 149*

G S MELVIN (comedian)
1926 *Eve's Film Review 279*
1936 *Variety Parade*
(Butcher) F
"The Old Fleecy Lined"
1940 *Cavalcade of Variety*
(reissue: *Variety Parade*)
1940 *Highlights of Variety*
(reissue: *Variety Parade*)
1943 *Down Melody Lane*
F (reissue: *Variety Parade*)
1948 *For Old Times Sake*
(reissue: *Variety Parade*)

THE MEMBERS (group)
1981 *Urgh! A Music War*
(White) F
"Offshore Banking Business"

THE MEN ABOUT TOWN (singing trio)
1949 *Nitwits on Parade*
(Adelphi) F

MENDEL'S COLLEGIANS (band)
1932 *Ideal Cinemagazine 315*
1932 *Ideal Cinemagazine 322*

MENDEL'S FEMALE SEXTETTE (singers)
1946 *Under New Management*
(Mancunian) F

**FELIX MENDELSSOHN AND HIS
HAWAIIAN SERENADERS** (band)
1938 *Pathetone 440*

"I Double Dare You"
1939 *Pathetone 504*
"Song of the Islands"
1940 *Pathetone 548*
"No Souvenirs"
1940 *Pathetone 557*
"String Harmony"
1941 *Pathetone 566*
"In the Mood"
1941 *Pathe Pictorial 282*
"Aloma"
1942 *Pathe Pictorial 322*
1943 *Pathe Pictorial 368*
1944 *Pathe Pictorial 417*
"Hula Girl"
1944 *Pathe Pictorial 440*
1944 *Demobbed*
(Mancunian) F
"Won't You Take Me Back to
Hawaii?"
"I'll Wait for You"
1946 *New Pictorial 105*
"Sophisticated Hula"
1947 *New Pictorial 124*
1947 *New Pictorial 158*
"Paradise Island"
1951 *Penny Points to Paradise*
(Adelphi) F
1952 *New Pictorial 366*
"Aloha Oe"

JULIE MENDEZ (dancer)
1959 *The Night We Dropped a Clanger*
(Rank) F
1965 *Traitor's Gate*
(Summit) F
1968 *Duffy*
(Columbia) F

MENDOS SISTERS (entertainers)
1948 *The Big Show*
(Rayant)

TOM MENNARD (comedian)
1972 *The Flesh and Blood Show*
(Tigon) F
1973 *Tiffany Jones*
(Hemdale) F

YEHUDI MENUHIN (violin)
1946 *The Magic Bow*
(Gainsborough) F
"Romance"
"Devil's Trill"
"La Ronde des Lutins"
"Campanella"
"Caprice No. 20"
"Violin Concerto No. 1"
1968 *Music*
(Warner-Pathe)

MABEL MERCER (singer)
1936 *Everything Is Rhythm*
(Rock) F

"Since Black Minnie's Got the Blues"
1936 *Tropical Trouble*
(City) г

TONY MERCER (bass)
1963 *It's All Happening*
(British Lion) F
"Whittling Time Away"

LU ANNE MEREDITH (singer)
1937 *Sing As You Swing*
(Rock) F
"Calling All Stars"

GLADYS MERREDEW (child impressions)
1933 *Pathe Pictorial 796*
"Idle Dreams"
1934 *Pathetone 214*
"Baby's View"
1936 *Pathe Pictorial NS 18*
"Cows and Fishes"

BILLY MERRIN AND HIS COMMANDERS
(band)
1933 *Ideal Cinemagazine 373*
1935 *In Town Tonight*
(British Lion) F
1935 *Cheerio*
(Fidelity)
"Cheerio"
"Shine"
"Tiger Rag"
1936 *The Show's the Thing*
(Fidelity)
"Miracles Sometimes Happen"
1938 *The Dance of Death*
(Fidelity) F

TOM MERRY (cartoonist)
1895 *Tom Merry Lightning Cartoonist 1-4*
(Acres) S

MATHEA MERRYFIELD (dancer)
1935 *She Shall Have Music*
(Twickenham) F

THE MERSEYBEATS (group)
1964 *Just For You*
(British Lion) F
1964 *Swinging UK*
(Baim)
"Fools Like Me"
"Don't Turn Around"

BILLY MERSON (comedian)
1915 *Billy's Spanish Love Spasm*
(Homeland)
1915 *The Man in Possession*
(Homeland)
1915 *The Only Man*
(Homeland)
1916 *The Terrible Tec*
(Homeland)
1916 *The Tale of a Shirt*
(Homeland)

1916 *The Perils of Pork Pie*
(Homeland)
1916 *Billy's Stormy Courtship*
(Homeland)
1917 *Billy the Truthful*
(Homeland)
1917 *Billy Strikes Oil*
(Homeland)
1922 *Eve's Film Review 50*
"The Whirl of the World"
1922 *Eve's Film Review 61*
1925 *Eve's Film Review 203*
"Rose Marie"
1926 *Eve's Film Review 252*
"Umbrellas and Ice Cream"
1926 *Billy Merson in Russian Opera*
(Phonofilm)
1926 *Billy Merson Singing Desdemona*
(Phonofilm)
1926 *Billy Merson in his Harry Lauder Burlesque*
(Phonofilm)
"Scotland's Whiskey"
1928 *Eve's Film Review 357*
1930 *Comets*
(Alpha) F
"The Spaniard That Blighted My Life"
1931 *Bill and Coo*
(BIP) F
"The Photo of the Girl I Left Behind"
"Down Where the Breezes"
1935 *Pathetone 290*
"The Spaniard That Blighted My Life"
1936 *Pathe Pictorial NS 4*
"I'll B.B.C.-ing You"
"It's My Mother's Birthday Today"
1937 *Pathe Pictorial NS 46*
"A Bouncing Baby"
1937 *Pathetone 385*
"Desdemona"
1937 *The Show Goes On*
(ATP) F
1937 *Riding High*
(British Lion) F
"Let Us Pretend"
"Old Black Chloe"
1938 *Chips*
(BFA) F
1938 *Scruffy*
(Vulcan) F
1938 *Cavalcade of the Stars*
(Coronel)

YVONNE MERTENS (dancer)
1932 *Ideal Cinemagazine 333*
"Finger Dance"
1932 *Ideal Cinemagazine 337*
"Machine Dance"

HENRI MERTON (conjurer)
1931 *Ideal Cinemagazine 292*

174

JESSICA MERTON
see **BERNARD DE GAUTIER AND JESSICA MERTON**

THE MERTON PARKAS (group)
1979   *Steppin' Out*
(White)
"You Need Wheels"

METAXA GIRLS (dancers)
1937   *Starlight Parade*
(Viking)
1940   *Showtime*
(reissue: *Starlight Parade*)

GERALD METCALFE (singer)
1944   *Starlight Serenade*
(Federated) F

JEAN METCALFE (broadcaster)
1944   *New Pictorial 21*

THE METEORS (group)
1980   *Meteor Madness*
(Osiris)

MICHAELSON (cartoonist)
1933   *Ideal Cinemagazine 375*
1937   *West End Frolics*
(Ace) F

MICHEL (xylophonist)
1931   *Ideal Cinemagazine 285*
"The Dancing Xylophonist"

MICHEL AND ARNOVA (adagio)
1937   *West End Frolics*
(Ace) F

MICHEL AND HERO (xylophonists)
1939   *Pathetone Parade of 1939*
F

CLIFF MICHELMORE (broadcaster)
1963   *A Jolly Bad Fellow*
(British Lion) F

BRYAN MICHIE (broadcaster)
1937   *Let's Make a Night of It*
(ABPC) F
1943   *Battle for Music*
(Strand) F
1944   *Starlight Serenade*
(Federated) F
1949   *The Magnet*
(Ealing) F

C H MIDDLETON (broadcaster)
1938   *In Your Garden*
(Newhall) S
1940   *Band Waggon*
(Gainsborough) F
1940   *The Backyard Front*
(British Films)

1944   *New Pictorial 2*
"B.B.C. Gardening Expert"

VERNON MIDGELEY (baritone)
1985   *Hitler's SS: Portrait in Evil*
(Cannon) F

WALTER MIDGELEY (tenor)
1944   *My Ain Folk*
(Butcher) F
"My Ain Folk"
"Annie Laurie"
"Comin' Thro' the Rye"
"Mary"
"Road to the Isles"
"Loch Lomond"

JULIA MIGENES (singer)
1990   *The Krays*
(Rank) F

MIGIL FIVE (group)
1964   *Swinging UK*
(Baim)
"Mocking Bird Hill"
"Long Tall Sally"

BARBARA MILES AND MAXWELL STEWART (dancers)
1924   *Eve's Film Review 147*
"Foxtrot"
1924   *Eve's Film Review 193*
"Waltz"
1925   *Eve's Film Review 203*
"Foxtrot"
1925   *Eve's Film Review 218*
"Charleston"

MICHAEL MILES (television personality)
1961   *Dentist on the Job*
(Anglo) F

HELENA MILLAIS (comedienne)
1929   *Pathe Magazine 2*

ALEC MILLAR
see **PHYLLIS HAYLOR AND ALEC MILLAR**

JOAN MILLER (television personality)
1937   *Pathe Pictorial NS 56*

MAX MILLER (comedian)
1933   *The Good Companions*
(Gaumont) F
1933   *Channel Crossing*
(Gaumont) F
1933   *Friday the Thirteenth*
(Gainsborough) F
1934   *Princess Charming*
(Gaumont) F
1935   *Things Are Looking Up*
(Gainsboroough) F
1936   *Educated Evans*
(Warner) F

1936 *Get Off My Foot*
(Warner) F
1937 *Take It From Me*
(Warner) F
1937 *Don't Get Me Wrong*
(Warner) F
1938 *Thank Evans*
(Warner) F
1938 *Everything Happens to Me*
(Warner) F
"Everything Happens to Me"
"At the Bathing Parade"
1939 *The Good Old Days*
(Warner) F
1939 *Hoots Mon*
(Warner) F
"Mary From the Dairy"
"The Charabanc Song"
1942 *Asking for Trouble*
(British National) F
1945 *New Pictorial 57*

WALTER MILLER (singer)
1909 *Isn't It Lovely to Be in Love?*
(Cinephone)

MILLIE (singer)
1964 *Just For You*
(British Lion) F
"Sugar Dandy"
1964 *Swinging UK*
(Baim)
"My Boy Lollipop"
"Oh Henry"

PRIMROSE MILLIGAN (comedienne)
1946 *Amateur Night*
(Renown)

SPIKE MILLIGAN (comedian)
1951 *Penny Points to Paradise*
(Adelphi) F
1951 *London Entertains*
(New Realm) F
1951 *Let's Go Crazy*
(Adelphi) F
1952 *Down Among the Z Men*
(New Realm) F
1956 *Case of the Mukkinese Battlehorn*
(Archway)
1960 *The Running Jumping and Standing
Still Film*
(British Lion)
1960 *Watch Your Stern*
(Anglo) F
1960 *Suspect*
(British Lion) F
1961 *Invasion Quartet*
(MGM) F
1961 *What a Whopper*
(Regal) F
1961 *Spike Milligan on Treasure Island
WC2*
(British Lion)

1961 *Spike Milligan Meets Joe Brown*
(British Lion)
1962 *Postman's Knock*
(MGM) F
1966 *Fish and Milligan*
(New Realm)
1969 *The Bed Sitting Room*
(UA) F
1969 *The Magic Christian*
(Grand) F
1969 *The Undertakers*
(Paramount) F
1971 *The Magnificent Seven Deadly Sins*
(Tigon) F
1972 *Rentadick*
(Rank) F
1972 *Alice's Adventures in Wonderland*
(TCF) F
1972 *The Cherry Picker*
(Rank) F
1973 *Adolf Hitler My Part in His Downfall*
(UA) F
1973 *Digby the Biggest Dog in the World*
(Rank) F
1974 *Man About the House*
(Hammer) F
1975 *The Great McGonagall*
(Tigon) F
1977 *The Hound of the Baskervilles*
(Hemdale) F
1979 *Monty Python's Life of Brian*
(CIC) F
1983 *Yellowbeard*
(Hemdale) F

MARY MILLINGTON (nude model)
1976 *Keep It Up Downstairs*
(EMI) F
1976 *Intimate Games*
(Tigon) F
1977 *Come Play With Me*
(Tigon) F
1978 *The Playbirds*
(Tigon) F
1978 *What's Up, Superdoc?*
(Blackwater) F
1979 *Confessions from the David Galaxy
Affair*
(Tigon) F
1979 *Queen of the Blues*
(Tigon) F
1980 *The Great Rock 'n' Roll Swindle*
(Virgin) F

ANNETTE MILLS (songs and piano)
1933 *Pathetone 194*

BERTRAM MILLS' CIRCUS
1947 *Circus Boy*
(GFD) F

GARRY MILLS (singer)
1961 *Spike Milligan on Treasure Island
WC2*

(British Lion)
"Treasure Island"

NAT MILLS AND BOBBIE (comedy)
1935 *Equity Musical Revue 3*
(British Lion)
1935 *Equity Musical Revue 6*
(British Lion)
"King Charles and Nell Gwyn"
1939 *Jail Birds*
(Butcher) F

MILLS AND BROWNING (eccentric dancers)
1935 *Pathe Pictorial 902*
"How Do I Know It's Saturday?"

MILLS BROTHERS (quartette)
1937 *Sing As You Swing*
(Rock) F
"Solitude"
"Nagasaki"
1940 *Swing Tease*
(reissue: *Sing As You Swing*)

SYD MILLWARD AND HIS NITWITS
(comedy band)
1940 *Pathe Pictorial 247*
"St Louis Blues"
1949 *Nitwits on Parade*
(Adelphi) F
1952 *For Your Entertainment 3*
(Gaumont)
"Surprise Symphony"
1952 *For Your Entertainment 4*
(Gaumont)
"Poet and Peasant"

MILNE SISTERS (dancers)
1931 *Eve's Film Review 548*
1932 *Eve's Film Review 559*

LA MILO (poseuse)
1906 *La Milo*
(Urban)

MILOVAN AND SERENA (circus act)
1972 *Vampire Circus*
(Hammer) F

JACK MILROY (comedian)
1949 *Bless 'Em All*
(Adelphi) F
"Maggie Cock-a-Bendy"

BILLY MILTON (songs and piano)
(films as actor not listed)
1933 *Ideal Cinemagazine 380*
1933 *Aunt Sally*
(Gainsborough) F
"You Ought to See Sally on
Sunday"
1935 *Pathe Pictorial 924*
"Fruity Flute"
1936 *Pathetone 312*

"No Thrill"
1937 *Saturday Night Revue*
(Pathe) F
"It Was Such a Glorious Night"
"Together"
1938 *Pathe Pictorial NS 143*
"Time to Go"

THE MINDBENDERS (group)
1966 *To Sir With Love*
(Columbia) F
"Off and Running"
"Stealing My Love from Me"
"It's Getting Harder All the Time"

ANGELO MINGHETTI (tenor)
1934 *Pathetone 224*
"Nina"

CHARLES MINGUS (musician)
1962 *All Night Long*
(Rank) F

MINIATURE PIANO SYMPHONY
1935 *Pathe Pictorial 920*

THE MINI-PIANO EIGHT
1937 *Spinning a Yarn*
(Ace Cinemagazine)

**MINI-PIANO ENSEMBLE OF 14
JUVENILES**
1937 *Talking Feet*
(Baxter) F
"William Tell"
"When Day Is Done"
"Miss Annabelle Lee"
1941 *Twinkling Fingers*
(reissue: *Talking Feet*)

MIRA AND KARINOFF (dancers)
1932 *Pathetone 106*

**FREDDIE MIRFIELD AND HIS GARBAGE
MEN** (comedy band)
1951 *Let's Go Crazy*
(Adelphi) F
"Poet and Peasant"
"Dark Eyes"

ADRIAN MITCHELL (poet)
1965 *Wholly Communion*
(Lorrimer)

GEORGE MITCHELL SINGERS
1955 *Eric Winstone Band Show*
(Hammer)
1959 *Music With Max Jaffa*
(Zonic)
1963 *It's All Happening*
(British Lion) F
"It's Summer"
"Once Upon a Time in Venice"
"Watching All the World Go By"

GEORGE MITCHELL SWING CHOIR
1949   *It's a Wonderful Day*
       (Equity) F
       "It's a Wonderful Day"
       "Peel Rides Again"
       "Big Noise from Winnetka"

LESLIE MITCHELL (broadcaster)
1937   *The Sky's the Limit*
       (GFD) F
1951   *Lady Godiva Rides Again*
       (London) F
1953   *Grand National Night*
       (Renown) F
1959   *The Heart of a Man*
       (Rank) F

MALCOLM MITCHELL TRIO (singers)
1954   *Star of My Night*
       (Rank) F
1956   *Parade of the Bands*
       (Hammer)

MOCCESSEN (contortionist)
1898   *Moccessen the Human Snake*
       (Cinematograph)

MODERNAIRES (dancers)
1939   *Pathe Pictorial NS 165*
1945   *Don Chicago*
       (British National) F

MODERNIQUES (quartette)
1933   *Pathetone 195*
       "Tiger Rag"
1933   *Musical Film Revue 2*
       (British Lion)
       "Tiger Rag"
1934   *Pathetone 202*
       "St Louis Blues"
1935   *Equity Musical Revue 2*
       (British Lion)
       "I Heard"
1935   *Equity Musical Revue 5*
       (British Lion)
       "Sentimental Gentleman from
       Georgia"
1935   *Equity Musical Revue 6*
       (British Lion)

ALBERT MODLEY (comedian)
1941   *Bob's Your Uncle*
       (Butcher) F
       "Hey Little Hen"
1950   *Up for the Cup*
       (Byron) F
1951   *Take Me To Paris*
       (Byron) F

MONTY MODLYN (broadcaster)
1969   *Under the Table You Must Go*
       (Butcher) F

BENNO MOISEIWITSCH (piano)
1943   *Battle for Music*
       (Strand) F
       "Piano Concerto No. 2"

THE MOJOS (group)
1964   *Every Day's a Holiday*
       (Grand National) F

CLIFFORD MOLLISON (comedian)
1929   *Express Love*
       (Alpha)
1930   *Eve's Film Review 458*
       "Here Comes the Bride"
1930   *Almost a Honeymoon*
       (BIP) F
1933   *Lucky Number*
       (Gaumont) F
       "Wish for Happiness"
1933   *Meet My Sister*
       (Pathe) F
1933   *A Southern Maid*
       (BIP) F
1934   *Luck of a Sailor*
       (BIP) F
1934   *Freedom of the Seas*
       (BIP) F
1934   *Give Her a Ring*
       (BIP) F
       "Come On and Love"
       "The Lamp of Love"
       "Let the Bells Ring"
1934   *Mr Cinders*
       (BIP) F
       "Just a Blue Sky"
       "I Can Get Used to You"
1934   *Radio Parade of 1935*
       (BIP) F
1935   *Royal Cavalcade*
       (BIP) F
1939   *Blind Folly*
       (RKO) F
1951   *Scrooge*
       (Renown) F
1956   *The Baby and the Battleship*
       (British Lion) F
1961   *Mary Had a Little...*
       (UA) F
1969   *Oh What a Lovely War*
       (Paramount) F
1972   *That's Your Funeral*
       (Hammer) F
1973   *Love Thy Neighbour*
       (Hammer) F
1974   *Frankenstein and the Monster from
       Hell*
       (Hammer) F

NEWMAN MOND (trick billiards)
1937   *Pathe Pictorial NS 75*
1939   *Pathe Pictorial NS 188*
1939   *Pathetone 482*
1940   *Pathe Pictorial 229*
1941   *Pathetone Parade of 1941*
       F (reissue: *Pathetone 482*)

1943   *Pathe Pictorial 385*

ZOOT MONEY (singer)
1968   *Popdown*
        (New Realm) F
1978   *The Waterloo Bridge Handicap*
        (Paramount)
1979   *Porridge*
        (ITC) F
1980   *Breaking Glass*
        (GTO) F
1981   *Riding High*
        (Klinger) F
1981   *Take It Or Leave It*
        (GTO) F
1982   *Who Dares Wins*
        (Rank) F
1982   *The Pirates of Penzance*
        (UIP) F
1983   *Bullshot*
        (Handmade) F
1984   *Scandalous*
        (Hemdale)
1984   *Supergirl*
        (Columbia) F
1985   *Billy the Kid and the Green Baize
        Vampire*
        (Zenith) F
1986   *Absolute Beginners*
        (Palace) F

MARIE MONIGHETTI (singer)
1930   *Comets*
        (Alpha) F

BOB MONKHOUSE (comedian)
1952   *The Secret People*
        (Ealing) F
1956   *All In Good Fun*
        (Butcher) F
1958   *Carry On Sergeant*
        (Anglo) F
1960   *Dentist in the Chair*
        (Renown) F
1961   *Dentist on the Job*
        (Anglo) F
1961   *Weekend With Lulu*
        (Hammer) F
1962   *She'll Have To Go*
        (Anglo) F
1966   *Thunderbirds Are Go*
        (UA) F
1968   *The Bliss of Mrs Blossom*
        (Paramount) F
1970   *Simon Simon*
        (Tigon) F
1983   *Out of Order*
        (UIP)

PHYLLIS MONKMAN (comedienne)
see also **THE CO-OPTIMISTS**
1913   *Persian Dance Eightpence a Mile*
        (Kineplastikon)
1927   *On With the Dance*
        (Parkinson)

1929   *The Co-Optimists*
        (New Era) F
1929   *Blackmail*
        (BIP) F
1939   *The Good Old Days*
        (Warner) F
1939   *Young Man's Fancy*
        (Ealing) F
        "When the Band Begins to Play"
1942   *Uncensored*
        (GFD) F
1946   *Carnival*
        (Two Cities) F
1949   *Diamond City*
        (GFD) F

VICTORIA MONKS (singer)
1906   *Love Song*
        (Chronophone)

MATT MONRO (singer)
1965   *Pop Gear*
        (Pathe) F
1967   *Go With Matt Monro*
        (Pathe)

**BERNARD MONSHIN AND HIS RIO
TANGO BAND**
1933   *Pathe Pictorial 779*
        "La Cumparsita"
1935   *Pathetone 263*
        "Madame You're Lovely"
1936   *Pathetone 307*
        "A Rose in Her Hair"
1936   *Pathe Pictorial NS 11*
        "Tabu"

JANET MONTANA (striptease)
1970   *All the Way Up*
        (Anglo) F

MARIAN MONTGOMERY (singer)
1967   *Go With Matt Monro*
        (Pathe)

MONTPARNASSE BALLET (dancers)
1959   *Jack the Ripper*
        (Regal) F

THE MONTREALS (trick cyclists)
1942   *Pathe Pictorial 346*

HAL MONTY (comedian)
1949   *Bless 'Em All*
        (Adelphi) F
        "Hi De Hi"
        "What More Can I Say?"
1949   *Skimpy in the Navy*
        (Adelphi) F
        "Capito"
        "Bell Bottom Trousers"

MONTY PYTHON
see **GRAHAM CHAPMAN, JOHN CLEESE,
ERIC IDLE, TERRY JONES** and **MICHAEL
PALIN**

NORAH MOODY (impressionist)
1949 *Nitwits on Parade*
(Adelphi) F
(as Charles Boyer, Jimmy Durante)

GEORGE MOON AND BURTON BROWN
(comedians)
1945 *What Do We Do Now?*
(Grand National) F

KEITH MOON (drummer)
see also **THE WHO**
1971 *200 Motels*
(UA) F
1973 *That'll Be the Day*
(EMI) F
1973 *Radio Wonderful*
(Goodtimes) F
1974 *Stardust*
(EMI) F
1975 *Tommy*
(Stigwood) F
"Fiddle About"
"Tommy's Holiday Camp"

ALEX MOORE (dancer)
1932 *Ideal Cinemagazine 337*

BRIAN MOORE (television commentator)
1969 *Bloomfield*
(TCF) F

DUDLEY MOORE (comedian)
1966 *The Wrong Box*
(Columbia) F
1967 *Thirty Is a Dangerous Age, Cynthia*
(Columbia) F
1967 *Bedazzled*
(TCF) F
1969 *The Bed Sitting Room*
(UA) F
1969 *Monte Carlo or Bust*
(Paramount) F
1972 *Alice's Adventures in Wonderland*
(TCF) F
1977 *The Hound of the Baskervilles*
(Hemdale) F
1985 *Santa Claus*
(Rank) F
1992 *Blame It on the Bellboy*
(Warner) F

JANE MOORE
see **BILLY REVEL AND JANE MOORE**

MANDY MOORE (singer)
1985 *Parker*
(Virgin) F

CHARLES MOPPETT (singer)
1906 *The Heart Bowed Down*
(Chronophone)

MIKE MORAN (singer)
1985 *Water*
(Rank) F

ROSIE MORAN (acrobatic dancer)
1930 *Pathetone 28*
1930 *Eve's Film Review 491*
1931 *Ideal Cinemagazine 268*

KENNETH MORE (comedian)
(films as actor not listed)
1936 *Full Steam*
(Ace) F
1936 *Bottle Party*
(Ace) F
1937 *Windmill Revels*
(Ace) F
1937 *Carry On London*
(Ace) F

ERIC MORECAMBE AND ERNIE WISE
(comedians)
1965 *The Intelligence Men*
(Rank) F
1966 *That Riviera Touch*
(Rank) F
1967 *The Magnificent Two*
(Rank) F
1970 *Simon Simon*
(Tigon) F

AIRTO MOREIRA (singer)
1996 *Glastonbury: The Movie*
(Starlight) F
"Improv No. 1"

ED MORELLE (conjurer)
1937 *Pathe Pictorial NS 84*
"The Mad Magician"

GENE MORELLE (musical saw)
1930 *Pathetone 12*

IVOR MORETON AND DAVE KAYE
(pianists)
1936 *Everything Is Rhythm*
(Rock) F
"Make Some Music"
1938 *Pathetone 436*
"Peter Pan"
1947 *New Pictorial 123*
"Boogie Bash"
1947 *New Pictorial 137*
"I Love to Sing"
"Bless You"

ROBERT MORETON (comedian)
1942 *In Which We Serve*
(Two Cities) F

1951 *One Wild Oat*
(Eros) F
1956 *Tons of Trouble*
(Renown) F

GLADYS MORGAN (Welsh comedienne)
1963 *The Wild Affair*
(7 Arts) F

MORGAN AND STONE (banjo)
1932 *Ideal Cinemagazine 342*

ELSIE MORISON (singer)
1952 *The Story of Gilbert and Sullivan*
(London) F

ERIC MORLEY (compère)
1957 *These Dangerous Years*
(ABPC) F

SHERIDAN MORLEY (broadcaster)
1996 *The Leading Man*
(J&M) F

MORONI AND LESLIE (acrobatic dancers)
1928 *British Screen Tatler 2*

LIBBY MORRIS (comedienne)
1960 *Climb Up the Wall*
(New Realm) F
1967 *The Plank*
(Rank) F
1967 *Two for the Road*
(TCF) F
1969 *The Adding Machine*
(Universal) F

LILY MORRIS (comedienne)
1930 *Elstree Calling*
(BIP) F
"Why Am I Always the Bridesmaid?"
"Only a Working Man"
1931 *Pathetone 61*
"The Old Apple Tree"
1932 *Pathe Pictorial 729*
"Don't Have Any More"
1934 *Those Were the Days*
(BIP) F
"My Old Man"
1934 *Pathetone Parade*
F (reissue: *Pictorial 729*)
1934 *Radio Parade of 1935*
(BIP) F
"We Won't Say Good Morning"
"We're Not Quite What We Used To
Be"
1941 *I Thank You*
(Gainsborough) F
"Waiting at the Church"

MARGARET MORRIS DANCERS
1922 *Around the Town 139*
(Gaumont)

MONTE MORRIS (tap-dancer)
1939 *Pathe Pictorial NS 176*
"Me, Myself and I"

VAN MORRISON (singer)
1981 *Van Morrison in Ireland*
(Angle)

MOSCOW SINGERS
1942 *Pathe Pictorial 332*
1943 *Pathe Pictorial 369*
"Comrades"

JENNIFER MOSS (singer)
1963 *Live It Up*
(Rank) F
"Please Let It Happen to Me"

JAMES MOSSMAN (broadcaster)
1964 *Masquerade*
(UA) F

MOTHERS OF INVENTION (group)
1971 *200 Motels*
(UA) F

JOHN MOTSON (television commentator)
1979 *Yesterday's Hero*
(EMI) F

TED MOULT (broadcaster)
1983 *Bullshot*
(Handmade) F

MOUTH ORGAN MASTERS
1931 *Pictorial 705*
"Gladys"

MOYA (child organist)
1939 *Pathe Pictorial NS 171*

GEORGE MOZART (comedian)
1913 *Coney as Peacemaker*
(Hepworth)
1913 *Coney Gets the Glad Eye*
(Hepworth)
1913 *Coney, Ragtimer*
(Hepworth)
1927 *Mr George Mozart the Famous
Comedian*
(Phonofilm)
1929 *Pathe Magazine 24*
1930 *Domestic Troubles*
(Gainsborough)
1932 *Indiscretions of Eve*
(BIP) F
1936 *Polly's Two Fathers*
(Hammer)
1936 *Strange Cargo*
(Paramount) F
1936 *Two On a Doorstep*
(Paramount) F
1936 *Cafe Mascot*
(Paramount) F

1936　*Song of Freedom*
(Hammer) F
1936　*Bank Messenger Mystery*
(Hammer) F
1936　*Full Speed Ahead*
(Paramount) F
1937　*Overcoat Sam*
(Baxter) F

MUD (group)
1975　*Never Too Young To Rock*
(GTO) F
"Never Too Young To Rock"
"Dynamite"
"Tiger Feet"
"The Cat Crept In"
"Rocket"
1975　*Side By Side*
(GTO) F
"Side By Side"

MALCOLM MUGGERIDGE (television
personality)
1959　"*I'm All Right Jack*"
(British Lion) F
1963　*Heavens Above*
(British Lion) F
1967　*Herostratus*
(BFI) F

FRANK MUIR (writer)
1948　*The Clouded Crystal*
(Butcher) F
1953　*Innocents in Paris*
(Romulus) F

RENATE MULLER (German singer)
1931　*Sunshine Susie*
(Gainsborough) F
"Today I Feel So Happy"
1932　*Marry Me*
(Gainsborough) F
"Marry Me"
"A Little Sunshine"
"Wonderful to Me"

BROWNING MUMMERY (tenor)
1934　*Evensong*
(Gaumont) F
"I Wait for You"
"Santa Lucia"
"La Traviata"

HILDA MUNDY
see **BILLY CARYLL AND HILDA MUNDY**

ALEX MUNRO (Scottish comedian)
1973　*Holiday On the Buses*
(Hammer) F

RONNIE MUNRO (piano)
1938　*Lassie from Lancashire*
(British National) F

PATRICE MUNSEL (soprano)
1953　*Melba*
(UA) F
"Ave Maria"
"Comin' Thro' the Rye"
"On Wings of Song"
"Is This the Beginning of Love?"
"Serenade"

RICHARD MURDOCH (comedian)
1937　*Over She Goes*
(ABPC) F
"We Police Are Wonderful"
1938　*The Terror*
(ABPC) F
1940　*Pathe Gazette 36*
(with Arthur Askey)
1940　*Band Waggon*
(Gainsborough) F
1940　*Charley's (Big-Hearted) Aunt*
(Gainsborough) F
1941　*The Ghost Train*
(Gainsborough) F
1941　*I Thank You*
(Gainsborough) F
1944　*One Exciting Night*
(Columbia) F
1945　*New Pictorial 45*
1946　*New Pictorial 80*
1948　*It Happened in Soho*
(Chisnell) F
1949　*Golden Arrow*
(Renown) F
1950　*New Pictorial 297*
"Much Binding in the Marsh"
1955　*Mr Therm's Review*
(Gas) ADVERT
1959　*Strictly Confidential*
(Rank) F
1960　*Not a Hope in Hell*
(Archway) F
1969　*Under the Table You Must Go*
(Butcher) F
1988　*Whoops Apocalypse*
(Virgin) F

MURGATROYD AND WINTERBOTTOM
(comedians) (Ronald Frankau and Tommy
Handley)
see also **RONALD FRANKAU, TOMMY
HANDLEY**
1935　*Pathetone 275*
1936　*Pathe Pictorial NS 3*
1938　*Two Men in a Box*
(Ace) F
1939　*Pathetone Parade of 1940*
F

**MRS MURGATROYD AND MRS
WINTERBOTTOM** (comedy) (Rene Roberts
and Jean Allistone)
1937　*Pathe Pictorial NS 52*
"This is the Rhythm for Me"

BILLY MURRAY (singer)
  1907 *Harrigan*
        (Chronophone)

CHIC MURRAY (Scottish comedian)
  1967 *Casino Royale*
        (Columbia) F
  1975 *Secrets of a Door to Door Salesman*
        (New Realm) F
  1975 *Ups and Downs of a Handyman*
        (Target) F
  1975 *I'm Not Feeling Myself Tonight*
        (New Realm) F
  1977 *What's Up, Nurse?*
        (Variety) F
  1978 *What's Up, Superdoc?*
        (Blackwater) F
  1979 *Can I Come Too?*
        (New Realm) F
  1981 *Gregory's Girl*
        (ITC) F

COLIN MURRAY
see **GRACE CLARKE AND COLIN MURRAY**

PETE MURRAY (singer and disc jockey)
  1944 *Time Flies*
        (Gainsborough) F
  1946 *Caravan*
        (Gainsborough) F
  1947 *Hungry Hill*
        (Two Cities) F
  1948 *Portrait from Life*
        (Gainsborough) F
  1958 *6.5 Special*
        (Anglo) F
  1959 *This Other Eden*
        (Dalton) F
  1960 *A Taste of Money*
        (Danziger) F
  1960 *Transatlantic*
        (Danziger) F
  1960 *Escort For Hire*
        (Danziger) F
  1962 *Behave Yourself*
        (Baim) F
  1962 *Design for Loving*
        (Danziger) F
  1962 *It's Trad Dad*
        (Columbia) F
  1963 *The Cool Mikado*
        (Baim) F

  1965 *Is Your I.Q. O.K.?*
        (Baim)
  1968 *Otley*
        (Columbia) F
  1969 *Under the Table You Must Go*
        (Butcher) F
  1970 *Cool It Carol*
        (Miracle) F
  1970 *Simon Simon*
        (Tigon) F
  1973 *Radio Wonderful*
        (Goodtimes) F

RUBY MURRAY (singer)
  1956 *It's Great To Be Young*
        (ABPC) F
  1956 *A Touch of the Sun*
        (Eros) F
        "In Love"
        "O'Malley's Tango"

WEBSTER MURRAY (cartoonist)
  1931 *Pathetone 85*

MUSAIRE (instrumentalist)
  1937 *Pathe Pictorial NS 49*
        "The Fleet's in Port Again"
  1938 *Pathe Pictorial NS 111*
        "Bird Song at Eventide"

JOSEPH MUSCANT AND HIS BAND
  1933 *Pathe Pictorial 818*
        "Liszt Melodies"

MUSIC HALL BOYS (comedy songs)
  1937 *Variety Hour*
        (Fox) F
  1938 *Lassie from Lancashire*
        (British National) F
        "There Is a Tavern in the Town"

RUTH AND ELLA MYLES (acrobats)
  1935 *Pathe Pictorial 923*
  1937 *Pathetone Parade of 1938*
        F (reissue: *Pictorial 923*)

MYRA AND ELLEN (skaters)
  1938 *Pathe Pictorial NS 121*

MYSTIC (group)
  1973 *Horror Hospital*
        (Balch) F
        "Mask of Death"

NADEARJA (dancer)
1932 *Ideal Cinemagazine 341*

PRINCESS NADJI (entertainer)
1903 *Nadji the Hindoo Marvel*
(Paul)

NALDI TRIO (entertainers)
1933 *Aunt Sally*
(Gainsborough) F

MARGUERITE NAMARA (soprano)
1931 *Gypsy Blood*
(BIP) F
"If I Love You"

NANETTE (contortionist)
1936 *Pathe Pictorial NS 3*
1937 *Windmill Revels*
(Ace) F
1939 *Pathe Pictorial NS 189*
"Toy Trumpeter"
1942 *Pathe Pictorial 305*

HEDDLE NASH (singer)
1945 *For You Alone*
(Butcher) F
"For You Alone"
"At Dawning"

NASHVILLE TEENS (group)
1965 *Pop Gear*
(Pathe) F
"Tobacco Road"
"Google Eye"
1965 *Gonks Go Beat*
(Anglo) F
1965 *Be My Guest*
(Rank) F
"Whatcha Gonna Do About It?"

SAN NATANO AND HIS ROMAINE BAND
1933 *Ideal Cinemagazine 391*

NATASHA AND LORENZ (dancers)
1936 *Cabaret Nights 1*
(Highbury)

BEN NATHAN (comedian)
1898 *The Fatal Letter*
(Mutoscope)

NATIONAL YOUTH ORCHESTRA
1959 *The Lady Is a Square*
(ABPC) F
"Beethoven's Piano Concerto"
"Ave Maria"
1966 *The National Youth Orchestra of Great Britain*
(Anvil)
"Dvorak's Overture"

OSCAR NATZKE (bass)
1946 *Meet the Navy*
(British National) F
1946 *Meet the Navy On Tour*
(British National)
"Shenandoah"
"Blow the Man Down"

GRETE NATZLER (soprano)
1934 *The Scotland Yard Mystery*
(BIP) F
1935 *The Student's Romance*
(BIP) F
"There's a Smile in the Skies"
"Oh Lassie Come"
"I Lost My Heart in Heidelberg"
"Marching Along"

(CHARLIE) NAUGHTON AND (JIMMY) GOLD (comedians)
see also **THE CRAZY GANG**
1933 *Sign Please*
(Gaumont)
1933 *My Lucky Star*
(W&F) F
1935 *Cock o' the North*
(Butcher) F
1936 *Highland Fling*
(Fox) F
1937 *Wise Guys*
(Fox) F
1938 *Highlights of Variety 11*
(reissue: *Cock o' the North*)
1943 *Down Melody Lane*
F (reissue: *Cock o' the North*)

NAVARRE (impressionist)
1936 *Stars On Parade*
(Butcher) F
(as Maurice Chevalier)
"Valentine" (as Richard Tauber)
"Thine In My Heart"
"Valentine"
"Song of the Volga Boatmen"
"I Hear You Calling Me"
"The Moon Is Tired of Shining"
1936 *Shipmates o' Mine*
(Butcher) F
1938 *Highlights of Variety 7*
(reissue: *Stars On Parade*)
1938 *Highlights of Variety 8*
(reissue: *Shipmates o' Mine*)
1938 *Pathe Pictorial NS 110*
(as Maurice Chevalier: "Valentine")
(as Richard Tauber: "Thine In My Heart")

LEON NAVARRE AND PARTNER (adagio)
1947 *New Pictorial 165*

KATHLEEN NAYLOR (singer)
1939 *The Mikado*
(GFD) F

ROBERT NAYLOR (tenor)
1934 *Pathetone 242*
      "For Love of You"
1935 *Abdul the Damned*
      (BIP) F

RUTH NAYLOR (singer)
1936 *Sunshine Ahead*
      (Baxter) F

YOUSSOU N'DOUR (singer)
1987 *The Secret Policeman's Third Ball*
      (Virgin) F
      "Biko"
      "Voices of Freedom"

ANNA NEAGLE (song and dance)
(films as actress not listed)
1932 *Goodnight Vienna*
      (B&D) F
      "Dear Little Waltz"
      "My Pretty Flowers"
1933 *The Little Damozel*
      (Wilcox) F
      "What More Can I Ask?"
      "The Dream Is Over"
      "Brighter Than the Sun"
1933 *Bitter Sweet*
      (B&D) F
      "I'll See You Again"
      "The Call of Life"
      "A Sweet Little Cafe"
1934 *The Queen's Affair*
      (B&D) F
      "Tonight"
      "I Love You So"
      "When I Hear Your Voice"
      "Fisherman's Waltz"
1934 *Nell Gwyn*
      (Wilcox) F
      "Gillie-whack-a-day"
      "Merrymakers Dance"
1935 *Peg of Old Drury*
      (Wilcox) F
      "A Little Dash of Dublin"
      "Kiss Me Goodnight"
1936 *Limelight*
      (Wilcox) F
      "The Sandman's Serenade"
      "The Whistling Waltz"
      "Celebrating"
1937 *London Melody*
      (Wilcox) F
      "The Eyes of the World Are on You"
      "Jingle of the Jungle"
1946 *Piccadilly Incident*
      (Wilcox) F
      "Boogie Woogie Moonshine"
      "Piccadilly 1944"
      "Jealousy"
      "If You Were the Only Girl in the World"
1947 *The Courtneys of Curzon Street*
      (Wilcox) F

      "Roses of Picardy"
      "A Broken Doll"
      "Whispering"
      "Ramona"
      "Soldiers in the Park"
      "The Honeysuckle and the Bee"
      "Lili Marlene"
      "A Place of My Own"
      "Haste to the Wedding"
1948 *Spring in Park Lane*
      (Wilcox) F
      "The Moment I Saw You"
1949 *Maytime in Mayfair*
      (Wilcox) F
      "Do I Love You?"
1954 *Lilacs in the Spring*
      (Republic) F
      "The Moment I Saw You"
      "Dance Little Lady"
1955 *King's Rhapsody*
      (Wilcox) F
      "The Gates of Paradise"
      "Some Day My Heart Will Awake"
      "The Years Together"

WILLER NEAL (Irish tenor)
1945 *Old Mother Riley at Home*
      (British National) F
1949 *Old Mother Riley's New Venture*
      (Renown) F
      "I'll Take You Home Again Kathleen"
1950 *Old Mother Riley Headmistress*
      (Renown) F
1951 *Old Mother Riley's Jungle Treasure*
      (Renown) F

MAGDA NEELD (singer)
1935 *She Shall Have Music*
      (Twickenham) F
      "Santa Lucia"

NIGEL NEILSEN (singer)
1950 *Stranger At My Door*
      (Monarch) F

KOLIA NEJIN (singer)
1932 *Pathetone 139*
      "Song of the Steppes"

SYLVIA NELLS (singer)
1936 *Whom the Gods Love*
      (ATP) F

BILLY NELSON (comedian)
1935 *Look Up and Laugh*
      (ATP) F
1937 *The Penny Pool*
      (Mancunian) F
      "Julie and Myrtle"
1938 *Calling All Crooks*
      (Mancunian) F

JIMMY NERVO AND TEDDY KNOX
(comedians)
see also **THE CRAZY GANG**
- 1926 *Nervo and Knox*
  (Phonofilm)
- 1928 *The Rising Generation*
  (Westminster) F
- 1930 *Alf's Button*
  (Gaumont) F
- 1930 *Eve's Film Review 499*
  "Excuse Me"
- 1931 *Eve's Film Review 501*
  "Here and There"
- 1932 *Camera Cocktales 3*
  (reissue: *Nervo and Knox*)
- 1936 *It's In the Bag*
  (Warner) F
- 1936 *Skylarks*
  (Reunion) F
- 1938 *Cavalcade of the Stars*
  (Coronel)
- 1946 *New Pictorial 72*
  "Golf"

MAX AND HARRY NESBITT (comedy
songs)
- 1926 *Yid Nesbitt*
  (Phonofilm)
- 1930 *Pathetone 23*
  "My Baby's Got Red Hair"
  "Stars and Stripes"
- 1931 *Pathetone 44*
  "I've Got a Feeling I'm Falling"
  "I Want to Be Happy"
- 1931 *Old Soldiers Never Die*
  (BIP) F
  "Momma Loves Poppa"
- 1931 *Motley and Melody*
  (Warner)
- 1934 *Pathetone Parade*
  F (reissue: *Pathetone 44*)
- 1934 *Screen Vaudeville*
  (Vaudeville)
- 1935 *Pathetone 282*
  "Mademoiselle"
  "That Certain Thing"
- 1937 *Film Fare*
  (Ambassador)
- 1939 *Pathe Pictorial NS 154*
  "Georgia's Got a Moon"

NEW ORDER (group)
- 1985 *Perfect Kiss*
  (Palace)

THE NEW PARIS LIDO CLUB BAND
- 1928 *The New Paris Lido Club Band*
  (Phonofilm)

THE NEW TEMPERANCE SEVEN (band)
- 1970 *Games That Lovers Play*
  (Border) F

THE NEW TZIGANE ORCHESTRA
- 1937 *Bobbin About*
  (Ace Cinemagazine)
  "Hungarian Medley"

BILLY AND ELSA NEWELL (entertainers)
- 1933 *Ideal Cinemagazine 374*

RAYMOND NEWELL (baritone)
- 1931 *Pathetone 74*
  "Over the Rolling Sea"
- 1931 *Pathetone 82*
  "Leanin'"
- 1932 *Pathetone 93*
  "Red Rose"
- 1932 *Pathe Pictorial 721*
  "The Sergeant Major On Parade"
- 1932 *Pathe Pictorial 748*
  "The Tinker"
- 1932 *Pathetone 129*
  "Watch the Navy"
- 1933 *Pathe Pictorial 795*
  "I'll Go My Way"
- 1934 *Pathetone 201*
  "Rags Bottles or Bones"
- 1934 *Pathe Pictorial 852*
  "The Pavement Artist"
- 1934 *Pathe Pictorial 864*
  "Lay of the Pirate"
- 1934 *Music Hall*
  (Realart) F
  "With a Smile on Your Lips"
- 1935 *Pathetone 298*
  "Harvester"
- 1936 *Pathe Pictorial 937*
  "Dear England Mine"
- 1937 *Variety Hour*
  (Fox) F
- 1937 *Pathe Pictorial NS 80*
  "The Shepherd"
- 1938 *Pathetone 443*
- 1939 *Pathetone 474*
  "Slowcoach"
- 1939 *Pathetone Parade of 1939*
  F (reissue: *Pathetone 201*)
- 1941 *Pathe Pictorial 277*
  "London Will Rise Again"
- 1941 *Pathe Pictorial 295*
  "Follow the Plough"
- 1943 *Pathe Pictorial 387*
  "Our Land"

BOB NEWHART (American comedian)
- 1968 *Hot Millions*
  (MGM) F

ANTHONY NEWLEY (singer)
(films as actor not listed)
- 1959 *Idle on Parade*
  (Columbia) F
  "Idle on Parade"
  "Idle Rock-a-Boogie"
  "I've Waited So Long"
  "Saturday Night Rock-a-Boogie"

1960 *Jazzboat*
(Columbia) F
"Someone to Love"
"On Our Own"
"Don't Talk to Me About Love"
"I Wanna Jive Tonight"
1960 *In the Nick*
(Columbia) F
"Must Be"
"In the Nick"
1960 *Let's Get Married*
(Eros) F
"Let's Get Married"
"Do You Mind?"
"Confessions"
1969 *Can Heironymus Merkin Ever Forget Mercy Humppe and Find True Happiness?*
(Universal) F
"I'm All I Need"
"When You Gotta Go"
"Oh What a Son of a Bitch I Am"
"If All the World's a Stage"
"Piccadilly Lily"
"Sweet Love Child"
"Once Upon a Time"

NEWMAN, WHEELER AND YVONNE (acrobats)
1937 *Pathe Pictorial NS 73*

ZOE NEWTON (model)
1955 *No Love for Judy*
(Archway) F
1955 *I Am a Camera*
(Remus) F

OLIVIA NEWTON-JOHN (singer)
1970 *Toomorrow*
(Rank) F
"You're My Baby Now"

NICHOLAS (conjurer)
1939 *Pathe Pictorial NS 151*

PORJAI NICHOLAS (striptease)
1974 *Confessions of a Window Cleaner*
(Columbia) F

NICHOLAS BROTHERS (tap-dancers)
1937 *Calling All Stars*
(British Lion) F
"Za Zu Za Zu"
1947 *New Pictorial 165*
"Florida Special"

NICHOLL SISTERS (dancers)
1933 *Ideal Cinemagazine 388*
1937 *Pathe Pictorial NS 59*
"La Gaiety" (balloons)
1937 *Pathe Pictorial NS 81*
"June Roses" (fans)

HORATIO NICHOLLS (composer)
1928 *Evo's Film Review 358*

HOWARD NICHOLS (conjurer)
1931 *Ideal Cinemagazine 295*
1932 *Ideal Cinemagazine 309*

JOY NICHOLS (singer)
1956 *Not So Dusty*
(Eros) F
"Telling Me What to Do"
1957 *A King in New York*
(Archway) F
"The Sadness Goes On"

NICOL AND MARTIN (trick cyclists)
1940 *Garrison Follies*
(Butcher) F

NIGHT (group)
1981 *The Monster Club*
(ITC) F

ANNE NIGHTINGALE (broadcaster)
1973 *Radio Wonderful*
(Goodtimes) F
1978 *Home Before Midnight*
(EMI) F

ANDREA NIJINSKI (dancer)
1930 *Song of Soho*
(BIP) F

THE NILE PLAYERS (harp septette)
1933 *Musical Film Revue*
(British Lion) S
"Lullabye of the Leaves"
"Danny Boy"

WALTER NILSSON (unicyclist)
1931 *Ideal Cinemagazine 286*

JULIAN NIMAN AND HIS BOYS (band)
1937 *The Penny Pool*
(Mancunian) F
"So Say All of Us"
"Keep Fit"

GYPSY NINA (singer)
1936 *Murder at the Cabaret*
(Paramount) F
1938 *Pathetone 453*
"Waltz of the Gypsies"
1938 *Take Off That Hat*
(Viking) F
1942 *Pathetone Parade of 1942*
F (reissue: *Pathetone 453*)

999 (group)
1981 *Urgh! A Music War*
(White) F
"Homicide"

188

POLA NIRENSKA (dancer)
1940   *Hullo Fame*
        (British Films) F

NISELLE AND ILSTER (pianists)
1948   *New Pictorial 204*
        "Melody in F"

JOHNNY NIT (tap-dancer)
1930   *Black and White*
        (Gainsborough)
        "S'posin'"
1930   *Darkie Melodies*
        (Gainsborough)
1932   *Pathe Pictorial 751*
1933   *Taking Ways*
        (Sound City) F
1935   *The Morals of Marcus*
        (Realart) F
1935   *Hello Sweetheart*
        (Warner) F
1936   *Everything Is Rhythm*
        (Rock) F
        "Since Black Minnie's Got the Blues"

THE NITESHADES (group)
1965   *Be My Guest*
        (Rank) F
        "Be My Guest"

DAVID NIXON (conjurer)
1954   *Variety Half Hour*
        (Baim)
1960   *The Spider's Web*
        (Danziger) F
1962   *What's in a Flame?*
        (Gas) ADVERT
1965   *Pathe Pictorial 557*

DENNIS NOBLE (baritone)
1930   *Spanish Eyes*
        (MGM) F
1933   *Pathetone 147*
        "The One Girl"
1934   *Pathetone 211*
        "London River"
1934   *Pathetone 231*
        "Island of June"
1936   *Pathe Pictorial NS 28*
        "Limehouse"
1937   *Pathetone 401*
1938   *Pathetone 420*
        "The Phantom Fleet"
1938   *Pathe Pictorial NS 139*
        "When the Guards Go Marching By"
1939   *Pathetone 501*
        (reissue: *Pathetone 420*)
1940   *Pathetone 514*
        "The Little Ships"

PATSY ANN NOBLE (singer)
1963   *Live It Up*
        (Rank) F
        "Accidents Will Happen"

1966   *Death Is a Woman*
        (Pathe) F

PETER NOBLE (television personality)
1957   *The Naked Truth*
        (Rank) F
1959   *Make Mine a Million*
        (British Lion) F
1963   *Live It Up*
        (Rank) F

GERALD NODIN (baritone)
1936   *Pathetone 332*
        "Devonshire Cream and Cider"
1937   *Pathetone 387*
        "I Wish I Was Single Again"
1937   *Pathe Pictorial NS 53*
        "The Bargee"
1938   *Pathe Pictorial NS 126*
        "Roadways"
1939   *Pathetone 481*

KLAUS NOMI (singer)
1981   *Urgh! A Music War*
        (White) F
        "Total Eclipse"

NONI AND HORACE (musical clowns)
1930   *Comets*
        (Alpha) F

NONI AND PARTNER (musical clowns)
1936   *Variety Parade*
        (Butcher) F
1938   *Take Off That Hat*
        (Viking) F
1938   *Pathe Pictorial NS 137*
        "You're Driving Me Crazy"
1940   *Highlights of Variety 14*
        (reissue: *Variety Parade*)
1940   *Cavalcade of Variety*
        (reissue: *Variety Parade*)

VALENTINE NONYELA (singer)
1991   *Young Soul Rebels*
        (BFI) F
1994   *Welcome II the Terrordome*
        (Metro Tartan) F
        "Black and White"

PETER NOONE (singer)
see also **HERMAN'S HERMITS**
1968   *Mrs Brown You've Got a Lovely
        Daughter*
        (MGM) F
1975   *Never Too Young To Rock*
        (GTO) F

CLEO NORDLI (dancer)
1937   *Cafe Colette*
        (ABFD) F

EDGAR NORFIELD (cartoonist)
1943   *Pathe Pictorial 368*

JOSE NORMAN AND HIS RUMBEROS
(band)
  1938 *Pathe Pictorial NS 108*
        "Cubana"

NORMAN AND ARNOLD (singers)
  1931 *Pathetone 51*
        "One Minute of Heaven"

NORMAN AND MYRTILL (acrobats)
  1928 *Eve's Film Review 376*

JUMPING JACK NORRIS (dancer)
  1968 *Popdown*
        (New Realm) F

EDMUND NORTON
see **THE SINGING TAXI DRIVER**

NORWICH TRIO (musicians)
  1937 *Variety Hour*
        (Fox) F

JAMILLA NOVOTNA (song and dance)
  1936 *The Last Waltz*
        (Warwick) F
        "Believe Me I'm Quite Sincere"
        "The Magic Waltz"

REITA NUGENT (contortionist)
  1928 *Eve's Film Review 371*
        "So This Is Love"

GARY NUMAN (singer)
  1981 *Urgh! A Music War*
        (White) F
        "Down in the Park"

RUDOLPH NUREYEV (Russian dancer)
  1963 *An Evening with the Royal Ballet*
        (BHE) F
        "Les Sylphides"
        "Aurora's Wedding"
  1966 *Romeo and Juliet*
        (Rank) F
  1972 *I Am a Dancer*
        (EMI) F
        "Les Sylphides"
        "Field Figures"
        "Marguerite and Armand"
        "Sleeping Beauty"
  1977 *Valentino*
        (UA) F

THOMAS NYE (singer)
  1906 *Little Nell*
        (Chronophone)

MICHAEL O'BRIEN (Irish baritone)
1942   *Pathe Pictorial 306*
        "Paddy McGinty's Goat"

PAT O'BRIEN (Irish tenor)
1936   *Stars On Parade*
        (Butcher) F
        "That Old-Fashioned Mother of
        Mine"

CHRIS O'BRIEN'S CARIBBEANS (band)
1957   *The Tommy Steele Story*
        (Anglo) F

CAVAN O'CONNOR (Irish tenor)
1936   *Ourselves Alone*
        (BIP) F
        "Rose of Tralee"
        "Wearing of the Green"
        "Eileen Mavourneen"
1946   *Under New Management*
        (Mancunian) F
        "Little Sprig of Shamrock"
1949   *A Touch of Shamrock*
        (New Realm)
1954   *In Melodious Mood*
        (Paramount)
        "Killarney"

HAZEL O'CONNOR (singer)
1975   *Girls Come First*
        (New Realm) F
1977   *Double Exposure*
        (Columbia) F
1980   *Breaking Glass*
        (GTO) F
        "Have You Seen the Writing on the
        Wall?"
        "Monsters in Disguise"
        "Come Into the Air"
        "Big Brother"
        "Who Needs It"
        "Will You?"
        "Eighth Day"
        "Top of the Wheel"
        "Whoever Writes the Song Calls the
        Tune"
        "I Am the Black Man"
        "Give Me an Inch"
        "If Only"
        "One More Time"
1986   *Car Trouble*
        (Double Helix) F

RORY O'CONNOR (Irish singer)
1937   *Kathleen Mavourneen*
        (Butcher) F

JIMMY O'DEA (Irish comedian)
1922   *The Casey Millions*
        (Irish) F
1922   *Cruiskeen Lawn*
        (Irish) F

1922   *Wicklow Gold*
        (Irish) F
1935   *Jimmy Boy*
        (Baxter) F
1938   *Blarney*
        (ABFD) F
1938   *Penny Paradise*
        (ATP) F
        "Thirty Thousand Pounds"
        "Biddy Mulligan"
1939   *Let's Be Famous*
        (ATP) F
        "The Minstrel Boy"
1957   *The Rising of the Moon*
        (Warner) F
1961   *Johnny Nobody*
        (Columbia) F

TALBOT O'FARRELL (Irish singer)
1930   *Pathetone 31*
        "Casey's Charabanc"
1933   *Born Lucky*
        (MGM) F
1937   *Kathleen Mavourneen*
        (Butcher) F
1937   *Rose of Tralee*
        (Butcher) F
        "Down On Finnegan's Farm"
1938   *Pathetone 423*
1938   *Lily of Laguna*
        (Butcher) F
        "When Flanagan Went to Spain"
1938   *Little Dolly Daydream*
        (Butcher) F
        "Little Dolly Daydream"
        "The Lisp of a Baby's Prayer"
1941   *Highlights of Variety 19*
        (reissue: *Lily of Laguna*)
1942   *Rose of Tralee*
        (Butcher) F
1943   *Highlights of Variety 25*
        (reissue: *Lily of Laguna*)

DAVE AND JOE O'GORMAN (comedians)
1932   *Pathetone 114*
1935   *Pathetone 301*
1936   *Pictorial Revue*
        F (reissue: *Pathetone 301*)
1936   *Variety Parade*
        (Butcher) F

O'LEARY, TRACY AND O'LEARY (dancers)
1936   *Pathe Pictorial NS 33*

BIRRELL O'MALLEY (Welsh tenor)
1932   *Land of My Fathers*
        (Heale)
1932   *Hills of My Old Welsh Home*
        (Heale)
1932   *One Bright Summer Morning*
        (Heale)
1932   *Bells of Aberdovy*
        (Heale)

PAT O'MALLEY (Irish singer)
1935 *Pathetone 277*
      "Believe It Beloved"
1935 *Pathetone 287*
      "Orchids for My Lady"

ZELMA O'NEAL (American singer)
1934 *Freedom of the Seas*
      (BIP) F
1934 *Give Her a Ring*
      (BIP) F
      "Come On and Love"
1934 *Mr Cinders*
      (BIP) F
      "Just a Blue Sky"
      "I Can Get Used to You"
      "Spread a Little Happiness"
1934 *There Goes Susie*
      (Pathe) F
1935 *Spring In the Air*
      (Pathe) F
1935 *Joy Ride*
      (City) F
1937 *Let's Make a Night of It*
      (ABPC) F
      "Honeybunch"

DENNIS O'NEIL (Irish tenor)
1931 *No Lady*
      (Gaumont) F
1933 *General John Regan*
      (B&D) F
1934 *Danny Boy*
      (Butcher) F
      "Come Back to Erin"
      "The Mountains o' Mourne"
1935 *Variety*
      (Butcher) F
      "Have You Got Another Girl Like
      Mary?"
1935 *Father O'Flynn*
      (Butcher) F
      "Father O'Flynn"
1937 *Kathleen Mavourneen*
      (Butcher) F

PADDIE O'NEIL (comedienne)
1944 *New Pictorial 24*
1951 *Penny Points to Paradise*
      (Adelphi) F
1965 *The Early Bird*
      (Rank) F
1969 *The Adding Machine*
      (Universal) F

PEGGY O'NEIL (singer)
1929 *Pathe Magazine 2*
      "Merry Merry"

CON O'NEILL (Irish singer)
1989 *Dancin' Thru' the Dark*
      (Palace)
      "So Many People"
      "Shoeshine"
      "Dancin' Thru' the Dark"

ALFRED O'SHEA (singer)
1936 *Pathe Pictorial NS 34*
      "Gentle Maiden"

TESSIE O'SHEA (comedienne)
1944 *The Way Ahead*
      (Two Cities) F
      "If You Were the Only Girl in the
      World"
1946 *London Town*
      (GFD) F
      "The Hampstead Way"
      "My Heart Goes Crazy"
      "And So Would I"
      "Any Old Iron"
1948 *Holidays With Pay*
      (Mancunian) F
      "Strolling Along by the Seaside"
      "He Isn't Much to Look At"
1949 *Somewhere in Politics*
      (Mancunian) F
      "Spade and Bucket"
1950 *The Blue Lamp*
      (Ealing) F
      "There Isn't Enough To Go Round"
      "I'm Looking for a Lad Once More"
1954 *Tonight in Britain*
      (Pathe)
1957 *The Shiralee*
      (MGM) F
1960 *Tonight's the Nite*
      (reissue: *Holidays With Pay*)
1969 *The Best House in London*
      (MGM) F
      "The Birds of London Town"

PETER O'SULLEVAN (television
commentator)
1997 *Shooting Fish*
      (Gruber) F

AL OAKES AND HIS THREE STOOGES
(comedy)
1934 *Crazy People*
      (British Lion) F

OLLY OAKLEY (banjo)
1927 *Olly Oakley*
      (Phonofilm)
1932 *Musical Medley 5*
      (reissue: *Olly Oakley*)

GENE OCTOBER (singer)
1978 *Jubilee*
      (Cinegate) F
1985 *Number One*
      (Lutebest) F
1986 *Caravaggio*
      (BFI) F

BILL ODDIE (comedian)
1967 *The Plank*
      (Rank) F

1976 *Pleasure at Her Majesty's*
(Amnesty) F
"Funky Gibbon"
"Lumberjack Song"

OHIO TRIO (musicians)
1928 *Ohio Trio*
(Phonofilm)
1932 *Musical Medley 5*
(reissue: *Ohio Trio*)

OINGO BOINGO (group)
1981 *Urgh! A Music War*
(White) F
"Ain't This the Life"

OLD MOSCOW BALALAIKA ORCHESTRA
1934 *Forbidden Territory*
(Gaumont) F

MIKE OLDFIELD (singer)
1982 *The Essential Mike Oldfield*
(Holmes)

DEREK OLDHAM (baritone)
1934 *On the Air*
(British Lion) F
1934 *The Broken Rosary*
(Butcher) F
"Ave Maria"
1935 *City Of Beautiful Nonsense*
(Butcher) F
"Ave Maria"
"Sally in Our Alley"
"Summer Night"
"Bless You"
1935 *Charing Cross Road*
(British Lion) F
"Roadway of Romance"
1936 *Melody of My Heart*
(Butcher) F
"Whisper in Your Dreams"
"I Give You My Love"
1941 *Highlights of Variety 24*
(reissue: *The Broken Rosary*)

BARRIE OLIVER (dancer)
1922 *Eve's Film Review 79*
"Flirtation Foxtrot" (with Olivette)
1922 *Eve's Film Review 80*
"Exhibition Waltz" (with Olivette)
1926 *Eve's Film Review 246*
(with Doreen Read)
1926 *British Screen Magazine*
"Charleston"
1928 *Eve's Film Review 358*
"Table Top Toes" (with Betty Bolton)
1928 *Eve's Film Review 371*
"Baltimore Dance" (with Beryl
Yvette)
1930 *The Musical Beauty Shop*
(PDC)
1930 *The New Waiter*
(PDC)

JOHN OLIVER (bass)
1932 *Pathe Pictorial 743*
"Father O'Flynn"

VIC OLIVER (comedian)
1935 *Pathetone 289*
"Stars and Stripes"
1935 *Pathetone 297*
"Nice Morning"
1936 *Rhythm in the Air*
(Fox) F
1937 *Who's Your Lady Friend?*
(ABFD) F
1938 *Around the Town*
(British Lion) F
1938 *Meet Mr Penny*
(British National) F
1940 *Room for Two*
(Grand National) F
1941 *He Found a Star*
(GFD) F
1941 *Hi Gang*
(Gainsborough) F
1944 *Give Us the Moon*
(Gainsborough) F
1945 *I'll Be Your Sweetheart*
(Gainsborough) F
1948 *For Old Times Sake*
(Butcher)
1954 *Behind the Scenes 2*
(Gas) ADVERT

OLIVER AND WICKS (pianists)
1936 *Cabaret Nights 1*
(Highbury)

OLIVETTE (dancer)
1922 *Eve's Film Review 79*
"Flirtation Foxtrot"
1922 *Eve's Film Review 80*
"Exhibition Waltz"
1930 *Not So Quiet on the Western Front*
(BIP) F
1930 *Kiss Me Sergeant*
(BIP) F
1930 *Why Sailors Leave Home*
(BIP) F
1931 *What a Night*
(BIP) F
1937 *Boys Will Be Girls*
(Fuller) F

VICTOR OLOFF SEXTETTE (musicians)
1931 *Pathe Pictorial 708*
"When Dawn Breaks Through"

OLSEN'S SEA LIONS (animal act)
1935 *Variety*
(Butcher) F
1937 *The Show Goes On*
(ATP) F
1937 *Highlights of Variety 3*
(reissue: *Variety*)

OMAR (acrobatic dancer)
1935 *Cock o' the North*
(Butcher) F

OMAR (singer)
1996 *Glastonbury: The Movie*
(Starlight) F
"There's Nothing Like This"

YOKO ONO (singer)
1970 *Let It Be*
(UA) F
1972 *Imagine*
(Vaughan) F
"Mind Train"
"Midsummer New York"
"Mrs Lennon"

DAVID OPENSHAW (singer)
1930 *London Melody*
(British Screen) F

PAUL ORAH
see **VIOLET DURRANT AND PAUL ORAH**

ORANGE BUTTERFLY (group)
1970 *Groupie Girl*
(Eagle) F

**ORCHESTRAL MANOEUVRES IN THE
DARK** (group)
1981 *Urgh! A Music War*
(White) F
"Enola Gay"

THE ORCHIDS (group)
1964 *Just For You*
(British Lion) F
"Mr Scrooge"

BERYL ORDE (impressionist)
1934 *Pathe Pictorial 823*
1934 *Radio Parade of 1935*
(BIP) F
(as Jimmy Durante, Mae West,
Mabel Constanduros)
1935 *In Town Tonight*
(British Lion) F
1937 *Sing As You Swing*
(Rock) F
(as Greta Garbo, Mae West, Jean
Harlow, Ned Sparks)
1939 *Pathetone 478*
(as Mabel Constanduros, Western
Brothers)
1941 *Pathetone Parade of 1941*
F (reissue: *Pathetone 478*)
1943 *The Dummy Talks*
(British National) F
"Teasing"
"Oh Johnny" (as Nellie Wallace,
Martha Raye)
1946 *As Others See Us*
(Merlin)

THE ORIENTAL BROTHERS (balancers)
1939 *Pathetone 493*

ORLANDO (dancer)
1973 *The Lindsay Kemp Circus*
(Scottish Arts Council)
"Just a Regular Man"
1990 *The Garden*
(Basilisk) F

CURLY ORMEROD (guitar)
1939 *Eddie Carroll and his Boys*
(Inspiration)
"Sweet Sue"

ORPHEUM OCTET (singers)
1935 *Wedding Eve*
(Astor) F

TOM ORRELLO AND MIMI
1939 *Pathe Pictorial NS 178*

BERT OSBORNE AND HIS BAND
1937 *Sticking to the Facts*
(Ace Cinemagazine)
1937 *Wood You Believe It*
(Ace Cinemagazine)

CHIEF OSKENONTON (American Indian
broadcaster)
1936 *Pathetone 325*

ADRIANA OTERO (singer)
1936 *Melody of My Heart*
(Butcher) F

JOHN OTWAY (singer)
1981 *Urgh! A Music War*
(White) F
"Cheryl's Going Home"

OUMANSKY BALLET (dancers)
1928 *Phototone 15*

THE OUTLAWS (group)
1963 *Live It Up*
(Rank) F
"Law and Disorder"

HARRY OWENS AND HIS BAND
1946 *Wot No Gangsters*
(New Realm) F

OZI AND GLESNE (Welsh singers)
1981 *The Mouse and the Woman*
(Facelift) F

OZRIC TENTACLES (group)
1996 *Glastonbury: The Movie*
(Starlight) F
"Jurassic Shift"

PABLO (conjurer)
  1938   *Pathe Pictorial NS 106*

JACK PADBURY AND HIS COSMO CLUB SIX (band)
  1929   *Pathe Magazine 1*
         "Just a Little Jazz"
  1931   *Ideal Cinemagazine 265*
  1933   *Pathetone 162*
         "It Don't Mean a Thing"
         "Sure of Everything But You"

DAPHNE PADEL (broadcaster)
  1950   *Twenty Questions Murder Mystery*
         (Grand National) F
  1952   *Murder On the Air*
         F (reissue: *Twenty Questions Murder Mystery*)

IGNACE JAN PADEREWSKI (Polish pianist)
  1937   *Moonlight Sonata*
         (UA) F
         "Moonlight Sonata"
         "Polonaise"
         "Second Hungarian Rhapsody"
         "Minuet"
  1943   *The Charmer*
         (reissue: *Moonlight Sonata*)

GAIL PAGE (singer)
  1945   *What Do We Do Now?*
         (Grand National) F

PAGE AND JEWITT (trick cyclists)
  1933   *Eve's Film Review 652*

PETER PAGET (characters)
  1934   *Pathe Pictorial 840*
         "Uriah Heep"

VIVIENNE PAGET (blues singer)
  1940   *At the Havana*
         (New Realm)

OTTO PAGOTTI
  see **CELEBRITY TRIO**

PAICE, ASHTON AND LORD (group)
  1979   *Lifespan*
         (ITC)

ELAINE PAIGE (singer)
  1978   *Adventures of a Plumber's Mate*
         (Alpha) F

LUELLA PAIKIN (soprano)
  1929   *Favourite Airs*
         (BSFP)
         "Rigoletto"
         "Lo Hear the Gentle Lark"
         "Londonderry Air"

MONA PAIVA (dancer)
  1920   *Around the Town 12*
         (Gaumont)
         "Harem Dance"

MICHAEL PALIN (comedian)
  1971   *And Now For Something Completely Different*
         (Columbia) F
  1975   *Monty Python and the Holy Grail*
         (EMI) F
  1976   *Pleasure at Her Majesty's*
         (Amnesty) F
         "Dead Parrot Sketch"
         "Court Room Sketch"
         "Lumberjack Song"
  1977   *Jabberwocky*
         (Columbia) F
  1979   *Monty Python's Life of Brian*
         (CIC) F
  1980   *The Secret Policeman's Ball*
         (Tigon) F
  1981   *Time Bandits*
         (UIP) F
  1982   *The Secret Policeman's Other Ball*
         (UIP) F
  1983   *The Missionary*
         (Handmade) F
  1983   *Crimson Permanent Assurance*
         (UIP)
  1983   *Monty Python's The Meaning of Life*
         (UIP) F
  1983   *Monty Python Live at the Hollywood Bowl*
         (Handmade) F
  1984   *A Private Function*
         (Handmade) F
  1984   *The Dress*
         (UIP)
  1985   *Brazil*
         (TCF) F
  1988   *A Fish Called Wanda*
         (Prominent) F
  1991   *American Friends*
         (Prominent) F
  1996   *Fierce Creatures*
         (Universal) F
  1996   *The Wind in the Willows*
         (Allied) F

ANITA PALLENBERG (model)
  1970   *Performance*
         (Warner) F

EDDIE PALMER (novachord)
  1944   *Starlight Serenade*
         (Federated) F

GASTON PALMER (French juggler)
  1936   *The Three Maxims*
         (Wilcox) F
  1937   *Pathetone 373*
  1937   *Pathe Pictorial NS 77*
  1939   *Pathe Pictorial NS 158*

1941 *Pathe Pictorial 265*
1943 *Pathe Pictorial 384*
1945 *I Didn't Do It*
(Columbia) F

LILLI PALMER (singer)
(films as actress not listed)
1937 *Good Morning Boys*
(Gainsborough) F
"Baby Whatcha Gonna Do Tonight?"
1937 *Sunset in Vienna*
(Wilcox) F
"Sunset in Vienna"
"We'll Never Run Short of Love"

SID PALMER (comedian)
1939 *Music Hall Parade*
(Butcher) F

DAVID PALTENGHI (dancer)
1952 *The Black Swan*
(Stereo)
1954 *Harmony Lane*
(Eros)
"Swan Lake"
1956 *Invitation to the Dance*
(MGM) F

PAN (group)
1996 *Glastonbury: The Movie*
(Starlight) F
"Glasters"

PAN AFRICAN ORCHESTRA, GHANA
1991 *Ama*
(Efiri) F

MAJA PAPANDOPOLOU (singer)
1972 *England Made Me*
(Hemdale) F

PAQUITA AND BILLDAINITA (dancers)
1928 *Phototone 11*
"La Provinciera"

NORRIE PARAMOR (pianist)
1961 *The Frightened City*
(Anglo) F
"I Laughed at Love"
1962 *Band of Thieves*
(Rank) F

PARIS SISTERS (singers)
1962 *It's Trad Dad*
(Columbia) F
"Now That We Are Through With Love"

PHIL PARK (musician)
1944 *New Pictorial 34*
1945 *A Holiday Ramble*
(Renown)

MERLE PARK (ballerina)
1963 *An Evening with the Royal Ballet*
(BHE) F

AUDREY PARKER (singer)
1937 *Arty Egg Samples*
(Ace Cinemagazine)
"One Kiss Before We Part"

DON PARKER AND HIS BAND
1926 *Eve's Film Review 246*

MICHAEL PARKINSON (television personality)
1974 *Madhouse*
(EMI) F

JACK PARNELL (drums)
1946 *London Town*
(GFD) F
"The Hampstead Way"
1950 *The Blue Lamp*
(Ealing) F
1950 *Dance Hall*
(Ealing) F
"Courtin'"
1963 *Just For Fun*
(Columbia) F

PARR AND PARR (dancers)
1930 *Eve's Film Review 498*
1930 *Pathetone 37*

HARRY PARRY AND HIS RADIO RHYTHM CLUB SEXTET
1942 *Pathe Pictorial 320*
1943 *Pathe Pictorial 381*
1943 *Swingonometry*
(Inspiration)
"Tiger Rag"
"Honeysuckle Rose"
"Whistler's Mother-in-Law"
1943 *Harry Parry and his Radio Rhythm Sextet*
(Inspiration)
1945 *What Do We Do Now?*
(Grand National) F
1947 *New Pictorial 132*
"Honeysuckle Rose"

NICHOLAS PARSONS (comedian)
1950 *Full Circle*
(Eclipse)
1955 *Simon and Laura*
(Rank) F
1955 *An Alligator Named Daisy*
(Rank) F
1956 *Brothers in Law*
(Tudor) F
1956 *The Long Arm*
(Ealing) F
1957 *Happy Is the Bride*
(Soskin) F

1964 *Every Day's a Holiday*
(Grand National) F
1964 *Murder Ahoy*
(MGM) F
1966 *The Ghost Goes Gear*
(Pathe) F
1966 *The Wrong Box*
(Columbia) F
1967 *Don't Raise the Bridge, Lower the River*
(Shenson) F
1971 *Danger Point*
(Damor) F
1974 *The Best of Benny Hill*
(EMI) F
1976 *Spy Story*
(Shonteff) F

DON PARTRIDGE (one-man band)
1968 *Popdown*
(New Realm) F
1968 *Otley*
(Columbia) F
"Homeless Bones"

PASCALINE (striptease)
1960 *Beat Girl*
(Renown) F

PASCO AND CAMPO (acrobats)
1932 *Ideal Cinemagazine 320*

PAT AND EDDY (dancers)
1930 *We Two*
(Morgan)

MAY PATTERSON (tap-dancer)
1939 *Discoveries*
(Vogue) F

OTTILIE PATTERSON (singer)
1955 *Momma Don't Allow*
(BFI)
"The Blues Knocking On My Door"
1962 *It's Trad Dad*
(Columbia) F
"Down By the Riverside"
"When the Saints Go Marching In"
1962 *Chris Barber Bandstand*
(British Lion)
"Mamma He Treats Your Daughter Mean"
"Can't Afford To Do It"

TINO PATTIERA (Italian tenor)
1928 *Phototone 4*
"Tosca"
1928 *Phototone 10*
"Pagliacci"

THE PATTON BROTHERS (entertainers)
1971 *Top of the Bill*
(Butcher) F

BETTY PAUL (singer)
1950 *Let's Have a Murder*
(Mancunian) F
"Hold Me in Your Arms Again"

JOHN E. PAUL AND THE BLUE MOUNTAIN BOYS (group)
1968 *The Strange Affair*
(Paramount) F

THE PAVIANS (balancers)
1942 *Pathe Pictorial 302*

ANNA PAVLOVA (ballerina)
1921 *Celebrities of the Dance*
(Gaumont)
1930 *Pathetone 27*
1930 *Eve's Film Review 487*
1935 *The Immortal Swan*
(Ace) F
"Invitation to the Waltz"
"Giselle"
"Don Quixote"
"The Dying Swan"
"Californian Poppy"
"Radino"

JEREMY PAXMAN (television presenter)
1979 *The Kids Are Alright*
(Rose) F

GRAHAM PAYN (boy soprano)
1932 *Pathe Pictorial 724*
"I Hear You Calling Me"
1932 *Pathe Pictorial 736*
"In an Old-Fashioned Town"
1934 *Love Mirth Melody*
(Mancunian) F
1935 *Musical Medley*
(Mancunian)
1940 *Music Hall Personalities 14*
(reissue: *Musical Medley*)

JACK PAYNE AND HIS DANCE ORCHESTRA
1929 *Jazztime*
(BIP)
"Ever So Goosey"
"My Sin"
"I'll Never Ask for More"
1929 *Pathe Magazine 8*
1930 *Symphony in Two Flats*
(Gainsborough) F
"Give Me Back My Heart"
1932 *Say It With Music*
(B&D) F
"Say It With Music"
"Love Is the Sweetest Thing"
"Good Morning Mr Sun"
"I'll Do My Best to Make You Happy"
"Smile and Sing Your Cares Away"
1935 *Pathe Pictorial 880*
"Tiger Rag"

1936 *Sunshine Ahead*
(Baxter) F
"Sunshine Ahead"
"All Jolly Pirates"

JACK PAYNE AND HIS HOTEL CECIL BAND
1927 *Syncopated Melodies*
(Parkinson)

JOHN PAYNE'S CHOIR
1934 *Radio Parade of 1935*
(BIP) F
1938 *Lily of Laguna*
(Butcher) F
"The Banshee"
1938 *Follow Your Star*
(Belgrave) F
"De Lawd Loves His People to Sing"

RICHARD PAYNE (hypnotist)
1948 *New Pictorial 235*

TOM PAYNE AND VERA HILLIARD
(comedy)
1930 *Pathe Magazine 20*
1930 *Pathetone 40*
1931 *Payne and Hilliard*
(Pathe)
"The Women I've Had At My Feet"
1936 *Queen of Hearts*
(ATP) F

EDDIE PEABODY AND HIS BEACHCOMBERS (band)
1938 *Pathe Pictorial NS 123*
"When I Grow Too Old to Dream"
"Listen to the Mocking Bird"
1938 *Pathetone 446*
"Song of the Islands"

ROLAND PEACHY AND HIS BAND
1938 *Pathetone 444*
"Rosita"

PRINCESS PEARL (singer)
1936 *Everything Is Rhythm*
(Rock) F
"Man of My Dreams"
"Without Love"
"Sky High Honeymoon"

BOB AND ALF PEARSON (singers)
1932 *Pathe Pictorial 741*
"By the Fireside"
1932 *Pathe Pictorial 760*
"The Clouds Will Soon Roll By"
1932 *Pathe Pictorial 764*
"Old Time Medley"
1933 *Pathetone 183*
"My Goodbye to You"
1933 *Pathe Pictorial 777*
"Lord You Made the Night Too Long"

1933 *Pathe Pictorial 790*
"What Would You Like for Breakfast?"
1933 *Pathe Pictorial 796*
"Old Father Thames"
1933 *Pathe Pictorial 819*
"Sunday Down in Old Caroline"
1934 *Pathe Pictorial 879*
"London on a Rainy Night"
1936 *Pathe Pictorial 928*
"Misty Islands of the Highlands"
1937 *Pathe Pictorial NS 50*
"Did Your Mother Come From Ireland?"
1938 *Pathetone 419*
"Pride of Tipperary"
1971 *Top of the Bill*
(Butcher) F

THE JUGGLING PEARSONS (jugglers)
1938 *Pathe Pictorial NS 130*

DON PEDRO AND HIS BAND
1937 *Pathe Pictorial NS 90*
"Gypsy Airs"

EDA PEEL (singer)
1944 *Give Me the Stars*
(British National) F

JOHN PEEL (disc jockey)
1973 *Radio Wonderful*
(Goodtimes) F
1977 *A Bridge Too Far*
(UA) F

PEEL AND CURTIS (comedians)
1940 *Music Hall Personalities 14*

DONALD PEERS (singer)
1942 *The Balloon Goes Up*
(New Realm) F
"I'll Soon Be Coming Home"
"Keep Looking for the Rainbow"
"You've Gotta Smile"
1952 *Sing Along With Me*
(British Lion) F
"Take My Heart"
"If You Smile at the Sun"
"Hoop Diddle-i-do-ra-li-ay"
"Down at the Old Village Hall"
"I Left My Heart in a Valley in Wales"

STAN PELL AND STAN LITTLE (comedy)
1936 *Dodging the Dole*
(Mancunian) F
1938 *Music Hall Personalities 5*
(reissue: *Dodging the Dole*)

NOBERTO PENA (guitarist)
1974 *Three for All*
(Fox-Rank) F

BOB PENDER (stilt-walker)
1904 *Hands Up, or Captured By Highwaymen*
(Gaumont)
1910 *The Travelling Stiltwalkers*
(Gaumont)

PENGE FORMATION DANCERS
1959 *Make Mine a Million*
(British Lion) F
1988 *It Couldn't Happen Here*
(Entertainment) F

CHARLES PENROSE (comedian)
1936 *Calling the Tune*
(Phoenix) F
"The Laughing Policeman"
1937 *The Derelict*
(Gover) F
1939 *The Dark Eyes of London*
(Pathe) F
1939 *Hospital Hospitality*
(Renown)
1947 *Miranda*
(GFD) F

FRANK PEPPER (entertainer)
1954 *Variety Half Hour*
(Baim)

HARRY S. PEPPER (piano)
see also **THE CO-OPTIMISTS**
1929 *The Co-Optimists*
(New Era) F
1933 *Radio Parade*
(BIP) F
1934 *Kentucky Minstrels*
(Realart) F
1936 *Sunshine Ahead*
(Baxter) F

TOM PEPPER (comedian)
1987 *Business As Usual*
(Cannon) F

ELSIE PERCIVAL (dancer)
1930 *Elsie Percival and Ray Raymond*
(Gainsborough)
1930 *Big Business*
(Fox) F

LANCE PERCIVAL (comedian)
1961 *Raising the Wind*
(Anglo) F
1961 *The Devil's Daffodil*
(British Lion) F
1962 *Postman's Knock*
(MGM) F
1962 *Twice Round the Daffodils*
(Anglo) F
1962 *Carry On Cruising*
(Anglo) F
1963 *It's All Over Town*
(British Lion) F

1963 *Hide and Seek*
(Spectrum) F
1963 *The VIPs*
(MGM) F
1964 *The Yellow Rolls Royce*
(MGM) F
1965 *The Big Job*
(Anglo) F
1965 *You Must Be Joking*
(Columbia) F
1965 *Joey Boy*
(British Lion) F
1968 *Mrs Brown You've Got a Lovely Daughter*
(MGM) F
"Any Old Iron"
1970 *There's a Girl in My Soup*
(Columbia) F
1971 *The Magnificent 6½*
(CFF) SERIAL
1971 *Up Pompeii*
(EMI) F
1971 *Up the Chastity Belt*
(EMI) F
1972 *Up the Front*
(EMI) F
1972 *Our Miss Fred*
(EMI) F
1974 *The Boy With Two Heads*
(CFF) F
1977 *Confessions from a Holiday Camp*
(Columbia) F
1978 *Rosie Dixon Night Nurse*
(Columbia) F

PERCIVAL AND HILL (entertainers)
1928 *Percival and Hill*
(Phonofilm)

BILLY PERCY (comedian)
1934 *Love Mirth Melody*
(Mancunian) F
1956 *Ramsbottom Rides Again*
(British Lion) F

PERE UBU (group)
1981 *Urgh! A Music War*
(White) F
"Birdies"

ROSE PERFECT (soprano)
1933 *Pathetone 169*
"Song of Songs"

PERMAN'S BEAR (animal act)
1902 *Perman's Equestrian Bear*
(Warwick)

JEAN PERRIE AND MARIE COLORES
(acrobats)
1930 *Eve's Film Review 458*

HARRY PERRY AND MILLICENT RAY
(dancers)
  1912 *Ragtime Texas Tommy*
        (Selsior)

HARRY PERRY AND ROSIE SLOMAN
(dancers)
  1913 *Spanish-American Quickstep*
        (Selsior)

STEVE PERRY (singer)
  1963 *Take Six*
        (British Lion)
        "Ginny Come Lately"

VIC PERRY (pickpocket)
  1955 *Timeslip*
        (Anglo) F
  1956 *Raiders of the River*
        (CFF) SERIAL
  1964 *Mozambique*
        (British Lion) F

PET SHOP BOYS (group)
  1988 *It Couldn't Happen Here*
        (Entertainment) F
        "It Couldn't Happen Here"
        "Suburbia"
        "It's a Sin"
        "West End Girls"
        "Rent"
        "Two Divided by Zero"
        "King's Cross"
        "One More Chance"
        "Wake Up"
        "Always on My Mind"
        "What Have I Done To Deserve
        This?"

PETER (boy singer)
  1945 *Here Comes the Sun*
        (Baxter) F
        "You Never Miss Your Mother"

PETER AND GORDON (singers)
  1964 *Just For You*
        (British Lion) F
        "Leave Me Alone"
  1965 *Pop Gear*
        (Pathe) F
        "World Without Love"

JOE PETERMAN (comedian)
  1919 *The Lads of the Village*
        (Atlantic) F
  1920 *The Glad Eye*
        (Reardon) F
  1933 *Pathe Pictorial 810*

LAURI PETERS (American singer)
  1963 *Summer Holiday*
        (ABPC) F
        "A Swinging Affair"
        "Is This Me Here?"

SYLVIA PETERS (television personality)
  1950 *Shooting Stars*
        (Anglo)

PETITE ASCOTS (child tap-dancers)
  1936 *British Lion Varieties 1; 3; 4; 7*

PETITE POUPEE (strong girl)
  1941 *Pathe Pictorial 284*

PEGGY PETRONELLA (singer)
see also **THE CO-OPTIMISTS**
  1929 *The Co-Optimists*
        (New Era) F

**PETRULENGRO AND HIS GYPSY GIRLS'
BAND**
  1937 *Pathe Pictorial NS 51*

NORMAN PETT (cartoonist)
  1943 *Pathe Pictorial 395*
  1944 *New Pictorial 23*

PEVERI (tenor)
  1929 *Pathe Pictorial M 8*
        "Tenor on Stilts"

PHAROS (juggler and conjurer)
  1911 *Pharos the Wonder Worker*
        (Tress)

PHILHARMONIC STRING QUARTETTE
  1936 *Calling the Tune*
        (Phoenix) F

DON PHILLIPE AND PARTNER (specialty)
  1940 *Pathetone 559*
        "Modes While You Wait"

JEAN PHILIPPE (singer)
  1960 *Jazzboat*
        (Columbia) F
        "Oui Oui"

ARLENE PHILLIPS' HOT GOSSIP (dancers)
  1979 *The Golden Lady*
        (Target) F

EMO PHILLIPS (American comedian)
  1987 *The Secret Policeman's Third Ball*
        (Virgin) F

FRANK PHILLIPS (broadcaster)
  1943 *Pictorial Revue of 1943*
        (Pathe) F
  1954 *The Runaway Bus*
        (Eros) F
  1955 *The Dam Busters*
        (ABPC) F
  1955 *The Quatermass Experiment*
        (Hammer) F
  1959 *"I'm All Right Jack"*
        (British Lion) F
  1963 *It Happened Here*
        (UA) F

MILLICENT PHILLIPS (child singer)
1935　*Pathe Pictorial 901*
　　　"Little Brown Owl"
1939　*Pathe Pictorial NS 156*
　　　"On Wings of Song"

NORMAN PHILLIPS SAXOPHONE TRIO
(musicians)
1936　*Mewsical Airs*
　　　(Ace Cinemagazine)
1937　*Mewsical Gems*
　　　(Ace Cinemagazine)

WOOLF PHILLIPS AND THE SKYROCKETS
(band)
1949　*Vote for Huggett*
　　　(Gainsborough) F
　　　"Compliments Will Get You
　　　Nowhere"

PHROSO (Trevillion) (specialty)
1903　*The Mysterious Mechanical Toy*
　　　(Gaumont)

PIANO SEXTETTE
1940　*Laugh It Off*
　　　(British National) F

THE PIANOVILLES (musicians)
1936　*Pathetone 329*
　　　"Goody Goody"

PICCADILLY HOBOES (buskers)
1937　*More Wire Less Talk*
　　　(Ace Cinemagazine)

PICCADILLY REVELS GIRLS (dancers)
1926　*British Screen Magazine*

PICCADILLY PLAYERS (band)
1929　*Pathe Magazine 7*

ALFRED PICCAVER (tenor)
1932　*Pathetone 99*
1934　*A Garland of Song*
　　　(APD)

MIRTO PICCHI (tenor)
1948　*Broken Journey*
　　　(GFD) F

PICKARD'S CHINESE SYNCOPATORS
(band)
1935　*Dance Band*
　　　(BIP) F
　　　"Nagasaki"
　　　"Chinatown"
　　　"Sing Song Girl"

WILFRED PICKLES (broadcaster)
1948　*Thee and Me*
　　　(COI)
1954　*The Gay Dog*
　　　(Eros) F

1959　*Serious Charge*
　　　(Eros) F
1963　*Billy Liar*
　　　(Anglo) F
1966　*The Family Way*
　　　(British Lion) F
1972　*For the Love of Ada*
　　　(Tigon) F

MOLLY PICON (American comedienne)
1937　*Let's Make a Night of It*
　　　(ABPC) F

THE PIDDINGTONS (mind readers)
1950　*The Piddingtons*
　　　(Pathe)

BURTON PIERCE (tap-dancer)
1938　*Crackerjack*
　　　(Gainsborough) F
　　　"Interpretations in Tempo"

LA PILLINA (dancer)
1951　*Pandora and the Flying Dutchman*
　　　(Romulus) F

PIM'S COMEDY NAVY (comedy acrobats)
1941　*Bob's Your Uncle*
　　　(Butcher) F

**EUGENE PINI AND HIS TANGO
ORCHESTRA**
1936　*B.B.C. Musicals 6*
　　　(Inspiration)
　　　"La Paloma"
1937　*Calling All Stars*
　　　(British Lion) F
1938　*Melodies of the Moment*
　　　(Inspiration)
1938　*Sweet Devil*
　　　(GFD) F
1939　*Radio Nights*
　　　(reissue: *B.B.C. Musicals 6*)
1948　*The Flamingo Affair*
　　　(Inspiration) F
　　　"La Passionara"
1948　*Eugene Pini and his Orchestra*
　　　(Inspiration)
1949　*Music Parade*
　　　(reissue: *Eugene Pini and his
　　　Orchestra*)
1951　*Mirth and Melody*
　　　(reissue: *title unknown*)
1952　*Blonde for Danger*
　　　(reissue: *The Flamingo Affair*)

PINK FLOYD (group)
1967　*Tonite Let's All Make Love in
　　　London*
　　　(Lorrimer) F
1967　*Pathe Pictorial 665*
　　　"Scarecrow"
1982　*Pink Floyd: The Wall*
　　　(UIP) F

PIPE BAND OF THE SCOTS GUARDS
1938 *Bonnie Scotland Calls You*
      (ABPC)

ARCHIE PITT (comedian)
1929 *Eve's Film Review 421*
1934 *Danny Boy*
      (Butcher) F
1935 *Barnacle Bill*
      (Butcher) F
      "I'll Meet You By the Blue Lagoon"
1936 *Excuse My Glove*
      (ABFD) F

JACK PLANT (singer)
1935 *Pathe Pictorial 876*
      "Isle of Capri"
      "What a Difference a Day Makes"
1939 *Pathetone 502*
1939 *Pathe Pictorial NS 150*

THE PLAYBOYS (group)
1977 *Black Joy*
      (Hemdale) F

PLAZA BOYS (acrobatic dancers)
1930 *Al Fresco*
      (Gainsborough)
1930 *Black and White*
      (Gainsborough)
1930 *Amateur Night in London*
      (PDC) F

THE PLEBS (group)
1965 *Be My Guest*
      (Rank) F

ALEC PLEON (comedian)
1949 *School for Randle*
      (Mancunian) F
1950 *Over the Garden Wall*
      (Mancunian) F
1960 *Teacher's Pest*
      (reissue: *School for Randle*)
1960 *The Three Who Flungs*
      (reissue: *School for Randle*)
1971 *Up the Chastity Belt*
      (EMI) F

GRACE POGGI (dancer)
1935 *Heat Wave*
      (Gainsborough) F
1935 *Ten Minute Alibi*
      (British Lion) F

EDDIE POLA (pianist)
1934 *Pathe Pictorial 823*
      "Jazz Justice"
1936 *Sunshine Ahead*
      (Baxter) F
1937 *Catch As Catch Can*
      (Fox) F
1938 *Hey Hey USA*
      (Gainsborough) F

1939 *The Outsider*
      (ABPC) F
1939 *Pathe Pictorial NS 173*
      "Twisted Tunes"
1939 *Pathe Pictorial NS 180*
      "Twisted Tunes"
1939 *Pathetone 505*
      "Twisted Tunes"

POLICE (group)
1981 *Urgh! A Music War*
      (White) F
      "Driven to Tears"
      "Roxanne"
      "So Lonely"

POLISH MILITARY CHOIR
1943 *Scottish Mazurka*
      (Technique)

ARTHUR POND (comedian)
1934 *Love Mirth Melody*
      (Mancunian) F
1935 *Musical Medley*
      (Mancunian)
1940 *Music Hall Personalities 15*
      (reissue: *Musical Medley*)

BRIAN POOLE AND THE TREMELOES
(group)
1963 *Just For Fun*
      (Columbia) F
      "Keep On Dancing"
1964 *Swinging UK*
      (Baim)
      "Do You Love Me?"
1964 *UK Swings Again*
      (Baim)
      "Someone"

DAVID POOLE AND MARYON LANE
(dancers)
1954 *Dance Little Lady*
      (Renown) F

IGGY POP (singer)
1986 *Sid and Nancy*
      (Zenith) F
1990 *Hardware*
      (Palace) F
      "Cold Metal"

FRED POPLAR (comedian)
1899 *My Pal*
      (Warwick)

PORNO FOR PYROS (group)
1996 *Glastonbury: The Movie*
      (Starlight) F
      "Porno For Pyros"

JOEY PORTER
see **JACK WILLIAMS AND JOEY PORTER**

LINDA PORTER (singer)
1947　*When You Come Home*
　　　(Butcher) F
　　　"When You Come Home"

URIEL PORTER (singer)
1941　*He Found a Star*
　　　(GFD) F
　　　"Waiting"
1942　*Gert and Daisy Clean Up*
　　　(Butcher) F
　　　"Coaling"

PORTERJINSKY'S RUSSIAN CHOIR
1938　*Make a Note of It*
　　　(Ace Cinemagazine)

GEORGE POSFORD (composer)
1944　*Pathe Pictorial 421*
　　　"Room 504"

GILLIE POTTER (comedian)
1932　*Ideal Cinemagazine 345*
　　　"Member for Hogsnorton"
1934　*Death at Broadcasting House*
　　　(Phoenix) F
1943　*Pathe Gazette 1*
　　　(MOI)
1945　*The Burning Question*
　　　(Worldwide)

JIMMY POWELL (singer)
1963　*Just For Fun*
　　　(Columbia) F
　　　"Everyone But You"

SANDY POWELL (comedian)
1930　*Sandy the Fireman*
　　　(Warner)
1930　*Pathetone 10*
　　　"The Careless Caretaker"
1930　*Pathetone 22*
　　　"The Music Lesson"
1931　*Pathetone 64*
　　　"Sandy MP"
1931　*Sandy the Lost Policeman*
　　　(Warner)
1932　*The Third String*
　　　(WP) F
1934　*Pathetone Parade*
　　　F (reissue: *Pathetone 22*)
1935　*Can You Hear Me, Mother?*
　　　(British Lion) F
1937　*It's a Grand Old World*
　　　(British Lion) F
　　　"It's a Grand Old World"
1937　*Leave It To Me*
　　　(British Lion) F
1938　*I've Got a Horse*
　　　(British Lion) F
　　　"I'm Getting On Nicely Thank You"
　　　"Hear All See All Say Nowt"
1939　*Home From Home*
　　　(British Lion) F

1939　*All At Sea*
　　　(British Lion) F
　　　"Oh Ain't It Grand To Be in the
　　　Navy?"
1948　*Cup Tie Honeymoon*
　　　(Mancunian) F
　　　"Love Is Just a Game"

SANDY POWELL'S HARMONICA BAND
1936　*Soft Lights and Sweet Music*
　　　(British Lion) F
　　　"La Rêve Passe"

POWELL AND PAGE (cyclists)
1932　*Ideal Cinemagazine 333*

IRENE PRADOR (singer)
1937　*Figures Can Lie*
　　　(Ace Cinemagazine)
1937　*Let's Make a Night of It*
　　　(ABPC) F
　　　"For Only You"
1958　*The Snorkel*
　　　(Hammer) F

LOU PRAEGER AND HIS BAND
1942　*Pathe Pictorial 339*
　　　"Jive Dance"
1946　*Dancing Thru*
　　　(Angel) F
　　　"The Lambeth Walk"
　　　"Palais Glide"
　　　"Jive"

NONY PRAGER (acrobat)
1938　*Pathe Pictorial 918*

JOHN PRATT (comedian)
1946　*Meet the Navy*
　　　(British National) F
　　　"You'll Get Used To It"
1946　*Meet the Navy On Tour*
　　　"You'll Get Used To It"

PRESCO AND CAMPO (comedy acrobats)
1940　*Pathetone 512*
1942　*Pathetone Parade of 1942*
　　　F (reissue: *Pathetone 512*)

BILLY PRESTON (singer)
1970　*Let It Be*
　　　(UA) F

HARRY PRESTON (musician)
1932　*Pathetone 98*
　　　"Serenade Erotik"

MIKE PRESTON (singer)
1960　*Climb Up the Wall*
　　　(New Realm) F
　　　"Try Again"

THE PRETTY THINGS (group)
1966   *The Pretty Things*
       (Amanda)
       "Midnight to Six Man"
       "Can't Stand the Pain"
       "Me Needing You"
1969   *What's Good for the Goose*
       (Tigon) F
1981   *The Monster Club*
       (ITC) F

GISELLE PREVILLE (singer)
1950   *The Dancing Years*
       (ABPC) F
       "Waltz of My Heart"
       "My Life Belongs to You"
       "I Can Give You the Starlight"

ALAN PRICE (musician)
see also **THE ANIMALS**
1973   *O Lucky Man*
       (Memorial) F
       "O Lucky Man"
       "Poor People"
       "Keep That Smile On Your Face"
       "On and On"
       "There's Always Someone"
       "Money/Justice"
       "My Hometown"
       "Everyone Changes"
1975   *Alfie Darling*
       (EMI) F

PETER PRICE (comedian)
1985   *No Surrender*
       (Palace) F

THE PRIDE OF ERIN BAND
1938   *Caught Knapping*
       (Ace Cinemagazine)
       "Irish Jig Medley"

J B PRIESTLEY (author)
1943   *Battle for Music*
       (Strand) F
1944   *They Came to a City*
       (Ealing) F

ARTHUR PRINCE AND JIM (ventriloquist)
1921   *Around the Town 76*
       (Gaumont)
1931   *Gaumont Sound Mirror*
1933   *Pathetone 160*
1933   *Pathetone 170*

1933   *Pathetone 175*
1933   *Pathetone 186*
       "All the Nice Girls Love a Sailor"
1934   *Pathetone Parade*
       F (reissue: *Pathetone 186*)
1934   *Pathetone 203*
       "Student Song"
1935   *In Town Tonight*
       (British Lion) F
1935   *Arthur Prince and Jim*
       (National Government)
1936   *Pathe Pictorial NS 27*
1936   *Pathetone Parade of 1936*
       F (reissue: *Pathetone 203*)
1936   *Twenty-One Today*
       (Albany) F
1939   *Pathe Pictorial 186*
1939   *Pathetone Parade of 1939*
       F (reissue: *Pictorial NS 27*)
1940   *Pathe Pictorial 212*
1940   *Pathe Pictorial 233*
1942   *Pathetone Parade of 1942*
       F (reissue: *Pictorial 233*)

EDNA PRINCE (singer)
1930   *Harmony Heaven*
       (BIP) F

PRINCE TWINS (song and dance)
1930   *Al Fresco*
       (Gainsborough)
       "Sweet Music"
       "Come On Baby"
       "I'm Just in the Mood Tonight"

TOMMY PRIOR (comedian)
1934   *Pathe Pictorial 845*
       "A Bundle of Cheek"
1934   *Love Mirth Melody*
       (Mancunian) F

PERCY PRYDE (phonofiddle)
1928   *Percy Pryde and his Phonofiddle*
       (Phonofilm)
       "William Tell"

RENE PUGNET AND CLIVE RICHARDSON
(pianists)
1938   *Pathetone 448*
       "Dizzy Fingers"

JIMMY PURSEY (singer)
1980   *Rude Boy*
       (Tigon) F

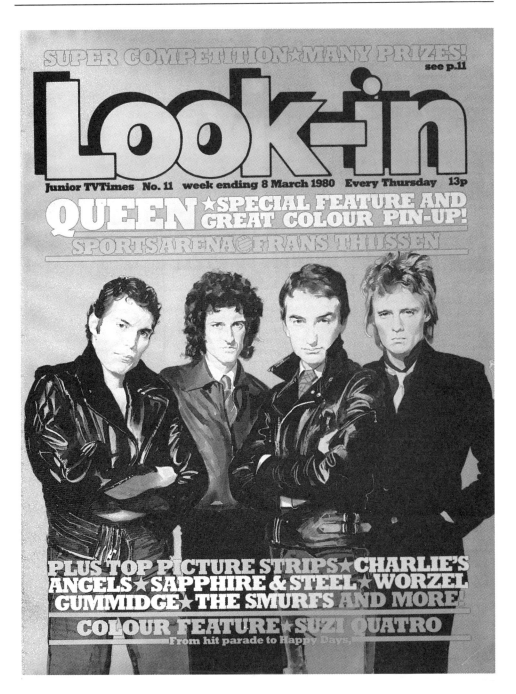

QUEEN MARY DANCE BAND
1937 *Pathe Pictorial 101*
        "The Fleet's in Port Again"

QUEEN'S HALL LIGHT ORCHESTRA
1936 *Calling the Tune*
        (Phoenix) F (conductor Sir Henry
        Wood)
        "Ride of the Valkyries"
        "Shepherds Hey"
        "Peer Gynt"

CAROLINE QUENTIN (comedienne)
1983 *Party Party*
        (F&G) F

1985 *Billy the Kid and the Green Baize
        Vampire*
        (Zenith) F

TOMMY QUICKLY AND THE REMO FOUR
(group)
1965 *Pop Gear*
        (Pathe) F
        "Humpty Dumpty"

QUINTESSENCE (group)
1973 *Glastonbury Fayre*
        (Goodtimes) F

RABELLO (juggler)
1936 *Pathetone 308*
1937 *Concert Party*
(Ace) F

OSCAR RABIN AND HIS ROMANY BAND
1937 *Pathe Pictorial NS 77*
"Rural Rhythm"
1939 *Pathetone 485*
"Nice People"
"Hold Tight"
1943 *Pictorial Revue of 1943*
F (reissue: *Pathetone 485*)
1944 *Starlight Serenade*
(Federated) F
"Frenesi"
"Perfidia"
"Hawaiian War Chant"
1950 *Variety Makers*
(reissue: *Starlight Serenade*)

STEVE RACE (piano)
1948 *Calling Paul Temple*
(Butcher) F
"What's Cooking?"
"Lady on the Loose"

JACK RADCLIFFE (Scottish comedian)
1955 *Geordie*
(British Lion) F

RADIO RASCALS (impressionists)
1939 *Discoveries*
(Vogue) F
"A Shanty in Old Shanty Town"

RADIO REVELLERS (singers)
1938 *Pathetone 406*
"There Is a Tavern in the Town"
1938 *Pathe Pictorial NS 108*
"Sweet Sue"
1949 *High Jinks in Society*
(Adelphi) F

RADIO THREE (singers)
1935 *Pathe Pictorial 889*
"I'm Gonna Wash My Hands of You"
1935 *Pathe Pictorial 902*
"Blue Moon"
"Blue Skies"
1936 *Radio Favourites*
(Publicity) ADVERT
1936 *Variety Parade*
(Butcher) F
"These Foolish Things"
1937 *Okay For Sound*
(Gainsborough) F
"Okay For Sound"
1940 *Cavalcade of Variety*
(reissue: *Variety Parade*)

ANNA RAEBURN (broadcaster)
1978 *The Rise and Fall of Ivor Dickie*
(DUK) F

THE RAELETS (singers)
1964 *Ballad in Blue*
(Warner) F

R.A.F. DANCE ORCHESTRA
1941 *Pathe Gazette 13*
"I Cried For You"
1944 *We the People*
(Independent)

RAGOLI (balancer)
1932 *Ideal Cinemagazine 324*

JOHN RAKER AND NAT LEWIS (dancers)
1913 *Way Down the Mississippi*
(Selsior)

JAN RALFINI AND HIS BAND
1942 *Pathe Pictorial 347*
"Pennsylvania Polka"

RANI RAMA (Siamese dancer)
1931 *Ideal Cinemagazine 274*
"Virginal Offering"

RAMAR AND JEANNE (dancers)
1928 *Eve's Film Review 357*
"Dance of the Mermaids"

MARIE RAMBERT'S CORPS DE BALLET
(dancers)
see also **THE BALLET RAMBERT**
1932 *Dance Pretty Lady*
(BIP) F
1946 *Woman to Woman*
(British National) F

REX RAMER (novelty musician)
1949 *Nitwits on Parade*
(Adelphi) F

HAROLD RAMSAY (organ)
1936 *Sunshine Ahead*
(Baxter) F
1942 *Pathe Pictorial 317*

FREDERICK RANALOW (baritone)
1927 *The King's Highway*
(Stoll) F
"The Beggar's Opera"
1933 *The Lost Chord*
(Butcher) F
"The Lost Chord"
1934 *Autumn Crocus*
(ATP) F

FREDDY RANDALL AND HIS BAND
1956 *Parade of the Bands*
(Hammer)

HARRY RANDALL (comedian)
1900 *The Rats*
(Warwick)

LESLIE RANDALL (comedian)
1960 *Just Joe*
(Archway) F
1963 *Mystery Submarine*
(British Lion) F
1963 *Billy Liar*
(Anglo) F
1990 *The Garden*
(Basilisk) F

PAMELA RANDALL (singer)
1937 *Rhythm Racketeer*
(Rock) F
1939 *A Window in London*
(GFD) F

FRANK RANDLE (comedian)
1940 *Somewhere in England*
(Mancunian) F
1942 *Somewhere in Camp*
(Mancunian) F
"Ilkley Moor Baht 'At"
1942 *Somewhere on Leave*
(Mancunian) F
1943 *Somewhere in Civvies*
(Mancunian) F
1945 *Home Sweet Home*
(Mancunian) F
1946 *Randle and All That*
(reissue: *Home Sweet Home*)
1946 *Randle Remembers*
(reissue: *Home Sweet Home*)
1947 *When You Come Home*
(Butcher) F
1948 *Holidays With Pay*
(Mancunian) F
1949 *Somewhere in Politics*
(Mancunian) F
1949 *School for Randle*
(Mancunian) F
1953 *It's a Grand Life*
(Mancunian) F
1960 *Full House*
(reissue: *Somewhere in Politics*)
1960 *Teacher's Pest*
(reissue: *School for Randle*)
1960 *The Three Who Flungs*
(reissue: *School for Randle*)
1960 *Bella's Birthday*
(Mancunian) (reissue: *School for Randle*)
1960 *Seaside Frolics*
(reissue: *Holidays With Pay*)
1960 *Tonight's the Nite*
(reissue: *Holidays With Pay*)

MANNY RANDLE (musician)
1928 *Phototone 3*

ELSIE RANDOLPH (song and dance)
1929 *Eve's Film Review 438*
"Follow Through"
1931 *Eve's Film Review 511*
"Stand Up and Sing"

1931 *Rich and Strange*
(BIP) F
1932 *Life Goes On*
(B&D) F
1932 *Brother Alfred*
(BIP) F
1933 *Yes Mr Brown*
(B&D) F
1933 *Night of the Garter*
(B&D) F
1933 *That's a Good Girl*
(B&D) F
"Fancy Our Meeting"
"Now That I've Found You"
1936 *This'll Make You Whistle*
(Wilcox) F
"This'll Make You Whistle"
"The Wrong Rhumba"
"I'm in a Dancing Mood"
"My Red Letter Day"
1937 *Smash and Grab*
(GFD) F
1950 *Cheer the Brave*
(Apex) F
1972 *Frenzy*
(Universal) F

ERIC RANDOLPH (singer)
1929 *Musical Moments*
(BIP)
1929 *A Song or Two*
(BIP)

ESTHER RANTZEN (television personality)
1979 *The Music Machine*
(Target) F

THE RAPID FOUR (acrobats)
1940 *Pathe Pictorial 222*

THE RAPIERS (group)
1965 *He Who Rides a Tiger*
(British Lion) F

RAS ANGELS AND RAS MESSENGERS
(group)
1981 *Burning an Illusion*
(BFI) F
"Militant Works"
"Righteous Warriors"
"Tribulations"

ALBERTA RASCH DANCERS
1932 *Pathetone 140*
"Wild Violets"

RAWICZ AND LANDAUER (pianos)
1937 *The Street Singer*
(ABPC) F
1937 *The Sky's the Limit*
(GFD) F
1945 *Home Sweet Home*
(Mancunian) F

GORDON RAY GIRLS (dancers)
1931 *Ideal Cinemagazine 265*
1937 *The Penny Pool*
(Mancunian) F
"Keep Fit"
"So Say All of Us"
1937 *Talking Feet*
(Baxter) F
"Tapping Out Rhythm"
1944 *Rainbow Round the Corner*
(Berkeley) F
1944 *A Night of Magic*
(Berkeley) F

LA RAY (acrobatic dancer)
1931 *Ideal Cinemagazine 266*

MILLICENT RAY
see **HARRY PERRY AND MILLICENT RAY**

OSWALD RAY (paper tearing)
1936 *Play Fare*
(Ace Cinemagazine)

RENE RAY (singer)
(films as actress not listed)
1938 *Mountains o' Mourne*
(Butcher) F
"Danny Boy"
"Dear Little Shamrock"
"The Mountains o' Mourne"

TED RAY (comedian)
1933 *Ideal Cinemagazine 357*
1934 *Radio Parade of 1935*
(BIP) F
"The Canary"
1943 *Pathe Gazette 11*
"Dig for Victory"
1950 *A Ray of Sunshine*
(Adelphi) F
1952 *Meet Me Tonight*
(GFD) F
"Has Anybody Seen Our Ship?"
1954 *Escape By Night*
(Eros) F
1956 *My Wife's Family*
(ABPC) F
1959 *The Crowning Touch*
(Butcher) F
1959 *Carry On Teacher*
(Anglo) F
1959 *Please Turn Over*
(Anglo) F

CAROL RAYE (soprano)
1945 *Waltz Time*
(British National) F
"The Heavenly Waltz"
"This Land of Mine"
"Only to You"
"Call to Arms"
1946 *Spring Song*
(British National) F

"Spring Song"
"Love Again"
"I Can't Make Up My Mind"
"Just For You"
"Jitterbug Song"
"All Pull Together"

HARRY RAYE AND BILLIE MAYE (dancers)
1927 *Eve's Film Review 310*
"Waltz of the Kiss"

HELEN RAYE (singer)
1935 *Equity Musical Revue 8*
(British Lion)
"One Tiny Tear"
1935 *Equity Musical Revue 9*
(British Lion)
"In the Valley of the Moon"

HELEN RAYMOND (singer)
see also **CAVENDISH THREE**
1936 *Pathe Pictorial NS 31*
"Okay For Sound"

**MAURICE RAYMOND AND HIS
CONTINENTAL BAND**
1932 *Ideal Cinemagazine 341*
(with Nadearja)
1932 *Ideal Cinemagazine 347*
"Gypsy Moon"
1933 *Ideal Cinemagazine 354*
1933 *Pathetone 182*

RAY RAYMOND (singer)
1930 *Elsie Percival and Ray Raymond*
(Gainsborough)

JEANNE REVEL
see **RONNIE BOYER AND JEANNE REVEL**

RAYMOND REVUEBAR GIRLS (dancers)
1981 *Paul Raymond's Erotica*
(Brent) F

RAYMONDE AND HIS BANJO BAND
1936 *Pathe Pictorial NS 14*
"Blaze Away"
1937 *Pathe Pictorial NS 76*
"Stars and Stripes"

RALPH READER (singer)
1934 *The Blue Squadron*
(Warner) F
1936 *Limelight*
(Wilcox) F
1937 *Splinters in the Air*
(Wilcox) F
"Those Dear Old Tivoli Days"
1937 *The Gang Show*
(Wilcox) F
"Children of the New Regime"
"I've Got a Rainbow in My Heart"
"Birds of a Feather"
"With a Twinkle in Your Eye"

212

"Crest of a Wave"
1942 *Coastal Command*
(Crown) F
"Crest of a Wave"
1952 *Derby Day*
(Wilcox) F
1957 *These Dangerous Years*
(ABPC) F
1961 *Summer Show*
(Archway)

READING AND GRANTLEY (trampoline act)
1941 *Old Mother Riley's Circus*
(British National) F
1941 *Pathe Pictorial 291*
1952 *For Your Entertainment 3*
(Gaumont)
1954 *Variety Half Hour*
(Baim)

ALBERT REBLA (juggler)
1920 *Forty Winks*
(Thespian)
1920 *Who Laughs Last*
(Thespian)
1929 *The Celestial City*
(BIF) F
1930 *Just For a Song*
(Gainsborough) F
1930 *The New Waiter*
(PDC)
1932 *The Midshipmaid*
(Gainsborough) F
1933 *Soldiers of the King*
(Gainsborough) F
1933 *Ideal Cinemagazine 362*
1935 *Pity the Poor Rich*
(ABFD)
1935 *While Parents Sleep*
(UA) F
1935 *Pathe Pictorial 885*
1936 *Twenty-One Today*
(Albany) F
1937 *Pathetone 359*
1938 *Pathe Pictorial NS 123*
1943 *Pictorial Revue of 1943*
F (reissue: *Pictorial 123*)

LOU REED (singer)
1987 *The Secret Policeman's Third Ball*
(Virgin) F
"Tell It to Your Heart"
"Biko"
"Voices of Freedom"

BILLY REEVES (comedian)
1930 *Jerry Builders*
(PDC)

JOAN REGAN (singer)
1955 *Just For You*
(Hammer)
1958 *6.5 Special*
(Anglo) F
"I'll Close My Eyes"

1958 *Hello London*
(Regal) F
"When You Know Someone Loves You"

MICHAEL REGAN AND ANNE (comedy)
1940 *Pathe Pictorial 223*

CHARLIE AND BILLIE REGO (comedy)
1930 *Amateur Night in London*
(PDC) F
1930 *Jerry Builders*
(PDC)

BILLY REID AND THE LONDON ACCORDION BAND
1932 *Pathetone 121*
"Daisy Bell"
"Two Lovely Black Eyes"
1933 *Pathe Pictorial 781*
"Bohemian Memories"
1937 *Pathetone Parade of 1938*
F (reissue: *Pictorial 781*)
1937 *Saturday Night Revue*
(Pathe) F

MIKE REID (comedian)
1972 *Steptoe and Son*
(EMI) F

NOLA REID (dancer)
1936 *Pathe Pictorial NS 10*
"Can Can"
1936 *Pathe Pictorial NS 25*
"Devil Dance"
1937 *Spirit of Variety*
(Exclusive)

TERRY REID (singer)
1973 *Glastonbury Fayre*
(Goodtimes) F

TEDDY REILLY (singer)
1936 *Hearts of Humanity*
(Baxter) F

REILLY AND COMFORT (singers)
1933 *Aunt Sally*
(Gainsborough) F

ENA REISS (soprano)
1930 *Ena Reiss*
(Gainsborough)

JEAN REMA (tap-dancer)
1936 *Pathe Pictorial NS 4*
"The Lady in Red"
"Bye Bye Blues"
1936 *Pathe Pictorial NS 24*
"Rhumba"

RENARA (piano)
1943 *Swingonometry*
(Inspiration)

"Tiger Rag"
"Yours"
"How Green Was My Valley"

DEREK RENCHER (ballet dancer)
1966 *Romeo and Juliet*
(Rank) F

HUGH RENE (Hebrew comedian)
1934 *Pathe Pictorial 846*
"My Idea of a Girl"
1936 *Pathe Pictorial 934*
"Inventions"

RENE AND BEBE (fan dancers)
1933 *Pathetone 179*

RENOFF AND RENOVA (dancers)
1928 *Eve's Film Review 383*
"Indian Dance"

RESISTA (specialty)
1937 *Pathe Pictorial NS 86*

ELLA RETFORD (singer)
1914 *Ella Retford At Home*
(Kearton)
1937 *Derby and Joan*
(Rock) F
1939 *Poison Pen*
(ABPC) F
1943 *Variety Jubilee*
(Butcher) F
"Take Me Back to Blighty"
"Pack Up Your Troubles"
"Tipperary"
1945 *I'll Be Your Sweetheart*
(Gainsborough) F
1948 *Noose*
(Pathe) F
1949 *Paper Orchid*
(Columbia) F
1950 *Shadow of the Past*
(Columbia) F

BILLY REVEL AND JANE MOORE (comedy)
1929 *Eve's Film Review 432*
"Classicitus Burlesque"

ETHEL REVNELL AND GRACIE WEST
(comedy)
1935 *Father O'Flynn*
(Butcher) F
1937 *Calling All Stars*
(British Lion) F
"Good Old Wedding Ring"
"Red Sails in the Sunset"
"Sweet Adeline"
1939 *So This Is London*
(TCF) F
1942 *The Balloon Goes Up*
(New Realm) F
"The Balloon Goes Up"
"We Do See Life"
"Winnie the Wench on the Winch"

1943 *Up With the Lark*
(New Realm) F
"Up With the Lark"
1943 *Highlights of Variety 25*
(reissue: *Father O'Flynn*)
1940s *Ask My Mummy*
(Lintas) ADVERT

BILLY REY (comedian)
1938 *Pathe Pictorial NS 93*

MONTE REY (tenor)
1936 *Pathe Pictorial NS 11*
1937 *Pathe Pictorial NS 85*
"Shake Hands with a Millionaire"

REX REYMER (novelty musician)
1949 *Nitwits on Parade*
(Adelphi) F

REYMOS (harp)
1932 *Pathetone 131*
1933 *Pathe Pictorial 772*
"The Bells of St Mary's"

JOHN REYNDERS AND HIS BAND
1931 *Out of the Blue*
(BIP) F
"Out of the Blue to You"
1937 *Saturday Night Revue*
(Pathe) F

BILLY RHODES AND CHIKA LAINE
(comedy adagio)
1949 *Skimpy in the Navy*
(Adelphi) F

MILTON RHODES (busker)
1956 *Cabaret Nights 4*
(Highbury)

RHODES AND STEPHENS (comedy)
1940 *Music Hall Personalities 13*
(reissue: *title unknown*)

GYPSY RHOUMA (dancer)
1929 *Pathe Pictorial 7*
1930 *Alf's Button*
(Gaumont) F

RHYTHM ACES (singers)
1935 *Pathe Pictorial 914*
"Oh By Jingo"

RHYTHM GIRLS (singers)
1931 *Pathetone 41*

RHYTHM SISTERS (singers)
1936 *Pathe Pictorial 935*
"Weather Man"
1937 *Pathetone 360*
"South Sea Island Magic"
1937 *Feather Your Nest*
(ATP) F
"The Robin Told Me So"

1938   *Around the Town*
        (British Lion) F

BERTHA RICARDO (comedy)
  1936   *Dodging the Dole*
          (Mancunian) F

RONA RICARDO (comedy)
  1933   *Cleaning Up*
          (British Lion) F

PAUL RICH (singer)
  1944   *We the People*
          (Independent)

ROY RICH (broadcaster)
  1942   *Pathetone Parade of 1942*
          F

RICH AND GALVIN (dancers)
  1927   *Pathe Pictorial 480*
          "The More We Are Together"
  1932   *Ideal Cinemagazine 308*
  1932   *Money Talks*
          (BIP) F

CLIFF RICHARD (singer)
  1959   *Serious Charge*
          (Eros) F
          "Living Doll"
          "Mad About You"
          "No Turning Back"
          "Chinchilla"
  1959   *Expresso Bongo*
          (British Lion) F
          "Shrine on the Second Floor"
          "Voice in the Wilderness"
          "Love"
  1961   *The Young Ones*
          (ABPC) F
          "Got a Funny Feeling"
          "Nothing's Impossible"
          "Friday Night"
          "The Young Ones"
          "Lessons in Love"
          "We've Got a Show"
          "Where Did You Get That Hat?"
          "Captain Jinjah"
          "Living Doll"
          "The Girl in Your Arms"
          "All for One"
          "We Say Yeah"
          "The Savage"
  1963   *Summer Holiday*
          (ABPC) F
          "Summer Holiday"
          "Every Girl Is Beautiful"
          "Bachelor Boy"
          "A Swinging Affair"
          "Dancing Shoes"
          "Next Time"
          "Big News"
          "Stranger in Town"
          "All at Once"

"Seven Days to a Holiday"
"Let Us Take You for a Ride"
"Really Waltzing"
  1964   *Wonderful Life*
          (Elstree) F
          "Wonderful Life"
          "We Love a Movie"
          "All Kinds of People"
          "Youth and Experience"
          "Home"
          "On the Beach"
          "What've I Gotta Do?"
          "A Matter of Moments"
          "A Girl in Every Port"
          "A Little Imagination"
          "In the Stars"
          "Do You Remember?"
  1966   *Finders Keepers*
          (UA) F
          "Finders Keepers"
          "The Washerwoman"
          "La La La"
          "Time Drags By"
          "Oh Señorita"
          "Paella"
          "Fiesta"
  1967   *Two a Penny*
          (Worldwide) F
          "Two a Penny"
          "I'll Love You For Ever Today"
          "Questions"
          "Lonely Girl"
          "And Me"
          "Twist and Shout"
          "Wake Up"
          "Cloudy"
          "Red Rubber Ball"
          "Close to Kathy"
          "Rattler"
  1971   *His Land*
          (Worldwide) F
          "One in Bethlehem"
          "His Land"
          "He's Everything to Me"
          "Jerusalem"
          "The New 23rd"
          "Keep Me Where Love Is"
  1973   *Take Me High*
          (EMI) F
          "Take Me High"
          "It's Only Money"
          "Why?"
          "Life"
          "Driving"
          "The Game"
          "Midnight Blue"
          "Brumberger Duet"
          "The Anti-Brotherhood of Man"
          "Winning"
          "Join the Band"
          "The Word Is Love"
          "There's Too Much Love"

KEITH RICHARD (guitarist)
see also **THE ROLLING STONES**
1979   *The Kids Are Alright*
        (Rose) F

DARROL RICHARDS (singer)
1933   *Facing the Music*
        (BIP) F
        "Faust"

ALBERT RICHARDSON (singer)
1933   *Song of the Plough*
        (Sound City) F
        "The Old Sow"

CLIVE RICHARDSON
see **TONY LOWRY AND CLIVE
RICHARDSON** and **RENE PUGNET AND
CLIVE RICHARDSON**

FOSTER RICHARDSON (baritone)
1933   *Musical Film Revue*
        (British Lion) S
1936   *Railroad Rhythm*
        (Carnival)
1937   *Pathetone 358*
        "Captain Mac"

JOYCE RICHARDSON (singer)
1934   *Radio Parade of 1935*
        (BIP) F

MARK RICHARDSON (singer)
1965   *Dateline Diamonds*
        (Rank) F

HARRY RICHMAN (American singer)
1938   *Kicking the Moon Around*
        (Vogue) F
        "Two Bouquets"
        "You're What's the Matter With Me"
        "Mayfair Merry Go Round"

FIONA RICHMOND (striptease)
1974   *Barry McKenzie Holds His Own*
        (EMI) F
1975   *Exposé*
        (Norfolk) F
1977   *Hardcore*
        (Target) F
1978   *Let's Get Laid*
        (Target) F
        "You Turn My Legs To Water"
1987   *Eat the Rich*
        (Comic Strip) F

ROBIN RICHMOND (organ)
1944   *Rainbow Round the Corner*
        (Berkeley) F
        "Black Eyes"
1949   *Murder at the Windmill*
        (Grand National) F
        "Two Little Dogs"
1940s *Animal Antics*
        (International)

"Felix Keeps On Walking"
"Run Rabbit Run"

PAUL RICO AND HIS MEXICANS (band)
1940   *Pathetone 535*
        "March España"

PHILIP RIDGEWAY AND JEAN MELVILLE
(singers)
1936   *Pathe Pictorial 930*
        "Paint and Powder"
        "Talking in My Sleep"

JOHN RIDLEY AND ANN DE NYS (singers)
1947   *New Pictorial 129*

FREDDIE RIGBY (comedian)
1914   *Buying a Horse*
        (Lucrative)
1914   *Bill Posting*
        (Lucrative)

RIGHT SAID FRED (group)
1994   *Solitaire for Two*
        (Solitaire)
        "She's My Missis"

PAT RIGNOLD
see **CAVENDISH THREE**

RIGOLETTO BROTHERS (comedy)
1933   *Taking Ways*
        (Sound City) F

RIGOLLO (specialty)
1910   *Rigollo the Man of Many Faces*
        (Urban)

RIKSARAJ (group)
1996   *Glastonbury: The Movie*
        (Starlight) F
        "Krish"

RINGLE BROTHERS AND RENEE
(acrobats)
1933   *Pathe Pictorial 773*

RINTALLA (Finnish soprano)
1940   *Pathe Pictorial 206*
        "There Goes My Dream"

RIO AND THE ROBOTS (group)
1982   *Listen to London*
        (White) F

RIOS AND SANTOS (acrobats)
1936   *Sunshine Ahead*
        (Baxter) F
1937   *Sing As You Swing*
        (Rock) F
1938   *Lassie from Lancashire*
        (British National) F

RIOS BROTHERS (specialty)
1962 *The Main Attraction*
(MGM) F

BOB RIPA (boy juggler)
1929 *Gaumont Mirror 118*

JACKIE RIPPER
see **GERRY GERRARD AND JACKIE RIPPER**

ARTHUR RISCOE (comedian)
1920 *Horatio's Deception*
(Gaumont)
1920 *The Other Dog's Day*
(Gaumont)
1920 *Oh Jemima*
(Gaumont)
1920 *The Bitten Biter*
(Gaumont)
1932 *For the Love of Mike*
(BIP) F
1933 *Going Gay*
(Windsor) F
1933 *For Love of You*
(Windsor) F
1933 *Pathetone 147*
1936 *Public Nuisance No. 1*
(GFD) F
"Spring"
"Between You and Me and the Carpet"
"Since I Met Her"
"Hotsy Totsy"
1937 *The Street Singer*
(ABPC) F
1937 *Paradise for Two*
(London) F
1938 *Pathe Pictorial NS 124*
1940 *Pathetone 520*
1941 *Kipps*
(TCF) F

JOHNNIE RISCOE (comedian)
1937 *Pathe Pictorial NS 83*

CYRIL RITCHARD (singer)
1929 *Blackmail*
(BIP) F
"Miss Up-to-Date"
1948 *The Winslow Boy*
(London) F
"Who Were You With Last Night?"

CYRIL RITCHARD AND MADGE ELLIOTT
(dancers)
1927 *On With the Dance*
(Parkinson)
1929 *Eve's Film Review 410*
"Love"
1931 *Eve's Film Review 523*
"The Millionaire Kid"

W. E. RITCHIE (trick cyclist)
1899 *Ritchie, Tramp Cyclist*
(Warwick)

MAX RIVERS (dancer)
1924 *Eve's Film Review 182*
1927 *Eve's Film Review 326*
(with Janette Gilmore)
1928 *Eve's Film Review 380*

MAX RIVERS' RADIO GIRLS (dancers)
1935 *Pathe Pictorial 886*

MAX RIVERS' TROCADERO GIRLS
(dancers)
1929 *Eve's Film Review 405*
"Stepping Out"
1930 *Greek Street*
(Gaumont) F
"Undress Parade"
1931 *Who Killed Doc Robin?*
(Gainsborough) F
1932 *That Night in London*
(London) F
1932 *Camera Cocktales 5*
(Hallmark)
1933 *Cleaning Up*
(British Lion) F

ELENA RIZZIERI (soprano)
1949 *The Glass Mountain*
(Renown) F

THE ROAD STARS (buskers)
1966 *The Vanishing Busker*
(Ritz)

A. D. ROBBINS (trick cyclist)
1902 *Robbins, Champion of All Champions*
(Warwick)

CHARLIE ROBBINS (comedian)
1931 *Pathetone 50*

HARRY ROBBINS (xylophone)
1932 *Ideal Cinemagazine 330*
1933 *Ideal Cinemagazine 351*
1933 *Pathe Pictorial 793*
1933 *Pathetone 180*
1934 *Music Hall*
(Realart) F
1936 *Stage Coaching*
(Ace Cinemagazine)
1937 *Shooting Stars*
(Viking) F
"Robbin' Harry"

ROBERTA (fan dancer)
1950 *A Ray of Sunshine*
(Adelphi) F

STELLA ROBERTA (singer)
1939   *French Without Tears*
(Two Cities) F
1939   *Pathetone 502*

ARTHUR ROBERTS (comedian)
1924   *Gaumont Graphic*
1927   *Arthur Roberts No. 1*
(Phonofilm)
1927   *Topsey Turvey*
(Phonofilm)

BETTY AND FREDDIE ROBERTS (dancers)
1938   *Pathe Pictorial NS 110*
"Vienna City of My Dreams"

KIM ROBERTS (singer)
1963   *Live It Up*
(Rank) F
"Loving Me This Way"

LESLIE ROBERTS (dancer)
1937   *O.H.M.S.*
(Gaumont) F
1939   *Pathetone 469*
(with Eda Peel)

LESLIE ROBERTS' TELEVISION GIRLS
(dancers)
1953   *Forces Sweetheart*
(New Realm) F
"Charlie Chaplin Dance"

PADDY ROBERTS (singer)
1961   *Spike Milligan on Treasure Island WC2*
(British Lion)

RENE ROBERTS
see **MRS MURGATROYD AND MRS WINTERBOTTOM**

ROBERTS' SILHOUETTE QUINTETTE
(dancers)
1937   *Signal Services*
(Ace Cinemagazine)

B A ROBERTSON (singer)
1981   *The Monster Club*
(ITC) F
"Sucker for Your Love"

FYFE ROBERTSON (television personality)
1961   *What a Whopper*
(Regal) F

MAX ROBERTSON (television personality)
1959   *Friends and Neighbours*
(British Lion) F

STUART ROBERTSON (baritone)
1933   *Bitter Sweet*
(B&D) F
"Tokay"

1935   *Peg of Old Drury*
(Wilcox) F
1936   *Millions*
(Wilcox) F
1936   *As You Like It*
(Fox) F
1937   *Splinters in the Air*
(Wilcox) F
"Watching the Stars"
"The Sunshine of Your Smile"
"Sweet and Low"
"Flying High"
1937   *The Gang Show*
(Wilcox) F
"That Song in My Heart"

PAUL ROBESON (bass)
1935   *Sanders of the River*
(London) F
"Canoe Song"
"Killing Song"
"Love Song"
"Congo Lullabye"
1936   *Song of Freedom*
(Hammer) F
"Song of Freedom"
"Sleepy River"
"Lonely Road"
"Black Emperor"
"Joshua Fit de Battle of Jericho"
"Stepping Stones"
"Ma Curly-Headed Babby"
"I Got a Robe"
1937   *Big Fella*
(British Lion) F
"Lazin'"
"Roll Up Sailor Man"
"You Didn't Oughta Do Such Things"
"I Don't Know What's Wrong"
"River Steals My Folks From Me"
1937   *King Solomon's Mines*
(Gaumont) F
"Climbing Up"
"Ho Ho"
1937   *Jericho*
(UA) F
"Golden River"
"My Way"
"Deep Desert"
"Holy Night"
"Shortenin' Bread"
1937   *My Song Goes Forth*
(Ambassador)
1939   *Proud Valley*
(Ealing) F
"Deep River"
"All Through the Night"
"Land of My Fathers"
"Wales"
"Ebenezer"
"Lord God Abraham"

GEORGE ROBEY (comedian)
1900 *The Rats*
      (Warwick)
1913 *And Very Nice Too*
      (Kineplastikon)
1913 *Good Queen Bess*
      (Kineplastikon)
1914 *George Robey Turns Anarchist*
      (Burns)
1916 *£66.13.9¾ for Every Man Woman and Child*
      (Ideal)
1916 *Blood Tells*
      (Ideal)
1917 *Doing His Bit*
      (Ideal)
1918 *George Robey's Day Off*
      (Stoll)
1918 *The Cure for Potato Blight*
      (Ministry of Food)
1922 *Eve's Film Review 32*
      "Jack and the Beanstalk"
1923 *The Rest Cure*
      (Stoll) F
1923 *One Arabian Night*
      (Stoll) F
1923 *Don Quixote*
      (Stoll) F
1923 *Harlequinade*
      (Stoll)
1924 *The Prehistoric Man*
      (Stoll) F
1928 *The Barrister*
      (Phonofilm)
1928 *Safety First*
      (Phonofilm)
1929 *The Bride*
      (BSFP)
1929 *Mrs Mephistopheles*
      (BSFP)
1930 *Pathetone 16*
1931 *Ideal Cinemagazine 269*
1932 *The Temperance Fete*
      (MGM) F
1932 *Marry Me*
      (Gainsborough) F
1933 *Don Quixote*
      (UA) F
1934 *Chu Chin Chow*
      (Gainsborough) F
      "Any Time's Kissing Time"
1935 *Birds of a Feather*
      (Baxter) F
1935 *Royal Cavalcade*
      (BIP) F
1936 *Men of Yesterday*
      (Baxter) F
1936 *Calling the Tune*
      (Phoenix) F
      "Safety First"
      "In Other Words"
1936 *Southern Roses*
      (GFD) F
1937 *Pathe Pictorial NS 50*
      "Stamps"

1939 *A Girl Must Live*
      (GFD) F
1940 *Camp Concert*
      (reissue: *Men of Yesterday*)
1942 *Salute John Citizen*
      (British National) F
1943 *Variety Jubilee*
      (Butcher) F
      "I Stopped I Looked and I Listened"
1943 *They Met in the Dark*
      (GFD) F
1944 *Highlights of Variety 27*
      (reissue: *Variety Jubilee*)
1945 *Waltz Time*
      (British National) F
1945 *Henry V*
      (GFD) F
1945 *The Trojan Brothers*
      (British National) F
1952 *The Pickwick Papers*
      (Renown) F

THE ROBINIS (dancers)
1937 *Okay For Sound*
      (Gainsborough) F

JENNIE ROBINS (singer)
1933 *One Precious Year*
      (B&D) F
      "A Glad New Year"

PHYLLIS ROBINS (singer)
1935 *The Lad*
      (Twickenham) F
1935 *Variety*
      (Butcher) F
      "This Thing Called Love"
      "When I Grow Up"
1936 *Murder at the Cabaret*
      (Paramount) F
      "Powder Blues"
      "Forgotten Woman"
1937 *Shooting Stars*
      (Viking) F
      "I Saw a Ship Asailing"
      "Boo Hoo"
      "The Meanest Thing You Did to Me"
      "I Took My Harp to a Party"
1940 *Pathetone 520*
1940 *Cavalcade of Variety*
      (reissue: *Variety*)
1943 *Down Melody Lane*
      F (reissue: *Variety*)
1946 *Gaiety George*
      (Embassy) F
      "The Pretty Little Girl From Nowhere"
1947 *They Made Me a Fugitive*
      (Warner) F
      "Caress Me"

BILLY ROBINSON (comedian)
1938 *Pathe Pictorial 451*

CARDEW (DOUGLAS) ROBINSON
(comedian)
- 1956 *Fun at St Fanny's*
(British Lion) F
- 1959 *"I'm All Right Jack"*
(British Lion) F
- 1959 *The Navy Lark*
(TCF) F
- 1960 *Let's Get Married*
(Eros) F
- 1960 *Light Up the Sky*
(British Lion) F
- 1960 *Piccadilly Third Stop*
(Rank) F
- 1962 *Hair of the Dog*
(Rank) F
- 1962 *Waltz of the Toreadors*
(Rank) F
- 1963 *Ladies Who Do*
(British Lion) F
- 1963 *Father Came Too*
(Rank) F
- 1963 *The Young Detectives*
(CFF) S
- 1964 *Go Kart Go*
(CFF) F
- 1965 *I Was Happy Here*
(Rank) F
- 1967 *Smashing Time*
(Paramount) F
- 1968 *Carry On Up the Khyber*
(Rank) F
- 1969 *Where's Jack?*
(Paramount) F
- 1969 *The Nine Ages of Nakedness*
(Orb) F
- 1969 *The Magnificent 6½*
(CFF) SERIAL
- 1970 *Hoverbug*
(CFF) F
- 1971 *The Magnificent Seven Deadly Sins*
(Tigon) F
- 1977 *Come Play With Me*
(Tigon) F
- 1977 *What's Up, Nurse?*
(Variety) F

ERIC ROBINSON (television personality)
- 1948 *Things Happen at Night*
(Renown) F

ROBERT ROBINSON (television personality)
- 1964 *French Dressing*
(Kenwood) F

TOM ROBINSON (singer)
- 1980 *The Secret Policeman's Ball*
(Tigon) F
"Glad To Be Gay"
- 1982 *The Secret Policeman's Other Ball*
(UIP) F
"I Shall Be Released"

CARSON ROBISON AND HIS PIONEERS
(cowboy band)
- 1932 *Pathetone 142*
"Wyoming"
- 1933 *Pathe Pictorial 799*
"Sittin' by the River"
- 1933 *Pathetone 185*
"Good Time in New Orleans"
- 1936 *Pathetone 353*
"Sleepy Rio Grande"
- 1937 *Variety Hour*
(Fox) F

THE ROCKIN' BERRIES (group)
- 1965 *Pop Gear*
(Pathe) F
"What in the World"
"He's in Town"

ALFRED RODE AND HIS TZIGANE BAND
- 1931 *Carnival*
(B&D) F
- 1932 *The Blue Danube*
(B&D) F
"The Blue Danube"
- 1934 *Temptation*
(Gaumont) F
- 1936 *Gypsy Melody*
(Wardour) F
"Second Hungarian Rhapsody"

CLODAGH RODGERS (singer)
- 1963 *Just For Fun*
(Columbia) F
"Sweet Boy"
- 1963 *It's All Over Town*
(British Lion) F
"My Love Will Still Be There"

NICOLETTE ROEG (singer)
- 1946 *Under New Management*
(Mancunian) F
"Little Sprig of Shamrock"

LEON ROGEE (instrumentalist)
- 1933 *Ideal Cinemagazine 360*

CHARLES 'BUDDY' ROGERS (singer)
- 1935 *Dance Band*
(BIP) F
"Lovey Dovey"
"The Valparaiso"
"I Hate to Say Good Night"
"Twelfth Street Rag"
- 1936 *Once in a Million*
(BIP) F
- 1937 *Let's Make a Night of It*
(ABPC) F
"Something in My Eye"
"Why Don't You Come Down to Earth?"

HARRY ROGERS (Hebrew comedian)
- 1930 *Amateur Night in London*
(PDC) F

HOWARD ROGERS (comedian)
1929   *Pathe Magazine 12*
1938   *Calling All Crooks*
       (Mancunian) F

JIMMY ROGERS (conjurer)
1939   *Pathe Pictorial NS 151*

SIMONE ROGERS (singer)
1935   *Cock o' the North*
       (Butcher) F

WILL ROGERS (American comedian)
1927   *Tiptoes*
       (British National) F

MARIKA ROKK (dancer)
1930   *Kiss Me Sergeant*
       (BIP) F
1930   *Eve's Film Review 455*
       "Slow Motion Dance"
1930   *Why Sailors Leave Home*
       (BIP) F

CHERRY ROLAND (singer)
1963   *Just For Fun*
       (Columbia) F
       "Just For Fun"

TUTTA ROLF (dancer)
1936   *Rhythm in the Air*
       (Fox) F
       "Walking the Beam"

THE ROLLING STONES (group)
see also **MICK JAGGER, KEITH RICHARD,
BILL WYMAN**
1967   *Tonite Let's All Make Love in
       London*
       (Lorrimer) F
       "Standing in the Shadows"
1968   *Sympathy for the Devil*
       (Connoisseur) F
       "Sympathy for the Devil"
1983   *Undercover*
       (Palace)
       "Undercover of the Night"

PAUL ROLLO, EARLE AND CAROLE
(skaters)
1939   *Pathetone 460*
1941   *Pathetone Parade of 1941*
       F (reissue: *Pathetone 460*)

DUDLEY ROLPHE (singer)
1931   *Ideal Cinemagazine 275*
       "What Would You Do?"
1935   *It's a Bet*
       (BIP) F
1938   *Lily of Laguna*
       (Butcher) F
       "Lily of Laguna"
1941   *Highlights of Variety 21*
       (reissue: *Lily of Laguna*)

ROMA T. ROMA (comedienne)
1898   *He and She*
       (Mutoscope)

VICTOR ROMERO (singer)
1981   *Burning an Illusion*
       (BFI) F
       "You Can't Be Roots in Football
       Boots"

ROMILLY CHOIR
1936   *Hearts of Humanity*
       (Baxter) F

MICHAEL RONNI (dancer)
1936   *Murder at the Cabaret*
       (Paramount) F
1938   *Romance of Dancing*
       (Highbury) S

LINDA RONSTADT (American singer)
1982   *The Pirates of Penzance*
       (UIP) F

ANNIE ROONEY (singer)
1934   *Love Mirth Melody*
       (Mancunian) F

ROOSTERS CONCERT PARTY
1937   *French Leave*
       (Pathe) F

FRED ROPER AND HIS MIDGETS
1936   *Pathe Pictorial 939*
       "Parade of the Toys"

REX ROPER (rope/whip)
1936   *Pathetone 305*
       "Okay Toots"
1937   *Melody and Romance*
       (British Lion) F

JOHN RORKE (comedy singer)
1935   *Variety*
       (Butcher) F
       "Champagne Charlie"
       "My Little Lot"
1935   *Lieutenant Daring RN*
       (Butcher) F
       "Sailors Don't Care"
1943   *Variety Jubilee*
       (Butcher) F
       "Arf a Pint of Ale"
1944   *Highlights of Variety 28*
       (reissue: *Variety Jubilee*)
1946   *Under New Management*
       (Mancunian) F

EDMUNDO ROS AND HIS RUMBA BAND
1945   *Flight from Folly*
       (Warner) F
       "The Majorca"
1945   *What Do We Do Now?*
       (Grand National) F

1946 *Night Boat to Dublin*
(ABPC) F
1948 *Here Come the Huggetts*
(Gainsborough) F
1952 *Judgement Deferred*
(Group 3) F
"My Favourite Samba"
"No No Lolita"
"With a Kiss and a Sigh"
1957 *Edmundo Ros Half Hour*
(Hammer)
"Mayfair Mambo"
"John Peel Samba"
"Monte Carlo"
1962 *The Primitives*
(Border) F

ROSARITA (dancer)
1936 *Murder at the Cabaret*
(Paramount) F
1939 *Traitor Spy*
(Pathe) F

CLARKSON ROSE (comedian)
1957 *Davy*
(Ealing) F

JULIAN ROSE (Hebrew comedian)
1932 *Pathe Pictorial 760*
1932 *Money Talks*
(BIP) F

PAT ROSE AND HIS MAJESTIC ORCHESTRA
1935 *Kiddies On Parade*
(Majestic) F

ARTHUR ROSEBERY'S SWINGTETTE
(band)
1933 *Pathetone 169*
"Song of Songs"
1935 *Pathe Pictorial 919*
"Babies On Parade"
1939 *Pathetone 469*
1942 *Pathe Pictorial 349*
1943 *Pathe Pictorial 383*

ARTHUR ROSEBERY'S SYMPHONIC SYNCOPATED ORCHESTRA
1930 *Big Business*
(Fox) F

ROSERAY AND CAPELLA (dancers)
1929 *Eve's Film Review 395*

ROSETTE
1937 *Pathe Pictorial NS 65*
"Delyse"

VAL ROSING (singer)
1933 *Aunt Sally*
(Gainsborough) F
1935 *In Town Tonight*
(British Lion) F

1936 *One Good Turn*
(Fuller) F
"Come Swing With Me"
"One Persian Night"
1937 *Feather Your Nest*
(ATP) F
"Leaning on a Lamp Post"
1937 *Pathetone 363*
"Polka Dot Swing"
"Hiawatha's Lullabye"

EMPEROR ROSKO (disc jockey)
1973 *Radio Wonderful*
(Goodtimes) F
1975 *Flame*
(VPS) F

ALEC ROSS (dancer)
1923 *Watch Your Steps*
(Hepworth)
"Foxtrot"
"Tango"

ANNIE ROSS (singer)
1955 *Look At Life*
(Rank)
"Don't Say Goodbye"
1972 *Straight On Till Morning*
(Hammer) F
1974 *Dead Cert*
(UA) F
1975 *Alfie Darling*
(EMI) F
1979 *Yanks*
(UA) F

JONATHAN ROSS (television personality)
1989 *The Tall Guy*
(Virgin) F
1997 *Spice World*
(Fragile) F

LYNDA ROSS (singer)
1946 *Under New Management*
(Mancunian) F

ROSS AND BENNETT (comedy)
1939 *Pathe Pictorial NS 175*

ROSS AND SARGENT (dancers)
1931 *Pathetone 46*
"Seven Veils"

PATRICIA ROSSBOROUGH (pianist)
1929 *Song Copation*
(BIP)
"Walking With Susie"
"Funny That Way"
"You Can't Make Me Feel Blue"
1929 *Musical Medley*
(BIP)
1933 *Pathe Pictorial 787*
"Liebestraum"

1935 *Pathetone 288*
"Melody in F"
1939 *Pathetone Parade of 1940*
F (reissue: *Pathetone 288*)

PERCY ROSSITER (conjurer)
1926 *Pathe Pictorial 447*

ANNELIESE ROTHENBERGER (soprano)
1962 *Der Rosenkavalier*
(Rank) F

JOHNNY ROTTEN (singer)
see also **THE SEX PISTOLS**
1980 *The Great Rock 'n' Roll Swindle*
(Virgin) F

THOMAS ROUND (singer)
1952 *The Story of Gilbert and Sullivan*
(London) F
"Trial by Jury"
"The Mikado"

ROBERT ROUNSEVILLE (singer)
1951 *Tales of Hoffmann*
(London) F

HARRY ROUNTREE (cartoonist)
1931 *Ideal Cinemagazine 292*

JACK ROWALL AND MISS HALL (dancers)
1929 *British Screen Tatler 30*

SANDY ROWAN (Scottish comedian)
1935 *Pathetone 281*
1937 *Pathetone Parade of 1938*
F (reissue: *Pathetone 281*)

FRANK ROWE
see **EDITH ALBORD AND FRANK ROWE**

THE ROXY ROLLERS (group)
1979 *Steppin' Out*
(White)

DEREK ROY (comedian)
1950 *Come Dance With Me*
(Columbia) F

HARRY ROY AND HIS BAND
1933 *Pathetone 192*
1934 *Pathe Pictorial 849*
1936 *Everything Is Rhythm*
(Rock) F
"Dismal Moan"
"You're the Last Word in Love"
"Since Black Minnie's Got the Blues"
"Make Some Music"
"Man of My Dreams"
"Life Is Empty"
"The Internationale"
"Wa Wa Daddle O"
"Sky High Honeymoon"
"No Words or Anything"
"Cheerful Blues"

1937 *Rhythm Racketeer*
(Rock) F
"Rhythm Racketeer"
"I Fell in Love with a Poster"
"Seven Different Sweeties a Week"
"You Struck the Right Note"
1939 *Pathe Pictorial 192*
"Run Rabbit Run"
1940s *Floor Show*
(reissue: *Everything Is Rhythm*)
1940s *Cabaret Time*
(reissue: *Rhythm Racketeer*)

HARRY ROY'S ROYALISTS (singers)
1943 *Pathe Pictorial 372*
"Spring Is Here"

HARRY ROY'S TIGER RAGAMUFFINS
(band)
1942 *Pathe Pictorial 343*
1943 *Pathe Pictorial 366*

ROY AND ALF (animal imitators)
1937 *Pathe Pictorial NS 46*

THE ROYAL BALLET
1963 *An Evening with the Royal Ballet*
(BHE) F
1966 *Romeo and Juliet*
(Rank) F
1972 *I Am a Dancer*
(EMI) F
1979 *Stories from a Flying Trunk*
(Sands) F

ROYAL BALLET OF COPENHAGEN
1972 *I Am a Dancer*
(EMI) F

ROYAL ENGINEERS' BAND
1936 *Pathe Pictorial NS 18*

ROYAL KILTIE JUNIORS (dancers)
1951 *The Kilties Are Coming*
(Adelphi) F
1953 *Lads and Lassies On Parade*
(reissue: *The Kilties Are Coming*)

ROYAL MERRY FOUR (singers)
1934 *Love Mirth Melody*
(Mancunian) F

ROYAL NAVAL SINGERS
1935 *Pathetone 274*
1936 *Pathetone 328*
"Bound for the Rio Grande"
1938 *Pathetone 432*
"Billy Boy"

**ROYAL OPERA HOUSE COVENT GARDEN
CHORUS** (singers)
1938 *The Singing Cop*
(Warner) F

1957 *Davy*
(Ealing) F
"The Meistersingers"

ROYAL PHILHARMONIC ORCHESTRA
1971 *200 Motels*
(UA) F

EARL ROYCE AND THE OLYMPICS (group)
1964 *Ferry Cross the Mersey*
(UA) F
"Shake a Tail Feather"

LITA ROZA (singer)
1955 *Cyril Stapleton and the Show Band*
(Hammer)
1955 *Cast a Dark Shadow*
(Eros) F
"Leave Me Alone"
1979 *My Way Home*
(BFI) F

THE RUBETTES (group)
1975 *Never Too Young To Rock*
(GTO) F
"Never Too Young To Rock"
"Sugar Baby Love"
"Tonight"
"Juke Box Jive"
1975 *Side By Side*
(GTO) F
"I Can Do It"

PROFESSOR RUBINS (conjurer)
1927 *Pathe Pictorial 497*

BILLY RUSSELL (comedian)
1938 *Take Off That Hat*
(Viking) F
1951 *The Man in the White Suit*
(Ealing) F
1952 *Judgement Deferred*
(Group 3) F
1968 *Negatives*
(Crispin) F

1969 *I Start Counting*
(UA) F

RAE RUSSELL (harp)
1934 *Pathetone 231*
"Humoresque"

WENSLEY RUSSELL (singer)
1936 *Melody of My Heart*
(Butcher) F
"A Butcher's Love Song"

JOHN RUTLAND (comic songs)
1968 *A Little of What You Fancy*
(Border) F
"My Old Brown Hat"
"I'm Henery the Eighth I Am"
"What a Mouth"
"Ginger You're Barmy"
"Oh Saturday"
"Boiled Beef and Carrots"
"Any Old Iron"
"We Made Her Pull the Whole Lot Home"
"The Longer You Linger"

MARION RYAN (singer)
1956 *Eric Winstone's Stagecoach*
(Hammer)
1963 *It's All Happening*
(British Lion) F
"You Are Maximum Plus"
"Love a Man"

SLIM RYDER (clown cyclist)
1943 *Variety Jubilee*
(Butcher) F
1944 *Highlights of Variety 26*
(reissue: *Variety Jubilee*)
1949 *William Comes To Town*
(UA) F

WINNIE RYLAND (contortionist)
1939 *Pathetone Parade of 1940*
F

SABRINA (model)
1956 *Ramsbottom Rides Again*
       (British Lion) F
1957 *Just My Luck*
       (Rank) F
1957 *Blue Murder at St Trinian's*
       (British Lion) F
1959 *Make Mine a Million*
       (British Lion) F

SADE (singer)
1986 *Absolute Beginners*
       (Palace) F

HAROLD SADLER AND HIS ORCHESTRA
1937 *Heads You Win*
       (Ace Cinemagazine)

ARTHUR SALISBURY AND THE SAVOY HOTEL ORCHESTRA
1935 *Pathe Pictorial 894*
       "Poems"

THE SALISBURY SINGERS
1929 *Gentlemen the Chorus 1*
       (BSFP)
       "Come Landlord"
       "My Bonnie Lies Over the Ocean"
1929 *Gentlemen the Chorus 2*
       (BSFP)
       "John Peel"
       "Who's That A-calling?"
1932 *Camera Cocktales 3*
       (reissue: *Gentlemen the Chorus 1*)
1932 *Musical Medley 4*
       (reissue: *Gentlemen the Chorus 2*)

ADAM SALKELD (singer)
1996 *Glastonbury: The Movie*
       (Starlight) F
       "Fairground"
       "Riddim"

MARCELLA SALTZER
1936 *International Revue*
       (Medway) F

SAM APPLE PIE (group)
1970 *Toomorrow*
       (Rank) F

JULIE SAMUEL
see **ALAN KLEIN AND JULIE SAMUEL**

FRED SANBORN (xylophonist)
1933 *Ideal Cinemagazine 358*
1935 *Pathe Pictorial 925*
       "Hungarian Rhapsody"

SCOTT SANDERS (comedian)
1937 *Talking Feet*
       (Baxter) F
1941 *The Common Touch*
       (British National) F

1943 *Playtime for Workers*
       (Federated) F
       "Rolling Round the World"
       "The Japanese, the Jerries and the Wops"
1945 *Murder in Reverse*
       (British National) F
1954 *Lilacs in the Spring*
       (Republic) F
1956 *Not So Dusty*
       (Eros) F

SANDERS TWINS (dancers)
1938 *Stepping Toes*
       (Baxter) F

GEORGE SANDIFORD
see **THE SINGING BAKERY BOY**

ALBERT SANDLER (violin)
1928 *Phototone 2*
       "Schubert's Serenade"
1928 *Phototone 5*
       "Czardas"
1930 *Comets*
       (Alpha) F
1930 *Pathetone 10*
       "Hungarian Dance"
1932 *Pathetone 92*
       "Gypsy Selection"
1932 *Pathetone 97*
       "An Old Violin"
1932 *Pathetone 132*
       "A Song in the Night"
1932 *Pathe Pictorial 749*
       "Black Eyes"
1933 *Musical Film Revue*
       (British Lion) S
       "Barcarolle"
       "Hungarian Dance"
1935 *Equity Musical Revue Series*
       (British Lion)
       "Tell Me Tonight"
1935 *The Small Man*
       (Baxter) F
1935 *Pathetone 252*
1936 *Here and There*
       (Baxter)
1937 *Pathe Pictorial NS 60*
       "Toreador Song"
1938 *Pathetone 412*
       "Passing Clouds"
1939 *Pathetone Parade of 1939*
       F
       "Melody at Dusk"
1939 *Pathetone Parade of 1940*
       F (reissue: *Pathetone 252*)
1943 *Pathetone Parade of 1943*
       F (reissue: *Pathetone 412*)
1945 *For You Alone*
       (Butcher) F
       "Flight of the Bumblebee"
1945 *Waltz Time*
       (British National) F
1945 *New Pictorial 53*

ALBERT SANDLER AND THE PALM COURT ORCHESTRA
1946 *I'll Turn To You*
(Butcher) F
"Scrub Brothers Scrub"

MIGUEL SANDOVAL (singer)
1986 *Sid and Nancy*
(Zenith) F
"I Wanna Job (One That Satisfies)"
1986 *Straight to Hell*
(Island) F

CHRIS SANDS (clown cyclist)
1952 *For Your Entertainment 1; 2*
(Gaumont)

JOSIE SANTOI AND ROMA CLARKE
(singers)
1935 *Musical Medley*
(Mancunian)

MALCOLM SARGENT (conductor)
1943 *Battle for Music*
(Strand) F
"La Colinda"
"Fifth Symphony"
"Carnival Romain"

MIKE SARNE (singer)
(films as actor not listed)
1964 *Every Day's a Holiday*
(Grand National) F
"Every Day's a Holiday"
"Love Me Please"
"Say You Do"
"Indubitably Me"
1964 *A Place to Go*
(British Lion) F
"A Place to Go"
"Out and About"

LESLIE SARONY (comedian)
see also **THE TWO LESLIES**
1927 *On With the Dance*
(Parkinson)
1928 *Hot Water and Vegetabuel*
(Phonofilm)
1929 *Pathe Magazine 11*
"I Lift Up My Finger"
1930 *Eve's Film Review 465*
"Rio Rita"
1931 *Pathetone 66*
"Icicle Joe"
"Roaming Through the Roses"
1931 *Pathetone 89*
"I'm Happy When I'm Hiking"
"Oh Mr Constabule"
1932 *Pathetone 141*
"Toasts"
1933 *Pathetone 156*
"Wheezy Anna"
1933 *Pathetone 189*
"Peggoty Leg"

1933 *Soldiers of the King*
(Gainsborough) F
"A Jolly Good Sporting Lot"
1934 *Rolling in Money*
(Fox) F
1935 *Wedding Eve*
(Astor) F
1935 *Where's George?*
(B&D) F
1936 *Sunshine Ahead*
(Baxter) F
1958 *Noddy in Toyland*
(Luckwell) F
1965 *Game for Three Losers*
(Anglo) F
1976 *It Shouldn't Happen to a Vet*
(EMI) F
1983 *Crimson Permanent Assurance*
(UIP)
1984 *Give My Regards to Broad Street*
(UK) F

SYLVIA SARTRE (singer)
1940 *At the Havana*
(New Realm)
"Blue Moments"
"Old Man Swing"

WALTER SAULL'S SCOTIA SINGERS
1947 *Comin' Thro' the Rye*
(Adelphi) F

JENNIFER SAUNDERS (comedienne)
1985 *The Supergrass*
(Comic Strip) F
1987 *Eat the Rich*
(Comic Strip) F
1987 *More Bad News*
(Comic Strip) F
1988 *The Strike*
(Palace) F
1995 *In the Bleak Midwinter*
(Rank) F
1997 *Spice World*
(Fragile) F

MARION SAUNDERS (singer)
1946 *London Town*
(GFD) F
"If Spring Were Only Here to Stay"
1949 *Melody in the Dark*
(Adelphi) F
"Our Time Is Now"

MERVYN SAUNDERS (singer)
1941 *Pathe Pictorial 298*
"The Voice of Romance"
1942 *Pathe Pictorial 307*

JIMMY SAVILE (television personality)
1963 *Just For Fun*
(Columbia) F
1964 *Ferry Cross the Mersey*
(UA) F

1965 *Pop Gear*
(Pathe) F
1973 *Radio Wonderful*
(Goodtimes) F

SAVOIR (entertainer)
1954 *Variety Half Hour*
(Baim)

SAVOY HAVANA BAND
1927 *Syncopated Melodies*
(Parkinson)
1929 *After Many Years*
(Savana) F

SAVOY HOTEL BAND
1930 *Comets*
(Alpha) F

SAVOY ORPHEANS BAND
1932 *Pathetone 103*
"A Hundred Per Cent"

SAXES AND SEVENS DANCE BAND
1931 *Ideal Cinemagazine 291*

AL SAXON (singer)
1964 *Just For You*
(British Lion) F

ALVIN SAXON'S MURRAY CLUB BAND
1936 *Strange Cargo*
(Paramount) F

ALEXEI SAYLE (comedian)
1979 *Repeater*
(Welsh Arts) F
1982 *The Secret Policeman's Other Ball*
(UIP) F
1983 *The Comic Strip*
(UK)
1985 *The Supergrass*
(Comic Strip) F
1985 *The Bride*
(Columbia) F
1987 *Didn't You Kill My Brother?*
(Comic Strip) F
1988 *The Strike*
(Palace) F
1988 *Whoops Apocalypse*
(Virgin) F
1992 *Carry On Columbus*
(Comedy House) F

SCAFFOLD (group)
see also **ROGER McGOUGH**
1972 *Plod*
(Crown)

TITO SCHIPA (tenor)
1950 *Soho Conspiracy*
(New Realm) F

JOSEPH SCHMIDT (tenor)
1034 *My Song Goes Round the World*
(BIP) F
"My Song Goes Round the World"
"The Linden Tree"
"Santa Lucia"
"O Paradise"
"Mourning"
"Osteria Lied"
"Frag Nicht"
"Lenisches Gluck"
1936 *A Star Fell From Heaven*
(BIP) F
"A Star Fell Out of Heaven"
"I Hear You Calling Me"
"I'm Happy When It's Raining"
"La Cœur de la Vie"
"I'll Sing a Song of Love to You"
"Wine and Waltz"
"Excelsior"

HETTY SCHNEIDER QUARTET (group)
1968 *Popdown*
(New Realm) F

ANDREW SCHOFIELD (singer)
1985 *No Surrender*
(Palace) F
"We're Gonna Die"
1986 *Sid and Nancy*
(Zenith) F
"I'm Not Your Stepping Stone"
"God Save the Queen"
"Anarchy in the UK"
"No Feelings"
"Holidays in the Sun"
"Pretty Vacant"
"Problems"

JOHNNY SCHOFIELD (whistler)
(films as actor not listed)
1933 *Heads We Go*
(BIP) F
"Whistling Under the Moon"

MAX SCHUMANN (piano)
1937 *Pathe Pictorial NS 88*
"Poet and Peasant"
1939 *Pathe Pictorial NS 146*
"Zampa in Rhythm"

ELIZABETH SCHWARZKOPF (soprano)
1954 *Svengali*
(Renown) F
1962 *Der Rosenkavalier*
(Rank) F

FREDDIE SCHWEITZER (musical clown)
1935 *She Shall Have Music*
(Twickenham) F
"Blaze Away"
1940 *Band Waggon*
(Gainsborough) F
1943 *Old Mother Riley Overseas*
(British National) F

SCOTS KILTIES BAND (juveniles)
1937 *Talking Feet*
(Baxter) F
1937 *Saturday Night Revue*
(Pathe) F

SCOTS MILITARY EX-GUARDS BAND
1943 *Pathe Pictorial 873*
"Welsh Medley"

BILLY 'UKE' SCOTT (singer)
1944 *Rainbow Round the Corner*
(Berkeley) F
"Learning to Play the Uke"
"I've Got a Girl Friend"
"Manhattan Blues"
"Ragtime Mandarin"
"A Million Little Raindrops"
"California Here I Come"
1944 *Night of Magic*
(Berkeley) F
"On the Beautiful Banks of the Nile"
1946 *Rainbow Rhythm*
(reissue: *Rainbow Round the
Corner*)

**DOUGLAS SCOTT AND HIS DEBONAIR
BOYS** (dancers)
1951 *Happy Go Lovely*
(ABP) F

KEVIN SCOTT (singer)
1963 *The Cool Mikado*
(Baim) F
"A Wandering Minstrel"
"Here's a How d'ye Do"
"Were You Not To Koko Plighted"

MALCOLM SCOTT (comedian)
1913 *How a Housekeeper Lost Her
Character*
(Magnet)

MILLICENT SCOTT (striptease)
1968 *Curse of the Crimson Altar*
(Tigon) F

VICKI SCOTT (striptease)
1978 *Adventures of a Plumber's Mate*
(Alpha) F
1978 *What's Up, Superdoc?*
(Blackwater) F

SCOTT AND WHALEY (comedians)
1933 *Pathe Pictorial 798*
1934 *On the Air*
(British Lion) F
1934 *Kentucky Minstrels*
(Realart) F
"Oh Lordy"
"Louisiana Lou"
1936 *Pathetone Parade of 1936*
F (reissue: *Pathe Pictorial 798*)

1937 *Shooting Stars*
(Viking) F
1938 *Take Off That Hat*
(Viking) F

BILLY SCOTT-COOMBER (singer)
1933 *Pathe Pictorial 780*
"Four Leaf Clover"
1933 *Pathe Pictorial 786*
"There's a Light in Your Window"
1936 *Sunshine Ahead*
(Baxter) F

**BILLY SCOTT-COOMBER AND HIS EIGHT
ROYAL MOUNTIES** (singers)
1939 *Pathetone 459*
"A Perfect Day"
"When Day Is Done"

**BILLY SCOTT-COOMBER AND HIS
SINGING GRENADIERS** (singers)
1940 *Pathetone 518*

**SCOTTISH CO-OPERATIVE WHOLESALE
SOCIETY BAND**
1932 *Pathe Pictorial 762*
"Scotch Medley"
1933 *Pathe Pictorial 791*
"The Joker"

SCOVELL AND WHELDON (singers)
1927 *Scovell and Wheldon*
(Phonofilm)
"Ukulele Lullabye"
"Fresh Milk Comes From Cows"
1933 *Pathe Pictorial 800*
"Girl in the Little Green Hat"
1933 *Pathetone 181*
"Calm Waters"
1934 *Pathetone 199*
"Noah's Ark"
1934 *Pathetone 203*
"A Cup of Coffee"

CLIFFORD SEAGRAVE (acrobatic dancer)
1936 *Murder at the Cabaret*
(Paramount) F

ADDIE SEAMON
see **CHARLES FORSYTHE, ADDIE
SEAMON AND ELEANOR FARRELL**

PHIL SEAMON'S JAZZ GROUP
1958 *The Golden Disc*
(Butcher) F
"Lower Deck"

THE SEARCHERS (group)
1964 *Saturday Night Out*
(Compton) F

HARRY SECOMBE (comedian/singer)
1949 *Helter Skelter*
(Gainsborough) F

1951 *Penny Points to Paradise*
(Adelphi) F
1951 *London Entertains*
(New Realm) F
1952 *Down Among the Z Men*
(New Realm) F
1953 *Forces Sweetheart*
(New Realm) F
"All Through the Year"
"One Love One Lifetime"
"She Knows Me"
1954 *Svengali*
(Renown) F
1957 *Davy*
(Ealing) F
"My World Is Your World"
"Nessun Dorma"
1959 *Jet Storm*
(British Lion) F
1968 *Oliver*
(Columbia) F
"Oliver"
"Boy for Sale"
1969 *The Bed Sitting Room*
(UA) F
1970 *Rhubarb*
(Warner) F
1970 *Doctor in Trouble*
(Rank) F
1971 *The Magnificent Seven Deadly Sins*
(Tigon) F
1972 *Sunstruck*
(EMI) F

SECOND GENERATION (dancers)
1975 *Side By Side*
(GTO) F

SECOND HAND (group)
1969 *Death May Be Your Santa Claus*
(Amanda) F

SECRET AFFAIR (group)
1979 *Steppin' Out*
(White)
"Time for Action, Glory Boys"

SENOR SEDELLI (singer)
1930 *Gypsy Land*
(Gainsborough)
"Gypsy Melody"

SELBIN TROUPE (acrobats)
1902 *The Selbin Troupe of Marvellous Clever Acrobats*
(Warwick)

THE SELECTER (group)
1981 *Dance Craze*
(Osiris) F
"Three Minute Hero"
"Missing Words"
"On My Radio"
"Too Much Pressure"

LOUISE SELKIRK'S LADIES ORCHESTRA
1935 *Play Up the Band*
(City) F

GATTY SELLARS (organ)
1931 *Pathetone 56*
"Temple Gates"
1936 *Scenes in Harmony*
(Fidelity)
1936 *An Ocean Tempest*
(Fidelity)
1936 *A Cornish Idyll*
(Fidelity)

ENID SELLERS
see **JOE BISSETT AND ENID SELLERS**

PETER SELLERS (comedian)
1951 *Penny Points to Paradise*
(Adelphi) F
1951 *Let's Go Crazy*
(Adelphi) F
1951 *Burlesque on Carmen*
[commentary]
1951 *London Entertains*
(New Realm) F
1952 *Down Among the Z Men*
(New Realm) F
1953 *Super Secret Service*
(New Realm) F
1954 *Orders Are Orders*
(British Lion) F
1955 *John and Julie*
(Group 3) F
1955 *The Ladykillers*
(Ealing) F
1956 *Case of the Mukkinese Battlehorn*
(Archway)
1956 *The Man Who Never Was*
(TCF) F (voice)
1956 *The Smallest Show On Earth*
(British Lion) F
1957 *Cold Comfort*
(Saxon)
1957 *Insomnia Is Good For You*
(ABP)
1957 *Dearth of a Salesman*
(ABP)
1957 *The Naked Truth*
(Rank) F
1958 *Up the Creek*
(British Lion) F
1958 *Tom Thumb*
(MGM) F
1959 *Carlton Browne of the F.O.*
(British Lion) F
1959 *The Mouse That Roared*
(Columbia) F
1959 *"I'm All Right Jack"*
(British Lion) F
1959 *Battle of the Sexes*
(British Lion) F
1960 *Two Way Stretch*
(British Lion) F

1960	*The Running Jumping and Standing Still Film* (British Lion)	
1960	*Climb Up the Wall* (New Realm) F	
1960	*Never Let Go* (Rank) F	
1960	*The Millionairess* (TCF) F	
1961	*Mr Topaze* (TCF) F	
1961	*Only Two Can Play* (British Lion) F	
1962	*The Road to Hong Kong* (UA) F	
1962	*Lolita* (MGM) F	
1962	*Waltz of the Toreadors* (Rank) F	
1962	*The Dock Brief* (MGM) F	
1962	*The Wrong Arm of the Law* (British Lion) F	
1963	*Heavens Above* (British Lion) F	
1963	*Dr Strangelove Or: How I Learned to Stop Worrying and Love the Bomb* (Columbia) F	
1964	*A Shot in the Dark* (UA) F	
1966	*The Wrong Box* (Columbia) F	
1967	*Casino Royale* (Columbia) F	
1967	*The Bobo* (Warner) F	
1969	*The Magic Christian* (Grand) F	
1970	*Hoffman* (Warner) F	
1970	*Simon Simon* (Tigon) F	
1970	*There's a Girl in My Soup* (Columbia) F	
1972	*Alice's Adventures in Wonderland* (TCF) F	
1973	*The Blockhouse* (Galactacus) F	
1973	*Ghost in the Noonday Sun* (Columbia) F	
1974	*Soft Beds Hard Battles* (Rank) F	
1974	*The Optimists of Nine Elms* (Scotia) F	
1975	*The Great McGonagall* (Tigon) F	
1975	*Return of the Pink Panther* (UA) F	
1976	*The Pink Panther Strikes Again* (UA) F	
1978	*Revenge of the Pink Panther* (UA) F	
1982	*Trail of the Pink Panther* (UA) F	

EMILIE SELLS AND FRITZ YOUNG (acrobats)
1901   *Acrobatic Performance* (Paul)

HARRY SELTZER (comedian)
1945   *Cabaret* (Empire) F

DORITA SENSIER (singer)
1962   *Guns of Darkness* (Warner) F

SERENA (striptease)
1973   *The Lovers* (British Lion) F

SERENADE QUINTET (band)
1938   *What a Spread* (Ace Cinemagazine)

SERENO AND JUNE (acrobatic dancers)
1934   *Pathe Pictorial 851* "Fairy Dreams Waltz"
1936   *Pictorial Revue* F (reissue: *Pathe Pictorial 851*)

SERPENTELLO (contortionist)
1897   *Serpentello* (Velograph)

JOHN SESSIONS (comedian)
1984   *The Bounty* (Bounty) F
1986   *Castaway* (EMI) F
1988   *Whoops Apocalypse* (Virgin) F
1989   *Henry V* (Renaissance) F
1991   *The Pope Must Die* (Palace) F
1995   *In the Bleak Midwinter* (Rank) F
1996   *The Scarlet Tunic* (Scarlet)
1996   *The Adventures of Pinocchio* (Allied) F

DON SESTES (singer)
1935   *Pathetone 271*
1935   *Pathetone 284*

SEVEN ELLIOTTS (singers)
1936   *Pathe Pictorial NS 22* "Alice Blue Gown" "Good Ship Lollipop"

SEVEN IMESON BROTHERS (band)
1949   *It's a Wonderful Day* (Equity) F

SEVEN ROYAL HINDUSTANIS (musicians)
1938　*Calling All Crooks*
　　　(Mancunian) F
1940　*Music Hall Personalities 13*
　　　(reissue: *Calling All Crooks*)

SEVEN THUNDERBOLTS (acrobats)
1935　*In Town Tonight*
　　　(British Lion) F
1936　*British Lion Varieties 8*

SEVEN VOLANTES (acrobats)
1952　*For Your Entertainment 2; 3*
　　　(Gaumont)
　　　"A Life on the Ocean Wave"

THE SEX PISTOLS (group)
1980　*The Great Rock 'n' Roll Swindle*
　　　(Virgin) F
　　　"The Great Rock 'n' Roll Swindle"
　　　"God Save the Queen"
　　　"Anarchy in the UK"
　　　"No Feelings"
　　　"Pretty Vacant"
　　　"Bodies"
　　　"Holidays in the Sun"
　　　"Belsen Was a Gas"
　　　"Silly Thing"
　　　"Lonely Boy"
　　　"Watcha Gonna Do About It?"
　　　"Johnny B. Goode"
　　　"Something Else"
　　　"C'mon Everybody"
　　　"No Fun"
　　　"My Way"
　　　"Friggin' in the Riggin'"

BARRY SEYMOUR (entertainer)
1938　*Revue Parade*
　　　(Ace) F

CONSTANCE SEYMOUR
see **ANDREA MEAZZA AND CONSTANCE
SEYMOUR**

LYNN SEYMOUR (ballerina)
1972　*I Am a Dancer*
　　　(EMI) F
1993　*Wittgenstein*
　　　(BFI) F

SYD SEYMOUR (comedian)
1928　*Eve's Film Review 348*
　　　"Eccentricity"

SYD SEYMOUR AND HIS MAD HATTERS
(comedy band)
1930　*Just For a Song*
　　　(Gainsborough) F
1934　*Pathetone 217*
　　　"On a Steamer Coming Over"
1936　*Happy Days Are Here Again*
　　　(Argyle) F
　　　"Put Me Among the Girls"

　　　"Fall In and Follow Me"
　　　"Auld Lang Syne"
　　　"Spring"
　　　"Melancholy Baby"
1938　*Happy Days Revue*
　　　F (reissue: *Happy Days Are Here
　　　Again*)
1939　*The Mad Hatter*
　　　(reissue: *Happy Days Are Here
　　　Again*)

THE SHADOWS (group)
1959　*Expresso Bongo*
　　　(British Lion) F
　　　"Bongo Blues"
1961　*The Young Ones*
　　　(ABPC) F
1963　*Summer Holiday*
　　　(ABPC) F
　　　"Bachelor Boy"
　　　"Foot Tapper"
　　　"Round and Round"
1964　*Wonderful Life*
　　　(Elstree) F
1964　*Rhythm 'n' Greens*
　　　(Pathe)
1966　*Finders Keepers*
　　　(UA) F

CHARLES SHADWELL (conductor)
1943　*Variety Jubilee*
　　　(Butcher) F
　　　"Richmond Hill"
　　　"The Spice of Life"
1945　*New Pictorial 55*
1948　*The Big Show*
　　　(Rayant)

HARRY SHALSON (singer)
1927　*Harry Shalson the Popular
　　　Entertainer*
　　　(Phonofilm)
　　　"You Go Too Far"

SHAMROCK SINGERS AND DANCERS
1946　*Under New Management*
　　　(Mancunian) F

DEL SHANNON (singer)
1962　*It's Trad Dad*
　　　(Columbia) F
　　　"You Never Talked About Me"

ERNEST SHANNON (impersonator)
1936　*Variety Parade*
　　　(Butcher) F
　　　(as Claude Hulbert, Gordon Harker,
　　　George Robey)
1940　*Pathe Pictorial 235*
1940　*Highlights of Variety 17*
　　　(reissue: *Variety Parade*)
1940　*Cavalcade of Variety*
　　　(reissue: *Variety Parade*)

SHANTI (group)
1996 *Glastonbury: The Movie*
(Starlight) F
"Trolls of Excess"

HELEN SHAPIRO (singer)
1961 *Look At Life*
(Rank)
"Walking Back to Happiness"
1962 *Play It Cool*
(Anglo) F
"I Could Cry My Heart Out"
"I Don't Care"
1962 *It's Trad Dad*
(Columbia) F
"Let's Talk About Love"
"Sometime Yesterday"
"Ring-a-Ding"
1968 *A Little of What You Fancy*
(Border) F
"The Boy I Love"
"Don't Dilly Dally on the Way"

REGINALD SHARLAND (dancer)
1926 *Eve's Film Review 290*
"Twinkling Toes"

JOHN SHARMAN (broadcaster)
1942 *We'll Meet Again*
(Columbia) F

CEDRIC SHARPE (cello)
1933 *Ideal Cinemagazine 377*
"Midsummer Morn"
1943 *Highlights of Variety 25*
"Love's Old Sweet Song"

CEDRIC SHARPE AND HIS SEXTETTE
1936 *B.B.C. Musicals 1*
(Inspiration)
"Father O'Flynn"

AL SHAW (guitar)
1939 *Pathe Pictorial 183*
"Aloha Oe"

AL SHAW AND HIS BAND
1933 *Ideal Cinemagazine 367*
1933 *Ideal Cinemagazine 378*

ALEC SHAW (bird impressions)
1932 *Pathe Pictorial 753*
1937 *Footlights*
(Ace) F

SANDIE SHAW (singer)
1986 *Absolute Beginners*
(Palace) F
1987 *Eat the Rich*
(Comic Strip) F

SYDNEY SHAW (mouth organ)
1941 *The Common Touch*
(British National) F

MOIRA SHEARER (dancer)
1948 *The Red Shoes*
(Archers) F
1951 *Tales of Hoffmann*
(London) F
1955 *The Man Who Loved Redheads*
(British Lion) F
1960 *Peeping Tom*
(Anglo) F

GEORGE SHEARING (piano)
1943 *Theatre Royal*
(Baxter) F
1948 *Stephane Grappelly and His Quintet*
(Inspiration)
"Sweet Georgia Brown"
1954 *Magic of Music*
(Carisbrooke)
"Lullabye of Birdland"

STAN SHEDDON AND THE PLAYTIMERS
(band)
1943 *Playtime for Workers*
(Federated) F
"South Rampart Street Parade"
"It Ain't Whatcha Do"
"United We Stand"
"Home On the Range"

CHRIS SHEEN
see **VIC FORD AND CHRIS SHEEN**

THE SHEFFIELD CHOIR
1931 *Pathetone 48*

DOUG SHELDON (singer)
1964 *Just For You*
(British Lion) F

GENE SHELDON (banjo)
1937 *Television Talent*
(Alexander) F
"Can't You See It In My Eyes?"
1940 *The Banjo Fool*
(reissue: *Television Talent*)

**HORACE SHELDON AND HIS
ORCHESTRA**
1935 *Variety*
(Butcher) F
1935 *Lieutenant Daring RN*
(Butcher) F
"Sunnyside Lane"
"Sailor's Hornpipe"
"Lads in Navy Blue"
"Red River Valley"
1936 *Shipmates o' Mine*
(Butcher) F

ELIZABETH SHELLEY
1957 *Edmundo Ros Half Hour*
(Hammer)

ANNE SHELTON (singer)
1941   *Jeannie*
       (GFD) F
       "Take Me"
1942   *King Arthur Was a Gentleman*
       (Gainsborough) F
       "Why Can't It Happen To Me?"
1943   *Miss London Limited*
       (Gainsborough) F
       "You Too Can Have a Lovely
       Romance"
       "A Fine How Do You Do"
       "The 8.50 Choo Choo"
       "If You Could Only Cook"
1944   *Bees in Paradise*
       (Gainsborough) F
       "Don't Ever Leave Me"
       "Keep a Sunbeam in Your Pocket"
1950   *Come Dance With Me*
       (Columbia) F

ERNEST H. SHEPARD (cartoonist)
1946   *New Pictorial 75*
1974   *Mr Shepard & Mr Milne*
       (Hemdale)

**HORACE SHEPHERD AND HIS
SYMPHONY ORCHESTRA**
1939   *Radio Nights*
       (Inspiration)
       "Festive March"

LEON SHERKOT (mime)
1935   *Dance Band*
       (BIP) F
1948   *Merry Go Round*
       (Federated) F
1950   *Variety Makers*
       (reissue: *Merry Go Round*)

HAL SHERMAN (comedy dancer)
1926   *London's Famous Cabarets*
       (Parkinson)
1926   *Eve's Film Review 246*
1927   *The Glad Eye*
       (Gaumont) F

NED SHERRIN (broadcaster)
1992   *Orlando*
       (Electric) F

SHERRY BROTHERS (quintette)
1936   *Pathe Pictorial NS 2*
       "Love's Old Sweet Song"
1937   *Pathe Pictorial NS 59*
       "Sailor Where Art Thou?"
       "Hilly Billy Blues"

ELLA SHIELDS (singer)
1930   *Pathetone 38*
       "Adeline"
1936   *Men of Yesterday*
       (Baxter) F
       "Burlington Bertie"

1937   *Pathe Pictorial NS 41*
       "I'm Not All There"
       "Burlington Bertie"
1938   *Cavalcade of the Stars*
       (Coronel)
1940   *Camp Concert*
       (reissue: *Men of Yesterday*)

IVY SHILLING (dancer)
1920   *Around the Town 9*
       (Gaumont)

JUDY SHIRLEY (singer)
1937   *Pathe Pictorial NS 83*
       "Where's the Sun"
       "Kiss Myself Goodbye"
1938   *Pathe Pictorial NS 122*
       "I'm Saving the Last Waltz for You"

JEAN SHRIMPTON (model)
1967   *Privilege*
       (Universal) F

ANTOINETTE SIBLEY (ballerina)
1963   *An Evening with the Royal Ballet*
       (BHE) F

SICANIA ORCHESTRA
1932   *Gaumont Sound Mirror 74*

LES SILVAS (acrobats)
1938   *Pathe Pictorial NS 132*

SILVER SPURS (group)
1985   *Shadey*
       (Mainline) F

PHIL SILVERS (American comedian)
1967   *Follow That Camel*
       (Rank) F
1979   *There Goes the Bride*
       (Lonsdale) F

MR AND MRS VICTOR SILVESTER
(dancers)
1927   *The Black Bottom*
       (Triangle)
1928   *Eve's Film Review 361*
       "Argentine Tango"

**VICTOR SILVESTER AND HIS BALLROOM
ORCHESTRA**
1939   *Pathetone 483*
       "I'm Just Wild About Harry"
       "The Lady in Red"

ALAN SIMPSON
see **RAY GALTON AND ALAN SIMPSON**

JACK SIMPSON (xylophone)
1933   *Pathe Pictorial 830*
       "On the Track"
1935   *Pathetone 291*

1936 *Pathe Pictorial NS 34*
"Versatile Solo"
1938 *Pathe Pictorial NS 114*
"Sweet Sue"
1939 *Pathe Pictorial 176*
"Another Track"

JACK SIMPSON AND HIS BEACHCOMBERS (band)
1939 *Pathetone 480*

JACK SIMPSON AND HIS SEXTET
1940 *Pathe Pictorial 234*
1941 *Pathe Pictorial 259*
1942 *Pathe Pictorial 316*
1942 *Pathe Pictorial 327*
1943 *Pathe Pictorial 357*
"I Mean You"
1944 *Pathe Pictorial 405*
"Spooks"
1944 *Pathe Pictorial 432*
"Pop Goes the Weasel"
1946 *Strawberry Roan*
(British National) F
1948 *Nothing Venture*
(Baxter) F

JACK SIMPSON AND HIS TANGO BAND
1936 *Pathetone 321*
"Marilou"

GEORGE SIMS
1938 *On Velvet*
(AIP) F

PETER SINCLAIR (Scottish comedian)
1939 *Pathetone 466*
"My Lady Crinoline"
1940 *Pathetone 547*
1940 *Pathe Pictorial 203*
"Laird of Cockpen"
1941 *Pathe Pictorial 266*
"Mothers of the Motherland"
1945 *The Man From Morocco*
(British Lion) F
1951 *The Kilties Are Coming*
(Adelphi) F
"Cock o' the North"
"The Wind That Shakes the Barley"
1953 *Lads and Lassies On Parade*
(reissue: *The Kilties Are Coming*)
1954 *Escape By Night*
(Eros) F
1954 *Trouble in the Glen*
(Republic) F
1955 *Cross Channel*
(Republic) F
1957 *Let's Be Happy*
(ABPC) F
1957 *Zoo Baby*
(Rank) F
1959 *Web of Suspicion*
(Danziger) F

1959 *In the Wake of a Stranger*
(Butcher) F
1959 *The Heart of a Man*
(Rank) F
1961 *Court Martial of Major Keller*
(Danziger) F
1965 *Invasion*
(Anglo) F

THE SINGING BAKERY BOY (George Sandiford)
1938 *Pathe Pictorial NS 140*
"Why Have You Stolen My Heart?"

THE SINGING CARPENTER (Jimmy Kelley)
1938 *Pathe Pictorial NS 95*
"When My Dreamboat Comes Home"

THE SINGING CHARLADY
1936 *Cabaret Nights 4*
(Highbury)

THE SINGING COOK (Rosina Dixon)
1936 *Cabaret Nights 4*
(Highbury)
1937 *Pathe Pictorial NS 41*
"My Dear Soul"

THE SINGING LADY
1935 *Pathe Pictorial 916*
"Mighty Lak' a Rose"

THE SINGING TAXI DRIVER (Edmund Norton)
1938 *Pathe Pictorial NS 93*
"For You Alone"

VALERIE SINGLETON (television personality)
1978 *The Chiffy Kids*
(CFF)
1978 *Valerie Singleton Introduces*
(CFF)

SIOUXSIE AND THE BANSHEES (group)
1978 *Jubilee*
(Cinegate) F
"Love In a Void"

SIRDANI (conjurer)
1931 *Ideal Cinemagazine 282*
"The Glass Eater"
1934 *Pathe Pictorial 862*
"The Human Ostrich"
1939 *Pathetone 506*
"Musical Moments"

NOBLE SISSLE AND HIS BAND
1931 *Pathetone 42*
"Happy Feet"
"Little White Lies"

PETER SISSONS (television personality)
1997   *Spice World*
       (Fragile) F

EDITH SITWELL (poet)
1927   *Edith Sitwell*
       (Phonofilm)

SIX CAN-CAN DANCERS
1935   *Variety*
       (Butcher) F
1937   *Highlights of Variety 2*
       (reissue: *Variety*)
1944   *Highlights of Variety 27*
       (reissue: *Variety*)

SIX HARMONISTS (singers)
1937   *Pathe Pictorial NS 67*
       "Keep the Home Fires Burning"
1939   *Pathe Pictorial NS 156*
       "When You're Smiling"

SIX LADY HARPISTS
1935   *Equity Musical Revue 3*
       (British Lion)
       "Speak to Me of Love"
1935   *Equity Musical Revue 5*
       (British Lion)
       "Spring Song"
1935   *Equity Musical Revue 6*
       (British Lion)
       "Waltz by Durand"

SKAFISH (group)
1981   *Urgh! A Music War*
       (White) F
       "Sign of the Cross"

SKATING AVALONS (roller skates)
1943   *The Dummy Talks*
       (British National) F
1946   *Walking On Air*
       (Piccadilly) F

SKATING BARODAS (roller skates)
1949   *Sawdust Cabaret*
       (GFD)

SKATING JEWELS (roller skates)
1935   *Pathetone 278*
1937   *Pathetone Parade of 1938*
       F (reissue: *Pathetone 278*)

SKATING SAYERS (roller skates)
1954   *Harmony Lane*
       (Eros)

SKATING TYPHOONS (roller skates)
1948   *International Circus Revue*
       (Butcher) F

PETER SKELLERN (pianist)
1984   *Lassiter*
       (Rank) F

HAL SKELLY (American dancer)
1926   *Eve's Film Review 246*

MARGERY SKELLY (dancer)
1904   *Modern Stage Dances*
       (Paul)

SLADE (group)
1975   *Flame*
       (VPS) F
       "How Does It Feel?"
       "Them Monkeys Can't Swing"
       "So Far So Good"
       "Summer Song"
       "OK Yesterday Was Yesterday"
       "Far Far Away"
       "This Girl"
       "Lay It Down"
       "Heaven Knows"
       "Standing on the Corner"

FRANK SLATER (cartoonist)
1931   *Ideal Cinemagazine 289*
       (draws Jack Buchanan)
1931   *Ideal Cinemagazine 293*
       (draws Jack Hulbert)
1931   *Ideal Cinemagazine 296*
       (draws G B Shaw)
1932   *Ideal Cinemagazine 301*
       (draws Ramsay MacDonald)
1932   *Ideal Cinemagazine 303*
       (draws Marlene Dietrich)
1932   *Ideal Cinemagazine 311*
       (draws George Arliss)
1932   *Ideal Cinemagazine 317*
       (draws Ralph Lynn)
1932   *Ideal Cinemagazine 323*
       (draws Joan Crawford)
1932   *Ideal Cinemagazine 328*
       (draws Gordon Harker)
1932   *Ideal Cinemagazine 346*
       (draws Lilian Braithwaite)
1933   *Ideal Cinemagazine 355*
       (draws Charles Laughton)
1933   *Ideal Cinemagazine 366*
       (draws Henry VIII)
1937   *Pathetone 399*
       (draws Leslie Henson)
1938   *Pathe Pictorial NS 124*
       (draws Arthur Riscoe)
1938   *Striking Gold*
       (Ace Cinemagazine)
       (draws Hildegarde)

TONY SLATTERY (comedian)
1989   *How To Get Ahead in Advertising*
       (Handmade) F
1992   *The Crying Game*
       (Palace) F
1992   *Peter's Friends*
       (Renaissance) F
1992   *Carry On Columbus*
       (Comedy House) F

1994 *To Die For*
(Metro) F
1997 *Up "n" Under*
(Touchdown) F

TOD SLAUGHTER (melodrama)
(films as actor not listed)
1936 *Pathetone 314*
1937 *Pathe Pictorial NS 67*
1938 *Pathe Pictorial NS 131*
"Sweeney Todd"
"Maria Marten"

WAYNE SLEEP (dancer)
1969 *The Virgin Soldiers*
(Columbia) F
1971 *Tales of Beatrix Potter*
(EMI) F
1979 *The First Great Train Robbery*
(Starling) F

PHILIP SLESSOR (broadcaster)
1949 *Golden Arrow*
(Renown) F

SLIK (group)
1975 *Never Too Young To Rock*
(GTO) F
"Never Too Young To Rock"
"Boogiest Band in Town"

THE SLITS (group)
1978 *Jubilee*
(Cinegate) F

ODA SLOBODSKAYA (Russian singer)
1936 *Whom the Gods Love*
(ATP) F

ROSIE SLOMAN (dancer)
see also **HARRY PERRY AND ROSIE SLOMAN**
1913 *Spanish-American Quickstep*
(Selsior)
1913 *The Cowboy Twist*
(Selsior)

JOAN SMALL (singer)
1957 *Rock You Sinners*
(Small) F
"You Can't Say I Love You"

SMALL FACES (group)
1965 *Dateline Diamonds*
(Rank) F
"It's Too Late"
"Come On Children"
"I've Got Mine"
"Whatcha Gonna Do About It?"
1967 *Tonite Let's All Make Love in London*
(Lorrimer) F

SMART AND GREY (jugglers)
1934 *Pathe Pictorial 834*

BILLY SMART'S CIRCUS
1967 *Berserk*
(Columbia) F

BILL SMITH (tenor)
1943 *Playtime for Workers*
(Federated) F
"When You and I Were Young, Maggie"
"Annie Laurie"
"Comin' Thro' the Rye"

CLAY SMITH
see **JOYCE BARBOUR AND CLAY SMITH**

DALE SMITH (baritone)
1929 *Gentlemen the Chorus 1*
(BSFP)
"Come Landlord"
"My Bonnie Lies Over the Ocean"
1929 *Gentlemen the Chorus 2*
(BSFP)
"John Peel"
"Who's That A-calling?"
1931 *Pathetone 54*
"Shenandoah"
1932 *Camera Cocktales 3*
(reissue: *Gentlemen the Chorus 1*)
1932 *Musical Medley 4*
(reissue: *Gentlemen the Chorus 2*)

EDDIE SMITH AND GIRL FRIEND (comedy)
1933 *Pathe Pictorial 803*

MAVIS SMITH (singer)
1929 *A Song or Two*
(BIP)

MEL SMITH (comedian)
1980 *Bloody Kids*
(British Lion) F
1980 *Babylon*
(Diversity) F
1983 *Bullshot*
(Handmade) F
1983 *Slayground*
(EMI) F
1985 *Number One*
(Lutebest) F
1985 *Morons From Outer Space*
(EMI) F
1985 *Restless Natives*
(Oxford) F
1986 *Royal Flush*
(Linkwood) ADVERT
1989 *Wilt*
(LWT) F
1989 *The Wolves of Willoughby Chase*
(Subatomic) F
1996 *Twelfth Night*
(Renaissance) F

MURIEL SMITH (singer)
1953 *Moulin Rouge*
(Romulus) F

RAYMOND SMITH (ventriloquist)
1938 *Calling All Crooks*
(Mancunian) F
1940 *Music Hall Personalities 14*
(reissue: *Calling All Crooks*)

TOM SMITH AND HIS HARMONICA BAND
1935 *Pathe Pictorial 901*
"Classical Overture"

WEAVER SMITH (conjurer)
1952 *Say Abracadabra*
(Butcher)

TOM SMOTHERS (American comedian)
1979 *There Goes the Bride*
(Lonsdale) F

JOHN SNAGGE (broadcaster)
1944 *2000 Women*
(GFD) F
1963 *It Happened Here*
(UA) F
1969 *The Magic Christian*
(Grand) F

LEONARD SNELLING (singer)
1936 *The Three Maxims*
(Wilcox) F

**DON SOLLASH AND HIS ROCKIN'
HORSES** (group)
1957 *Rock You Sinners*
(Small) F
"Rockin' the Blues"

MARIA SOLVEG AND KATTA STERNA
(dancers)
1926 *Eve's Film Review 260*
"Mirror Dance"

CLAIRE SOMBERT (dancer)
1956 *Invitation to the Dance*
(MGM) F

DEBROY SOMERS AND HIS BAND
1929 *Piccadilly*
(BIP) F
1933 *Aunt Sally*
(Gainsborough) F
"We All Go Riding on a Rainbow"
"You Ought to See Sally on
Sunday"
1934 *Music Hall*
(Realart) F
"Ain't Misbehavin'"
"So Shy"
"1812 Overture"
1934 *Kentucky Minstrels*
(Realart) F

1935 *Royal Cavalcade*
(BIP) F
"How You Gonna Keep Them Down
on the Farm?"
"Whispering"
1936 *Stars On Parade*
(Butcher) F
"Say It While Dancing"
"Sweet Nothings"
"Flight of the Bumblebee"
"Stepping Out"
"Tannhäuser"
"The Moon Is Tired of Shining"
1937 *Shooting Stars*
(Viking) F
1937 *Feather Your Nest*
(ATP) F
"Leaning on a Lamp Post"
1938 *Highlights of Variety 7; 9*
(reissue: *Stars On Parade*)
1939 *Co-operette*
(CWS) ADVERT
"There Is a Co-op in the Town"
1940 *Showtime*
(reissue: *Shooting Stars*)
1946 *Radio Rhythm*
(reissue: *Stars On Parade*)

JIMMY SOMERVILLE (singer)
1992 *Orlando*
(Electric) F
"Coming"
"Eliza Is the Fairest Queen"

MICHAEL SOMES (dancer)
1947 *The Little Ballerina*
(CFF) F
1960 *The Royal Ballet*
(Rank) F
"Swan Lake"
"Firebird"
"Ondine"
1966 *Romeo and Juliet*
(Rank) F
1972 *I Am a Dancer*
(EMI) F

RAY SONE (singer)
1964 *Just For You*
(British Lion) F
"Teenage Valentino"

SOUNDS INCORPORATED (group)
1962 *It's Trad Dad*
(Columbia) F
"Spaceship to Mars"
1963 *Just For Fun*
(Columbia) F
"Go"
1963 *Live It Up*
(Rank) F
"Keep Moving"
1965 *Pop Gear*
(Pathe) F

"William Tell"
"Rinky Dink"

LILLIAN SOUTHCOTE (strong woman)
1938 *Pathe Pictorial NS 112*

SOUTHERN BELLES (dancers)
1902 *Southern Belles and Cissy Heath in a Coon Dance*
(Warwick)
1902 *Southern Belles Specialty Dance*
(Warwick)

SOUTHERN SISTERS (singers)
1933 *Pathetone 176*
"Dinah"

THE SOUTHERNERS (group)
1972 *Showcase*
(Butcher) F

LESLIE SOUTHGATE TRIO (musicians)
1937 *Peas and Plenty*
(Ace Cinemagazine)

VICTOR SOVERALL (tenor)
1958 *6.5 Special*
(Anglo) F
"Say Goodbye Now"

NANCY SPAIN (broadcaster)
1963 *Live It Up*
(Rank) F

BOBBY SPARROW (dancer)
1974 *Just One More Time*
(New Realm) F

THE SPECIALS (group)
1981 *Dance Craze*
(Osiris) F
"Nite Klub"
"Too Much Too Young"
"Concrete Jungle"
"Man at C & A"

FRED SPENCER (comedian)
1930 *Pathe Pictorial M 28*
"Mrs Arris on the Tube"

THE SPICE GIRLS (group)
1997 *Spice World*
(Fragile) F
"Say You'll Be There, Mama"
"Too Much"
"Do It"
"Denying"
"Stop"
"Who Do You Think You Are?"
"Lady Is a Vamp"
"Saturday Night Divas"
"Two Become One"
"Never Give Up on the Good Times"
"Wannabe"

"Spice Up Your Life"
"Girl Power"
"Viva Forever"

SPIRITUALIZED (group)
1996 *Glastonbury: The Movie*
(Starlight) F
"Clear Rush"

SPLODGENESSABOUNDS (group)
1981 *Urgh! A Music War*
(White) F
"Two Little Boys"

SPONOOCH (group)
1979 *Steppin' Out*
(White)

THE SPOTNICKS (group)
1963 *Just For Fun*
(Columbia) F
"My Bonnie Lies Over the Ocean" ·

THE SPRINGFIELDS (singers)
1963 *Just For Fun*
(Columbia) F
"Little Boat"
1963 *It's All Over Town*
(British Lion) F
"Down and Out"
"Moraca Mamba"

SPRITELY AND MERRY (comedy)
1935 *Pathe Pictorial 905*

LESLIE SPURLING
1936 *Piccadilly Playtime*
(Ace) F
1937 *Carry On London*
(Ace) F
1937 *Uptown Revue*
(Ace) F
1937 *Footlights*
(Ace) F
1938 *Revue Parade*
(Ace) F

MEL B. SPURR (comedy)
1897 *The Village Blacksmith*
(Paul)

THE SQUADRONNAIRES (band)
1943 *Breathing Space*
(Strand)
"In the Mood"
1946 *New Pictorial 86*
"Rustle of Swing"
1949 *High Jinks in Society*
(Adelphi) F
1952 *Melody Time*
(International)
"Never Make Eyes"
"My Heart Sings"

1952 *New Pictorial 389*
"Apple Honey"
"Riot In Rio"

CHRIS SQUIRE (guitar)
1976 *Fish Out of Water*
(Pleasant)
"Hold Out Your Hand"
"You By My Side"

J. H. SQUIRE'S CELESTE OCTET
1928 *J. H. Squire's Celeste Octet*
(Phonofilm)
"Memories of Tchaikowsky"
1930 *Pathetone 11*
"Song of the Waterfall"
1931 *Pathe Pictorial 705*
"Curfew Time"
1932 *Musical Medley 2*
(reissue: *J. H. Squire's Celeste Octet*)

J. H. SQUIRE'S TRIO
1937 *Pathe Pictorial NS 43*
"Mazurka Brilliante"

EDNA SQUIRE-BROWN (exotic dancer)
1931 *Eve's Film Review 525*
"Dance of the Hoops"
1938 *Romance of Dancing*
(Highbury) S

DOROTHY SQUIRES (singer)
1956 *Stars in Your Eyes*
(British Lion) F
"With All My Heart"
"Without You"
"My Boy"
"I Saw the Look in Your Eyes"

GRANVILLE SQUIRES (ventriloquist)
1946 *Bad Company*
(New Realm) F

ST. DAVID'S SINGERS
1932 *Pathe Pictorial 732*
"Jolly Roger"
1932 *Pathe Pictorial 747*
"Italian Salad"
1932 *Pathe Pictorial 767*
"The Blue Danube"
1939 *Pathe Pictorial NS 146*
"Zion"
1943 *I'll Walk Beside You*
(Butcher) F
"Love's Old Sweet Song"
"Drink To Me Only"

ST. GALL'S SCHOOL CHOIR
1938 *Devil's Rock*
(Burger) F

IVY ST. HELIER (singer)
1933 *Bitter Sweet*
(B&D) F
"If Love Were All"
"Kiss Me Before You Go Away"
1938 *The Singing Cop*
(Warner) F
1945 *Henry V*
(GFD) F
1948 *London Belongs To Me*
(GFD) F

ST. LOUIS UNION (group)
1966 *The Ghost Goes Gear*
(Pathe) F

STADLER AND ROSE (acrobatic dancers)
1933 *Eve's Film Review 618*

STAINLESS STEPHEN (comedian)
1933 *Radio Parade*
(BIP) F
1939 *Pathe Gazette 76*
"ENSA Concert"

MICHAEL STANDING (broadcaster)
1940 *Band Waggon*
(Gainsborough) F

STANELLI (comedian)
1930 *Greek Street*
(Gaumont) F
1933 *Ideal Cinemagazine 356*
1933 *Pathe Pictorial 797*
"Do Not Trust Him Gentle Maiden"
1934 *Radio Parade of 1935*
(BIP) F
"Peter Peter"
1935 *Pathetone 254*
"Peter Peter"
1935 *Pathetone 262*
"Topsy"
1936 *Hearts of Humanity*
(Baxter) F
1937 *Pathe Pictorial NS 80*
1937 *Pathetone 369*
(with Jim Emery)
1937 *Pathetone Parade of 1938*
F (reissue: *Pathetone 359*)
1939 *Pathe Pictorial NS 155*
1940 *Fiddlers All*
(reissue: *title unknown*)
1941 *Pathe Pictorial 256*
1943 *Pathe Pictorial 360*
1943 *Old Mother Riley Overseas*
(British National) F
1944 *Give Me the Stars*
(British National) F
1949 *Adventures of Jane*
(Eros) F

STANELLI AND EDGAR (comedy violinists)
1930 *Pathetone 29*
"A Tiny Tea Shop"

1931 *Pathetone 43*
"Sunny Side of the Street"
1931 *Pathetone 54*
"Don't Talk"
1931 *The Fiddle Fanatics*
(Warner)
1932 *Pathetone 128*
"Auf Wiedersehen"
1932 *Ideal Cinemagazine 301*
1932 *Ideal Cinemagazine 321*
1933 *Radio Parade*
(BIP) F
1933 *Musical Film Revue*
(British Lion) S
1936 *British Lion Varieties 1*
"Get Out and Get Under the Moon"

STANELLI AND HIS BAND
1937 *Pathe Pictorial NS 80*
"Dreaming"
"Destiny"
"Nights of Gladness"

JACK STANFORD (eccentric dancer)
1932 *Ideal Cinemagazine 300*
1935 *Pathe Pictorial 897*
"Hungarian Rhapsody"
1937 *Pathe Pictorial NS 70*
"I'm Nuts About Screwy Music"
1939 *Music Hall Parade*
(Butcher) F
"I'm Nuts About Screwy Music"
1940 *Cavalcade of Variety*
(reissue: *Music Hall Parade*)

STANFORD AND MACNAUGHTON
(comedy)
1937 *Saturday Night Revue*
(Pathe) F

LITTLE STANLEY (cartoonist)
1898 *Little Stanley Lightning Cartoonist*
(Cinematograph)

PHYLLIS STANLEY (singer)
1933 *Musical Film Revue*
(British Lion) S
"Minnie the Moocher"
1934 *Leave It To Blanche*
(Warner) F
1935 *Equity Musical Revue 7*
(British Lion)
"That's My Home"
1935 *Hello Sweetheart*
(Warner) F
1937 *Command Performance*
(Grosvenor) F
1937 *Side Street Angel*
(Warner) F
1938 *St Martin's Lane*
(ABPC) F
1942 *The Next of Kin*
(Ealing) F

1942 *We'll Smile Again*
(British National) F
1943 *They Met in the Dark*
(GFD) F
"Toddle Along"
1944 *One Exciting Night*
(Columbia) F
1948 *Good Time Girl*
(GFD) F
1948 *Look Before You Love*
(GFD) F
1949 *That Dangerous Age*
(London) F

STANLEY AND BAIN (duettists)
1907 *Tala the Indian Love Song*
(Chronophone)

VIVIAN STANSHALL (singer)
see also **THE BONZO DOG DOO DAH BAND**
1977 *Black Joy*
(Hemdale) F
1980 *Sir Henry at Rawlinson End*
(Charisma) F

CLIFFORD STANTON (impressionist)
1936 *Pathe Pictorial NS 23*
1937 *Pathe Pictorial NS 57*
(as Claude Dampier, Ralph Lynn, Robertson Hare)
1938 *Pathetone 424*
"Colonel Bogey"
1939 *Pathetone 469*
1944 *Pathe Pictorial 441*
1952 *Down Among the Z Men*
(New Realm) F

ARTHUR STAPLES (singer)
1908 *Following in Father's Footsteps*
(Chronophone)

CYRIL STAPLETON AND THE SHOW BAND
1955 *Cyril Stapleton and the Show Band*
(Hammer)
"Mexican Hat Dance"
"A Smile is Worth a Million Tears"
"Lucky Strike"
"I'll Close My Eyes"
"Blue Tail Fly"
"Oranges and Lemons"
1955 *Just For You*
(Hammer)
"Just For You"

ALVIN STARDUST
see **SHANE FENTON**

STARDUSTERS DANCE ORCHESTRA
1949 *Melody in the Dark*
(Adelphi) F
"Welcome Inn"
"Gay Doggie"
"Our Time Is Now"

AL STARITA (saxophone)
1928   *Phototone 2*
     "At Dawning"
1928   *Phototone 7*
     "Lanette"

RUDY STARITA (musician)
1930   *Pathetone 36*
     "Lover Come Back to Me"
     (vibraphone)
1931   *Pathetone 67*
     "That Rhumba Rhythm"
     (vibraphone)
1934   *Pathetone 222*
     (with the Four Bright Sparks)
1936   *Pathe Pictorial 936*
     "Roses of Picardy" (octarimba)
1936   *Pathetone 326*
     "Song of the Islands" (electric
     guitar)
1938   *Pathe Pictorial NS 96*
     "Evensong" (octovibraphone)
1940   *Pathetone 531*
     "Eighteenth Century Drawing Room"
     (vibraharp)
1942   *Pathe Pictorial 324*

RUDY STARITA AND HIS MARIMBA BAND
1935   *Pathetone 299*
     "Aloha Oe"
     "Cuban Moonlight"
1937   *Let's Make a Night of It*
     (ABPC) F
1939   *Pathetone Parade of 1939*
     F (reissue: *Pathetone 299*)

FREDDIE STARR (comedian)
1977   *The Squeeze*
     (Warner) F

RINGO STARR (musician)
see also **THE BEATLES**
1969   *The Magic Christian*
     (Grand) F
1971   *200 Motels*
     (UA) F
1972   *Born to Boogie*
     (Apple) F
1973   *That'll Be the Day*
     (EMI) F
1973   *Ziggy Stardust and the Spiders from
     Mars*
     (EMI) F
1975   *Lisztomania*
     (Warner) F
1979   *The Kids Are Alright*
     (Rose) F
1982   *The Cooler*
     (UIP)
1984   *Give My Regards to Broad Street*
     (UK) F
     "Yesterday"
     "Here, There and Everywhere"
     "Wanderlust"

     "Not Such a Bad Boy"
     "No Values"
     "So Bad"
     "Ballroom Dancing"
1985   *Water*
     (Rank) F

JOHN STEBBEN (baritone)
1941   *Pathe Pictorial 281*
     "Your England and Mine"

STEEL PULSE (group)
1981   *Urgh! A Music War*
     (White) F
     "Ku Klux Klan"

MARY STEELE (singer)
1958   *The Golden Disc*
     (Butcher) F
     "Before We Say Goodnight"

TOMMY STEELE (singer)
1957   *Kill Me Tomorrow*
     (Renown) F
     "Rock With the Cave Man"
     "Rebel Rock"
1957   *The Tommy Steele Story*
     (Anglo) F
     "A Handful of Songs"
     "Elevator Rock"
     "Doomsday Rock"
     "Butterfingers"
     "Take Me Back Baby"
     "I Like"
     "You Gotta Go"
     "Water Water"
     "It's Fun Finding Out About London"
     "Will It Be You?"
     "Cannibal Pot"
     "Two Eyes"
     "Build Up"
     "Time to Kill"
     "Teenage Party"
1958   *The Duke Wore Jeans*
     (Anglo) F
     "It's All Happening"
     "What Do You Do?"
     "Family Tree"
     "Happy Guitar"
     "Hair Down Hoe Down"
     "Princess"
     "Photograph"
     "Thanks a Lot"
     "Knees Up Mother Brown"
1959   *Tommy the Toreador*
     (ABPC) F
     "Take a Ride With Me"
     "That's Fiesta"
     "Singing Time"
     "Where's the Birdie?"
     "Little White Bull"
     "Amanda"
     "Tommy the Toreador"

1960   *Light Up the Sky*
        (British Lion) F
        "Touch It Light"
1963   *It's All Happening*
        (British Lion) F
        "Dream Maker"
        "You Are Maximum Plus"
        "Egg and Chips"
1967   *Half a Sixpence*
        (Paramount) F
        "Half a Sixpence"
        "Flash Bang Wallop"
        "She's Too Far Above Me"
        "All in the Name of Economy"
        "Money to Burn"
        "This Is My World"
        "If the Rain's Got to Fall"
1969   *Where's Jack?*
        (Paramount) F

STEELEYE SPAN (group)
1973   *Radio Wonderful*
        (Goodtimes) F

STEFFANI'S SIXTEEN SINGING SCHOLARS
1935   *Pathe Pictorial 882*
        "Love's Old Sweet Song"

STEFFANI'S THIRTY SILVER SONGSTERS
1936   *Dodging the Dole*
        (Mancunian) F
1937   *Music Hall Personalities 1*
        (reissue: *Dodging the Dole*)
1940   *Music Hall Personalities 16*
        (Butcher) (reissue: *Dodging the Dole*)
1945   *What Do We Do Now?*
        (Grand National) F

JOHN STEIN AND HIS RUMBA BAND
1935   *Pathe Pictorial 922*
        "El Castanero"
1937   *Pathetone 357*
        "Sous les Toits de Paris"
1938   *Pathe Pictorial NS 97*
        "Santa Lucia"

JOHN STEIN AND HIS TZIGANE GYPSY ORCHESTRA
1933   *Ideal Cinemagazine 382*

JERRY STEINER (entertainer)
1928   *Phototone 16*

ELSA STENNING (soprano)
1937   *Pathetone 394*
        "Parlez Moi d'Amour"
1938   *Pathetone 450*
        "Ma Curly Headed Babby"
1938   *Pathe Pictorial NS 106*
        "Love Is a Duet"
1939   *Pathe Pictorial NS 147*
        "Mighty Lak' a Rose"

1939   *Pathe Pictorial NS 181*
        "La Paloma"

PAMELA STEPHENSON (comedienne)
1977   *Stand Up Virgin Soldiers*
        (Warner) F
1978   *The Comeback*
        (Heritage) F
1982   *The Secret Policeman's Other Ball*
        (UIP) F
        "Cash or I'll Strip Sketch"
1983   *Monty Python Live at the Hollywood Bowl*
        (Handmade) F
1983   *Superman III*
        (Warner) F
1984   *Bloodbath at the House of Death*
        (EMI) F
1984   *Scandalous*
        (Hemdale) F

KATTA STERNA
see **MARIA SOLVEG AND KATTA STERNA**

STETSON (juggler)
1932   *Ideal Cinemagazine 307*
1935   *Pathetone 273*
1937   *Pathe Pictorial NS 66*
1938   *Something On Account*
        (Ace Cinemagazine)
1939   *Pathetone Parade of 1939*
        F (reissue: *Pictorial NS 66*)
1940   *Pathe Pictorial 225*

JOHN STEVENS
see **DORIS BARRY AND JOHN STEVENS**

MADGE STEVENS (singer)
1934   *Love Mirth Melody*
        (Mancunian) F

DONALD STEWART (singer)
1935   *First a Girl*
        (Gaumont) F
        "Little Silkworm"
        "I Can Wiggle My Ears"
1936   *Accused*
        (UA) F
        "Rendezvous in Paradise"
1936   *Soft Lights and Sweet Music*
        (British Lion) F
        "South American Joe"

ED STEWART (disc jockey)
1976   *Ed Stewart Introduces*
        (CFF)

MAXWELL STEWART AND HIS BALLROOM MELODY (band)
see also **BARBARA MILES AND MAXWELL STEWART**
1939   *Pathe Pictorial NS 163*
        "Cherokee"

ROD STEWART (singer)
1980 *Breaking Glass*
      (GTO) F

SONNY STEWART'S SKIFFLE KINGS
1958 *The Golden Disc*
      (Butcher) F
      "Let Me Lie"

STEWART AND VALE (comedy)
1936 *British Lion Varieties 5*

ROBERT STICKLING (stilt dancer)
1926 *Eve's Film Review*
      "Charleston"

STING (singer)
1979 *Quadrophenia*
      (Who) F
1980 *Radio On*
      (BFI) F
      "Three Steps to Heaven"
1982 *The Secret Policeman's Other Ball*
      (UIP) F
      "Message in a Bottle"
      "I Shall Be Released"
1982 *Brimstone and Treacle*
      (Walker) F
1985 *The Bride*
      (Columbia) F
1985 *Plenty*
      (RKO) F
1987 *Stormy Monday*
      (Palace) F
1988 *The Adventures of Baron
      Munchausen*
      (Columbia) F
1995 *The Grotesque*
      (Xingu) F

FRANCINE STOCK (television presenter)
1992 *Damage*
      (Entertainment) F

STOKES AND HOLLOWAY (comedy songs)
1931 *Pathetone 73*
      "Blue Again"
1931 *Pathetone 87*
      "I'm Yours"

CHRISTOPHER STONE (broadcaster)
1932 *Gaumont Sound Mirror 77*
1933 *Radio Parade*
      (BIP) F
1936 *In Town Tonight*
      (British Commercial) ADVERT
1936 *The Missing Record*
      (British Commercial) ADVERT

LEW STONE AND HIS BAND
1937 *The Street Singer*
      (ABPC) F
1937 *Melody and Romance*
      (British Lion) F

1937 *Intimate Relations*
      (Tudor) F
1946 *Appointment With Crime*
      (British National) F

**LEW STONE AND THE MONSEIGNEUR
ORCHESTRA**
1932 *Goodnight Vienna*
      (B&D) F
1932 *It's a King*
      (B&D) F
1932 *The Love Contract*
      (B&D) F
1933 *Yes Mr Brown*
      (B&D) F
1933 *The King's Cup*
      (B&D) F
1933 *Just My Luck*
      (B&D) F
1933 *Up for the Derby*
      (B&D) F
1933 *Bitter Sweet*
      (B&D) F
      "I'll See You Again"

MARK STONE (comedian)
1938 *On Velvet*
      (AIP) F

PADDY STONE (dancer)
1955 *Value for Money*
      (Rank) F
1957 *The Good Companions*
      (ABPC) F
1958 *6.5 Special*
      (Anglo) F
      "Ice Blue"

REG STONE (female impersonator)
1929 *Splinters*
      (B&D) F
      "I'll Be Getting Along"
      "There's Room in My Heart"
1931 *Splinters in the Navy*
      (Twickenham) F

REGINALD STONE (organ)
1940 *Pathe Pictorial 217*
      "Bells Across the Meadow"
1940 *Pathetone 550*
      "Rosita"

FRED STOREY (comedian)
1896 *The Soldier's Courtship*
      (Paul)
1899 *Specialty Dance by Fred Storey*
      (Warwick)
1914 *Rip Van Winkle*
      (Climax)

STRAD AND HIS NEWSBOYS (specialty)
1937 *Saturday Night Revue*
      (Pathe) F

LESLIE STRANGE (impersonator)
1940 *Pathe Pictorial 238*
(as Adolf Hitler, Jack Hulbert, Stan Laurel)

RENEE STRANGE (puppeteer)
1940 *Pathe Pictorial 247*
1952 *New Pictorial 375*
1952 *Pulling Strings*
(New Realm)

VAN STRATEN AND HIS PICCADILLY DANCE BAND
1940 *Pathetone 528*
"I'll Send You My Love Letter"
1943 *Up With the Lark*
(New Realm) F

VAN STRATTEN (whip)
1938 *Pathe Pictorial NS 142*

EUGENE STRATTON (singer)
1899 *A Game of Cards*
(Vitascope)

THE STRAWBS (group)
1972 *Grave New World*
(Schulman) F
"Benedictus"
"Hey Little Man"
"Is It Today, Lord?"
"New World"
"The Flower and the Young Man"
"Ah Me Ah My"
"On Growing Older"
"Tomorrow"
"Journey's End"

BARBRA STREISAND (American singer)
1983 *Yentl*
(MGM/UA) F

CAPTAIN STRELSKY AND HIS BAND
1937 *Pathetone 371*

STRELSKY'S COSSACKS (Russian band)
1930 *Comets*
(Alpha) F
1934 *Forbidden Territory*
(Gaumont) F

PHIL STRICKLAND (entertainer)
1934 *Love Mirth Melody*
(Mancunian) F

STROBLE (mouth organ)
1932 *Pathetone 113*

JOE STRUMMER (musician)
see also **THE CLASH**
1986 *Straight to Hell*
(Island) F
"Yakety Yak"
"Ambush at Mystery Rock"

BINKIE STUART (juvenile)
1936 *Keep Your Seats Please*
(ATP) F
"You've Got Me Standing on Tip of My Toes"
1937 *Splinters in the Air*
(Wilcox) F
1937 *Moonlight Sonata*
(UA) F
1937 *Our Fighting Navy*
(Wilcox) F
1937 *Rose of Tralee*
(Butcher) F
"Daddy Wouldn't Buy Me a Bow-Wow"
1937 *Little Miss Somebody*
(Butcher) F
"Then I Wiggle Down in Bed"
1938 *Little Dolly Daydream*
(Butcher) F
"Teddy Bear's Picnic"
1938 *My Irish Molly*
(ABPC) F
"Farmyard Frolics"

UNA STUBBS (dancer)
1963 *Summer Holiday*
(ABPC) F
1963 *The King's Breakfast*
(FM)
1964 *Wonderful Life*
(Elstree) F
1965 *Three Hats for Lisa*
(Anglo) F
1967 *Mister Ten Per Cent*
(ABP) F
1968 *Till Death Us Do Part*
(British Lion) F
1969 *Bachelor of Arts*
(Paramount)
1973 *Penny Gold*
(Fanfare) F
1973 *Pianorama*
(MGM)
1974 *Bedtime with Rosie*
(LIP) F

DARYL STUERMER (guitarist)
1982 *The Secret Policeman's Other Ball*
(UIP) F
"In the Air Tonight"

EDWIN STYLES (comedian)
1931 *Ideal Cinemagazine 279*
"Almost a Musician"
1932 *Ideal Cinemagazine 314*
1934 *Road House*
(Gaumont) F
1934 *On the Air*
(British Lion) F
1936 *B.B.C. Musicals 1*
(Inspiration)
1937 *The £5 Man*
(Fox) F

1937 *Patricia Gets Her Man*
(Warner) F
1947 *Making the Grade*
(Inspiration)
(reissue: *B.B.C. Musicals 1*)
1951 *The Lady With a Lamp*
(Wilcox) F
1952 *Derby Day*
(Wilcox) F
1952 *Penny Princess*
(GFD) F
1954 *The Weak and the Wicked*
(ABPC) F
1956 *Up in the World*
(Rank) F

SU-YEE TROUPE (Chinese acrobats)
1935 *Lieutenant Daring RN*
(Butcher) F

PENNY SUGG (singer)
1971 *Nicholas and Alexandra*
(Columbia) F

"SUGGS" (GRAHAM McPHERSON) (singer)
see also **MADNESS**
1989 *The Tall Guy*
(Virgin) F

DOROTHY SUMMERS (comedienne)
1943 *It's That Man Again*
(Gainsborough) F
1943 *Mrs Mopp Finds Out*
ADVERT
1943 *Mrs Mopp Entertains*
ADVERT
1943 *Mrs Mopp at Work*
ADVERT
1943 *Mrs Mopp's Birthday*
ADVERT
1943 *Mrs Mopp Asks Why*
ADVERT
1952 *No Haunt for a Gentleman*
(Apex) F

FREDDY SUMMERS (comedian)
1936 *Pal o' Mine*
(RKO) F

JILL SUMMERS (singer)
1945 *What Do We Do Now?*
(Grand National) F

CONCHITA SUPERVA (Spanish singer)
1934 *Evensong*
(Gaumont) F

SURF PUNKS (group)
1981 *Urgh! A Music War*
(White) F
"My Beach"

SCREAMING LORD SUTCH (singer)
1973 *The London Rock and Roll Show*
(Pleasant) F

HANNEN SWAFFER (journalist)
1934 *Death at Broadcasting House*
(Phoenix) F
1935 *Late Extra*
(Fox) F
1941 *Spellbound*
(UA) F
1946 *Passing Clouds*
(reissue: *Spellbound*)

HAL SWAIN (saxophone)
1928 *Eve's Film Review 356*
"Words and Music"

HAL SWAIN AND HIS KIT KAT BAND
1930 *Al Fresco*
(Gainsborough)
"Sweet Music"
"Sarah Jane"
"Come On Baby"
"I'm Just in the Mood Tonight"
1930 *Black and White*
(Gainsborough)
"Doing the Low Down"
1930 *Classic v Jazz*
(Gainsborough)
"Mickey Mouse"
"Tchaikowsky Medley"

HAL SWAIN AND HIS SAX-O-FIVE
1930 *Hal Swain and his Sax-O-Five*
(Gainsborough)

HAL SWAIN AND HIS SAXOPHONE BAND
1936 *Pathe Pictorial NS 34*
"When the Poppies Bloom Again"
"The Fleet's in Port Again"
1937 *Pathe Pictorial NS 64*

HAL SWAIN AND HIS SWING SISTERS
1939 *Pathe Pictorial 193*
"Smile When You Say Goodbye"

JOFFRE SWALES QUARTET
1981 *The Mouse and the Woman*
(Facelift) F

SWAN AND LEIGH (jugglers)
1952 *For Your Entertainment 3*
(Gaumont)

SWEATY BETTY (group)
1970 *Groupie Girl*
(Eagle) F

NORA SWINBURNE (singer)
(films as actress not listed)
1938 *Lily of Laguna*
(Butcher) F
"Mighty Lak' a Rose"

"Charmaine"
"If You Could Care For Me"

SWINGING BLUE JEANS (group)
1964 *UK Swings Again*
(Baim)
1964 *Sound of a City*
(Rank)

LES SWINGLES (singers)
1966 *Pathe Pictorial 623*

ERIC SYKES (comedian)
1954 *Orders Are Orders*
(British Lion) F
1956 *Charley Moon*
(British Lion) F
1960 *Watch Your Stern*
(Anglo) F
1961 *Very Important Person*
(Rank) F
1961 *Invasion Quartet*
(MGM) F
1962 *Village of Daughters*
(MGM) F
1962 *Kill or Cure*
(MGM) F
1963 *Heavens Above*
(British Lion) F
1964 *The Bargee*
(Warner) F
1964 *One Way Pendulum*
(UA) F
1965 *Those Magnificent Men in Their Flying Machines*
(TCF) F
1965 *Rotten to the Core*
(British Lion) F

1965 *The Liquidator*
(MGM) F
1966 *The Spy With a Cold Nose*
(Paramount) F
1967 *The Plank*
(Rank) F
1968 *Shalako*
(Warner) F
1969 *Monte Carlo or Bust*
(Paramount) F
1970 *Rhubarb*
(Warner) F
1972 *The Alf Garnett Saga*
(Columbia) F
1973 *You Had Better Go In Disguise*
(Lynach) F
1975 *Theatre of Blood*
(UA) F
1983 *The Boys in Blue*
(Rank) F
1984 *Gabrielle and the Doddleman*
(CFF) F
1986 *Absolute Beginners*
(Palace) F
1993 *Splitting Heirs*
(Prominent) F

FRED SYLVESTER AND HIS MIDGETS
(specialty)
1927 *Eve's Film Review*
1933 *Pathetone 193*

FRED SYLVESTER AND NEPHEW
(specialty)
1942 *Pathe Pictorial 340*
1943 *The Dummy Talks*
(British National) F

AL TABOR AND HIS BAND
1937   *Pathe Pictorial NS 44*
        "Organ Grinder's Swing"

HARRY TAFT (comedian)
1930   *Pathetone 30*
        "Hold It"

TAMARA (trapezist)
1932   *Eve's Film Review 598*

TAMAROFF AND TAMARA (dancers)
1939   *Pathe Pictorial NS 159*

VALERIE TANDY
see **MARGARET HARRIS AND VALERIE TANDY**

TANIA (pianist)
1941   *Pathe Pictorial 309*

TANITA AND MARIO (acrobatic dancers)
1932   *Pathe Pictorial 756*

"LOS TARANTOS" FLAMENCO COMPANY
1967   *The Bobo*
        (Warner) F

JIMMY TARBUCK (comedian)
1967   *The Plank*
        (Rank) F
1969   *Twinky*
        (Rank) F

SUZETTE TARRI (comedienne)
1937   *Pathe Pictorial NS 90*
1938   *Pathe Pictorial NS 103*
1938   *Pathetone 430*
1938   *Pathe Pictorial NS 139*
1943   *Pictorial Revue of 1943*
        F (reissue: *Pictorial 139*)
1943   *Somewhere in Civvies*
        (Mancunian) F
        "Somebody's Kisses"

TARZAN AND PONGO (circus)
1948   *International Circus Revue*
        (Butcher) F

BILLY TASKER (comedian)
1930   *His First Car*
        (PDC) F

HARRY TATE (comedian)
1899   *Harry Tate Grimaces*
        (Warwick)
1899   *Harry Tate Impersonations*
        (Warwick)
1927   *Motoring*
        (ICC) F
1932   *Her First Affaire*
        (Sterling) F
1933   *Counsel's Opinion*
        (London) F

1933   *My Lucky Star*
        (W&F) F
1933   *I Spy*
        (BIP) F
1934   *Happy*
        (BIP) F
1934   *Pathe Pictorial 842*
        "How Are You?"
1934   *Pathetone 221*
        "Billiards"
1934   *Pathetone 226*
        "Mixed Ginx"
1935   *Royal Cavalcade*
        (BIP) F
1935   *Look Up and Laugh*
        (ATP) F
1935   *Midshipman Easy*
        (Ealing) F
1935   *Hyde Park Corner*
        (Grosvenor) F
1936   *Soft Lights and Sweet Music*
        (British Lion) F
        "Motoring"
1936   *Keep Your Seats Please*
        (ATP) F
1936   *Variety Parade*
        (Butcher) F
1937   *Take a Chance*
        (Grosvenor) F
1937   *Wings of the Morning*
        (Fox) F
1937   *Sam Small Leaves Town*
        (BSS) F
1937   *Storm in a Teacup*
        (London) F

HARRY TATE JR (comedian)
1934   *Pathe Pictorial 842*
1934   *Pathetone 221*
1934   *Pathetone 226*
1936   *Variety Parade*
        (Butcher) F
1943   *A Bicycle Made For Two*
        (Rover) ADVERT
1979   *It Happened in Leicester Square*
        (Benstead) F

RICHARD TAUBER (tenor)
1933   *Pathetone 184*
        "Serenade"
1934   *Pathetone 219*
        "Salutation of the Morning"
1934   *Blossom Time*
        (BIP) F
        "Love Comes at Blossom Time"
        "First Love"
        "Red Rose"
        "Impatience"
        "Dearest Maiden"
        "Once There Lived a Lady Fair"
        "The Question"
        "Love Lost For Ever More"
1935   *Heart's Desire*
        (BIP) F

"Heart's Desire"
"My World Is Gold"
"Let Me Awaken Your Heart"
"Vienna City of My Dreams"
"A Message Sweet as Roses"
"Farewell"
"Devotion"
"All Hope Is Ended"
1936 *Land Without Music*
(Capitol) F
"You Must Have Music"
"Heaven in a Song"
"Simple Little Melody"
"March of Musicians"
"Smile for Me"
"Sleepy"
"Fernando"
1937 *Pagliacci*
(Capitol) F
"Prologue"
"Such a Game"
"On With the Motley"
"Serenade"
"Sleep Song"
1945 *Waltz Time*
(British National) F
"Break of Day"
1946 *Lisbon Story*
(British National) F
"Pedro the Fisherman"
"French Folk Song"

MARTIN TAUBMANN (electrodist)
1938 *Pathetone 455*
"Music From the Air"

CECIL TAYLOR (dancer)
1913 *The Tango Dance*
(Sphinx)

MARJORIE TAYLOR (singer)
1937 *The Ticket of Leave Man*
(King) F
"On Wings of Song"
"Cherry Ripe"
"Standchen"

MAURICE TAYLOR (singer)
1943 *Playtime for Workers*
(Federated) F
"Carry Me Back to the Lone Prairie"
"Home On the Range"
"United We Stand"

NEVILLE TAYLOR (singer)
1960 *Climb Up the Wall*
(New Realm) F

PAT TAYLOR (singer)
1936 *The Artful Dodger*
(Ace Cinemagazine)
"Spring Don't Mean a Thing"

PHIL TAYLOR (skater)
1933 *Pathetone 190*

**PHYLLIS TAYLOR AND CHARLES
GRIMSHAW** (dancers)
1938 *Pathe Pictorial 115*

SHAW TAYLOR (television personality)
1977 *Adventures of a Private Eye*
(Salon) F
1978 *The Medusa Touch*
(ITC) F

LUDMILLA TCHERINA (Russian ballerina)
1948 *The Red Shoes*
(Archers) F
1951 *Tales of Hoffmann*
(London) F
1955 *Oh Rosalinda*
(ABPC) F
1959 *Honeymoon*
(British Lion) F

TELEVISION TOPPERS (dancers)
1952 *Down Among the Z Men*
(New Realm) F
1954 *Harmony Lane*
(Eros)
1957 *After the Ball*
(Romulus) F
1959 *Make Mine a Million*
(British Lion) F

TEMPERANCE SEVEN (band)
1962 *It's Trad Dad*
(Columbia) F
"Dream Away Romance"
"Everybody Loves My Baby"
1963 *Take Me Over*
(Columbia) F
1966 *The Wrong Box*
(Columbia) F

WILFRED TEMPLE (baritone)
1929 *Splinters*
(B&D) F
"At Gretna Green"
1930 *The Yellow Mask*
(BIP) F
"A Million Dreams"
"I Left My Heart With You"
1931 *Splinters in the Navy*
(Twickenham) F
"We Didn't Know What to Say"

ALEC TEMPLETON (pianist)
1935 *The Deputy Drummer*
(Columbia) F
"Rhapsody in Pink"
1935 *She Shall Have Music*
(Twickenham) F
"Merry Month of May"

MAX TEMPLETON (shadowgrapher)
1936 *Pathe Pictorial NS 31*

TEN DURHAM PITMEN (singers)
1933 *Pathe Pictorial 821*
      "Toy Grenadiers"

TEN TROMBONEERS (musicians)
1933 *Musical Film Revue*
      (British Lion) S

JOSIE TERENA (strong woman)
1941 *Pathe Pictorial 257*

JOSEPH TERMINI (violinist)
1926 *Joe Termini the Somnolent Melodist*
      (Phonofilm)
1939 *Pathetone 487*
      "Some of These Days"
      "St Louis Blues"

BILLY TERNENT AND HIS ORCHESTRA
1953 *Out of the Bandbox*
      (New Realm)

TERRI AND PATLANZKI (dancers)
1937 *A Corking Story*
      (Ace Cinemagazine)
      "Mexican Dance"

ELLALINE TERRISS (singer)
1907 *My Indian Anna*
      (Chronophone)
1907 *Glow Little Glow Worm*
      (Chronophone)
1913 *Seymour Hicks and Ellaline Terriss*
      (Zenith)
      "Bumble Bee Sting"
      "If I Were a Boy"
      "Alexander's Ragtime Band"
1914 *Always Tell Your Wife*
      (Zenith)
1917 *Masks and Faces*
      (Ideal) F
1922 *Eve's Film Review 74*
      "Listeners In"
1927 *Blighty*
      (Gainsborough) F
1927 *Land of Hope and Glory*
      (Napoleon) F

TERRY-THOMAS (comedian)
1939 *Sam Goes Shopping*
      (Publicity)
1948 *Lucky Mascot*
      (UA) F
      "It's the Greatest Business in the
      World"
      "Somebody Blew My Bluebird's
      Egg"
1948 *A Date With a Dream*
      (Grand National) F
1949 *Melody Club*
      (Eros) F
1951 *What's Cooking?*
      (Regent) ADVERT

1951 *That's Odd*
      (Carisbrooke)
1952 *The Queen Steps Out*
      (Carisbrooke)
1956 *Private's Progress*
      (Charter) F
1956 *The Green Man*
      (Grenadier) F
1956 *Brothers in Law*
      (Tudor) F
1957 *Lucky Jim*
      (Charter) F
1957 *Blue Murder at St Trinian's*
      (British Lion) F
1957 *The Naked Truth*
      (Rank) F
1957 *Happy Is the Bride*
      (Soskin) F
1958 *Tom Thumb*
      (MGM) F
1959 *Carlton Browne of the F.O.*
      (British Lion) F
1959 *Too Many Crooks*
      (Rank) F
1959 *"I'm All Right Jack"*
      (British Lion) F
1959 *School for Scoundrels*
      (ABPC) F
1960 *Make Mine Mink*
      (Rank) F
1960 *His and Hers*
      (Sabre) F
1961 *A Matter of W.H.O.*
      (Foray) F
1962 *Operation Snatch*
      (Keep) F
1962 *Kill or Cure*
      (MGM) F
1963 *The Mouse on the Moon*
      (UA) F
1963 *Wild Affair*
      (7 Arts) F
1963 *Terry-Thomas in Tuscany*
      (Thomkin)
1965 *Those Magnificent Men in Their
      Flying Machines*
      (TCF) F
1965 *You Must Be Joking*
      (Columbia) F
1966 *Anglers Choice*
      (Town) ADVERT
1966 *Our Man in Marrakesh*
      (Towers) F
1966 *The Sandwich Man*
      (Rank) F
1967 *Jules Verne's Rocket to the Moon*
      (Anglo) F
1967 *Don't Raise the Bridge, Lower the
      River*
      (Shenson) F
1969 *Arthur? Arthur!*
      (Gallu) F
1971 *The Abominable Dr Phibes*
      (AIP) F

1972   *Dr Phibes Rises Again*
        (AIP) F
1972   *Tho Cherry Picker*
        (Rank) F
1973   *Vault of Horror*
        (Amicus) F
1975   *Spanish Fly*
        (Winkle) F
1975   *The Bawdy Adventures of Tom
        Jones*
        (Chobridge) F
1975   *Side By Side*
        (GTO) F
1977   *Hound of the Baskervilles*
        (Hemdale) F

TERRY TWINS (comedians)
1920   *The Fordington Twins*
        (Gaumont) F

TERRY'S JUVENILES (song and dance)
1935   *She Shall Have Music*
        (Twickenham) F
1938   *Chips*
        (BFA) F
1938   *Around the Town*
        (British Lion) F

LUISA TETRAZIN (Italian soprano)
1921   *Around the Town*
        (Gaumont)

TEXAS TED AND HIS RANCH BOYS (trio)
1937   *Taking the Cake*
        (Ace Cinemagazine)
        "I'm a High-Faluting Puncher"

THAT CERTAIN TRIO (singers) (Patrick
Waddington, William Walker, Peggy
Cochrane)
1931   *Pathetone 57*
        "Cheerful Little Earful"

**CHARLES THEBAULT AND DOREEN
BEAHAN** (dancers)
1942   *Pathe Pictorial 305*
        "Waltz"
1942   *Pathe Pictorial 310*
        "Quickstep"
1946   *Dancing Thru*
        (Angel) F

THELMINA (novelty)
1920s   *Eve's Film Review*
        "The Electric Woman"

TERENCE THEOBALD (dancer)
1955   *King's Rhapsody*
        (Wilcox) F

JOE THIERS (saxophone)
1928   *Joe Thiers' Saxotette*
        (Phonofilm)
1932   *Musical Medley 1*
        (reissue: *Joe Thiers' Saxotette*)

BONITA THOMAS (striptease)
1971   *Villain*
        (EMI) F

DILLWYN THOMAS (boy soprano)
1937   *The Gang Show*
        (Wilcox) F
        "Mother Machree"
        "Danny Boy"
1937   *Pathe Pictorial NS 57*
        "Vienna City of My Dreams"

HUW THOMAS (television personality)
1964   *The First Men in the Moon*
        (Columbia) F
1966   *The Ghost Goes Gear*
        (Pathe) F

SONNY THOMAS (dancer)
1946   *Walking On Air*
        (Piccadilly) F

TERRY THOMAS
see **TERRY-THOMAS**

WYNFORD VAUGHAN THOMAS
(broadcaster)
1955   *John and Julie*
        (Group 3) F

EDNA THOMPSON (blues singer)
1936   *Digging for Gold*
        (Ace) F
1936   *Full Steam*
        (Ace) F
1936   *Bottle Party*
        (Ace) F
1937   *Snuff Said*
        (Ace Cinemagazine)
        "A Dogseye View of Love"

THOMPSON TWINS (singers)
1982   *Listen to London*
        (White) F

BILLY THORBURN AND HIS BAND
1933   *Pathe Pictorial 786*
        "There's a Light in Your Window"
1936   *Pathe Pictorial NS 31*
        "Okay For Sound"
1937   *Pathe Pictorial NS 55*
        "There's a New World"
1937   *Talking Feet*
        (Baxter) F
1938   *Stepping Toes*
        (Baxter) F

GEORGE THORNE (singer)
1907   *Tit Willow*
        (Cinematophone)

PHIL THORNTON (singer)
1996   *Glastonbury: The Movie*
        (Starlight) F
        "Rainbow Chant"

THREE ACCORDION KINGS
1936 *British Lion Varieties 1*
       "Selection from Faust"
1936 *British Lion Varieties 3*
       "East of the Sun"
       "Never Say Never Again Again"
       "Some of These Days"
1936 *British Lion Varieties 7*
       "Overture to Trieste"

THREE ADMIRALS (comedy singers)
1933 *Aunt Sally*
       (Gainsborough) F
       "My Wild Oat"
       "We All Go Riding on a Rainbow"
       "You Ought to See Sally on
       Sunday"
1936 *Pathetone 337*
       "All Over Italy"
1937 *Pathetone 393*
       "Love Marches On"
1938 *Pathetone 435*
       "Don't Send My Daddy to Dartmoor"
1938 *Pathe Pictorial NS 141*
       "The Riding Academy"
1938 *Around the Town*
       (British Lion) F

THREE AUSTINS (circus)
1948 *International Circus Revue*
       (Butcher) F

THREE AUSTRALIAN BOYS (singers)
1933 *Ideal Cinemagazine 355*
1936 *Pathe Pictorial NS 14*
       "Away in Killarney"
1936 *British Lion Varieties 2*
       "Turn On the Music"
1936 *British Lion Varieties 7*
       "For You Madonna"
1936 *British Lion Varieties 9*
       "Heads or Tails"
1936 *Cabaret Nights 2*
       (Highbury)
1936 *Cabaret Nights 6*
       (Highbury)

THREE BELLS (group)
1966 *The Ghost Goes Gear*
       (Pathe) F

THREE BLUE NOTES (musicians)
1937 *Pathe Pictorial NS 56*
       "Japanese Sandman"

THREE BONDS (acrobats)
1932 *Ideal Cinemagazine 328*
1932 *Pathe Pictorial 764*

THREE BULVONOS (acrobats)
1938 *Pathe Pictorial NS 119*

THE THREE CANADIAN BACHELORS
see **CANADIAN BACHELORS**

THREE CUTIES (dancers)
1936 *Pathetone 309*
       "The Girl With the Dreamy Eyes"

THREE DIAMOND BROTHERS (comedy)
1934 *Give Her a Ring*
       (BIP) F
1937 *Knights for a Day*
       (Pathe) F

THREE DOTS (dancers)
1938 *Stepping Toes*
       (Baxter) F

THREE EDDIES (dancers)
1930 *Elstree Calling*
       (BIP) F
       "Dance Around in Your Bones"
1931 *Pathetone 59*
       "Jerusalem Morning"

THREE EMERALDS (dancers)
1935 *Pathe Pictorial 905*
       "Sweet Sue"

THREE EQUALS (dancers)
1926 *Eve's Film Review 256*

THREE GINX (singers)
1935 *Hello Sweetheart*
       (Warner) F
1936 *It's Love Again*
       (Gaumont) F
1939 *Discoveries*
       (Vogue) F
1939 *Pathe Pictorial 195*
       "Tan Tan Tivvy"
1940 *Sailors Three*
       (Ealing) F
       "All Over the Place"

THREE GIRLIES (acrobats)
1936 *Pathe Pictorial NS 13*

THREE HERON SISTERS (singers)
1937 *Keeping the Piece*
       (Ace Cinemagazine)

THREE IN HARMONY (singers)
1938 *Pathe Pictorial NS 131*
       "I Can't Give You Anything But
       Love"

THREE JOKERS (comedy acrobats)
1939 *Music Hall Parade*
       (Butcher) F
1952 *For Your Entertainment 1*
       (Gaumont)

THREE KNAVES (acrobats)
1937 *Pathe Pictorial NS 71*
1937 *Punch's Punches*
       (Ace Cinemagazine)

THREE LITTLE WORDS (dancers)
1937 *Okay For Sound*
(Gainsborough) F

THREE LOOSE SCREWS (comedy acrobats)
1935 *Pathetone 292*
"Dinah"
"I Want to Ring Bells"
1936 *Pathetone 316*
"I'll Never Say Never Again"

THREE MACS (comedy)
1898 *The Three Macs*
(Riley)

THREE MATAS (balancers)
1939 *Pathe Pictorial NS 192*

THREE MAXWELLS (singers)
1940 *Laugh It Off*
(British National) F
"Anybody Can Dance"

THREE MISSOURIS (comedy acrobats)
1900 *The Flying Scots*
(Warwick)
1902 *The Three Missouris*
(Warwick)

THREE MONARCHS (harmonicas)
1952 *For Your Entertainment 1; 2*
(Gaumont)

THREE NAGELS (acrobats)
1936 *Variety Parade*
(Butcher) F

THREE NEW YORKERS (jugglers)
1936 *Pathetone 317*
1939 *Pathetone Parade of 1940*
F (reissue: *Pathetone 317*)

THREE RADIO ROGUES (impressionists)
1935 *In Town Tonight*
(British Lion) F
1936 *British Lion Varieties 1*
"The Man on the Flying Trapeze"
1936 *British Lion Varieties 2*
"They Cut Down the Old Pine Tree"
1936 *British Lion Varieties 8*
"Sweethearts Forever"

THREE RASCALS (singers)
1927 *Three Rascals and a Piano*
(Phototone)

THREE RHYTHM BROTHERS (singers)
1936 *Soft Lights and Sweet Music*
(British Lion) F
"Ridin' Up the River Road"
"We Can't Find the Tiger Any More"
1940 *Under Your Hat*
(Grand National) F
"We Can't Find the Tiger Any More"

THREE SAILORS (comedy)
1932 *Pathe Pictorial 740*
1934 *Radio Parade of 1935*
(BIP) F

THREE SISTERS (singers)
1937 *Pathe Pictorial NS 78*
"California Here I Come"

THREE STARS (dancers)
1936 *Pathetone 324*
"Star Spangled Banner"

THREE TORINIS (acrobats)
1953 *New Pictorial 465*

THREE VIRGINIANS (singers)
1930 *Pathetone 15*
"Mighty Lak' a Rose"
1940 *Pathetone 521*
"Beer Barrel Polka"

THUNDERCLAP NEWMAN (group)
1971 *Not Tonight Darling*
(Border) F
"Hollywood Dream"
"Hollywood One"

TIFFANY SISTERS (striptease)
1971 *Not Tonight Darling*
(Border) F

TILLER GIRLS (dancers)
1898 *The Mascots*
(Chard)
1898 *Girls Playing Leapfrog*
(Chard)
1899 *Tiller's Six Diamonds*
(Warwick)
1901 *Tiller Group of Dancers*
(Warwick)
1901 *Girls Indulging in a Pillow Fight*
(Warwick)
1927 *On With the Dance*
(Parkinson)
1927 *British Screen Magazine*
1927 *Eve's Film Review*
1927 *The Arcadians*
(Gaumont) F
1927 *On With the Dance*
(Parkinson)
1928 *A Little Bit of Fluff*
(BIP) F
1930 *Comets*
(Alpha) F
1930 *Raise the Roof*
(BIP) F
1933 *Pathe Pictorial 818*
1934 *Screen Vaudeville*
(Vaudeville)
1935 *In Town Tonight*
(British Lion) F

JOHN TILLEY (comedian)
1934 *The Motor Magnate*
      (Electa)
1934 *Pathetone 230*

VESTA TILLEY (singer)
1900 *The Midnight Son*
      (Phono-Bio-Tableaux)
1900 *Algy the Piccadilly Johnny*
      (Phono-Bio-Tableaux)
1900 *Louisiana Lou*
      (Phono-Bio-Tableaux)
1907 *Please Mister Conductor*
      (Chronophone)
1914 *Vesta Tilley At Home*
      (Kearton)
1916 *The Girl Who Loves a Soldier*
      (Samuelson) F

JOHNNY TILLOTSON (singer)
1963 *Just For Fun*
      (Columbia) F
      "Judy Judy"

FRED TILSON (singer)
1937 *The Penny Pool*
      (Mancunian) F
      "Keep Fit"

ANDREW TIMOTHY (broadcaster)
1952 *Down Among the Z Men*
      (New Realm) F

TIN PAN ALLEY TRIO (singers)
1938 *Pathe Pictorial NS 100*
      "Horsey Horsey"
1938 *Around the Town*
      (British Lion) F

TINA OF HAWAII (singer)
1938 *Beginnings and Ends*
      (Ace Cinemagazine)

TITANIC CINQ (group)
1995 *The Run of the Country*
      (Rank) F
      "Oh Boy!"
      "Stay"
      "I Need a Pickaxe To Break Your
      Heart of Stone"

TOM TITT (cartoonist)
1931 *Ideal Cinemagazine 274*

FRANK TITTERTON (tenor)
1932 *Pathetone 103*
      "Yeoman's Wedding Song"
1932 *Pathetone 135*
      "You Brought My Heart the
      Sunshine"
1932 *Pathetone 143*
      "Dark-Haired Marie"
1932 *Pathe Pictorial 741*
      "Friend of Mine"

1933 *Pathetone 158*
      "Because"
1933 *Pathe Pictorial 801*
      "Once in a Blue Moon"
1933 *Waltz Time*
      (Gaumont) F
1934 *Song at Eventide*
      (Butcher) F
      "Evensong"
      "For You Alone"
      "Sanctuary of the Heart"
1935 *Barnacle Bill*
      (Butcher) F
1935 *Wedding Eve*
      (Astor) F
1936 *Twenty-One Today*
      (Albany) F

TOADSTOOL (group)
1996 *Glastonbury: The Movie*
      (Starlight) F
      "Bottleneck"
      "Piazza"

SANDI TOKSVIG (comedienne)
1988 *Paris by Night*
      (British Screen) F

QUENTIN AND KENNETH TOD (dancers)
1931 *Ideal Cinemagazine 291*
      "Can Can"

DIANE TODD (singer)
1958 *6.5 Special*
      (Anglo) F
      "Come to My Arms"
      "It's a Wonderful Thing"
      "You Are My Favourite Dream"

TOGO (Chinese juggler)
1936 *Song in Soho*
      (Ace) F
1937 *Pathe Pictorial NS 42*

TOLEDO, ELLY AND JEAN (acrobats)
1937 *Pathe Pictorial NS 51*
      "March of the Little Soldiers"

TORALF TOLLEFSON (accordion)
1939 *Pathetone 476*
      "Invitation to the Waltz"
1940 *Pathetone 517*
      "Is That the Way to Treat a
      Sweetheart?"

ALFREDO TOMASINI (Canadian baritone)
1936 *Pathe Pictorial NS 37*
      "Crown of the Year"
1938 *Pathe Pictorial NS 118*
      "The Old Black Mare"

JEAN BAPTISTE TONER (musician)
1939 *Pathe Pictorial NS 148*
      "The Blue Danube"

1940 *Pathe Pictorial 218*
"Nocturne"

SYDNEY TORCH (organ)
1933 *Pathe Pictorial 814*
1955 *On With the Dance*
(Carisbrooke)

THE TORNADOES (skaters)
1940 *Pathe Pictorial 200*

THE TORNADOS (group)
1963 *Just For Fun*
(Columbia) F
"All the Stars in the Sky"
1963 *Farewell Performance*
(Rank) F
"The Ice Cream Man"
1964 *UK Swings Again*
(Baim)
"Blue Beat"

HELLA TOROS (soprano)
1940 *Pathetone 560*
"I Thank You For Love"

TAMARA TOUMANOVA (ballerina)
1956 *Invitation to the Dance*
(MGM) F
1970 *The Private Life of Sherlock Holmes*
(UA) F

TOVARICH TRIO (equilibrists)
1944 *Pathe Pictorial 415*

F. H. TOWNSEND (cartoonist)
1920 *Around the Town 8*
(Gaumont)

PETE TOWNSHEND (singer)
see also **THE WHO**
1975 *Tommy*
(Stigwood) F
"Captain Walker It's a Boy"
"Amazing Journey"
1980 *The Secret Policeman's Ball*
(Tigon) F
"Pinball Wizard"
"Won't Get Fooled Again"

SIMON TOWNSHEND (singer)
1975 *Tommy*
(Stigwood) F
"Extra Extra"
"Miracle Cure"

TOY AND WING (Chinese dancers)
1948 *No Orchids for Miss Blandish*
(Renown) F

WENDY TOYE (dancer)
1927 *Eve's Film Review 333*
1935 *Invitation to the Waltz*
(BIP) F

1956 *On the Twelfth Day*
(British Lion)

JOHNNY TRABER'S TROUPE
(funambulists)
1979 *Moonraker*
(UA) F

SID TRACEY AND BESSIE HAY (dancers)
1927 *On With the Dance*
(Parkinson)
1927 *The Arcadians*
(Gaumont) F
1932 *Eve's Film Review 565*
1940 *Pathetone 556*
"The World Is Waiting for the
Sunrise"

ARTHUR TRACY (tenor)
1936 *Limelight*
(Wilcox) F
"Marta"
"Stranded"
"Stay Awhile"
"The Whistling Waltz"
"The Sandman's Serenade"
"Farewell Sweet Señorita"
"Nirewana"
"We Were Meant to Meet Again"
"La Donna e Mobile"
1937 *The Street Singer*
(ABPC) F
"Halfway to Heaven"
"Street Serenade"
"Haroun El Raschid"
1937 *Command Performance*
(Grosvenor) F
"My Gypsy Dream Girl"
"Dance Gypsy Dance"
"Trees"
"Toreador Song"
"Whistling Gypsy"
"Danny Boy"
"Marta"
"The Old Oaken Bucket"
"Daisy Bell"
"Genevieve"
"Jolly Great Lumps of Duff"
1938 *Follow Your Star*
(Belgrave) F
"Laugh Clown Laugh"
"Misty Islands of the Highlands"
"Goldilocks"
"Waltz for Those in Love"
"It's My Mother's Birthday Today"
"De Lawd Loves His People To
Sing"

TRAFFIC (group)
1967 *Here We Go Round the Mulberry
Bush*
(UA) F
"Here We Go Round the Mulberry
Bush"

"Utterly Simple"
"Am I What I Was?"
1973 *Glastonbury Fayre*
(Goodtimes) F
"Gimme Some Loving"

JACK TRAIN (impressionist)
1942 *King Arthur Was a Gentleman*
(Gainsborough) F
1943 *It's That Man Again*
(Gainsborough) F
1943 *Miss London Limited*
(Gainsborough) F
1946 *Gaiety George*
(Embassy) F
1946 *As Others See Us*
(Merlin)
1947 *What's Yours*
(Grand National)
1948 *Colonel Bogey*
(GFD) F
1950 *Twenty Questions Murder Mystery*
(Grand National) F
1952 *Murder On the Air*
F (reissue: *Twenty Questions Murder Mystery*)
1964 *Catacombs*
(Parroch) F

ARTHUR TRAVERS (singer)
1933 *Musical Film Revue*
(British Lion) S
1935 *Equity Musical Revue 7*
(British Lion)

DAVE LEE TRAVIS (disc jockey)
1973 *Radio Wonderful*
(Goodtimes) F

TREASURE CHEST (go-go girls)
1968 *Popdown*
(New Realm) F

TREBLE TAPPERS (comedy dancers)
see also **THE WIERE BROTHERS**
1933 *Pathe Pictorial 811*
"Hot Lips"

BRUCE TRENT (singer)
1940 *Band Waggon*
(Gainsborough) F

IVY TRESMAND (dancer)
1920 *Around the Town 10*
(Gaumont)
"The Red Mill"
1920 *Around the Town 28*
(Gaumont)
"Breton Dance"
1922 *Eve's Film Review 42*
"Lady of the Rose"

TED TREVOR AND DINAH HARRIS
(dancers)
1920 *Around the Town*
(Gaumont)
1922 *Eve's Film Review 58*
"Waltz"
1922 *Eve's Film Review 61*
"One Step"
1923 *Eve's Film Review 124*
"Exhibition Step"

TOMMY TREVOR AND PARTNER (jugglers)
1940 *Pathe Pictorial 245*

TRICKY DICKY (singer)
1963 *What a Crazy World*
(Hammer) F

TOMMY TRINDER (comedian)
1938 *Almost a Honeymoon*
(ABPC) F
1938 *Save a Little Sunshine*
(Pathe) F
1939 *She Couldn't Say No*
(ABPC) F
1940 *Laugh It Off*
(British National) F
"Sarternoon"
"Laugh It Off"
"If You Were the Only Girl in the World"
1940 *Sailors Three*
(Ealing) F
"All Over the Place"
"A Happy Go Lucky Song"
1941 *Eating Out with Tommy Trinder*
(Strand)
1941 *The Foreman Went to France*
(Ealing) F
"The Smoke Goes Up the Chimney"
1942 *The Bells Go Down*
(Ealing) F
1942 *Pathe Pictorial 347*
1944 *Champagne Charlie*
(Ealing) F
"Champagne Charlie"
"The Old Folks at Home"
"Hit Him on the Boko"
"Half of Half and Half"
"Ale Old Ale"
"Burgundy Claret and Port"
"I'm One of the Brandy and Seltzer Boys"
"Everything Will Be Lovely"
"The Man on the Flying Trapeze"
1944 *Fiddlers Three*
(Ealing) F
"Sweet Fanny Adams"
"There's No Place Like Rome"
"You Never Can Tell"
"Ay Ay Ay Ay"
1945 *New Pictorial 42*
1945 *New Pictorial 45*

1949   *Bitter Springs*
        (Ealing) F
1955   *You Lucky People*
        (Adelphi) F
1959   *Make Mine a Million*
        (British Lion) F
1964   *The Beauty Jungle*
        (Rank) F
1969   *Under the Table You Must Go*
        (Butcher) F
1974   *Barry McKenzie Holds His Own*
        (EMI) F

MICHAEL TRIPP (dancer)
1928   *Eve's Film Review 379*
        "Good News"
        "Varsity Drag"

TROCADERO GIRLS (dancers)
1937   *The Price of Folly*
        (Pathe) F

TROISE AND HIS BANJOLIERS (band)
1933   *Pathe Pictorial 811*
        "At Sundown"
1933   *Pathe Pictorial 817*
        "Banjo On My Knee"
        "Jingle Bells"

TROISE AND HIS MANDOLIERS (band)
1932   *Pathetone 140*
        "Gypsy Moon"
1933   *Pathe Pictorial 790*
        "Nothing But a Lie"
1936   *Sunshine Ahead*
        (Baxter) F
1936   *Pathetone Parade of 1936*
        F (reissue: *Pictorial 811*)
1939   *Pathetone 479*
        "Romany"

THE TROLES (group)
1965   *Gonks Go Beat*
        (Anglo) F

DORIS TROY (singer)
1973   *Radio Wonderful*
        (Goodtimes) F

W. L. TRYTEL'S DANCE BAND
1927   *W. L. Trytel's Dance Band*
        (Phonofilm)

DICK TUBB (comedian)
1934   *The Old Curiosity Shop*
        (BIP) F
1936   *Digging for Gold*
        (Ace) F
1937   *Concert Party*
        (Ace) F
1938   *Follow Your Star*
        (Belgrave) F

SOPHIE TUCKER (American singer)
1926   *Eve's Film Review*

1930   *Pathetone 27*
        "No-One But the Right Man"
1930   *Eve's Film Review 488*
        "Follow a Star"
1934   *Pathetone 222*
        "Some of These Days"
1934   *Gay Love*
        (British Lion) F
        "Louisville Lady"
        "My Extraordinary Man"
        "Hotcha Joe"

EDDIE 'TENPOLE' TUDOR (singer)
1980   *The Great Rock 'n' Roll Swindle*
        (Virgin) F
        "Who Killed Bambi?"
        "Rock Around the Clock"
1986   *Absolute Beginners*
        (Palace) F
        "Ted Ain't Dead"
1986   *Sid and Nancy*
        (Zenith) F
1986   *Straight to Hell*
        (Island) F
1988   *Drowning by Numbers*
        (Allarts) F

TOMMY TUNE (American dancer)
1972   *The Boy Friend*
        (MGM) F

CHESTER TUNIS (musical bottles)
1938   *Pathe Pictorial NS 134*
        "The Fleet's in Port Again"
        "Another Little Drink"

ALAN TURNER (singer)
1909   *Love's Old Sweet Song*
        (Cinephone)

HAROLD TURNER (dancer)
1952   *The Dancing Fleece*
        (Crown)

JOAN TURNER (comedienne)
1985   *No Surrender*
        (Palace) F
1989   *Scandal*
        (Palace) F

MARGARET TURNER (tap-dancer)
1937   *Pathe Pictorial NS 85*
        "Swing for Sale"

TINA TURNER (American singer)
1975   *Tommy*
        (Stigwood) F
        "Acid Queen"

TURNER TWINS (tap-dancers)
1933   *Pathe Pictorial 794*
        "Mardi Gras"
1934   *Pathe Pictorial 832*
        "42nd Street"

TWELVE ARISTOCRATS (tap-dancers)
1937   *Calling All Stars*
       (British Lion) F
       "I Will Be Happy"

TWELVE JACKSON GIRLS (dancers)
1952   *For Your Entertainment 2; 3*
       (Gaumont)
       "A-hunting We Will Go"
       "Jolly Good Luck"
       "The Girl I Left Behind Me"
       "The Army of Today's All Right"

TWENTY TINY TAPPERS (juveniles)
1938   *Chips*
       (BFA) F

THE TWICE AS MUCH (group)
1967   *Tonite Let's All Make Love in London*
       (Lorrimer) F

TWILIGHT BLONDES (dancers)
1935   *Off the Dole*
       (Mancunian) F

TWO CHARLADIES (comedy)
1938   *Around the Town*
       (British Lion) F

TWO CODOLBANS (cymbalum)
1950   *New Pictorial 291*
       "Tico Tico"

TWO EDDIES (balancers)
1940   *Pathetone 532*
1941   *Pathe Pictorial 297*

TWO JAYS (comedy dancers)
1936   *Dodging the Dole*
       (Mancunian) F
1936   *International Revue*
       (Medway) F

THE TWO LESLIES (singers)
see also **LESLIE HOLMES, LESLIE SARONY**
1933   *Pathetone 171*
       "Billy Played His Old Trombone"
1935   *Pathe Pictorial 890*
       "Teas, Light Refreshments and Minerals"

1936   *Sunshine Ahead*
       (Baxter) F
1936   *Here and There*
       (Baxter)
1937   *Pathe Pictorial NS 45*
       "Forty Four Thousand and Five"
1937   *Pathe Pictorial NS 61*
       "The Dart Song"
1938   *Pathetone 407*
       "I'm a Little Prairie Flower"
1939   *Pathe Pictorial NS 160*
       "There Ain't No Magic in Moonlight"
1939   *Pathetone Parade of 1940*
       F (reissue: *Pathetone 407*)
1940   *Pathe Pictorial 226*
1942   *Pathe Pictorial 337*
1942   *Pathetone Parade of 1942*
       F (reissue: *Pictorial 226*)
1943   *Pathe Pictorial 389*
       "Won't It Be Wonderful?"
       "I Lift Up My Finger"
1944   *Pathe Pictorial 434*
1947   *When You Come Home*
       (Butcher) F

TWO NEW YORKERS (singers)
1936   *Pathetone 348*

TWO RASCALS (singers)
1931   *Pathetone 52*
       "Meyer What a Liar"
       "Say It While Dancing"

TWO SPALLAS (Jim and Masie) (acrobats)
1943   *Pathe Pictorial 362*

GRANT TYLER (boy accordionist)
1941   *Danny Boy*
       (Butcher) F
       "A Bicycle Made For Two"
       "Savoy Scottish Medley"
       "Bless 'Em All"
       "Auld Lang Syne"
       "Love's Old Sweet Song"

TZIGANSKY CHOIR
1937   *Cafe Colette*
       (ABFD) F

WONDERFUL THINGS

by Harold Rome

FROM the Film

Wonderful Things

starring

Frankie VAUGHAN & **Jeremy SPENSER**

Produced by
ANNA NEAGLE

Directed by
HERBERT WILCOX

An Associated British-Anna Neagle
Production

Distributed by
Associated British-Pathe Ltd

CHAPPELL & CO. LTD.
50 NEW BOND STREET
LONDON, W.I

CHAPPELL & CO. INC. NEW YORK
BY ARRANGEMENT WITH FLORENCE MUSIC COMPANY

44-247

2/- NET

MADE IN ENGLAND

UB40 (group)
1981 *Urgh! A Music War*
(White) F
"Madame Medusa"
1988 *The Yob*
(Palace) F
"Hit It"
"Sing Our Own Song"

GALINA ULANOVA (Russian ballerina)
1946 *Dancing Thru*
(Angel) F
"Swan Lake"
1957 *The Bolshoi Ballet*
(Rank) F
"The Dying Swan"
"Giselle"

STANLEY UNWIN (comedian)
1956 *Fun at St Fanny's*
(British Lion) F
1958 *Further Up the Creek*
(Hammer) F
1960 *Inn for Trouble*
(Eros) F
1961 *Carry On Regardless*
(Anglo) F
1962 *Hair of the Dog*
(Rank) F
1966 *Press for Time*
(Rank) F
1968 *Chitty Chitty Bang Bang*
(UA) F

MIDGE URE (singer)
1982 *The Secret Policeman's Other Ball*
(UIP) F
"I Shall Be Released"

GRAHAM USHER (ballet dancer)
1963 *An Evening with the Royal Ballet*
(BHE) F

V.5. BAND
1995 *Small Faces*
(Skyline) F
"Till the End of the Day"
"Tongs YaBass"

THE VACQUEROS (group)
1965 *Gonks Go Beat*
(Anglo) F

HENRY VADDEN (juggler)
1939 *Pathe Pictorial NS 145*

VADIM TRIO (dancers)
1932 *Ideal Cinemagazine 329*

VALENCIA TRIO (adagio)
1952 *The Gambler and the Lady*
(Hammer) F

DICKIE VALENTINE (singer)
1958 *6.5 Special*
(Anglo) F
"King of Dixieland"
"Come to My Arms"

THE VALJOHNS (entertainers)
1971 *Top of the Bill*
(Butcher) F

VALKEIRER AND BRADLEY (singers)
1937 *Model Man*
(Ace Cinemagazine)
"Goodbye Hawaii"

MADAME VALLI (singer)
1930 *Gypsy Land*
(Gainsborough)
"Heart of a Romany"
"Gypsy Melody"

VALMAR TRIO (balancers)
1933 *Pathetone 185*

AUGUSTE VAN BIENE (cello)
1896 *The Broken Melody*
(Collings)
1907 *The Blind Violinist*
(Chronophone)
1907 *The Broken Melody*
(Chronophone)

REBECCA VAN DER POST STRING QUARTETTE
1993 *Shopping*
(Rank)
"Eine Kleine Nachtmusik"

VAN HORN AND INEZ (dancers)
1932 *Eve's Film Review 578*

THE VANCOUVER BOYS BAND
1934 *Pathe Pictorial 852*
"Triumphal March"
1934 *Pathe Pictorial 859*
"The World Is Waiting for the Sunrise"
1939 *Pathetone 490*

VANDA AND VLADIMIR (dancers)
1932 *Gaumont Sound Mirror 78*

ALMA VANE (singer)
1929 *Musical Moments*
(BIP)
1929 *A Song or Two*
(BIP)
1929 *An Arabian Night*
(BIP)

DENISE VANE (contortionist)
1936 *Pathe Pictorial NS 15*
1937 *Pathe Pictorial NS 47*
"The Blue Danube"

MARIA VAR (singer)
1947 *Master of Bankdam*
        (GFD) F
        "The Fire of Your Love"
1949 *Silent Dust*
        (ABPC) F

REG VARNEY (comedian)
1952 *Miss Robin Hood*
        (Group 3) F
1965 *Joey Boy*
        (British Lion) F
1966 *The Great St Trinian's Train Robbery*
        (British Lion) F
1971 *On the Buses*
        (Hammer) F
1972 *Mutiny On the Buses*
        (Hammer) F
1972 *Go For a Take*
        (Rank) F
1972 *The Best Pair of Legs in the Business*
        (EMI) F
        "Strollin'"
        "Home Town"
        "Tickle My Fancy"
        "I Do Like To Be Beside the Seaside"
        "The Virgin Queen"
1973 *Holiday On the Buses*
        (Hammer) F

VASHTI (group)
1967 *Tonite Let's All Make Love in London*
        (Lorrimer) F

VAUDEVILLE GIRLS (dancers)
1933 *Ideal Cinemagazine 371*
        "After Dark"

ELIZABETH VAUGHAN (singer)
1982 *Victor Victoria*
        (UIP) F

FRANKIE VAUGHAN (singer)
1956 *Ramsbottom Rides Again*
        (British Lion) F
        "Ride Ride Again"
        "This Is the Night"
1957 *These Dangerous Years*
        (ABPC) F
        "These Dangerous Years"
        "Cold Cold Shower"
        "Isn't This a Lovely Evening?"
1958 *Wonderful Things*
        (ABPC) F
        "Wonderful Things"
        "Little Fishes"
1958 *Pathe Pictorial 211*
1959 *The Lady Is a Square*
        (ABPC) F
        "Honey Bunny Baby"
        "That's My Doll"

"Ave Maria"
"The Lady Is a Square"
1959 *The Heart of a Man*
        (Rank) F
        "The Heart of a Man"
        "Walking Tall"
        "Sometime Somewhere"
        "My Boy Flat Top"
1963 *It's All Over Town*
        (British Lion) F
        "Give Me the Moonlight"
        "Wouldn't You Like It?"
        "Alley Alley O"
        "Gonna Be a Good Boy Now"
        "It's All Over Town"

NORMAN VAUGHAN (comedian)
1965 *Doctor in Clover*
        (Rank) F
1965 *You Must Be Joking*
        (Columbia) F
1969 *Twinky*
        (Rank) F
1969 *Bachelor of Arts*
        (Paramount)
1977 *Come Play With Me*
        (Tigon) F
1991 *Hear My Song*
        (Palace) F

TONY VAUGHAN (singer)
1939 *Discoveries*
        (Vogue) F
        "Santa Lucia"
        "It Began in Eden"

BOBBY VEE (singer)
1962 *Play It Cool*
        (Anglo) F
        "At a Time Like This"
1963 *Just For Fun*
        (Columbia) F
        "Night Has a Thousand Eyes"
        "All You Gotta Do Is Touch Me"

VLADIMIR VEGA (musician)
1994 *Ladybird Ladybird*
        (Parallax) F

SENORITA VELASCO (Spanish dancer)
1898 *Castanet Dance*
        (Cinematograph)
1898 *Hat Dance*
        (Cinematograph)

LUPE VELEZ (American singer)
1936 *Gypsy Melody*
        (Wardour) F
        "Doina"
1937 *Mad About Money*
        (Morgan) F
        "Dusting the Stars"

**VENICE OPERA HOUSE ORCHESTRA
AND CHORUS**
1949   *The Glass Mountain*
        (Renown) F

PEARL VENTERS (juvenile)
1939   *Discoveries*
        (Vogue) F
        "I'll Always Remember You Smiling"
        "My Home in the Highland Hills"

VERA-ELLEN (American dancer)
1951   *Happy Go Lovely*
        (ABP) F
        "Mackintosh's Wedding"
        "One Two Three"
        "Piccadilly Ballet"
        "Would You Could You"
1957   *Let's Be Happy*
        (ABPC) F
        "I'm Going to Scotland"
        "Let's Be Happy"

AL VERDI AND THELMA LEE (comedy
musicians)
1937   *Pathetone 390*
        "Dinah"
        "Poet and Peasant"

VIRGINIA VERNON (entertainer)
1971   *Top of the Bill*
        (Butcher) F

THE VERNONS GIRLS (singers)
1963   *Just For Fun*
        (Columbia) F
        "Just Another Girl"

VERONICA (acrobatic dancer)
1933   *Pathe Pictorial 784*
        "Do It Again"
1937   *Starlight Parade*
        (Viking)

THE VERSATILE THREE (singers)
1934   *Pathe Pictorial 868*
        "Sweet Sue"

VERUSCHKA (model)
1967   *Blow-Up*
        (MGM) F
1985   *The Bride*
        (Columbia) F

THE VERVE (group)
1996   *Glastonbury: The Movie*
        (Starlight) F
        "Gravity Grave"

VESTA (xylophone)
1938   *Pathe Pictorial NS 135*
        "Bye Bye Blues"

SGT. VICCARI AND THE G.I. BAND
1945   *I Live in Grosvenor Square*
        (ABPC) F

SID VICIOUS (bass player)
see also **THE SEX PISTOLS**
1980   *The Great Rock 'n' Roll Swindle*
        (Virgin) F

EDWARD VICTOR (entertainer)
1935   *Variety*
        (Butcher) F
        "Shadows from the Past"

VESTA VICTORIA (singer)
1902   *Grace Darling*
        (Warwick)
1934   *Broken Rosary*
        (Butcher) F
        "Waiting at the Church"
1937   *The Schooner Gang*
        (Butcher) F
        "The Old Tin Kettle"
        "For You"
1938   *The Dance of Death*
        (Fidelity) F
1941   *Highlights of Variety 24*
        (reissue: *The Broken Rosary*)

VICTORIA GIRLS (dancers)
1928   *The Victoria Girls*
        (Phonofilm)
1928   *The Victoria Girls Skipping*
        (Phonofilm)
1931   *Stepping Stones*
        (Benstead) F
1932   *Musical Medley 1*
        (reissue: *The Victoria Girls*)
1932   *Musical Medley 6*
        (reissue: *The Victoria Girls Skipping*)

**FRANZ VIENNA AND HIS RADIO THEATRE
ORCHESTRA**
1935   *Pathe Pictorial 883*
        "One Night in Napoli"

VIENNA BOYS CHOIR
1934   *Unfinished Symphony*
        (Cine) F

VIENNA PHILHARMONIC CHOIR
1934   *Unfinished Symphony*
        (Cine) F

VIENNESE SINGERS
1937   *Fizzy Facts*
        (Ace Cinemagazine)
1938   *Striking Gold*
        (Ace Cinemagazine)
        "The Blue Danube"

VIENNESE SINGING SISTERS
1937   *Pathetone 397*
1938   *Pathetone 454*
        "Memories of Chopin"

THE VIEWERS (group)
1981 *The Monster Club*
(ITC) F

GENE VINCENT (American singer)
1962 *It's Trad Dad*
(Columbia) F
"Spaceship to Mars"
1963 *Live It Up*
(Rank) F
"Temptation Baby"

ROBBIE (ENOCH) VINCENT (comedian)
1940 *Somewhere in England*
(Mancunian) F
1942 *Somewhere in Camp*
(Mancunian) F
1942 *Somewhere on Leave*
(Mancunian) F
1943 *Happidrome*
(Aldwych) F
"We Want a Little Song"

VINE, MORE AND NEVARD (singers)
1936 *Pathe Pictorial NS 36*
"We've Only Got Three Minutes"
1937 *Pathe Pictorial NS 71*
"The Bob Song"
1938 *Pathetone 437*
"Mr Middleton Says Its Right"

IVOR VINTNOR (dancer)
1927 *The Arcadians*
(Gaumont) F

1936 *Variety Parade*
(Butcher) F
(with Ann Gordon)

VIOLINDA (violin)
1940 *Pathe Pictorial 199*

VISCOUNT (performing dog)
1939 *Pathe Pictorial 161*

THE VISCOUNTS (group)
1963 *Take Six*
(British Lion)
"Let's Twist Again"

CRISTIAN VOGEL (singer)
1996 *Glastonbury: The Movie*
(Starlight) F
"Stone Flute"

VOLGA SINGERS (sextette)
1930 *The Volga Singers*
(Gainsborough)

LES VOLGAS (balancers)
1934 *Pathe Pictorial 857*

HILDE VON STOLTZ (German singer)
1934 *My Heart Is Calling*
(Gaumont) F

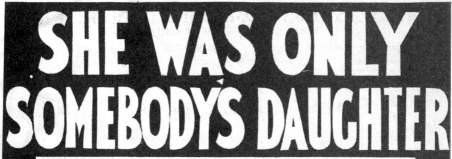

THE ORIGINAL AND AUTHENTIC VERSION OF THE NEW RHYMING CRAZE

SHE WAS ONLY SOMEBODYS DAUGHTER

(Poor Little Orphan Child)

Written Composed and Featured by

The WESTERN BROS.
(KEN. & GEORGE)

The Peter Maurice Music Co. Ltd.

Copyright in all Countries.

All Rights Reserved.

Nº 1156.

6D net.

THE WACKERS (group)
    1964   *Swinging UK*
            (Baim)
            "Love or Money"

PATRICK WADDINGTON (singer)
see also **THAT CERTAIN TRIO**
    1932   *Pathe Pictorial 719*
            "I Found You Little Girl"
    1946   *Gaiety George*
            (Embassy) F
            "Maytime is Made for Love"
            "One Love"

WAIATA MAORI CHOIR (singers)
    1937   *Among Best Sellers*
            (Ace Cinemagazine)

CHERRY WAINER (organ)
    1960   *Girls of Latin Quarter*
            (New Realm) F
    1960   *Climb Up the Wall*
            (New Realm) F

DOUGLAS WAKEFIELD (comedian)
    1933   *This Week of Grace*
            (Realart) F
    1935   *Look Up and Laugh*
            (ATP) F
    1937   *The Penny Pool*
            (Mancunian) F
            "Break the News to Mother"
            "Julie and Myrtle"
    1938   *Calling All Crooks*
            (Mancunian) F
            "Daphne and Me"
    1939   *Highlights of Variety 13*
            (reissue: *The Penny Pool*)
    1940   *Highlights of Variety 18*
            (reissue: *Calling All Crooks*)
    1940   *Spy for a Day*
            (Two Cities) F
    1941   *Music Hall Personalities*
            (reissue: *Highlights of Variety*)

OLIVER WAKEFIELD (comedian)
    1936   *Pathe Pictorial NS 40*
    1937   *French Leave*
            (Pathe) F
    1937   *Let's Make a Night of It*
            (ABPC) F
    1937   *There Was a Young Man*
            (Fox) F
    1938   *Pathetone 439*
    1939   *Shipyard Sally*
            (TCF) F
    1941   *Variety Interlude*
            (Publicity) ADVERT
    1942   *Let the People Sing*
            (British National) F
    1942   *The Peterville Diamond*
            (Warner) F
    1943   *Pictorial Revue of 1943*
            F (reissue: *Pathetone 439*)

RICK WAKEMAN (musician)
see also **YES**
    1975   *Lisztomania*
            (Warner) F
    1976   *White Rock*
            (Worldmark) F

HAROLD WALDEN (comedian)
    1948   *Cup Tie Honeymoon*
            (Mancunian) F

RONALD WALDMAN (broadcaster)
    1946   *Dancing Thru*
            (Angel) F
    1954   *Behind the Scenes*
            (Gas) S
    1955   *Man of the Moment*
            (Rank) F

MAX WALDORF (entertainer)
    1933   *Pathe Pictorial 794*

WALDORF BRASS QUINTET (musicians)
    1939   *Pathetone 492*
            "A Perfect Day"
    1940   *Pathe Pictorial 209*
            "Black Eyes"

BOB DANVERS WALKER (broadcaster)
    1989   *Resurrected*
            (Hobo) F

DAPHNE WALKER (skater)
    1938   *Pathetone 452*
    1946   *Mind Your Step*
            (Argo)
    1946   *Women and Sport*
            (Butcher)

FRANK WALKER AND HIS B.B.C. OCTET
(band)
    1936   *Pathe Pictorial NS 13*
            "The Clockwork Two Seater"
    1938   *Still Life*
            (Ace Cinemagazine)
    1938   *Talking Shop*
            (Ace Cinemagazine)
    1938   *Mapping Things Out*
            (Ace Cinemagazine)
            "The Bee's Wedding"

JOCK WALKER (Scottish comedian)
    1929   *Pathe Magazine 14*
    1929   *Pathe Magazine 24*

NORAH WALKER
see **ERNEST BELCHER AND NORAH
WALKER**

SYD WALKER (comedian)
    1924   *Old Bill Through the Ages*
            (Ideal) F
    1935   *Royal Cavalcade*
            (BIP) F

1936 *Public Nuisance No. 1*
(GFD) F
1937 *Let's Make a Night of It*
(ABPC) F
1937 *Over She Goes*
(ABPC) F
1938 *Oh Boy*
(ABPC) F
1938 *Hold My Hand*
(ABPC) F
1938 *Sweet Devil*
(GFD) F
1939 *The Gang's All Here*
(ABPC) F
1939 *What Would You Do, Chums?*
(British National) F
1939 *I Killed the Count*
(British National) F
1943 *Pathe Pictorial 355*
"The Scrap Chap"
1944 *Save No. 1; 3*
(National Savings)

WHIMSICAL WALKER (clown)
1928 *Gaumont Mirror*

WILLIAM WALKER
see **THAT CERTAIN TRIO**

MAX WALL (comedian)
1931 *Ideal Cinemagazine 281*
"The Boy with the Obedient Feet"
1934 *On the Air*
(British Lion) F
1938 *Save a Little Sunshine*
(Pathe) F
1940 *Pathe Pictorial 220*
"Goodbye Sally"
1941 *Pathe Pictorial 261*
1950 *Come Dance With Me*
(Columbia) F
1951 *Mirth and Melody*
(Inspiration)
1951 *That's Odd*
(Carisbrooke)
1955 *Odds and Ends*
(Carisbrooke)
1968 *Chitty Chitty Bang Bang*
(UA) F
1969 *The Nine Ages of Nakedness*
(Orb) F
1975 *Max Wall Funny Man*
(GTO) F
1976 *One of Our Dinosaurs Is Missing*
(Disney) F
1977 *Jabberwocky*
(Columbia) F
1977 *The Hound of the Baskervilles*
(Hemdale) F
1979 *Hanover Street*
(Columbia) F
1979 *Film*
(BFI)

1987 *Little Dorrit*
(Sands) F
1988 *We Think the World of You*
(Cinecom)
1988 *Strike It Rich*
(Flamingo)

WALL OF VOODOO (group)
1981 *Urgh! A Music War*
(White) F
"Can't Make Love"

IAN WALLACE (singer)
1949 *Floodtide*
(GFD) F
1951 *Assassin for Hire*
(Anglo) F
1952 *The Story of Gilbert and Sullivan*
(London) F
1958 *Tom Thumb*
(MGM) F
1960 *Dentist in the Chair*
(Renown) F
1985 *Plenty*
(RKO) F

NELLIE WALLACE (comedienne)
1902 *Biograph Dramatised Songs*
(Biograph) S
1902 *A Lady's First Lesson on the Bicycle*
(Williamson)
1920 *Why Men Leave Home*
(Alliance) F
1924 *Eve's Film Review 150*
"The Whirl of the World"
1928 *Gaumont Mirror*
1931 *Ideal Cinemagazine 271*
1931 *Ideal Cinemagazine 295*
1933 *The Wishbone*
(Sound City) F
1934 *Radio Parade of 1935*
(BIP) F
"We Won't Say Good Morning"
"We're Not Quite What We Used to Be"
1935 *Variety*
(Butcher) F
1937 *Highlights of Variety 5*
(reissue: *Variety*)
1937 *Boys Will Be Girls*
(Fuller) F
"Lo Hear the Gentle Lark"
1937 *Hoarding Treasure*
(Ace Cinemagazine)
1938 *Cavalcade of the Stars*
(Coronel)

BOB WALLIS AND HIS STORYVILLE JAZZ MEN (band)
1962 *It's Trad Dad*
(Columbia) F
"Aunt Flo"
"Bellissima"
1963 *Two Left Feet*
(British Lion) F

SHANI WALLIS (singer)
1956 *The Extra Day*
(British Lion) F
1956 *Ramsbottom Rides Again*
(British Lion) F
"This Is the Night"
1957 *A King in New York*
(Archway) F
1968 *Oliver*
(Columbia) F
"Oom Pah Pah"
"As Long As He Needs Me"
"It's a Fine Life"

WALSH AND BARKER (duet)
1935 *Equity Musical Revue 2*
(British Lion)
1935 *Pathetone 295*
"Dennis the Menace from Venice"
1936 *Pathetone 303*
"Winter Wonderland"
1936 *Pathetone 311*
"Dance Dolores"
1936 *Pathetone 320*
"On Top of a Bus"
1937 *Pathetone 369*
"The Duchess is Learning the
Rumba"
1937 *Pathetone 382*
"Here Comes Tomorrow"
1937 *Pathetone 392*
"I Like a Little Girl Like That"
1937 *Pathetone 404*
"Never Blow Your Whistle in the
Park"
1938 *Pathe Pictorial NS 104*
"The Value of a Smile"
1938 *Pathe Pictorial NS 140*
"Cruise Minded Women"
1938 *Pathetone 457*
1939 *Pathe Pictorial 185*
"I'll Get By"
1941 *Pathe Pictorial 254*
"It's Still Being Done"

WALSH BROTHERS (singers)
1930 *The Walsh Brothers*
(Gainsborough)

RONALD WALTERS (singer)
1937 *The Minstrel Boy*
(Butcher) F
"Moonlight Madonna"
"Sweet Muchacha"

WALTER WALTERS (ventriloquist)
1941 *Pathetone 569*

KENT WALTON (television personality)
1959 *The Heart of a Man*
(Rank) F
1964 *Swinging UK*
(Baim)
1964 *UK Swings Again*
(Baim)

ALBERT AND LES WARD (comedy
musicians)
1948 *Lucky Mascot*
(UA) F
"Black Eyes"

ARTHUR L. WARD AND HIS BAND
1935 *Off the Dole*
(Mancunian) F

DIANA WARD (singer)
1935 *She Shall Have Music*
(Twickenham) F
"Moaning Minnie"

DOROTHY WARD (singer)
1921 *Around the Town*
(Gaumont)
"Jack and the Beanstalk"
1925 *Eve's Film Review 207*
1931 *Pathetone 80*
"The Same As We Used To Do"
1931 *Eve's Film Review 515*
"The Belle of New York"
1939 *Pathe Gazette 76*
"Do It Again"

THE HEDLEY WARD TRIO (singers)
1952 *Melody Time*
(International)
"Daisy Bell"

PATRICK WARD (tenor)
1939 *A Tramp in Killarney*
(Fraternity)

PAULINE WARD (tap-dancer)
1935 *Pathetone 300*
1936 *Pathe Pictorial NS 6*

PHYLLIS WARD (cartoonist)
1932 *Ideal Cinemagazine 325*

POLLY WARD (song and dance)
1927 *This Marriage Business*
(FBO) F
1928 *Shooting Stars*
(BIF) F
1930 *Harmony Heaven*
(BIP) F
"We're in Harmony Heaven"
1930 *Alf's Button*
(Gaumont) F
1932 *His Lordship*
(UA) F
1934 *Kentucky Minstrels*
(Realart) F
1934 *The Old Curiosity Shop*
(BIP) F
1935 *It's a Bet*
(BIP) F
1936 *Shipmates o' Mine*
(Butcher) F
"You're Driving Me Crazy"

1936 *Annie Laurie*
(Butcher) F
"Strolling Through the Heather"
1936 *Show Flat*
(Paramount) F
1937 *Feather Your Nest*
(ATP) F
1937 *Television Talent*
(Alexander) F
1938 *Thank Evans*
(Warner) F
1938 *St Martin's Lane*
(ABPC) F
1938 *Hold My Hand*
(ABPC) F
"Hold My Hand"
"As Long As I Can Look At You"
1938 *It's In the Air*
(ATP) F
1939 *Highlights of Variety*
(reissue: *Shipmates o' Mine*)
1940 *Bulldog Sees It Through*
(ABPC) F
1942 *Women Aren't Angels*
(ABPC) F

WARDEN AND WEST (dame comedians)
1936 *Digging for Gold*
(Ace) F
1936 *Full Steam*
(Ace) F
1936 *Bottle Party*
(Ace) F
1936 *Piccadilly Playtime*
(Ace) F
1936 *Song in Soho*
(Ace) F
1937 *Windmill Revels*
(Ace) F
1937 *Carry On London*
(Ace) F
1937 *West End Frolics*
(Ace) F
1937 *Uptown Revue*
(Ace) F
1937 *Concert Party*
(Ace) F
1937 *Footlights*
(Ace) F
1937 *Pathe Pictorial NS 82*
1938 *Two Men in a Box*
(Ace) F
1938 *Swing*
(Ace) F
1938 *The Interrupted Rehearsal*
(Ace) F
1938 *Behind the Tabs*
(Ace) F
1938 *Spotlight*
(Ace) F
1939 *Pathe Pictorial 184*

JACK WARMAN (comedian)
1930 *Jerry Builders*
(PDC)
1937 *Pathe Pictorial NS 60*
1937 *Pathe Pictorial NS 72*
1938 *Pathe Pictorial NS 105*
"The Girl I Left Behind Me"

JACK WARNER (comedian)
(films as actor not listed)
1939 *Pathetone 494*
1940 *Pathetone 534*
"The Railway Lines"
1940 *Pathe Pictorial 225*
1943 *The Dummy Talks*
(British National) F
"'At's a Nice Ats' 'At 'At Is"

(JACK) WARNER AND (JEFF) DARNELL
(comedians)
1936 *Pathetone 344*
"Cookhouse Call"
"Just a Pair of Foreign
Legionnaires"
1940 *Pathetone 526*
(reissue: *Pathetone 344*)

BETTY WARREN (singer)
1942 *Secret Mission*
(GFD) F
1943 *Variety Jubilee*
(Butcher) F
"The Twi-Twi-Twilight"
"Has Anybody Here Seen Kelly?"
1943 *They Met in the Dark*
(GFD) F
1944 *Champagne Charlie*
(Ealing) F
"Come On Algernon"
"Not in Front of Baby"
"Hunting After Dark"
1950 *So Long At the Fair*
(GFD) F

JOHN WARREN (conjurer)
1904 *Up To His Tricks*
(Biograph)
1933 *Eve's Film Review 611*
1933 *Eve's Film Review 625*

THE WARRIORS (group)
1964 *Just For You*
(British Lion) F

BEN WARRISS (comedian)
see also **JIMMY JEWEL AND BEN
WARRISS**
1971 *Top of the Bill*
(Butcher) F

ELSIE AND DORIS WATERS (comedy)
1933 *Radio Parade*
(BIP) F

1941 *Gert and Daisy's Weekend*
(Butcher) F
"I've Got Sixpence"
"Goodnight Children Everywhere"
"Kiss Me Goodnight Sergeant
Major"
"Won't We Have a Party?"
"She's a Lily But Only by Name"
1942 *Gert and Daisy Clean Up*
(Butcher) F
"We'll Shout Hooray Again"
"Salvage"
"Home Sweet Home Again"
"Little Gypsy of the Seven Seas"
1942 *Pathe Gazette 50*
"The Save Song"
1943 *It's In the Bag*
(Butcher) F

TREVOR WATKINS (singer)
1929 *Pathe Magazine 4*
1936 *B.B.C. Musicals 3*
(Inspiration)

BOBBY WATSON (sword dancer)
1959 *Music With Max Jaffa*
(Zonic)

HARRY WATSON (animal act)
1902 *Harry Watson's Pony Tumbling Act*
(Warwick)
1902 *Watson's Clown and Dogs Tug of War*
(Warwick)

JACK WATSON (comedian)
(films as actor not listed)
1945 *Pathe Radio Music Hall*

VERNON WATSON (comedian)
see also **NOSMO KING**
1922 *Eve's Film Review 57*
(as George Robey, Harry Weldon,
Fred Emney)
1926 *Eve's Film Review 249*

JOHNNY WATSON'S PERFORMING DOGS
1939 *Pathe Pictorial NS 162*

GILLIAN WATT (dancer)
1963 *Jungle Street*
(Theatrecraft) F

JOHN WATT (broadcaster)
1937 *Saturday Night Revue*
(Pathe) F
1942 *We'll Meet Again*
(Columbia) F

ANDREW WATTS (tenor)
1992 *Orlando*
(Electric) F
"Where E'er You Walk"

PHILIP WATTS AND HIS BAND
1937 *Puff Puff*
(Ace Cinemagazine)

QUEENIE WATTS (singer)
1962 *Sparrows Can't Sing*
(Carthage) F
1964 *Portrait of Queenie*
(British Lion)
1966 *Alfie*
(Paramount) F
"Goodbye Dolly Gray"
1967 *Up the Junction*
(Paramount) F
1967 *Poor Cow*
(Vic) F
1971 *All Coppers Are...*
(Rank) F
1972 *Steptoe and Son*
(EMI) F
1973 *Holiday On the Buses*
(Hammer) F
1973 *Keep It Up, Jack*
(Blackwater) F
1976 *Schizo*
(Walker) F
1976 *Intimate Games*
(Tigon) F
1977 *Come Play With Me*
(Tigon) F
1979 *Confessions from the David Galaxy Affair*
(Tigon) F

RUBY WAX (television personality)
1981 *Chariots of Fire*
(TCF) F
1981 *Shock Treatment*
(TCF) F
1985 *Water*
(Rank) F
1987 *Eat the Rich*
(Comic Strip) F
1987 *The Secret Policeman's Third Ball*
(Virgin) F
1997 *The Borrowers*
(PolyGram) F

JERRY WAYNE (singer)
1955 *As Long As They're Happy*
(Rank) F
"You Started Something"
"Be My Guest"
"Liza's Eyes"
"I Don't Know Whether to Laugh or
Cry"

MABEL WAYNE (composer)
1935 *Pathetone 253*
"Her Majesty the Baby"

NAUNTON WAYNE (comedian)
(films as actor not listed)
1932 *Pathe Pictorial 739*
"A Little Tact"

1932	*Pathe Pictorial 749*	
	"Butting In"	
1932	*Ideal Cinemagazine 313*	
1932	*The First Mrs Fraser*	
	(Sterling) F	
1933	*Going Gay*	
	(Windsor) F	
1933	*For Love of You*	
	(Windsor) F	
1938	*Pathetone 438*	

TONY WAYNE AND HIS BAND
1950 *Round Rainbow Corner*
(Sanders)

WEB (group)
1971 *Bread*
(Salon) F

ELIZABETH WEBB (singer)
1946 *Appointment With Crime*
(British National) F
1946 *Wanted for Murder*
(TCF) F
"A Voice in the Night"
1952 *A Voice in the Night*
(reissue: *Wanted for Murder*)

KURT WEGENER (singer)
1945 *Waltz Time*
(British National) F
"Little White Horse"

THE WEINTRAUBS
1938 *Pathetone 418*

FRANK WEIR AND HIS BAND
1946 *Happy Family*
(British Foundation)
1956 *Parade of the Bands*
(Hammer)

LEONARD WEIR
1959 *Make Mine a Million*
(British Lion) F

ELISABETH WELCH (singer)
1934 *Death at Broadcasting House*
(Phoenix) F
"Lazy Lady"
1936 *Soft Lights and Sweet Music*
(British Lion) F
"Yesterday's Thrill"
1936 *Song of Freedom*
(Hammer) F
"Sleepy River"
1937 *Calling All Stars*
(British Lion) F
"Nightfall"
1937 *Big Fella*
(British Lion) F
"One Kiss"
"Harlem in My Heart"

1937 *Over the Moon*
(London) F
"Red Hot Annabelle"
1938 *Around the Town*
(British Lion) F
1942 *Alibi*
(British Lion) F
1944 *Fiddlers Three*
(Ealing) F
"Drums in My Heart"
1945 *Dead of Night*
(Ealing) F
"The Hullabaloo"
1971 *Girl Stroke Boy*
(Virgin) F
1978 *Revenge of the Pink Panther*
(UA) F
1979 *Arabian Adventure*
(EMI) F
1980 *The Tempest*
(Boyd) F
"Stormy Weather"

JAMES WELCH (comedian)
1913 *Recitation*
(Kineplastikon)
1916 *When Knights Were Bold*
(London) F
1916 *The New Clown*
(Ideal) F

HARRY WELCHMAN (baritone)
1915 *Verdict of the Heart*
(Clarendon) F
1915 *Mr Lyndon at Liberty*
(London) F
1916 *A Princess of the Blood*
(Clarendon) F
1916 *The Lyons Mail*
(Ideal) F
1920 *The House on the Marsh*
(London) F
1920 *The Holiday Husband*
(Alliance) F
1920 *Around the Town 9*
(Gaumont)
1920 *Around the Town 10*
(Gaumont)
1922 *Eve's Film Review 42*
"Lady of the House"
1932 *Maid of the Mountains*
(BIP) F
"A Bachelor Gay Am I"
"There's No Day Like Today"
"The Keys to My Heart"
"True Love"
1933 *A Southern Maid*
(BIP) F
"Here's to Those We Love"
"Love's Cigarette"
1936 *The Last Waltz*
(Warwick) F
"The Laughing Cavalier"
"I Like Your Dimples"

"Believe Me I'm Quite Sincere"
"The Mirror Song"
"The Magic Waltz"
1941 *The Common Touch*
(British National) F
1942 *This Was Paris*
(Warner) F
1943 *The Gentle Sex*
(GFD) F
1943 *The Life and Death of Colonel Blimp*
(GFD) F
1945 *Waltz Time*
(British National) F
1946 *Lisbon Story*
(British National) F
1946 *Loyal Heart*
(British National) F
1947 *Green Fingers*
(British National) F
1952 *Judgement Deferred*
(Group 3) F
1954 *Eight O'Clock Walk*
(British Lion) F
1954 *Mad About Men*
(GFD) F

MAISIE WELDON (impressionist)
1941 *Pathe Pictorial 286*
1949 *Melody in the Dark*
(Adelphi) F

LJUBA WELITSCH (singer)
1953 *The Man Between*
(London) F

DON WELLER BAND
1987 *Stormy Monday*
(Palace) F

SYLVIA WELLING (soprano)
1946 *I'll Turn To You*
(Butcher) F
"I'll Turn To You"
"The Little Damozel"
1947 *Comin' Thro' the Rye*
(Adelphi) F
"Comin' Thro' the Rye"
"Ye Banks and Braes"
"O Whistle and I'll Come"
"Charlie Is My Darling"

CHRISTINE WELSFORD (fan dancer)
1949 *Murder at the Windmill*
(Grand National) F

JANE WELSH (singer)
1938 *Little Dolly Daydream*
(Butcher) F
"Here, There, Everywhere"
"Don't You Come Any More"
"I Know That Love Is Somewhere"

WELSH LADIES CHOIR
1939 *Pathe Pictorial NS 172*
"Bells of Aberdovy"
1939 *Pathetone 461*
"All Through the Night"

HENRY WENDON (tenor)
1934 *Pathetone 233*
"Passing By"

GRACIE WEST
see **ETHEL REVNELL AND GRACIE WEST**

THE WESTERN BROTHERS (Kenneth and
George) (comedians)
1931 *Gaumont Sound Mirror*
1932 *Pathetone 101*
"It Was All Hushed Up"
1932 *Pathetone 117*
1932 *Pathe Pictorial 761*
"She Was Only Somebody's
Daughter"
1932 *Pathe Pictorial 788*
"Play the Game Cads"
1933 *Pathetone 186*
"In the Parlour When the Company's
Gone"
1933 *One Precious Year*
(B&D) F
"Wearing His Old School Tie"
1934 *Mister Cinders*
(BIP) F
"I Think of You Dear"
"Aren't We All?"
1934 *The Way Of Youth*
(B&D) F
1934 *Radio Parade of 1935*
(BIP) F
"Weather Forecast"
1936 *Soft Lights and Sweet Music*
(British Lion) F
"After All That"
"Don't Be a Cad"

WESTERN THEATRE BALLET COMPANY
1964 *Mods and Rockers*
(Anglo)

WESTMINSTER ABBEY CHOIR
1934 *Danny Boy*
(Butcher) F
"Bird Song at Eventide"
1934 *Song at Eventide*
(Butcher) F
"Sanctuary of the Heart"

WESTMINSTER GLEE SINGERS
1927 *Westminster Glee Singers*
(Phonofilm)
1932 *Musical Medley 3*
(reissue: *Westminster Glee Singers*)

WESTMINSTER MORRIS MEN (dancers)
1966 *The Great St Trinian's Train Robbery*
(British Lion) F

BERT WESTON (comedian)
1937 *Pathetone 366*
1938 *Pathe Pictorial NS 133*

LESLIE WESTON (comedian)
1931 *Pathetone 86*
1932 *Pathe Pictorial 734*
1932 *Pathe Pictorial 747*
1932 *Pathe Pictorial 765*
1934 *Pathetone 245*
1935 *Pathe Pictorial 921*
1936 *Pathe Pictorial NS 19*
1937 *Pathetone 366*
1938 *Pathe Pictorial 120*
1939 *Pathetone 503*

WESTON AND VINE (comedy)
1936 *Cabaret Nights 4*
(Highbury)

HARRY WHANSLAW (puppets)
1936 *Pathe Pictorial NS 18*

(JIMMY) WHEELER AND (ERNIE) WILSON
(comedians)
1938 *Pathe Pictorial NS 138*

ALBERT WHELAN (comedian)
1928 *An Intimate Interlude*
(BSFP)
1930 *Pathetone 37*
"She's My Secret Passion"
1930 *O.K. Chief*
(BIP)
1930 *The Man From Chicago*
(BIP) F
1931 *Pathetone 55*
1933 *Matinee Idol*
(UA) F
1934 *Anything Might Happen*
(Realart) F
1935 *Dance Band*
(BIP) F
1936 *Educated Evans*
(Warner) F
1936 *Stars On Parade*
(Butcher) F
1937 *Action for Slander*
(ATP) F
1937 *The Girl in the Taxi*
(ABFD) F
1937 *Mad About Money*
(Morgan) F
"The Stolen Melody"
1938 *Thank Evans*
(Warner) F
1940 *Pathe Pictorial 210*
"The Love Bug"
"I Belong to Glasgow"
1943 *Candlelight in Algeria*
(British Lion) F
1944 *English Without Tears*
(GFD) F

1956 *Keep It Clean*
(Eros) F

ANGELA WHELDON (singer)
1942 *Pathe Pictorial 323*

ALAN WHICKER (television personality)
1960 *The Angry Silence*
(British Lion) F
1969 *The Magic Christian*
(Grand) F

JAY WHIDDEN AND HIS MELODY MAKERS
1926 *Eve's Film Review 249*

WHIRLWIND SKATERS (specialty)
1937 *Calling All Stars*
(British Lion) F

NANCY WHISKEY (folk songs)
1957 *The Tommy Steele Story*
(Anglo) F
"Freight Train"
1958 *The Golden Disc*
(Butcher) F
"Johnny O"

FRANCIS WHITE (conjurer)
1938 *Pathe Pictorial NS 94*

IRIS KIRK WHITE
see **IRIS KIRKWHITE**

LEE WHITE (dancer)
1921 *Around the Town*
(Gaumont)
"Penguin Dance"

STAN WHITE (singer)
1949 *Bless 'Em All*
(Adelphi) F
"I'll Be Seeing You"
"Boom"
"Victory Waltz"

TAM WHITE (singer)
1990 *Paper Mask*
(Enterprise)

THE WHITE COONS (concert party)
1908 *A Visit to the Seaside*
(Kinemacolor)
1934 *Kentucky Minstrels*
(Realart) F

WHITE, TREVOR AND DAWN (dancers)
1941 *Pathe Pictorial 257*

PAUL WHITEMAN AND HIS BAND
1926 *London*
(British National) F

WHITESNAKE (group)
1978 *Snake Bite*
(New Realm)

JACK WHITING (song and dance)
1938 *Sailing Along*
(Gaumont) F
"My Heart Skips a Beat"
"My River"

MARIA WHITTAKER (model)
1988 *Tank Malling*
(Parkfield) F
1988 *Whoops Apocalypse*
(Virgin) F

THE WHO (group)
1975 *Tommy*
(Stigwood) F
"Bernie's Holiday Camp"
"Fiddle About"
"Sparks"
"Sally Simpson"
"Listening to You"
"'51 Is Going To Be a Good Year"
"What About the Boy?"
"Christmas"
"Do You Think It's All Right?"
"Cousin Kevin"
"Today It Rained Champagne"
"There's a Doctor"
"Go To the Mirror"
"Tommy, Can You Hear Me?"
"Smash the Mirror"
"We're Not Gonna Take It"
"Eyesight to the Blind"
"Deceived"
1979 *The Kids Are Alright*
(Rose) F
"My Generation"
"Can't Explain"
"Baba O'Riley"
"Tommy, Can You Hear Me?"
"Pinball Wizard"
"We're Not Gonna Take It [See Me, Feel Me]"
"Substitute"
"I'm a Boy"
"Pictures of Lily"
"I Can See for Miles"
"Magic Bus"
"Happy Jack"
"A Quick One While He's Away"
"Sparks"
"Who Are You?"
"Won't Get Fooled Again"
"Long Live Rock"
"Shout and Shimmy"
"Young Man Blues"
"Anyway Anyhow Anywhere"
"Success Story"
"Heatwave"
"Cobwebs and Strange"
"Barbara Ann"
"Roadrunner"

1979 *Quadrophenia*
(Who) F
"Anyway Anyhow Anywhere"
"My Generation"
1982 *Face Dances*
(UIP)

IRIS WHYTE
see **IRIS KIRKWHITE**

WALTER WIDDOP (singer)
1933 *The Song You Gave Me*
(BIP) F

WIERE BROTHERS (comedy dancers)
see also **TREBLE TAPPERS**
1931 *Pathetone 68*
1933 *Pathe Pictorial 811*
"Hot Lips"

FRANK WIGNALL (baritone)
1932 *Pathe Pictorial 738*
"Stonecracker John"
1932 *Pathe Pictorial 769*
"The Veteran"
1938 *Pathe Pictorial NS 124*
"Bert the Bosun"

JAY WILBUR AND HIS BAND
1941 *Hi Gang*
(Gainsborough) F
"Hi Gang"
"We Chose the Air Force"

KEITH WILBUR (singer)
1933 *Radio Parade*
(BIP) F
1937 *Uptown Revue*
(Ace) F

NAN WILD (singer)
1927 *Nan Wild*
(Phonofilm)

MARTY WILDE (singer)
1959 *Jet Storm*
(British Lion) F
1961 *The Hellions*
(Columbia) F
1963 *What a Crazy World*
(Hammer) F
"A Layabout's Lament"
"Oh What a Family"
"Independence"
1974 *Stardust*
(EMI) F

GILBERT WILKINSON (cartoonist)
1938 *Pathe Pictorial NS 109*

TOYAH WILLCOX (singer)
1978 *Jubilee*
(Cinegate) F

1979 *Quadrophenia*
(Who) F
1980 *The Tempest*
(Boyd) F
1981 *Urgh! A Music War*
(White) F
"Dance"

WILLE BROTHERS (balancers)
1901 *The Famous Wille Brothers*
(Warwick)

ARTHUR WILLIAMS (tenor)
1936 *Pathe Pictorial 926*
"My Little Welsh Home"
1936 *Pathe Pictorial NS 32*
"Rose of Tralee"

BILLY WILLIAMS (violin)
1937 *Behind the Screen*
(Ace Cinemagazine)

BRANSBY WILLIAMS (characterisations)
(films as actor not listed)
1928 *Grandfather Smallweed*
(Phonofilm)
1928 *Scrooge*
(Phonofilm)
1932 *Pathe Pictorial 750*
1940 *Pathe Pictorial 230*

CHARLIE WILLIAMS (comedian)
1973 *Man At the Top*
(Hammer) F

DANNY WILLIAMS (singer)
1962 *Play It Cool*
(Anglo) F
"Who Can Say?"
1963 *It's All Happening*
(British Lion) F
"On a Day Without You"

DORIAN WILLIAMS (television
commentator)
1980 *High Rise Donkey*
(CFF) F

E. H. WILLIAMS' MERRIE MEN (minstrels)
1899 *The Famous Merrie Men*

JACK WILLIAMS AND JOEY PORTER
(comedians)
1933 *Post Haste*
(Gaumont)
1933 *Tooth Will Out*
(Gaumont)

JOHN WILLIAMS (guitarist)
1980 *The Secret Policeman's Ball*
(Tigon) F
"Won't Get Fooled Again"
"Cavatina"

MARILYN WILLIAMS (singer)
1941 *Pathe Pictorial 260*
"I Can't Love You Any More"

NORA WILLIAMS (blues singer)
1935 *In Town Tonight*
(British Lion) F

NORMAN WILLIAMS (bass)
1930 *Pathetone 24*
"Myself When Young"
1932 *Pathe Pictorial 718*
"My Old Kentucky Home"

**WALTER WILLIAMS AND WINNIE
COLLINS** (singers)
1926 *I Can't Take You Out of My Dreams*
(Phonofilm)
1926 *I Don't Believe You're in Love With
Me*
(Phonofilm)

DAVE WILLIS (Scottish comedian)
1938 *Save a Little Sunshine*
(Pathe) F
"Everything in France is Hunky
Dory"
"Down in the Deep Blue Sea"
1939 *Me and My Pal*
(Pathe) F
"Keep On Moving Along"
"Tyrolean Yodel"
1949 *Slick Tartan*
(Equity) F

RITA WILLIS (singer)
1936 *The Show's the Thing*
(Fidelity)

WINCEY WILLIS (television personality)
1988 *Consuming Passions*
(Vestron) F

BERTHA WILLMOTT (singer)
1935 *Variety*
(Butcher) F
"Ta-Ra-Ra-Boom-De-Ay"
"Tipperary"
"Who Were You With Last Night?"
1937 *Highlights of Variety 2*
(reissue: *Variety*)
1943 *Millions Like Us*
(GFD) F
"Just Like the Ivy"
"Waiting at the Church"

GERRY WILMOTT (broadcaster)
1942 *They Flew Alone*
(RKO) F
1942 *One of Our Aircraft Is Missing*
(British National) F
1942 *The First of the Few*
(GFD) F
1942 *Pathe Pictorial 308*

1943 *Yellow Canary*
(RKO) F
1943 *Playtime for Workers*
(Federated) F
1944 *Candles at Nine*
(British National) F
1944 *Dreaming*
(Baxter) F
1945 *I Live in Grosvenor Square*
(ABPC) F
1947 *Plenty Questions*
(Butcher)
1947 *Holiday Camp*
(Gainsborough) F

BERT WILSON (comedian)
1938 *Pathe Pictorial NS 133*
"The Singing Drunk"

ERNIE WILSON
see **(JIMMY) WHEELER AND (ERNIE) WILSON**

MARIE WILSON (trick cyclist)
1941 *Pathetone 568*
1942 *Pathe Pictorial 321*

ROBERT WILSON (tenor)
1937 *Pathe Pictorial NS 84*
"Annie Laurie"
1938 *Pathe Pictorial NS 107*
"An Old-Fashioned Town"
1938 *Pathetone 433*
"Bonnie Mary of Argyle"
1938 *Pathetone 442*
"For You Alone"
1938 *Pathe Pictorial NS 136*
"Passing By"
1939 *Pathe Pictorial NS 159*
"Loch Lomond"
1939 *Pathetone 486*
"Who Is Sylvia?"
1939 *Pathetone 505*
"Hail Caledonia"
1939 *Pathetone Parade of 1940*
F (reissue: *Pathetone 433*)
1940 *Pathe Pictorial 224*
"Homing"
1940 *Pathe Pictorial 229*
"The Cameron Men"
1941 *Pathe Pictorial 250*
"I Thought I Heard You Singing"
1941 *Pathe Pictorial 275*
"Ye Banks and Braes"
1942 *Pathetone Parade of 1942*
F (reissue: *Pictorial 275*)
1942 *Pathe Pictorial 313*
"So Deep Is the Night"
1942 *Pathe Pictorial 332*
"Intermezzo"
1942 *Pathe Pictorial 352*
"Misty Island"
1943 *Pathe Pictorial 392*
"I Met an Angel"

1944 *Pathe Pictorial 430*
"Always"
1944 *Pathe Pictorial 438*
"I Dream of Jeannie"

ROSE WILSON (singer)
1931 *Pathetone 87*

WILSON, KEPPEL AND BETTY (burlesque dance)
1933 *Pathetone 164*
"Ballet Egyptienne"
1934 *On the Air*
(British Lion) F
1935 *In Town Tonight*
(British Lion) F
1936 *Soft Lights and Sweet Music*
(British Lion) F
1943 *Variety Jubilee*
(Butcher) F
1944 *Starlight Serenade*
(Federated) F
1944 *Highlights of Variety 25; 26*
(reissue: *Variety Jubilee*)
1948 *For Old Times Sake*
(reissue: *Variety Jubilee*)
1950 *Variety Makers*
(reissue: *Starlight Serenade*)
1950 *A Ray of Sunshine*
(Adelphi) F

WILSON SISTERS
1950 *Round Rainbow Corner*
(Sanders)

ROBB WILTON (comedian)
1928 *The Fire Brigade*
(Phonofilm)
1930 *Pathetone 18*
1932 *Pathetone 99*
1932 *Pathetone 107*
"The Policeman"
1932 *Pathetone 113*
"The Prison Governor"
1932 *Pathetone 123*
"The Army"
1932 *Pathetone 144*
"The Magistrate"
1933 *Pathetone 180*
"Back Answers"
1934 *Pathe Pictorial 822*
"The Lion Hunter"
1934 *Pathetone 204*
"The Police Station"
1934 *Pathetone 209*
"The Fire Station"
1934 *Pathetone 215*
"The Hunter"
1934 *Pathe Pictorial 849*
"In the Jungle"
1934 *Love Life and Laughter*
(ATP) F
1934 *Pathetone 243*
"An Embankment Cameo"

1934 *Pathetone Parade*
F (reissue: *Pathetone 209*)
1935 *Pathetone 258*
"The Local Magistrate"
1935 *The Silent Passenger*
(ABFD) F
1935 *Look Up and Laugh*
(ATP) F
1935 *A Fire Has Been Arranged*
(Twickenham) F
1936 *Pathe Pictorial NS 5*
"The Solicitor"
1936 *Pathetone 347*
"The K.C."
1936 *Stars On Parade*
(Butcher) F
1936 *Don't Rush Me*
(PDC) F
1936 *Pathetone Parade of 1936*
F (reissue: *title unknown*)
1936 *Pictorial Revue*
F (reissue: *title unknown*)
1936 *Servants All*
(Fox) F
1937 *Fine Feathers*
(British Films) F
1938 *Chips*
(BFA) F
1938 *Break the News*
(GFD) F
1938 *Highlights of Variety 8*
(reissue: *Stars On Parade*)
1938 *Pathe Pictorial NS 107*
"Don't Tell a Soul"
1939 *Pathetone Parade of 1939*
F (reissue: *title unknown*)
1939 *Pathetone 496*
1939 *The Gang's All Here*
(ABPC) F
1939 *Pathetone Parade of 1940*
F (reissue: *Pathetone 496*)
1940 *Pathe Pictorial 197*
"Mr Muddlecombe JP"
1940 *Pathe Pictorial 202*
"Mr Muddlecombe JP"
1940 *Pathe Pictorial 237*
"Flat Irons"
1941 *Pathetone Parade of 1941*
F (reissue: *Pathetone 204*)
1942 *Pathetone Parade of 1942*
F (reissue: *title unknown*)
1943 *Pictorial Revue of 1943*
F (reissue: *Pictorial 202*)
1955 *The Love Match*
(Group 3) F

THE WINDMILL GIRLS (dancers)
1936 *Digging for Gold*
(Ace) F
1936 *Full Steam*
(Ace) F
1936 *Bottle Party*
(Ace) F

1936 *Piccadilly Playtime*
(Ace) F
1936 *Song in Soho*
(Ace) F
"Escalator Squiggle"
1937 *Windmill Revels*
(Ace) F
1937 *Carry On London*
(Ace) F
1937 *West End Frolics*
(Ace) F
"Hunting Ballet"
1937 *Uptown Revue*
(Ace) F
1937 *Concert Party*
(Ace) F
1937 *Footlights*
(Ace) F
1938 *Two Men in a Box*
(Ace) F
1938 *Swing*
(Ace) F
1938 *Revue Parade*
(Ace) F
1938 *The Interrupted Rehearsal*
(Ace) F
1938 *Behind the Tabs*
(Ace) F
1938 *Spotlight*
(Ace) F
1946 *New Pictorial 109*
1946 *Pathe News*
1949 *Murder at the Windmill*
(Grand National) F
"The King's Night Out"
"Mexico"
"Life Should Go With a Swing"

CHARLES WINGROVE (singer)
1906 *Goodbye Sweet Marie*
(Chronophone)
1906 *Serenade from Faust*
(Chronophone)

ANONA WINN (singer)
1929 *Pathe Magazine 10*
"A Precious Thing Called Love"
1934 *On the Air*
(British Lion) F

GODFREY WINN (broadcaster)
1927 *Blighty*
(Gainsborough) F
1937 *Personality Parade*
1937 *Snuff Said*
(Ace Cinemagazine)
1956 *Eyewitness*
(Rank) F
1961 *Very Important Person*
(Rank) F
1963 *Billy Liar*
(Anglo) F
1964 *The Bargee*
(Warner) F

1966 *The Great St Trinian's Train Robbery*
(British Lion) F
1971 *Up the Chastity Belt*
(EMI) F

MAURICE WINNICK AND HIS ORCHESTRA
1930 *Piccadilly Nights*
(FBO) F
1931 *Pathetone 63*
"Sing Something Simple"
1933 *Pathe Pictorial 770*
"I Don't Want to Go to Bed"
"Roll Along Kentucky Moon"
1934 *Give Her a Ring*
(BIP) F
"Giving You the Stars"
1934 *Gay Love*
(British Lion) F
1937 *Thunder In the City*
(UA) F
1938 *Around the Town*
(British Lion) F

FLORENCE WINSTON (singer)
1928 *Laugh Clown Laugh*
(Edibellotone)

ERIC WINSTONE AND HIS BAND
1945 *Don Chicago*
(British National) F
1952 *Highlights of Radio*
(Arrow)
1955 *Eric Winstone Band Show*
(Hammer)
1956 *Eric Winstone's Stagecoach*
(Hammer)

ERIC WINSTONE AND HIS SWING QUARTETTE
1943 *Pathe Pictorial 379*

MARIUS B. WINTER (musician)
1931 *Pathetone 51*
"A Farmyard Symphony"

MARIUS B. WINTER AND HIS ORCHESTRA
1932 *Indiscretions of Eve*
(BIP) F

MYRTLE WINTER (dancer)
1932 *Pathe Pictorial 740*
"Dance of the Butterfly"

BERNIE WINTERS (comedian)
see also **MIKE AND BERNIE WINTERS**
1955 *Dollars for Sale*
(Adelphi) F
1959 *Idle on Parade*
(Columbia) F
1960 *Jazzboat*
(Columbia) F
1960 *Let's Get Married*
(Eros) F

1960 *In the Nick*
(Columbia) F
1961 *Johnny Nobody*
(Columbia) F
1962 *Play It Cool*
(Anglo) F
1970 *Simon Simon*
(Tigon) F
1979 *Confessions from the David Galaxy Affair*
(Tigon) F
1982 *Mary Millington's World Striptease Extravaganza*
(Tigon) F

JOAN WINTERS (singer)
1943 *Variety Jubilee*
(Butcher) F
"Richmond Hill"
1943 *Highlights of Variety 25*
(reissue: *Variety Jubilee*)
1945 *New Pictorial 55*

MIKE AND BERNIE WINTERS (comedy duo)
see also **BERNIE WINTERS**
1958 *6.5 Special*
(Anglo) F
1963 *The Cool Mikado*
(Baim) F
1969 *Given the Right Contacts You Can Go Anywhere*
(Lucas)

DALE WINTON (comedian)
1995 *Trainspotting*
(Figment) F

STEVIE WINWOOD (singer)
1966 *The Ghost Goes Gear*
(Pathe) F

NORA WIPP (belly dancer)
1971 *Up the Chastity Belt*
(EMI) F

THE WIRENGARDS (acrobats)
1952 *New Pictorial 360*

WISBECH MALE CHOIR
1932 *Pathe Pictorial 738*
"Sailors Chorus"
1932 *Pathe Pictorial 745*
"Heaven"

NORMAN WISDOM (comedian)
1948 *A Date With a Dream*
(Grand National) F
1953 *Trouble in Store*
(Two Cities) F
"Don't Laugh At Me"
1953 *Meet Mr Lucifer*
(Ealing) F
1954 *One Good Turn*
(Rank) F
"Please Opportunity"

1955 *As Long As They're Happy*
(Rank) F
"Don't Laugh At Me"
1955 *Man of the Moment*
(Rank) F
"Man of the Moment"
"Dream for Sale"
"Beware"
"Yodelee Yodelay"
1956 *Up in the World*
(Rank) F
"Up in the World"
"Talent"
"Boy Meets Girl"
1957 *Just My Luck*
(Rank) F
1958 *The Square Peg*
(Rank) F
1959 *Follow a Star*
(Rank) F
"Follow a Star"
"Give Me a Night in June"
"I Love You"
"Early One Morning"
"I'll Sing You a Song"
"You Deserve a Medal for That"
"The Square Song"
"I Want to Go to Heaven for the
Weekend"
1960 *The Bulldog Breed*
(Rank) F
1960 *There Was a Crooked Man*
(UA) F
1961 *The Girl On the Boat*
(UA) F
1962 *On the Beat*
(Rank) F
1963 *A Stitch in Time*
(Rank) F
1965 *The Early Bird*
(Rank) F
1966 *The Sandwich Man*
(Rank) F
1966 *Press for Time*
(Rank) F
1969 *What's Good for the Goose*
(Tigon) F
1992 *Double X*
(String of Pearls) F

ERNIE WISE
see **ERIC MORECAMBE AND ERNIE WISE**

LEON WOIZIKOWSKI BALLET
1935 *She Shall Have Music*
(Twickenham) F
1936 *A Woman Alone*
(UA) F

GENE WOLFF (bass-baritone)
1934 *Pathe Pictorial 835*
"Wagon Wheels"

THE WONDERFUL WORLD (group)
1996 *Glastonbury: The Movie*
(Starlight) F
"Danger Zone"
"Three Days in the Country"
"Bicycle Song"

EVA MAY WONG (juggler)
1940 *Pathe Pictorial 209*

BARBARA WOOD (dancer)
1936 *Pathe Pictorial NS 19*
1938 *Pathe Pictorial NS 138*
"I've Got a Feeling You're Fooling"

BRENTON WOOD (singer)
1968 *Popdown*
(New Realm) F

EDNA WOOD (song and dance)
1936 *Bottle Party*
(Ace) F
1936 *Song in Soho*
(Ace) F
1937 *Windmill Revels*
(Ace) F
1937 *West End Frolics*
(Ace) F
1937 *Uptown Revue*
(Ace) F
1937 *Footlights*
(Ace) F
1938 *Swing*
(Ace) F
1938 *Two Men in a Box*
(Ace) F

HAYDN WOOD (musician)
1931 *Gaumont Sound Mirror*
1935 *The Small Man*
(Baxter) F
1946 *New Pictorial 90*
"Roses of Picardy"

SIR HENRY WOOD (conductor)
1936 *Calling the Tune*
(Phoenix) F
"Shepherds Hey"
"Ride of the Valkyries"
1938 *Pathetone 451*

JOHN WOOD (singer)
1937 *Over She Goes*
(ABPC) F
"I Breathe on Windows"
"Side By Side"
"Country Wedding"
1938 *Hold My Hand*
(ABPC) F
"As Long As I Can Look At You"
"Spring Time"
"Hold My Hand"

VICTORIA WOOD (comedienne)
1982   *The Secret Policeman's Other Ball*
(UIP) F
"I've Had It Up To Here With Men"
1996   *The Wind in the Willows*
(Allied) F

WEE GEORGIE WOOD (comedian)
1919   *Convict 99*
(Samuelson) F
1928   *Two Little Drummer Boys*
(Samuelson) F
1930   *The Black Hand Gang*
(BIP) F
1936   *Variety Parade*
(Butcher) F
1971   *Top of the Bill*
(Butcher) F

WENDY WOOD (singer)
1932   *Gaumont Sound Mirror 69*

CORBET WOODALL (television personality)
1973   *Don't Just Lie There, Say
Something!*
(Rank) F
1978   *Carry On Emmanuelle*
(Hemdale) F
1979   *The World Is Full of Married Men*
(New Realm) F

ERIC WOODBURN (baritone)
1934   *Pathe Pictorial 866*
"Legion of the Lost"
1934   *Pathe Pictorial 872*
"Coaling"
1935   *Pathe Pictorial 911*
"Boots Boots"
1936   *Pictorial Revue*
F (reissue: *Pictorial 866*)
1936   *Digging for Gold*
(Ace) F
1936   *Full Steam*
(Ace) F
1936   *Bottle Party*
(Ace) F
1936   *Piccadilly Playtime*
(Ace) F
1937   *West End Frolics*
(Ace) F
1937   *Uptown Revue*
(Ace) F
1937   *Footlights*
(Ace) F
1938   *Swing*
(Ace) F
1938   *Two Men in a Box*
(Ace) F
1939   *Pathetone 468*
"La Marseillaise"
1939   *Pathetone 489*
"Texas Dan"
1941   *Pathe Pictorial 276*
"Peeping Tom"

1942   *Pathetone Parade of 1942*
F (reissue: *Pathetone 408*)
1952   *You're Only Young Twice*
(ABFD) F

TOMMY WOODROOFFE (broadcaster)
1939   *Sword of Honour*
(Butcher) F
1943   *The Volunteer*
(Archers) F

MIDDLETON WOODS (comedian)
1931   *Ideal Cinemagazine 288*

TERRY WOODS
see **RON KAVANA AND TERRY WOODS**

GYPSY WOOLF (singer)
1907   *Navaho*
(Chronophone)

GLYN WORSNIP (television personality)
1967   *I Like Birds*
(Border) F

PEREGRINE WORSTHORNE (journalist)
1967   *Tell Me Lies*
(Ronorus) F

PLOTEN J WORTH (violin)
1933   *Ideal Cinemagazine 385*
"The Swan"

JOHNNY WORTHY AND BERTIE JARRETT
(song and dance)
1946   *Walking On Air*
(Piccadilly) F
"Walking On Air"
"Harlem Jamboree"
"I Don't Know How to Swing"
"St Louis Blues"
"Carolina"
"Honeysuckle Rose"
"Solitude"
"Ain't She Sweet?"
"Basin Street Blues"
"Frankie and Johnny"

ALFRED WRIGHT AND COMPANY
(comedy)
1941   *Bob's Your Uncle*
(Butcher) F

BELINDA WRIGHT (ballerina)
1953   *The Nutcracker*
(Group 3)
1970   *The Nutcracker Suite*
(Carlyle)

BERT WRIGHT (juggler)
1940   *Pathe Pictorial 224*

HAL WRIGHT AND HIS CIRCUS
1938   *Calling All Crooks*
(Mancunian) F

HARRY WRIGHT (comedian)
  1923   *Early Birds*
         (Brouett)
  1923   *Mumming Birds*
         (Brouett)
  1923   *Jail Birds*
         (Brouett)

HUNTLY WRIGHT (comedian)
  1926   *Eve's Film Review 275*

JULIA WRIGHT (singer)
  1971   *Dr Jekyll and Sister Hyde*
         (Hammer) F

LAWRENCE WRIGHT (composer)
  1938   *Pathe Pictorial NS 122*
         "I'm Saving the Last Waltz for You"

STEVE WRIGHT (disc jockey)
  1994   *Funny Man*
         (Nomad) F

JOHN WRIGHT'S MARIONETTES
  1949   *Britannia Mews*
         (TCF) F

BEN WRIGLEY (comedian)
  1949   *Melody in the Dark*
         (Adelphi) F
  1949   *High Jinks in Society*
         (Adelphi) F

BILL WYMAN (musician)
see also **THE ROLLING STONES**
  1987   *Eat the Rich*
         (Comic Strip) F

BRUCE WYNDHAM (broadcaster)
  1976   *Not Now Comrade*
         (EMI) F

STOCK WYNN (entertainer)
  1938   *More Than Positive*
         (Ace Cinemagazine)

WISH WYNNE (child impersonator)
  1930   *Pathe Magazine 37*
  1931   *Gaumont Sound Mirror*

MARK WYNTER (singer)
  1963   *Just For Fun*
         (Columbia) F
         "Just For Fun"
         "Vote for Me"
         "Happy with You"
  1964   *Just For You*
         (British Lion) F
  1969   *Haunted House of Horror*
         (Tigon) F
         "Responsibility"
  1975   *Red*
         (TCF) F

Yana

X (group)
1981 *Urgh! A Music War*
(White) F
"Beyond and Back"

X-PRODUCTIONS (group)
1996 *Glastonbury: The Movie*
(Starlight) F
"Pretty Pictures"

XENIA AND ASHTON (dancers)
1930 *Eve's Film Review 494*

XENIA AND BOYER (dancers)
1937 *The Minstrel Boy*
(Butcher) F
"Tango Town"

XTC (group)
1981 *Urgh! A Music War*
(White) F
"Respectable Street"

YACHT CLUB BOYS (American comedy)
1934 *Pathetone 240*
"Madame You're Lovely"
"We're Glad to Be in London"

YANA (singer)
1955 *The Cockleshell Heroes*
(Columbia) F
"The London I Love"
1955 *The Ship That Died of Shame*
(Ealing) F
"We'll Meet Again"
1957 *Zarak*
(Columbia) F
"Climb Up the Wall"
1957 *Interpol*
(Columbia) F

THE YARDBIRDS (group)
1967 *Blow-Up*
(MGM) F
"Stroll On"

HAL YATES (singer)
1936 *Pathetone 352*
"My Blue Heaven"
1937 *Pathetone 365*
"Serenade in the Night"
1938 *Pathe Pictorial NS 135*
"The World Is Waiting for the Sunrise"
1940 *Pathe Pictorial 243*
"I Hear You Calling Me"

HAL YATES AND COOPER LAWLEY
(singers)
1933 *Pathetone 182*
"The Grass Is Getting Greener"
1933 *Pathe Pictorial 816*
"When Irish Eyes Are Smiling"

TOMMY YEARDYE (singer)
1960 *Climb Up the Wall*
(New Realm) F

YES (group)
1973 *Yessongs*
(Fair) F
"All Good People"
"The Clap"
"Roundabout"
"Yours Is No Disgrace"
"Wurm"
"Close to the Edge"

YOLANDE, ELVA AND DOROTHY (dancers)
1938 *Pathe Pictorial NS 131*

TRACEY YORKE (striptease)
1968 *Strip Poker*
(Miracle) F

YORKE AND BRIAN (singers)
1932 *Pathe Pictorial 754*
"Let's Drift Away to Dreamer's Bay"

ARTHUR YOUNG (pianist)
1934 *Radio Parade of 1935*
(BIP) F
1935 *Pity the Poor Rich*
(ABFD)

ARTHUR YOUNG AND GEOFFREY GAUNT
(pianists)
1928 *Phototone 13*
"Piano Duet"

DAN YOUNG (comedian)
1932 *The New Hotel*
(PDC) F
1935 *Off the Dole*
(Mancunian) F
1936 *Dodging the Dole*
(Mancunian) F
1937 *Music Hall Personalities 1*
(reissue: *Dodging the Dole*)
1938 *Calling All Crooks*
(Mancunian) F
1939 *Highlights of Variety 13; 15; 18*
(reissue: *Off the Dole; Dodging the Dole; Calling All Crooks*)
1940 *Somewhere in England*
(Mancunian) F
1942 *Somewhere in Camp*
(Mancunian) F
1942 *Somewhere on Leave*
(Mancunian) F
1944 *Demobbed*
(Mancunian) F
1946 *Under New Management*
(Mancunian) F
1948 *Honeymoon Hotel*
(reissue: *Under New Management*)
1948 *Cup Tie Honeymoon*
(Mancunian) F

1948 *Holidays With Pay*
(Mancunian) F
1949 *School for Randle*
(Mancunian) F
1950 *Over the Garden Wall*
(Mancunian) F
1953 *It's a Grand Life*
(Mancunian) F
1960 *Teacher's Pest*
(reissue: *School for Randle*)
1960 *The Three Who Flungs*
(reissue: *School for Randle*)
1960 *Bella's Birthday*
(Mancunian) (reissue: *School for Randle*)
1960 *Tonight's the Nite*
(reissue: *Holidays With Pay*)

DOUGLAS YOUNG
see **NAN KENWAY AND DOUGLAS YOUNG**

FRITZ YOUNG
see **EMILIE SELLS AND FRITZ YOUNG**

JIMMY YOUNG (singer and disc jockey)
1951 *Lady Godiva Rides Again*
(London) F
1968 *Otley*
(Columbia) F

1973 *Radio Wonderful*
(Goodtimes) F

MURIEL YOUNG (television personality)
1959 *"I'm All Right Jack"*
(British Lion) F

THE YOUNG CHINA TROUPE (jugglers)
1952 *Meet Me Tonight*
(GFD) F

YOUNGMAN AND HIS CZARDAS BAND
1938 *Pathe Pictorial NS 121*

IGOR YOUSKEVITCH (dancer)
1956 *Invitation to the Dance*
(MGM) F

THE YUK CHINGS (Chinese acrobats)
1939 *Pathe Pictorial NS 148*

YVETTE (dancer)
1932 *The First Mrs Fraser*
(Sterling) F

YVONNE (acrobatic dancer)
1944 *Pathe Pictorial 407*

FRANK ZAPPA (singer)
1971 *200 Motels*
(UA) F

NICHOLAS ZEFF (strong man)
1939 *Pathe Pictorial NS 151*

BENJAMIN ZEPHANIAH (Reggae performer)
1988 *Time and Judgement*
(Ceddo) F

THE ZEPHYRS (group)
1965 *Be My Guest*
(Rank) F
"She Laughed"

ANNE ZIEGLER (soprano)
1935 *Pathetone 294*
"I Give My Heart"
1936 *Pathetone 318*
"A Song in the Night"
1936 *Faust Fantasy*
(Publicity) F
1936 *Chinese Cabaret*
(Bijou) F
1944 *Demobbed*
(Mancunian) F

"So Deep Is the Night"
"Love's Old Sweet Song"
"I Hear You Calling Me"
"Until"
1945 *Waltz Time*
(British National) F
"You Will Return to Vienna"
1946 *The Laughing Lady*
(British National) F
"Laugh at Life"
"Love Is the Key"

ZOLA BROTHERS (clowns)
1949 *Horsecapades*
(GFD)
1949 *Sawdust Cabaret*
(GFD)

THE ZOMBIES (group)
1965 *Bunny Lake Is Missing*
(Columbia) F
"Just Out of Reach"

ZURA (group)
1996 *Glastonbury: The Movie*
(Starlight) F
"Wanna Dan"
"Ruftek Wiggle"

1 2 3 4 5 6 7	RONALD FRANKAU
007	THE BODYSNATCHERS
8.50 Choo Choo, The	ANNE SHELTON
10.15 Saturday Night	THE CURE
12th Caller	CABBAGE HEAD
42nd Street	TURNER TWINS
'51 Is Going To Be a Good Year	THE WHO
1812 Overture	DEBROY SOMERS AND HIS BAND
1919 March	KENNY BALL AND HIS JAZZMEN

A

ABC Song, The	
	FRANCIS LANGFORD'S SINGING SCHOLARS
Abide With Me *(1948)*	EVELYN McCABE
Abide With Me *(1949)*	JOSEF LOCKE
Absent Friends	ROBERT ASHLEY
Absolute Beginners	DAVID BOWIE
Accidents Will Happen	PATSY ANN NOBLE
Ach So Fromm	JAN KIEPURA
Acid Queen	TINA TURNER
Acrobatic Waltz	MARQUE AND MARQUETE
Across the Great Divide	
	BIG BILL CAMPBELL AND HIS ROCKY
	MOUNTAINEERS
Across the Universe	THE BEATLES
Act Naturally	THE BEATLES
Adeline	ELLA SHIELDS
Adios Muchachos	
	GERALDO AND HIS GAUCHO TANGO ORCHESTRA
Adventures of Bunny	LEONARD HENRY
Ae Fond Kiss	TREFOR JONES
Afgar	ALICE DELYSIA
Africana, L'	BENJAMINO GIGLI
After All That	THE WESTERN BROTHERS
After All These Years	JESSIE MATTHEWS
After Dark	VAUDEVILLE GIRLS
After the Ball *(1932)*	ELSA LANCHESTER
After the Ball *(1936)*	STANLEY LUPINO
After the Ball *(1957)*	PAT (PATRICIA) KIRKWOOD
After the Rain	VERA LYNN
After the War	RONALD FRANKAU
After Tomorrow	THE COCKNEYS
After Tonight We Say Goodbye	GRACIE FIELDS
After You've Gone	CHARLIE KUNZ
Ah Me Ah My	THE STRAWBS
A-hunting We Will Go	TWELVE JACKSON GIRLS
Aida	JAN KIEPURA
Ain't It Nice?	ELGA COLLINS
Ain't Misbehavin' *(1930)*	TEDDY BROWN
Ain't Misbehavin' *(1934)*	
	DEBROY SOMERS AND HIS BAND
Ain't She Dainty?	CICELY COURTNEIDGE
Ain't She Sweet? *(1926)*	
	DICK HENDERSON (senior)
Ain't She Sweet? *(1946)*	
	JOHNNY WORTHY AND BERTIE JARRETT
Ain't She Sweet? *(1946)*	
	LAUDERIC CATON AND HIS RHYTHM SWINGTETTE
Ain't This the Life	OINGO BOINGO
Air Raid *(2 films)*	FOUR ACES
Airs and Graces	GASTON AND ANDREE
Aladdin	CHARLES AUSTIN; CLARICE MAYNE
Albert and the Lion *(1935)*	STANLEY HOLLOWAY
Albert and the Lion *(1942)*	MARRIOTT EDGAR

Ale Old Ale	TOMMY TRINDER
Alexander's Ragtime Band *(1913)*	
	SIR SEYMOUR HICKS
Alexander's Ragtime Band *(1913)*	
	ELLALINE TERRISS
Algy the Piccadilly Johnnie	
	PAT (PATRICIA) KIRKWOOD
Alice Blue Gown	SEVEN ELLIOTTS
All at Once	CLIFF RICHARD
All By Myself	LORRAE DESMOND
All for a Shilling a Day	CICELY COURTNEIDGE
All for One	CLIFF RICHARD
All God's Chillun	KENTUCKY SINGERS
All Good People	YES
All Hope Is Ended	RICHARD TAUBER
All I Do Is Dream of You	CHARLIE KUNZ
All I Want Is You *(1964)*	JOHNNY LEYTON
All I Want Is You *(1970)*	THE BEATLES
All I Want To Do Is Sing	
	MR ACKER BILK AND THE PARAMOUNT JAZZ BAND
All in Favour	GEORGE ELRICK
All in the Name of Economy	TOMMY STEELE
All Jolly Pirates	
	JACK PAYNE AND HIS DANCE ORCHESTRA
All Kinds of People	CLIFF RICHARD
All Over Italy	THREE ADMIRALS
All Over the Place	THREE GINX; TOMMY TRINDER
All Over the World	HERMAN'S HERMITS
All Pull Together	CAROL RAYE
All Scotch	NORAH BLANEY
All the Nice Girls Love a Sailor *(1933)*	
	ARTHUR PRINCE AND JIM
All the Nice Girls Love a Sailor *(1970)*	
	HETTY KING
All the Stars in the Sky	THE TORNADOS
All the Time	ROY CASTLE
All the World Loves a Fat Girl	TERRY DAY
All the Young Dudes	DAVID BOWIE
All the Young Punks	THE CLASH
All Things Bright and Beautiful	
	GRIMETHORPE COLLIERY BAND
All Those in Favour of Swing	JOY CONWAY
All Through the Night *(1931)*	
	GLANHOWY SINGERS
All Through the Night *(1939; 2 films)*	
	PAUL ROBESON; WELSH LADIES CHOIR
All Through the Night *(1953)*	
	LONDON WELSH ASSOCIATION CHORAL SOCIETY
All Through the Year	
	HY HAZELL; HARRY SECOMBE
All You Gotta Do Is Touch Me	BOBBY VEE
All You Need Is Love	THE BEATLES
Alley Alley O	FRANKIE VAUGHAN
Alma Llamera	
	ISABELITA ALONSO AND MILO AMADO
	ESTUDIANTINA
Almost a Musician	EDWIN STYLES
Aloha Oe *(1930)*	GAINSBOROUGH GIRLS
Aloha Oe *(1935)*	
	RUDY STARITA AND HIS MARIMBA BAND
Aloha Oe *(1936)*	AMBROSE AND HIS ORCHESTRA
Aloha Oe *(1939)*	AL SHAW
Aloha Oe *(1944)*	DAPHNE DAY
Aloha Oe *(1952; 2 films)*	
	MARIE DE VERE DANCERS; FELIX MENDELSSOHN
	AND HIS HAWAIIAN SERENADERS

Aloha Waikiki

HALLAM HAWAIIAN GUITAR PLAYERS

Aloma

FELIX MENDELSSOHN AND HIS HAWAIIAN SERENADERS

Alone and Afraid — ELSIE CARLISLE
Alone With My Dreams — JACK BUCHANAN
Alouette — JEAN CAVALL
Altogether Now — THE BEATLES
Always — ROBERT WILSON
Always on My Mind — PET SHOP BOYS
Am I What I Was? — TRAFFIC
Amanda — TOMMY STEELE
Amazing Journey — PETE TOWNSHEND
Ambush at Mystery Rock — JOE STRUMMER
Americana Stray Cat Blues — DAVID ESSEX
Amor Navigo — DON AZPIAZU AND HIS BAND
Amore Baciami — PAT BOONE
Anarchy in the UK (1980) — THE SEX PISTOLS
Anarchy in the UK (1986)

GLEN MATLOCK; ANDREW SCHOFIELD

And I Love Her — THE BEATLES
And Me — CLIFF RICHARD
And So Do I — CAVENDISH THREE
And So Would I — TESSIE O'SHEA
Andy the Handy Man — GEORGE FORMBY
Angel Face — GLITTER BAND
Angelino Piccolino — EVE BECKE
Anima-e-Care

WINSTON LEE AND HIS ORCHESTRA

Anna from Anacapresi — GRACIE FIELDS
Annie Laurie (1930) — JOSEPH HISLOP
Annie Laurie (1933) — JACK HODGES
Annie Laurie (1937) — ROBERT WILSON
Annie Laurie (1943) — BILL SMITH
Annie Laurie (1944) — WALTER MIDGELEY
Another Girl — THE BEATLES
Another Little Drink — CHESTER TUNIS
Another Misunderstanding — ABE AND MAWRUSS
Another Tear Falls — GENE McDANIELS
Another Track — JACK SIMPSON
Anti-Brotherhood of Man, The — CLIFF RICHARD
Any Broken Hearts to Mend

SANDY MacPHERSON

Any Old Iron (2 films: 1936, 1941)

HARRY CHAMPION

Any Old Iron (1946) — SID FIELD; TESSIE O'SHEA
Any Old Iron (1968; 2 films)

LANCE PERCIVAL; JOHN RUTLAND

Any Time at All — THE BEATLES
Any Time's Kissing Time — GEORGE ROBEY
Any Way the Wind Blows

SID FIELD; SCOTTY (ALASTAIR) McHARG

Anybody Can Dance

DARVILLE AND SHIRES; JOAN DAVIS DANCERS; THREE MAXWELLS

Anyone Can Be a Millionaire — JOHNNY BRANDON
Anyway Anyhow Anywhere (2 films) — THE WHO
Apple Honey — THE SQUADRONNAIRES
Aren't We All? — THE WESTERN BROTHERS
Arf a Pint of Ale — JOHN RORKE
Argentine Tango (1928)

SANTOS CASANI AND JOSE LENNARD; PHYLLIS HAYLOR AND ALEC MILLAR; MR AND MRS VICTOR SILVESTER

Argentine Tango (1930)

RAMON CORTEZ AND FLORA HARTE

Army, The — ROBB WILTON
Army of Today's All Right, The (1952)

TWELVE JACKSON GIRLS

Army of Today's All Right, The (1957)

PAT (PATRICIA) KIRKWOOD

Around and About — CHARLIE KUNZ
A-Roving — GERRARD QUARTET
Art's Theme

ART BAXTER AND HIS ROCKIN' SINNERS

As I Take My Morning Promenade — JANE CARR
As Long As He Needs Me — SHANI WALLIS
As Long As I Can Look At You

POLLY WARD; JOHN WOOD

As the World Falls Down — DAVID BOWIE
Asher Bara — RAY McVAY BAND
Ask a Policeman — THE BARBOUR BROTHERS
Asleep in the Deep — EMMANUEL LIST
Asp — PETER COOK
At a Time Like This — BOBBY VEE
At Dawning (1928) — AL STARITA
At Dawning (1945) — HEDDLE NASH
At Gretna Green

CARROLL GIBBONS AND HIS ORCHESTRA; WILFRED TEMPLE

At Home — NAN KENWAY AND DOUGLAS YOUNG
At Sundown — TROISE AND HIS BANJOLIERS
At the Bar — COLLINSON AND DEAN
At the Bathing Parade — MAX MILLER
At the Dawning of the Day — JOHN McCORMACK
At the End of the Day

LITTLEWOODS' GIRLS CHOIR

At Trinity Church — TOM COSTELLO
'At's a Nice Ats' 'At 'At Is — JACK WARNER
Au Revoir — BENNETT AND WILLIAMS
Au Revoir Dear Old Pal — BUD FLANAGAN
Auf Wiedersehen (2 films)

GRETA KELLER; STANELLI AND EDGAR

Auld Lang Syne (1929) — SIR HARRY LAUDER
Auld Lang Syne (1930) — JOSEPH HISLOP
Auld Lang Syne (1936)

SYD SEYMOUR AND HIS MAD HATTERS

Auld Lang Syne (1941) — GRANT TYLER
Aunt Flo

BOB WALLIS AND HIS STORYVILLE JAZZ MEN

Auntie Maggie's Remedy — GEORGE FORMBY
Auntie's Got Ants in Her Pants — LOUIS DE VRIES
Aurora's Wedding

MARGOT FONTEYN; RUDOLPH NUREYEV

Autobahn — TONY KINSEY QUARTET
Autumn Lake — LED ZEPPELIN
Autumn Leaves

WALFORD HYDEN AND HIS MAGYAR ORCHESTRA

Autumn Sunshine

ALFREDO CAMPOLI AND REGINALD KING

Avalanche — LEONARD COHEN
Ave Maria (1934; 2 films)

JAN KIEPURA; DEREK OLDHAM

Ave Maria (1935; 2 films)

THOMAS (TOM) BURKE; DEREK OLDHAM

Ave Maria (1949) — JOSEF LOCKE
Ave Maria (1953) — PATRICE MUNSEL

Ave Maria *(1959)*
NATIONAL YOUTH ORCHESTRA; FRANKIE VAUGHAN
Awake Awake   LENI LYNN
Away in Killarney   THREE AUSTRALIAN BOYS
Ay Ay Ay Ay   TOMMY TRINDER

B

Baba O'Riley   THE WHO
Babes in the Wood   DOLLY SISTERS
Babies On Parade
ARTHUR ROSEBERY'S SWINGTETTE
Baby   HARRY HUDSON AND HIS BAND
Baby Let Me Take You Home   THE ANIMALS
Baby Lover   PETULA CLARK
Baby Strange   MARC BOLAN AND T. REX
Baby That's All   THE HOLLIES
Baby Whatcha Gonna Do Tonight?
LILLI PALMER
Baby You're So Good to Me
GERRY AND THE PACEMAKERS
Baby's View   GLADYS MERREDEW
Bachelor Boy   CLIFF RICHARD; THE SHADOWS
Bachelor Gay Am I, A   HARRY WELCHMAN
Bacio, Il   MAX GELDRAY
Back Answers   ROBB WILTON
Back Door Man   THE BLUES BAND
Back in the USSR *(1979)*   ELTON JOHN
Back in the USSR *(1991)*
PAUL AND LINDA McCARTNEY
Bad Reputation   JOAN JETT
Ball Dancer, The   LINDSAY KEMP
Ballad of Lucy Jordan, The
MARIANNE FAITHFULL
Ballet Egyptienne   WILSON, KEPPEL AND BETTY
Ballet from Faust   LOCARNO FOUR
Balling the Jack   JIMMY JEWEL
Balloon Goes Up, The
ETHEL REVNELL AND GRACIE WEST
Ballroom Dancing *(1929)*
SANTOS CASANI AND JOSE LENNARD
Ballroom Dancing *(1984)*
LINDA McCARTNEY; PAUL McCARTNEY; RINGO STARR
Balmoral Melody   MURRAY CAMPBELL
Baltimore Dance   BARRIE OLIVER
Band Master's Daughter, The   BETTY CHESTER
Band on the Run   PAUL AND LINDA McCARTNEY
Band That Jack Built, The
JACK HYLTON AND HIS BAND
Band Waggon   JACK HYLTON AND HIS BAND
Banjo On My Knee   TROISE AND HIS BANJOLIERS
Banshee, The   JOHN PAYNE'S CHOIR
Barbara Ann   THE WHO
Barbarian, The   EMERSON, LAKE AND PALMER
Barcarolle   ALBERT SANDLER
Bargee, The   GERALD NODIN
Barmaid at the Rose and Crown, The
GEORGE FORMBY
Barrers in the Walworth Road, The
NORMAN LONG
Barrow Song, The   JACK HODGES
Basin Street Blues
JOHNNY WORTHY AND BERTIE JARRETT
Bats in the Belfry   BILLY MAYERL

Battle, The   JACK BUCHANAN
B.B.C. Gardening Expert   C H MIDDLETON
Be Like the Kettle and Sing   VERA LYNN
Be My Guest *(1955)*   JERRY WAYNE
Be My Guest *(1965)*   THE NITESHADES
Beale Street Blues
KENNY BALL AND HIS JAZZMEN
Beat Girl   THE JOHN BARRY SEVEN
Beat of a Brother Heart, The   JOHNNY LEYTON
Beat of the Drum, The   EIGHT MASTERSINGERS
Beauty Prize, The
DOROTHY DICKSON; LESLIE HENSON
Because   FRANK TITTERTON
Bee Song, The *(2 films)*   ARTHUR ASKEY
Bee's Wedding, The
FRANK WALKER AND HIS B.B.C. OCTET
Beer Barrel Polka   THREE VIRGINIANS
Beethoven's Fifth Symphony
LONDON PHILHARMONIC ORCHESTRA
Beethoven's Piano Concerto
NATIONAL YOUTH ORCHESTRA
Before We Met   GITTA ALPAR
Before We Say Goodnight   MARY STEELE
Beggar's Opera, The   FREDERICK RANALOW
Behold Behold   MALCOLM MacEACHERN
Believe It Beloved   PAT O'MALLEY
Believe It Or Not   JACK AND DAPHNE BARKER
Believe Me I'm Quite Sincere
JAMILLA NOVOTNA; HARRY WELCHMAN
Bell Bottom George   GEORGE FORMBY
Bell Bottom Trousers   HAL MONTY
Belle of New York, The   DOROTHY WARD
Belle with the Bells, The   ANNA MAC
Bellissima
BOB WALLIS AND HIS STORYVILLE JAZZ MEN
Bells Across the Meadow   REGINALD STONE
Bells of Aberdovy   WELSH LADIES CHOIR
Bells of St Mary's, The *(1932)*
MUSICAL DAWSON AND HIS CANARY CHOIR
Bells of St Mary's, The *(1933)*   REYMOS
Bells of St Mary's, The *(1939)*
GERRY FITZGERALD
Belsen Was a Gas   THE SEX PISTOLS
Bench Beneath the Tree, A
THE HOUSTON SISTERS
Bend It   DAVE DEE, DOZY, BEAKY, MICK AND TICH
Benedictus   THE STRAWBS
Bermondsey Bounce   HUMPHREY LYTTELTON
Bernie's Holiday Camp   THE WHO
Bert the Bosun   FRANK WIGNALL
Besame Mucho   THE BEATLES
Best Show in Town, The   PATTI BOULAYE
Best Things in Life, The   CHILI BOUCHIER
Better Off Dead   ELTON JOHN
Betty in Mayfair   EVELYN LAYE
Betty Slow Drag   DINAH KAYE
Between You and Me and the Carpet
FRANCES DAY; ARTHUR RISCOE
Beware   NORMAN WISDOM
Beyond and Back   X
Biceps Muscle and Brawn   GEORGE FORMBY
Bicycle Made For Two, A   GRANT TYLER
Bicycle Song   THE WONDERFUL WORLD
Biddy Mulligan   JIMMY O'DEA
Big Apple   EARL AND JOSEPHINE LEACH

Big Brother	HAZEL O'CONNOR
Big Chief Tom Tom	EVELYN DALL
Big Grand Coolie Dam	LONNIE DONEGAN
Big Hearted Arthur *(2 films)*	ARTHUR ASKEY
Big News	CLIFF RICHARD
Big Noise from Winnetka	
	GEORGE MITCHELL SWING CHOIR
Big Ship	
HENRY HALL AND THE B.B.C. DANCE ORCHESTRA	
Big Shot	THE BEAT
Big Stiff, The	ALEC HALES
Big'ead	MAX BYGRAVES
Biko	
PETER GABRIEL; YOUSSOU N'DOUR; LOU REED	
Billiards	HARRY TATE
Billy Boy *(1937)*	GERRARD QUARTET
Billy Boy *(1938)*	ROYAL NAVAL SINGERS
Billy Played His Old Trombone	
	THE TWO LESLIES
Billykins and His Dinah	BETTY FIELDS
Bird of Love Divine *(1932)*	MAVIS BENNETT
Bird of Love Divine *(1936)*	ADELE DIXON
Bird on a Wire	LEONARD COHEN
Bird Song at Eventide *(1934)*	
	WESTMINSTER ABBEY CHOIR
Bird Song at Eventide *(1938)*	MUSAIRE
Bird Song at Eventide *(1939)*	FRANK BIRD
Birdie Out of a Cage	
CICELY COURTNEIDGE; JACK HULBERT	
Birdies	PERE UBU
Birds of a Feather	RALPH READER
Birds of London Town, The	TESSIE O'SHEA
Birthday	PAUL AND LINDA McCARTNEY
Black and White	VALENTINE NONYELA
Black Arabs Medley	THE BLACK ARABS
Black Bottom	
EDWARD BLUNT AND MARGERY JACKSON;	
	MILDRED MELROSE
Black Dog	LED ZEPPELIN
Black Emperor	PAUL ROBESON
Black Eyed Susan Brown	
	SYD AND MAX HARRISON
Black Eyes *(1932)*	ALBERT SANDLER
Black Eyes *(1933)*	DE GROOT
Black Eyes *(1934)*	
ALFREDO AND HIS GYPSY BAND	
Black Eyes *(1937)*	
MANTOVANI AND HIS TIPICA ORCHESTRA	
Black Eyes *(1940)*	WALDORF BRASS QUINTET
Black Eyes *(1944)*	ROBIN RICHMOND
Black Eyes *(1948)*	ALBERT AND LES WARD
Black Girl	FOUR PENNIES
Black Ice Ballet	SONJA HENIE
Black Magic	ZAIDEE JACKSON
Black Money	CULTURE CLUB
Black Shadows	ALBERTA HUNTER
Blaze Away *(1935)*	FREDDIE SCHWEITZER
Blaze Away *(1936)*	
RAYMONDE AND HIS BANJO BAND	
Blaze Away *(1991)*	JOSEF LOCKE
Bleed For Me	THE DEAD KENNEDYS
Bless 'Em All *(1941)*	GRANT TYLER
Bless 'Em All *(1949)*	MAX BYGRAVES
Bless This House *(1943)*	HELEN HILL
Bless This House *(1945)*	DAVID DAVIES

Bless You *(1935)*	DEREK OLDHAM
Bless You *(1947)*	
IVOR MORETON AND DAVE KAYE	
Bless You for Being an Angel	CHARLIE KUNZ
Blind Corner	RONNIE CARROLL
Blow the Man Down *(1946)*	OSCAR NATZKE
Blow the Man Down *(1955)*	ROSE ALBA
Blow Your Head	PAT LEACOCK
Blue Again	STOKES AND HOLLOWAY
Blue Beat	THE TORNADOS
Blue Danube, The *(1931)*	
ALFREDO AND HIS GYPSY BAND	
Blue Danube, The *(1932; 2 films)*	
ALFRED RODE AND HIS TZIGANE BAND;	
	ST. DAVID'S SINGERS
Blue Danube, The *(1935)*	
	JACK HYLTON AND HIS BAND
Blue Danube, The *(1937)*	DENISE VANE
Blue Danube, The *(1938)*	VIENNESE SINGERS
Blue Danube, The *(1939)*	JEAN BAPTISTE TONER
Blue Danube, The *(1943)*	LESLIE JEFFRIES TRIO
Blue Danube Swing	
	BILLY COTTON AND HIS BAND
Blue Devil	KATHLEEN GIBSON
Blue Dragoons	LANCE FAIRFAX
Blue Eyes	EVELYN LAYE
Blue Mediterranean Sea	FRANCES DAY
Blue Moments	SYLVIA SARTRE
Blue Moon	RADIO THREE
Blue Nile Blues	
	WILLIAM HODGSON AND HIS BAND
Blue Rhythm	SYDNEY KYTE AND HIS BAND
Blue Roses	GEORGE CLARKE
Blue Skies	RADIO THREE
Blue Tail Fly	
CYRIL STAPLETON AND THE SHOW BAND	
Bluebells of Scotland	HERMAN DAREWSKI
Blues, The	BETTY ASTELL
Blues Knocking On My Door, The	
CHRIS BARBER AND HIS JAZZ BAND; OTTILIE	
	PATTERSON
Bluest Kind of Blues, The	
	TONY KINSEY QUARTET
Bob Song, The	VINE, MORE AND NEVARD
Bobbikins' Lullaby	MAX BYGRAVES
Bobbing Up and Down Like This	
	CHARLIE CHESTER
Bodies	THE SEX PISTOLS
Body and Soul	
AMBROSE AND HIS ORCHESTRA; SAM BROWNE	
Bohème, La	EVELYN LAYE
Bohemian Memories	
BILLY REID AND THE LONDON ACCORDION BAND;	
	LONDON ACCORDION BAND
Boiled Beef and Carrots	JOHN RUTLAND
Bond Street	TED HEATH AND HIS MUSIC
Bongo Blues	THE SHADOWS
Bonnie Mary of Argyle	ROBERT WILSON
Bonnie Wee Thing *(1930)*	JOSEPH HISLOP
Bonnie Wee Thing *(1947)*	TREFOR JONES
Boo Hoo	PHYLLIS ROBINS
Boodle	JUNE
Boogie Bash	IVOR MORETON AND DAVE KAYE
Boogie Woogie Moonshine	ANNA NEAGLE
Boogiest Band in Town	SLIK

Boom STAN WHITE
Boomps-a-Daisy
JACK HYLTON AND HIS BAND, PAT (PATRICIA)
KIRKWOOD
Boots Boots (1932) ROBERT EASTON
Boots Boots (1935) ERIC WOODBURN
Border Ballad
GLASGOW PHILHARMONIC MALE VOICE CHOIR
Born With a Smile on My Face
STEPHANIE DE SYKES
Botany Bay SHIRLEY ABICAIR
Bottleneck TOADSTOOL
Bouncing Baby, A BILLY MERSON
Bound for the Rio Grande
ROYAL NAVAL SINGERS
Bow Wow THE CO-OPTIMISTS
Boy for Sale HARRY SECOMBE
Boy I Love, The HELEN SHAPIRO
Boy Meets Girl (1942)
PERCIVAL MACKEY AND HIS BAND
Boy Meets Girl (1956) NORMAN WISDOM
Boy Meets Girl (1958)
DON LANG AND HIS FRANTIC FIVE
Boy Needs a Girl, A JOHNNY LEYTON
Boy on the Beach, The CAROL DEENE
Boy with the Obedient Feet, The MAX WALL
Boys Don't Cry THE CURE
Brave Hearts EVELYN LAYE
Brazilly Willy MARIE DE VERE DANCERS
Bread and Cheese and Kisses LUPINO LANE
Break of Day RICHARD TAUBER
Break the News to Mother
DOUGLAS WAKEFIELD
Breath Away From Heaven, A
GEORGE HARRISON
Breton Dance IVY TRESMAND
Bright Side of Life ERIC IDLE
Bright Silvery Light of the Moon, The
RICHARD HAYWARD
Brighter Than the Sun ANNA NEAGLE
Brighton Rock
TONY CROMBIE AND HIS ROCKETS
Britain All the Way SIDNEY BURCHALL
Britain I Am With Thee BARRINGTON HOOPER
Britannia Rag WINIFRED ATWELL
Broken Doll, A ANNA NEAGLE
Broken English MARIANNE FAITHFULL
Brothers Brothers JOE BROWN
Brown Skin Girl
DICK CHARLESWORTH AND HIS CITY GENTS
Brumberger Duet CLIFF RICHARD
Bubbling Over With Love BETTY ASTELL
Buffoon (2 films) TEDDY BROWN
Bugginses, The
MABEL CONSTANDUROS; MICHAEL HOGAN
Build Up TOMMY STEELE
Bumble Bee Sting
SIR SEYMOUR HICKS; ELLALINE TERRISS
Bundle of Cheek, A TOMMY PRIOR
Burgundy Claret and Port TOMMY TRINDER
Burlington Bertie (2 films) ELLA SHIELDS
Burmese Hand Dance LAURIE DEVINE
Bus Conductor, The NORMAN LONG
Business Figures COLLINSON AND DEAN
Butcher's Love Song, A WENSLEY RUSSELL

Butterfingers TOMMY STEELE
Butterfly Song EVELYN LAYE
Butting In NAUNTON WAYNE
By Myself JUDY GARLAND
By the Fireside BOB AND ALF PEARSON
By the Side of the Zuyder Zee
MACARI AND HIS DUTCH SERENADERS
By the Way
CICELY COURTNEIDGE; JACK HULBERT
Bye and Bye VERA LYNN
Bye Bye Blackbird JOCK McKAY
Bye Bye Blues (1936) JEAN REMA
Bye Bye Blues (1938) VESTA

C

Cabaret Rhumba BERNARDI
Cabin in the Pines (1934) HARMONY KINGS
Cabin in the Pines (1935) TEDDY BROWN
Caesar's Wife FRANCES DAY
Cafe Mozart Waltz (2 films) ANTON KARAS
Cake Walk
LEWIS HARDCASTLE'S DUSKY SYNCOPATERS
California Here I Come (1937) THREE SISTERS
California Here I Come (1944)
BILLY 'UKE' SCOTT
Californian Poppy ANNA PAVLOVA
Caliope Yodel HARMONY KINGS
Call Me Home
DAGENHAM GIRL PIPERS; WILLIAM HEUGHEN
Call of Life, The ANNA NEAGLE
Call to Arms CAROL RAYE
Calling All Cars FOUR ACES
Calling All Stars
FLOTSAM AND JETSAM; LU ANNE MEREDITH
Calm Waters SCOVELL AND WHELDON
Calypso Rock 'n' Roll GEORGE BROWN
Cameron Men, The ROBERT WILSON
Camille CARL BRISSON
Caminto
GERALDO AND HIS GAUCHO TANGO ORCHESTRA
Campanella (1933) COSSACK CHOIR
Campanella (1946) YEHUDI MENUHIN
Campbells Are Coming, The (1930)
GLASGOW ORPHEUS CHOIR
Campbells Are Coming, The (1944)
TONY LOWRY AND CLIVE RICHARDSON
Camptown Races FREDDIE AND THE DREAMERS
Can Can (1931) QUENTIN AND KENNETH TOD
Can Can (1936) NOLA REID
Can-Can (1943)
DOREEN ASHTON'S JUBILEE TROUPE
Can-Can (1946)
PAULINE GRANT BALLET COMPANY
Can You Forgive Me? KARL DENVER TRIO
Can't Afford To Do It
CHRIS BARBER AND HIS JAZZ BAND; OTTILIE
PATTERSON
Can't Buy Me Love (1964) THE BEATLES
Can't Buy Me Love (1991)
PAUL AND LINDA McCARTNEY
Can't Explain THE WHO
Can't Make Love WALL OF VOODOO
Can't Stand the Pain THE PRETTY THINGS

Can't We Talk It Over?
BILLY GERHARDI AND HIS BAND
Can't You See It In My Eyes?   GENE SHELDON
Canadian Capers   TEDDY BROWN
Canary, The *(1934)*   TED RAY
Canary, The *(1947)*   BILL HALL TRIO
Candy Floss   TERRY DENE
Cannibal Pot   TOMMY STEELE
Canoe Song   PAUL ROBESON
Capito   HAL MONTY
Caprice No. 20   YEHUDI MENUHIN
Captain Jinjah   CLIFF RICHARD
Captain Mac   FOSTER RICHARDSON
Captain Walker It's a Boy   PETE TOWNSHEND
Careless Caretaker, The   SANDY POWELL
Careless Sneezer, The   CYRIL FLETCHER
Caress Me   PHYLLIS ROBINS
Carina   RAY ELLINGTON QUARTET
Carmelita
GERALDO AND HIS GAUCHO TANGO ORCHESTRA
Carmen   BENJAMINO GIGLI
Carnival Nights   LILYAN, DANIA AND MALO
Carnival of Venice   KENNY BAKER
Carnival Romain
LONDON PHILHARMONIC ORCHESTRA; MALCOLM
SARGENT
Carolina   JOHNNY WORTHY AND BERTIE JARRETT
Carolina Cotton Town Blues   BETTY LANCASTER
Carpet Crawl   GENESIS
Carranga, The   JACK BUCHANAN
Carrie From Lancasheer   HAL JONES
Carry Me Back to the Lone Prairie
MAURICE TAYLOR
Carry That Weight   PAUL AND LINDA McCARTNEY
Casbah   CLYDE VALLEY STOMPERS
Casey's Charabanc   TALBOT O'FARRELL
Cash or I'll Strip Sketch
GRAHAM CHAPMAN; PAMELA STEPHENSON
Castanero, El
JOHN STEIN AND HIS RUMBA BAND
Cat, The   THE BLUES BAND
Cat Crept In, The
BOB KERR'S WHOOPEE BAND; MUD
Cat Duet   BOBBY HOWES
Catch the Wind   DONOVAN
Catch Us If You Can   DAVE CLARK FIVE
Cavatina   JOHN WILLIAMS
Celebrating
BOBBIE AND VIRGINIA; GERALDO AND HIS
ORCHESTRA; HIPPODROME GIRLS; ANNA NEAGLE
Challenge, The   BILL McGUFFIE
Chamber Music   SYDNEY HOWARD
Champ, The   TED HEATH AND HIS MUSIC
Champagne Charlie *(1935)*   JOHN RORKE
Champagne Charlie *(1944)*   TOMMY TRINDER
Changes   DAVID BOWIE
Changing of the Guard, The *(1933)*
FLOTSAM AND JETSAM
Changing of the Guard, The *(1937)*
FLOTSAM AND JETSAM; MALCOLM MacEACHERN
Changing of the Guard, The *(1944)*
MALCOLM MacEACHERN
Charabanc Song, The   MAX MILLER
Chariot Choogle   MARC BOLAN AND T. REX

Charleston *(1925; 2 films)*
BEE JACKSON; BARBARA MILES AND MAXWELL
STEWART
Charleston *(1926; 3 films)*
PHYLLIS HAYLOR AND ALEC MILLAR; BARRIE
OLIVER; ROBERT STICKLING
Charleston *(1927)*
SANTOS CASANI AND JOSE LENNARD; RENEE
FOSTER
Charleston Blues   SANTOS CASANI
Charlie Chaplin Dance
LESLIE ROBERTS' TELEVISION GIRLS
Charlie Is My Darling   SYLVIA WELLING
Charlot's Masquerade
ANTON DOLIN; BEATRICE LILLIE
Charlotte Sometimes   THE CURE
Charm   TERRY DENE
Charm of Life   LOUISE BROWN
Charmaine   NORA SWINBURNE
Charming Chloe   IWAN DAVIES
Chasing the Moon   ERIC COATES
Che Gelida Manina   JAN KIEPURA
Cheer Up   STANLEY LUPINO
Cheerful Blues   HARRY ROY AND HIS BAND
Cheerful Little Earful   THAT CERTAIN TRIO
Cheerio   BILLY MERRIN AND HIS COMMANDERS
Chelsea Hotel   LEONARD COHEN
Cherie   GRACIE FIELDS
Cherokee *(1939)*
MAXWELL STEWART AND HIS BALLROOM MELODY
Cherokee *(1952)*   MARIE DE VERE DANCERS
Cherokee *(1960)*
DILL JONES AND HIS ALL STARS
Cherokee *(1961)*   TED HEATH AND HIS MUSIC
Cherry Ripe   MARJORIE TAYLOR
Cheryl's Going Home   JOHN OTWAY
Chicken Town   JOHN COOPER CLARKE
Children of the New Regime   RALPH READER
Children of the Revolution
MARC BOLAN AND T. REX
Chilling Down   DAVID BOWIE
Chinatown   PICKARD'S CHINESE SYNCOPATORS
Chinchilla   CLIFF RICHARD
Chinese Laundry Blues
BERYL FORMBY; GEORGE FORMBY
Chinese Nights   JACK HODGES
Chinky Blues   BILLY KAY
Choc Ice   LULU AND THE LUVVERS
Choo Choo   JACK HYLTON AND HIS BAND
Christmas   THE WHO
Christmas Day in the Cookhouse
BILLY BENNETT
Christmas Greetings to Forces Everywhere
VERA LYNN
Christmas Star   PATRICIA BREDIN
Christopher Columbus's Sister
THE ACE QUINTET
Christopher Robin   GRACIE FIELDS
Chu Chin Chow of China
MALCOLM MacEACHERN
Church of the Poison Mind   CULTURE CLUB
Churchmouse on the Spree
HENRY HALL AND THE B.B.C. DANCE ORCHESTRA
Cinderella   CLARICE MAYNE
Cinderella's Wedding   JUBILEE DUETTISTS

Cindy's Birthday
SHANE FENTON AND THE FENTONES
Cinema Show, The GENESIS
Clap, The YES
Clap Hands *(2 films)* CHARLIE KUNZ
Clarence That's My Beau DORIS HARE
Classical Overture
TOM SMITH AND HIS HARMONICA BAND
Classicitus Burlesque
BILLY REVEL AND JANE MOORE
Clear Rush SPIRITUALIZED
Climb Up the Wall YANA
Climbing Up PAUL ROBESON
Clo-Clo BILLY LEONARD
Clock on the Wall, The TONY KINSEY QUARTET
Clockwork Two Seater, The
FRANK WALKER AND HIS B.B.C. OCTET
Close to Kathy CLIFF RICHARD
Close to Me THE CURE
Close to the Edge YES
Close Your Eyes *(2 films)*
GERALDO AND HIS GAUCHO TANGO ORCHESTRA;
LESLIE A HUTCHINSON
Clouds Will Soon Roll By, The
BOB AND ALF PEARSON
Cloudy CLIFF RICHARD
Clowns in Clover *(1927)* JACK HULBERT
Clowns in Clover *(1928)*
CICELY COURTNEIDGE; JACK HULBERT
C'mon Everybody THE SEX PISTOLS
Coaling *(1934)* ERIC WOODBURN
Coaling *(1942)* URIEL PORTER
Cobwebs and Strange THE WHO
Cock o' the North PETER SINCLAIR
Cockaigne Overture *(1934)*
FINNISH NATIONAL ORCHESTRA
Cockaigne Overture *(1943)*
SIR ADRIAN BOULT; LONDON PHILHARMONIC
ORCHESTRA
Cockney Lady, A RITA BRUNSTROM
Cod Liver Oil IAN McELHINNEY
Cœur de la Vie, La JOSEPH SCHMIDT
Cohen the Crooner MAX BACON
Cold Cold Shower FRANKIE VAUGHAN
Cold Metal IGGY POP
Colinda, La
LONDON PHILHARMONIC ORCHESTRA; MALCOLM
SARGENT
Colinette *(1931; 2 films)*
RONALD FRANKAU; LEONARD GOWINGS
Collette CARL BRISSON
Colonel Bogey *(1937)*
KITKAT SAXOPHONE RASCALS
Colonel Bogey *(1938)* CLIFFORD STANTON
Colonel Bogey *(1955)* HANWELL SILVER BAND
Colonel Bogey *(1996)*
GRIMETHORPE COLLIERY BAND
Comber Ballad, The RICHARD HAYWARD
Come Again THE AU PAIRS
Come Back to Erin *(1934)* DENNIS O'NEIL
Come Back to Erin *(1937)* JOHN McCORMACK
Come Back to Erin *(1938)*
THOMAS (TOM) BURKE
Come Back to Me BENJAMINO GIGLI
Come Back to Sorrento JOSEF LOCKE
Come In and Be Loved TERRY DENE

Come Into the Air HAZEL O'CONNOR
Come Landlord
THE SALISBURY SINGERS; DALE SMITH
Come On Algernon BETTY WARREN
Come On and Love
CLIFFORD MOLLISON; ZELMA O'NEAL
Come On and Stomp HUMPHREY LYTTELTON
Come On Baby
PRINCE TWINS; HAL SWAIN AND HIS KIT KAT BAND
Come On Children SMALL FACES
Come On In THE BLUES BAND
Come On Let's Go
WAYNE GIBSON AND THE DYNAMIC SOUNDS
Come On Little Dixie
DAVE EDMUNDS AND THE STRAY CATS
Come Outside ALAN KLEIN
Come Swing With Me VAL ROSING
Come to My Arms
DIANE TODD; DICKIE VALENTINE
Come to the Happidrome HARRY KORRIS
Complete Control THE CLASH
Comin' Thro' the Rye *(1930)* JOSEPH HISLOP
Comin' Thro' the Rye *(1943)* BILL SMITH
Comin' Thro' the Rye *(1944)* WALTER MIDGELEY
Comin' Thro' the Rye *(1947)* SYLVIA WELLING
Comin' Thro' the Rye *(1953)* PATRICE MUNSEL
Coming JIMMY SOMERVILLE
Coming Round the Mountain
BIG BILL CAMPBELL AND HIS ROCKY
MOUNTAINEERS
Coming Up PAUL AND LINDA McCARTNEY
Compliments Will Get You Nowhere
WOOLF PHILLIPS AND THE SKYROCKETS
Comrades MOSCOW SINGERS
Concerto for Two JACK LEON AND HIS BAND
Concerto in A Minor EILEEN JOYCE
Concerto in D Major
LONDON SYMPHONY ORCHESTRA
Concrete Jungle THE SPECIALS
Confessions ANTHONY NEWLEY
Congo Lullabye PAUL ROBESON
Connie You're a Caution PADDY BROWNE
Considering
AL BOWLLY; ROY FOX AND HIS BAND
Convent Bells THE ASPIDISTRAS
Convoy MALCOLM MacEACHERN
Cookhouse Call
(JACK) WARNER AND (JEFF) DARNELL
Co-Op Shop, The GRACIE FIELDS
Coppelia FALLOW TWINS
Coraleen JOHN GARRICK
Cornish Rhapsody HARRIET COHEN
Coronation Bells
BAND OF THE ROYAL ARTILLERY
Coseita FLORA LE BRETON
Cosmic Dancer MARC BOLAN AND T. REX
Cossack March
FODEN'S MOTOR WORKS PRIZE BAND
Coster Rhumba EVELYN DALL
Count Your Blessings *(1950)*
LUTON GIRLS' CHOIR
Count Your Blessings *(1991)* JOSEF LOCKE
Count Your Blessings and Smile
GEORGE FORMBY

Country and Western Supersong, The
BILLY CONNOLLY
Country Wedding
STANLEY LUPINO; JOHN WOOD
County Clare   ROBERT ASHLEY
Court Room Sketch
GRAHAM CHAPMAN; JOHN CLEESE; PETER COOK;
TERRY JONES; MICHAEL PALIN
Courtin'   JACK PARNELL
Cousin Kevin   THE WHO
Cows and Fishes   GLADYS MERREDEW
Cracked Actor   DAVID BOWIE
Crawl Home   CABBAGE HEAD
Crazy Baldhead BOB MARLEY AND THE WAILERS
Crazy Crazes   KENNY LYNCH
Crazy Horse Saloon, The   JOHNNY LEYTON
Crazy Little Mixed Up Heart
JEAN (JEANNIE) CARSON
Crazy People
TERENCE McGOVERN AND HIS NOVELTY
ORCHESTRA
Crazy with Love   JACK BUCHANAN
Crest of a Wave (2 films)   RALPH READER
Crippled Inside   JOHN LENNON
Crocodile Crawl, The
KEN MacINTOSH AND HIS BAND
Crocodile Rock   ELTON JOHN
Crocodile Tears   HARRY GREEN
Crooner, The   RONALD FRANKAU
Crooners' Corner
BILLY BISSETT AND HIS CANADIAN BAND
Crosshands Boogie   THUNDERCLAP JONES
Crown of the Year   ALFREDO TOMASINI
Crown Prince of Arcadia, A   CARL BRISSON
Cruise Minded Women   WALSH AND BARKER
Cry   JACK BUCHANAN
Cry Upon My Shoulder   DICKIE BENNETT
Cry Wolf   FRANK IFIELD
Cuban Moonlight
RUDY STARITA AND HIS MARIMBA BAND
Cuban Pete   FRANK KING AND HIS ORCHESTRA
Cuban Rhythm   CORTEZ AND PEGGY
Cubana   JOSE NORMAN AND HIS RUMBEROS
Cumparsita, La (1928)
DE VINARAN, ORLOFF AND CASADO
Cumparsita, La (1933)
BERNARD MONSHIN AND HIS RIO TANGO BAND
Cumparsita, La (1950)
GERALDO AND HIS ORCHESTRA
Cup of Coffee, A   SCOVELL AND WHELDON
Curfew Time   J. H. SQUIRE'S CELESTE OCTET
Cut   THE CURE
Czardas   ALBERT SANDLER
Czechoslovakian Love   BOBBY HOWES

D

Daddy Wouldn't Buy Me a Bow-Wow (1934)
JESSIE MATTHEWS
Daddy Wouldn't Buy Me a Bow-Wow (1937)
BINKIE STUART
Daisy Bell (1932)
BILLY REID AND THE LONDON ACCORDION BAND
Daisy Bell (1937)   ARTHUR TRACY
Daisy Bell (1952)   THE HEDLEY WARD TRIO

Dance   TOYAH WILLCOX
Dance Around in Your Bones   THREE EDDIES
Dance Dolores   WALSH AND BARKER
Dance from Othello
COLERIDGE-TAYLOR ORCHESTRA
Dance Gypsy Dance   ARTHUR TRACY
Dance Hall   TED HEATH AND HIS MUSIC
Dance Little Lady   ANNA NEAGLE
Dance Magic   DAVID BOWIE
Dance of the Butterfly   MYRTLE WINTER
Dance of the Hoops   EDNA SQUIRE-BROWN
Dance of the Mermaids   RAMAR AND JEANNE
Dance of the Raindrops   TEDDY BROWN
Dance of the Tartars   THE BOLSHOI BALLET
Dance of the Wooden Dolls
GAINSBOROUGH GIRLS
Dance Variation
SANTOS CASANI AND JOSE LENNARD
Dancin' Thru' the Dark   CON O'NEILL
Dancing Accordionist, The   GLUM
Dancing on the Ceiling   JESSIE MATTHEWS
Dancing Shoes   CLIFF RICHARD
Dancing Tambourine   TEDDY BROWN
Dancing Through Life   LADDIE CLIFF
Dancing With My Shadow   TEDDY BROWN
Dancing Xylophonist, The   MICHEL
Danger By My Side   KIM DARVOS
Danger Zone   THE WONDERFUL WORLD
Daniel   ELTON JOHN
Danny Boy (1933; 2 films)
LANCE FAIRFAX; THE NILE PLAYERS
Danny Boy (1934)   DOROTHY DICKSON
Danny Boy (1935)   DANNY MALONE
Danny Boy (1937; 2 films)
DILLWYN THOMAS; ARTHUR TRACY
Danny Boy (1938)   RENE RAY
Danny Boy (1939)   GRACIE FIELDS
Danny Boy (1948)   EVELYN McCABE
Danny Boy (1996)
GRIMETHORPE COLLIERY BAND
Danse Apache   ALEXIS AND DORRANO
Danse Poupette   BETTY BUCKNELL
Danza, La   JAN KIEPURA
Daphne and Me   DOUGLAS WAKEFIELD
Daring Young Man, The   GEORGE FORMBY
Dark Eyes
FREDDIE MIRFIELD AND HIS GARBAGE MEN
Dark-Haired Marie   FRANK TITTERTON
Darling I Love You   GEORGE CLARKE
Darling Je Vous Aime Beaucoup JEAN CAVALL
Dart Song, The   THE TWO LESLIES
Dashing White Sergeant, The
GLASGOW ORPHEUS CHOIR
Davy Jones   PERCY AND MARY HONRI
Dazed and Confused   LED ZEPPELIN
Dea Sancta   DAVID ESSEX
Dead Parrot Sketch
JOHN CLEESE; MICHAEL PALIN
Dear Dear Dear   JESSIE MATTHEWS
Dear England Mine   RAYMOND NEWELL
Dear Little Billy   LADDIE CLIFF
Dear Little Shamrock (1934)   JOHN GARRICK
Dear Little Shamrock (1938)
PERCIVAL MACKEY AND HIS BAND; RENE RAY

Dear Little Waltz

     JACK BUCHANAN; ANNA NEAGLE

Dear Love

     THOMAS (TOM) BURKE; SYDNEY HOWARD

Dear Old Pals   PERCY MANCHESTER

Dear Old Southland   JULES BLEDSOE

Dearest Maiden   RICHARD TAUBER

Death or Glory   GRIMETHORPE COLLIERY BAND

Deathless Army, The *(2 films)*   LANCE FAIRFAX

Deceived   THE WHO

Deep Desert   PAUL ROBESON

Deep Dream River   ROBERT ASHLEY

Deep River   PAUL ROBESON

Deep Waters   PATRICK COLBERT

Delivering the Morning Milk   GEORGE FORMBY

Delyse   ROSETTE

Dennis the Menace from Venice *(1935)*

     WALSH AND BARKER

Dennis the Menace from Venice *(1936)*

     HARRIETTE HUTCHINS

Denying   THE SPICE GIRLS

Desdemona   BILLY MERSON

Destiny   STANELLI AND HIS BAND

Devil Dance   NOLA REID

Devil May Care   ROBERT EASTON

Devil's Awa' wi' the Exciseman, The

     ALEX HENDERSON

Devil's Trill   YEHUDI MENUHIN

Devonshire Cream and Cider   GERALD NODIN

Devotion   RICHARD TAUBER

Dicky Bird Hop *(2 films)*   RONALD GOURLAY

Did You Get That Out of a Book?   BINNIE HALE

Did Your First Wife Ever Do That?

     MARIE KENDALL

Did Your Mother Come From Ireland?

(2 films)

  FRED CONYNGHAM; BOB AND ALF PEARSON

Didn't We?   TONY KINSEY QUARTET

Dig a Pony   THE BEATLES

Dig for Victory   TED RAY

Dig It   THE BEATLES

Diga Diga Doo

  AMBROSE AND HIS ORCHESTRA; DORCHESTER
     GIRLS

Dimples   CROSS SECTION

Dinah *(1933)*   SOUTHERN SISTERS

Dinah *(1935; 2 films)*

  NINA MAE McKINNEY; THREE LOOSE SCREWS

Dinah *(1936)*   PEGGY COCHRANE

Dinah *(1937)*   AL VERDI AND THELMA LEE

Dinah *(1939)*   PAT (PATRICIA) KIRKWOOD

Ding Dong Daddy   THE HAZEL MANGEAN GIRLS

Dinner for One Please, James *(1938)*

     JIMMY KENNEDY AND MICHAEL CARR

Dinner for One Please, James *(1961)*

     TONY KINSEY QUARTET

Dirty Work at the Crossroads   ALBERT BURDON

Disco Dancer   PATTI BOULAYE

Dismal Moan   HARRY ROY AND HIS BAND

Divertimento   ELEKTRA QUARTET

Dixie   GEORGIAN SINGERS

Dixie Boogie   WINIFRED ATWELL

Dixieland Rock

  ART BAXTER AND HIS ROCKIN' SINNERS

Dizzy Fingers *(1936)*   FREDDIE BAMBERGER

Dizzy Fingers *(1938)*

     RENE PUGNET AND CLIVE RICHARDSON

Do I Love You?   ANNA NEAGLE

Do It   THE SPICE GIRLS

Do It Again *(1933)*   VERONICA

Do It Again *(1939)*   DOROTHY WARD

Do It For Me   ROY CASTLE

Do Not Trust Him Gentle Maiden   STANELLI

Do the Old Soft Shoe   BILLY FURY

Do the Rock-Steady   THE BODYSNATCHERS

Do the Runaround   JUNE CLYDE

Do You Love Me?

     BRIAN POOLE AND THE TREMELOES

Do You Mind?   ANTHONY NEWLEY

Do You Really Want To Hurt Me?

     CULTURE CLUB

Do You Remember?   CLIFF RICHARD

Do You Think It's All Right?   THE WHO

Dogseye View of Love, A   EDNA THOMPSON

Doina   LUPE VELEZ

Doing the Low Down

  GAINSBOROUGH GIRLS; HAL SWAIN AND HIS KIT
     KAT BAND

Doing the Unstuck   THE CURE

Doll, The   FLORA LE BRETON

Doll Dance   THE BOSWELL TWINS

Dolls on Parade   AVANT BROTHERS

Don Juan

  THE BRITISH WOMEN'S SYMPHONY ORCHESTRA

Don Quixote   ANNA PAVLOVA

Don't Ask Me Any Questions

  JACK HYLTON AND HIS BAND; BRYAN LAWRANCE

Don't Be a Cad   THE WESTERN BROTHERS

Don't Be Like That   MIGUEL GALVAN

Don't Blame Me   FLORENCE DESMOND

Don't Cry When We Say Goodbye

     GERALDO AND HIS ORCHESTRA

Don't Dilly Dally on the Way   HELEN SHAPIRO

Don't Ever Leave Me *(1944)*   ANNE SHELTON

Don't Ever Leave Me *(1949)*   PETULA CLARK

Don't Forget Me

  FRANK KING AND HIS ORCHESTRA; ROSALIND
     MELVILLE

Don't Give a Good Gosh Darn

     JESSIE MATTHEWS

Don't Have Any More   LILY MORRIS

Don't Laugh At Me *(2 films)*   NORMAN WISDOM

Don't Let Me Be Misunderstood   THE ANIMALS

Don't Let Me Down   THE BEATLES

Don't Let the River Run Dry

     LESLIE A HUTCHINSON

Don't Let's Sing About the War

     RONALD FRANKAU

Don't Move   GLEN MASON

Don't Put a Thing in Writing   EVELYN DALL

Don't Say Goodbye   ANNIE ROSS

Don't Send My Boy to Prison   NELSON KEYS

Don't Send My Daddy to Dartmoor

     THREE ADMIRALS

Don't Take Your Love From Me

     ANDY CAVELL AND THE SAINTS

Don't Talk   STANELLI AND EDGAR

Don't Talk to Me About Love   ANTHONY NEWLEY

Don't Tell a Soul   ROBB WILTON

Don't Turn Around   THE MERSEYBEATS

Don't You Come Any More   JANE WELSH

Don't You Cry When We Say Goodbye
VIOLET LORAINE
Don't You Understand? HEINZ
Donkey Laugh TARRANT BAILEY JR
Donna e Mobile, La (1931) JAN KIEPURA
Donna e Mobile, La (1936) ARTHUR TRACY
Doomsday Rock TOMMY STEELE
Dos and Donts in Dance
SANTOS CASANI AND JOSE LENNARD
Double Trouble THE BROOK BROTHERS
Down Among the Dead Men
STANLEY HOLLOWAY
Down Among the Z Men CAROLE CARR
Down and Out THE SPRINGFIELDS
Down at Holiday Inn HERMAN'S HERMITS
Down at the Old Bull and Bush
PERCY AND MARY HONRI
Down at the Old Village Hall DONALD PEERS
Down By the Riverside
CHRIS BARBER AND HIS JAZZ BAND; OTTILIE
PATTERSON
Down Forget-Me-Not Lane
BILLY DE HAVEN AND DANDY PAGE
Down in a Flowery Vale
GLASGOW ORPHEUS CHOIR
Down in Our Village in Somerset
NORMAN LONG
Down in the Deep Blue Sea DAVE WILLIS
Down in the Park GARY NUMAN
Down in the Valley BEVERLEY SISTERS
Down Love Lane
THE CO-OPTIMISTS; STANLEY HOLLOWAY; ELSA
MacFARLANE
Down Old Lover's Lane
RICHARD DABSON AND HIS ORCHESTRA
Down On Finnegan's Farm TALBOT O'FARRELL
Down South ARCHIE GALBRAITH
Down the Hillbilly Trail PATRICK COLBERT
Down Where the Breezes
NAN KENNEDY; BILLY MERSON
Drake Is Going West THE MASTERSINGERS
Dream Away Romance TEMPERANCE SEVEN
Dream for Sale NORMAN WISDOM
Dream Is Over, The ANNA NEAGLE
Dream Lover DAVID ESSEX
Dream Maker TOMMY STEELE
Dreaming (2 films: 1933, 1944)
BUD FLANAGAN AND CHESNEY ALLEN
Dreaming (1934) FAY COMPTON
Dreaming (1937) STANELLI AND HIS BAND
Dreaming of Thee CYRIL FLETCHER
Drifting With the Tide MARJORIE DALE
Drink To Me Only (1926) GWEN FARRAR
Drink To Me Only (1931) THE BELLS
Drink To Me Only (1938)
EARL AND JOSEPHINE LEACH
Drink To Me Only (1943) ST. DAVID'S SINGERS
Driven to Tears POLICE
Driving CLIFF RICHARD
Drover, The SIDNEY BURCHALL
Drums in My Heart ELISABETH WELCH
Drums of the Desert
WILLIAM HODGSON AND HIS BAND
Dubarry, The GITTA ALPAR
Duchess is Learning the Rumba, The
WALSH AND BARKER

Duke Insists, The
REGINALD FORESYTHE AND HIS BAND
Dusting the Stars
MARY COLE; JEAN COLIN; HARRY LANGDON;
LUPE VELEZ
Dvorak's Overture
NATIONAL YOUTH ORCHESTRA
D'Ye Ken John Peel BILLY MAYERL
Dying Swan, The (1922) KARINA
Dying Swan, The (1935) ANNA PAVLOVA
Dying Swan, The (1957)
THE BOLSHOI BALLET; GALINA ULANOVA
Dynamite MUD
Dynamo LES HOBEAUX

E

E Lucevan le Stelle THOMAS (TOM) BURKE
Each Hour of Every Day NANCY LOGAN
Each Night I Make a Song for You MARY ELLIS
Early in the Morning BETTY FIELDS
Early One Morning NORMAN WISDOM
East of the Sun (1936)
THREE ACCORDION KINGS
East of the Sun (1937) TURNER LAYTON
Eastern Dance SHEILA DEXTER
Eastward Ho VIOLET LORAINE
Easy Life THE BODYSNATCHERS
Ebenezer PAUL ROBESON
Eccentricity SYD SEYMOUR
Echoes of the Past DR. DIDGE
Eclipse, The ALFRED LESTER
Ee by Gum GRACIE FIELDS
Egg and Chips TOMMY STEELE
Eh Deh Oh CHARLIE CREED-MILES
Eighteenth Century Drawing Room
RUDY STARITA
Eighth Day HAZEL O'CONNOR
Eightsome Reel
TONY LOWRY AND CLIVE RICHARDSON
Eileen Alanah THOMAS (TOM) BURKE
Eileen Mavourneen (1936) CAVAN O'CONNOR
Eileen Mavourneen (1947) JAMES ETHERINGTON
Eileen Ogh DANNY MALONE
El Salvador PAUL BRADY; JACKSON BROWNE
Eleanor Rigby (1968) THE BEATLES
Eleanor Rigby (1984) PAUL McCARTNEY
Eleanor Rigby (1991)
PAUL AND LINDA McCARTNEY
Electric Woman, The THELMINA
Elevator Rock TOMMY STEELE
Eleven More Months (1932) RUSSELL JONES
Eleven More Months (1937)
AMBROSE AND HIS ORCHESTRA; LESLIE CAREWE
Elfin Folly GASTON AND ANDREE
Elisir d'Amour BENJAMINO GIGLI
Eliza Is the Fairest Queen JIMMY SOMERVILLE
Elvira MANTOVANI AND HIS TIPICA ORCHESTRA
Embankment Cameo, An ROBB WILTON
Emperor of Lancashire, The GEORGE FORMBY
Empire Depends On You, The (2 films)
CICELY COURTNEIDGE
Encore CARROLL GIBBONS AND HIS ORCHESTRA
End, The (1991) PAUL AND LINDA McCARTNEY
End (1993) THE CURE

End of a Perfect Day, The   EVELYN LAYE
End of the Road, The *(2 films)*
    SIR HARRY LAUDER
Endos, Los   GENESIS
Enola Gay
    ORCHESTRAL MANOEUVRES IN THE DARK
ENSA Concert   STAINLESS STEPHEN
Entangled   GENESIS
Equestrian Statue
    THE BONZO DOG DOO DAH BAND
Escalator Squiggle   THE WINDMILL GIRLS
Eton Boating Song   REGINALD FOORT
Evensong *(1934)*   FRANK TITTERTON
Evensong *(1938)*   RUDY STARITA
Ever Since I Met Lucy   JIMMY LLOYD
Ever So Goosey
    JACK PAYNE AND HIS DANCE ORCHESTRA
Every Day Away from You
    THE BARRIE SISTERS/TWINS
Every Day's a Holiday   MIKE SARNE
Every Girl Is Beautiful   CLIFF RICHARD
Every Little Bit of Me
    CHARLES FORSYTHE, ADDIE SEAMON AND
    ELEANOR FARRELL
Every Little Thing   SPENCER DAVIS GROUP
Every Move You Make   JIGSAW
Every Time We Say Goodbye   ANNIE LENNOX
Every Which Way   THE JOHN BARRY SEVEN
Everybody Dance   CICELY COURTNEIDGE
Everybody Loves My Baby
    TEMPERANCE SEVEN
Everybody's Dancing   GITTA ALPAR
Everybody's Got Love   KENNY LYNCH
Everyone But You   JIMMY POWELL
Everyone Changes   ALAN PRICE
Everything Happens to Me   MAX MILLER
Everything I Have Is Yours   CHARLIE KUNZ
Everything in France is Hunky Dory
    DAVE WILLIS
Everything in Life   GITTA ALPAR
Everything Stops for Tea   JACK BUCHANAN
Everything Will Be Lovely   TOMMY TRINDER
Everything's in Rhythm with My Heart
    JESSIE MATTHEWS
Excelsior   JOSEPH SCHMIDT
Excuse Me   JIMMY NERVO AND TEDDY KNOX
Exhibition One Step
    JACK HYLTON AND HIS BAND
Exhibition Step   TED TREVOR AND DINAH HARRIS
Exhibition Waltz *(1922)*
    BARRIE OLIVER; OLIVETTE
Exhibition Waltz *(1927)*   FOWLER AND TAMARA
Exodus   BOB MARLEY AND THE WAILERS
Extra Day, The   DENNIS LOTIS
Extra Extra   SIMON TOWNSHEND
Eyes of the World Are on You, The
    GERALDO AND HIS ORCHESTRA; ANNA NEAGLE
Eyesight to the Blind   ERIC CLAPTON; THE WHO
Ezekiel Saw the Wheel   FOUR MUSKETEERS

F

Fabulous Golden Boy, The   MAX BYGRAVES
Faery Chorus *(2 films)*
    GLASGOW ORPHEUS CHOIR

Fair and Square Man, A   CICELY COURTNEIDGE
Fairground   ADAM GALKELD
Fairies' Gavotte   RAIE DA COSTA
Fairy, The   RONALD FRANKAU
Fairy Dreams Waltz   SERENO AND JUNE
Faith   THE CURE
Fall In and Fly   BILLY COTTON AND HIS BAND
Fall In and Follow Me
    IDA BARR; SYD SEYMOUR AND HIS MAD HATTERS
Fall In and Follow the Band   GRACIE FIELDS
Fall in Love *(1958)*   GLEN MASON
Fall in Love *(1964)*
    GERRY AND THE PACEMAKERS
Family Tree   TOMMY STEELE
Famous Blue Raincoat   LEONARD COHEN
Fan Dance   THE ADAMS SISTERS
Fancy Our Meeting
    JACK BUCHANAN; ELSIE RANDOLPH
Fancy Pants   KENNY
Fanlight Fanny   GEORGE FORMBY
Far Away from Everybody   JILL DAY
Far Far Away   SLADE
Far Off Place, The   DANA
Farewell *(1932)*   NANCY BROWN
Farewell *(1935)*   RICHARD TAUBER
Farewell Sweet Señorita
    BOBBIE AND VIRGINIA; GERALDO AND HIS
    ORCHESTRA; ARTHUR TRACY
Farmyard Frolics   BINKIE STUART
Farmyard Symphony, A   MARIUS B. WINTER
Farther Up the Road   JEFF BECK; ERIC CLAPTON
Fascination Street   THE CURE
Father O'Flynn *(1932)*   JOHN OLIVER
Father O'Flynn *(1934)*
    JOHN GARRICK; STANLEY HOLLOWAY
Father O'Flynn *(1935)*
    THOMAS (TOM) BURKE; DENNIS O'NEIL
Father O'Flynn *(1936)*
    WILLIAM HEUGHEN; CEDRIC SHARPE AND HIS
    SEXTETTE
Faust *(1933)*   DARROL RICHARDS
Faust *(1936)*   GEORGE BAKER; WEBSTER BOOTH
Faust *(1937)*   RONALD FRANKAU
Faust *(1938)*   KEITH FALKNER
Feet Fun and Fancy   JOHNNY HUDGINS
Felix Keeps On Walking   ROBIN RICHMOND
Fernando   RICHARD TAUBER
Ferry Cross the Mersey
    GERRY AND THE PACEMAKERS
Festive March
    HORACE SHEPHERD AND HIS SYMPHONY
    ORCHESTRA
Few Kisses Ago, A   DENNIS LOTIS
Fiddle About   KEITH MOON; THE WHO
Field Figures   RUDOLPH NUREYEV
Fiesta   CLIFF RICHARD
Fifth Symphony   MALCOLM SARGENT
Fight For Your Rights   MCKOY
Find the Lady   JACK HULBERT
Find Yourself Another Fool   THE BLUES BAND
Finders Keepers   CLIFF RICHARD
Fine How Do You Do, A
    EVELYN DALL; ANNE SHELTON
Fingal's Cave   LONDON SYMPHONY ORCHESTRA
Finger Dance   YVONNE MERTENS
Fingers Crossed   MAX BYGRAVES

Finlandia FINNISH NATIONAL ORCHESTRA
Fire Brigade, The
          BUDDY BRADLEY'S RHYTHM GIRLS
Fire of Your Love, The MARIA VAR
Fire Station, The ROBB WILTON
Firebird MARGOT FONTEYN; MICHAEL SOMES
First Call of Spring BENNETT AND WILLIAMS
First Love RICHARD TAUBER
First Lullaby, The ROBERT ASHLEY
Firty Fahsand Quid NORMAN LONG
Fisherman's Waltz
          TREFOR JONES; ANNA NEAGLE
Fit as a Fiddle (2 films)
          JEAN MELVILLE; FOUR MUSKETEERS
Flamenco RUSS CONWAY
Flamenco Bongo RAY ELLINGTON QUARTET
Flamme d'Amour CHRISTIANNE DE MURIN
Flash Bang Wallop TOMMY STEELE
Flat Irons ROBB WILTON
Fledermaus, Die
          LONDON SYMPHONY ORCHESTRA
Fleet's in Port Again, The (1936)
          HAL SWAIN AND HIS SAXOPHONE BAND
Fleet's in Port Again, The (1937; 2 films)
          MUSAIRE; QUEEN MARY DANCE BAND
Fleet's in Port Again, The (1938)
          CHESTER TUNIS
Fleet's Not in Port Very Long, The
  BAND OF H.M. ROYAL MARINES; PETER DAWSON
Flies Crawled Up the Window, The
          JACK HULBERT
Flight of the Bumblebee (1936)
          DEBROY SOMERS AND HIS BAND
Flight of the Bumblebee (1945)
          ALBERT SANDLER
Flight of the Bumblebee (1948) WINNIE BARNES
Flirtation THE DIAMONDOS
Flirtation Foxtrot BARRIE OLIVER; OLIVETTE
Floral Dance, The (1932) GEORGE BAKER
Floral Dance, The (1933) THE MASTERSINGERS
Floral Dance, The (1996)
          GRIMETHORPE COLLIERY BAND
Florida Special NICHOLAS BROTHERS
Flower, The LINDSAY KEMP
Flower and the Young Man, The THE STRAWBS
Flowers That Bloom in the Spring, The
          FRANKIE HOWERD; STUBBY KAYE
Fly on a Windshield GENESIS
Flying High STUART ROBERTSON
Flying Through the Rain
          BUD FLANAGAN AND CHESNEY ALLEN
Fold Your Wings of Love Around Me
          MARY ELLIS; TREFOR JONES
Follow a Star (1930)
          A W BASKCOMB; CLAUDE HULBERT; JACK
                    HULBERT; SOPHIE TUCKER
Follow a Star (1959) NORMAN WISDOM
Follow the Drum PATRICIA BURKE
Follow the Plough RAYMOND NEWELL
Follow Through
          LESLIE HENSON; ELSIE RANDOLPH
Following in Father's Footsteps
          PAT (PATRICIA) KIRKWOOD
Folly to be Wise
          CICELY COURTNEIDGE; NELSON KEYS

Fonso My Hot Spanish Knight BETTY FIELDS
Fool on the Hill PAUL AND LINDA McCARTNEY
Foolish I Know JOOLS HOLLAND
Fools Like Me THE MERSEYBEATS
Foot Tapper THE SHADOWS
Football on Wheels
          HARVARD, MORTIMER AND KENDRICK
For Better For Worse
          EDMUND (TED) HOCKRIDGE
For Love of You (1933) FRANCO FORESTA
For Love of You (1934) ROBERT NAYLOR
For No One PAUL McCARTNEY
For Nothing GENE GERRARD
For Only You IRENE PRADOR
For You (1937) VESTA VICTORIA
For You (1958) MICHAEL HOLLIDAY
For You Alone (1931) THOMAS (TOM) BURKE
For You Alone (1934; 2 films)
          FAY COMPTON; ARMAND GONET; FRANK
                              TITTERTON
For You Alone (1938; 2 films)
          THE SINGING TAXI DRIVER; ROBERT WILSON
For You Alone (1945) HEDDLE NASH
For You, Blue THE BEATLES
For You Madonna (2 films)
          JOE LOSS AND HIS ORCHESTRA;
                    THREE AUSTRALIAN BOYS
Forest, A THE CURE
Forever THE FILBERTS
Forget Me Not EDEN KANE
Forgive Me For Dreaming EDNA KAYE
Forgotten Woman PHYLLIS ROBINS
Fortune Hunter, The TOPLISS GREEN
Forty Four Thousand and Five
          THE TWO LESLIES
Four Leaf Clover BILLY SCOTT-COOMBER
Foxtrot (1923) ALEC ROSS
Foxtrot (2 films: 1924, 1925)
          BARBARA MILES AND MAXWELL STEWART
Foxtrot (1926) FRANKLYN GRAHAM AND BARBARA
Frag Nicht JOSEPH SCHMIDT
Frankie and Johnny (1946)
          JOHNNY WORTHY AND BERTIE JARRETT
Frankie and Johnny (1962)
  MR ACKER BILK AND THE PARAMOUNT JAZZ BAND
Franklin D. Roosevelt Jones
          AMBROSE AND HIS ORCHESTRA; EVELYN DALL
Fraternise PERCIVAL MACKEY AND HIS BAND
Fred Fanakapan GRACIE FIELDS
Free BUD FLANAGAN AND CHESNEY ALLEN
Freight Train
  CHAS McDEVITT SKIFFLE GROUP; NANCY WHISKEY
French Folk Song RICHARD TAUBER
French Tango
          SANTOS CASANI AND JOSE LENNARD
Frenesi
  BERYL DAVIS; OSCAR RABIN AND HIS ROMANY
                              BAND
Fresh Milk Comes From Cows
          SCOVELL AND WHELDON
Friday I'm in Love THE CURE
Friday Night CLIFF RICHARD
Friend of Mine (1932) FRANK TITTERTON
Friend of Mine (1978) MIKE McKENZIE
Friggin' in the Riggin' THE SEX PISTOLS
From One Minute to Another JACK BUCHANAN

From the Edge of the Deep Green Sea
THE CURE
Fruity Flute BILLY MILTON
Fun and Fancy CASA AND LENN
Fun of the Fayre EVELYN LAYE
Funerailles ROGER DALTREY
Funiculi Funicula NORAH COLTON
Funky Gibbon BILL ODDIE
Funny Face FRED CONYNGHAM
Funny Little Clown MAX BYGRAVES
Funny Man MAX BYGRAVES
Funny That Way
BOBBIE ALDERSON; PATRICIA ROSSBOROUGH

G

Gaiety, La NICHOLL SISTERS
Galway Bay ARTHUR LUCAN AND KITTY McSHANE
Game, The CLIFF RICHARD
Gang Bang BLACK LACE
Gangway JESSIE MATTHEWS
Garage MATTHEW BALLESTER
Garageland THE CLASH
Garden in Granada ROBERT ASHLEY
Garden Where the Praeties Grow, The
GABRIEL LAVELLE
Gates of Paradise, The ANNA NEAGLE
Gaucho Tango SANTOS CASANI
Gay Doggie STARDUSTERS DANCE ORCHESTRA
Gay Highway, The (1933) ROBERT EASTON
Gay Highway, The (1939) SIDNEY BURCHALL
General's Fast Asleep, The
JOE LOSS AND HIS ORCHESTRA
Genevieve ARTHUR TRACY
Gentle Flowers PAT (PATRICIA) KIRKWOOD
Gentle Maiden (1936) ALFRED O'SHEA
Gentle Maiden (1955) RONALD CHESNEY
Georgia (2 films)
NAT GONELLA AND HIS GEORGIANS
Georgia's Got a Moon MAX AND HARRY NESBITT
Get Along Little Dogie ROY FOX AND HIS BAND
Get Back (1970) THE BEATLES
Get Back (1991) PAUL AND LINDA McCARTNEY
Get Cracking GEORGE FORMBY
Get It On MARC BOLAN AND T. REX
Get Out and Get Under the Moon
STANELLI AND EDGAR
Get the Feel Right PATTI BOULAYE
Get Up Early in the Morning FREDDY CANNON
Get Up Stand Up
BOB MARLEY AND THE WAILERS
Get Your Friends to Do It FRED CONYNGHAM
Get Your Hair Cut HARRY BRUNNING
Ghetto Tension CATHERINE COFFEY
Giddy Up GRACIE FIELDS
Gigolette FAY COMPTON
Gillie-whack-a-day ANNA NEAGLE
Gimme Some Loving TRAFFIC
Gimme Some Truth JOHN LENNON
Ginger You're Barmy JOHN RUTLAND
Ginny Come Lately STEVE PERRY
Girl I Left Behind Me, The (1938) JACK WARMAN
Girl I Left Behind Me, The (1952)
TWELVE JACKSON GIRLS
Girl in Every Port, A CLIFF RICHARD

Girl in the Clogs and Shawl, The BETTY FIELDS
Girl in the Little Green Hat
SCOVELL AND WHELDON
Girl in Your Arms, The CLIFF RICHARD
Girl Like Nina, A MARTA LABARR
Girl of My Dreams SONJA HENIE
Girl Power THE SPICE GIRLS
Girl With the Dreamy Eyes, The (1936)
THREE CUTIES
Girl With the Dreamy Eyes, The (1938)
AL AND BOB HARVEY
Girls Girls Girls DENNIS LOTIS
Girls of the Old Brigade BEATRICE LILLIE
Giselle (1935) ANNA PAVLOVA
Giselle (1952) LONDON SYMPHONY ORCHESTRA
Giselle (1957)
THE BOLSHOI BALLET; GALINA ULANOVA
Giselle (1968)
GRAND BALLET CLASSIQUE DE FRANCE
Give Her a Little Kiss CARL BRISSON
Give It to Father PAT (PATRICIA) KIRKWOOD
Give Me a Chance to Dance JACK BILLINGS
Give Me a Mustang and a Rifle
RONALD FRANKAU
Give Me a Night in June NORMAN WISDOM
Give Me an Inch HAZEL O'CONNOR
Give Me Back My Heart
JACK PAYNE AND HIS DANCE ORCHESTRA
Give Me It THE CURE
Give Me Love KENNY LYNCH
Give Me the Moonlight FRANKIE VAUGHAN
Giving You the Stars
JOE LEIGH; MAURICE WINNICK AND HIS
ORCHESTRA
Glad New Year, A
CASA NOVA GIRLS; JENNIE ROBINS
Glad To Be Gay TOM ROBINSON
Gladys MOUTH ORGAN MASTERS
Glamorous Night (2 films)
TREFOR JONES; MARY ELLIS
Glass Eater, The SIRDANI
Glass Mountain, The TITO GOBBI
Glass of Golden Bubbles, A
GEORGE BAKER; EVELYN LAYE
Glass of Sherry Wine, A STANLEY HOLLOWAY
Glasters PAN
Glorious Devon JOSEPH FARRINGTON
Gloriously Russian MILLICENT MARTIN
Glory of Love, The (2 films)
SAM BROWNE; DON GALVAN
Go SOUNDS INCORPORATED
Go Fetch Me a Pint of Wine JOSEPH HISLOP
Go To the Mirror THE WHO
God Bless Our King
BRITISH LEGION CITY OF LONDON MILITARY BAND
God Save the King
BAND OF H.M. SCOTS GUARDS
God Save the Queen (1968) NAT JACKLEY
God Save the Queen (1980) THE SEX PISTOLS
God Save the Queen (1986)
GLEN MATLOCK; ANDREW SCHOFIELD
God Send You Back to Me
JULIAS LADIES CHOIR
Going Home THE BLUES BAND
Gold and Silver Waltz CLEMSON AND VALERIE

Golden Age, The — TERRY DENE
Golden River — PAUL ROBESON
Golden Slumbers — PAUL AND LINDA McCARTNEY
Golden Striker, The — TONY KINSEY QUARTET
Goldilocks — ARTHUR TRACY
Golf — JIMMY NERVO AND TEDDY KNOX
Golfer's Glide, The — TONY MARTIN
Golfing Blues — GERLYS AND LYSIA
Gondola Gondola — PAT BOONE
Gondoliers, The
  OWEN BRANNIGAN; MARTYN GREEN
Gonna Be a Good Boy Now — FRANKIE VAUGHAN
Good Day Sunshine
  PAUL AND LINDA McCARTNEY
Good Luck — GITTA ALPAR
Good Morning — TEDDY JOYCE AND HIS BAND
Good Morning Mr Sun
  JACK PAYNE AND HIS DANCE ORCHESTRA
Good Morning to You — CARLYLE COUSINS
Good News — MICHAEL TRIPP
Good Night Binkie — GEORGE FORMBY
Good Old Wedding Ring
  ETHEL REVNELL AND GRACIE WEST
Good Ship Lollipop — SEVEN ELLIOTTS
Good Time in New Orleans
  CARSON ROBISON AND HIS PIONEERS
Goodbye (2 films) — JOSEF LOCKE
Goodbye Again — JACK HULBERT
Goodbye Dolly Gray (1935) — TESSA DEANE
Goodbye Dolly Gray (1966) — QUEENIE WATTS
Goodbye Hawaii — VALKEIRER AND BRADLEY
Goodbye Little Yellow Bird — THE CRAZY GANG
Goodbye Sally — MAX WALL
Goodie Goodie — MEGGIE EATON
Goodnight (1933) — BEBE DANIELS
Goodnight (1938) — JACK BARTY
Goodnight But Not Goodbye — CHARLIE KUNZ
Goodnight Children Everywhere
  ELSIE AND DORIS WATERS
Goodnight Little Fellow — GEORGE FORMBY
Goodnight Sweetheart (1937) — DOREEN
Goodnight Sweetheart (1950)
  GERALDO AND HIS ORCHESTRA
Goodnight Vienna (2 films) — JACK BUCHANAN
Goody Goody — THE PIANOVILLES
Google Eye — NASHVILLE TEENS
Gopak (1938) — BEBE CAPLAN
Gopak (1939) — LONDON AMATEUR ORCHESTRA
Gospel of Love, The — BETTY DRIVER
Got a Date with an Angel — BOBBY HOWES
Got a Funny Feeling — CLIFF RICHARD
Got to Dance My Way to Heaven
  JESSIE MATTHEWS
Got to Get You Into My Life
  PAUL AND LINDA McCARTNEY
Got to Get Your Photo in the Press
  GEORGE FORMBY
Got You On My Mind — KENNY BAKER
Gotta Get Away Now — JOYCE BLAIR
Gotta Have Rain — MAX BYGRAVES
Gotta See Baby Tonight
MR ACKER BILK AND THE PARAMOUNT JAZZ BAND
Grandad's Flannelette Nightshirt
  GEORGE FORMBY
Grandfather's Bagpipes — GRACIE FIELDS

Grannie — NAN KENWAY AND DOUGLAS YOUNG
Grass Is Getting Greener, The
  HAL YATES AND COOPER LAWLEY
Gravity Grave — THE VERVE
Great Rock 'n' Roll Swindle, The
  THE SEX PISTOLS
Greatest Mistake of My Life, The
  GERRY FITZGERALD
Greeks Had a Word For It, The
  CHARLES B COCHRAN'S YOUNG LADIES
Greensleeves — LITTLEWOODS' GIRLS CHOIR
Greenstuff — THE BLUES BAND
Growing Old Together — IDA BARR
Guarding the Home of the Home Guard
  GEORGE FORMBY
Gypsy, The (1938) — HUGHIE DIAMOND
Gypsy, The (1960)
  DILL JONES AND HIS ALL STARS
Gypsy Airs — DON PEDRO AND HIS BAND
Gypsy Dan — BERNARD DUDLEY
Gypsy Love — MAGDA KUN
Gypsy Melody — SENOR SEDELLI; MADAME VALLI
Gypsy Moon (1932; 2 films)
  DON CARLOS; MAURICE RAYMOND AND HIS
  CONTINENTAL BAND; TROISE AND HIS
  MANDOLIERS
Gypsy Moon (1938)
  GAU DE VITO AND HIS LADIES BAND
Gypsy Played, The — MARY ELLIS
Gypsy Selection — ALBERT SANDLER
Gypsy Song — LORRAINE LA FOSSE

H

Habanera — LORRAINE LA FOSSE
Hail Caledonia — ROBERT WILSON
Hail Women of History — BOBBY HOWES
Hair Down Hoe Down — TOMMY STEELE
Half a Pint of Ale — GUS ELEN
Half a Sixpence — TOMMY STEELE
Half a World Away — KAY CAVENDISH
Half and Half — JESSIE MATTHEWS
Half of Everything Is Yours — ARTHUR ASKEY
Half of Half and Half — TOMMY TRINDER
Halfway to Heaven (1928) — MIGUEL GALVAN
Halfway to Heaven (1937) — ARTHUR TRACY
Hall of Memory Medley
  GERALDO AND HIS ORCHESTRA
Hampstead Way, The
  SID FIELD; TESSIE O'SHEA; JACK PARNELL
Hand Me Down My Walkin' Shoes
  KENNY BALL AND HIS JAZZMEN
Hand Me Down My Walking Cane (1936)
  FOUR ACES
Hand Me Down My Walking Cane (1958)
  KING BROTHERS
Handful of Songs, A — TOMMY STEELE
Hang On To Happiness
  JACK LEWIS'S SINGING SCHOLARS
Hang On To Yourself — DAVID BOWIE
Hannah — THE HILLBILLIES
Happy — STANLEY LUPINO
Happy Days Are Here Again
  THE HOUSTON SISTERS
Happy Ending — GRACIE FIELDS

Happy Feet   NOBLE SISSLE AND HIS BAND
Happy Go Lucky   JUNE
Happy Go Lucky Song, A   TOMMY TRINDER
Happy Go Lucky You BAMBERGER AND BISHOP
Happy Guitar   TOMMY STEELE
Happy in the Morning
  HENRY HALL AND THE B.B.C. DANCE ORCHESTRA
Happy Jack   THE WHO
Happy with You   MARK WYNTER
Harbour Lights (1937; 2 films)
       GEDDES BROTHERS; MACARI AND HIS DUTCH
                                    SERENADERS
Harbour Lights (1938)
            JIMMY KENNEDY AND MICHAEL CARR
Harbour Lights (1951)   FIVE SMITH BROTHERS
Hard Day's Night, A   THE BEATLES
Hard Times Come Again No More
                               BETTY FIELDS
Harem Dance   MONA PAIVA
Harlem   EDDIE CARROLL AND HIS BAND
Harlem in My Heart   ELISABETH WELCH
Harlem Jamboree
  LAUDERIC CATON AND HIS RHYTHM SWINGTETTE;
       JOHNNY WORTHY AND BERTIE JARRETT
Harlem Rhythm   BUCK AND BUBBLES
Harlemania   JESSIE MATTHEWS
Harlequin Dance   THE ADAJIO TRIO
Haroun El Raschid   ARTHUR TRACY
Harp That Once Through Tara's Halls, The
  (1936)   RICHARD HAYWARD
Harp That Once Through Tara's Halls, The
  (1947)   JAMES ETHERINGTON
Harry Lime Theme (3 films)   ANTON KARAS
Harvester   RAYMOND NEWELL
Has Anybody Here Seen Kelly? (1934)
                              FLORRIE FORDE
Has Anybody Here Seen Kelly? (1937)
                            REGINALD FOORT
Has Anybody Here Seen Kelly? (1943)
                             BETTY WARREN
Has Anybody Here Seen Kelly? (1956)
               PAT (PATRICIA) KIRKWOOD
Has Anybody Seen Our Ship?   TED RAY
Haste to the Wedding   ANNA NEAGLE
Hatters, The   THE BUCKLEYS
Haul the Timber   PATRICK COLBERT
Havana
    JACK JACKSON AND HIS BAND; CLAIRE LUCE
Have I Told You Lately That I Love You?
       PETULA CLARK; JOHNNY DENIS AND NETTA
                                     ROGERS
Have Nagila   RAY McVAY BAND
Have You Got Another Girl Like Mary?
                             DENNIS O'NEIL
Have You Heard This One?   GEORGE FORMBY
Have You Seen the Writing on the Wall?
                           HAZEL O'CONNOR
Hawaiian War Chant (1944)
       OSCAR RABIN AND HIS ROMANY BAND
Hawaiian War Chant (1956)
               TED HEATH AND HIS MUSIC
He Ain't Done Right by Our Nell
                             NORAH BLANEY
He Isn't Much to Look At   TESSIE O'SHEA
He's a Dangerous Man   GWEN FARRAR

He's All Right When You Know Him
                            CHARLES COBURN
He's Dead But He Won't Lie Down
                              GRACIE FIELDS
He's Everything to Me   CLIFF RICHARD
He's Gone   TAMARA DESNI
He's Got the Whole World In His Hands
                            THE BACHELORS
He's in Town   THE ROCKIN' BERRIES
He's Sent in the Army   THE GANG OF FOUR
Head Over Heels in Love   JESSIE MATTHEWS
Heads or Tails (3 films)
            FOUR CROTCHETS; JOE LOSS AND HIS
       ORCHESTRA; THREE AUSTRALIAN BOYS
Hear All See All Say Nowt   SANDY POWELL
Hear My Song Violetta   JOSEF LOCKE
Heart Breaker   LED ZEPPELIN
Heart of a Man, The   FRANKIE VAUGHAN
Heart of a Romany   MADAME VALLI
Heart's Desire   RICHARD TAUBER
Heartbreak Hotel   DICKIE BENNETT
Hearts Never Know   GITTA ALPAR
Hearts of Oak   SHERMAN FISHER GIRLS
Heathen   BOB MARLEY AND THE WAILERS
Heatwave   THE WHO
Heaven (1932)   CHARLIE AND SONIA
Heaven (1996)   WISBECH MALE CHOIR
Heaven in a Song   RICHARD TAUBER
Heaven Is Round the Corner   LENI LYNN
Heaven Knows   SLADE
Heaven Will Be Heavenly
    JACK HYLTON AND HIS BAND; PAT (PATRICIA)
                                   KIRKWOOD
Heaven Will Protect an Honest Girl
                              GRACIE FIELDS
Heavenly Waltz, The   CAROL RAYE
Hello Bluebird   JUDY GARLAND
Hello Hello I'm Back Again   GARY GLITTER
Hello London   SONJA HENIE
Hello to the Sun   ARTHUR ASKEY
Help   THE BEATLES
Her Bathing Suit Never Got Wet
                          BEVERLEY SISTERS
Her Golden Hair Was Hanging Down Her
  Back   JUNE CLYDE
Her Majesty the Baby   MABEL WAYNE
Her Name Is Mary   PERCY MANCHESTER
Here and There JIMMY NERVO AND TEDDY KNOX
Here Come the Warm Jets   BRIAN ENO
Here Comes the Bride
       JEAN COLIN; CLIFFORD MOLLISON
Here Comes the Show
              VIC LEWIS AND HIS ORCHESTRA
Here Comes the Sun
       BUD FLANAGAN AND CHESNEY ALLEN
Here Comes Tomorrow   WALSH AND BARKER
Here I Go Again   THE HOLLIES
Here, There and Everywhere
       PAUL McCARTNEY; RINGO STARR
Here, There, Everywhere   JANE WELSH
Here We Go Again   AL AND BOB HARVEY
Here We Go Round the Mulberry Bush
                                 TRAFFIC
Here's a Health Unto His Majesty
                         STANLEY HOLLOWAY

Here's a How d'ye Do
    JACQUELINE JONES; KEVIN SCOTT
Here's to the Best of Us   TREFOR JONES
Here's to the Ladies   GORDON HOLDOM
Here's to the Next Time *(3 films)*
  HENRY HALL AND THE B.B.C. DANCE ORCHESTRA
Here's to Those We Love   HARRY WELCHMAN
Here's to You   HENRI GARAT
Here's To You, Here's To Me
    BUD FLANAGAN AND CHESNEY ALLEN
Hey Bulldog   THE BEATLES
Hey Jude   PAUL AND LINDA McCARTNEY
Hey Little Hen   ALBERT MODLEY
Hey Little Man   THE STRAWBS
Hey There Circus Clown
    THE HOUSTON SISTERS
Hi De Hi *(1937)*   STANLEY HOLLOWAY
Hi De Hi *(1949)*   HAL MONTY
Hi Gang
  GREEN SISTERS; JAY WILBUR AND HIS BAND
Hi Heel Sneakers   CROSS SECTION
Hiawatha's Lullabye   VAL ROSING
Hibernian Lament   AVRIL ANGERS
High   THE CURE
High Society
MR ACKER BILK AND THE PARAMOUNT JAZZ BAND
Highgate Hill   PERCY MANCHESTER
Highland Swing   MARIO 'HARP' LORENZI
Hiking   TOMMY HANDLEY
Hilarity   BILLY MAYERL
Hill Billy Willy   GEORGE FORMBY
Hills, The   TREFOR JONES
Hills of Donegal, The *(1943)*   DELYA
Hills of Donegal, The *(1947)*
    JAMES ETHERINGTON
Hilly Billy Blues   SHERRY BROTHERS
His Land   CLIFF RICHARD
Hit Him on the Boko   TOMMY TRINDER
Hit It   UB40
Hitting the High Spots Now   GEORGE FORMBY
HMS Pinafore   MARTYN GREEN
Ho Ho   PAUL ROBESON
Hold Everything   GEORGE GEE
Hold It   HARRY TAFT
Hold Me   REGGIE BRISTOW AND HIS BAND
Hold Me Close to Your Heart
    BERNARD CLIFTON
Hold Me in Your Arms Again   BETTY PAUL
Hold My Hand
  STANLEY LUPINO; POLLY WARD; JOHN WOOD
Hold on to Love   TONY MARTIN
Hold Out Your Hand   CHRIS SQUIRE
Hold Tight OSCAR RABIN AND HIS ROMANY BAND
Hold Your Hand Out Naughty Boy *(1929)*
    CARROLL GIBBONS AND HIS ORCHESTRA
Hold Your Hand Out Naughty Boy *(1934)*
    FLORRIE FORDE
Holidays in the Sun *(1980)*   THE SEX PISTOLS
Holidays in the Sun *(1986)*
    GLEN MATLOCK; ANDREW SCHOFIELD
Hollywood Dream   THUNDERCLAP NEWMAN
Hollywood One   THUNDERCLAP NEWMAN
Holy City, The   GRACIE FIELDS
Holy Night   PAUL ROBESON
Home *(1937)*   PERCY AND MARY HONRI

Home *(1945)*   IRENE MANNING
Home *(1964)*   CLIFF RICHARD
Home Before Midnight   JIGSAW
Home Guard Blues   GEORGE FORMBY
Home On the Range *(1934)*   THE HILLBILLIES
Home On the Range *(1943)*
STAN SHEDDON AND THE PLAYTIMERS; MAURICE
    TAYLOR
Home Sweet Home *(1928)* HERSCHEL HENLERE
Home Sweet Home *(1948)*   AVRIL ANGERS
Home Sweet Home Again *(1942)*
    ELSIE AND DORIS WATERS
Home Sweet Home Again *(1943)*   VERA LYNN
Home Town *(1944)*
    BUD FLANAGAN AND CHESNEY ALLEN
Home Town *(1972)*   REG VARNEY
Homeless Bones   DON PARTRIDGE
Homicide   999
Homing   ROBERT WILSON
Honey Bunny Baby   FRANKIE VAUGHAN
Honey Coloured Moon   HILDEGARDE
Honey On My Mind
    ARTHUR ASKEY; EVELYN DALL
Honey You Can't Love Two   DIANA DECKER
Honeybunch   ZELMA O'NEAL
Honeysuckle and the Bee, The *(1940)*
    JEAN COLIN
Honeysuckle and the Bee, The *(1947)*
    ANNA NEAGLE
Honeysuckle Rose *(1943)*
  IRENE CUTTER; HARRY PARRY AND HIS RADIO
    RHYTHM CLUB
Honeysuckle Rose *(1946)*
LAUDERIC CATON AND HIS RHYTHM SWINGTETTE;
  JOHNNY WORTHY AND BERTIE JARRETT
Honeysuckle Rose *(1947)*
  HARRY PARRY AND HIS RADIO RHYTHM CLUB
    SEXTET
Honeysuckle Rose *(1948)*
    MAURICE ARNOLD SEXTET; DINAH KAYE
Hoop Diddle-i-do-ra-li-ay   DONALD PEERS
Hornpipe Song   DANNY LIPTON TRIO
Horsey Horsey *(2 films)*
HENRY HALL AND THE B.B.C. DANCE ORCHESTRA;
    BOB MALLIN; TIN PAN ALLEY TRIO
Hot as Hades
  DUKE ELLINGTON AND THE COTTON CLUB BAND
Hot Lips   TREBLE TAPPERS; WIERE BROTHERS
Hot Love   MARC BOLAN AND T. REX
Hotcha   RONALD FRANKAU
Hotcha Joe   SOPHIE TUCKER
Hotsy Totsy   FRANCES DAY; ARTHUR RISCOE
House Beautiful, The
    REGINALD KING AND HIS ORCHESTRA
House in the Sky   PETULA CLARK
House of the Rising Sun, The   THE ANIMALS
How About Me for You?
    JEAN (JEANNIE) CARSON
How Are You?   HARRY TATE
How Come You Do Me Like You Do?
    FOUR BRIGHT SPARKS
How Deep Is the Ocean?
    LESLIE A HUTCHINSON
How Do I Know It's Saturday?
    MILLS AND BROWNING
How Do You Sleep?   JOHN LENNON

How Does a Fresh Fish Wish? VIOLET LORAINE
How Does It Feel? SLADE
How Green Was My Valley RENARA
How Happy the Lover GRACIE FIELDS
How Many Times? DICKIE BENNETT
How You Gonna Keep Them Down on the
Farm? DEBROY SOMERS AND HIS BAND
How're We Doing?
TERENCE McGOVERN AND HIS NOVELTY
ORCHESTRA
Hula Girl
FELIX MENDELSSOHN AND HIS HAWAIIAN
SERENADERS
Hullabaloo, The ELISABETH WELCH
Hully Gully
JET HARRIS AND THE JETBLACKS; TONY MEEHAN
Human Ostrich, The SIRDANI
Humoresque RAE RUSSELL
Humpty Dumpty
TOMMY QUICKLY AND THE REMO FOUR
Hundred Per Cent, A SAVOY ORPHEANS BAND
Hungarian Dance (1930) ALBERT SANDLER
Hungarian Dance (1932) TOM JONES
Hungarian Dance (1933) ALBERT SANDLER
Hungarian Dance (1939) LESLIE JEFFRIES
Hungarian Medley (1937)
THE NEW TZIGANE ORCHESTRA
Hungarian Medley (1938)
DOROTHY HOLBROOK AND HER HARMONY
HUSSARS
Hungarian Rhapsody (1930) BALAM
Hungarian Rhapsody (1935; 2 films)
FRED SANBORN; JACK STANFORD
Hungarian Rhapsody (1952)
LESLIE JEFFRIES AND HIS ORCHESTRA
Hunter, The ROBB WILTON
Hunting After Dark
STANLEY HOLLOWAY; BETTY WARREN
Hunting Ballet THE WINDMILL GIRLS
Hunting Melody
FODEN'S MOTOR WORKS PRIZE BAND
Hunting Song JOHN GARRICK
Hunting the Fox ROY FOX AND HIS BAND
Hylton Stromp, The
JACK HYLTON AND HIS BAND

I

I Am the Black Man HAZEL O'CONNOR
I Am the Monarch of the Sea JUDY GARLAND
I Belong to Glasgow ALBERT WHELAN
I Breathe on Windows
CLAIRE LUCE; JOHN WOOD
I Can Do It THE RUBETTES
I Can Get Used to You
CLIFFORD MOLLISON; ZELMA O'NEAL
I Can Give You the Starlight GISELLE PREVILLE
I Can See for Miles THE WHO
I Can Tell It By My Horoscope
GEORGE FORMBY
I Can Wiggle My Ears
JESSIE MATTHEWS; DONALD STEWART
I Can't Forget the Days When I Was Young
ALICE LLOYD
I Can't Get Along Without You TAMARA DESNI

I Can't Give You Anything But Love (1928)
PAT AND TERRY KENDAL
I Can't Give You Anything But Love (1935)
CHARLIE KUNZ
I Can't Give You Anything But Love (1938)
THREE IN HARMONY
I Can't Give You Anything But Love (1943)
JIMMY JEWEL AND BEN WARRISS
I Can't Love You Any More MARILYN WILLIAMS
I Can't Make Up My Mind CAROL RAYE
I Can't Stand It DAVE CLARK FIVE
I Could Cry My Heart Out HELEN SHAPIRO
I Could Go For You DAN BROOKS
I Could Go On Singing JUDY GARLAND
I Could Make a Good Living at That
GEORGE FORMBY
I Couldn't Be Mean To You
ORD HAMILTON AND HIS 20TH CENTURY BAND
I Couldn't Let the Stable Down
GEORGE FORMBY
I Cried All Night GAMBLERS
I Cried For You R.A.F. DANCE ORCHESTRA
I Did Not Know MAESTRO SINGERS
I Did What You Told Me ADAM FAITH
I Do Like a Little Drop of Gin
STANLEY HOLLOWAY
I Do Like To Be Beside the Seaside
REG VARNEY
I Don't Care HELEN SHAPIRO
I Don't Care What You Used To Be
DICK HENDERSON (senior)
I Don't Know How to Swing
JOHNNY WORTHY AND BERTIE JARRETT
I Don't Know What's Wrong PAUL ROBESON
I Don't Know Whether to Laugh or Cry
JACK BUCHANAN; JERRY WAYNE
I Don't Know Why CHARLIE KUNZ
I Don't Like GEORGE FORMBY
I Don't Like Mondays
JOHNNY FINGERS; BOB GELDOF
I Don't Wanna Get Hot EVELYN DALL
I Don't Want to Be a Soldier JOHN LENNON
I Don't Want to Climb a Mountain
THE HOUSTON SISTERS
I Don't Want to Go to Bed (1932)
STANLEY LUPINO
I Don't Want to Go to Bed (1933)
MAURICE WINNICK AND HIS ORCHESTRA
I Double Dare You
PAULA GREEN; FELIX MENDELSSOHN AND HIS
HAWAIIAN SERENADERS
I Dream of Jeannie ROBERT WILSON
I Feel the Same Way Too
JOE BROWN; SUSAN MAUGHAN
I Fell in Love with a Poster
HARRY ROY AND HIS BAND
I Found a New Moon (2 films) BOB LIVELY
I Found the Right Girl
BILLY COTTON AND HIS BAND
I Found You PEGGY COCHRANE
I Found You Little Girl PATRICK WADDINGTON
I Fought the Law THE CLASH
I Give My Heart (2 films)
GITTA ALPAR; ANNE ZIEGLER
I Give You My Love DEREK OLDHAM

304

I Got a Robe	PAUL ROBESON
I Got a Woman	THE BLACK KNIGHTS
I Guess I'll Have To Change My Plan	
	BINNIE BARNES
I Guess I'm Not the Type	LIND JOYCE
I Had a Dream	RUSS HAMILTON
I Hate the Morning	JACK BUCHANAN
I Hate to Say Good Night	
	CHARLES 'BUDDY' ROGERS
I Hate You	GRACIE FIELDS
I Hate You, Alfie Hitchens	SUSAN MAUGHAN
I Have a Song to Sing, O!	MARTYN GREEN
I Hear You Calling Me *(1932)*	GRAHAM PAYN
I Hear You Calling Me *(1936; 2 films)*	
	NAVARRE; JOSEPH SCHMIDT
I Hear You Calling Me *(1940)*	HAL YATES
I Hear You Calling Me *(1944)*	
	WEBSTER BOOTH; ANNE ZIEGLER
I Heard	MODERNIQUES
I Heard a Robin Singing	LUTON GIRLS' CHOIR
I Heard You Singing	RAYMOND ALLEN
I Hunger For You	JACK HULBERT
I Just Couldn't Tell Him	EVE BECKE
I Know Love	MARIE BRYANT
I Know Myself Too Well	CAROLE LANDIS
I Know That Love Is Somewhere	JANE WELSH
I Know Two Bright Eyes	THOMAS (TOM) BURKE
I Know What I Like	GENESIS
I Laughed at Love	NORRIE PARAMOR
I Left My Heart in a Valley in Wales	
	DONALD PEERS
I Left My Heart in Budapest	
	MANTOVANI AND HIS TIPICA ORCHESTRA
I Left My Heart With You	WILFRED TEMPLE
I Lift Up My Finger *(1929)*	LESLIE SARONY
I Lift Up My Finger *(1936)*	STANLEY LUPINO
I Lift Up My Finger *(1943)*	THE TWO LESLIES
I Like	TOMMY STEELE
I Like a Little Girl Like That	
	WALSH AND BARKER
I Like Animals	BILLY FURY
I Like Singing	DOROTHEE BAROONE
I Like the Way You Dance	SAMMY DAVIS JR
I Like Your Dimples	HARRY WELCHMAN
I Live for Love	MARTA LABARR
I Lost My Heart in Heidelberg	GRETE NATZLER
I Love a Lassie *(1929)*	SIR HARRY LAUDER
I Love a Lassie *(1937)*	
	MORTON FRASER AND HIS HARMONICA GANG
I Love a Lassie *(1940)*	REGINALD FOORT
I Love Her All the More	
	DICK HENDERSON (senior)
I Love It When You Call Me Names	
	JOAN ARMATRADING
I Love Me	DOUGLAS BYNG
I Love the Moon *(1932)*	CRITERION REVELLERS
I Love the Moon *(1937)*	FRED CONYNGHAM
I Love the Moon *(1946)*	LENI LYNN
I Love to Sing *(1943)*	VERA LYNN
I Love to Sing *(1947)*	
	IVOR MORETON AND DAVE KAYE
I Love You	NORMAN WISDOM
I Love You Love Me Love	GARY GLITTER
I Love You So *(2 films)*	
	EVE BECKE; ANNA NEAGLE

I Love You Too	FOURMOST
I Love You Very Much Madame	JOHN HENDRIK
I, Me, Mine	THE BEATLES
I Mean You	
	BETTY KENT; JACK SIMPSON AND HIS SEXTET
I Met an Angel	ROBERT WILSON
I Must Be Dreaming	GWEN CATLEY
I Need a Pickaxe To Break Your Heart of	
Stone	TITANIC CINQ
I Need You	THE BEATLES
I Never Cried So Much in All My Life	
	GRACIE FIELDS
I Once Had a Heart, Marguerita	DON GALVAN
I Once Was a Very Abandoned Person	
	RUTLAND BARRINGTON
I Played on my Spanish Guitar	
	GEORGE FORMBY
I Promised to be Home by Nine	
	GEORGE FORMBY
I Ran into Love	BETTY DRIVER
I Remember You	FRANK IFIELD
I Saw a Ship Asailing	PHYLLIS ROBINS
I Saw Her Standing There	
	PAUL AND LINDA McCARTNEY
I Saw Stars *(1934)*	CHARLIE KUNZ
I Saw Stars *(1935)*	
	MANTOVANI AND HIS TIPICA ORCHESTRA
I Saw the Look in Your Eyes	
	DOROTHY SQUIRES
I Send My Love With These Roses	
	JOHN DUDLEY
I Shall Be Released	
	SHEENA EASTON; TOM ROBINSON; STING;
	MIDGE URE
I Shall Remember Tonight	CARROLL GIBBONS
I Shot the Sheriff	
	BOB MARLEY AND THE WAILERS
I Should Have Known Better	THE BEATLES
I Should Shay Sho	HAL JONES
I Stopped I Looked and I Listened	
	GEORGE ROBEY
I Thank You For Love	HELLA TOROS
I Think I Can	JACK BUCHANAN
I Think of You Dear	THE WESTERN BROTHERS
I Think You're Swell	BILLY FURY
I Thought I Heard You Singing	
	ROBERT WILSON
I Took My Harp to a Party	PHYLLIS ROBINS
I Travel the Road *(1932)*	GEORGE BAKER
I Travel the Road *(1944)*	SIDNEY BURCHALL
I Wait for You	
	EVELYN LAYE; BROWNING MUMMERY
I Wanna Be Your Dog	GLEN MATLOCK
I Wanna Jive Tonight	ANTHONY NEWLEY
I Wanna Job (One That Satisfies)	
	MIGUEL SANDOVAL
I Want a Good Time Bad	ELSIE CARLISLE
I Want a Little Doggie	LIND JOYCE
I Want to Be Discovered, Mr Levis	DORIS HARE
I Want to Be Happy	MAX AND HARRY NESBITT
I Want to Be Loved	PETER BERNARD
I Want to Cling to Ivy	JACK HULBERT
I Want to Go to Heaven for the Weekend	
	NORMAN WISDOM
I Want to Ring Bells	THREE LOOSE SCREWS

I Was Anything But Sentimental
CICELY COURTNEIDGE
I Was Christened with a Horse Shoe
GEORGE FORMBY
I Was in the Mood   HILDEGARDE
I Will Be Happy   TWELVE ARISTOCRATS
I Wish I Had a Bigger Word Than Love
MELVILLE GIDEON
I Wish I Was Back on the Farm
GEORGE FORMBY
I Wish I Was Single Again   GERALD NODIN
I Won't Do the Conga
DON MARINO BARETTO AND HIS RHUMBA BAND;
CICELY COURTNEIDGE; JACK HULBERT
I Wonder Where My Baby Is Tonight
BARRI CHAT AND TERRI GARDNER
I'd Do It with a Smile   GEORGE FORMBY
I'd Like a Dream Like That   GEORGE FORMBY
I'd Pick Piccadilly   PAT (PATRICIA) KIRKWOOD
I'll Always Have Time for You
BUD FLANAGAN AND CHESNEY ALLEN
I'll Always Remember You Smiling
PEARL VENTERS
I'll B.B.C.-ing You   BILLY MERSON
I'll Be Getting Along
CARROLL GIBBONS AND HIS ORCHESTRA;
REG STONE
I'll Be Seeing You   STAN WHITE
I'll Be the Lucky One   FRED CONYNGHAM
I'll Be There to Stand by You   BILLY FURY
I'll Be Your Sweetheart   TESSA DEANE
I'll Build a Fence Around You   STANLEY LUPINO
I'll Close My Eyes (1955)
CYRIL STAPLETON AND THE SHOW BAND
I'll Close My Eyes (1958)   JOAN REGAN
I'll Close My Eyes (1960)
RAY ELLINGTON QUARTET
I'll Cry Instead   THE BEATLES
I'll Do My Best to Make You Happy
JACK PAYNE AND HIS DANCE ORCHESTRA
I'll Get By   WALSH AND BARKER
I'll Go My Way   RAYMOND NEWELL
I'll Love You For Ever Today   CLIFF RICHARD
I'll Meet You By the Blue Lagoon   ARCHIE PITT
I'll Never Ask for More
JACK PAYNE AND HIS DANCE ORCHESTRA
I'll Never Feel This Way Again   FRANK IFIELD
I'll Never Say Never Again (2 films)
FOUR JOKERS; THREE LOOSE SCREWS
I'll See You Again
ANNA NEAGLE; LEW STONE AND THE
MONSEIGNEUR ORCHESTRA
I'll Send You My Love Letter
VAN STRATEN AND HIS PICCADILLY DANCE BAND
I'll Settle for You
DONALD CLIVE; DIANA DECKER
I'll Sing a Song of Love to You
JOSEPH SCHMIDT
I'll Sing My Way   JOSEPHINE BAKER
I'll Sing You a Song   NORMAN WISDOM
I'll Soon Be Coming Home   DONALD PEERS
I'll Stay With You
CARROLL GIBBONS AND THE SAVOY ORPHEANS;
JESSIE MATTHEWS

I'll Take You Home Again Kathleen (1948)
JOSEF LOCKE
I'll Take You Home Again Kathleen (1949)
WILLER NEAL
I'll Take You Home Again Kathleen (1952)
LESLIE JEFFRIES AND HIS ORCHESTRA
I'll Take You Home Again Kathleen (1991)
JOSEF LOCKE
I'll Tumble 4 Ya   CULTURE CLUB
I'll Turn To You
JOHN McHUGH; SANDY MacPHERSON;
SYLVIA WELLING
I'll Wait for You (1944)
FELIX MENDELSSOHN AND HIS HAWAIIAN
SERENADERS
I'll Wait for You (1964)
GERRY AND THE PACEMAKERS
I'll Walk Beside You (1942)   ROBERT ASHLEY
I'll Walk Beside You (1943)
JOHN McHUGH; SYLVIA MARRIOTT
I'm a Boy   THE WHO
I'm a Failure   GRACIE FIELDS
I'm a High-Faluting Puncher
TEXAS TED AND HIS RANCH BOYS
I'm a Little Pimp   JUICY LUCY
I'm a Little Prairie Flower   THE TWO LESLIES
I'm a Wolf on My Mother's Side   ARTHUR ASKEY
I'm Afraid to Love You   MAX BYGRAVES
I'm All I Need   ANTHONY NEWLEY
I'm All In   EVELYN DALL
I'm as Happy as a Sand Boy   GEORGE FORMBY
I'm Feeling Happy
DAN DONOVAN; HENRY HALL AND THE B.B.C.
DANCE ORCHESTRA
I'm Free   ROGER DALTREY
I'm Getting On Nicely Thank You
SANDY POWELL
I'm Glad   CREAM
I'm Glad I Met You
GENE GERRARD; JESSIE MATTHEWS
I'm Going to Scotland   VERA-ELLEN
I'm Going to Stick by My Mother
GEORGE FORMBY
I'm Gonna Love That Guy   KAY CAVENDISH
I'm Gonna Sing a Song   SAM MAYO
I'm Gonna Wash My Hands of You (1935; 2
films)
NAT GONELLA AND HIS GEORGIANS; RADIO THREE
I'm Gonna Wash My Hands of You (1936)
TEDDY JOYCE AND HIS BAND
I'm Gonna Wrap You Up   DENNIS LOTIS
I'm Happy Just to Dance with You
THE BEATLES
I'm Happy When I'm Hiking   LESLIE SARONY
I'm Happy When It's Raining   JOSEPH SCHMIDT
I'm Henery the Eighth I Am   JOHN RUTLAND
I'm in a Dancing Mood
JACK BUCHANAN; ELSIE RANDOLPH
I'm in Love   RENEE DYMOTT
I'm in Love for the Very First Time
JEAN (JEANNIE) CARSON
I'm in Love with my Life   MARTA LABARR
I'm in Love with Susan   RONALD FRANKAU
I'm in Love with the Band   NINA MAE McKINNEY
I'm Into Something Good   HERMAN'S HERMITS

I'm Just in the Mood Tonight
PRINCE TWINS; HAL SWAIN AND HIS KIT KAT BAND
I'm Just Wild About Harry *(1933)*
BILLY COTTON AND HIS BAND
I'm Just Wild About Harry *(1939)*
VICTOR SILVESTER AND HIS BALLROOM
ORCHESTRA
I'm Leaving Dear Old Ireland
STANLEY HOLLOWAY
I'm Looking for a Lad Once More
TESSIE O'SHEA
I'm Looking for You
CARROLL GIBBONS AND THE SAVOY ORPHEANS;
JESSIE MATTHEWS
I'm Making Headway Now   GEORGE FORMBY
I'm Ninety Four Today   WILL FYFFE
I'm Nobody's Sweetheart Now
PAT (PATRICIA) KIRKWOOD
I'm Not All There   ELLA SHIELDS
I'm Not Your Stepping Stone
GLEN MATLOCK; ANDREW SCHOFIELD
I'm Nuts About Screwy Music *(2 films)*
JACK STANFORD
I'm on Fire   CHELSEA
I'm One of the Brandy and Seltzer Boys
TOMMY TRINDER
I'm Only Me   ARTHUR ASKEY
I'm Popeye the Sailor Man
BILLY 'POPEYE' COSTELLO
I'm Saving the Last Waltz for You
JUDY SHIRLEY; LAWRENCE WRIGHT
I'm Sending a Letter to Santa Claus
GRACIE FIELDS
I'm Shy   GEORGE FORMBY
I'm Singing to a Million   BEBE DANIELS
I'm So Happy to Be Back Home   BINNIE HALE
I'm So Happy When I Cry   LESLIE FULLER
I'm So Used to You Now   AL BOWLLY
I'm Still Dreaming   JACK BUCHANAN
I'm Terribly British   RONALD FRANKAU
I'm the Girl the Forces Fight For   HY HAZELL
I'm Your Sweetheart Maybe   HY HAZELL
I'm Yours   STOKES AND HOLLOWAY
I've Fallen in Love   CICELY COURTNEIDGE
I've Got a Feeling   THE BEATLES
I've Got a Feeling I'm Falling
MAX AND HARRY NESBITT
I've Got a Feeling You're Fooling
BARBARA WOOD
I've Got a Girl Friend   BILLY 'UKE' SCOTT
I've Got a Hole in My Pocket   FRANK IFIELD
I've Got a Hunch   BETTY DRIVER
I've Got a Man   KENNY BAKER
I've Got a Rainbow in My Heart RALPH READER
I've Got a Robe   FRISCO
I've Got a Sweetie on the Radio GWEN FARRAR
I've Got Mine   SMALL FACES
I've Got Sixpence   ELSIE AND DORIS WATERS
I've Got the Eye   LYNN BRETON
I've Got the Jitterbugs   GRACIE FIELDS
I've Got the World on a String   BETTY ASTELL
I've Got the Wrong Man   ZAIDEE JACKSON
I've Gotta Horse   BILLY FURY
I've Had It Up To Here With Men
VICTORIA WOOD

I've Just Seen a Face   THE BEATLES
I've Lost My Rhythm   EVELYN DALL
I've Never Seen a Straight Banana
DICK HENDERSON (senior)
I've Only Come Down for the Day   SAM MAYO
I've Waited So Long   ANTHONY NEWLEY
Ice Blue   PADDY STONE
Ice Cream Man, The   THE TORNADOS
Ich Liebe Dich My Dear   ARMAND CRABBE
Icicle Joe   LESLIE SARONY
Idle Days   LOUISE GOFFIN
Idle Dreams   GLADYS MERREDEW
Idle on Parade   ANTHONY NEWLEY
Idle Rock-a-Boogie   ANTHONY NEWLEY
If All the World's a Stage   ANTHONY NEWLEY
If Anything Happened to You
AL BOWLLY; ROY FOX AND HIS BAND
If I Could Only Find Her   CARL BRISSON
If I Fell   THE BEATLES
If I Had a Girl Like You   GEORGE FORMBY
If I Had a Hammer   JOHNNY B. GREAT
If I Had My Way
CARROLL GIBBONS AND HIS ORCHESTRA
If I Love You   MARGUERITE NAMARA
If I Was Anything But Sentimental
JACK HULBERT
If I Were a Boy   ELLALINE TERRISS
If I Won the Penny Pool   ALAN DEAN
If It Weren't for the Likes of Us Chaps
THE CO-OPTIMISTS
If It's to Last   LESLIE A HUTCHINSON
If Love Were All   IVY ST. HELIER
If My Heart Says Sing
JUNE CLYDE; JACK JACKSON AND HIS BAND
If Night Should Fall   GERRY FITZGERALD
If Only   HAZEL O'CONNOR
If Spring Were Only Here to Stay
MARION SAUNDERS
If the Rain's Got to Fall   TOMMY STEELE
If This Is Love   CAROLE CARR
If You Are Out to Give a Party
CICELY COURTNEIDGE
If You Could Care For Me *(1938)*
NORA SWINBURNE
If You Could Care For Me *(1939)*
REGINALD KING AND HIS ORCHESTRA
If You Could Only Cook   ANNE SHELTON
If You Don't Want the Goods GEORGE FORMBY
If You Hadn't Gone Away   NORAH BLANEY
If You Haven't Got a Train
THE HOUSTON SISTERS
If You Smile at the Sun   DONALD PEERS
If You Were the Only Girl in the World *(1937)*
VIOLET LORAINE
If You Were the Only Girl in the World *(1939)*
VIOLET LORAINE
If You Were the Only Girl in the World *(1940)*
JEAN COLIN; TOMMY TRINDER
If You Were the Only Girl in the World *(1944)*
TESSIE O'SHEA
If You Were the Only Girl in the World *(1946)*
ANNA NEAGLE
If You Would Learn to Live   JACK BUCHANAN
If You're Walking My Way DOROTHY DICKSON
If Your Father Only Knew   LES ALLEN

Ilkley Moor Baht 'At (1937) STANLEY HOLLOWAY
Ilkley Moor Baht 'At (1942) FRANK RANDLE
Ill Wind TED HEATH AND HIS MUSIC
Imagine (1972) JOHN LENNON
Imagine (1987) CHET ATKINS; MARK KNOPFLER
Imagine Me Imagine You FOX
Imagine Me in the Maginot Line
  GEORGE FORMBY
Imagine My Embarrassment PETER BERNARD
Imagine That JANET KAY
Impatience RICHARD TAUBER
Improv No. 1 AIRTO MOREIRA
In a Cloister Garden FOUR MUSKETEERS
In a Little Garage RONALD FRANKAU
In a Little Lancashire Town GRACIE FIELDS
In a Little Wigan Garden GEORGE FORMBY
In a Monastery Garden (1935)
  ARGENTINE ACCORDION BAND
In a Monastery Garden (1938)
  MUSICAL DAWSON AND HIS CANARY CHOIR
In a Paradise for Two
  PATRICIA ELLIS; JACK HULBERT
In a Persian Market (2 films)
MR ACKER BILK AND THE PARAMOUNT JAZZ BAND
In an Old-Fashioned Town GRAHAM PAYN
In Between Age, The SHEILA BUXTON
In Between Days (2 films) THE CURE
In Cellar Cool (1928) EMMANUEL LIST
In Cellar Cool (1929)
  CARROLL GIBBONS AND HIS ORCHESTRA
In Cellar Cool (1932) ROBERT EASTON
In Cellar Cool (1937)
  KITKAT SAXOPHONE RASCALS
In Love RUBY MURRAY
In Love for the Very First Time
  KEN MacINTOSH AND HIS BAND
In My Heart of Hearts
HENRY HALL AND THE B.B.C. DANCE ORCHESTRA;
  HILDEGARDE
In My Little Snapshot Album GEORGE FORMBY
In Old Vienna CARL BRISSON
In Other Words GEORGE ROBEY
In the Air HILDEGARDE
In the Air Tonight
  PHIL COLLINS; DARYL STUERMER
In the Garden TOMMY HANDLEY
In the Jungle ROBB WILTON
In the Mood (1941; 2 films)
PEGGY DESMOND; FELIX MENDELSSOHN AND HIS
  HAWAIIAN SERENADERS
In the Mood (1943) THE SQUADRONNAIRES
In the Mood (1944)
  MORTON FRASER AND HIS HARMONICA GANG
In the Mood (1947)
  MORTON FRASER AND HIS HARMONICA GANG
In the Mood (1965)
  JOE LOSS AND HIS ORCHESTRA
In the Nick ANTHONY NEWLEY
In the Parlour When the Company's Gone
  THE WESTERN BROTHERS
In the Shade of the Old Apple Tree
  PETULA CLARK
In the Spring GITTA ALPAR
In the Springtime
  LADDIE CLIFF; STANLEY LUPINO

In the Stars CLIFF RICHARD
In the Sweet Bye and Bye DUKES OF DIXIELAND
In the Twilight GEORGIA COLEMAN
In the Valley of the Moon HELEN RAYE
Independence MARTY WILDE
Indian Dance RENOFF AND RENOVA
Indubitably Me MIKE SARNE
Inner London Violence BAD MANNERS
Intermezzo ROBERT WILSON
Internationale, The HARRY ROY AND HIS BAND
Interpretations in Tempo BURTON PIERCE
Intro to the Rock
  RORY BLACKWELL AND THE BLACKJACKS
Inventions HUGH RENE
Invictus TREFOR JONES
Invitation to the Waltz (1935) ANNA PAVLOVA
Invitation to the Waltz (1939)
  TORALF TOLLEFSON
Iolanthe MARTYN GREEN
Ireland in Spring JOHN GARRICK
Ireland, Mother Ireland THOMAS (TOM) BURKE
Irish Emigrant, The THOMAS (TOM) BURKE
Irish Jig Medley THE PRIDE OF ERIN BAND
Is It Today, Lord? THE STRAWBS
Is It True What They Say About Dixie?
  DON GALVAN
Is That the Way to Treat a Sweetheart?
  TORALF TOLLEFSON
Is This Me Here? LAURI PETERS
Is This the Beginning of Love?
  PATRICE MUNSEL
Island of June DENNIS NOBLE
Isle of Capri (1934)
  WILHELM CROSS; GRETA KELLER
Isle of Capri (1935) JACK PLANT
Isle of Capri (1960)
  DILL JONES AND HIS ALL STARS
Isle of Man GEORGE FORMBY
Isle of Mull (2 films) GLASGOW ORPHEUS CHOIR
Isn't Love a Funny Thing?
  BERYL FORMBY; GEORGE FORMBY
Isn't This a Lovely Evening? FRANKIE VAUGHAN
It Ain't No Fault of Mine
  ROY FOX AND HIS BAND; NAT GONELLA
It Ain't Whatcha Do (1939)
  EDDIE CARROLL AND HIS BAND
It Ain't Whatcha Do (1943)
  CAVENDISH THREE; STAN SHEDDON AND THE
  PLAYTIMERS
It All Belongs to You JACK BUCHANAN
It Always Starts to Rain
  LESLIE HOLMES; CLAY KEYES
It Began in Eden TONY VAUGHAN
It Could Be GEORGE FORMBY
It Couldn't Happen Here PET SHOP BOYS
It Doesn't Cost a Dime VERA LYNN
It Doesn't Cost a Thing to Smile
  BUDDY BRADLEY'S RHYTHM GIRLS
It Don't Do Nothin' But Rain
  GWEN FARRAR; BILLY MAYERL
It Don't Mean a Thing
  JACK PADBURY AND HIS COSMO CLUB SIX
It Happens Every Day EDDIE ELLIS
It Is Only a Tiny Garden RAYMOND ALLEN
It Isn't That One MAX BYGRAVES

It Serves You Right   GEORGE FORMBY
It Was All Hushed Up   THE WESTERN BROTHERS
It Was Such a Glorious Night   BILLY MILTON
It's a Beautiful Day   SIDNEY BURCHALL
It's a Crazy World
     DON LANG AND HIS FRANTIC FIVE
It's a Fine Life   SHANI WALLIS
It's a Fine Thing to Sing   SIR HARRY LAUDER
It's a Grand Old World   SANDY POWELL
It's a Great Big Shame   GUS ELEN
It's a Miracle   CULTURE CLUB
It's a Pity to Say Goodnight
     ERIC DELANEY AND HIS BAND
It's a Sin   PET SHOP BOYS
It's a Sin To Tell a Lie (2 films)
     JACK BUTLER; KATHLEEN GIBSON
It's a Small World   BEBE DANIELS
It's a Wonderful Day
     GEORGE MITCHELL SWING CHOIR
It's a Wonderful Thing   DIANE TODD
It's All Happening   TOMMY STEELE
It's All Over Town   FRANKIE VAUGHAN
It's All Too Much   THE BEATLES
It's Been a Long Time   ANDY ELLISON
It's Derby Day   STANLEY LUPINO
It's For You   THE CO-OPTIMISTS
It's Fun Finding Out About London
     TOMMY STEELE
It's Getting Harder All the Time
     LULU; THE MINDBENDERS
It's Gonna Be a Good War   JIM DALE
It's Gonna Be Alright
     GERRY AND THE PACEMAKERS
It's In the Air   GEORGE FORMBY
It's Just the Gypsy in My Soul   THE KENTONES
It's Legal   THE JOHN BARRY SEVEN
It's Like Old Times   VERA LYNN
It's Love (1936)   CARSON SISTERS
It's Love (1943)   CHRISTIANNE DE MURIN
It's Love Again   JESSIE MATTHEWS
It's My Mother's Birthday Today (1936; 2 films)
     JIMMY FLETCHER; BILLY MERSON
It's My Mother's Birthday Today (1938)
     ARTHUR TRACY
It's Nice To Be Out in the Morning
     HERMAN'S HERMITS
It's Only Love   THE BEATLES
It's Only Money   CLIFF RICHARD
It's So Hard   JOHN LENNON
It's So Hard to be Good   LOUISE CORDET
It's Still Being Done   WALSH AND BARKER
It's Summer
     DAI FRANCIS; GEORGE MITCHELL SINGERS
It's the Greatest Business in the World
     TERRY-THOMAS
It's the Rhythm in Me
     AMBROSE AND HIS ORCHESTRA; EVELYN DALL
It's the Same Old World
     TERENCE McGOVERN AND HIS NOVELTY
     ORCHESTRA
It's Too Late   SMALL FACES
It's Trad Dad   CHRIS BARBER AND HIS JAZZ BAND
It's True   CILLA BLACK
It's Up To You   WILL MAHONEY
Italian Salad   ST. DAVID'S SINGERS

J

Jack and the Beanstalk (1921) DOROTHY WARD
Jack and the Beanstalk (1922)
     JAY LAURIER; CLARICE MAYNE; GEORGE ROBEY
Jack o' Diamonds   LONNIE DONEGAN
Jack's Ashore
     HAZEL ASCOT; BAND OF H.M. ROYAL MARINES
Jacob's Magic Banana   CABBAGE HEAD
Jacob's Magic Banana   BUNG LUNG
Jamming   BOB MARLEY AND THE WAILERS
Janie Jones   THE CLASH
Japanese Sandman (1933)
     HARRY BENTLEY; CHARLIE KUNZ
Japanese Sandman (1937) THREE BLUE NOTES
Japanese, the Jerries and the Wops, The
     SCOTT SANDERS
Jazz Justice   EDDIE POLA
Jazznochracy   JACK HART AND HIS BAND
Je Suis Seule Ce Soir   JEAN CAVALL
Jealous Guy   JOHN LENNON
Jealousy (1943; 2 films)
     CAVENDISH THREE; MARIO DE PIETRO
Jealousy (1946)   ANNA NEAGLE
Jeepster   MARC BOLAN AND T. REX
Jerusalem (1971)   CLIFF RICHARD
Jerusalem (1996) GRIMETHORPE COLLIERY BAND
Jerusalem Morning   THREE EDDIES
Jewel Song   JOSÉ COLLINS
Jimmy Brown
     LES COMPAGNONS DE LA CHANSON
Jingle Bells   TROISE AND HIS BANJOLIERS
Jingle Jangle Thingamajig   KEYNOTES
Jingle of the Jungle
     GERALDO AND HIS ORCHESTRA; ANNA NEAGLE
Jitterbug Song   CAROL RAYE
Jive   LOU PRAEGER AND HIS BAND
Jive Dance   LOU PRAEGER AND HIS BAND
Jockey Dance   BARBARA CHETHAM
Joe McDormell
     RON KAVANA AND TERRY WOODS
John Peel (1929)
     THE SALISBURY SINGERS; DALE SMITH
John Peel (1933)   THE MASTERSINGERS
John Peel (1939)   FOUR ACES
John Peel Samba
     EDMUNDO ROS AND HIS RUMBA BAND
Johnny B. Goode   THE SEX PISTOLS
Johnny I Hardly Knew You   RICHARD HAYWARD
Johnny O
CHAS McDEVITT SKIFFLE GROUP; NANCY WHISKEY
Join the Army   HAZEL ASCOT
Join the Band   CLIFF RICHARD
Joker, The
SCOTTISH CO-OPERATIVE WHOLESALE SOCIETY
     BAND
Jolly Good Company   JACK HULBERT
Jolly Good Luck (1938)   TESSA DEANE
Jolly Good Luck (1952)
     TWELVE JACKSON GIRLS
Jolly Good Luck to the Girl Who Loves a
   Soldier   PAT (PATRICIA) KIRKWOOD
Jolly Good Sporting Lot, A   LESLIE SARONY
Jolly Great Lumps of Duff   ARTHUR TRACY
Jolly Roger   ST. DAVID'S SINGERS

Jolly Song, The   LYLE EVANS
Joshua Fit de Battle of Jericho PAUL ROBESON
Journey's End   THE STRAWBS
Judy Judy   JOHNNY TILLOTSON
Juju
  HENRY HALL AND THE B.B.C. DANCE ORCHESTRA
Juke Box Jive
  BOB KERR'S WHOOPEE BAND; THE RUBETTES
Julie and Myrtle
      BILLY NELSON; DOUGLAS WAKEFIELD
Juliette *(2 films)*   FOUR PENNIES
June Night on Marlow Reach
          REGINALD KING QUARTET
June Roses   NICHOLL SISTERS
Jungle Love   CHARMIAN INNES
Jurassic Shift   OZRIC TENTACLES
Just a Blue Sky
     CLIFFORD MOLLISON; ZELMA O'NEAL
Just a Catchy Little Tune   GRACIE FIELDS
Just a Little Bit Too Long   DAVID ESSEX
Just a Little Jazz *(2 films)*
  MURRAY GOODMAN AND HIS NEW YORKERS;
  JACK PADBURY AND HIS COSMO CLUB SIX
Just a Little Medley
  CARUSO AND HIS NEW YORK SYNCOPATERS
Just a Pair of Foreign Legionnaires
  (JACK) WARNER AND (JEFF) DARNELL
Just a Regular Man   ORLANDO
Just an Old Sprig of Shamrock
      MRS JACK HYLTON AND HER BOYS
Just Another Girl   THE VERNONS GIRLS
Just as Fat   CHARLIE CREED-MILES
Just By Your Example   JESSIE MATTHEWS
Just For Fun CHERRY ROLAND; MARK WYNTER
Just for the Fun of It   FRANCES DAY
Just For You *(1946)*   CAROL RAYE
Just For You *(1955)*
  CYRIL STAPLETON AND THE SHOW BAND
Just For You *(1975)*   GLITTER BAND
Just Heaven   JACK BUCHANAN
Just Humming Along CRITERION REVELLERS
Just in Time   DORRIE DENE
Just Like Heaven   THE CURE
Just Like Me   SPENCER DAVIS GROUP
Just Like the Ivy *(3 films: 1933, 1934, 1936)*
         MARIE KENDALL
Just Like the Ivy *(1943)* BERTHA WILLMOTT
Just Little Bits and Pieces
  HENRY HALL AND THE B.B.C. DANCE ORCHESTRA
Just Out of Reach   THE ZOMBIES
Just Whisper I Love You JACK BUCHANAN
Just You Wait and See *(1948)*
        STANLEY HOLLOWAY
Just You Wait and See *(1963)*   JOE BROWN

K

Kansas City   THE BEATLES
Karma Chameleon   CULTURE CLUB
Kasbek ALFREDO CAMPOLI AND REGINALD KING
Kashmiri Song MANTOVANI AND HIS TRIO
Kathleen Mavourneen *(2 films)*
        THOMAS (TOM) BURKE
Katya the Dancer   GENE GERRARD
K.C., The   ROBB WILTON

Kedron   GLASGOW ORPHEUS CHOIR
Keep a Sunbeam in Your Pocket
        ANNE SHELTON
Keep Cool Calm and Collect EVELYN DALL
Keep Fit *(2 films)*
  GEORGE FORMBY; JULIAN NIMAN AND HIS BOYS;
      GORDON RAY GIRLS; FRED TILSON
Keep It Clean   TONIA BERN
Keep It For Me   CATHERINE HOWE
Keep It Under Your Hat
  CICELY COURTNEIDGE; JACK HULBERT
Keep Looking for the Rainbow DONALD PEERS
Keep Me Where Love Is   CLIFF RICHARD
Keep Moving   SOUNDS INCORPORATED
Keep On Dancing
     BRIAN POOLE AND THE TREMELOES
Keep On Moving Along   DAVE WILLIS
Keep On the Bright Side   JACK HULBERT
Keep That Smile On Your Face ALAN PRICE
Keep the Home Fires Burning *(1934)*
        EVELYN LAYE
Keep the Home Fires Burning *(1937)*
        SIX HARMONISTS
Keep the Home Fires Burning *(1943)*
        TESSA DEANE
Keep Your Seats Please GEORGE FORMBY
Kerb Step, The   BOBBY HOWES
Kerry Dance PERCIVAL MACKEY AND HIS BAND
Keys to My Heart, The
  NANCY BROWN; HARRY WELCHMAN
Kick Me When I'm Down   JIGSAW
Kid Boots   LESLIE HENSON
Kids! Kids!   JACK BARTY
Killarney *(1937)*   JOHN McCORMACK
Killarney *(1939)*   ROBERT ASHLEY
Killarney *(1954)*   CAVAN O'CONNOR
Killing an Arab   THE CURE
Killing Song   PAUL ROBESON
King Charles and Nell Gwyn
       NAT MILLS AND BOBBIE
King of Dixieland   DICKIE VALENTINE
King's Cross   PET SHOP BOYS
King's Night Out, The THE WINDMILL GIRLS
Kiss Me FRANZ CONDE AND HIS BEGUINES
Kiss Me Before You Go Away IVY ST. HELIER
Kiss Me Goodnight *(1935)* ANNA NEAGLE
Kiss Me Goodnight *(1937)* PATRICIA ELLIS
Kiss Me Goodnight Sergeant Major
      ELSIE AND DORIS WATERS
Kiss Me Honey Honey MARCELLE DUPREY
Kiss Myself Goodbye   JUDY SHIRLEY
Kisses Can Lie   LYN CORNELL
Kissin'
  MR ACKER BILK AND THE PARAMOUNT JAZZ BAND
Kitchen EVAN DANDO AND THE LEMONHEADS
Kitten on the Keys FAIRCHILD AND LINDHOLM
Kleine Nachtmusik, Eine
  REBECCA VAN DER POST STRING QUARTETTE
Knees Up Mother Brown *(1950)*
      GERALDO AND HIS ORCHESTRA
Knees Up Mother Brown *(1958)* TOMMY STEELE
Knife Edge EMERSON, LAKE AND PALMER
Knight for My Nights, A   EARTHA KITT
Knight Riding, A AMBROSIAN SINGERS

Knocked 'em in the Old Kent Road
KEARNEY AND BROWNING
Krish RIKSARAJ
Ku Klux Klan STEEL PULSE
Kyoto Song THE CURE

L

La Dee Dah JACKIE DENNIS
La La La (1934) CONTINENTAL TRIO
La La La (1966) CLIFF RICHARD
La La La Song, The CORONA BOYS AND GIRLS
Lac des Cygnes, Le THE BOLSHOI BALLET
Ladies of the Gaiety HY HAZELL
Ladies of the Night
ALEC ALEXANDER AND HIS MELODY BOYS
Lads in Navy Blue
HORACE SHELDON AND HIS ORCHESTRA
Lady Craved Excitement, The HY HAZELL
Lady in Red, The (1936) JEAN REMA
Lady in Red, The (1939)
VICTOR SILVESTER AND HIS BALLROOM
ORCHESTRA
Lady Is a Square, The FRANKIE VAUGHAN
Lady Is a Vamp THE SPICE GIRLS
Lady Known as Sal, The BEBE DANIELS
Lady Luck LESLIE HENSON
Lady Mary GEORGE GROSSMITH
Lady of Spain (1932)
GERALDO AND HIS GAUCHO TANGO ORCHESTRA
Lady of Spain (1960) RAY ELLINGTON QUARTET
Lady of the Crinoline
ALEC ALEXANDER AND HIS MELODY BOYS
Lady of the House HARRY WELCHMAN
Lady of the Rose IVY TRESMAND
Lady on the Loose CELIA LIPTON; STEVE RACE
Lady's Maid Is Always in the Know, The
ANDRE CHARLOT GIRLS
Laird of Cockpen PETER SINCLAIR
Lambeth Walk, The (2 films: 1938, 1939)
LUPINO LANE
Lambeth Walk, The (1946)
LOU PRAEGER AND HIS BAND
Lamp of Love, The CLIFFORD MOLLISON
Lancashire Blues GRACIE FIELDS
Land of Hope and Glory (1928) ETHEL HOOK
Land of Hope and Glory (1931)
SIR EDWARD ELGAR
Land of Hope and Glory (1932)
B.B.C. SYMPHONY ORCHESTRA; SIR ADRIAN
BOULT
Land of Hope and Glory (1940) GRACIE FIELDS
Land of My Fathers (1931) GLANHOWY SINGERS
Land of My Fathers (1939) PAUL ROBESON
Land of My Fathers (1953)
LONDON WELSH ASSOCIATION CHORAL SOCIETY
Lanette AL STARITA
Largo el Factotum TITO GOBBI
Lassie from Lancashire (1934) FLORRIE FORDE
Lassie from Lancashire (1935; 2 films)
ANITA LOWE; LUTON SILVER PRIZE BAND
Last Night I Dreamed MAX BYGRAVES
Last Night's Kisses SAM BROWNE
Last Rose of Summer, The (2 films)
CHARLOTTE ALLEN AND JOHNNY BRODERICK;
JOHN GARRICK

Last Roundup, The LANCE FAIRFAX
Last Supper Sketch JOHN CLEESE
Last Waltz, The JOSÉ COLLINS
Laugh at Life WEBSTER BOOTH; ANNE ZIEGLER
Laugh Clown Laugh ARTHUR TRACY
Laugh It Off TOMMY TRINDER
Laughing Cavalier, The (1935) ROBERT EASTON
Laughing Cavalier, The (1936)
HARRY WELCHMAN
Laughing Policeman, The CHARLES PENROSE
Law and Disorder THE OUTLAWS
Lawd Loves His People to Sing, De
JOHN PAYNE'S CHOIR; ARTHUR TRACY
Lawd You Made the Night Too Long
IKE HATCH
Lawdy Miss Clawdy THE BEATLES
Lay It Down SLADE
Lay of the Pirate RAYMOND NEWELL
Layabout's Lament, A MARTY WILDE
Laziest Girl in Town, The MARLENE DIETRICH
Lazin' PAUL ROBESON
Lazy Lady ELISABETH WELCH
Lead Me On CHRIS BARBER AND HIS JAZZ BAND
Leader of the Gang GARY GLITTER
Leaf of Life, A CLARICE MAYNE
League of Notions DOLLY SISTERS
Leanin' (1931) RAYMOND NEWELL
Leanin' (1937) BRYN GWYN
Leaning on a Lamp Post
GEORGE FORMBY; VAL ROSING; DEBROY
SOMERS AND HIS BAND
Leap Year Waltz MOYRA FRASER
Learn How to Sing a Love Song BETTY DRIVER
Learning to Play the Uke BILLY 'UKE' SCOTT
Leave a Little Love for Me JACK BUCHANAN
Leave Me Alone (1955) LITA ROZA
Leave Me Alone (1964) PETER AND GORDON
Leave the Pretty Girls Alone LEN BERMAN
Leave the Rest to Nature AL BOWLLY
Legion of the Lost ERIC WOODBURN
Leicester Square Rag
IVY BENSON AND HER ALL GIRLS ORCHESTRA
Lenisches Gluck JOSEPH SCHMIDT
Lessons in Love CLIFF RICHARD
Let Her Go JOE BROWN
Let It Be (1970) THE BEATLES
Let It Be (1991) PAUL AND LINDA McCARTNEY
Let It Be Me DAVID ESSEX
Let It Rain JUNE CLYDE
Let Me Awaken Your Heart RICHARD TAUBER
Let Me Dream JEAN (JEANNIE) CARSON
Let Me Gaze (1932) NANCY BROWN
Let Me Gaze (1933) STANLEY LUPINO
Let Me Give My Happiness to You
JESSIE MATTHEWS
Let Me Go On Dreaming GERRY FITZGERALD
Let Me Lie SONNY STEWART'S SKIFFLE KINGS
Let Me Tell You HARRY KORRIS
Let the Bells Ring CLIFFORD MOLLISON
Let the Bulgine Run
KNELLER HALL MILITARY BAND
Let the Great Big World Keep Turning (1934)
VIOLET LORAINE
Let the Great Big World Keep Turning (1937)
MARIE LAVARRE

311

Let the World Go Drifting By	VIOLET LORAINE
Let Us Pretend	BILLY MERSON
Let Us Take You for a Ride	CLIFF RICHARD
Let's All Go to Mary's House	
	DICK HENDERSON (senior)
Let's All Go Up in the Sky	
	MRS JACK HYLTON AND HER BOYS
Let's Be Happy	TONY MARTIN; VERA-ELLEN
Let's Be in Love	ELSIE BROWN
Let's Be Sentimental	
	GENE GERRARD; JESSIE MATTHEWS
Let's Dance (2 films)	
EVELYN DALL; JOE LOSS AND HIS ORCHESTRA;	
MANTOVANI AND HIS TIPICA ORCHESTRA	
Let's Do the Samba	
	ROBERTO INGLEZ AND HIS ORCHESTRA
Let's Drift Away to Dreamer's Bay	
	YORKE AND BRIAN
Let's Fall in Love	THOMAS (TOM) BURKE
Let's Get Hold of Hitler	
ARTHUR ASKEY; CHARLES FORSYTHE, ADDIE	
SEAMON AND ELEANOR FARRELL	
Let's Get Married	ANTHONY NEWLEY
Let's Get Together Again	GLITTER BAND
Let's Go To Bed (2 films)	THE CURE
Let's Go Wild	RONALD FRANKAU
Let's Have Another One	TEDDY BROWN
Let's Kiss and Make Up	FRED CONYNGHAM
Let's Paint the Town	BILLY FURY
Let's Put Some People to Work	
	JACK BUCHANAN
Let's Spend the Night Together	DAVID BOWIE
Let's Talk About Love	HELEN SHAPIRO
Let's Twist Again	
	BOSCOE HOLDER; THE VISCOUNTS
Let's You and I Rock	
	TONY CROMBIE AND HIS ROCKETS
Letting in the Sunshine	ALBERT BURDON
Lido Lady	JACK HULBERT
Liebestraum (1930)	MAURICE COLE
Liebestraum (1932)	TOM JONES
Liebestraum (1933)	
EDDIE COLLIS AND THE ARISTOCRATS; PATRICIA	
ROSSBOROUGH	
Liebestraum (1946)	JOHN McHUGH
Life	CLIFF RICHARD
Life Is a Circus	
THE CRAZY GANG; BUD FLANAGAN AND CHESNEY	
ALLEN; MICHAEL HOLLIDAY	
Life Is Empty	HARRY ROY AND HIS BAND
Life Is Nothing Without Music	
FRED HARTLEY AND HIS QUINTET; JESSIE	
MATTHEWS	
Life on the Ocean Wave, A (1936)	
	SHERMAN FISHER GIRLS
Life on the Ocean Wave, A (1952)	
	SEVEN VOLANTES
Life on the Ocean Wave, A (1955)	
	HANWELL SILVER BAND
Life Should Go With a Swing	
DONALD CLIVE; THE WINDMILL GIRLS	
Life's a Joker	LANCE FAIRFAX
Lifetime Isn't Long Enough, A	JOYCE BLAIR
Light as Air	STANLEY LUPINO
Light Cavalry Overture	ERNESTO JACONELLI
Light Out of Darkness	RAY CHARLES

Lighterman Tom	ROBERT LAYTON
Lights of London	ROBERT ASHLEY
Like Clones	HOT GOSSIP
Like Dreamers Do	THE APPLEJACKS
Like Magic	SHANE FENTON
Lilac Domino Waltz, The	JUNE KNIGHT
Lili Marlene	ANNA NEAGLE
Lily of Laguna (1934; 2 films)	
	HARRY BEDFORD; G H ELLIOTT
Lily of Laguna (1938)	DUDLEY ROLPHE
Lily of Laguna (1940)	TOM E FINGLASS
Lily of Laguna (1943)	TOM E FINGLASS
Lily of Laguna (1944)	STANLEY HOLLOWAY
Limehouse	DENNIS NOBLE
Limehouse Blues	
	AMBROSE AND HIS ORCHESTRA
Linden Tree, The	JOSEPH SCHMIDT
Linger Awhile	
	BUD FLANAGAN AND CHESNEY ALLEN
Lion Hunter, The	ROBB WILTON
Lip Up Fatty	BAD MANNERS
Lisp of a Baby's Prayer, The	TALBOT O'FARRELL
Listen On	THE ALLEY CATS
Listen to the Mocking Bird	
EDDIE PEABODY AND HIS BEACHCOMBERS	
Listeners In	ELLALINE TERRISS
Listening to You	THE WHO
Liszt Melodies JOSEPH MUSCANT AND HIS BAND	
Little Bit of Heaven, A	WILL MAHONEY
Little Bit Off the Top, A (2 films)	
	HARRY BEDFORD
Little Boat	THE SPRINGFIELDS
Little Brown Jug	GEORGIAN SINGERS
Little Brown Owl (1931)	ANN BURGESS
Little Brown Owl (1935)	MILLICENT PHILLIPS
Little Chick	TONY KINSEY QUARTET
Little Children	
	BILLY J. KRAMER AND THE DAKOTAS
Little Damozel, The	SYLVIA WELLING
Little Dash of Dublin, A	ANNA NEAGLE
Little Dolly Daydream (1938)	TALBOT O'FARRELL
Little Dolly Daydream (1940)	TOM E FINGLASS
Little Fishes	FRANKIE VAUGHAN
Little Friend	BETTY FIELDS
Little Girl	JACK HULBERT
Little Girl in Blue	DICK JAMES
Little Girl What Now?	FREDDIE LATHAM
Little Grey Home in the West	LENI LYNN
Little Gypsy of the Seven Seas	
	ELSIE AND DORIS WATERS
Little Imagination, A	CLIFF RICHARD
Little Lady Make Believe	DON GALVAN
Little Liza Jane	
	CHRIS BARBER AND HIS JAZZ BAND
Little Lost Tune, The	JEAN COLIN
Little Loving, A	FOURMOST
Little Nelly Kelly	JUNE
Little of What You Fancy, A	
	MARIE LLOYD JUNIOR
Little Robin Told Me, A	
BILLY BISSETT AND HIS CANADIAN BAND	
Little Ships, The	DENNIS NOBLE
Little Silkworm	
JESSIE MATTHEWS; DONALD STEWART	

Little Sprig of Shamrock
    PERCIVAL MACKEY AND HIS BAND; CAVAN
    O'CONNOR; NICOLETTE ROEG
Little Sunshine, A   RENATE MULLER
Little Tact, A   NAUNTON WAYNE
Little White Bull   TOMMY STEELE
Little White Horse   KURT WEGENER
Little White Lies   NOBLE SISSLE AND HIS BAND
Live and Let Die   PAUL AND LINDA McCARTNEY
Live It Up   HEINZ
Lively Up Yourself
        BOB MARLEY AND THE WAILERS
Living Doll *(2 films)*   CLIFF RICHARD
Living in Clover *(1932)*   JACK BUCHANAN
Living in Clover *(1936)*   STANLEY LUPINO
Liza You Are My Dona   STANLEY HOLLOWAY
Liza's Eyes   JERRY WAYNE
Lo Hear the Gentle Lark *(1929)* LUELLA PAIKIN
Lo Hear the Gentle Lark *(1937)*
                    NELLIE WALLACE
Local Magistrate, The   ROBB WILTON
Loch Lomond *(1930; 2 films)*
    GLASGOW ORPHEUS CHOIR; JOSEPH HISLOP
Loch Lomond *(1933)*
    GLASGOW PHILHARMONIC MALE VOICE CHOIR
Loch Lomond *(1936)*   MAURICE CHEVALIER
Loch Lomond *(1939)*   ROBERT WILSON
Loch Lomond *(1944)*   WALTER MIDGELEY
Loch Ness Monster, The   LESLIE HOLMES
Locomotion, The   JACKIE AND THE RAINDROPS
Lohengrin   BAND OF THE ROYAL ARTILLERY
Lollipops   MARIO DE PIETRO
London   ROBERT CHIGWELL
London Bridge   ERIC COATES
London I Love, The *(1941)* ROBERT ASHLEY
London I Love, The *(1955)*   YANA
London is a Fine Town   TOPLISS GREEN
London on a Rainy Night
         BOB AND ALF PEARSON
London River   DENNIS NOBLE
London Town *(1929)*   THE CO-OPTIMISTS
London Town *(1936)*   STANLEY LUPINO
London Will Rise Again   RAYMOND NEWELL
London's Burning   THE CLASH
Londonderry Air *(1929)*   LUELLA PAIKIN
Londonderry Air *(1930)*
        GLASGOW ORPHEUS CHOIR
Londonderry Air *(1935)*   MARIO DE PIETRO
Londonderry Air *(1938; 2 films)*
    THOMAS (TOM) BURKE; REGINALD FOORT
Londoner and the Hun, The
         FLOTSAM AND JETSAM
Loneliness   GITTA ALPAR
Loneliness in My Heart   BERYL DAVIS
Lonely Am I   NANCY BROWN
Lonely Avenue   THE BLUES BAND
Lonely Boy   THE SEX PISTOLS
Lonely City   JOHNNY LEYTON
Lonely Girl   CLIFF RICHARD
Lonely Road   PAUL ROBESON
Long and Winding Road *(1970)* THE BEATLES
Long and Winding Road *(1984)*
        PAUL McCARTNEY
Long and Winding Road *(1991)*
    PAUL AND LINDA McCARTNEY

Long Live Rock *(1973)*   BILLY FURY
Long Live Rock *(1979)*   THE WHO
Long Long Trail, The   ALONZO ELLIOTT
Long Tall Sally   MIGIL FIVE
Longer You Linger, The   JOHN RUTLAND
Longshoreman, The   BERNARD DUDLEY
Look Don't Touch   FRANK IFIELD
Look to the Left   MARC BOLAN AND T. REX
Look Up and Laugh   GRACIE FIELDS
Looking Around Corners JESSIE MATTHEWS
Looking Back   SPENCER DAVIS GROUP
Looking for Someone   DAVID ESSEX
Looking on the Bright Side   GRACIE FIELDS
Lord and Lady Whozis   JESSIE MATTHEWS
Lord God Abraham   PAUL ROBESON
Lord High Executioner, The FRANKIE HOWERD
Lord Mayor's Coachman, The
          SIDNEY BURCHALL
Lord You Made the Night Too Long
        BOB AND ALF PEARSON
Lord You've Been Good to Me
    CHRIS BARBER AND HIS JAZZ BAND
Lose Your Inhibitions Twist   CHUBBY CHECKER
Lost Chord, The *(1928)*   HERSCHEL HENLERE
Lost Chord, The *(1933)*
    TUDOR DAVIS; FREDERICK RANALOW
Lost My Rhythm AMBROSE AND HIS ORCHESTRA
Loudly Proclaim
  LONDON WELSH ASSOCIATION CHORAL SOCIETY
Louisiana Lou   SCOTT AND WHALEY
Louisville Lady   SOPHIE TUCKER
Love *(1929)*
LADDIE CLIFF; STANLEY LUPINO; CYRIL RITCHARD
              AND MADGE ELLIOTT
Love *(1934)*   GRACIE FIELDS
Love *(1959)*   CLIFF RICHARD
Love a Man   MARION RYAN
Love Again   CAROL RAYE
Love Bug, The   ALBERT WHELAN
Love Comes at Blossom Time
         RICHARD TAUBER
Love If You Will Come to Me
        AMBROSIAN SINGERS
Love In a Void SIOUXSIE AND THE BANSHEES
Love Is a Bore   CLEO LAINE
Love Is a Dream   ALAN DAVID
Love Is a Duet   ELSA STENNING
Love Is a Song   EVELYN LAYE
Love Is Everywhere   GRACIE FIELDS
Love Is Just a Game
      BETTY JUMEL; SANDY POWELL
Love Is Like a Cigarette
    JOE LOSS AND HIS ORCHESTRA; VERA LYNN
Love Is the Key
    WEBSTER BOOTH; ANNE ZIEGLER
Love Is the Sweetest Thing
    JACK PAYNE AND HIS DANCE ORCHESTRA
Love Kills   THE CIRCLE JERKS
Love Life and Laughter   GRACIE FIELDS
Love Lost For Ever More RICHARD TAUBER
Love Marches On   THREE ADMIRALS
Love Me Little Love Me Long   JILL DAY
Love Me Please   MIKE SARNE
Love or Money   THE WACKERS
Love Remembers Everything ROBERT ASHLEY

Love Song	PAUL ROBESON
Love to be Let or Sold	BINNIE BARNES
Love Twist	CULTURE CLUB
Love Will Find a Way	NANCY BROWN
Love's a Racketeer	CHILI BOUCHIER
Love's Cigarette	HARRY WELCHMAN
Love's Dream	ROGER DALTREY
Love's Glamour	ERIC MARSHALL
Love's Melody	FRANCES DAY
Love's Old Sweet Song (1928)	ETHEL HOOK
Love's Old Sweet Song (1933)	LESLIE DAY
Love's Old Sweet Song (1934)	EVELYN LAYE
Love's Old Sweet Song (1935)	
STEFFANI'S SIXTEEN SINGING SCHOLARS	
Love's Old Sweet Song (1936; 2 films)	
BASYL; SHERRY BROTHERS	
Love's Old Sweet Song (1937)	
BERTIE KENDRICK	
Love's Old Sweet Song (1941)	GRANT TYLER
Love's Old Sweet Song (1943; 2 films)	
CEDRIC SHARPE; ST. DAVID'S SINGERS	
Love's Old Sweet Song (1944)	
WEBSTER BOOTH; ANNE ZIEGLER	
Love's Serenade	HARRY AND GRAY
Lover Come Back to Me	RUDY STARITA
Lovers	FRANK IFIELD
Lovey Dovey	
JUNE CLYDE; CHARLES 'BUDDY' ROGERS	
Lovin' On My Mind (2 films)	FRANK IFIELD
Loving Me This Way	KIM ROBERTS
Low Backed Car, The	JAMES ETHERINGTON
Lower Deck	PHIL SEAMON'S JAZZ GROUP
Lucky Five	RUSS CONWAY
Lucky for Me	JESSIE MATTHEWS
Lucky Strike (1955)	
CYRIL STAPLETON AND THE SHOW BAND	
Lucky Strike (1960)	RAY ELLINGTON QUARTET
Lucy in the Sky with Diamonds	THE BEATLES
Lullaby (1936)	BENJAMINO GIGLI
Lullaby (1993)	THE CURE
Lullabye of Birdland	GEORGE SHEARING
Lullabye of the Leaves (1932)	
THOMAS (TOM) BURKE	
Lullabye of the Leaves (1933)	
THE NILE PLAYERS	
Lullabye of the Leaves (1936)	JACK COURTNEY
Lumberjack Song	
GRAHAM CHAPMAN; JOHN CLEESE; PETER COOK;	
BARRY HUMPHRIES; NEIL INNES; TERRY JONES;	
BILL ODDIE; MICHAEL PALIN	
Lying Argument, A	COLLINSON AND DEAN

M

Ma Curly-Headed Babby (1936)	
PAUL ROBESON	
My Curly Headed Babby (1938)	
ELSA STENNING	
Macbeth	RONALD FRANKAU
MacDougall McNab and McKay	
FRED CONYNGHAM	
Machine Dance	YVONNE MERTENS
Mackintosh's Wedding	JOAN HEAL; VERA-ELLEN
MacNamara's Band	STANLEY HOLLOWAY
Macushla (1931)	LANCE FAIRFAX

Macushla (1935)	THOMAS (TOM) BURKE
Macushla (1949)	JOSEF LOCKE
Mad About You	CLIFF RICHARD
Mad Magician, The	ED MORELLE
Mad March Hare	GEORGE FORMBY
Madame Medusa	UB40
Madame Pompadour	EVELYN LAYE
Madame You're Lovely (1934)	
YACHT CLUB BOYS	
Madame You're Lovely (1935)	
BERNARD MONSHIN AND HIS RIO TANGO BAND	
Maddalena	MARTA EGGERTH
Made You	ADAM FAITH
Mademoiselle	MAX AND HARRY NESBITT
Madness	MADNESS
Madonna	JACK COOPER
Mae Time	FLORENCE DESMOND
Maggie Cock-a-Bendy	JACK MILROY
Maggie's Farm	THE BLUES BAND
Magic Bus	THE WHO
Magic Flute, The	
SIR THOMAS BEECHAM; LONDON PHILHARMONIC	
ORCHESTRA	
Magic of You, The	SONJA HENIE
Magic Waltz, The	
JAMILLA NOVOTNA; HARRY WELCHMAN	
Magistrate, The	ROBB WILTON
Main Attraction, The	PAT BOONE
Maire My Girl (1932)	TREFOR JONES
Maire My Girl (1933)	THOMAS (TOM) BURKE
Majorca, The (1945)	
PAT (PATRICIA) KIRKWOOD; EDMUNDO ROS AND	
HIS RUMBA BAND	
Make Hay While the Moon Shines	
STANLEY LUPINO	
Make It Soon	FRANK IFIELD
Make Me Good	
DAVE EDMUNDS AND THE STRAY CATS	
Make Some Music	
IVOR MORETON AND DAVE KAYE; HARRY ROY	
AND HIS BAND	
Make the Punishment Fit the Crime	
STUBBY KAYE	
Making a Record at HMV	GRACIE FIELDS
Malgré Tout	
HERMANOS DENIZ AND HIS CUBAN RHYTHM BAND	
Mambo Rat	CABBAGE HEAD
Mamma He Treats Your Daughter Mean	
CHRIS BARBER AND HIS JAZZ BAND; OTTILIE	
PATTERSON	
Mammy	HARRY BRUNNING
Mammy's Little Fellow	FAYRE SISTERS
Man About Town	JACK MELFORD
Man and his Music, A	JACK JACKSON
Man at C & A	THE SPECIALS
Man for Me, The	FLORENCE DESMOND
Man from Harlem, The	
BILLY COTTON AND HIS BAND	
Man from Nowhere, The	
JET HARRIS AND THE JETBLACKS	
Man of My Dreams	
PRINCESS PEARL; HARRY ROY AND HIS BAND	
Man of the Moment	NORMAN WISDOM
Man on the Flying Trapeze, The (1936)	
THREE RADIO ROGUES	

Man on the Flying Trapeze, The *(1944)* TOMMY TRINDER
Man Who Broke the Bank, The *(4 films: 1934, 1934, 1936, 1943)* CHARLES COBURN
Man Who Broke the Bank, The *(1938)* GRACIE FIELDS
Manhattan Blues BILLY 'UKE' SCOTT
Many Happy Returns
  HENRY HALL AND THE B.B.C. DANCE ORCHESTRA
Marakech ANDY GUTHRIE
Marc's Intro MARC BOLAN AND T. REX
March España PAUL RICO AND HIS MEXICANS
March of Musicians RICHARD TAUBER
March of the Cameron Men TOM KINNIBURGH
March of the Little Soldiers
  TOLEDO, ELLY AND JEAN
Marche Militaire MANSELL AND LING
Marching Along GRETE NATZLER
Marching Song JACK BUCHANAN
Mardi Gras TURNER TWINS
Marguerite and Armand
  MARGOT FONTEYN; RUDOLPH NUREYEV
Maria from Bahia
HERMANOS DENIZ AND HIS CUBAN RHYTHM BAND
Maria Marten TOD SLAUGHTER
Marianne LEONARD COHEN
Marigold *(3 films)* BILLY MAYERL
Marilou JACK SIMPSON AND HIS TANGO BAND
Marriage of Figaro
SIR THOMAS BEECHAM; LONDON PHILHARMONIC ORCHESTRA
Marry Me RENATE MULLER
Marseillaise, La ERIC WOODBURN
Marta *(1936; 2 films)*
  BENJAMINO GIGLI; ARTHUR TRACY
Marta *(1937)* ARTHUR TRACY
Mary WALTER MIDGELEY
Mary From the Dairy *(1939)* MAX MILLER
Mary From the Dairy *(1971)* CHARLIE CHESTER
Mary Morison TREFOR JONES
Mary Rose GRACIE FIELDS
Maryland
  TERRY LIGHTFOOT AND HIS NEW ORLEANS JAZZ BAND
Masculine Women and Feminine Men
  NORAH BLANEY
Mask of Death MYSTIC
Mastersingers, The
  B.B.C. SYMPHONY ORCHESTRA
Match for Two, A THE HOUSTON SISTERS
Matter of Moments, A CLIFF RICHARD
Maureen O'Dare PERCY MANCHESTER
Maxwell's Silver Hammer THE BEATLES
May All Your Troubles Be Little Ones
  JUNE CLYDE; JACK HYLTON AND HIS BAND; BRYAN LAWRANCE
May I Have the Next Romance With You
  JESSIE MATTHEWS
Maybe Baby BERYL FORMBY; GEORGE FORMBY
Maybe Me Maybe You THE CO-OPTIMISTS
Mayfair Mambo
  EDMUNDO ROS AND HIS RUMBA BAND
Mayfair Merry Go Round
AMBROSE AND HIS ORCHESTRA; HARRY RICHMAN
Mayoress, The DOUGLAS BYNG

Maytime is Made for Love
  PATRICK WADDINGTON
Mazurka Brilliante J. H. SQUIRE'S TRIO
Me and My Dog FRANCES DAY
Me and My Girl LUPINO LANE
Me, Myself and I MONTE MORRIS
Me Needing You THE PRETTY THINGS
Mean Mistreater
  CHRIS BARBER AND HIS JAZZ BAND
Meanest Thing You Did to Me, The
  PHYLLIS ROBINS
Medley MARIO 'HARP' LORENZI
Meeting You DICK KALLMAN
Meistersingers, The
  ROYAL OPERA HOUSE COVENT GARDEN CHORUS
Melancholy Baby *(1936; 2 films)*
  AL BOWLLY; SYD SEYMOUR AND HIS MAD HATTERS
Melancholy Baby *(1954)* KENNY BAKER
Melodious Melodies FOUR ADMIRALS
Melody at Dawn GRACIE FIELDS
Melody at Dusk ALBERT SANDLER
Melody in F *(1934)* SYDNEY KYTE AND HIS BAND
Melody in F *(1935)* PATRICIA ROSSBOROUGH
Melody in F *(1937)* NORMAN EVANS
Melody in F *(1948)* NISELLE AND ILSTER
Melody Maker, The
  JACK HYLTON AND HIS BAND; PAT (PATRICIA) KIRKWOOD
Melody of My Heart LORRAINE LA FOSSE
Melting Pot CULTURE CLUB
Member for Hogsnorton GILLIE POTTER
Memo for Turner MICK JAGGER
Memories of Chopin
  VIENNESE SINGING SISTERS
Memories of Tchaikowsky
  J. H. SQUIRE'S CELESTE OCTET
Memory's Garden JOHN HENDRIK
Men AMANDA BARRIE
Men of Harlech *(1931)* GLANHOWY SINGERS
Men of Harlech *(1963)*
  IVOR EMMANUEL; DAVID KERNAN
Men Oh How I Hate Them FRANCES DAY
Mendelssohn's Violin Concerto
  ALFREDO CAMPOLI
Merci Beaucoup TEDDY JOHNSON
Mère, La ERIC IDLE
Merry Merry PEGGY O'NEIL
Merry Moments A W BASKCOMB; W H BERRY
Merry Month of May ALEC TEMPLETON
Merry Wives of Windsor
  LONDON SYMPHONY ORCHESTRA
Merrymakers Dance ANNA NEAGLE
Message in a Bottle STING
Message Sweet as Roses, A RICHARD TAUBER
Metropole Midnight Follies
  JOAN CARR; EDDIE CHILDS; BOBBY HOWES; ELSA MacFARLANE
Mexican Dance TERRI AND PATLANZKI
Mexican Hat Dance
  CYRIL STAPLETON AND THE SHOW BAND
Mexico THE WINDMILL GIRLS
Meyer What a Liar TWO RASCALS
Mice and Men GLASGOW ORPHEUS CHOIR

Mickey Mouse
THE BARRIE SISTERS/TWINS; HAL SWAIN AND HIS KIT KAT BAND
Midgets   DESMOND LANE
Midinette, La   LUCIENNE AND ASHOUR
Midnight Blue   CLIFF RICHARD
Midnight Follies (1922)
NORAH BLANEY; CICELY COURTNEIDGE; GWEN FARRAR; JACK HULBERT
Midnight Follies (1926)   BOBBY HOWES
Midnight Madness
JEAN CARSON; KEN MacINTOSH AND HIS BAND
Midnight to Six Man   THE PRETTY THINGS
Midshipmaid, The   DAVY BURNABY
Midsummer Morn   CEDRIC SHARPE
Midsummer New York   YOKO ONO
Midway Rhythm
SANTOS CASANI AND JOSE LENNARD
Mighty Lak' a Rose (1930)   THREE VIRGINIANS
Mighty Lak' a Rose (1935)   THE SINGING LADY
Mighty Lak' a Rose (1938)   NORA SWINBURNE
Mighty Lak' a Rose (1939)   ELSA STENNING
Mikado, The
OWEN BRANNIGAN; MARTYN GREEN; THOMAS ROUND
Milano   LESLIE HOLMES
Militant Works
RAS ANGELS AND RAS MESSENGERS
Million Dreams, A   WILFRED TEMPLE
Million Little Raindrops, A   BILLY 'UKE' SCOTT
Million Tears, A
BUD FLANAGAN AND CHESNEY ALLEN
Millionaire Kid, The
LADDIE CLIFF; BARRY LUPINO; CYRIL RITCHARD AND MADGE ELLIOTT
Millions of Kisses
PERCIVAL MACKEY AND HIS BAND
Milton's SexRap   CHARLIE CREED-MILES
Mind How You Go Across the Road
BOBBY HOWES
Mind Train   YOKO ONO
Miner from Asia Minor, The   RONALD FRANKAU
Minnie the Moocher   PHYLLIS STANLEY
Minstrel Boy, The (1937; 2 films)
FRED CONYNGHAM; JOHN GARRICK
Minstrel Boy, The (1939)   JIMMY O'DEA
Minstrels of 1922
GUS CHEVALIER; GENE GERRARD
Minuet (1937)   IGNACE JAN PADEREWSKI
Minuet (1943)   REGINALD KING QUARTET
Miracle Cure   SIMON TOWNSHEND
Miracles Sometimes Happen
BILLY MERRIN AND HIS COMMANDERS
Mirror Dance (1926)
MARIA SOLVEG AND KATTA STERNA
Mirror Dance (1939)   THE BOSWELL TWINS
Mirror in the Bathroom   THE BEAT
Mirror Song, The   HARRY WELCHMAN
Miss Annabelle Lee (1935; 2 films)
CHARLIE KUNZ
Miss Annabelle Lee (1937)
MINI-PIANO ENSEMBLE OF 14 JUVENILES
Miss In Between   CRAIG DOUGLAS
Miss Me Blind   CULTURE CLUB
Miss Up-to-Date   CYRIL RITCHARD
Miss Whatshername   STANLEY LUPINO

Missing Words   THE SELECTER
Mister Man   CULTURE CLUB
Misty Island   ROBERT WILSON
Misty Islands of the Highlands (1936)
BOB AND ALF PEARSON
Misty Islands of the Highlands (1938)
ARTHUR TRACY
Misty Islands of the Highlands (1940)
THE BELLS; BENNETT AND WILLIAMS
Mixed Ginx   HARRY TATE
Mixed Melody   JEAN MELVILLE
Moaning Minnie
JACK HYLTON AND HIS BAND; DIANA WARD
Moby Dick   LED ZEPPELIN
Mocking Bird Hill   MIGIL FIVE
Model Worker   MAGAZINE
Modern Romeo, A   DIANA DECKER
Modes While You Wait
DON PHILLIPE AND PARTNER
Moment I Saw You, The (1933)
CICELY COURTNEIDGE
Moment I Saw You, The (2 films: 1948, 1954)
ANNA NEAGLE
Momma Don't Allow
CHRIS BARBER AND HIS JAZZ BAND; LONNIE DONEGAN
Momma Loves Poppa MAX AND HARRY NESBITT
Money/Justice   ALAN PRICE
Money to Burn   TOMMY STEELE
Monsters in Disguise   HAZEL O'CONNOR
Montasara, La   TITO GOBBI
Monte Carlo
EDMUNDO ROS AND HIS RUMBA BAND
Montreal, The   JACK BUCHANAN
Monument   KENNY LYNCH
Moon and I, The   JACQUELINE JONES
Moon at Sea   SAM COSTA
Moon for Sale   ROBERT ASHLEY
Moon Has Raised Her Lamp Above, The
JOHN GARRICK
Moon Is Tired of Shining, The
NAVARRE; DEBROY SOMERS AND HIS BAND
Moon or No Moon   JESSIE MATTHEWS
Moon Remembers, The   BETTY DRIVER
Moonage Daydream   DAVID BOWIE
Moonlight and a Prairie Sky   JOSEF LOCKE
Moonlight and Music   FRANCES DAY
Moonlight in Mexico   VIRGINIA DAWN
Moonlight Madonna
PERCIVAL MACKEY AND HIS BAND; RONALD WALTERS
Moonlight Sonata (1930)   MARK HAMBOURG
Moonlight Sonata (1937)
IGNACE JAN PADEREWSKI
Moraca Mamba   THE SPRINGFIELDS
More Humane Mikado, A   STUBBY KAYE
More We Are Together, The RICH AND GALVIN
Most Beautiful Thing in My Life, The
HERMAN'S HERMITS
Moth, The (2 films)   ARTHUR ASKEY
Mother and Son   ROGER DALTREY
Mother Machree (1937)   DILLWYN THOMAS
Mother Machree (1993)   DONAL BYRNE
Mother, What'll I Do Now?   GEORGE FORMBY
Mothers of the Motherland   PETER SINCLAIR
Motoring   HARRY TATE

Mountain Lovers	LORNA MARTIN
Mountains o' Mourne, The *(1934)*	
	DENNIS O'NEIL
Mountains o' Mourne, The *(1937; 2 films)*	
FRED CONYNGHAM; BRYAN LAWRANCE	
Mountains o' Mourne, The *(1938)*	
PERCIVAL MACKEY AND HIS BAND; RENE RAY	
Mountains o' Mourne, The *(1941)*	
	PERCY MANCHESTER
Mourning	JOSEPH SCHMIDT
Move On	DAVE CLARK FIVE
Mozart's 10th Symphony	
LONDON PHILHARMONIC ORCHESTRA	
Mr Middleton Says Its Right	
	VINE, MORE AND NEVARD
Mr Muddlecombe JP *(2 films)*	ROBB WILTON
Mr Pastry at the Circus	RICHARD HEARNE
Mr Pottle	NAN KENWAY AND DOUGLAS YOUNG
Mr Scrooge	THE ORCHIDS
Mr Wu's a Window Cleaner Now	
	GEORGE FORMBY
Mrs Arris on the Tube	FRED SPENCER
Mrs Binns's Twins	GRACIE FIELDS
Mrs Brown You've Got a Lovely Daughter	
	HERMAN'S HERMITS
Mrs Lennon	YOKO ONO
Much Binding in the Marsh	
SAM COSTA; KENNETH HORNE; RICHARD	
	MURDOCH
Murmuring Breezes	LEONARD GOWINGS
Murmurs of Spring	
ALFREDO CAMPOLI AND REGINALD KING;	
	REGINALD KING
Music From the Air	MARTIN TAUBMANN
Music Hath Charms *(2 films)*	
HENRY HALL AND THE B.B.C. DANCE ORCHESTRA;	
	STANLEY HOLLOWAY
Music is the Cure	SYDNEY HOWARD
Music Lesson, The	SANDY POWELL
Musical Moments	SIRDANI
Must Be	ANTHONY NEWLEY
My Ain Folk	LORNA MARTIN; WALTER MIDGELEY
My Attraction	JUNE MALO
My Awful Past	STANLEY LUPINO
My Baby's Got Red Hair	
	MAX AND HARRY NESBITT
My Bally Eyeglass	TOM CLARE
My Beach	SURF PUNKS
My Beloved	JACK BUCHANAN
My Blue Heaven	HAL YATES
My Bonnie Lies Over the Ocean *(1929)*	
THE SALISBURY SINGERS; DALE SMITH	
My Bonnie Lies Over the Ocean *(1963)*	
	THE SPOTNICKS
My Boy	DOROTHY SQUIRES
My Boy Flat Top	FRANKIE VAUGHAN
My Boy Lollipop	MILLIE
My British Buddy	IRVING BERLIN
My Canary Has Circles Under His Eyes	
	ELSIE CARLISLE
My Dear Soul	THE SINGING COOK
My Death	DAVID BOWIE
My Extraordinary Man	SOPHIE TUCKER
My Favourite Samba	
EDMUNDO ROS AND HIS RUMBA BAND	

My First Love Song	GRACIE FIELDS
My First Thought Is You	GITTA ALPAR
My First Thrill	
JUNE CLYDE; SONNY FARRAR; JACK HYLTON AND	
	HIS BAND; BRYAN LAWRANCE
My Four British Tailors	
	RONNY GRAHAM; TREFOR JONES
My Generation *(2 films)*	THE WHO
My Girl's a Yorkshire Girl	
	LUTON SILVER PRIZE BAND
My Girl's Face	LADDIE CLIFF; THE CO-OPTIMISTS
My Goodbye to You	BOB AND ALF PEARSON
My Guy's Come Back	
	ERIC DELANEY AND HIS BAND
My Gypsy Dream Girl	ARTHUR TRACY
My Hat's on the Side of My Head	
	JACK HULBERT
My Heart Belongs To Daddy	FRANCES ASHMAN
My Heart Goes Crazy	TESSIE O'SHEA
My Heart Is Always Calling	JAN KIEPURA
My Heart Is Full of Sunshine	JAN KIEPURA
My Heart Is Irish	DENIS MARTIN
My Heart Is Saying	
	ADELPHI GIRLS; HELEN BURNELL
My Heart Sings	THE SQUADRONNAIRES
My Heart Skips a Beat	
	JESSIE MATTHEWS; JACK WHITING
My Heart Will Be Dancing	
	MICHAEL BARTLETT; JUNE KNIGHT
My Heart Will Never Sing Again	
	ROBERT ASHLEY
My Heart Wouldn't Beat Again	
JOE LOSS AND HIS ORCHESTRA; VERA LYNN	
My Home in the Highland Hills	PEARL VENTERS
My Home in Tralee	EVELYN LAYE
My Hometown	ALAN PRICE
My Idea of a Girl	HUGH RENE
My Ideal	CARL BRISSON
My Irish Song	DAN DONOVAN
My Lady Crinoline	PETER SINCLAIR
My Lady's Eyes	THE CO-OPTIMISTS
My Life Belongs to You	GISELLE PREVILLE
My Life in Politics/The Media	
	THE CO-CREATORS
My Little Black Dove	NINA MAE McKINNEY
My Little Bottom Drawer	GRACIE FIELDS
My Little Girl	THE CRICKETS
My Little Irish Gig	JOHN GARRICK
My Little Lot	JOHN RORKE
My Little Welsh Home	ARTHUR WILLIAMS
My Little Wooden Hut	JESSIE MATTHEWS
My Love For You *(1937)*	GRACIE FIELDS
My Love For You *(1951)*	VERA LYNN
My Love Forever	GERRY AND THE PACEMAKERS
My Love Is Like a Red Red Rose	
	TREFOR JONES
My Love She's But a Lassie Yet	
	ALEX HENDERSON
My Love Will Still Be There	CLODAGH RODGERS
My Old Brown Hat	JOHN RUTLAND
My Old Dutch	
LEON CORTEZ AND HIS COSTER PALS	
My Old Kentucky Home	NORMAN WILLIAMS
My Old Man	LILY MORRIS

My Old Man's a Dustman NAT JACKLEY; MARGERY MANNERS
My One and Only FRED CONYNGHAM
My Prayer VERA LYNN
My Pretty Flowers ANNA NEAGLE
My Red Letter Day ELSIE RANDOLPH
My River JESSIE MATTHEWS; JACK WHITING
My Shadow's Where My Sweetheart Used to
Be JOE LOSS AND HIS ORCHESTRA
My Sheep Dog and I JOHN GARRICK
My Ship MARY ELLIS
My Sin JACK PAYNE AND HIS DANCE ORCHESTRA
My Son BEBE DANIELS
My Song for You JAN KIEPURA
My Song Goes Round the World
JOSEPH SCHMIDT
My Song of Love DAWN LESLEY
My S.O.S. to You TURNER LAYTON
My Southern Maid BEBE DANIELS
My Sunshine Is You
GERALDO AND HIS GAUCHO TANGO ORCHESTRA
My Sweet GERTRUDE LAWRENCE
My Tender Flower JOHN GARRICK
My Treasure FAY COMPTON
My Unlucky Day GRACIE FIELDS
My Way (1937) PAUL ROBESON
My Way (1980) THE SEX PISTOLS
My Way (1986) GLEN MATLOCK
My What a Different Night
CICELY COURTNEIDGE
My Wife's Family ERNIE LOTINGA
My Wild Oat
CICELY COURTNEIDGE; LESLIE HOLMES;
THREE ADMIRALS
My Word He Is a Naughty Boy
PAT (PATRICIA) KIRKWOOD
My World Is Gold RICHARD TAUBER
My World Is Your World HARRY SECOMBE
Myself When Young NORMAN WILLIAMS

N

Nagasaki (1935)
PICKARD'S CHINESE SYNCOPATORS
Nagasaki (1936) ART GREGORY AND HIS BAND
Nagasaki (1937) MILLS BROTHERS
Nancy LEONARD COHEN
Naples Your Song Is Everywhere JAN KIEPURA
Napoleon's Hat CICELY COURTNEIDGE
Narrative Calypso
TOMMY EYTLE'S CALYPSO BAND
Natural Thing to Do, The SALLY BARNES
Naval Pact, A COLLINSON AND DEAN
Ne Ne Na Na Nu Nu BAD MANNERS
Near and Yet So Far EVELYN LAYE
Nellie Dean CANADIAN BACHELORS
Nelly Bly RICHARD HAYWARD
Nessun Dorma HARRY SECOMBE
Never Blow Your Whistle in the Park
WALSH AND BARKER
Never Enough THE CURE
Never Give Up on the Good Times
THE SPICE GIRLS
Never Make Eyes THE SQUADRONNAIRES

Never Say Never Again Again (1936)
THREE ACCORDION KINGS
Never Say Never Again Again (1937)
DANNY LIPTON TRIO
Never Too Young To Rock
SCOTT FITZGERALD; GLITTER BAND; MUD;
THE RUBETTES; SLIK
New Colonial March EDDIE BOWERS
New Foxtrot, The
SANTOS CASANI AND JOSE LENNARD
New Orleans Street Parade
CHRIS BARBER AND HIS JAZZ BAND
New Tango SANTOS CASANI AND JOSE LENNARD
New 23rd, The CLIFF RICHARD
New Waltz, The
SANTOS CASANI AND JOSE LENNARD
New World THE STRAWBS
New Year's Day WILL FYFFE
New York Scene, The MILLICENT MARTIN
Next Time CLIFF RICHARD
Nice Morning VIC OLIVER
Nice People
OSCAR RABIN AND HIS ROMANY BAND
Nice Quiet Day, A ALICK McLEAN
Nigger Strut CLEMSON AND VALERIE
Night Before, The THE BEATLES
Night Boat to Cairo MADNESS
Night Has a Thousand Eyes BOBBY VEE
Night Like This, A (1932)
AL BOWLLY; ROY FOX AND HIS BAND
Night Like This, A (1987) THE CURE
Night Like This, A (1993) THE CURE
Nightfall ELISABETH WELCH
Nightingale Sang in Berkeley Square, A
(1940) BERNARD CLIFTON
Nightingale Sang in Berkeley Square, A
(1961) DILL JONES AND HIS ALL STARS
Nightmare CRAZY WORLD OF ARTHUR BROWN
Nights of Gladness STANELLI AND HIS BAND
Nila THE ADAJIO TRIO
Nina ANGELO MINGHETTI
Nirewana TILLY LOSCH; ARTHUR TRACY
Nite Klub THE SPECIALS
No Feelings (1980) THE SEX PISTOLS
No Feelings (1986)
GLEN MATLOCK; ANDREW SCHOFIELD
No Fun THE SEX PISTOLS
No Funny Business GERTRUDE LAWRENCE
No More Lonely Nights PAUL McCARTNEY
No More Trouble
BOB MARLEY AND THE WAILERS
No More You BETTY ASTELL
No No Lolita
EDMUNDO ROS AND HIS RUMBA BAND
No One But Me JERRY LEE LEWIS
No One But the Right Man SOPHIE TUCKER
No One Is Ever Lost PATTI BOULAYE
No One to Care for Me EVE BECKE
No Other Love Like Yours BILLY FURY
No Quarter LED ZEPPELIN
No Reason THE CLASH
No Song About Love EVELYN DALL
No Souvenirs
FELIX MENDELSSOHN AND HIS HAWAIIAN
SERENADERS

No Thrill BILLY MILTON
No Time Like the Present
  HENRY HALL AND THE B.B.C. DANCE ORCHESTRA
No Turning Back CLIFF RICHARD
No Values
  LINDA McCARTNEY; PAUL McCARTNEY;
  RINGO STARR
No Woman No Cry
  BOB MARLEY AND THE WAILERS
No Words or Anything
  HARRY ROY AND HIS BAND
Noah's Ark SCOVELL AND WHELDON
Nobody Discovers Me
  SONNY FARRAR; BUNTY MEADOWS
Nobody Knows the Trouble I've Seen (1928)
  FRISCO
Nobody Knows the Trouble I've Seen (1954)
  KENNY BAKER
Nobody Loves a Fairy When She's Forty
  VIC FORD AND CHRIS SHEEN
Nobody's Sweetheart
  TERENCE McGOVERN AND HIS NOVELTY
  ORCHESTRA
Nocturne JEAN BAPTISTE TONER
Nola FOUR FLASH DEVILS
Not for the Want of Trying PETULA CLARK
Not in Front of Baby BETTY WARREN
Not Such a Bad Boy
  PAUL McCARTNEY; RINGO STARR
Nothing But a Lie (2 films)
  DON CARLOS; TROISE AND HIS MANDOLIERS
Nothing Can Worry Me Now
  PAT (PATRICIA) KIRKWOOD
Nothing Means Nothing Anymore
  THE ALLEY CATS
Nothing on Earth
  JUNE CLYDE; JACK HYLTON AND HIS
  BAND
Nothing's Impossible CLIFF RICHARD
Noughts and Crosses GEORGE FORMBY
Now Ain't That Wonderful? WILL FYFFE
Now and Then CLEO LAINE
Now I Have Found You GITTA ALPAR
Now I Understand FRANCES DAY
Now Is the Time for Love
  JEAN (JEANNIE) CARSON
Now That I've Found You
  JACK BUCHANAN; ELSIE RANDOLPH
Now That We Are Through With Love
  PARIS SISTERS
Now That You're Gone
  BILLY GERHARDI AND HIS BAND
Now's the Time THE HOLLIES
Nowhere Man THE BEATLES
Nubecitas CLELIA MATANIA
Nun Me Sceta JAN KIEPURA
Nursery Suite SIR EDWARD ELGAR
Nut Rocker EMERSON, LAKE AND PALMER

O

O Lucky Man ALAN PRICE
O Madonna JAN KIEPURA
O Paradise JOSEPH SCHMIDT
O Sole Mio JAN KIEPURA
O Star of Eve ANDRE LEDOR

O Whistle and I'll Come SYLVIA WELLING
O'Malley's Tango RUBY MURRAY
Occhi Puri Che Incante MARTA EGGERTH
Octopus's Garden THE BEATLES
Of a' the Airts (1930) JOSEPH HISLOP
Of a' the Airts (1947) TREFOR JONES
Of Love CRAIG DOUGLAS
Off and Running LULU; THE MINDBENDERS
Off to Philadelphia (1935) NEIL McKAY
Off to Philadelphia (1938) THOMAS (TOM) BURKE
Offshore Banking Business THE MEMBERS
Oft in the Stilly Night (1937) JOHN GARRICK
Oft in the Stilly Night (1949) JOSEF LOCKE
Oh Ain't It Grand To Be in the Navy?
  SANDY POWELL
Oh Bondage Up Yours GLEN MATLOCK
Oh Boy! TITANIC CINQ
Oh By Jingo RHYTHM ACES
Oh Darling THE BEATLES
Oh Dem Golden Slippers GEORGIAN SINGERS
Oh Don't the Wind Blow Cold
  GEORGE FORMBY
Oh Henry MILLIE
Oh How I Hate to Get Up in the Morning
  IRVING BERLIN
Oh Johnny (1940) ANN LENNER
Oh Johnny (1943) BERYL ORDE
Oh Johnny Teach Me to Dance
  CHARLES FORSYTHE, ADDIE SEAMON AND
  ELEANOR FARRELL
Oh Lassie Come GRETE NATZLER
Oh Lordy SCOTT AND WHALEY
Oh Mr Constabule LESLIE SARONY
Oh Mr Hemingway HETTY BROWNING
Oh My Love JOHN LENNON
Oh Oh Antonio FLORRIE FORDE
Oh Papa PERCY AND MARY HONRI
Oh Saturday JOHN RUTLAND
Oh Señorita CLIFF RICHARD
Oh So Beautiful JEAN COLIN
Oh the Fairies BARRY CRYER
Oh What a Family MARTY WILDE
Oh What a Girl STANLEY LUPINO
Oh What a Son of a Bitch I Am
  ANTHONY NEWLEY
Oh Yoko JOHN LENNON
Oh You Nasty Man NOSMO KING AND HUBERT
Oh You Naughty Men GRACIE FIELDS
Oh! You Pretty Things DAVID BOWIE
OK Yesterday Was Yesterday SLADE
Okay For Sound (1936)
  HELEN RAYMOND; BILLY THORBURN AND HIS
  BAND
Okay For Sound (1937) RADIO THREE
Okay Toots REX ROPER
Old Apple Tree, The (1931) LILY MORRIS
Old Apple Tree, The (1937)
  LEON CORTEZ AND HIS COSTER PALS
Old Barty TOPLISS GREEN
Old Black Chloe BILLY MERSON
Old Black Mare, The ALFREDO TOMASINI
Old Bull and Bush, The FLORRIE FORDE
Old Cornet NAT GONELLA AND HIS GEORGIANS
Old Dog and the Young Dog, The
  FRANCES DAY
Old English Fan Dance EDNA MAUDE

Old Faithful (1934)   THE HILLBILLIES
Old Faithful (1935)
             SID BUCKMAN; ROY FOX AND HIS BAND
Old-Fashioned Girl, An
                   GWEN FARRAR; BILLY MAYERL
Old-Fashioned Love Song, An   EVE CHAPMAN
Old-Fashioned Town, An   ROBERT WILSON
Old Father Thames   BOB AND ALF PEARSON
Old Fleecy Lined, The   G S MELVIN
Old Folks at Home, The (1929)
          CARROLL GIBBONS AND HIS ORCHESTRA
Old Folks at Home, The (1944)
                              TOMMY TRINDER
Old Kettledrum   PETER DAWSON
Old Lady of Armentières   SIDNEY BURCHALL
Old Man Mose Is Dead
             NAT GONELLA AND HIS GEORGIANS
Old Man of Killyburn Brae, The
                           RICHARD HAYWARD
Old Man Swing   SYLVIA SARTRE
Old Oaken Bucket, The   ARTHUR TRACY
Old Organ Blower, The   ROBERT EASTON
Old Pal   LUPINO LANE
Old Pine Tree, The   THE HILLBILLIES
Old Shep   THE HILLBILLIES
Old Sow, The (1929)   GOTHAM QUARTETTE
Old Sow, The (1933)   ALBERT RICHARDSON
Old Time Medley   BOB AND ALF PEARSON
Old Tin Kettle, The   VESTA VICTORIA
Old Town Hall, The   THE HILLBILLIES
Old Violin, An (1932; 2 films)
              OLIVE GROVES; ALBERT SANDLER
Old Violin, An (1942)   VERA FLORENCE
'Oles   NORMAN LONG
Olive Oil   MALCOLM MacEACHERN
Oliver   HARRY SECOMBE
On a Day Without You   DANNY WILLIAMS
On a Steamer Coming Over
          SYD SEYMOUR AND HIS MAD HATTERS
On and On   ALAN PRICE
On Golf   BILLY BENNETT
On Growing Older   THE STRAWBS
On My Radio   THE SELECTER
On Our Own   ANTHONY NEWLEY
On the Air
          CARROLL GIBBONS AND HIS ORCHESTRA
On the Beach   CLIFF RICHARD
On the Beach at Bali Bali
                 NAT ALLEN AND HIS BAND
On the Beat   GEORGE FORMBY
On the Beautiful Banks of the Nile
                            BILLY 'UKE' SCOTT
On the Move   DAVE CLARK FIVE
On the Tips of My Toes FLORENCE DESMOND
On the Track   JACK SIMPSON
On the Wings of Dawn   EVELYN LAYE
On Top of a Bus   WALSH AND BARKER
On Top of the World   BETTY FIELDS
On Wings of Song (1937)   MARJORIE TAYLOR
On Wings of Song (1939)   MILLICENT PHILLIPS
On Wings of Song (1953)   PATRICE MUNSEL
On With the Motley   RICHARD TAUBER
Onaway Awake Beloved (2 films: 1931, 1939)
                              LANCE FAIRFAX

Onaway Awake Beloved (1933)
                            CHARLES MAYHEW
Once in a Blue Moon   FRANK TITTERTON
Once There Lived a Lady Fair RICHARD TAUBER
Once Upon a Dream   BILLY FURY
Once Upon a Time   ANTHONY NEWLEY
Once Upon a Time in Venice
     JOHN BOULTER; GEORGE MITCHELL SINGERS
Ondine   MARGOT FONTEYN; MICHAEL SOMES
One After 909   THE BEATLES
One and Only, The   CHESNEY HAWKES
One Girl, The   DENNIS NOBLE
One Good Tune Deserves Another
                            JACK BUCHANAN
One Hundred Years   THE CURE
One in a Crowd   RONALD FRANKAU
One in Bethlehem   CLIFF RICHARD
One Kiss   ELISABETH WELCH
One Kiss Before We Part   AUDREY PARKER
One Little Kiss from You   JESSIE MATTHEWS
One Love (1944)   VERA LYNN
One Love (1946)
           LENI LYNN; PATRICK WADDINGTON
One Love One Lifetime   HARRY SECOMBE
One Minute of Heaven   NORMAN AND ARNOLD
One More Chance   PET SHOP BOYS
One More Time (1969)   SAMMY DAVIS JR
One More Time (1980)   HAZEL O'CONNOR
One Morning in May
             GERALDO AND HIS ORCHESTRA
One Night Alone With You
                        COLLINSON AND DEAN
One Night in Napoli
       FRANZ VIENNA AND HIS RADIO THEATRE
                               ORCHESTRA
One Night With You   NINO MARTINI
One of the Ruins Cromwell Knocked About a
Bit (1936)   MARIE LLOYD JUNIOR
One of the Ruins Cromwell Knocked About a
Bit (1937)
       LEON CORTEZ AND HIS COSTER PALS
One of Us Can't Be Wrong   LEONARD COHEN
One Persian Night   VAL ROSING
One Step   TED TREVOR AND DINAH HARRIS
One Step Beyond   MADNESS
One Tiny Tear   HELEN RAYE
One Two Button Your Shoe   EMBASSY KIDS
One Two Three   VERA-ELLEN
Only a Northern Song   THE BEATLES
Only a Working Man   LILY MORRIS
Only an Old Rough Diamond
                       MALCOLM MacEACHERN
Only One, The   LULU AND THE LUVVERS
Only One Who's Difficult Is You, The
              JACK HYLTON AND HIS BAND;
              PAT (PATRICIA) KIRKWOOD
Only to You   CAROL RAYE
Onward We Go   JACK BUCHANAN
Oo La La   JACK BUCHANAN
Oom Pah Pah   SHANI WALLIS
Open   THE CURE
Open Road, The   SIDNEY BURCHALL
Operatic Medley   LESLIE JEFFRIES
Operation Jazzboat TED HEATH AND HIS MUSIC
Opportunity   MAX BYGRAVES

Oranges and Lemons
CYRIL STAPLETON AND THE SHOW BAND
Orchids for My Lady   PAT O'MALLEY
Organ Grinder's Swing *(2 films)*
EVELYN DALL; AL TABOR AND HIS BAND
Orphans of the Storm   GRACIE FIELDS
Orpheus in the Underworld   TEDDY BROWN
Orpheus Song   ROGER DALTREY
Osteria Lied   JOSEPH SCHMIDT
Othello   FRANCO FORESTA
Oui Oui   JEAN PHILIPPE
Our Land   RAYMOND NEWELL
Our Own Pictorial
NAN KENWAY AND DOUGLAS YOUNG
Our Sergeant Major   GEORGE FORMBY
Our Time Is Now
MARION SAUNDERS; STARDUSTERS DANCE
ORCHESTRA
Out and About   MIKE SARNE
Out in the Cold Cold Snow   GRACIE FIELDS
Out of the Blue
GENE GERRARD; JESSIE MATTHEWS
Out of the Blue to You
JOHN REYNDERS AND HIS BAND
Out of Town   MAX BYGRAVES
Over My Shoulder   JESSIE MATTHEWS
Over She Goes   LADDIE CLIFF; STANLEY LUPINO
Over the Rolling Sea   RAYMOND NEWELL
Overture to Trieste   THREE ACCORDION KINGS

P

Pack Up Your Troubles *(1934)*   FLORRIE FORDE
Pack Up Your Troubles *(1943)*   ELLA RETFORD
Paddy McGinty's Goat   MICHAEL O'BRIEN
Paella   CLIFF RICHARD
Pagan Love Song
TERENCE McGOVERN AND HIS NOVELTY
ORCHESTRA
Pagan Moon   THE MASTERSINGERS
Pagliacci *(1928)*   TINO PATTIERA
Pagliacci *(1932)*   THOMAS (TOM) BURKE
Pagliacci *(1933)*   FRANCO FORESTA
Paint and Powder *(2 films)*
JEAN MELVILLE; PHILIP RIDGEWAY AND
JEAN MELVILLE
Painting Rainbows
CANADIAN BACHELORS; CARROLL GIBBONS AND
HIS ORCHESTRA
Palais Glide   LOU PRAEGER AND HIS BAND
Palais Jive   TED HEATH AND HIS MUSIC
Paloma, La *(1925)*
ANDREA MEAZZA AND CONSTANCE SEYMOUR
Paloma, La *(1931)*   MARIO DE PIETRO
Paloma, La *(1936)*
EUGENE PINI AND HIS TANGO ORCHESTRA
Paloma, La *(1939)*   ELSA STENNING
Pandora   FRANCES ASHMAN
Parade of the Toys *(1936)*
FRED ROPER AND HIS MIDGETS
Parade of the Toys *(1938)*
JACK JACKSON AND HIS BAND
Paradise *(1935)*   BAMBERGER AND BISHOP
Paradise *(1963)*   TED HEATH AND HIS MUSIC

Paradise Island
FELIX MENDELSSOHN AND HIS HAWAIIAN
SERENADERS
Paranoia Paradise
WAYNE COUNTY AND THE ELECTRIC CHAIRS
Pardon Me   GEORGE FORMBY
Paris in My Heart   PATRICIA BURKE
Park Parade   IVOR KIRCHIN AND HIS BAND
Parlez Moi d'Amour   ELSA STENNING
Parliamentary Candidate, The   CHICK FARR
Parted   ESTELLE BRODY
Partisan   LEONARD COHEN
Paso Doble   FOWLER AND TAMARA
Passing By *(1938)*   ROBERT WILSON
Passing By *(1934)*   HENRY WENDON
Passing By *(1943)*   JOHN McHUGH
Passing By *(1944)*
TOMMY CRIDDLE; ANDREW FENNER
Passing Clouds
REGINALD KING; ALBERT SANDLER
Passionara, La
EUGENE PINI AND HIS TANGO ORCHESTRA
Path in the Forest, A   NINO MARTINI
Patricia   DOROTHY DICKSON
Pavement Artist, The   RAYMOND NEWELL
Peace at Last   ROGER DALTREY
Peace of Mind   GRACIE FIELDS
Peaceful Night   HAYDN HEMEREY SINGERS
Peanut Polka   DAVID LOBER
Peanut Vendor
AMBROSE AND HIS ORCHESTRA; SAM BROWNE
Pearl Fishers, The   FRANCO FORESTA
Peculiar Groove   FRANCES ASHMAN
Pedro the Fisherman   RICHARD TAUBER
Peel Rides Again
GEORGE MITCHELL SWING CHOIR
Peeping Round the Corners   GENE GERRARD
Peeping Tom   ERIC WOODBURN
Peer Gynt   QUEEN'S HALL LIGHT ORCHESTRA
Peggoty Leg   LESLIE SARONY
Peggy   HERSCHEL HENLERE
Penguin Dance   LEE WHITE
Pennsylvania Polka   JAN RALFINI AND HIS BAND
Penny Serenade
DILL JONES AND HIS ALL STARS
People's Army   BENDER
Perfect Day, A *(2 films)*
BILLY SCOTT-COOMBER AND HIS EIGHT ROYAL
MOUNTIES; WALDORF BRASS QUINTET
Perfidia
EDMUND (TED) HOCKRIDGE; OSCAR RABIN AND
HIS ROMANY BAND
Perfume Waltz   BEBE AND RENEE
Personality   LUPINO LANE
Pet   RAY ELLINGTON QUARTET
Pete the Postman   SIDNEY BURCHALL
Peter Pan   IVOR MORETON AND DAVE KAYE
Peter Peter *(1934; 2 films)*
HARRY HUDSON AND HIS BAND; STANELLI
Peter Peter *(1935; 2 films)*
REGGIE BRISTOW AND HIS BAND; STANELLI
Petticoat Lane   STANLEY HOLLOWAY
Phantom Fleet, The   DENNIS NOBLE
Phi-Phi   JUNE; JAY LAURIER; STANLEY LUPINO
Phil the Fluter's Ball   WILL MAHONEY

Photo of the Girl I Left Behind, The
BILLY MERSON
Photograph TOMMY STEELE
Piano Concerto in C Major DAME MYRA HESS
Piano Concerto No. 1 MARK HAMBOURG
Piano Concerto No. 2
CONSTANT LAMBERT; LONDON PHILHARMONIC
ORCHESTRA; BENNO MOISEIWITSCH
Piano Duet
ARTHUR YOUNG AND GEOFFREY GAUNT
Piazza TOADSTOOL
Piccadilly AMBROSE AND HIS ORCHESTRA
Piccadilly Ballet
JACK BILLINGS; DAVID LOBER; JONATHAN LUCAS;
VERA-ELLEN
Piccadilly Lily ANTHONY NEWLEY
Piccadilly 1944 ANNA NEAGLE
Piccadilly Playground
ROY FOX AND HIS BAND; VIOLET LORAINE
Piccadilly Ride
HENRY HALL AND THE B.B.C. DANCE ORCHESTRA
Piccadilly Stomp STÉPHANE GRAPPELLY
Picking All the Big Ones Out
STANLEY HOLLOWAY
Picture of Her SPENCER DAVIS GROUP
Pictures at an Exhibition
EMERSON, LAKE AND PALMER
Pictures of Lily THE WHO
Pictures of You THE CURE
Pierrette Cherie
ALFREDO CAMPOLI AND REGINALD KING;
CELEBRITY TRIO
Pig Tail Alley BETTY CHESTER
Piggy in the Mirror THE CURE
Pinball Wizard (1975) ELTON JOHN
Pinball Wizard (1979; 2 films)
ELTON JOHN; THE WHO
Pinball Wizard (1980) PETE TOWNSHEND
Pink Elephants CHARLIE KUNZ
Piper's Wedding, The TONY MARTIN
Pity the Fate AMBROSIAN SINGERS
Pity the Man Who Stands Alone
RONALD FRANKAU
Place of My Own, A ANNA NEAGLE
Place to Go, A MIKE SARNE
Plantation Medley
GENE ESSEN AND HIS CHICAGO VELLUM BOYS
Plastic Surgery ADAM ANT
Play for Today THE CURE
Play It Cool BILLY FURY
Play the Game Cads THE WESTERN BROTHERS
Play to Me Gypsy TEDDY BROWN
Play Up the Band STANLEY HOLLOWAY
Please Believe Me SAM BROWNE
Please Forgive and Forget RAY CHARLES
Please Let It Happen to Me (2 films)
ALAN DAVISON; JENNIFER MOSS
Please Mr Constable ARTY ASH
Please Opportunity NORMAN WISDOM
Please Sell No More Drink To My Father
ELSA LANCHESTER
Poacher, The STANLEY HOLLOWAY
Poems
ARTHUR SALISBURY AND THE SAVOY HOTEL
ORCHESTRA

Poet and Peasant (1937; 2 films)
MAX SCHUMANN; AL VERDI AND THELMA LEE
Poet and Peasant (1951)
FREDDIE MIRFIELD AND HIS GARBAGE MEN
Poet and Peasant (1952)
SYD MILLWARD AND HIS NITWITS
Police and Thieves THE CLASH
Police Station, The ROBB WILTON
Policeman, The (1932) ROBB WILTON
Policeman, The (1933) RONALD FRANKAU
Political Meeting, A FARR AND FARLAND
Political Satire, A RONALD FRANKAU
Politician CREAM
Polka Dot Swing VAL ROSING
Poll Parrot Rag BOBBIE 'UKE' HENSHAW
Polonaise (2 films)
MARK HAMBOURG; IGNACE JAN PADEREWSKI
Polonaise and Cracovienne
THE BOLSHOI BALLET
Pomp and Circumstance (1943)
LONDON PHILHARMONIC ORCHESTRA
Pomp and Circumstance (1996)
GRIMETHORPE COLLIERY BAND
Poor Butterfly CHARLIE KUNZ
Poor Little Locked-Up Me FLORA LE BRETON
Poor Man's Blues
CHRIS BARBER AND HIS JAZZ BAND
Poor People ALAN PRICE
Pop Goes the Weasel
JACK SIMPSON AND HIS SEXTET
Poppy W H BERRY
Porno For Pyros PORNO FOR PYROS
Possession SPENCER DAVIS GROUP
Post Horn Boogie TED HEATH AND HIS MUSIC
Post Horn Gallop (1936) FREDDIE FINCH
Post Horn Gallop (1943)
IVY BENSON AND HER ALL GIRLS ORCHESTRA
Postman's Holiday, The GUS ELEN
Powder Blues PHYLLIS ROBINS
Power to the People JOHN LENNON
Practise What You Preach EDDIE KELLAND
Precious Thing Called Love, A ANONA WINN
Prelude in C Sharp Minor MARK HAMBOURG
Preparatory School, The Public School, the
Varsity, The RONALD FRANKAU
Pretty Bird, A (2 films) ARTHUR ASKEY
Pretty Little Girl From Nowhere, The
PHYLLIS ROBINS
Pretty Pictures X-PRODUCTIONS
Pretty Vacant (1980) THE SEX PISTOLS
Pretty Vacant (1986)
GLEN MATLOCK; ANDREW SCHOFIELD
Pride of My Irish Home GENE CROWLEY
Pride of Tipperary BOB AND ALF PEARSON
Primary THE CURE
Prince, The MADNESS
Princess TOMMY STEELE
Princess Is Awakening, The EVELYN LAYE
Princess Jaune
LONDON PHILHARMONIC ORCHESTRA
Prison Governor, The ROBB WILTON
Prisoner, The THE CLASH
Problems (1965) AMANDA BARRIE
Problems (1986)
GLEN MATLOCK; ANDREW SCHOFIELD

Prologue	RICHARD TAUBER
Proposal, The	ARTHUR ASKEY
Provinciera, La	PAQUITA AND BILLDAINITA
Pull Down the Blind	JACK BUCHANAN
Punch Bowl Revue	SONNIE HALE
Puppet	ECHO AND THE BUNNYMEN
Puppets	BINNIE HALE; STANLEY LUPINO
Purcell's Evening Hymn	
	DURHAM CATHEDRAL CHOIR
Puritans, The	BENJAMINO GIGLI
Push	THE CURE
Push the Clouds Away	CHARLIE CREED-MILES
Puss Puss	BERT COOTE
Put It There	PAUL AND LINDA McCARTNEY
Put Me Among the Girls	
IDA BARR; SYD SEYMOUR AND HIS MAD HATTERS	
Put On Your Old Grey Bonnet	FOUR ACES

Q

Quand Même	JEAN CAVALL
Queen of Hearts	GRACIE FIELDS
Question, The	RICHARD TAUBER
Questions	CLIFF RICHARD
Quick One While He's Away, A	THE WHO
Quickstep	
CHARLES THEBAULT AND DOREEN BEAHAN	
Quiet Life	RAY DAVIES
Quiet Rendezvous	JEAN (JEANNIE) CARSON

R

Radino	ANNA PAVLOVA
Radio Red Cross Quiz (2 films)	
NAT ALLEN AND HIS BAND; LIONEL GAMLIN	
Radio Star, The	RITA BRUNSTROM
Rags Bottles or Bones	RAYMOND NEWELL
Ragtime Cowboy Joe	PETER BERNARD
Ragtime Mandarin	BILLY 'UKE' SCOTT
Railway Lines, The	JACK WARNER
Rain	PATRICK COLBERT
Rain Song	LED ZEPPELIN
Rainbow	GWEN FARRAR
Rainbow Chant	PHIL THORNTON
Rainbows In Your Tears	CRAIG DOUGLAS
Ramona	ANNA NEAGLE
Ranking Full Stop	THE BEAT
Rattler	CLIFF RICHARD
Raymonde Overture	DOREEN
Razor Blade Alley	MADNESS
Ready for Love	PATTI BOULAYE
Really Got a Hold on Me	THE BEATLES
Really Waltzing	CLIFF RICHARD
Rebel, The	JOSEPH FARRINGTON
Rebel Music	BOB MARLEY AND THE WAILERS
Rebel Rock	TOMMY STEELE
Red Hot Annabelle	ELISABETH WELCH
Red Hot Feet	
BERYL FORMBY; HARRY HUDSON AND HIS BAND	
Red Mill, The	IVY TRESMAND
Red River Valley	
HORACE SHELDON AND HIS ORCHESTRA	
Red Rose (1932)	RAYMOND NEWELL
Red Rose (1934)	RICHARD TAUBER
Red Rubber Ball	CLIFF RICHARD

Red Sails in the Sunset (1936)	
	FREDDIE BAMBERGER
Red Sails in the Sunset (1937)	
ETHEL REVNELL AND GRACIE WEST	
Red Sails in the Sunset (1938)	
JIMMY KENNEDY AND MICHAEL CARR	
Reginella	
MANTOVANI AND HIS TIPICA ORCHESTRA	
Remember Me	CLAIRE LUCE
Remember Me This Way	GARY GLITTER
Rendezvous in Paradise	
FLORENCE DESMOND; DONALD STEWART	
Rent	PET SHOP BOYS
Repeat It Again to Me	LORRAINE LA FOSSE
Respectable Street	XTC
Responsibility	MARK WYNTER
Rêve Passe, La (1935)	ROBERT CHISHOLM
Rêve Passe, La (1936)	
SANDY POWELL'S HARMONICA BAND	
Revival	CHRIS BARBER AND HIS JAZZ BAND
Revolution Rock	THE CLASH
Rhapsody in Pink	ALEC TEMPLETON
Rhumba (1936)	JEAN REMA
Rhumba (1946)	CHRIS GILL
Rhythm	THE HOUSTON SISTERS
Rhythm in the Alphabet	
JOE LOSS AND HIS ORCHESTRA	
Rhythm of My Heart	HAZEL ASCOT
Rhythm of the Road	GORDON LITTLE
Rhythm Racketeer	HARRY ROY AND HIS BAND
Rhythm's Okay in Harlem	
AMBROSE AND HIS ORCHESTRA	
Richmond Hill	
CHARLES SHADWELL; JOAN WINTERS	
Riddim	ADAM SALKELD
Ride of the Valkyries	
QUEEN'S HALL LIGHT ORCHESTRA; SIR HENRY WOOD	
Ride Ride Again	FRANKIE VAUGHAN
Ridin' Up the River Road	
THREE RHYTHM BROTHERS	
Riding Academy, The	THREE ADMIRALS
Riding Around on a Rainbow	
FLORENCE DESMOND; GEORGE FORMBY	
Riding in the TT Races	GEORGE FORMBY
Riding on the Clouds	GRACIE FIELDS
Righteous Warriors	
RAS ANGELS AND RAS MESSENGERS	
Rigoletto (1929)	LUELLA PAIKIN
Rigoletto (1936)	BENJAMINO GIGLI
Ring-a-Ding	HELEN SHAPIRO; CRAIG DOUGLAS
Ring Out the Bells	THE CRAZY GANG
Rinky Dink	SOUNDS INCORPORATED
Rio Rita	GEORGE GEE; LESLIE SARONY
Riot in Rio	THE SQUADRONNAIRES
River Sing Me a Song	PATRICK COLBERT
River Stay Away from My Door	BERNARDI
River Steals My Folks From Me	
	PAUL ROBESON
Road That Leads to You, The	
	LEONARD GOWINGS
Road to Mandalay	ROBERT EASTON
Road to the Isles (1936)	IAN McPHERSON
Road to the Isles (1944)	WALTER MIDGELEY
Roadhouse Revels	JACK HYLTON AND HIS BAND

Roadrunner	THE WHO
Roadway of Romance	
BELLE BAKER; JUNE CLYDE; DEREK OLDHAM	
Roadways	GERALD NODIN
Roaming Through the Roses	LESLIE SARONY
Robbin' Harry	HARRY ROBBINS
Robin Told Me So, The	RHYTHM SISTERS
Rock and Roll	LED ZEPPELIN
Rock and Roll Suicide	DAVID BOWIE
Rock With the Cave Man	TOMMY STEELE
Rock You Sinners	
ART BAXTER AND HIS ROCKIN' SINNERS	
Rocket	MUD
Rocketman	ELTON JOHN
Rockin' in Morocco	TED HEATH AND HIS MUSIC
Rockin' the Blues	
DON SOLLASH AND HIS ROCKIN' HORSES	
Rockin' with Rory	
RORY BLACKWELL AND THE BLACKJACKS	
Roll Along Kentucky Moon	
MAURICE WINNICK AND HIS ORCHESTRA	
Roll Dem Bones	FOUR MUSKETEERS
Roll On Tomorrow	
BUD FLANAGAN AND CHESNEY ALLEN	
Roll the Clouds Before You	LANCE FAIRFAX
Roll Up Sailor Man	PAUL ROBESON
Rollin' the Tymps	ERIC DELANEY AND HIS BAND
Rolling Round the World	SCOTT SANDERS
Rolling Stones	TOM KINNIBURGH
Romance (1936)	WEBSTER BOOTH
Romance (1946)	YEHUDI MENUHIN
Romany	TROISE AND HIS MANDOLIERS
Romany Tango	LOLITA AND CORTEZ
Romeo and Juliet	
LONDON PHILHARMONIC ORCHESTRA	
Ronde des Lutins, La	YEHUDI MENUHIN
Rondo	KENNY BALL AND HIS JAZZMEN
Room 504 (1941)	ROBERT ASHLEY
Room 504 (1944)	
BERYL DAVIS; GEORGE POSFORD	
Rosanne	DENNIS LOTIS
Rosary, The	LES ALLEN
Rose in Her Hair, A	
BERNARD MONSHIN AND HIS RIO TANGO BAND	
Rose Marie	EDITH DAY; BILLY MERSON
Rose of Tralee (1936; 2 films)	
CAVAN O'CONNOR; ARTHUR WILLIAMS	
Rose of Tralee (1937)	DANNY MALONE
Rose of Tralee (1938)	RICHARD HAYWARD
Roses of Picardy (1936)	RUDY STARITA
Roses of Picardy (1939)	
PERCIVAL MACKEY AND HIS BAND	
Roses of Picardy (1946)	HAYDN WOOD
Roses of Picardy (1947)	ANNA NEAGLE
Rosita (1938)	ROLAND PEACHY AND HIS BAND
Rosita (1940)	REGINALD STONE
Rosita (1961)	
HERMANOS DENIZ AND HIS CUBAN RHYTHM BAND	
Rough Ride	PAUL AND LINDA McCARTNEY
Roughrider	THE BEAT
Round About Regent Street	
DANNY LIPTON TRIO	
Round and Round	THE SHADOWS
Round the Back of the Arches	
BUD FLANAGAN AND CHESNEY ALLEN	

Round the Corner	
HERMAN'S HERMITS; STANLEY HOLLOWAY	
Roundabout	YES
Roundabout Goes Round, The	
IVY BENSON AND HER ALL GIRLS ORCHESTRA	
Roxanne	POLICE
Royal Blackbird, The	RICHARD HAYWARD
Ruddigore	MARTYN GREEN
Rudi Can't Fail	THE CLASH
Ruftek Wiggle	ZURA
Rule Britannia (1937)	
BAND OF H.M. ROYAL MARINES	
Rule Britannia (1978)	JORDAN
Rum Rum Rum	STANLEY HOLLOWAY
Rumba (1932)	JUNE AND NADIADJA
Rumba (1936)	CLEMSON AND VALERIE
Rumba (1937)	CHERIE AND DON ALASANDRO
Rumba Batumba	
SANTIAGO LOPEZ AND HIS RUMBA BAND	
Run Rabbit Run (1939)	
HARRY ROY AND HIS BAND	
Run Rabbit Run (1940s)	ROBIN RICHMOND
Runaround, The	
JACK HYLTON AND HIS BAND; THE MacKAY TWINS	
Runaway Love (1939)	BILLY MAYERL
Runaway Love (1940)	GEORGE GEE
Running Away	BOB MARLEY AND THE WAILERS
Running Commentary	CECIL JOHNSON
Running Scared	FOUR PENNIES
Running Up That Hill	
KATE BUSH; DAVID GILMOUR; NICK MASON	
Running Wild	DANNY LIPTON TRIO
Rural Rhythm	
OSCAR RABIN AND HIS ROMANY BAND	
Russian Rhapsody	
PAULINE GRANT BALLET COMPANY	
Rustle of Spring	JACK COURTNEY
Rustle of Swing	THE SQUADRONNAIRES

S

Sabre Dance (1949)	
JIMMY JEWEL AND BEN WARRISS	
Sabre Dance (1950)	
IVY BENSON AND HER ALL GIRLS ORCHESTRA	
Sadness Goes On, The	JOY NICHOLS
Safe European Home	THE CLASH
Safety First	GEORGE ROBEY
Said the Spider to the Fly	
JACK HARRIS AND HIS BAND; CLAIRE LUCE	
Sailing Along on a Carpet of Clouds	
JACK HYLTON AND HIS BAND; BRYAN LAWRANCE	
Sailing Sailing	THE ASPIDISTRAS
Sailor Where Art Thou?	SHERRY BROTHERS
Sailor's Hornpipe (1935)	
HORACE SHELDON AND HIS ORCHESTRA	
Sailor's Hornpipe (1936)	
SHERMAN FISHER GIRLS	
Sailors Chorus (1931)	GLANHOWY SINGERS
Sailors Chorus (1932)	WISBECH MALE CHOIR
Sailors Chorus (1935)	
KETTERING MADRIGAL MALE VOICE CHOIR	
Sailors Don't Care (1935)	JOHN RORKE
Sailors Don't Care (1937)	MARIE LAVARRE
Sally (2 films)	GRACIE FIELDS

Sally Ann   FREDDIE AND THE DREAMERS
Sally in Our Alley   DEREK OLDHAM
Sally Simpson   THE WHO
Salome   EVELYN DALL
Salt and Pepper   SAMMY DAVIS JR
Salutation of the Morning   RICHARD TAUBER
Salvage   ELSIE AND DORIS WATERS
Sam and his Musket   STANLEY HOLLOWAY
Sam Pick Up Thy Musket   THE CO-OPTIMISTS
Sam Small Goes Shopping
    STANLEY HOLLOWAY
Samba Sud   TERRY AND DORIC KENDAL
Same As We Used To Do, The
    DOROTHY WARD
Same Old Bus, The   JACK HULBERT
Same Old Road, The   BUNNY DOYLE
Same Old Story, The   FREDDIE LATHAM
San Diego Betty   KEITH FALKNER
San Felipe   LES ALLEN
Sanctuary of the Heart
    FRANK TITTERTON; WESTMINSTER ABBEY CHOIR
Sandman's Serenade, The
    ANNA NEAGLE; ARTHUR TRACY
Sandy MP   SANDY POWELL
Santa Lucia (1934; 2 films)
    EVELYN LAYE; BROWNING MUMMERY; JOSEPH
    SCHMIDT
Santa Lucia (1935)   MAGDA NEELD
Santa Lucia (1938)
    JOHN STEIN AND HIS RUMBA BAND
Santa Lucia (1939)   TONY VAUGHAN
Santa Lucia (1948)   JOHN LEWIS
Santa Lucia (1986)   EKOW ABBAN
Sarah Jane   HAL SWAIN AND HIS KIT KAT BAND
Sari Marais
    JOSEF MARAIS AND HIS BUSHVELD BOYS
Sarternoon   TOMMY TRINDER
Saturday Night Divas   THE SPICE GIRLS
Saturday Night Rock-a-Boogie
    ANTHONY NEWLEY
Saturday Nite Drag   TED HEATH AND HIS MUSIC
Savage, The   CLIFF RICHARD
Save a Little Sunshine
    PAT (PATRICIA) KIRKWOOD
Save a Prayer   DURAN DURAN
Save Song, The   ELSIE AND DORIS WATERS
Saving Saving   JACK HYLTON AND HIS BAND
Savoy Scottish Medley   GRANT TYLER
Say Goodbye Now   VICTOR SOVERALL
Say Hello to the Sun
    CHARLES FORSYTHE, ADDIE SEAMON AND
    ELEANOR FARRELL
Say It While Dancing (1931)   TWO RASCALS
Say It While Dancing (1936)
    DEBROY SOMERS AND HIS BAND
Say It With Music
    JACK PAYNE AND HIS DANCE ORCHESTRA
Say Tata to Your Tar   THE CRAZY GANG
Say the Word and It's Yours JESSIE MATTHEWS
Say to Yourself I Will Be Happy   AL BOWLLY
Say Yes   JACK HYLTON AND HIS BAND
Say You Do   MIKE SARNE
Say You Will Not Forget Me   BENJAMINO GIGLI
Say You'll Be There, Mama   THE SPICE GIRLS
Scarecrow   PINK FLOYD
Scheherazade   ANTON DOLIN; ANNA LUDMILLA

Schubert's Serenade   ALBERT SANDLER
Scotch and Polly   PAT (PATRICIA) KIRKWOOD
Scotch Medley
    SCOTTISH CO-OPERATIVE WHOLESALE SOCIETY
    BAND
Scotland's Whiskey   BILLY MERSON
Scrap Chap, The   SYD WALKER
Scrub Brothers Scrub
    ALBERT SANDLER AND THE PALM COURT
    ORCHESTRA
Sea Is the Life for Me, The   PETER DAWSON
Seaside Band, The   ARTHUR ASKEY
Second Chance   DOROTHY DICKSON
Second Hungarian Rhapsody (1936)
    ALFRED RODE AND HIS TZIGANE BAND
Second Hungarian Rhapsody (1937)
    IGNACE JAN PADEREWSKI
Secretive Sarah   JOCK McKAY
See Me Dance the Polka
    SYDNEY KYTE AND HIS BAND
See Me Feel Me   ROGER DALTREY
Selection from Faust THREE ACCORDION KINGS
Selling Out   SLIM GAILLARD
Send for Mrs Bartholomew
    CICELY COURTNEIDGE
Señorita   TINO FOLGAR
Sensation   ROGER DALTREY
Sentimental Gentleman from Georgia
    REGGIE BRISTOW AND HIS BAND; MODERNIQUES
Sentry Song   OWEN BRANNIGAN
Serenade (2 films: 1933, 1937)
    RICHARD TAUBER
Serenade (1933)   JOHN BROWNLEE
Serenade (1953)   PATRICE MUNSEL
Serenade Erotik   HARRY PRESTON
Serenade in the Night (2 films)
    AMBROSE AND HIS ORCHESTRA; SAM BROWNE;
    HAL YATES
Serenata   WEBSTER BOOTH
Sergeant Major On Parade, The
    RAYMOND NEWELL
Sergeant of the Line, A   NORMAN ALLIN
Sergeant Pepper PAUL AND LINDA McCARTNEY
Sergeant Pepper's Lonely Hearts Club Band
    THE BEATLES
Set Me Free   MAXINE BARRIE
Seven Day Weekend   GARY (U.S.) BONDS
Seven Days to a Holiday   CLIFF RICHARD
Seven Different Sweeties a Week
    HARRY ROY AND HIS BAND
Seven Veils   ROSS AND SARGENT
Seville   MEDRANO AND DONNE
Sewing on a Button   CHARLES HARRISON
Shadow Line   THE FLESHTONES
Shadow of the Man I Love   ROSE ALBA
Shadows from the Past   EDWARD VICTOR
Shady Grove   BILLY CONNOLLY
Shake a Tail Feather
    EARL ROYCE AND THE OLYMPICS
Shake Dog Shake   THE CURE
Shake Hands with a Millionaire (1937)
    MONTE REY
Shake Hands with a Millionaire (1939)
    ISSY BONN
Shake Rattle and Roll   THE BEATLES
Shall I Be an Old Man's Darling GRACIE FIELDS

Shallow Grave
JOHN CARMICHAEL AND HIS BAND
Shanty in Old Shanty Town, A
DUMP AND TONY; RADIO RASCALS
She (1936)   AMBROSE AND HIS ORCHESTRA
She (1996)   MARIANNE FAITHFULL
She Knows Me
FREDDIE FRINTON; HARRY SECOMBE
She Laughed   THE ZEPHYRS
She Loves You (2 films)   THE BEATLES
She Shall Have Music
JACK HYLTON AND HIS BAND; BRYAN LAWRANCE
She Was Only Somebody's Daughter
THE WESTERN BROTHERS
She Was Poor But She Was Honest
MAX BYGRAVES
She's a Lily But Only by Name
ELSIE AND DORIS WATERS
She's a Woman   THE BEATLES
She's Done It Again   HERMAN'S HERMITS
She's Everybody's Sweetheart Now
EMILIO COLOMBO'S TZIGANE BAND
She's Got Two of Everything GEORGE FORMBY
She's Lost Control   DEVO
She's My Missis   RIGHT SAID FRED
She's My Secret Passion   ALBERT WHELAN
She's Only Wax   FRED CONYNGHAM
She's Too Far Above Me   TOMMY STEELE
Sheik of Araby, The
IVOR KIRCHIN AND HIS BAND
Shenandoah (1931)   DALE SMITH
Shenandoah (1946)   OSCAR NATZKE
Shenandoah (1947)
FRED HARTLEY AND HIS QUINTET; ALVAR LIDDELL
Shepherd, The   RAYMOND NEWELL
Shepherds Hey
QUEEN'S HALL LIGHT ORCHESTRA; SIR HENRY
WOOD
Shine
ALICE AND JIMMY DEY; BILLY MERRIN AND HIS
COMMANDERS
Shine On Harvest Moon   LUNA BOYS
Shine Through My Dreams (1935)
TREFOR JONES
Shine Through My Dreams (1937) MARY ELLIS
Shipmates o' Mine   ROBERT EASTON
Shoe Shine Boy
MORTON FRASER AND HIS HARMONICA GANG
Shoeshine   CON O'NEILL
Shooting of Dan McGrew   BILLY BENNETT
Shop Girl, The   EVELYN LAYE; ALFRED LESTER
Shortenin' Bread   PAUL ROBESON
Shot of Rhythm and Blues, A
DAVE EDMUNDS AND THE STRAY CATS
Shout   LULU AND THE LUVVERS
Shout and Shimmy   THE WHO
Shout Hallelujah   JOSEPHINE EARLE
Shout It Out   GLITTER BAND
Shouted Out   SCOTT FITZGERALD
Shovel On a Few More Coals
BERNARD DUDLEY
Show Me the Way to Romance FRANCES DAY
Show's the Thing, The   GRACIE FIELDS
Shrine on the Second Floor   CLIFF RICHARD
Si Si Si   PAT BOONE

Sick and Tired of Hillbilly
CANADIAN BACHELORS
Side By Side (1935)   CHARLIE KUNZ
Side By Side (1937)
LADDIE CLIFF; STANLEY LUPINO; JOHN WOOD
Side By Side (1975)   MUD
Sidewalks of Cuba   TED HEATH AND HIS MUSIC
Siesta, La   DETURA AND MORELL
Sign of the Cross   SKAFISH
Silly Love Songs
LINDA McCARTNEY; PAUL McCARTNEY
Silly Thing   THE SEX PISTOLS
Silver Dream Machine   DAVID ESSEX
Simon the Cellarer   GRESHAM SINGERS
Simon Tov   RAY McVAY BAND
Simple Girl, A   SONYA CORDEAU
Simple Little Melody   RICHARD TAUBER
Simultaneous Steppers
VIOLET DURRANT AND PAUL ORAH
Since Black Minnie's Got the Blues
MABEL MERCER; JOHNNY NIT; HARRY ROY AND
HIS BAND
Since I Fell in Love With You
CARROLL GIBBONS AND HIS ORCHESTRA
Since I Met Her   ARTHUR RISCOE
Since I've Been Loving You   LED ZEPPELIN
Sing a Song of London   STANLEY HOLLOWAY
Sing a Song of Tomorrow Today
BUD FLANAGAN AND CHESNEY ALLEN
Sing As We Go (2 films)   GRACIE FIELDS
Sing As You Swing   EVELYN DALL
Sing Brothers
CARLYLE COUSINS; BOBBY HOWES
Sing Me a Baby Song   BILLIE BARNES
Sing Me a Swing Song   ALICE MANN
Sing Me Some of the Old Songs   JEAN COLIN
Sing Our Own Song   UB40
Sing Something Simple
MAURICE WINNICK AND HIS ORCHESTRA
Sing Song Girl
PICKARD'S CHINESE SYNCOPATORS
Sing Willow   GERTRUDE LAWRENCE
Singing Drunk, The   BERT WILSON
Singing Time   TOMMY STEELE
Sinking   THE CURE
Sippin' Cider
MR ACKER BILK AND THE PARAMOUNT JAZZ BAND
Sisters of Mercy   LEONARD COHEN
Sittin' by the River
CARSON ROBISON AND HIS PIONEERS
Sitting On a Cloud   EVELYN DALL
Sitting On a Rainbow   BETTY ASTELL
Sitting On the Ice in the Ice Rink
GEORGE FORMBY
Six Different Ways   THE CURE
Six Eight, The
SANTOS CASANI AND JOSE LENNARD
Six Five Jive, The   KING BROTHERS
Six Piano Jazz Symphony   DORIS ARNOLD
Skater's Waltz, The (1930)
SANTOS CASANI AND JOSE LENNARD
Skater's Waltz, The (1939)
LESLIE JEFFRIES AND HIS ORCHESTRA
Skater's Waltz, The (1940)   IRVING KAYE
Skater's Waltz, The (1944) ROBINSON CLEAVER

Skipper, The   SIDNEY BURCHALL
Skipper of the Mary Jane   ROBERT EASTON
Sky High Honeymoon
    PRINCESS PEARL; HARRY ROY AND HIS BAND
Slaidburn
    THE BRITISH STEEL STOCKSBRIDGE BAND
Sleep   MARIANNE FAITHFULL
Sleep Song   RICHARD TAUBER
Sleeping Beauty   RUDOLPH NUREYEV
Sleepy   RICHARD TAUBER
Sleepy Boy   DOROTHY DICKSON
Sleepy Lagoon (1944)   DAPHNE DAY
Sleepy Lagoon (1947)
    FRED HARTLEY AND HIS QUINTET; JESSIE
                        MATTHEWS
Sleepy Lagoon (1950)
         GERALDO AND HIS ORCHESTRA
Sleepy Rio Grande
    CARSON ROBISON AND HIS PIONEERS
Sleepy River
    PAUL ROBESON; ELISABETH WELCH
Slider, The   MARC BOLAN AND T. REX
Slipping Through My Fingers
                 JESSIE MATTHEWS
Slow Motion Dance   MARIKA ROKK
Slowcoach   RAYMOND NEWELL
Smash the Mirror   THE WHO
Smile and Sing Your Cares Away
    JACK PAYNE AND HIS DANCE ORCHESTRA
Smile and Whistle a Love Song JEAN MELVILLE
Smile At Me Just Once   JAN KIEPURA
Smile for Me   RICHARD TAUBER
Smile is Worth a Million Tears, A
    CYRIL STAPLETON AND THE SHOW BAND
Smile When You Say Goodbye
    HAL SWAIN AND HIS SWING SISTERS
Smoke Goes Up the Chimney, The
                TOMMY TRINDER
Snake Charmer of Old Bagdad
             HAPPY WANDERERS
Snake's Hips   THE BARRIE SISTERS/TWINS
Snakes and Ladders   TARRANT BAILEY JR
Snap   A W BASKCOMB; CLARICE MAYNE
So Bad
    LINDA McCARTNEY; PAUL McCARTNEY; RINGO
                        STARR
So Deep Is the Night (1940)
    RONNIE BOYER AND JEANNE REVEL
So Deep Is the Night (1942) ROBERT WILSON
So Deep Is the Night (1944)
    WEBSTER BOOTH; ANNE ZIEGLER
So Far So Good   SLADE
So Green   JACK BUCHANAN
So It Goes On   VERA LYNN
So Little Time   BERNARD CLIFTON
So Lonely   POLICE
So Many People   CON O'NEILL
So Must Our Love Remain   FRANCES DAY
So Near My Heart   DOROTHEE BAROONE
So Say All of Us
    JULIAN NIMAN AND HIS BOYS; GORDON RAY
                      GIRLS
So Shy
    DAN DONOVAN; DEBROY SOMERS AND HIS BAND
So That's the Way You Like It
            PETER COOK; TERRY JONES

So This Is Love   REITA NUGENT
So What?   SMILEY CULTURE
So Would I   BERYL DAVIS
Soldiers in the Park   ANNA NEAGLE
Soldiers of the King
    BAND OF H.M. GRENADIER GUARDS
Soldiers' Chorus, The   KEITH FALKNER
Solicitor, The   ROBB WILTON
Solitude (1937)   MILLS BROTHERS
Solitude (1946)
    JOHNNY WORTHY AND BERTIE JARRETT
Solveig's Song   ADELE DIXON
Sombrero   ELTON HAYES
Some Day   RONNIE BOYER AND JEANNE REVEL
Some Day My Heart Will Awake ANNA NEAGLE
Some Day We Shall Meet Again
                PATRICIA BURKE
Some of These Days (1934)   SOPHIE TUCKER
Some of These Days (1936)
         THREE ACCORDION KINGS
Some of These Days (1938)
       JOE DANIELS AND HIS BAND
Some of These Days (1939; 2 films)
    PAT (PATRICIA) KIRKWOOD; JOSEPH TERMINI
Some of These Days (1968)   TERRY DAY
Some Other Guy Now
    DAVE EDMUNDS AND THE STRAY CATS
Some People Like to Rock
           MARC BOLAN AND T. REX
Somebody   GENE GERRARD
Somebody Blew My Bluebird's Egg
               TERRY-THOMAS
Somebody Else   SHANE FENTON
Somebody Help Me
       KENNY AND THE WRANGLERS
Somebody Loves Me
    BARRI CHAT AND TERRI GARDNER
Somebody Soon
    CARROLL GIBBONS AND HIS ORCHESTRA
Somebody Stole My Girl
       BILLY COTTON AND HIS BAND
Somebody's Kisses   SUZETTE TARRI
Someone   BRIAN POOLE AND THE TREMELOES
Someone Stole My Baby   ERIC IDLE
Someone to Love   ANTHONY NEWLEY
Someplace Else   GEORGE HARRISON
Something Came and Got Me BETTY ASTELL
Something Else   THE SEX PISTOLS
Something in My Eye
         CHARLES 'BUDDY' ROGERS
Something Will Happen Today BOBBY HOWES
Sometime Somewhere   FRANKIE VAUGHAN
Sometime Yesterday   HELEN SHAPIRO
Somewhere a Voice is Calling JEAN ADRIENNE
Somewhere in England
    STANLEY KING; PERCIVAL MACKEY AND HIS BAND
Somewhere on Leave
       PERCIVAL MACKEY AND HIS BAND
Son, This Is She   JOHNNY LEYTON
Sonata Appassionata   DAME MYRA HESS
Song Doesn't Care, A   KEITH FALKNER
Song in the Night, A (1932)
       OLIVE GROVES; ALBERT SANDLER
Song in the Night, A (1936)   ANNE ZIEGLER
Song in Your Heart, A   GRACIE FIELDS

Song of Empire SIDNEY BURCHALL
Song of Freedom PAUL ROBESON
Song of India
MORTON FRASER AND HIS HARMONICA GANG
Song of Paradise CELEBRITY TRIO
Song of Songs (1932; 2 films)
DE GROOT; LEONARD GOWINGS
Song of Songs (1933)
ROSE PERFECT; ARTHUR ROSEBERY'S
SWINGTETTE
Song of Swanee TEX McLEOD
Song of the Farmer's Boy CHARLIE CHESTER
Song of the Flea NORMAN ALLIN
Song of the Geese THE FESTIVE FELLOWS
Song of the Highway TOM KINNIBURGH
Song of the Islands (1936) RUDY STARITA
Song of the Islands (1938)
EDDIE PEABODY AND HIS BEACHCOMBERS
Song of the Islands (1939)
FELIX MENDELSSOHN AND HIS HAWAIIAN
SERENADERS
Song of the Marching Men
NAT D. AYER; BAND OF H.M. COLDSTREAM
GUARDS
Song of the Open Country EDWARD COOPER
Song of the Steppes KOLIA NEJIN
Song of the Sunrise PATRICIA BURKE
Song of the Tramp TOM KINNIBURGH
Song of the Troubadour
REGINALD KING AND HIS ORCHESTRA
Song of the Volga Boatmen NAVARRE
Song of the Waterfall
J. H. SQUIRE'S CELESTE OCTET
Song Remains the Same, The LED ZEPPELIN
Song That is Calling Me Home, The
GRACE CLARKE AND COLIN MURRAY
Song You Gave To Me, The BEBE DANIELS
Songs My Mother Taught Me LAURI KENNEDY
Sonny Boy REGINALD FOORT
Sons o' Guns BOBBY HOWES
Sons of the Sea (1928)
A W BASKCOMB; TOM COSTELLO
Sons of the Sea (1934) CLAUDE HULBERT
Sophisticated Hula
FELIX MENDELSSOHN AND HIS HAWAIIAN
SERENADERS
Sospen Bach
LONDON WELSH ASSOCIATION CHORAL SOCIETY
Sous les Toits de Paris
JOHN STEIN AND HIS RUMBA BAND
South American Joe
AMBROSE AND HIS ORCHESTRA; DONALD
STEWART
South of the Border (1939) THE BELLS
South of the Border (1960)
DILL JONES AND HIS ALL STARS
South Rampart Street Parade
STAN SHEDDON AND THE PLAYTIMERS
South Sea Island Magic RHYTHM SISTERS
Southern Love NANCY BROWN
Souvenir of Love JESSIE MATTHEWS
Souvenirs LESLIE A HUTCHINSON
Space Ball Pitcher MARC BOLAN AND T. REX
Space Invaders HOT GOSSIP
Space Oddity DAVID BOWIE

Spaceship to Mars
SOUNDS INCORPORATED; GENE VINCENT
Spade and Bucket TESSIE O'SHEA
Spaniard That Blighted My Life, The (2 films)
BILLY MERSON
Spanish Dance MARJORIE DAY
Sparks (2 films) THE WHO
Speak to Me of Love (1934) JEAN ADRIENNE
Speak to Me of Love (1935) SIX LADY HARPISTS
Speak to Me Thora GRACIE FIELDS
Spice of Life, The CHARLES SHADWELL
Spice Up Your Life THE SPICE GIRLS
Spider's March TED HEATH AND HIS MUSIC
Spike Sullivan's Girl A C ASTOR
Spirit of Liberty AVANT BROTHERS
Spirit of the Dance EDNA MAUDE
Spooks JACK SIMPSON AND HIS SEXTET
Spoonful CREAM
S'posin' JOHNNY NIT
Spread a Little Happiness ZELMA O'NEAL
Spread Your Wings MALCOLM MacEACHERN
Spring (2 films)
ARTHUR RISCOE; SYD SEYMOUR AND HIS MAD
HATTERS
Spring All the Year Round JACK DONAHUE
Spring Don't Mean a Thing PAT TAYLOR
Spring Is Here HARRY ROY'S ROYALISTS
Spring Song (1934) DOUGLAS BYNG
Spring Song (1935) SIX LADY HARPISTS
Spring Song (1941) MOLLY FORBES
Spring Song (1946) CAROL RAYE
Spring Time STANLEY LUPINO; JOHN WOOD
Spring Water THE BOLSHOI BALLET
Springtime in County Clare GERRY FITZGERALD
Springtime in the Rockies (1930)
LOU ABELARDO
Springtime in the Rockies (1938)
BIG BILL CAMPBELL AND HIS ROCKY
MOUNTAINEERS
Spunk BARRY HUMPHRIES
Square Song, The NORMAN WISDOM
S.S. GEORGE HARRISON
St Louis Blues (1934)
THE MASTERSINGERS; MODERNIQUES
St Louis Blues (1937)
LARRY ADLER; CHAPPIE D'AMATO AND HIS BAND;
LUCILLE AND FRANK
St Louis Blues (1939) JOSEPH TERMINI
St Louis Blues (1940)
SYD MILLWARD AND HIS NITWITS
St Louis Blues (1946)
LAUDERIC CATON AND HIS RHYTHM SWINGTETTE;
JOHNNY WORTHY AND BERTIE JARRETT
Stairway to Heaven LED ZEPPELIN
Stamps GEORGE ROBEY
Stan the Man from Idaho TONY MARTIN
Stand Up and Sing ELSIE RANDOLPH
Standchen MARJORIE TAYLOR
Standing in the Shadows THE ROLLING STONES
Standing on the Corner SLADE
Star Fell Out of Heaven, A (2 films)
REGINALD FOORT; JOSEPH SCHMIDT
Star Spangled Banner (1935) TEDDY BROWN
Star Spangled Banner (1936) THREE STARS
Stardust (1937) LARRY ADLER
Stardust (1938) MORRIS LOGAN TRIO

Stardust *(1944)* PEGGY DESMOND
Stardust *(1974)* DAVID ESSEX
Stars and Stripes *(1930)*
MAX AND HARRY NESBITT
Stars and Stripes *(1935)* VIC OLIVER
Stars and Stripes *(1937)*
RAYMONDE AND HIS BANJO BAND
Stars and Stripes For Ever *(1935)*
BOBBIE 'UKE' HENSHAW
Stars and Stripes For Ever *(1937)*
GENE ESSEN AND HIS CHICAGO VELLUM BOYS
Stars in My Eyes PAT (PATRICIA) KIRKWOOD
Stars in the Skies, The BILLY FURY
Stars Still Remember, The THE BACHELORS
Stay TITANIC CINQ
Stay Awhile ARTHUR TRACY
Stay Free THE CLASH
Stay Out of My Dreams
REGGIE BRISTOW AND HIS BAND
Stealing My Love from Me
LULU; THE MINDBENDERS
Stein Stein JAY LAURIER
Stephane Blues STÉPHANE GRAPPELLY
Stepping Out *(1929)*
MAX RIVERS' TROCADERO GIRLS
Stepping Out *(1936)*
DEBROY SOMERS AND HIS BAND
Stepping Stones PAUL ROBESON
Stick Out Your Chin BETTY DRIVER
Still as the Night FRANK IVALLO
Still Waters ZOE GAIL
Stille Nacht DE BIERE
Stilt Dance FOUR ASTAIRES
Stolen Melody, The ALBERT WHELAN
Stone Flute CRISTIAN VOGEL
Stonecracker John FRANK WIGNALL
Stop THE SPICE GIRLS
Stop It I Like It CURLY PAT BARRY
Stop the Clock EVE BECKE
Stormy Weather *(1933)* MORTON DOWNEY
Stormy Weather *(1980)* ELISABETH WELCH
Story of Tina, The
HERMANOS DENIZ AND HIS CUBAN RHYTHM BAND
Stranded ARTHUR TRACY
Strange Day, A THE CURE
Stranger in Town CLIFF RICHARD
Stranger on the Shore
MR ACKER BILK AND THE PARAMOUNT JAZZ BAND
Streamline TARRANT BAILEY JR
Street in Old Seville, A AL AND BOB HARVEY
Street Serenade ARTHUR TRACY
String Harmony
FELIX MENDELSSOHN AND HIS HAWAIIAN
SERENADERS
String Quartet No. 14 AMADEUS QUARTET
Stripper, The THE JOHN BARRY SEVEN
Stroll On THE YARDBIRDS
Strollin' REG VARNEY
Strolling Along by the Seaside TESSIE O'SHEA
Strolling in the Park STANLEY HOLLOWAY
Strolling Through the Heather POLLY WARD
Strong Go On, The LANCE FAIRFAX
Student Song ARTHUR PRINCE AND JIM
Substitute THE WHO
Suburbia PET SHOP BOYS

Success Story THE WHO
Such a Game RICHARD TAUBER
Such a Lonely Number TONY MARTIN
Sucker for Your Love B A ROBERTSON
Sue Sue Sue G H ELLIOTT
Suffragette City DAVID BOWIE
Sugar Baby Love THE RUBETTES
Sugar Dandy MILLIE
Sugar Step SANTOS CASANI AND JOSE LENNARD
Sugartime JIM DALE
Summer Holiday CLIFF RICHARD
Summer Night DEREK OLDHAM
Summer Song SLADE
Sun Whose Rays, The KENNY BAKER
Sun Will Shine, The HENRI GARAT
Sunday Down in Old Caroline *(1933)*
BOB AND ALF PEARSON
Sunday Down in Old Caroline *(1934)*
HARMONY KINGS
Sunny Side of the Street STANELLI AND EDGAR
Sunnyside Lane
HORACE SHELDON AND HIS ORCHESTRA
Sunrise MARIE BURKE
Sunset in Vienna LILLI PALMER
Sunset Trail
JIMMY KENNEDY AND MICHAEL CARR
Sunshine Ahead
JACK PAYNE AND HIS DANCE ORCHESTRA
Sunshine of Your Smile, The *(1937)*
STUART ROBERTSON
Sunshine of Your Smile, The *(1943)*
VERA LYNN
Super Casanova HOT GOSSIP
Super Nature HOT GOSSIP
Supper's Ready GENESIS
Sur le Pont d'Avignon JEAN CAVALL
Sure of Everything But You
JACK PADBURY AND HIS COSMO CLUB SIX
Surely There's No Harm in a Kiss
BERYL FORMBY; GEORGE FORMBY
Surprise Symphony
SYD MILLWARD AND HIS NITWITS
Sus Blues THE BLUES BAND
Suzanne LEONARD COHEN
Suzy Parker THE BEATLES
Swan, The PLOTEN J WORTH
Swan Lake *(1946)* GALINA ULANOVA
Swan Lake *(1954)*
SVETLANA BERIOSOVA; DAVID PALTENGHI
Swan Lake *(1960)*
BRYAN ASHBRIDGE; MARGOT FONTEYN;
MICHAEL SOMES
Swan Song FLORENCE DE JONG
Swanee River *(1930)*
GAINSBOROUGH GIRLS; LEWIS HARDCASTLE'S
DUSKY SYNCOPATERS
Swanee River *(1938)* NINA MAE McKINNEY
Sweeney Todd TOD SLAUGHTER
Sweep JACK HULBERT
Sweet Adeline *(1929)* SYDNEY HOWARD
Sweet Adeline *(1937)*
ETHEL REVNELL AND GRACIE WEST
Sweet and Low *(1929)*
CARROLL GIBBONS AND HIS ORCHESTRA
Sweet and Low *(1937)* STUART ROBERTSON

Sweet Boy	CLODAGH RODGERS
Sweet Enniskillen	RICHARD HAYWARD
Sweet Fanny Adams	
	SONNIE HALE; TOMMY TRINDER
Sweet Georgia Brown	
	STÉPHANE GRAPPELLY; GEORGE SHEARING
Sweet Little Cafe, A	ANNA NEAGLE
Sweet Love Child	ANTHONY NEWLEY
Sweet Memories	DAVE CLARK FIVE
Sweet Muchacha	
	PERCIVAL MACKEY AND HIS BAND; RONALD WALTERS
Sweet Music	
	PRINCE TWINS; HAL SWAIN AND HIS KIT KAT BAND
Sweet Nothings	
	DEBROY SOMERS AND HIS BAND
Sweet Sue (1934)	THE VERSATILE THREE
Sweet Sue (1935)	THREE EMERALDS
Sweet Sue (1938; 2 films)	
	RADIO REVELLERS; JACK SIMPSON
Sweet Sue (1939)	
	EDDIE CARROLL AND HIS BAND; CURLY ORMEROD
Sweet Sue (1940)	
	PERCIVAL MACKEY AND HIS BAND
Sweetest Song in the World, The	
	GRACIE FIELDS
Sweethearts Forever	THREE RADIO ROGUES
Sweetmeat Joe	
	DAN DONOVAN; HENRY HALL AND THE B.B.C. DANCE ORCHESTRA
Swim Little Fish	GEORGE FORMBY
Swing	FRANCES DAY
Swing and Sway	
	EARL CARROLL AND HIS RADIO BOYS
Swing for Sale	MARGARET TURNER
Swing Madame	JACK BUCHANAN
Swing Momma	GEORGE FORMBY
Swing That Music	BILLY COTTON AND HIS BAND
Swing Your Way to Happiness	GRACIE FIELDS
Swinging Affair, A	
	LAURI PETERS; CLIFF RICHARD
Swinging Along	GEORGE FORMBY
Swinging in a Hammock	MAESTRO SINGERS
Swinging In Between	
	HENRY HALL AND THE B.B.C. DANCE ORCHESTRA
Swinging the Pick	FOUR ACES
Swistles	HAL BROWN
Swonderful	FRED CONYNGHAM
Sylphides, Les (1963)	
	MARGOT FONTEYN; RUDOLPH NUREYEV
Sylphides, Les (1972)	RUDOLPH NUREYEV
Sylvia (1930)	HUGHES MACKLIN
Sylvia (1933; 2 films)	
	FOUR MUSKETEERS; TOM JONES
Sympathy for the Devil	
	MICK JAGGER; THE ROLLING STONES
Symphonic Variations	EILEEN JOYCE
Symphony in Motion	MARION AND IRMA
Syncopation	BILLY MAYERL

T

Ta-Ra-Ra-Boom-De-Ay (1935)	
	BERTHA WILLMOTT
Ta-Ra-Ra-Boom-De-Ay (1938)	GRACIE FIELDS
Ta-Ra-Ra-Boom-De-Ay (1940)	EMPIRE GIRLS

Table Top Toes	BARRIE OLIVER
Taboo	JOHNNY LEYTON
Tabu (1936)	
	BERNARD MONSHIN AND HIS RIO TANGO BAND
Tabu (1941)	
	DON MARINO BARETTO AND HIS RHUMBA BAND
Taint	JACK HULBERT
Take a Pebble	EMERSON, LAKE AND PALMER
Take a Ride on the Roundabouts	
	BOB JOHNSTON
Take a Ride With Me	TOMMY STEELE
Take a Step	FRED CONYNGHAM
Take It Away	DAVID ESSEX
Take It Easy	LIONEL BLAIR; JIMMY CRAWFORD
Take Me	ANNE SHELTON
Take Me Back Baby	TOMMY STEELE
Take Me Back to Blighty (1943)	ELLA RETFORD
Take Me Back to Blighty (1962)	
	CICELY COURTNEIDGE
Take Me High	CLIFF RICHARD
Take My Hands	GITTA ALPAR
Take My Heart	DONALD PEERS
Take the World Exactly As You Find It	
	LESLIE A HUTCHINSON
Take This Train	LONG AND THE SHORT
Take Your Pick	FOUR ACES
Taking a Stroll Around the Park	
	MRS JACK HYLTON AND HER BOYS
Taking Out Time	SPENCER DAVIS GROUP
Tale, The	HUGH DUNCAN AND NAN HAY
Tale of Hilda Hose, The	CYRIL FLETCHER
Tale of Queenie Feather, The	CYRIL FLETCHER
Talent	NORMAN WISDOM
Tales from the Vienna Woods	
	LONDON SYMPHONY ORCHESTRA
Tales of Hoffmann	FRANCO FORESTA
Talking Feet	HAZEL ASCOT
Talking in My Sleep	
	PHILIP RIDGEWAY AND JEAN MELVILLE
Talking to the Moon About You	
	GEORGE FORMBY
Tally Ho	ROBERT EASTON
Tan Tan Tivvy	THREE GINX
Tango	ALEC ROSS
Tango Town	XENIA AND BOYER
Tannhäuser (1936)	
	DEBROY SOMERS AND HIS BAND
Tannhäuser (1939)	FLORENCE DE JONG
Tannhäuser (1990)	KIRI TE KANAWA
Tap Your Tootsies	JACK HULBERT
Tape	THE CURE
Tapping Out Rhythm	
	HAZEL ASCOT; GORDON RAY GIRLS
Tappitout	HERMAN DAREWSKI
Tchaikowsky Medley	
	HAL SWAIN AND HIS KIT KAT BAND
Tear, a Smile, a Sigh, A	
	ARTHUR LUCAN AND KITTY McSHANE
Tear It Up	THE CRAMPS
Teardrops Fell Like Rain	THE CRICKETS
Tears On My Pillow	
	FRANK KING AND HIS ORCHESTRA; ROSALIND MELVILLE
Teas, Light Refreshments and Minerals	
	THE TWO LESLIES

Teasing — BERYL ORDE
Ted Ain't Dead — EDDIE 'TENPOLE' TUDOR
Teddy Bear's Picnic — BINKIE STUART
Teenage Party — TOMMY STEELE
Teenage Turtles — BACK TO THE PLANET
Teenage Valentino — RAY SONE
Telegram Sam — MARC BOLAN AND T. REX
Television Dress Rehearsal — ANITA D'RAY
Tell It to Your Heart — LOU REED
Tell Me I'm Forgiven
 GERALDO AND HIS GAUCHO TANGO ORCHESTRA
Tell Me Tonight *(1932)* — JAN KIEPURA
Tell Me Tonight *(1935)* — ALBERT SANDLER
Tell Me Truly — GWEN CATLEY
Tell Me What You See — THE BEATLES
Tell Me When — THE APPLEJACKS
Tell Me Why *(1964)* — THE BEATLES
Tell Me Why *(1965)* — BILLY FURY
Telling Me What to Do — JOY NICHOLS
Temple Bells — BOBBY HOWES
Temple Gates — GATTY SELLARS
Temple Song — MALCOLM MacEACHERN
Temptation Baby — GENE VINCENT
Temptation Rag — MARIO DE PIETRO
Tenderfoot Song, The — TOMMY HANDLEY
Tenor on Stilts — PEVERI
Terpsichorean Acrobatics — GASTON AND ANDREE
Texas Dan — ERIC WOODBURN
Thanks a Lot — TOMMY STEELE
Thanks Very Much
 CARROLL GIBBONS AND HIS ORCHESTRA; MARION HARRIS
That Certain Thing — MAX AND HARRY NESBITT
That Coal Black Mammy of Mine — LADDIE CLIFF
That Dusty Western Trail — AVRIL ANGERS
That Lovely Weekend
 TED HEATH AND HIS MUSIC
That Old-Fashioned Mother of Mine
 PAT O'BRIEN
That Rhumba Rhythm — RUDY STARITA
That Song in My Heart — STUART ROBERTSON
That's as Far as It Goes — EVELYN DALL
That's Fiesta — TOMMY STEELE
That's How I Spell Ireland — JACK DALY
That's How I Write a Love Song
 RONALD FRANKAU
That's Motivation — DAVID BOWIE
That's My Doll — FRANKIE VAUGHAN
That's My Home — PHYLLIS STANLEY
That's No Way to Say Goodbye
 LEONARD COHEN
That's What I'm Trying to Say — HAL JONES
That's What Life Is Made Of
 REGGIE BRISTOW AND HIS BAND
Them Bellyful — BOB MARLEY AND THE WAILERS
Them Monkeys Can't Swing — SLADE
Then I Wiggle Down in Bed — BINKIE STUART
There Ain't No Magic in Moonlight
 THE TWO LESLIES
There Are More Heavens Than One
 DICK HENDERSON (senior)
There Goes My Dream — RINTALLA
There Is a Co-op in the Town
 DEBROY SOMERS AND HIS BAND

There Is a Tavern in the Town *(1938; 3 films)*
 GRACIE FIELDS; MUSIC HALL BOYS; RADIO REVELLERS
There Is a Tavern in the Town *(1950)*
 GERALDO AND HIS ORCHESTRA
There Is a Tavern in the Town *(1962)*
 TERRY LIGHTFOOT AND HIS NEW ORLEANS JAZZ BAND
There Isn't Any Limit — JACK BUCHANAN
There Isn't Enough To Go Round
 TESSIE O'SHEA
There'll Always Be an England — GLYN DAVIES
There'll Always Be Time for a Song — JEAN COLIN
There'll Still Be Love
 VIOLET LORAINE; ROY FOX AND HIS BAND
There's a Big Day Coming
 BUD FLANAGAN AND CHESNEY ALLEN
There's a Doctor — THE WHO
There's a Light in Your Window
 BILLY SCOTT-COOMBER; BILLY THORBURN AND HIS BAND
There's a Long Long Trail Awinding
 EVELYN LAYE
There's a New World *(1937)*
 BILLY THORBURN AND HIS BAND
There's a New World *(1944)* — VERA LYNN
There's a Part of America
 BUD FLANAGAN AND CHESNEY ALLEN
There's a Smile in the Skies — GRETE NATZLER
There's a Star in the Sky — STANLEY LUPINO
There's a Time and a Place — DENNIS LOTIS
There's Always Someone — ALAN PRICE
There's Another Trumpet Playing in the Sky
 BOBBIE COMBER
There's Life in the Old Girl Yet
 FIVE CHARLADIES
There's No Day Like Today — HARRY WELCHMAN
There's No Excusing Susan
 PEGGY COCHRANE; FRED CONYNGHAM; TEDDY JOYCE AND HIS BAND
There's No Place Like Rome — TOMMY TRINDER
There's No Time Like the Present — LEN BERMAN
There's Nothing Like This — OMAR
There's Room in My Heart
 CARROLL GIBBONS AND HIS ORCHESTRA; REG STONE
There's So Much I'm Wanting to Tell You
 STANLEY LUPINO
There's Something About a Soldier
 CICELY COURTNEIDGE
There's Something About You — CARL BRISSON
There's That Look in Your Eye
 JESSIE MATTHEWS
There's Too Much Love — CLIFF RICHARD
These Dangerous Years — FRANKIE VAUGHAN
These Foolish Things *(1936)* — RADIO THREE
These Foolish Things *(1937)* — TURNER LAYTON
These Foolish Things *(1948)*
 MAURICE ARNOLD SEXTET; DINAH KAYE
These Foolish Things *(1952)*
 LESLIE JEFFRIES AND HIS ORCHESTRA
They Can't Fool Me — GEORGE FORMBY
They Cut Down the Old Pine Tree
 THREE RADIO ROGUES
They Laughed When I Started to Play
 GEORGE FORMBY

They Say   FREDDIE LATHAM
They're Building Flats Where the Arches Used
    To Be   BUD FLANAGAN AND CHESNEY ALLEN
They're Gathering Flowers for Mother
           SAM COSTA
They're Tough Mighty Tough in the West
    BIG BILL CAMPBELL AND HIS ROCKY
           MOUNTAINEERS
Thine In My Heart *(2 films)*   NAVARRE
Things Are Looking Up   CICELY COURTNEIDGE
Think Pink   JESSICA MARTIN
Thinking to Myself About You
    PAT KAYE AND BETTY ANKERS
Thirty Thousand Pounds   JIMMY O'DEA
This Girl   SLADE
This Is My First Romance   SUSAN MAUGHAN
This Is My World   TOMMY STEELE
This Is the Missis
    MRS JACK HYLTON AND HER BOYS
This Is the Night
    FRANKIE VAUGHAN; SHANI WALLIS
This Is the Rhythm for Me *(1935)*
    PAMELA GREY AND PAT GREEN
This is the Rhythm for Me *(1937)*
    MRS MURGATROYD AND MRS WINTERBOTTOM
This Is the Time for Dancing
    HENRY HALL AND THE B.B.C. DANCE ORCHESTRA
This Is the World Calling   BOB GELDOF
This Is Worth Fighting For   SIDNEY BURCHALL
This Land of Mine   CAROL RAYE
This Little Island of Mine   GENE GERRARD
This One   PAUL AND LINDA McCARTNEY
This Thing Called Love *(1935)*   PHYLLIS ROBINS
This Thing Called Love *(1964)*
    GERRY AND THE PACEMAKERS
This Thing Called Sin
    PAT KAYE AND BETTY ANKERS
This'll Make You Whistle
    JACK BUCHANAN; ELSIE RANDOLPH
Thistledown   MICHAEL FARADAY
Thomas and Anne   ENGLISH QUARTETTE
Those Dear Old Tivoli Days   RALPH READER
Those Endearing Young Charms *(1934)*
           JOHN GARRICK
Those Endearing Young Charms *(1937; 3
    films)*
    FRED CONYNGHAM; JOHN GARRICK; JOHN
           McCORMACK
Those Endearing Young Charms *(1947)*
           JAMES ETHERINGTON
Those Endearing Young Charms *(1948)*
           FRED GROUTS
Thought Never Entered My Head, The
    HELEN BURNELL; JACK HULBERT
Thoughts   B.B.C. MYSTERY SINGER
Three Bears, The   RAY ELLINGTON QUARTET
Three Blind Mice   MAURICE ARNOLD SEXTET
Three Days in the Country
    THE WONDERFUL WORLD
Three Feet   COLLINSON AND DEAN
Three Imaginary Boys   THE CURE
Three Minute Hero   THE SELECTER
Three Steps to Heaven   STING
Three Wishes   JESSIE MATTHEWS
Through the Courtesy of Love
           JESSIE MATTHEWS

Throughout the Years   LENI LYNN
Ticket to Ride   THE BEATLES
Tickle My Fancy   REG VARNEY
Tico Tico *(1947)*   MARIO 'HARP' LORENZI
Tico Tico *(1950)*   TWO CODOLBANS
Tico Tico *(1952)*   MARIE DE VERE DANCERS
Tiddley Om Pom Pay   JESSIE MATTHEWS
Tiger Feet   MUD
Tiger Rag *(1933; 3 films)*
    MODERNIQUES; TERENCE McGOVERN AND HIS
           NOVELTY ORCHESTRA
Tiger Rag *(1935; 3 films)*
    NAT GONELLA AND HIS GEORGIANS; BILLY
    MERRIN AND HIS COMMANDERS; JACK PAYNE
           AND HIS DANCE ORCHESTRA
Tiger Rag *(1943)*
    HARRY PARRY AND HIS RADIO RHYTHM CLUB
           SEXTET; RENARA
Till All Your Dreams Come True
           LUTON GIRLS' CHOIR
Till the End of the Day   V.5. BAND
Till the Lights of London Shine Again
           BERYL DAVIS
Till the Right Time Comes   PATRICIA BREDIN
Till the Wheel Comes Off   THE CO-OPTIMISTS
Timber   JIMMY JEWEL AND BEN WARRISS
Time *(1965)*   DAVE CLARK FIVE
Time *(1973)*   DAVID BOWIE
Time *(1984)*   CULTURE CLUB
Time *(1996)*   MARIANNE FAITHFULL
Time Drags By   CLIFF RICHARD
Time for Action, Glory Boys   SECRET AFFAIR
Time Has Come, The   ADAM FAITH
Time to Go   BILLY MILTON
Time to Kill   TOMMY STEELE
Tingaling   LUCILLE MAPP
Tinker, The   RAYMOND NEWELL
Tinkle Tinkle Tinkle
    SONNIE HALE; JESSIE MATTHEWS
Tiny Tea Shop, A   STANELLI AND EDGAR
Tipica Stomp
    MANTOVANI AND HIS TIPICA ORCHESTRA
Tipperary *(1934; 2 films)*
    FLORRIE FORDE; EVELYN LAYE
Tipperary *(1935; 2 films)*
    JACK JUDGE; BERTHA WILLMOTT
Tipperary *(1943)*   ELLA RETFORD
Tit Willow   LIONEL BLAIR
To a Stream   JOSEPH HISLOP
To Find Your Dream   BILLY FURY
To Sir With Love   LULU
To You Cherie   MORGAN DAVIES
Toasts   LESLIE SARONY
Tobacco Road   NASHVILLE TEENS
Today I Feel So Happy *(1931)*
    JACK HULBERT; RENATE MULLER
Today I Feel So Happy *(1940)*   ARTHUR ASKEY
Today It Rained Champagne   THE WHO
Toddle Along   PHYLLIS STANLEY
Together   BILLY MILTON
Tokay   STUART ROBERTSON
Tom the Piper's Son
    BILLY COTTON AND HIS BAND
Tommy, Can You Hear Me? *(2 films)*   THE WHO
Tommy Gun   THE CLASH
Tommy the Toreador   TOMMY STEELE

Tommy's Holiday Camp — KEITH MOON
Tomorrow — THE STRAWBS
Tomorrow Is a Beautiful Day
    BUD FLANAGAN AND CHESNEY ALLEN
Tomorrow's Rainbow — LESLIE A HUTCHINSON
Tongs YaBass — V.5. BAND
Tonight *(1934)* — ANNA NEAGLE
Tonight *(1975)* — THE RUBETTES
Tonight Will Be Fine — LEONARD COHEN
Tonight You Belong to Me — ELGA COLLINS
Tonight You're Mine — GWEN CATLEY
Tony's in Town — JESSIE MATTHEWS
Tony's Wife — JACK HARRIS AND HIS BAND
Too Late — BILLY GERHARDI AND HIS BAND
Too Much — THE SPICE GIRLS
Too Much Pressure — THE SELECTER
Too Much Too Young — THE SPECIALS
Toodle Oodle Ay — PETULA CLARK
Top of the House — LANCE FAIRFAX
Top of the Wheel — HAZEL O'CONNOR
Topsy — STANELLI
Topsy Turvy Blues — THE HOUSTON SISTERS
Toreador Song *(1931)* — LANCE FAIRFAX
Toreador Song *(1937; 2 films)*
    ALBERT SANDLER; ARTHUR TRACY
Tosca — TINO PATTIERA
Total Eclipse — KLAUS NOMI
Touch It Light — BENNY HILL; TOMMY STEELE
Touch of Texas, A
    CHARLES FORSYTHE, ADDIE SEAMON AND
    ELEANOR FARRELL
Touch of Your Lips, The
    RONNIE BOYER AND JEANNE REVEL
Touquet, Le
    MACARI AND HIS DUTCH SERENADERS
Toy Balloon — PEGGY COCHRANE
Toy Drum Major, The — THE HOUSTON SISTERS
Toy Grenadiers — TEN DURHAM PITMEN
Toy Town Dance — BINNIE HALE
Toy Trumpeter — NANETTE
Traces of a Long Forgotten Time — JACK JONES
Train Gang — JOHNNY DANKWORTH AND HIS BAND
Train Kept Arolling, The — JIM DALE
Tramp's Sacrifice, The — TOMMY HANDLEY
Travatore, Il — FLORENCE DE JONG
Traviata, La
    EVELYN LAYE; BROWNING MUMMERY
Tread on the Tail of My Coat
    RICHARD HAYWARD
Treasure Island *(1936)*
    JOE LOSS AND HIS ORCHESTRA
Treasure Island *(1961)*
    THUNDERCLAP JONES; GARRY MILLS
Trees *(1932)* — BARRINGTON HOOPER
Trees *(1933)* — LESLIE A HUTCHINSON
Trees *(1934)* — ANDRE BALOG
Trees *(1936)* — FREDDIE BAMBERGER
Trees *(1937; 2 films)*
    REGINALD FOORT; ARTHUR TRACY
Trees *(1952)*
    LESLIE JEFFRIES AND HIS ORCHESTRA
Trek Song *(2 films)* — GRACIE FIELDS
Trenchtown Rock
    BOB MARLEY AND THE WAILERS
Trial by Jury — THOMAS ROUND

Tribulations — RAS ANGELS AND RAS MESSENGERS
Tristan and Isolde
    LONDON PHILHARMONIC ORCHESTRA
Triumphal March — THE VANCOUVER BOYS BAND
Trocadero Cabaret — GRIFFITHS BROTHERS
Trolls of Excess — SHANTI
Troubadour Song, The — DAVID KERNAN
Trouble in Paradise — HILDEGARDE
Trouble with Man, The — JAN AND KELLY
Troublesome Trumpet
    NAT GONELLA AND HIS GEORGIANS
Trouser Snake — THE FILBERTS
True Love — HARRY WELCHMAN
Trumpeter *(1933)* — THE MASTERSINGERS
Trumpeter *(1936)* — LANCE FAIRFAX
Trust — THE CURE
Trusting My Luck — JESSIE MATTHEWS
Try Again — MIKE PRESTON
Try Try Again — THE BOSWELL TWINS
Try Walking Backwards — PETULA CLARK
Tulip Time
    MACARI AND HIS DUTCH SERENADERS
Turkey in the Straw
    GENE ESSEN AND HIS CHICAGO VELLUM BOYS
Turmut Hoeing — ERNEST BUTCHER
Turn on the Love Light — STANLEY LUPINO
Turn On the Music — THREE AUSTRALIAN BOYS
Turned Out Nice Again — JACK AND EDDIE EDEN
Turned Up — LUPINO LANE
Turning the Town Upside Down
    GRACE BRADLEY
Tutti Frutti — MARC BOLAN AND T. REX
Twelfth Street Rag — CHARLES 'BUDDY' ROGERS
Twelve and a Tanner a Bottle — WILL FYFFE
Twi-Twi-Twilight, The *(1940)* — WARREN JENKINS
Twi-Twi-Twilight, The *(1943)* — BETTY WARREN
Twickenham Ferry — JUBILEE DUETTISTS
Twinkling Toes — REGINALD SHARLAND
Twist and Shout *(1965)* — THE BEATLES
Twist and Shout *(1967)* — CLIFF RICHARD
Twist Kid — BILLY FURY
Twist 'n' Crawl — THE BEAT
Twisted Tunes *(3 films)* — EDDIE POLA
Twisting the Night Away *(3 films)*
    FREDDIE AND THE DREAMERS; VINCE HILL;
    BOSCOE HOLDER
Two a Penny — CLIFF RICHARD
Two Become One — THE SPICE GIRLS
Two Bouquets
AMBROSE AND HIS ORCHESTRA; HARRY RICHMAN
Two Divided by Zero — PET SHOP BOYS
Two Eyes — TOMMY STEELE
Two Grenadiers — ERIC MARSHALL
Two Gun Dan — BILLY GERHARDI AND HIS BAND
Two Hearts that Beat in Waltz Time
    CARL BRISSON
Two Imps, The — KNELLER HALL MILITARY BAND
Two in a Bar — JACK HULBERT
Two Little Dogs
    DONALD CLIVE; ROBIN RICHMOND
Two Little Boys — SPLODGENESSABOUNDS
Two Lovely Black Eyes *(1932)*
    BILLY REID AND THE LONDON ACCORDION BAND
Two Lovely Black Eyes *(1934)*
    CHARLES COBURN

Two Lovely Black Eyes *(1936)*
PERCY AND MARY HONRI
Two Lovely Black Eyes *(1938)*   GRACIE FIELDS
Two of Us   THE BEATLES
Two Sinners   LESLIE A HUTCHINSON
Two Tired Eyes   LESLIE A HUTCHINSON
Typically English   MILLICENT MARTIN
Typically Japanese   MILLICENT MARTIN
Tyrolean Yodel   DAVE WILLIS
Tzinga Doodle Day   MAURICE CHEVALIER

U

Ukulele Lullabye   SCOVELL AND WHELDON
Ukulele Man, The   GEORGE FORMBY
Ulster Love Song   RICHARD HAYWARD
Umbrellas and Ice Cream
GEORGE CLARKE; BILLY MERSON
Unconditional Surrender   GEORGE FORMBY
Under a Banana Tree   PEGGY DESMOND
Under the Bazunka Tree   NORMAN LONG
Under the Blasted Oak   GEORGE FORMBY
Under the Double Eagle   THE DANCETTES
Under Your Hat   JACK HULBERT
Undercover of the Night   THE ROLLING STONES
Underground   DAVID BOWIE
Underneath the Arches *(2 films)*
THE CRAZY GANG
Underneath the Arches *(5 films)*
BUD FLANAGAN AND CHESNEY ALLEN
Undress Parade MAX RIVERS' TROCADERO GIRLS
Union Hall Poem   MARC BOLAN AND T. REX
United We Stand
STAN SHEDDON AND THE PLAYTIMERS; MAURICE
TAYLOR
Unlucky   JEAN (JEANNIE) CARSON
Unnatural History   BILLY BENNETT
Until   WEBSTER BOOTH; ANNE ZIEGLER
Until a Few Kisses Ago   JEAN CAVALL
Up in the World   NORMAN WISDOM
Up With the Lark
ETHEL REVNELL AND GRACIE WEST
Ups and Downs of Love, The FREDDY CANNON
Uriah Heep   PETER PAGET
U.S.A.   THE CLASH
Utterly Simple   TRAFFIC

V

Valentine *(2 films)*   NAVARRE
Valium   INVISIBLE SEX
Valley of the Moon   THE MASTERSINGERS
Valparaiso, The
JACK HOLLAND AND JUNE HART; CHARLES
'BUDDY' ROGERS
Value of a Smile, The   WALSH AND BARKER
Variations on a Fugue
LONDON SYMPHONY ORCHESTRA
Varsity Drag   MICHAEL TRIPP
Vaudeville's Big Boots   ALLY FORD
Venetian Serenade   BENJAMINO GIGLI
Verdi's March Triumphant
ISABELLA ROSATI CASSERINI
Veronica   HILDA HEATH
Versatile Solo   JACK SIMPSON
Very Thought of You, The *(1934)*   AL BOWLLY

Very Thought of You, The *(1935)* CHARLIE KUNZ
Veteran, The   FRANK WIGNALL
Vicar of Bray, The *(2 films)*
JACK BRADY AND HIS BAND; STANLEY HOLLOWAY
Vicar of Mirth, The   VIVIAN FOSTER
Victims   CULTURE CLUB
Victory Waltz   STAN WHITE
Vie en Rose, La   MARLENE DIETRICH
Vienna City of My Dreams *(1934; 2 films)*
FAY COMPTON; MANTOVANI AND HIS TIPICA
ORCHESTRA
Vienna City of My Dreams *(1935)*
RICHARD TAUBER
Vienna City of My Dreams *(1936)*
ELEANOR FAYRE
Vienna City of My Dreams *(1937)*
DILLWYN THOMAS
Vienna City of My Dreams *(1938)*
BETTY AND FREDDIE ROBERTS
Viennese Waltz   CHARLIE KUNZ
Vilanelle   MAURICETTE
Village Blacksmith, The   STANLEY HOLLOWAY
Violetera, La   GLORIA MARIVILLA
Violetta *(1939)*
MANTOVANI AND HIS TIPICA ORCHESTRA
Violetta *(1949)*   JOSEF LOCKE
Violin Concerto No. 1   YEHUDI MENUHIN
Violin in Vienna
MANTOVANI AND HIS TIPICA ORCHESTRA
Violin Song from Tina   TOM JONES
Virgin Queen, The   REG VARNEY
Virginal Offering   RANI RAMA
Virginia   PAT AND TERRY KENDAL
Viva Forever   THE SPICE GIRLS
Voce Poco Fa, Una   MARTA EGGERTH
Voi Che Sapete   ADELE LEIGH
Voice in the Night, A   ELIZABETH WEBB
Voice in the Old Village Choir
THOMAS (TOM) BURKE
Voice in the Wilderness   CLIFF RICHARD
Voice of Romance, The   MERVYN SAUNDERS
Voices of Freedom
JACKSON BROWNE; PETER GABRIEL; YOUSSOU
N'DOUR; LOU REED
Volare   DAVID BOWIE
Volga Boatman *(1937)*   REGINALD FOORT
Volga Boatman *(1963)*
MR ACKER BILK AND THE PARAMOUNT JAZZ BAND
Vote for Me   MARK WYNTER

W

Wa Wa Daddle O   HARRY ROY AND HIS BAND
Wagon Wheels   GENE WOLFF
Waiting   URIEL PORTER
Waiting at the Church *(1934)*   VESTA VICTORIA
Waiting at the Church *(1941)*   LILY MORRIS
Waiting at the Church *(1943)*
BERTHA WILLMOTT
Waiting for the Robert E. Lee   PETER BERNARD
Wake   LESLIE A HUTCHINSON
Wake Up *(1932)*   BETTY FIELDS
Wake Up *(1967)*   CLIFF RICHARD
Wake Up *(1988)*   PET SHOP BOYS
Wales   PAUL ROBESON

Walk, The *(2 films)* THE CURE
Walk Down the Road LANCE FAIRFAX
Walking Back to Happiness HELEN SHAPIRO
Walking On Air
JOHNNY WORTHY AND BERTIE JARRETT
Walking Tall FRANKIE VAUGHAN
Walking the Beam
JACK DONAHUE; TUTTA ROLF
Walking With Susie
BOBBIE ALDERSON; PATRICIA ROSSBOROUGH
Walpurgisnacht THE BOLSHOI BALLET
Walter, Walter GRACIE FIELDS
Waltz *(1922; 2 films)*
CARL HYSON AND PEGGY HARRIS; TED TREVOR
AND DINAH HARRIS
Waltz *(1924)*
BARBARA MILES AND MAXWELL STEWART
Waltz *(1939; 2 films)*
DRAPER AND LINDEN; ANNA MAC
Waltz *(1942)*
CHARLES THEBAULT AND DOREEN BEAHAN
Waltz by Durand SIX LADY HARPISTS
Waltz for Caroline SPENCER DAVIS GROUP
Waltz for Those in Love ARTHUR TRACY
Waltz of Delight GWEN CATLEY
Waltz of My Heart GISELLE PREVILLE
Waltz of the Flowers THE LEROYS
Waltz of the Gypsies GYPSY NINA
Waltz of the Kiss HARRY RAYE AND BILLIE MAYE
Waltzing Matilda FRANK IFIELD
Waltzing the Blues RAY ELLINGTON QUARTET
Wandering Minstrel, A *(1939)* KENNY BAKER
Wandering Minstrel, A *(1963)* KEVIN SCOTT
Wandering to Paradise FAY COMPTON
Wanderlust PAUL McCARTNEY; RINGO STARR
Wanna Dan ZURA
Wannabe THE SPICE GIRLS
War BOB MARLEY AND THE WAILERS
Warm Summer Day KETTY LESTER
Was That the Human Thing To Do?
BILLY GERHARDI AND HIS BAND
Wash Me in His Blood MAXINE BARRIE
Washerwoman, The
CORONA BOYS AND GIRLS; CLIFF RICHARD
Watch That Man DAVID BOWIE
Watch the Navy RAYMOND NEWELL
Watcha Gonna Do About It? THE SEX PISTOLS
Watching All the World Go By
GEORGE MITCHELL SINGERS
Watching the Stars STUART ROBERTSON
Water Boy EDRIC CONNOR
Water Water *(1933)* HENDERSON AND LENNOX
Water Water *(1957)* TOMMY STEELE
Waterlogged Spa ERIC BARKER
Way to Make It Hep, The ROY CASTLE
Way We Dance, The JIGSAW
Wayfarer TITO GOBBI
We All Go Riding on a Rainbow
CICELY COURTNEIDGE; DEBROY SOMERS AND
HIS BAND; THREE ADMIRALS
We Are One MAXINE BARRIE
We Can't Find the Tiger Any More *(1936)*
THREE RHYTHM BROTHERS
We Can't Find the Tiger Any More *(1940)*
CICELY COURTNEIDGE; JACK HULBERT; THREE
RHYTHM BROTHERS

We Chose the Air Force
SAM BROWNE; JAY WILBUR AND HIS BAND
We Didn't Know What to Say WILFRED TEMPLE
We Do See Life
ETHEL REVNELL AND GRACIE WEST
We Got the Beat THE GO GOS
We Like Eliza AL AND BOB HARVEY
We Love a Movie CLIFF RICHARD
We Made Her Pull the Whole Lot Home
JOHN RUTLAND
We Must All Stick Together TEDDY BROWN
We Police Are Wonderful RICHARD MURDOCH
We Say Yeah CLIFF RICHARD
We Three CECIL FREDERICK; HARRY KORRIS
We Want a Little Song *(1936)*
MRS JACK HYLTON AND HER BOYS
We Want a Little Song *(1943)*
ROBBIE (ENOCH) VINCENT
We Were Meant to Meet Again ARTHUR TRACY
We Won't Say Good Morning
LILY MORRIS; NELLIE WALLACE
We'll Always Give a Thought To You
JEAN COLIN
We'll Have a Country Wedding LADDIE CLIFF
We'll Meet Again *(1942)* VERA LYNN
We'll Meet Again *(1955)* YANA
We'll Never Run Short of Love LILLI PALMER
We'll Shout Hooray Again
ELSIE AND DORIS WATERS
We'll Smile Again
BUD FLANAGAN AND CHESNEY ALLEN
We're All Good Pals Together GRACIE FIELDS
We're Glad to Be in London YACHT CLUB BOYS
We're Gonna Die ANDREW SCHOFIELD
We're Gonna Hang Out the Washing *(1939)*
GEORGE ELRICK
We're Gonna Hang Out the Washing *(1958)*
BUD FLANAGAN AND CHESNEY ALLEN
We're in Harmony Heaven POLLY WARD
We're Not Gonna Take It
ROGER DALTREY; THE WHO
We're Not Gonna Take It [See Me, Feel Me]
THE WHO
We're Not Quite What We Used To Be
LILY MORRIS; NELLIE WALLACE
We're Tops on Saturday Night
AMBROSE AND HIS ORCHESTRA
We've Been a Long Time Gone
GEORGE FORMBY
We've Got a Hunch SONNIE HALE
We've Got a Show CLIFF RICHARD
We've Only Got Three Minutes
VINE, MORE AND NEVARD
Wear a Great Big Smile ELEANOR FAYRE
Wear a Straw Hat in the Rain LARRY ADLER
Wear Gloves JACK HULBERT
Wearing His Old School Tie
THE WESTERN BROTHERS
Wearing of the Green CAVAN O'CONNOR
Weather Forecast THE WESTERN BROTHERS
Weather Man *(2 films)*
HARRIETTE HUTCHINS; RHYTHM SISTERS
Wedding Bells Are Ringing for Sally A C ASTOR
Wedding in Paris EVELYN LAYE
Wedding of the Painted Doll BURTON BROWN

Wee Deoch and Doris, A   SIR HARRY LAUDER
Wee MacGregor, The   LARSEN BROTHERS
Wee Shup, The   RICHARD HAYWARD
Welcome   ROGER DALTREY
Welcome Inn   STARDUSTERS DANCE ORCHESTRA
Welsh Medley (1933)
   LESLIE BRIDGEWATER AND HIS HARP SEPTET
Welsh Medley (1943)
   SCOTS MILITARY EX-GUARDS BAND
Were You Not To Koko Plighted   KEVIN SCOTT
West End Girls   PET SHOP BOYS
What a Crazy World
   JOE BROWN; THE BRUVVERS; SUSAN MAUGHAN
What a Difference a Day Makes   JACK PLANT
What a Little Moonlight Can Do
   GERALDO AND HIS ORCHESTRA; VIOLET LORAINE
What a Mouth   JOHN RUTLAND
What a Whopper   ADAM FAITH
What About Me?   NORAH BLANEY
What About the Boy?   THE WHO
What Am I Going to Tell Them Tonight?
CLEO LAINE; JOHNNY DANKWORTH AND HIS BAND
What Are Little Girls Made Of?   BETTY ASTELL
What Are You Going to Do if Love Comes?
   BOBBY HOWES
What Do They Say of England?
   SIDNEY BURCHALL
What Do They Think of England Now?
   EMPIRE MILITARY BAND
What Do You Do?   TOMMY STEELE
What Do You Know About Love?
   EDDIE CARROLL AND HIS BAND; GWEN JONES
What Does It Get Me?   CICELY COURTNEIDGE
What Happens To Her?   EYES OF BLUE
What Harlem Means to Me
   HARRIETTE HUTCHINS
What Has England Done for Him?
   SYDNEY HOWARD
What Have I Done To Deserve This?
   PET SHOP BOYS
What Have We Got to Lose?
   BETTY ASTELL; REGGIE BRISTOW AND HIS BAND
What I Do I Do Well   GERTRUDE LAWRENCE
What in the World   THE ROCKIN' BERRIES
What Is This Thing?   FRANCES DAY
What Lancashire Thinks Today   ELSIE BROWN
What Love Means to Girls Like Me   MAISIE GAY
What Makes You So Adorable?
   LESLIE A HUTCHINSON
What More Can I Ask?   ANNA NEAGLE
What More Can I Say?   HAL MONTY
What Would You Do?   DUDLEY ROLPHE
What Would You Like for Breakfast?
   BOB AND ALF PEARSON
What's Cooking? (1948)   STEVE RACE
What's Cooking? (1960)   GLEN MASON
What's Going to Happen to Me?
   BOBBY HOWES
What's My Name?   THE CLASH
What's the Name of the Game?
   THE BREAKAWAYS; JOE BROWN
What've I Gotta Do?   CLIFF RICHARD
Whatcha Gonna Do About It? (2 films)
   NASHVILLE TEENS; SMALL FACES

Wheel of the Wagon, The
   JOE LOSS AND HIS ORCHESTRA
Wheels on Fire   THE BRIAN AUGER TRINITY
Wheezy Anna   LESLIE SARONY
When   DAVE CLARK FIVE
When Chelsea Won the Cup   NORMAN LONG
When Cupid Calls   GRACIE FIELDS
When Dawn Breaks Through
   VICTOR OLOFF SEXTETTE
When Day Is Done (1936)
   AMBROSE AND HIS ORCHESTRA
When Day Is Done (1937; 2 films)
   AMBROSE AND HIS ORCHESTRA; MARK
HAMBOURG; MINI-PIANO ENSEMBLE OF 14
   JUVENILES
When Day Is Done (1939)
   BILLY SCOTT-COOMBER AND HIS EIGHT ROYAL
   MOUNTIES
When Dreams Grow Old
   MANTOVANI AND HIS TIPICA ORCHESTRA
When Flanagan Went to Spain
   TALBOT O'FARRELL
When Gay Adventure Calls   EVELYN LAYE
When Gimble Hits the Cymbal   MAX BACON
When He Got It Did He Want It?   ZOE GAIL
When I Grow Too Old to Dream
   EDDIE PEABODY AND HIS BEACHCOMBERS
When I Grow Up   PHYLLIS ROBINS
When I Hear Your Voice   ANNA NEAGLE
When I Leave Old Glasgow Behind
   IAN McELHINNEY
When I Was Young   THE ANIMALS
When I'm Cleaning Windows (2 films)
   GEORGE FORMBY
When I'm Sixty Four   THE BEATLES
When Irish Eyes Are Smiling
   HAL YATES AND COOPER LAWLEY
When It's Sleepy Time Down South   BERNARDI
When King Arthur Rules Our Land
   GOTHAM QUARTETTE
When Lights Are Low
   ERIC DELANEY AND HIS BAND
When Love Comes My Way   MELVILLE GIDEON
When Love Has Passed You By   OLIVE LUCIUS
When Loves Are So Many   FRED CONYNGHAM
When My Dreamboat Comes Home
   THE SINGING CARPENTER
When Old Man Love Comes
   CICELY COURTNEIDGE
When That Yiddisher Band Plays an Irish
   Tune
   TEDDY ELBEN AND THE IRISH JEWZALEERS
When the Band Begins to Play
   PHYLLIS MONKMAN
When the Feeling Hits You   SAMMY DAVIS JR
When the Guards Go Marching By (1932)
   JACKSON GIRLS
When the Guards Go Marching By (1938)
   DENNIS NOBLE
When the Night Is Through   ANN LENNER
When the Poppies Bloom Again
   HAL SWAIN AND HIS SAXOPHONE BAND
When the Rain Comes Rolling Down
   EIGHT PIANO SYMPHONY
When the Rich Man Rides By
   GILBERT CHILDS; THE CO-OPTIMISTS

When the Saints Go Marching In
    CHRIS BARBER AND HIS JAZZ BAND; OTTILIE PATTERSON
When the Water Works Caught Fire
    GEORGE FORMBY
When We Feather Our Nest   GEORGE FORMBY
When We Were in the Forces   NAT JACKLEY
When Will I Be Loved?
    DAVE EDMUNDS AND THE STRAY CATS
When You and I Were Young, Maggie
    BILL SMITH
When You Came Along
    TED HEATH AND HIS MUSIC; DENNIS LOTIS
When You Come Home   LINDA PORTER
When You Gotta Go   ANTHONY NEWLEY
When You Gotta Sing   JESSIE MATTHEWS
When You Hear Music   JACK HULBERT
When You Know Someone Loves You
    JOAN REGAN
When You Know You're Not Forgotten
    THE BELLS
When You Smile   ANN GORDON
When You Wish Upon a Star
    EDMUND (TED) HOCKRIDGE
When You're Far Far Away   THE BACHELORS
When You're Smiling   SIX HARMONISTS
When You've Got a Little Springtime in Your
    Heart   JESSIE MATTHEWS
When Your Television Set Comes Home
    NORMAN LONG
Where Did You Get That Hat?   CLIFF RICHARD
Where Do Flies Go?   SAM MAYO
Where Do I Go From Here?   SAMMY DAVIS JR
Where E'er You Walk   ANDREW WATTS
Where the Mountains Meet the Sea
    MAESTRO SINGERS
Where There's You There's Me   JACK HULBERT
Where You Goin'?   RONNIE CARROLL
Where's Captain Kirk?   ATHLETICO SPIZZ '80
Where's the Birdie?   TOMMY STEELE
Where's the Sun   JUDY SHIRLEY
Which Way the Wind Blows   LOUISE CORDET
Whiffenpoof Song, The   BARRY CRYER
Whirl of the World, The (1922)   BILLY MERSON
Whirl of the World, The (1924) NELLIE WALLACE
Whiskers Song, The   GEORGE CLARKE
Whisper in Your Dreams   DEREK OLDHAM
Whispering (1934)   CHARLIE KUNZ
Whispering (1935)
    DEBROY SOMERS AND HIS BAND
Whispering (1943)   IVOR DENNIS
Whispering (1947)   ANNA NEAGLE
Whispering Whatnot, The   SAM MAYO
Whistle and Blow Your Blues Away
    CHARLES FORSYTHE, ADDIE SEAMON AND ELEANOR FARRELL
Whistle If You Want Me   LENA BROWN
Whistle My Love   BILLY COTTON AND HIS BAND
Whistle When You Want Me   BETTY DRIVER
Whistle While You Work   THE CRAZY GANG
Whistler's Mother-in-Law
    SHIRLEY LENNER; HARRY PARRY AND HIS RADIO RHYTHM CLUB SEXTET
Whistling and Whittling   BERYL DAVIS
Whistling Gypsy   ARTHUR TRACY
Whistling Rufus   KITKAT SAXOPHONE RASCALS

Whistling Under the Moon
    IRIS ASHLEY; JOHNNY SCHOFIELD
Whistling Waltz, The
    BOBBIE AND VIRGINIA; GERALDO AND HIS ORCHESTRA; ANNA NEAGLE; ARTHUR TRACY
White Boy   CULTURE CLUB
White Heat   JOE LOSS AND HIS ORCHESTRA
White Light/White Heat   DAVID BOWIE
White Man at Hammersmith Palais   THE CLASH
White Riot   THE CLASH
Whittling Time Away   TONY MERCER
Who Are You?   THE WHO
Who Can Say?   DANNY WILLIAMS
Who Could, We Could, We Two   LUPINO LANE
Who Do You Think You Are?   THE SPICE GIRLS
Who Is Sylvia? (1933)   ROY HENDERSON
Who Is Sylvia? (1939)   ROBERT WILSON
Who Killed Bambi?   EDDIE 'TENPOLE' TUDOR
Who Needs It   HAZEL O'CONNOR
Who Walked In?   RAQUELLE DORNE
Who Wears Short Shorts?
    FREDDIE AND THE DREAMERS
Who Were You With Last Night? (1935; 2
    films)   BOBBIE COMBER; BERTHA WILLMOTT
Who Were You With Last Night? (1948)
    CYRIL RITCHARD
Who's Been Polishing the Sun?   JACK HULBERT
Who's Foolish?   ANITA HARRIS
Who's Taking You Home Tonight?
    FREDDIE BAMBERGER
Who's That A-calling?
    THE SALISBURY SINGERS; DALE SMITH
Whoa Mare
    LEON CORTEZ AND HIS COSTER PALS
Whoever Writes the Song Calls the Tune
    HAZEL O'CONNOR
Whole Lotta Love   LED ZEPPELIN
Whole World In His Hands, The
    ADELAIDE HALL
Whoopee (2 films)
    JACK AND EDDIE EDEN; TEX McLEOD
Whose Turn Now?
    VIC LEWIS AND HIS ORCHESTRA
Why?   CLIFF RICHARD
Why Am I Always the Bridesmaid? LILY MORRIS
Why Am I Living?   JESS CONRAD
Why Can't It Happen To Me?   ANNE SHELTON
Why Can't We? (1933)   STANLEY LUPINO
Why Can't We? (1936)   STANLEY HOLLOWAY
Why Did I Have to Meet You?   GRACIE FIELDS
Why Did She Fall for the Leader of the Band?
    (1935)   JACK HYLTON AND HIS BAND
Why Did She Fall for the Leader of the Band?
    (1936)   PERCY AND MARY HONRI
Why Did You Say Goodbye?   JACK BILLINGS
Why Do They Always Pick On Me?
    SHEILA BERNETTE
Why Do They Always Say No?
    BARRI CHAT AND TERRI GARDNER
Why Don't Women Like Me?   GEORGE FORMBY
Why Don't You Come Down to Earth?
    CHARLES 'BUDDY' ROGERS
Why Don't You Love Me?   THE BLACKWELLS
Why Has a Cow Got Four Legs?
    CICELY COURTNEIDGE; JACK HULBERT

Why Have You Stolen My Heart? THE SINGING BAKERY BOY
Why Not Madame? STANLEY LUPINO
Why Oh Why? GERRY AND THE PACEMAKERS
Why Wasn't I Told? BOBBY HOWES
Width of a Circle DAVID BOWIE
Wild-Eyed Boy from Free Cloud, The DAVID BOWIE
Wild River FRANK IFIELD
Wild Violets ALBERTA RASCH DANCERS
Wild Weekend DAVE CLARK FIVE
Wild Wind JOHNNY LEYTON
Wildflower LOLITA AND CORTEZ
Will It Be You? TOMMY STEELE
Will She Be Waiting Up? DENNIS HOEY
Will Ye No Come Back Again LORNA MARTIN
Will You? HAZEL O'CONNOR
Will You Love Me When I'm Mutton? GRACIE FIELDS
William Tell (1928) PERCY PRYDE
William Tell (1936) RAYMOND BAIRD
William Tell (1937) MINI-PIANO ENSEMBLE OF 14 JUVENILES
William Tell (1938) REGINALD FOORT
William Tell (1944) REGINALD FOORT
William Tell (1965) SOUNDS INCORPORATED
William Tell (1996) GRIMETHORPE COLLIERY BAND
Willow in the Rain ROBERT ALBINI
Willow Twist, The THE JOHN BARRY SEVEN
Wind and the Rain, The JOHNNY DE LITTLE
Wind That Shakes the Barley, The PETER SINCLAIR
Wind's in the West, The CICELY COURTNEIDGE; CARLYLE COUSINS
Winding Road, The PETER DAWSON
Wine and Waltz JOSEPH SCHMIDT
Wine Women and Song TILLY LOSCH
Wings KEITH FALKNER
Wings of Sleep OLIVE GILBERT
Winnie the Wench on the Winch ETHEL REVNELL AND GRACIE WEST
Winning CLIFF RICHARD
Winter Wonderland (1935) TEDDY BROWN
Winter Wonderland (1936) WALSH AND BARKER
Wire Ways HERMAN DAREWSKI
Wireless, The TOMMY HANDLEY
Wise Old Horsey CECIL BROADHURST
Wish for Happiness CLIFFORD MOLLISON
Wish Me Luck As You Wave Me Goodbye (2 films) GRACIE FIELDS
Wishing Well TONIA BERN
Witches Song MARIANNE FAITHFULL
With a Kiss and a Sigh EDMUNDO ROS AND HIS RUMBA BAND
With a Smile on Your Lips RAYMOND NEWELL
With a Twinkle in Your Eye RALPH READER
With All My Heart (1934) JAN KIEPURA
With All My Heart (1943) VERA LYNN
With All My Heart (1956) DOROTHY SQUIRES
With Me Old Clay Pipe DAN DONOVAN
With My Little Ukulele GEORGE FORMBY
Within You DAVID BOWIE
Without a Shadow of a Doubt SHIRL CONWAY
Without a Song ROBERT ASHLEY

Without Love PRINCESS PEARL
Without the Moon KEITH FALKNER
Without You (1934) EVELYN LAYE
Without You (1956) DOROTHY SQUIRES
Woman Is Free BLONDE ON BLONDE
Women I've Had At My Feet, The TOM PAYNE AND VERA HILLIARD
Won't Get Fooled Again (1979) THE WHO
Won't Get Fooled Again (1980) PETE TOWNSHEND; JOHN WILLIAMS
Won't It Be Wonderful? THE TWO LESLIES
Won't We Have a Party? ELSIE AND DORIS WATERS
Won't You Take Me Back to Hawaii? FELIX MENDELSSOHN AND HIS HAWAIIAN SERENADERS
Wonder Child Xylophonist, The DOREEN
Wonderful Day BILLY FURY
Wonderful Life CLIFF RICHARD
Wonderful Things FRANKIE VAUGHAN
Wonderful to Me RENATE MULLER
Wooly Bully BAD MANNERS
Word Is Love, The CLIFF RICHARD
Words and Music HAL SWAIN
Work Is a Four-Letter Word CILLA BLACK
Working for the Mayor and Corporation NORMAN LONG
World Belongs to Me, The IVY BENSON AND HER ALL GIRLS ORCHESTRA; EVELYN DARVILLE
World Goes Around Just the Same, The PAT HYDE
World Is For the Young, The STANLEY HOLLOWAY
World Is Mine Tonight, The WEBSTER BOOTH
World Is Waiting for the Sunrise, The (1934) THE VANCOUVER BOYS BAND
World Is Waiting for the Sunrise, The (1938) HAL YATES
World Is Waiting for the Sunrise, The (1940) SID TRACEY AND BESSIE HAY
World May Pass Me By, The FOUR MUSKETEERS
World of Dreams MAX BYGRAVES
World Without Love PETER AND GORDON
Would You Could You VERA-ELLEN
Wouldn't It Be Good NIK KERSHAW
Wouldn't You Like It? FRANKIE VAUGHAN
Wrong Rhumba, The ELSIE RANDOLPH
Wun Lung Too THE CO-OPTIMISTS
Wurm YES
Wyoming CARSON ROBISON AND HIS PIONEERS

Y

Yakety Yak JOE STRUMMER
Yale, The SANTOS CASANI AND JOSE LENNARD
Ye Banks and Braes (1934) TOM KINNIBURGH
Ye Banks and Braes (1941) ROBERT WILSON
Ye Banks and Braes (1947) SYLVIA WELLING
Ye Banks and Braes (1958) JEAN (JEANNIE) CARSON
Years Together, The ANNA NEAGLE
Yellow Dog CHRIS BARBER AND HIS JAZZ BAND
Yellow Mask, The BOBBY HOWES

Yellow Submarine THE BEATLES
Yeoman's Wedding Song FRANK TITTERTON
Yes Ma'am REGGIE BRISTOW AND HIS BAND
Yes Madam BOBBY HOWES
Yes Mr Brown JACK BUCHANAN
Yes Suh NAT GONELLA AND HIS GEORGIANS
Yesterday (1965) THE BEATLES
Yesterday (1984)
PAUL McCARTNEY; RINGO STARR
Yesterday (1991) PAUL AND LINDA McCARTNEY
Yesterday's Dreams
BUD FLANAGAN AND CHESNEY ALLEN
Yesterday's Thrill ELISABETH WELCH
Yip-I-Addy-I-Ay REGINALD FOORT
Yodelee Yodelay NORMAN WISDOM
Yokel's Philosophy, A TOM KINNIBURGH
You JUDY GARLAND
You Are Maximum Plus
MARION RYAN; TOMMY STEELE
You Are My Favourite Dream DIANE TODD
You Are My Love Song (1937)
MICHAEL BARTLETT
You Are My Love Song (1943)
LESLIE A HUTCHINSON
You Are My Song Divine ALEXIS AND ISOLDE
You Bring Out the Savage in Me FRANCES DAY
You Brought My Heart the Sunshine
FRANK TITTERTON
You By My Side CHRIS SQUIRE
You Call It Madness, I Call It Love
RUSSELL JONES
You Can't Be Roots in Football Boots
VICTOR ROMERO
You Can't Go Wrong in These
GEORGE FORMBY
You Can't Have Everything
JIMMY JEWEL AND BEN WARRISS
You Can't Have Your Cake BETTY DRIVER
You Can't Keep a Good Dreamer Down
SID FIELD
You Can't Live Without Love FRANCES DAY
You Can't Make Me Feel Blue
BOBBIE ALDERSON; PATRICIA ROSSBOROUGH
You Can't Say I Love You JOAN SMALL
You Can't Stop Me From Dreaming
TED ANDREWS AND HIS GIRL FRIEND
You Deserve a Medal for That
NORMAN WISDOM
You Didn't Oughta Do Such Things
PAUL ROBESON
You Don't Have to Tell Me I Know
BETTY DRIVER
You Don't Know the Half of It BINNIE HALE
You Don't Need a Licence for That
GEORGE FORMBY
You Don't Understand JACK HULBERT
You Forgot Your Gloves JACK BUCHANAN
You Give Me Ideas BOBBY HOWES
You Go Too Far HARRY SHALSON
You Gotta Go TOMMY STEELE
You Have No Idea JOSEPHINE EARLE
You Kept Me Waiting DAVID ESSEX
You Know What King Arthur Said
ARTHUR ASKEY
You Know Who I Am LEONARD COHEN

You Like Me Too Much THE BEATLES
You Look So Sweet Madame
MAURICE CHEVALIER
You Made Me Mad
VIC LEWIS AND HIS ORCHESTRA
You Me and Love JAN KIEPURA
You Must Have a Heartache HARRY LEON
You Must Have Music RICHARD TAUBER
You Must Have This HAZEL ASCOT
You Need Wheels THE MERTON PARKAS
You Never Can Tell TOMMY TRINDER
You Never Miss Your Mother
BUD FLANAGAN AND CHESNEY ALLEN; PETER
You Never Talked About Me DEL SHANNON
You Ought to See Me on Saturday Night
SID FIELD
You Ought to See Sally on Sunday
CICELY COURTNEIDGE; BILLY MILTON; DEBROY
SOMERS AND HIS BAND; THREE ADMIRALS
You Really Got Me LOOT
You Should Be Set to Music BOBBY HOWES
You Started Something JERRY WAYNE
You Struck the Right Note
HARRY ROY AND HIS BAND
You Too Can Have a Lovely Romance
ANNE SHELTON
You Turn My Legs To Water FIONA RICHMOND
You Were There CHARLIE KUNZ
You Will Remember Vienna
ALFREDO AND HIS GYPSY BAND
You Will Return to Vienna
WEBSTER BOOTH; ANNE ZIEGLER
You'll Get Used To It (2 films) JOHN PRATT
You'll Love the Army EVELYN DALL
You'll Never Know VERA LYNN
You're a Liarty GEORGE FORMBY
You're Driving Me Crazy (1936) POLLY WARD
You're Driving Me Crazy (1938)
NONI AND PARTNER
You're Everything to Me GEORGE FORMBY
You're Going to Lose That Girl THE BEATLES
You're Good to Me
GERRY AND THE PACEMAKERS
You're in Kentucky Sure as You're Born
CHARLIE KUNZ
You're More than All the World to Me
GRACIE FIELDS
You're My Baby Now OLIVIA NEWTON-JOHN
You're My Decline and Fall
GERTRUDE LAWRENCE
You're My Everything YVETTE DARNAC
You're On My Mind All Day JACK DONAHUE
You're Only Dreaming
GERALDO AND HIS ORCHESTRA; HY HAZELL
You're Sweeter Than I Thought You Were
JACK HULBERT
You're the Last Word in Love
HARRY ROY AND HIS BAND
You're What's the Matter With Me
HARRY RICHMAN
You've Got Everything JACK HULBERT
You've Got Me Crying Again BETTY ASTELL
You've Got Me Standing on Tip of My Toes
BINKIE STUART

You've Got to be Smart in the Army
GRACIE FIELDS
You've Got to Hide Your Love Away
THE BEATLES
You've Got to Look Right for the Part
BILLY FURY
You've Got to Smile   GRACIE FIELDS
You've Gotta Beat Out the Rhythm
THE CO-OPTIMISTS
You've Gotta Smile   DONALD PEERS
You've Gotta Way   THE JOHN BARRY SEVEN
Young Man Blues   THE WHO
Young Ned of the Hill
RON KAVANA AND TERRY WOODS
Young Ones, The   CLIFF RICHARD
Your England and Mine   JOHN STEBBEN
Your Eyes Are So Tender   CARL BRISSON
Your Face in a Crowd   PADDY BROWNE

Your First Love   KEN MacINTOSH AND HIS BAND
Your First Love Was Your Last
JEAN (JEANNIE) CARSON
Your Way Is My Way
FLORENCE DESMOND; GEORGE FORMBY
Yours   SHIRLEY LENNER; RENARA
Yours Is No Disgrace   YES
Yours Sincerely   VERA LYNN
Youth and Experience   CLIFF RICHARD

Z

Za Zu Za Zu   NICHOLAS BROTHERS
Zampa in Rhythm   MAX SCHUMANN
Ziggy Stardust   DAVID BOWIE
Zion   ST. DAVID'S SINGERS
Zodiak, The
THE BRITISH STEEL STOCKSBRIDGE BAND

.